T0325016

Knowledge Management and Business Strategies:
Theoretical Frameworks and Empirical Research

El-Sayed Abou-Zeid
Concordia University, Canada

INFORMATION SCIENCE REFERENCE

Hershey · New York

Acquisitions Editor: Kristin Klinger
Development Editor: Kristin Roth
Senior Managing Editor: Jennifer Neidig
Managing Editor: Sara Reed
Copy Editor: April Schmidt
Typesetter: Michael Brehm
Cover Design: Lisa Tosheff
Printed at: Yurchak Printing Inc.

Published in the United States of America by
        Information Science Reference (an imprint of IGI Global)
        701 E. Chocolate Avenue, Suite 200
        Hershey PA 17033
        Tel: 717-533-8845
        Fax: 717-533-8661
        E-mail: cust@igi-global.com
        Web site: http://www.igi-global.com/reference

and in the United Kingdom by
        Information Science Reference (an imprint of IGI Global)
        3 Henrietta Street
        Covent Garden
        London WC2E 8LU
        Tel: 44 20 7240 0856
        Fax: 44 20 7379 0609
        Web site: http://www.eurospanonline.com

Library of Congress Cataloging-in-Publication Data

Knowledge management and business strategies : theoretical frameworks and empirical research / El-Sayed Abou-Zeid, editor.
      p. cm.
  Summary: "This book provides researchers and practitioners fundamental business and management knowledge by exploring relevant theoretical frameworks and the latest empirical research findings in the area of knowledge and knowledge management strategies and their formulation and alignment with organizations' competitive business strategies"--Provided by publisher.
  Includes bibliographical references and index.
  ISBN 978-1-59904-486-6 (hardcover) -- ISBN 978-1-59904-488-0 (ebook)
  1. Knowledge management. 2. Strategic planning. I. Abou-Zeid, El-Sayed.
  HD30.2.K636842 2008
  658.4'012--dc22
                            2007024483

British Cataloguing in Publication Data
A Cataloguing in Publication record for this book is available from the British Library.

All work contributed to this book set is new, previously-unpublished material. The views expressed in this book are those of the authors, but not necessarily of the publisher.

Table of Contents

Section I
Organizational Knowledge Management

Section II
Knowledge Management (KM) Strategies

Section III
Business and KM Strategies Alignment

Section IV
Selected Readings

Detailed Table of Contents

Section I
Organizational Knowledge Management

Chapter I

Drawing on systems thinking and complexity theory, this chapter conceptualizes organizations as complex adaptive systems within which knowledge ecologies may flourish. The implications of such reconceptualisation for organizational practice and changes in managerial orientations are shown to be novel offering significant potential towards a second order knowledge management.

Chapter II

This chapter presents an empirical study of impact of introducing knowledge management programs on firm performance. In the proposed model, knowledge distinctive competences are considered as the mediating variable, which constitute the foundation of the firm innovation capacity. Data collected from 222 firms from the Spanish biotechnology and telecommunication sectors are used to test the model.

Chapter III

Using a Web-based Delphi method, this chapter presents the results obtained after reaching a consensus among 100 knowledge leaders on their critical issues. These issues include the perceived knowledge management benefits and obstacles, the knowledge leaders' roles and skills, as well as the technologies they use for implementing knowledge management initiatives.

Section II
Knowledge Management (KM) Strategies

This chapter introduces external knowledge search strategy as a central element of an organizations overall knowledge management strategy. A conceptual framework for organizations involved in the external knowledge management activity has been developed. The framework identifies 10 search paths organizations may follow into the search space, four of which relate exclusively to external knowledge search.

The two paradigms that inform most of the knowledge transfer literature, the positivist and social construction paradigms, and their implications on strategy formulation, are discussed. Based on this dual paradigm logic this chapter proposes a classification system of the core knowledge transfer concepts, models and contexts that helps address issues of a strategic nature.

A system dynamics model is used to explore the dynamic relation between organizational learning, modularity, and strategic flexibility. Based on this model three core constituent elements of a learning-supporting knowledge management strategy, namely, boundary spanners and boundary objects, collaboration-supporting systems and participative scenario planning.

This chapter presents a socialization-based view to organization's knowledge strategy. According to this view, socialization diffuses an organization's knowledge strategy through values leadership and practice-led process redesign. Moreover, it has been argued that socialization results in durable, accessible processes, uniquely configured to business strategy.

Chapter VIII

This chapter investigates to what extent knowledge management technologies support and improve strategic innovation management to face the aforementioned problems successfully. A characterization scheme is developed to serve as a framework for the subsequent evaluation of knowledge management technologies in relation to strategic innovation management.

Section III
Business and KM Strategies Alignment

Chapter IX

This chapter discusses the concept of alignment in the context of knowledge management and presents a three-dimensional generic alignment reference framework. The first dimension pertains to business-related strategies while the second one pertains to information-related strategies. The third dimension pertains to knowledge-related strategies. The framework encompasses key issue relating to alignment in KM and presents a unified approach to knowledge strategic alignment.

Chapter X

This chapter proposes a three-layered service infrastructure that composes services from heterogeneous applications into specific knowledge management (KM) services. It argues that the alignment of KM strategy with business strategy can be achieved by introducing a service infrastructure that uses the concept of KM service in order to connect the customer-oriented materialization of strategic decisions on a conceptual level with their technical counterpart on the ICT level.

Chapter XI

This chapter proposes a theoretical basis for a knowledge strategy called artificial Ba and discusses how to develop a concrete, artificial Ba that supports the alignment of knowledge and business strategies. The proposed system is a complete "artifact", a supportive environment in which knowledge accumulates and is shared, a system that is built to activate existing knowledge and to support the creation of valuable new knowledge in an organization.

This chapter introduces an Activity Domain Theory-based view for guiding the alignment of business and knowledge strategies. In this view alignment is focused around the activity domain, which can be comprehended as a human work practice where socially organized actors process a work object into a required outcome

Section IV
Selected Readings

Although it is widely accepted that alignment of knowledge with corporate strategy is necessary, to date there have been few clear statements on what a knowledge strategy looks like and how it may be practically implemented. We argue that current methods and techniques to accomplish this alignment are severely limited, showing no clear description on how the alignment can be achieved. Core competencies, embodying an organization's practical know-how, are also rarely linked explicitly to actionable knowledge strategy. Viewing knowledge embedded in core competencies as a strategic asset, the paper uses a case study to show how a company's core competencies were articulated and verified for either inclusion or exclusion in the strategy. The study is representative of similar studies carried out across a range of organisations using a novel and practically proven method. This method, StratAchieve, was used here in a client situation to show how the core competencies were identified and tested for incorporation or not in the strategy. The paper concludes by considering the value of the approach for managing knowledge.

Knowledge Management (KM) has gained increasing attention since the mid-1990s. A KM strategy involves consciously helping people share and put knowledge into action. However, before an organization can realize the promise of KM, a fundamental question needs to be asked: What performance goal(s) is the organization trying to achieve? In this paper, we develop and offer a framework that provides a holistic view of the performance environment surrounding organizational knowledge work. We illustrate the KM framework using two organizational case studies. Then, based on the KM framework and further insights drawn from our case studies, we offer a series of steps that may guide and assist organizations and practitioners as they undertake KM initiatives. We further demonstrate the applicability of these steps by examining KM initiatives within a global software development company. We conclude with a discussion of implications for organizational practice and directions for future research.

It is widely acknowledged that an organizational knowledge management strategy is a desired precursor to the development of specific knowledge management (KM) initiatives. The development of such a strategy is often difficult in the face of a lack of organizational understanding about KM and other organizational constraints. This case study describes the issues involved in developing a new KM strategy for the Air Force Material Command (AFMC). It centers around the AFMC KM program manager, Randy Adkins, and his challenges in developing the future KM strategy direction for the AFMC enterprise. The case study begins with a description of the history of the AFMC KM program and the existing KM system, but then focuses primarily on issues to be considered in future strategy development such as maintaining top leadership support and understanding, conflict with the IT organization, funding cuts, future KM system configuration needs, and outsourcing of KM. The intent of this case is to demonstrate, using Randy Adkins and AFMC as an example, many common issues that can be encountered as leaders struggle to develop viable KM strategies.

While organizations continue to grapple with the implementation of knowledge management, there remains a need for empirical research into the practical difficulties they encounter. In this chapter, we investigate the challenges faced by one multinational telecommunications company in a postmerger environment. We develop an instrument to evaluate the knowledge sharing culture and information infrastructure, and by using qualitative and quantitative data from a survey of five European sites, we illustrate how managers can measure gaps between the effectiveness of current practices and their importance, and decide whether to direct resources toward changing employee attitudes, organizational practices, or knowledge management infrastructure. More significantly, we highlight the need for senior managers to be in agreement about the strategic direction of their business and the strategic alignment between business strategy and knowledge management strategy. Without such consensus, knowledge management is likely to remain at best a series of fragmented and unrelated initiatives at local levels.

By viewing strategy, whether business (B)-strategy or knowledge (K)-strategy, can be seen as a balancing act between the external domain (opportunities/threats) and the internal domain (capabilities/arrangements) of the firm, this paper develops a "KM Strategic Alignment Model" is presented. It also discusses the dynamics of alignment process.

Preface

The role of knowledge as a crucial asset for an enterprise's survival and advancement has been recognized by researchers and managers (e.g., von Krogh, Ichijo & Nonaka, 2000). Moreover, by having knowledge (intellectual resources), an organization can understand how to exploit and develop its traditional resources better than its competitors can, even if some or all of those traditional resources are not unique.

With the growing awareness of the crucial role that knowledge can play in gaining competitive advantage, two inter-related issues with regard to knowledge management (KM) initiatives have challenged executives: first, how to built competitive business strategy around a firm's intellectual resources and capabilities, that is, Knowledge (K) strategy, which is oriented toward understanding what knowledge is strategic and why, and second, how to develop KM strategy that guides and defines the processes and infrastructure (organizational and technological) for managing organizational knowledge.

However, the realization of business value from KM investments requires alignment between business (B) and K/KM strategies. The importance of alignment for effective organizational performance is now well-recognized. Alignment among two or more organizational dimensions, which may be defined as the extent to which these dimensions meet theoretical norms of mutual coherence, has been argued and empirically found to enhance performance.

The main purpose of this book is to bring together, in one book, relevant theoretical frameworks and latest empirical research findings in the area of K and KM strategies formulation and how to align them with an organization's B strategy.

The overall objectives of the book are to enable the reader to:

- Get an in-depth understanding of the role of organizational knowledge in gaining sustainable competitive advantage.
- Understand the different approaches to formulate K and KM strategies.
- Recognize the underlying theories behind B and K/KM strategies alignment.
- Provide executives theoretically-sound approaches for formulating business aligned K/KM strategies.

This book is divided into four sections: Organizational Knowledge Management, Knowledge Management (KM) Strategies, and Business and KM Strategies Alignment, and Selected Readings.

The first section, Organizational Knowledge Management, looks at some emerging views such as knowledge ecologies and second order knowledge management, and knowledge management leaders' top issues.

Drawing on systems thinking and complexity theory, the first chapter conceptualizes organizations as complex adaptive systems within which knowledge ecologies may flourish. The implications of such reconceptualization for organizational practice and changes in managerial orientations are shown to be novel offering significant potential towards a second order knowledge management.

The second chapter presents an empirical study of the impact of introducing knowledge management programs on firm performance. In the proposed model knowledge distinctive competences are considered as the mediating variable, which constitute the foundation of the firm innovation capacity. Data collected from 222 firms from the Spanish biotechnology and telecommunication sectors are used to test the model.

Using a Web-based Delphi method, the third chapter presents the results obtained after reaching a consensus among 100 knowledge leaders on their critical issues. These issues include the perceived knowledge management benefits and obstacles, the knowledge leaders' roles and skills, as well as the technologies they use for implementing knowledge management initiatives.

The main theme of the second section, Knowledge Management (KM) Strategies, is the different approaches to formulate K and/or KM strategies. In this context K/KM strategy can defined as "the way in which the firm balances its knowledge resources and knowledge processing capabilities with the knowledge required to create its products for the markets in a manner superior to its competitors" (Zack, 1999b, p. x). Since strategy, whether business (B) strategy or knowledge (K) strategy, can be seen as a balancing act between the *external domain* (opportunities/threats) and the *internal domain* (capabilities/arrangements) of the firm (strengths and weaknesses) (Henderson & Venkatraman, 1993; Zack, 1999a), the external and internal domains of K-strategy can be described as follows (Abou-Zeid, 2005).

The *external domain* of K-strategy involves three dimensions: *K-Scope* (what the firm must know), *K-Systemic Competencies* (what are the critical characteristics of the required knowledge), and *K-Governance* (how to obtain the required K-competencies). The first dimension, K-Scope, deals with the specific domains of knowledge that are critical to the firm's survival and advancement strategies. Survival strategies aim at securing current enterprise profitability, while advancement strategies aim for future profitability (von Krogh et al., 2000).

The second dimension of the K-strategy external domain is K systemic competencies. The focus of this dimension is the set of utilization-oriented characteristics of knowledge that could contribute positively to the creation of new business strategy or better support of existing business strategy. This set includes characteristics such as:

- **Accessibility**, the extent to which organizational knowledge is made available to its members regardless of time or location (Buckman, 1998);
- **Transferability**, the extent to which the newly acquired knowledge can be applied in other contexts, for example, organizational and cultural (Grant, 1996);
- **Appropriability**, the extent to which knowledge can be imitated. Things are said to have "strong" appropriability if they are difficult to reproduce by another organization. The converse is "weak" appropriability. A related concept is that of "sticky/slippery"; that is, sticky knowledge is such an integral part of a regime that it cannot be extracted in a meaningful whole (Grant, 1996; Narasimha, 2000);
- **Depth and breadth** (Narasimha, 2000);
- **Compositionality**, the amenability of knowledge to be synthesized from existing knowledge; and
- **Integratability**, the extent to which the newly acquired knowledge can be integrated with existing knowledge.

Finally, K-governance dimension deals with the selection and use of mechanisms for obtaining the required K competencies. The process could generate valuable information about their needs

The *internal domain* of K-strategy involves three dimensions: *Knowledge (K) processes*, *Knowledge (K)-infrastructures*, and *Knowledge (K)-skills*.

Knowledge (K)-processes, the first dimension of the K-strategy internal domain, can be classified into two main categories: *K-manipulating processes* and *K-enabling processes*. The first category, K-manipulating processes, includes all the organizational processes needed to change the state of organizational knowledge such as K-generation, K-mobilization, and K-application (Abou-Zeid, 2003). The second category, K-enabling processes, include organizational processes that support K-manipulating processes such as managing conversation, mobilizing knowledge activists, creating the right context, and globalizing local knowledge (von Krogh et al., 2000).

Organizational knowledge processes are socially interaction-intensive. They involve social interactions and direct communication and contact among individuals and among members of "communities of practice". Therefore, they require the presence of social capital. Social capital is "the sum of actual and potential resources embedded within, available through, and derived from the network of relationships possessed by a social unit" (Nahapier & Ghoshal, 1998). Recognizing the importance of social capital, Gold, Malhotra, and Segars (2001) have identified three key K-infrastructures, the second dimension of the K-strategy internal domain, that is, technical, structural, and cultural, that enable social capital. The *K-technical infrastructure* includes IT-enabled technologies that support KM activities such as business intelligence, collaboration and distributed learning, K-discovery, K-mapping, opportunity generation, and security. The *K-structural infrastructure* refers to the presence of enabling formal organization structures and the organization's system of rewards and incentives. Finally, the *K-cultural infrastructure* involves elements such as corporate vision and the organization's system of values (Gold et al., 2001).

The last dimension of the K-strategy internal domain is K-skills. KM processes are by their very nature multifaceted. They involve many dimensions such as technical, organizational and human. This characteristic of KM processes reflects on the nature of skills required to perform them. For example, Malhotra (1997) defines a senior knowledge executive, such as a chief knowledge officer (CKO) or an organizational knowledge architect, as the person who should have the combined capabilities of a business strategist, technology analyst, and a human resource professional. The ability to facilitate the on-going process of knowledge sharing and knowledge renewal, the ability to develop the human and cultural infrastructure that facilitates information sharing, and the ability to utilize the available technologies for serving the creation, sharing, and documentation of knowledge are some examples of the required skills.

Chapters IV and V deal with one of the dimensions of K-strategy external domain, namely K-governance. Chapter IV introduces external knowledge search strategy as a central element of an organizations overall knowledge management strategy. A conceptual framework for organizations involved in the external knowledge management activity has been developed. The framework identifies 10 search paths organizations may follow into the search space, four of which relate exclusively to external knowledge search.

On the other hand, Chapter V reviews recent literature on knowledge and knowledge transfer (KT) and discusses the two paradigms that inform most of the KT literature, namely, the positivist and social construction paradigms and their implications on strategy formulation. Based on this dual paradigm logic, this chapter proposes a classification system of the core knowledge transfer concepts, models, and contexts that helps address issues of a strategic nature.

Some of K-structural infrastructure related issues are addressed in Chapter VI. In this chapter a system dynamics model is used to explore the dynamic relation between organizational learning, modularity, and strategic flexibility. Based on this model, three core constituent elements of a learning-supporting knowledge management strategy, namely, boundary spanners and boundary objects, collaboration-supporting systems, and participative scenario planning.

With regard to K-cultural infrastructure related issues, Chapter VII presents a socialization-based view to organization's knowledge strategy. According to this view, socialization diffuses an organization's knowledge strategy through values leadership and practice-led process redesign. Moreover, it has been argued that socialization results in durable, accessible processes, uniquely configured to business strategy. A socialization approach integrates practice-level internal knowledge networks to support business processes and strategy, leveraging and exchanging knowledge more effectively than authoritative ("top-down") institutionalization.

As technology life cycles are decreasing and the amount of information available is already vast, identifying upcoming innovations and trends as early as possible becomes necessary to decrease uncertainty, implement technology leadership, and create competitive advantage. To this end Chapter VIII investigates to what extent knowledge management technologies support and improve strategic innovation management to face the aforementioned problems successfully. A characterization scheme is developed to serve as a framework for the subsequent evaluation of knowledge management technologies in relation to strategic innovation management.

The third section, Business and KM Strategies Alignment, introduces new approaches for achieving such alignment. In fact several authors clearly indicate the importance of mutually aligning business strategy and KM efforts and how this alignment helps enhance organizational performance (e.g., Earl, 2001; Ribbens, 1997). For example, Maier and Remus (2001, 2002, 2003) propose a process-oriented approach that considers market-oriented factors in a KM strategy. In this approach KM strategies can be described according to the process focus and type of business processes supported (Maier & Remus, 2001). The process focus can extend from a single business process to an organization-wide perspective, including all relevant business processes (core and service). The type of process is related to the identification of knowledge-intensive business processes. In addition, Sabherwal and Sabherwal (2003) empirically found that the cumulative abnormal stock market return (in the 5-day event window) due to a KM announcement is positively associated with the alignment between the firm's business strategy and the attributes of the KM initiative announced. They use four attributes to characterize KM initiatives: KM level, KM process, KM means, and knowledge source. KM level concerns the hierarchical grouping of individuals upon which the KM effort described in the announcement is focused. The KM processes (or K-manipulating processes) involve the sharing, utilization, or creation of knowledge while KM means involve organizational structural arrangements and technologies that are used to enable KM processes (Earl, 2001; Hansen, Nohria, & Tierney, 1999). Finally, knowledge source reflects where the knowledge originates from.

The concept of alignment in the context of knowledge management is discussed in Chapter IX which presents a three-dimensional generic alignment reference framework. The first dimension pertains to business-related strategies while the second one pertains to information-related strategies. The third dimension pertains to knowledge-related strategies. The framework encompasses key issue relating to alignment in KM and presents a unified approach to knowledge strategic alignment.

Chapter X proposes a three-layered service infrastructure that composes services from heterogeneous applications into specific knowledge management (KM) services. It argues that the alignment of KM strategy with business strategy can be achieved by introducing a service infrastructure that uses the concept of KM service in order to connect the customer-oriented materialization of strategic decisions on a conceptual level with their technical counterpart on the information communication technology (ICT) level.

Chapter XI proposes a theoretical basis for a knowledge strategy called artificial *Ba* and discusses how to develop a concrete, artificial *Ba* that supports the alignment of knowledge and business strategies. The proposed system is a complete "artifact", a supportive environment in which knowledge accumulates and is shared, a system that is built to activate existing knowledge and to support the creation of valuable new knowledge in an organization.

The activity domain theory-based view introduced in Chapter XII provides a new approach for guiding the alignment of business and knowledge strategies. In this view alignment is focused around the activity domain, which can be comprehended as a human work practice where socially organized actors process a work object into a required outcome

The 12 chapters and Selected Readings provide an overview of the most recent research in the area of K and KM strategies formulation and how to align them with an organization's B strategy. In addition, each chapter provides insight into possible future research directions.

REFERENCES

Abou-Zeid, E. (2003). Developing business aligned knowledge management strategy. In E. Coakes (Ed.), *Knowledge management: Current issues and challenges* (pp. 156-172). Hershey, PA: IRM Press.

Abou-Zeid, E.-S. (2005). Alignment of business and knowledge management strategies. In M. Khosrow-Pour (Ed.), *Encyclopedia of information science and technology* (Vol. 1, pp. 98-103). Hershey, PA: Idea Group.

Buckman, R. (1998). Lions, tigers and bears: Following the road from command and control to knowledge sharing. Retrieved May 25, 2007, from http://www.knowledge-nurture.com/

Earl, M. (2001). Knowledge management strategies: Toward a taxonomy. *Journal of Management Information Systems, 18*(1), 215-233.

Gold, A., Malhotra, A., & Segars, A. (2001). Knowledge management: An organizational capabilities perspective. *Journal of Management Information Systems, 18*(1), 185-214.

Grant, R. (1996, Winter). Toward a knowledge-based theory of the firm [Special issue]. *Strategic Management Journal, 17*, 109-112.

Hansen, M., Nohria, N., & Tierney, T. (1999). What's your strategy for managing knowledge? *Harvard Business Review, 77*(2), 106-119.

Henderson, J., & Venkatraman, N. (1993). Strategic alignment: Leveraging information technology for transforming organization. *IBM Systems Journal, 32*(1), 4-16.

Maier, R., & Remus, U. (2001). *Towards a framework for knowledge management strategies: Process-orientation as a new strategic starting point.* Paper presented at the 34th Annual Hawaii International Conference on System Sciences (HICSS-34).

Maier, R., & Remus, U. (2002). Defining process-oriented knowledge management strategies. *Knowledge and Process Management, 9*(2), 109-118.

Maier, R., & Remus, U. (2003). Implementing process-oriented knowledge management strategies. *Journal of Knowledge Management, 7*(4), 62-74.

Malhotra, Y. (1997). Profile of the ideal knowledge manager/architect. Retrieved May 25, 2007, from http://www.brint.com/wwwboard/messages/273.html

Nahapier, J., & Ghoshal, S. (1998). Social capital, intellectual capital, and the organizational advantage. *Academy of Management Review, 23*, 242-266.

Narasimha, S. (2000). Organizational knowledge, human resource management and sustained competitive advantage: Toward a framework. *CR, 10*(1), 123-135.

Ribbens, B.A. (1997). Organizational learning styles: Categorizing strategic predispositions from learning. *International Journal of Organizational Analysis, 5*(1), 59-73.

Sabherwal, R., & Sabherwal, S. (2003). How do knowledge management announcements affect firm value? A study of firms pursuing different business strategies. Retrieved May 25, 2007, from http://misrc. umn.edu/workshops/2003/fall/Sabherwal_100303.pdf

von Krogh, G., Ichijo, K., & Nonaka, I. (2000). *Enabling knowledge creation: How to unlock the mystery of tacit knowledge and release the power of innovation.* Oxford: Oxford University Press.

Zack, M.H. (1999a). Developing knowledge strategy. *California Management Review, 41*(3), 125-145.

Zack, M.H. (1999b). Introduction. In M.H. Zack (Ed.), *Knowledge and strategy* (pp. vii-xii). Boston: Butterworth Heinemann.

Acknowledgment

This book is the outcome of the generous knowledge sharing of the 24 authors who also took part in the reviewing process.

Section I
Organizational Knowledge Management

Chapter I
Knowledge Management:
From Management Fad
to Systemic Change

Shamim Bodhanya
University of KwaZulu-Natal, South Africa

ABSTRACT

This chapter demonstrates that despite a plurality of discourses related to knowledge, they are reduced to a single dominant discourse on knowledge management. It draws on systems thinking and complexity theory to reconceptualise organisations as complex adaptive systems within which knowledge ecologies may flourish. The focus thus shifts to knowing in situated action and on knowledge as a dynamic phenomenon. The chapter makes a contribution to strengthening the impact of the epistemology of action and that of a social-process perspective of knowledge. The approach presented has radical implications for knowledge management such that it becomes an enduring organisational intervention as opposed to a management fad. The implications for organisational practice and changes in managerial orientations are shown to be novel offering significant potential towards a second order knowledge management.

"If a system is behaving badly, consistently over a long period of time, and in spite of many variations in surrounding conditions, then something more than marginal tinkering is required to bring about improvement. Something within the system itself must change, to a new structure that brings forth a new behaviour."

—Meadows and Robinson (2002, p. 291)

INTRODUCTION

Knowledge management (KM) is increasingly becoming regarded as crucial to an organisation's success. I shall argue in this chapter that this may only be the case under certain conditions. If these conditions are not met knowledge management loses its promise and is reduced to a management fad. They require a change in assumptions as well as a particular set of managerial orientations. This in turn naturally has significance for organisational culture, change management and the roles of various organisational actors ranging from executives, managers and professionals to practitioners.

This chapter first summarises the major discourses around knowledge (Spender, 1996) and then considers how these translate into a dominant discourse on knowledge management. Second, it explores the set of assumptions that underpin conventional approaches to knowledge management which are based on this dominant discourse. These assumptions lead to what may be termed *first order* knowledge management that views knowledge as static and reified. First order knowledge management is characterised by a positivist approach that is based on an epistemology of possession (Assudani, 2005; Cook & Brown, 1999) or a perspective referred to as cognitive-possession (Chiva & Alegre, 2005). The chapter then draws on constructs from systems thinking and complexity theory to question the assumptions of first order knowledge management and to show how it is likely to be reduced to a management fad. Systems thinking highlights the importance of holism, worldview, boundary determinations,

synthesis, positive and negative feedback, balancing and reinforcing behaviour, relationship between systems structure and behaviour, generic behaviours that replicate across organisational processes and the distinction between short term and long term impacts. Complexity theory complements the perspectives of systems thinking by introducing the notions of nonlinear dynamics, fitness landscapes, co-evolution and co-creation, self-organising behaviour, as well as accentuating the phenomenon of emergence in organisations characterised by social complexity.

Collectively these perspectives enrich the intellectual armour that may be brought to bear on knowledge management by professionals, researchers and practitioners. This call on systems thinking and complexity theory is a way of reflecting how the plurality of discourses on knowledge may be translated into a more pluralistic discourse on knowledge management itself. The contribution of this chapter is an attempt to strengthen the impact of the epistemology of action (Assudani, 2005; Cook & Brown, 1999) and that of a social-process perspective of knowledge (Chiva & Alegre, 2005) on knowledge management.

The shift in focus based on systems thinking and complexity theory results in conceptualising the organisation as a complex adaptive system. Within such a conceptualisation, one refers to knowledge ecologies that are dynamic, self-organising and adaptive. This has radical implications for both strategy and knowledge management. Alignment between business and knowledge management strategies may not simply be designed and imposed, but may only be stimulated, through managing organisational context and interactions between actors within and outside an organisation. We may therefore refer to business and knowledge strategies as undergoing a process of co-evolution.

Finally, the chapter draws on these theoretical approaches and assumptions and their implications to show how they require a change in managerial orientations. This is a very practical matter that offers guidelines to managers on how to proceed in crafting both organisational and knowledge management strategy in a synergistic way such that knowledge management becomes a deep and enduring organisational intervention, rather than just a management fad. The title of this chapter refers to systemic change. This is exemplified in the quotation by Meadows and Robinson (2002) at the start of the chapter. Systemic change requires something more fundamental than just "marginal tinkering". It requires a fundamental change in the system's structure. When I refer to systemic change in KM, it is directed at two levels. The first is directed at KM which needs fundamental change at a systemic level as a field itself. The KM field as a system includes scholars, professionals, academic publishing outlets, boards of journals that publish on KM, consultants and practitioners and the relationships between them. It also includes the process and content of KM. If KM is to fulfill its promise, it has to shift from marginal tinkering of this system to a change in the structure of the system itself. Since the KM system as identified here is a human activity system that is socially constructed, one way of changing the structure of the system is to change the *assumptions* that underlie such a system. The second level at which I am referring to systemic change in KM is the application of KM within organisations and firms that involves a change within the organisation as a system, such that it is an enduring intervention, as opposed to a superficial change based on "marginal tinkering".

The objectives of this chapter are to:

• Indicate that despite multiple discourses on knowledge there is a dominant discourse when it is translated to KM
• Critique existing approaches to KM that are based on this dominant discourse
• Present key concepts from systems thinking and complexity theory
• Show how systems thinking and complexity theory enable us to conceptualise organisations as complex adaptive systems (CAS)
• Present the notion of knowledge ecologies embedded with CAS
• Show how CAS and knowledge ecologies offer us a more radical view of KM
• Consider their implications for organisational practice

BACKGROUND

Knowledge management is considered to be important for organisational success in the contemporary world, as knowledge is now accepted as a critical resource. Scholars and practitioners argue that competitive advantage relies primarily on knowledge based resources especially if they are not easily imitated (Nielson, 2005). This goes to the heart of the resource based view (RBV) of the firm (Eisenhardt & Martin, 2000). Thomas, Sussman, and Henderson (2001) note that much of the dialogue in strategic management revolves around the theme that performance differences across organisations may be attributed to asymmetries in knowledge. Knowledge may be exploited to acquire economic rents and to achieve competitive advantage, hence the need for the implementation of knowledge management. However, knowledge is multifaceted and is a complex phenomenon (Spender, 2005). This is evident from the multiple, sometimes overlapping, discourses about knowledge together with a variety of classifications and taxonomies. In this section, I summarise some of the salient issues and debates arising from these.

There has been much debate based on multiple, tenable philosophical positions on knowledge. These have not been resolved. The debate revolves around the interplay between ontology and epistemology, and hence the relationship between reality and knowledge of that reality. Depending on one's philosophical standpoint, one's view of knowledge will be different (Assudani, 2005). For example Spender (1996, p. 47) shows that a positivist theory of knowledge holds that "universal knowledge, true at all times and in all places is the highest grade of knowledge". Alternatively a social constructionist perspective will posit that knowledge is transitory, subjective, changes in time and space, based on interpretation of the human knower and embedded in the context in which the interpretation is occurring. The implications for KM are very different depending on the philosophical stance on which it is based.

Knowledge as a factor of production (Earl, 2001; Spender, 1996) is a discourse that has to some extent propeled KM. For much of the twentieth century, the primary input factors of production were considered to be land, machines, labour, and capital. In the early industrial era, labour referred primarily to physical or manual labour, but over time with the rise of the bureaucratic organisation, the focus shifted to include intellectual labour as managerial and professional skills became more important. However, it became increasingly clear that knowledge ought to be considered an input factor in its own right. Indeed knowledge may be considered a superior factor of production, as it determines how the other factors of production may be managed, configured, and coordinated (Zack, 1999).

A complementary but parallel development in the theory of organisation was that of the resource based view of the firm (Eisenhardt & Martin, 2000;

Teece, 2000; Zack, 1999). The RBV approach argues that sustainable competitive advantage in product and service markets arises as a result of the underlying resources that give rise to the products and services. These underlying resources will be a source of sustained economic rents if they are relatively immobile, rare, and inimitable. The resource based view is then one small step away from a focus on intellectual resources, competencies, and capabilities towards what may be termed a knowledge-based view of the firm.

One aspect of the organisational learning discourse focuses on the cognizing entity. If the individual is considered "logically and temporally" (Spender, 1996) prior to the group, then the act of cognizing is considered to be an individual one. In this sense, it is only the individual that learns. Organisational learning then only exists to the extent that individuals make their knowledge available to others through a process of sharing, and organisational learning becomes the overlap of what individuals know. Alternatively, if the individual is not logically and temporally prior to the group, there is no reason to accept why a group, collective, or the entire organisation cannot be a cognising entity in its own right. At minimum, we may accept that all new learning by individuals occurs within a social context that shapes what cues from the environment the individual pays attention to, and hence what new experiences the individual engages in and what the individual learns. As a result, the organisational context and perhaps organisational culture impacts learning even if the individual is the cognising unit.

The collective therefore at least shapes the learning that occurs within organisations. The importance of context and organisational culture brings in an additional dimension, that of identity. The identity of an individual is mediated, if not largely determined, by the context in which he or she is immersed. As such, the relationship between knowledge and identity also becomes important. Spender has argued persuasively that "both individuals and collectives have knowledge based identities" and that "it is not easy to determine which is logically and temporally prior" (Spender, 1996, p. 53). This discussion then brings us into the realm of a social perspective of learning which "implies that individuals are social beings who together construct an understanding of what they have around them, and learn from social interaction within social systems as organisations" (Chiva & Alegre, 2005). Since communities of practice engage in this kind of social learning embedded in practice, the literature associated with communities of practice may be considered part of this knowledge discourse (Wenger, McDermott, & Snyder, 2002; Wenger, 1998).

We may also consider the discourse that differentiates between alternate types of knowledge as opposed to making a distinction between knowledge and other factors of production, or between different philosophical views of knowledge. As a result this discourse readily lends itself to the construction of various knowledge typologies and classification schemes. The one that stands out prominently is the differentiation between explicit and tacit knowledge. Other classifications, for example, distinguish between procedural and declarative knowledge. The relationship between data, information, and knowledge may also be considered part of this discourse (Alavi & Leidner, 2001).

Perhaps the discourse about knowledge that is the most contentious is that about distinguishing between knowledge as an object, asset, stock, resource, or commodity and that of knowledge as a flow or as a process. When knowledge is an object, then it is reified and lends itself to be captured, codified, manipulated, and transferred. Alternatively, if knowledge is considered a process, it is no longer static and objectified. Rather it becomes a dynamic phenomenon. I shall show later in this chapter that if KM is to become enduring, there needs to be more emphasis on knowledge as a process. Another way to characterise this distinction is that of the *epistemology of possession* vs. the *epistemology of action* proposed by Cook and Brown (1999). They pick up on the

distinction between tacit knowledge and explicit knowledge on the one hand, and the distinction between individual and group knowledge on the other hand, and assert that these give rise to four distinct forms of knowledge each equal to the others. They class all four of these under an epistemology of possession, and assert that in addition to this, there is a need for a parallel epistemology of practice where ways of knowing become the focus. They contend that knowledge and knowing should not be seen as competing, but as complementary and mutually enabling. They further contend that the interplay of knowledge and knowing is a potentially generative phenomenon, where new knowledge and knowing arises in the use of knowledge as a tool of knowing within situated interaction within the social and physical world.

It should be clear from the above discussion that the literature on knowledge is diverse with multiple, overlapping discourses. It further shows that knowledge is a complex phenomenon. This is laudable. Unfortunately pluralism is lost somewhat in the resulting discourse on knowledge management, as the dominant discourse on KM is one that is based on the cognitive-possession perspective. The major exception to this is KM based on communities of practice which tends to be based on a social-process perspective, as it is related to social learning out of situated action embedded in practice. The dominant discourse on KM is based on the epistemology of possession and this is what I refer to as first order KM. It is a discourse that *reduces* the complexities of knowledge into a more objectified notion. This is exemplified by the following:

The reification of knowledge has grown more overt with the "objectified transferable commodity" envisaged by the **knowledge management approach,** *which treats knowledge as practically synonymous with information created, disseminated, and embedded in products, services, and systems.* (Gherardi, 2000, p. 213, emphases added)

In order to consider this form of reductionism, we may consider the knowledge perspectives and their implications by Alavi and Leidner (2001), who identify the various perspectives of knowledge as: (1) knowledge vis-à-vis data and information, (2) a state of mind, (3) an object, (4) a process, (5) access to information, and (6) capability. Despite this diversity of knowledge perspectives that seem to reflect the multiple discourses on knowledge, a closer examination of their implications for knowledge management show that they reduce to the cognitive-possession perspective. The set of implications for four of their six perspectives of knowledge all reduce to a focus on provision, access, retrieval, or exposing individuals to information. This includes their perspective of knowledge as a process. Their interpretation of knowledge as process is about a process of creation, sharing, and distributing knowledge. Despite an attempted distinction between knowledge as a stock and knowledge as a flow, their implications reduce to knowledge as an object where the focus is on the building up of a stock of knowledge while that of knowledge as a flow is more about movement or transfer of the objects of knowledge. Their perspective of knowledge as process is reduced to the transfer of a commodity. This is very different from knowledge as process as a dynamic phenomenon with a focus on the activity of *knowing* that was accentuated in the knowledge discourses referred to earlier.

Assudani (2005) draws on a diverse set of literature in demonstrating the plurality of perspectives and multiple discourses on knowledge and also makes reference to the epistemology of possession and the epistemology of action. She acknowledges the epistemology of action as one where knowledge is seen as a dynamic process. In her proposed framework, she refers to "knowledge of", "knowledge as process", and "knowledge from". She categorises both "knowledge of" and "knowledge from" under the epistemology of possession and "knowledge as a process" under

the epistemology of action. "Knowledge of" is in the sense of knowledge as an input factor. "Knowledge from" is the outcome in the form of innovation and organisational learning. However, in consideration of "knowledge as a process" in her framework, it becomes one of leveraging resources and transferring knowledge. A careful consideration shows that the notion of knowledge as process in her framework reduces to one of an organisational process of knowledge transfer. This is a very distinct notion from that of knowledge as process to mean a focus on the situated activity of *knowing*. The latter is understanding knowledge as a dynamic phenomenon, while her version is one of a transfer process and that of leveraging resources. An organisational process of knowledge transfer in this sense ultimately reduces to a reification of knowledge, where knowledge is an object, and knowledge transfers in the same way a commodity transfers. The point is that Asssudani, while acknowledging knowledge as a process distinct from knowledge as a stock and acknowledging the importance of the social process perspective reduces it in her framework into a cognitive-possession perspective. Despite venturing into the messiness and complexity of the multiple perspectives of knowledge, her framework gets co-opted into the dominant KM discourse, that of the epistemology of possession.

A similar argument may be made in relation to the taxonomy of schools of knowledge management proposed by Earl (2001). The four schools that are labeled under technocratic and economic are clearly based on a cognitive-possession perspective. A brave attempt is made in moving to a social process perspective in the three schools that are labeled behavioral. However, a close examination of the attributes under each of the schools reveals that they are primarily based on an epistemology of possession. The exception may be Earl's organisational school which tends to be akin to a community of practice approach. Once again, the discourse on KM does not reflect the pluralistic discourses on knowledge. Rather it gets co-opted into the dominant discourse on KM, that is, the epistemology of possession.

Conventional approaches to KM that arise out of this dominant discourse may be termed first order knowledge management. They are based on the following set of related assumptions:

- Knowledge is reified.
- Knowledge is useful when it is objective and certain. Spender (1996), presenting a thorough critique of this view, underlines how much organisational theorising is constrained to such a positivist theory of knowledge.
- Distinction between tacit and explicit knowledge (Nonaka & Takeuchi, 1995).
- Knowledge may be managed through KM.
- Knowledge identification is a search process.
- Knowledge construction is a process of configuration.
- KM comprises knowledge processes such as identification, generation, codification, and transfer (Alavi & Leidner, 2001).
- Business strategy may be formulated and implemented. This is a fundamental assumption across all strategic choice approaches to strategy and, at a minimum, will include the design, planning, positioning, and cultural schools of strategy (Mintzberg, Ahlstrand & Lampel, 1998).
- KM strategy may be formulated and implemented (Hansen, Nohria & Tierney, 1999; Zack, 1999).
- KM strategy must be aligned to the business strategy (Zack, 1999).

The last three assumptions above are typified and are clearly evident in the framework for formulating a knowledge management strategy offered by Earl (2001).

Knowledge is considered a "thing"; in other words, it is reified. We refer to knowledge as a critical resource, intellectual asset, or strategic asset (Teece, 2000). A common view that is presented is that of a hierarchical relationship between data, information, knowledge, and wisdom as articulated in the knowledge pyramid. A reification of knowledge renders it amenable to knowledge management, because it enables us to bound it, classify it, control it, and thereby manage it. It seems to be accepted as almost axiomatic within first order KM that knowledge may either be classified as tacit or explicit. This distinction is drawn from Polanyi and was popularised by Nonaka and Takeuchi (1995) who examined the relationships between explicit and tacit knowledge. They mapped them as dimensions on a set of axes to generate their knowledge spiral model. The key components of KM are a number of organisational processes related to knowledge. The knowledge spiral gives rise to four of these processes, namely socialisation (tacit-to-tacit), externalisation (tacit-to-explicit), combination (explicit-to-explicit), and internalisation (explicit-to-tacit). Alternatively, a slightly different set of knowledge-related processes may be considered. These comprise the identification, generation, capture, codification, and transfer of knowledge.

The knowledge generation process assumes that human actors generate new knowledge from existing stocks of knowledge, and as such, KM must focus on creating the conditions for knowledge generation to occur. Knowledge generation is dependent on first identifying existing knowledge. If knowledge is reified, then the knowledge generation process is a matter of searching for knowledge through a process of identification and then reusing existing knowledge as building blocks to construct new knowledge. The issue then becomes defining what the search space is and putting into place mechanisms for optimising the search. The search space is related to internal and external knowledge search. The internal search space may defined as a map of all existing knowledge residing within the organisation. It may be in the form of knowledge held by individuals (either tacit or explicit), or in the form of knowledge embodied in organisational blueprints, manuals of best practice, policies, procedures, and organisational practices. The latter is sometimes referred to as congealed knowledge. The external search space is somewhat more open ended, but may be described as that space which encompasses knowledge that resides outside the organisation, that could be used for organisational benefit. Some of the managerial prescriptions focused on the external search space will include benchmarking and customer relationship management (CRM), especially the form of CRM that seeks to detect patterns of customer behaviour and needs, by the data mining of extensive customer and public information.

The basic mechanisms of knowledge generation, whether based on internal or external search, are essentially a process of configuration, or perhaps more accurately reconfiguration. It is a new configuration of building blocks of existing knowledge either internal or external that may be regarded as new knowledge. It must be noted that these approaches rely on an assumption of knowledge as valuable only if it has connotations of certainty, objectivity, and codifiability. The importance of tacit knowledge is only recognised tangentially when it may be converted to a form that is manageable and controllable.

The process of knowledge codification takes existing knowledge and codifies it in a form that is amenable for transfer and use by others. The KM task here becomes one of identifying appropriate formats, conventions, and media for codifying knowledge. Once the knowledge is codified, we require a means for facilitating knowledge transfer. The underlying idea is that the codified knowledge is an asset that can be used to create value, and hence must be made accessible and transferred to those within the organisation that can apply (exploit) it for value creation. This leads to the next knowledge management task of instituting mechanisms for widespread knowledge transfer. The focus here is on technology based

storage and search solutions in the form of databases, knowledge stores, directories of experts, and best practices.

Ultimately, first order KM relies on knowledge processes such as knowledge identification, generation (or more accurately configuration), codification, capture, and transfer in order to develop human and social capital, as these are considered as important in facilitating productive activity (Lovas & Ghoshal, 2000). While the underlying notions of human and social capital are valuable because they represent the potentiality for new knowledge, capabilities and organisational novelty, it is unfortunate that the term *capital* is used. It has connotations of economic or financial capital, and as a result the focus shifts to the idea of a stock of capital that may be accumulated. This downplays the notion of ever changing relationships and hence an underlying dynamism that relates to the potentiality hidden behind human and social capital. Furthermore, the relationship with economic capital has the connotation of a stock that may be depleted with use, whereas it is commonly accepted that knowledge may actually appreciate with use. The feedback mechanisms that relate to economic and financial capital and those related to knowledge creation are very different and the dynamic relationships are equally different. The focus on human and social capital has resulted in a preoccupation with accounting type measures for human and social capital. As a result social capital is reduced to ideas about customer capital, investor capital, and employee capital. It loses its richness, especially related to issues such as trust embedded in social relationships.

The discussion of KM thus far relates mainly to the KM process but provides little insight into the KM content. How do managers, executives, and practitioners define what the appropriate knowledge that has to be generated is and what knowledge must be made available for widespread transfer? The response of first order KM to this question is that the organisation requires a KM strategy that will encompass both process and content elements. The required KM content will in turn depend on the business strategy. We therefore need to turn our attention to business strategy. Conventional approaches to strategy are primarily based on what may be termed strategic choice perspectives (Child, 1972; Stacey, 2003). This means that decision makers and executives may analyse the external environment, and then choose and design an appropriate strategy that will yield organisational success in such an environment. A strategic choice approach dictates that an organisation's KM strategy becomes one element of the overall business strategy, and there has to be alignment between the KM strategy and the business strategy (Earl, 2001; Hansen, Nohrie, & Tierney, 1999; Zack, 1999). The operative words in this perspective are *fit* and *alignment*. The organisation strategy or business strategy must have the relevant *fit* with the environment, and the knowledge strategy must *align* with the business strategy.

First order KM and its relation to business strategy as articulated in the preceding paragraphs has become accepted wisdom and is based on a number of assumptions that have not been questioned critically. It leads to an understanding of knowledge that is very static, and this is one of the reasons that KM faces the danger of becoming a management fad. Nielson (2005) examines KM by considering how the strategic management literature is divided into mainly the content and process streams of theoretical approaches. He highlights that the content approach may be criticised as "it adopts a static approach, regards competition as a zero-sum game, and neglects the context within which, and the processes whereby strategies are generated, selected and implemented" (p. 2). He goes on to highlight that the process stream of literature, in turn, "uses a rather static approach to the management of knowledge in network relationships in that it assumes knowledge to be universal, objective, transferable (when coded) and controllable in general" (p. 2), whereas knowledge is in fact dynamic and subjective.

In the next section, I examine the nature of management fads to provide support for the contention that first order KM is based on assumptions that are likely to reduce KM to a management fad. Thereafter, I proceed to draw on systems thinking and complexity theory to show how these theoretical approaches offer us a possibility to reconceptualise KM differently, such that it may lead to systemic change in a more enduring way.

FIRST ORDER KNOWLEDGE MANAGEMENT AS A MANAGEMENT FAD

If we are to understand why KM may be reduced to a management fad, it will be instructive to analyse what a management fad is. The dictionary (WordWeb 1.63, 2001) defines a fad as "an interest followed with exaggerated zeal". It is associated with a craze and is cult-like. The notion of cult should alert us to the dangers inherent in fads. Sterman (2002) states that "a fad, by definition, involves the temporary adoption of a new idea or product, followed by its abandonment" (p. 339). A management fad therefore constitutes an idea, model, concept, or methodology which generates high interest amongst practitioners, academics, and consultants that is adopted with an exaggerated zeal that feeds on itself, through word of mouth, herding behaviour, and bandwagon effects. It is fueled by hype about what it can achieve and about its benefits. The management fad would therefore typically have an extended "honeymoon period" as the phenomenon of interest grows exponentially, but this is followed by a rapid decline via a downward spiral as it unravels when it does not fulfill its promise, causes disillusionment, and is abandoned. We could therefore identify the life cycle of a fad as comprised typical overshoot and collapse behaviour. Quality circles, management by objectives (MBO), total quality management (TQM), business process re-engineering, and perhaps the balanced scorecard may be cited as examples of management approaches that have become management fads.

Sometimes the idea or concept is of merit, but disillusionment occurs because of a variety of effects not directly linked to the value of the concept itself. This may include incorrect application of the concept, extending it beyond what it is designed to achieve, making a gross simplification of the phenomenon that is embodied in the concept, or the concept is merely over-exploited for commercial purposes by those who jump on the bandwagon of its popularity. In this way, it is stripped of its richness and complexity rendering it impotent in relation to its promise. I suggest that first order KM makes a gross oversimplification by way of being wedded to an epistemology of possession. It is therefore subject to such devaluation, for some of these reasons, and especially because it has stripped away the richness and complexity of knowledge. As a result, although KM has enormous potential, it may be reduced to just another management fad unless there is a shift in our assumptions about the nature of knowledge, KM, strategy, and a change in managerial orientations in practice.

A hint about KM becoming a fad is provided in Nielson (2005) where he states, "Knowledge management has become somewhat of a buzzword and the term is used extensively in the business literature" (p. 1). As Spender (2005) highlights:

The bulk of the managerial excitement, and the core of the more accessible KM literature, approaches it as better identification and management of the organization's "knowledge assets" where that term implies some non-traditional type of resource .... customer and supplier relations, and goodwill, can be similarly considered. In this way KM seeks to extend our traditional notions of decision-making about the acquisition and allocation of tangible assets to cover intangible assets as well. The implication is that organizations contain or possess under-considered assets which may be strategically important, especially

if they are the source of sustainable economic rents. (p. 102)

He then goes on to speak of KM's radical possibility where he argues that "our theory of managing and of the firm/organization may need to go beyond the limits that its present certainty and rationality-oriented axioms allow" (p. 103).

In order for KM to fulfill its real promise and radical potential, and to contribute as an enduring organisational intervention, a more critical review is required of the assumptions that underpin first order KM. If knowledge is a thing, then it can be captured, codified, and transmitted. I argue against this reification of knowledge and assert that we have to approach knowledge as a much more dynamic phenomenon, with the focus shifting from knowledge to the act of *knowing* itself. This is consistent with the social-process view of knowledge. Knowledge is only generated in the act of knowing; everything else is information. In other words there is the perpetual potentiality for knowledge generation, but this is only transformed into actuality when information comes into contact with the human intellect. This happens in the act of knowing in the instant when there is sensemaking and interpretation. Maitlis (2005) defines sensemaking as "a process of social construction in which individuals attempt to interpret and explain sets of cues from their environments. This happens through the production of 'accounts'—discursive constructions of reality that interpret or explain—or through the activation of existing accounts" (p. 21).

This is taken from the point of view of a single act of knowing. In reality, human actors are constantly engaged in thought, and hence are engaged in sensemaking and interpretation at every instant, so knowledge is being regenerated afresh at every instant. This phenomenon of constant thought and action means that there is perpetual regenerating of knowledge. If we believe that knowledge is a thing, we lose sight of this dynamic phenomenon of the knower that is creating the knowledge at every instant. This may appear to be a semantic distinction of little theoretical or practical value. However the distinction is very significant, as it leads us to two very different views of KM. The most common is that of knowledge becoming reified and a *de facto* static phenomenon, and the second a much more dynamic view of knowing. We have already considered the former in the background of this chapter. The latter requires an ecological view of knowledge. A second order KM requires a philosophical approach in considering the dynamic interplay between knowledge and the knower and hence the epistemological considerations. In addition, more attention needs to be paid to the social interactions between actors since "knowledge is socially constructed; it is about ideas and meanings that have evolved through social interaction and communication" (Hearn, Rooney, & Mandeville, 2003, p. 239).

There is a large body of theoretical work in the area of organisational science that supports such epistemological considerations of knowledge as a dynamic phenomenon. I shall draw on two of these strands from organisational theory, namely systems thinking and complexity theory. These theoretical perspectives offer the opportunity to reconceptualise KM such that it is in conformity with an ecological view of knowledge, and indeed one that is embodied in a wider ecology, namely that of the social ecology of organising/organisations. This makes the relationship between KM and organisational or business strategy one that is very significant in the form of co-evolution.

TOWARDS SECOND ORDER KNOWLEDGE MANAGEMENT

Systems Thinking

Systems thinking (Jackson, 2003; Senge, 2006; Sterman, 2000; Vennix, 1999) is a well developed area of study spanning some 40 years and made up of a number of strands of effort. For the purposes of this chapter, I shall introduce only a few key concepts from systems thinking relevant to our purpose.

- **Holism:** Systems thinking is concerned about holism as opposed to reductionism. Reductionism is a way of understanding the world based on the understanding of the parts. If we decompose an entity into its constituent parts and analyse the parts we can get an understanding of the whole, by summing up our understanding of the parts. By contrast, systems thinking argues that we lose something when we decompose a system into its constituent parts. This is based on the fact that relationships and interactions between parts are of crucial importance to the system. We may refer to the position that by decomposing and analysing a system into parts we can understand the system as the *fallacy of analysis.*

- **Relationships:** In systems thinking, relationships and interactions are of critical importance. If we wish to understand a system, then we need to understand patterns of relationships. This calls on the skills of synthesis to counter the *fallacy of analysis.*

- **Boundary:** A distinction is made between a system and its environment. This raises the question of system boundaries that separate the system from its environment. Boundary considerations are of enormous significance in systems thinking. If the boundary of a system changes, the system itself changes. Wostenholme (2003) states that "boundaries are the one facet of organisations that are perhaps changed more often than any other" (p. 9).

- **Feedback:** A fundamental principle of a systems approach is that the system is comprised of multiple feedback loops that interact with each other. This is the source of the system's dynamic behaviour. We may distinguish between positive and negative feedback loops. A positive feedback loop is one where a change in the value of a variable feeds back and cascades throughout the system such that it causes a further change of that variable in the same direction. As such, a positive feedback loop is also a reinforcing loop. In other words, a positive feedback loop generates reinforcing behaviour. This is one source of turbulence as a system propelled by positive feedback could lead to exponential or explosive growth. This is what is commonly manifested as vicious or virtuous cycles. A negative feedback loop is one where a change in a value of a variable feeds back such that it causes the variable to change in the opposite direction. This is balancing feedback, as it tends to balance the initial change. A negative feedback loop generates goal-seeking behaviour.

- **Structure drives behaviour:** The structure of the system is embodied in the feedback relationships of the underlying variables of the system. It is this deep structure of the system that gives rise to the system behaviour. The implications of this are that system behaviour is endogenously generated and not directly generated from the environment as such. Signals from the environment could trigger one or more feedback loops that stimulates the endogenous behaviour of the system, but the system behaviour is not exogenous.
- **Time delays:** The feedback effects are not always instantaneous as there will be a variety of time delays within the system. This is a source of oscillation of system behaviour as it will overshoot and undershoot the goal.
- **Emergence:** A system has emergent properties, which arise out of the interactions of the parts. Such properties are holistic in the sense that they are properties of the whole and not of the parts themselves. It is the relationships between the parts that determine the emergent properties of the system. Examples of emergent properties

are the properties of wetness in water or the temperature of a substance.
- **Generic behaviours:** There are common patterns of system behaviour that replicate themselves under a variety of systems contexts and situations. Such generic behaviours include exponential growth, asymptotic growth and decline, s-shaped growth, overshoot and collapse, and so on. As an example, s-shaped growth is common in population dynamics, the spread of epidemics, and the diffusion of innovations (Sterman, 2000). As a result of these generic behaviours, systems theorists have identified a set of systems archetypes which serve as templates to understand such common behaviour patterns (Senge, 2006; Wostenholme, 2003).

Complexity Theory

Complexity theory (Anderson, 1999; Chiles, Meyer & Hench, 2006; Cilliers, 1998; Kurtz & Snowden, 2003; Lewin & Volberda, 1999; Morel & Ramanujam, 1999; Stacey, 2003) is not a single theory but rather an ensemble of ideas, concepts, and metaphors drawn primarily from the physical and natural sciences that are considered to be applicable to many kinds of complex systems, including social systems. I shall begin by offering a general definition of a complex adaptive system:

A complex adaptive system (CAS) is a system comprised of heterogeneous agents that interact locally with each other based on local schema, such that the behaviour of the system arises as a result of feedback relationships between the agents, and the system evolves as the schemata of the agents adapt based on the feedback.

The actual nature of agents will depend on the kind of system under consideration. For example, in chemical systems, the agents may be molecules, while in the case of a colony of ants, the agents are the individual ants. In social systems, the agents are usually taken to be individual human beings or groups of human beings. There are exceptions I shall consider later. Since the agents are able to adapt their schemata and their behaviours based on feedback through their interactions with other agents, the system has an adaptive capability. The heterogeneity of agents is important as it accentuates the diversity and plurality that make up the richness of CAS, and is especially important when applying CAS to social systems. It is important to note that no agent can understand the whole system, nor does any single agent or small group of agents direct the behaviour of the system. The behaviour of the system emerges from the interaction of agents through multiple, nonlinear feedback relationships.

The characteristics of CAS are explored below:

- **Fitness landscapes:** Each of the agents acts according to its own schema which would amongst others embody its payoff functions and try to maximise its fitness. As a result, we may conceptualise agents as traversing an imaginary fitness landscape. A traversal up the landscape to a higher level would correspond to increasing the agent's fitness. Similarly, traversal downwards will decrease the agent's fitness. One strategy that could be adopted is an adaptive walk. An agent traverses one step in a particular direction. If the step leads upwards, then the agent takes the step to a higher fitness level. If the step would cause a decrease in fitness, it retraces the last step of the traversal. The consequence of an adaptive walk strategy is that the agent could be caught at local peaks and hence will not achieve maximum fitness. The fitness landscape represents the environment of the single agent traversing a static landscape. However, it gets more interesting because the fitness landscape is constantly being adjusted and shaped as other agents act according to their own schemata and fitness functions, and hence are changing the

environment for the first agent. As a result, the composite fitness landscape across which all agents are traversing is constantly being deformed. In this sense then, the landscape is shifting, hence the payoff functions for individual agents are shifting, and thereby their schemata are being updated. Thus we have a constantly heaving and deforming landscape. The agents are therefore co-evolving with the environment. This is co-evolution at a microlevel.

- **Co-evolution:** The complex adaptive system is also co-evolving at a macrolevel. In the same way that individual agents traverse a fitness landscape, we may conceive of the system itself interacting with other systems and hence co-evolving with the macro-environment.

- **Emergence:** We have already considered emergent properties of a system from a systems thinking perspective. For example, in an organisational context, culture is an emergent property of an organisational system. A complexity theory view accentuates the importance of emergence to the extent that we may say that it is not just the properties of the system, but the system itself that emerges from the interactions between agents as they co-evolve with each other and with the environment.

- **Self-organisation:** CAS have the ability to self-organise to various system states. They have the tendency to gravitate to a state of self-organised criticality (Anderson, 1999; Morel & Ramanujam, 1999). This is a state poised at the edge of chaos between static order and chaos. As a result, they achieve a state of dynamic equilibrium. This is in contrast with a systems thinking view where the preoccupation is with a system achieving homeostasis or balance with the environment. This state is what Stacey (2003) refers to as bounded instability, or what others term the edge of chaos (Beinhocker, 1999).

ORGANISATIONS AS COMPLEX ADAPTIVE SYSTEMS

By drawing on systems thinking and especially complexity theory, we may now conceptualise an organisation as a complex adaptive system. We have reviewed the primary characteristics of an organisation as a system, and that of organisation as CAS and therefore have a sense of what the implications for organisations are. Before we proceed to what this means for KM, we need to examine the nature of agents in CAS in more detail. Most scholars that apply CAS to organisations automatically equate agents to human individuals. Stacey (2003), by contrast, suggests that the agents are narrative themes that are part of organisational discourse in his complex responsive process view of organisations. Similarly, some have considered Dawkin's memes as the agents that replicate (Price, 2004). I have no objections to these possibilities but believe that there is still merit in considering individuals as the agents. However, a more nuanced view is required where individuals are included in the definition, but they are not exclusively so. Other forms of agents would include groups of individuals, teams, departments, and human artifacts, as defined by Maxfield (2003). Artifacts include physical artifacts such as products, tools, machinery, as well as knowledge based ones such as plans, blueprints, procedures, and organisational routines. As a consequence, agents co-evolve with other agents as well as artifacts. This offers much richness when we now want to apply complexity theory to KM, as it sets the basis for understanding knowledge ecologies within and across organisations.

A knowledge ecology is a dynamic system of heterogeneous agents that interact with each other according to their schemata. The schemata are inextricably linked to each agent's propensity for interpretation and sensemaking on an on-going basis. Since interpretation and sensemaking are related to knowing in action, every act of interpretation and every act of sensemaking is in effect an actor creating knowledge. There are therefore multiple cognitive feedback loops being generated which in turn refresh the schemata according to which agents then act. In addition, human actors are constantly using ideational and physical artifacts with which they interact. As a result, agents are co-evolving with other agents as well as with the artifacts. The artifacts embody the knowledge of agents.

A natural ecology is an interdependent system of species that co-exist with each other. In other words, an ecology consists of agents that compete and cooperate with each other. The mechanism of Darwinian evolution would apply in a knowledge ecology. This means that the mechanisms of variation, retention, and selection apply (Lewin & Volberda, 1999). In order to survive, agents strive to increase their fitness. Agents that do not achieve a threshold limit of fitness will be selected out. As a result, there is continuous variation amongst the agents. The variation amounts to changing the fitness landscape for the individual agent. In addition, there is the possibility of mutation in an ecology. If the mutation increases the agent fitness, it will be retained and will tend to survive longer. Conversely, if the mutation decreases the fitness, the result of that mutation will be selected out in future generations. The dynamics of competition and collaboration all contribute to variation and mutation. In the case of a knowledge ecology, we may consider that knowledge structures are the primary agents. So it is knowledge structures that survive, vary, mutate, and are subject to retention and selection. The organisation is a complex adaptive system, comprised of other complex adaptive systems. We have seen earlier that complex adaptive systems comprise of heterogeneous agents, where groups of agents or indeed some of the agents are themselves complex adaptive systems in their own right. We have also seen that complex adaptive systems are highly networked systems that embody other CAS either partially or in their entirety. Knowledge structures do not constitute knowledge *per se*, but knowledge structures may get adapted through human sensemaking and interpretation. We now have a more nuanced view of an organisation as a complex adaptive system. It comprises of agents that include human beings, knowledge structures, and artifacts. A knowledge ecology then is a CAS within the CAS that is the organisation as a whole. We know from both systems thinking and complexity theory that if the relationships of the parts change, then the emergent properties of the system change. Since a knowledge ecology is a dynamic, ever changing, effervescent system, the relationships are undergoing constant change, and as a result the organisation is undergoing constant change and flux (Tsoukas & Chia, 2002).

There is still a deeper level of complexity, since the schemata of human agents are inextricably linked with the knowledge structures, but do not equate to the knowledge structures themselves. The knowledge structures are shared between organisational actors and get shaped in the collective, while the schemata are individual constructs that are influenced by the knowledge structures, and also inform and shape the knowledge structures themselves. An agent acts according to its schema—in the act of acting, the agent is drawing on the knowledge structures and is engaging in thought as thought and action may not be separated. This idea of the duality of thinking and action is consistent with the epistemology of action referred to in the earlier part of the chapter (Cook & Brown, 1999) which is about knowing in situated action embedded in practice. This is made clear by Gherardi (2000): "Practice is both our production of the world and the result of the world…The important contribution of this tradition to practice-based theorizing is its methodological insight that practice is a system of activities in which knowing is not separated from doing." (p. 215). Therefore, second order KM recognises that "the use of knowledge may not be separated from its creation" (Nielson, 2005, p. 9). In this act of thought, knowledge is being generated afresh which changes the knowledge structure somewhat as it is shaped by the new

knowledge that was just generated. But we have seen that the schema may also be changed by the knowledge structure. So this is a highly nonlinear dynamic process that almost defies description. This is confounded by the inclusion of artifacts as agents, and the artifacts also have a relationship to the knowledge structures.

First order KM is based on a strategic choice view of business strategy as identified earlier in the chapter. It should be clear that such a view is very problematic if we consider the implications of systems thinking and complexity theory. The environment is far too complex for any one person (or small group of people) to fully understand. The variety of feedback loops have a number of unintended consequences and as a result will confound the details of any strategy which we may design. The environment itself is changing through our actions and through the processes of co-evolution. As a result, our organisation is traversing a constantly changing, deforming, heaving landscape. Our actions, as well as those of our competitors and other actors, are changing the fitness landscape. The concept of *fit* would only apply if we have a static landscape that we are traversing. The strategic choice approach to strategic analysis, development, and implementation is therefore an outdated and inappropriate approach to strategy. A more dynamic approach to strategy that is much more processual is required. Alignment between business and knowledge management strategies may therefore not simply be designed and imposed, but may only be stimulated through managing organisational context and the interactions between actors within an outside the organisation. We may therefore also refer to business and knowledge management strategies as undergoing a process of co-evolution.

Implications for Organisational Practice

Thus far, we have considered how a second order KM may be achieved based on an organisation as a CAS which includes knowledge ecologies as embedded CAS. This has been based on the theoretical implications of systems thinking and complexity theory. The question now arises about what this means for KM in practice, and what guidelines may be available to managers on how to proceed in crafting both business and KM strategy in a way that KM becomes a deep and enduring organisational intervention. The change in assumptions heralded earlier in this chapter requires a concomitant change in managerial orientations in the move from first to second order KM.

Managerial Orientations

The prevailing managerial orientations in first order KM are in the form of managerial certainty and control. It is assumed that managers are capable of becoming objective observers who can stand outside a system, understand the system and the environment, and can design and implement strategy and associated programmes to change the organisation to achieve its goals and objectives. In relation to KM, once the manager understands the business strategy that has been designed and needs to be implemented, he may be able to identify the knowledge needs of the organisation, map out existing knowledge structures, and design and implement an appropriate KM strategy that is aligned to the business strategy (Earl, 2001; Zack, 1999).

The often unstated managerial orientations may be listed as:

- The manager as external observer of the system.
- Human identity and agency is relatively fixed and predetermined.
- Goals are unambiguous and relatively constant and enduring.
- Goals may be formulated by senior management through strategic choice.
- Goals are conveyed to other organisational actors by way of the strategy.

- Lower level goals are formulated by aligning to the strategy.
- Goals are achieved by implementation of business strategy.
- KM strategy is derived from and must be aligned to the business strategy.
- KM goals are defined and achieved by implementation of the KM strategy.
- Since a KM strategy is designed to implement organisational change, there has to be a concomitant change management plan.
- The organisational culture has to be conducive to KM, and therefore the change management also involves changing organisational culture.
- The manager is a change agent who must be instrumental in changing organisational culture.
- Organisational culture change like the rest of KM is a matter of design and implementation.

It should now be clear from systems thinking that these managerial orientations are based on reductionism, where it is assumed that the organisational world may be reduced to its constituent parts, optimised and fitted together again to achieve desired outcomes. The managerial orientations do not take into account feedback effects sufficiently.

Second order KM requires a fundamental shift in these managerial orientations. We have seen from the definition of CAS that no single agent or small group of agents can stand outside the system and direct it. It is therefore not possible for the manager to be an external observer and direct the system (Stacey, 2003). In a dynamic organisational context, goals are never unambiguous, not always shared and are not immutable. Much of the richness of organisations is emergent and subject to self-organisation as opposed to being subject to managerial control and certainty. The view that a culture conducive to KM has to be implemented through culture change and other change management programmes do not stand up to scrutiny because organisational culture is an emergent phenomenon (Frank & Furbach, 1999). Organisational culture is based on a historical process that emerges through the interactions of agents within the system over a long period of time.

In an organisation as a CAS, human identity is constantly evolving and shaped. Weick, Sutcliffe, and Obstfeld (2005) note that "from the perspective of sensemaking, who we think we are (identity) as organisational actors shapes what we enact and how we interpret, which affects what outsiders think we are (image) and how they treat us, which stabilizes or destabilizes our identity" (p. 416).

As a result, managerial orientations must shift from a preoccupation with the ordered, rational, analytical, and the fixed towards a tolerance of ambiguity, subjectivity, flux, and the transient nature of organisational life. Weick, Sutcliffe, and Obstfeld (2005) further state that "students of sensemaking understand that the order in organisational life comes just as much from the subtle, the small, the relational, the oral, the particular and the momentary, as it does from the conspicuous, the large, the substantive, the written, the general and the sustained" (p. 410).

These ideas from sensemaking are consistent with a complex adaptive systems view of organisations and particularly that of a knowledge ecology. The fear that this will lead to disorder and chaos is not warranted. There is order, but it is a dynamic, emergent order as a result of self-organising processes within a complex adaptive system. Such an emergent order, where system boundaries are defined by the system itself and lead to an emergent form of strategy, is exemplified in the statement by Eden and Ackerman (2000) that "patterns they enact inevitably take the organization in one strategic direction rather than another. Organisations do not act randomly without purpose" (p. 12).

Now that we have considered the required managerial orientations in second order KM, we may consider what managers comfortable with these orientations can do to implement KM in practice. The ecological and CAS view implies that we may "implement" KM but the nature of implementation is very different from what we would expect. There is no formula, recipe, or easy prescriptions on how to implement KM. Rather we have to create the organisational conditions where knowledge ecologies can emerge and flourish. What are such conditions, and how does the manager create them? This is a difficult task and would require much research. However, existing ideas from organisation science may help us in this regard. In this chapter, I shall present one approach, based on strategic conversation. I would urge others to apply their minds to push the boundaries in order to develop other approaches.

Within a framework of organisations as CAS, knowledge ecologies and co-evolution between business and KM strategy, the strategic role shifts to one of shaping the context out of which a strategy emerges. The context is partially defined by the changing schemata of agents, and the knowledge strategy is in itself an emergent one in an ecological fashion. The best that we can do is to facilitate rich interconnections between agents, increase agent diversity, and provide an enabling context for sensemaking and interpretation. The ontology is one of a socially constructed reality (Smircich & Stubbart, 1985). We therefore have to encourage multiplicity and pluralism. An increase in the diversity of agents together with opportunities for rich interconnection between agents provides the context from which new knowledge generation possibilities exist. One of the mechanisms at our disposal is that of strategic conversation. Strategic conversation is defined by Van der Heijden (1998) as "the sum total of all exchanges formal and informal taking place between members of the organisation concerning aspects of the position of the organisation in its external environment, and how this can be changed from the inside out."

Although this definition of strategic conversation highlights the importance of interactions, it belies an overly rational, analytical approach to why the conversation is strategic. The focus of the position of the organisation in its external environment is reminiscent of the positioning school of strategy (Mintzberg, Ahlstrand, & Lampel, 1998) which is firmly a strategic choice approach. This definition of strategic conversation although a good starting point is somewhat incongruent with a knowledge ecology approach. I therefore offer the following definition of strategic conversation that draws on Van der Heijden but such that is in conformity with an ecological approach:

Strategic conversation is the sum total of all exchanges and interactions (which may be mediated by artifacts), both formal and informal, taking place between members of the organisation, and between members of the organisation and external actors that stimulate cognitive re-interpretations of their organisational world and its relation to the environment.

This definition shows a shift in emphasis from Van der Heijden's definition in a number of respects. First, it moves away from strategic choice and its overly rational and analytical dominance. This renders it useful in an organisational and knowledge ecology context. Second, it shows that strategic conversation is not limited to internal interactions and hence gives it more of a co-evolutionary flavour, because strategic re-orientations may often be a result of such co-evolution of the organisation and the environment. Third, it brings in co-evolution at a microlevel between agents but, more importantly, following Maxfield (2003), it draws in the significance of artifacts and how they mediate the strategic conversation. Fourth, the definition highlights the importance of cognitive re-interpretations of the agents (Maxfield, 2003). This is significant because this is what leads to

generative relationships and that is what makes it *strategic*. In addition, it is the act of cognitive re-interpretation that focuses on the importance of sensemaking and interpretation.

Strategic conversation recognises that "every reality presents itself as an inter-subjective world which is shared with others," and that "humans not only construct reality in their minds, their behaviour also causes the reality in their minds to become reality in their environment" (Vennix, 1999, pp. 382-387) and it therefore provides a concrete mechanism for actors to create their own strategically relevant social reality in an emergent, self-organising way.

One of the primary managerial tasks therefore becomes that of instituting practices for strategic conversation as I have defined it above. There are already numerous organisational practices that encourage both formal and informal interactions and exchanges between organisational members. However, these practices have to be adapted slightly, first by adopting the new managerial orientations, and second by ensuring that these exchanges are in conformity with the definition of strategic conversation, as well as that of organisation as CAS. In addition, there are opportunities for the creation of many new organisational practices that stimulate and contribute to strategic conversation. Some examples of organisational practices that may be applied to stimulate strategic conversation include scenario building, future search conferences, knowledge cafes, social network stimulation, metaphor analyses, the application of systems dynamics generic infrastructures, or systems archetypes and various modeling approaches such as group model building, and a variety of others. For more details on some of these, the reader may refer to Van der Heijden (1998), Ringland (2002), Schwartz (1998), Weisbord (1992), Senge, Kleiner, Roberts, Ross, and Smith (1994), Morgan (1997), Vennix (1996), Bodhanya (2005), and Senge (2006).

The call for a reliance on strategic conversation, which appears open-ended, raises questions about the role of planning, goal setting, and human agency and control. In addition, does it mean that the manager has little or no role, and that he is subject to the dictates of fate in the form of selection and variation, from a Darwinian perspective? A complex adaptive system view of organisation does not negate human agency or volition. Human agents must and do act within the ambit of the power and agency that they have. However, no agent may be an outside observer that can stand outside of the system, understand the system and the environment, and design a solution that can then be imposed on the system. The agent has full power to act within his agency, but he has no control on how the system will respond. The systemic response is through the actions of other agents, within and outside the system. The agent therefore has agency and volition, but may not determine the outcome of acting on that agency and volition. Does this mean that there is no control? No, there is still control, but the control comes from the system itself, not from a single human actor or small group of actors. There is control through the process of self-organisation. This may appear to be a bitter pill to swallow. As human actors and managers, we are in a sense deluded by the extent to which we think we are in control. It calls for increased humility on the part of all of us as human actors. In a systemic world, we control less than we think, because the effects of our actions are subject to many feedback loops and nonlinear responses that are outside our sphere of influence and control.

Does this mean that planning and goals setting are futile? No, once again, this is not the case, but it calls for humility in our plans and our expectations of what they can achieve. Our plans are merely artifacts, and to the extent that they contribute to co-evolution, they do have a valuable role. However, this may call into question our criteria for what the value of a plan is, and what constitutes a good or a bad plan.

In reviewing the implications of second order KM for practice, we may note that it calls for a radically different set of managerial orientations, a different understanding of what constitutes strategy, planning and goal setting, different roles for managers and executives, and the need for organisational practices that are consistent with a socially constructed reality based on sensemaking, which is in conformity with a CAS and ecological perspective of organisations. This is well articulated in the following by Anderson (1999):

The task of those responsible for the strategic direction of an organization is not to foresee the future or to implement enterprise-wide adaptation programs, because non-linear systems react to direction in ways that are difficult to predict or control. Rather, such managers establish and modify the direction and the boundaries within which effective, improvised, self organized solutions can evolve. They set constraints upon local actions, observe outcomes, and tune the system by altering the constraints, all the while raising or lowering the amount of energy injected into the dissipative structure they are managing. (p. 228)

The Future of KM

It is likely that KM will follow the typical pattern of a management fad, if it continues on its current trajectory. The reasons for this have been explored earlier but relate primarily to the fact that it is wed to an epistemology of possession and its associated assumptions which entails a preoccupation with strategic choice at the level of business strategy, the notion of fit between the firm and its environment through its business strategy, and the alignment between KM strategy and business strategy. If KM is to avoid this fate and to move towards systemic change, it needs a change in perspective to what may be termed second order KM. This perspective eschews the reification of knowledge and sees it as a dynamic phenomenon, better understood as evolving in knowledge ecologies that are complex adaptive systems embedded within a larger complex adaptive system which is the organisation itself. This is consistent with the social process perspective and an epistemology of action embedded in practice.

This chapter has provided but merely a starting point towards second order KM. There are opportunities for further cross-fertilisation between existing accounts of knowledge management based on communities of practice (Wenger, 1998), as the assumptions underpinning social practice are closer to an ecological view, and may be reframed according to a complex adaptive systems perspective.

Other opportunities for further research was only hinted at in this chapter in relation to sensemaking and interpretation. By combining sensemaking approaches, together with emergent forms of strategy, and a socially constructed reality, we may move away from business strategy as strategic choice to strategic enactment which provides a more robust framework for emergent forms of strategy (Bodhanya, 2005). This coupled with concepts from complexity theory, in turn provides a rich intellectual resource to better understand co-evolution within organisational contexts, at micro- and macro-levels as well as co-evolution between business strategy and knowledge management strategy from an emergent and self-organising systems perspective. As a result, the key themes identified in this book will in themselves be enriched, and may also need to be reconceptualised or should I say will need to co-evolve.

Finally, future efforts in KM will need to identify specific organisational practices that are consistent with second order KM, and especially organisational practices that stimulate strategic conversation.

CONCLUSION

Knowledge management is increasingly becoming regarded as crucial to an organisation's success. I have argued in this chapter that conventional approaches to KM, which I termed first order KM, are in the danger of being reduced to a management fad. If KM is to fulfill its radical potential, it requires something more fundamental than just "marginal tinkering", by way of a fundamental change in system structure (Meadows & Robinson, 2002). This is possible if KM draws more heavily on the plurality, diversity, and multiplicity of discourses on knowledge, especially if it encourages the social-process perspective and epistemology of action that implies a focus on *knowing* in situated action embedded in practice (Gherardi, 2000). This in turn will require a shift in our underlying assumptions about knowledge, KM, strategy, and organisational theory, coupled with a change in managerial orientations. It may be achieved if we reconceptualise KM by drawing on systems thinking and complexity where we consider an organisation as a complex adaptive system, within which there are knowledge ecologies, that are in turn complex adaptive systems. From such a perspective, knowledge is a dynamic phenomenon that is created afresh in every instant in an emergent co-evolutionary way. This perspective means that there are no easy approaches to KM, no recipes or formulae. It further implies that we have to let go of our assumptions of certainty and control, and to become tolerant of ambiguity and uncertainty. It does not mean that such a perspective leads to anarchy, chaos, or randomness. On the contrary, there is bounded behaviour by way of emergence and self-organisation. It is difficult to be prescriptive in managing knowledge ecologies but we can still influence the system and its boundaries as Anderson (1999) states: "rather than shaping the pattern that constitutes a strategy, managers shape the context within which it emerges" (p. 229).

Managers and practitioners may shy away from the approaches presented in this chapter with disdain because although it may appear to have theoretical relevance, there appears to be less practical guidance and hence leaves them at a loss on how to do KM. Yes, there is no silver bullet on how to do KM, but it does not mean that there is no practical guidance on how to proceed. A very powerful mechanism that was introduced in this chapter was that of strategic conversation. Managers and human actors in an organisation need to find ways of stimulating strategic conversation, which acts as a boundary setting mechanism, allows them to shape the context of the organisation, and to tune various organisational parameters that will contribute to organisational diversity, pluralism, and more spontaneous forms of creativity that offers enormous potential.

A framework based on CAS and knowledge ecologies may seem to limit managerial prerogative. This is not the case, but it does require letting go of control to the dictates of self-organisation and organisational emergence. While this may appear restrictive, on the contrary, it is very liberating, as it opens up entirely new possibilities, novelty, and innovation and therein lies the radical potential of second order KM, which ought to be exciting and exhilarating for KM practitioners and scholars alike.

FUTURE RESEARCH DIRECTIONS

This chapter has made but a small start in defining possibilities towards a second order knowledge management. It has introduced a number of concepts that though somewhat interdisciplinary have already found their way into organization science in a variety of ways. Each of these offers potential direction for further research, theoretical exploration as well as implications for practice. In this section, I sketch out what some of these possibilities may embrace.

The basic conceptual underpinnings of this chapter were that of systems thinking and complexity theory. Each one of these on there own offers rich possibilities for future exploration in relation to understanding knowledge as a dynamic phenomenon and in reflecting the plurality of dis-

courses of knowledge in re-conceptualised second order knowledge management. For example, there are a variety of other strands in systems thinking, not covered in this chapter, such as soft operational research (soft OR), soft systems approaches, the viable system model (VSM), and critical systems thinking and practice. Although these are generic in the sense that they are normally applied to bring about organisational improvement in the form of organisational intervention, they may be applied in a way that contributes specifically to knowledge management and the stimulating of knowledge ecologies.

Additional ideas from complexity theory may also be subject to further research in relation to knowing in situated action. For example, although this chapter introduced the concepts of emergence and self-organisation, their full potential has not yet been mapped out.

There is now a well-established literature on sensemaking in organisational contexts. There is little cross-pollination between sensemaking approaches and that of a CAS view of organisational life. Soft OR and soft systems approaches draw on multiple perspectives of and interpretation by individual actors. By bringing these perspectives together with that of sensemaking, there is an opportunity for extending our understanding of the social-process perspective of knowledge.

In discussing ecologies of knowledge, I introduced the relationship between knowledge structures and agent schemata. This is an area that requires much further development. What exactly is a knowledge structure? How does it form? How does an agent schema shape knowledge structures and *vice versa*? This relates to managerial and organisational cognition. In order to gain a better understanding of the dynamic nature of knowledge structures, we may draw on systems diagramming and cognitive mapping techniques. In addition, we may draw on dialogue mapping and associated software.

It was shown in this chapter that complex adaptive systems comprise of interacting heterogeneous agents that co-evolve with each other and with ideational and physical artifacts. A further conceptualisation of this is possible by relating this to concepts from structuration theory.

One of the difficulties of taking a CAS and knowledge ecologies view raised in the chapter is that of translating this into practical mechanisms for knowledge management. As was highlighted, it is not possible to offer formulae and recipes for KM, because of the dynamic approach focusing on knowing in situated action. I offered strategic conversation as one mechanism that managers and practitioners could apply. There is a need for much further work on developing novel approaches, mechanisms, and tools for managers and practitioners to be able to operate in the context of knowledge ecologies embedded within complex adaptive systems. These could extend and further develop the concept of strategic conversation as defined and presented in this chapter. Alternatively, it would be a useful endeavour to consider other mechanisms that may or may not be complementary to strategic conversation. For example, there is a body of research and practice referred to as whole systems change, which could be productively pursued to identify such mechanisms. This includes search conferences, future search, appreciative inquiry, and other forms of participatory large group processes. Other possibilities include the use of narrative and story-telling techniques within organisational settings.

Finally, it is important to note that given the nature of the phenomena under question, the research possibilities and opportunities addressed above would have to be based on a naturalistic inquiry paradigm. A positivist research agenda is unlikely to provide benefit, because by definition we are working with rich interactions, high levels of complexity, and interdependencies. In this type of context, it is not possible to isolate dependent and independent variables let alone define and operationalise them precisely. As such, the research agenda will in all likelihood draw on phenomenological case study approaches, action research, or grounded theory research.

ACKNOWLEDGMENT

The author wishes to thank the two anonymous reviewers for their challenging critique and for their suggestions to improve this chapter.

REFERENCES

Alavi, M., & Leidner, D.E. (2001). Review: Knowledge management and knowledge management systems: Conceptual foundations and research issues. *MIS Quarterly, 25*(1), 107-136.

Anderson, P. (1999). Complexity theory and organization science. *Organization Science, 10*(3), 216-232.

Assudani, R.H. (2005). Catching the chameleon: Understanding the elusive term "knowledge". *Journal of Knowledge Management, 9*(2), 31-44.

Beinhocker, E. (2000). On the origin of strategies. *The McKinsey Quarterly, 4*, 167-176.

Bodhanya, S.A. (2005, June). *Strategy making: Traversing complexity and turbulence.* Paper presented at the 7th International Conference on Foresight Management in Corporations and Public Organisations—New Visions for Sustainability, Helsinki, Finland.

Child, J. (1972). Organizational structure, environment and performance: The role of strategic choice. *Sociology, 6*, 1-22.

Chiles, T.H., Meyer, A.D., & Hench, T.J. (2004). Organizational emergence: The origin and transformation of Branson, Missouri's musical theaters. *Organization Science, 15*(5), 499-519.

Chiva, R., & Alegre, J. (2005). Organizational learning and organizational knowledge: Towards the integration of two approaches. *Management Learning, 36*(1), 49-68.

Cilliers, P. (1998). *Complexity and postmodernism*. London: Routledge.

Cook, S.D.N., & Brown, J.S. (1999). Bridging epistemologies: The generative dance between organizational knowledge and organizational knowing. *Organization Science, 10*(4), 381-400.

Earl, M. (2001). Knowledge management strategies: Toward a taxonomy. *Journal of Management Information Systems, 18*(1), 215-233.

Eden, C., & Ackermann, F. (2000). Mapping distinctive competencies: A systemic approach. *Journal of Operational Research Society, 51*, 12-20.

Eisenhardt, K.M., & Martin, J.A. (2000). Dynamic capabilities: What are they? *Strategic Management Journal, 21*, 1105-1121.

Frank, K.A., & Fahrbach, K. (1999). Organization culture as a complex system: Balance and information in models of influence and selection. *Organization Science, 10*(3), 253-277.

Gherardi, S. (2000). Practice based theorizing on learning and knowing in organizations. *Organization, 7*(2), 211-223.

Hansen, T.M., Nohria, N., & Tierney, T. (1999, March-April). What's your strategy for managing knowledge? *Harvard Business Review*, pp. 106-116.

Hearn, G., Rooney, D., & Mandeville, T. (2003). Phenomenological turbulence and innovation in knowledge systems. *Prometheus, 21*(2), 231-245.

Jackson, M.C. (2003). *Systems thinking: Creative holism for managers*. Chichester: John Wiley & Sons.

Kurtz, C.F., & Snowden, D.J. (2003). The new dynamics of strategy: Sense making in a complex and complicated world. *IBM Systems Journal, 24*(3), 462-483.

Lewin, A.Y., & Volberda, H.W. (1999). Prolegomena on coevolution: A framework for research on strategy and new organizational forms. *Organization Science, 10*(5), 519-534.

Lovas, B., & Ghoshal, S. (2000). Strategy as guided evolution. *Strategic Management Journal, 21*, 875-896.

Maitlis, S. (2005). The social processes of organizational sensemaking. *Academy of Management Journal, 48*(1), 21-49.

Maxfield, R.R. (2003). Complexity and organization management. In D.S. Alberts & T.J. Czerwinski (Eds.), *Complexity, global politics and national security*. Washington, DC: National Defence University. Retrieved May 15, 2007, from http://www.ndu.edu/inss/books/books%20-%201998/Complexity,%20Global%20Politics%20and%20Nat'l%20Sec%20-%20Sept%2098/index.html

Meadows, D.H., & Robinson, J.M. (2002). The electronic oracle: Computer models and social decisions. *System Dynamics Review, 18*(2), 271-308.

Mintzberg, H., Ahlstrand, B., & Lampel, J. (1998). *Strategy safari: The complete guide through the wilds of strategic management*. London: FT Prentice Hall.

Morel, B., & Ramanujam, R. (1999). Through the looking glass of complexity: The dynamics of organizations as adaptive and evolving systems. *Organization Science, 10*(3), 278-293.

Morgan, G. (1997). *Images of organization*. Thousand Oaks, CA: Sage Publications.

Nonaka, I., & Takeuchi, H. (1995). *The knowledge creating company: How Japanese companies create the dynamics of innovation*. New York: Oxford University Press.

Nielson, B.B. (2005). Strategic knowledge management research: Tracing the co-evolution of strategic management and knowledge management perspectives. *Competitiveness Review, 15*(1), 1-13.

Price, I. (2004). Complexity, complicatedness and complexity: A new science behind organizational intervention? *E:CO, 6*(1-2), 40-48.

Ringland, G. (2002). *Scenarios in business.* West Sussex: John Wiley & Sons.

Schwartz, P. (1998). *The art of the long view: Planning for the future in an uncertain world.* West Sussex: John Wiley & Sons.

Senge, P.M. (2006). *The fifth discipline: The art and practice of the learning organisation.* London: Random House.

Senge, P., Kleiner, A., Roberts, C., Ross, R., & Smith, B. (1994). *The fifth discipline fieldbook: Strategies and tools for building a learning organisation.* New York: Currency Doubleday.

Smircich, L., & Stubbart, C. (1985). Strategic management in an enacted world. *Academy of Management Review, 10*(4), 724-736.

Spender, J.C. (1996). Making knowledge the basis of a dynamic theory of the firm. *Strategic Management Journal, 17,* 45-62.

Spender, J.C. (2005). Review article: An essay of the state of knowledge management. *Prometheus, 1,* 101-116.

Stacey, R.D. (2003). *Strategic management and organisational dynamics: The challenge of complexity* (4th ed.). Harlow: Prentice-Hall.

Sterman, J.D. (2000). *Business dynamics: Systems thinking and modeling for a complex world.* London: William Heinemann.

Teece, D.J. (2000). Strategies for managing knowledge assets: The role of firm structure and industrial context. *Long Range Planning, 33,* 35-54.

Thomas, J.B., Sussman, S.W., & Henderson, J.C. (2004). Understanding "strategic learning": Linking organizational learning, knowledge management and sensemaking. *Organization Science, 12*(3), 331-345.

Tsoukas, H., & Chia, R. (2002). On organizational becoming: Rethinking organizational change. *Organization Science, 13*(5), 567-582.

Van der Heijden, K. (1998). *Scenarios: The art of strategic conversation.* Chichester: John Wiley & Sons.

Vennix, J.A.M. (1996). *Group model building: Facilitating team learning using system dynamics.* Chichester, UK: John Wiley & Sons.

Weick, K.E., Sutcliffe, K.M., & Obstfeld, D. (2005). Organizing and the process of sensemaking. *Organization Science, 16*(4), 409-421.

Weisbord, M.R. (1992). *Discovering common ground.* San Francisco: Berret-Koehler.

Wenger, E. (1998). *Communities of practice: Learning, meaning and identity.* Cambridge: Cambridge University Press.

Wenger, E. C., McDermott, R., & Snyder, W. M. (2002). *Cultivating communities of practice.* Boston: Harvard Business School

Wordweb 1.63. (2001). *Fad entry.* Retrieved from http://wordweb.info/

Wostenholme, E.F. (2003). Towards the definition and use of a core set of archetypal structures in system dynamics. *System Dynamics Review, 19*(1), 7-26.

Zack, M.H. (1999). Developing a knowledge strategy. *California Management Review, 41*(3), 125-145.

Additional Reading

Allen, P.M., Strathern, M., & Baldwin, J.S. (2006). Evolutionary drive: New understanding of change in socio-economic systems. *E:CO, 8*(2), 2-19.

Anderson, P., Meyer, A., Eisenhardt, K., Carley, K., & Pettigrew, A. (1999). Introduction to the special issue: applications of complexity theory to organization science. *Organization Science, 10*(3), 233-236.

Boje, D.M. (2001). *Narrative methods for organizational & communication research*. London: Sage.

Boulding, K.E. (2004). General systems theory: The skeleton of science. *E:CO, 6*(1-2), 127-139.

Charmaz, K. (2000). Grounded theory: Objectivist and constructivist methods. In N.K. Denzin & Y.S. Lincoln (Eds.), *Handbook of qualitative research* (2nd ed., pp. 509-535). Thousand Oaks, CA: Sage.

Cilliers, P. (2000). Knowledge, complexity and understanding. *Emergence, 2*(4), 7-13.

Conklin, J. (2006). *Dialogue mapping: Building shared understanding of wicked problems*. Chichester: Wiley.

Dagnino, G.B. (2004). Complex systems as key drivers for the emergence of a resource- and capability-based interorganizational network. *E:CO, 6*(1-2), 61-68.

Diaz, C.J.D. (2004). The political significance of small things. *E:CO, 6*(1-2), 49-54.

Dooley, K.J., & Van de Ven, A.H. (1999). Explaining complex organizational dynamics. *Organization Science, 10*(3), 358-372.

Eisenhardt, K.M. (1989). Building theories from case study research. *Academy of Management Review, 14*(4), 532-550.

Eoyang, G.H. (2004). The practitioner's landscape. *E:CO, 6*(1-2), 55-60.

Fitzgerald, L.A., & van Eijnatten, F.M. (2002). Reflections: Chaos in organizational change. *Journal of Organizational Change Management, 15*(4), 402-411.

Flood, R.L. (2006). The relationship of "systems thinking" to action research. In P. Reason & H. Bradbury (Eds.), *Handbook of action research* (Concise paperback ed., pp. 117-128). London: Sage.

Flyvbjerg, B. (2006). Five misunderstandings about case study research. *Qualitative Inquiry, 12*(2), 219-245.

Goulding, C. (1998). Grounded theory: the missing methodology on the interpretivist agenda. *Qualitative Market Research: An International Journal, 1*(1), 50-57.

Grandori, A., & Kogut, B. (2002). Dialogue on organization and knowledge. *Organization Science, 13*(3), 224-231.

Grinyer, P.H. (2000). A cognitive approach to group strategic decision taking: a discussion of evolved practice in the light of received research results. *Journal of the Operational Research Society, 51*, 21-35.

Hargadon, A., & Fanelli, A. (2002). Action and possibility: Reconciling dual perspectives of knowledge in organizations. *Organization Science, 13*(3), 290-302.

Jackson, M.C. (2000). *Systems approaches to management*. New York: Kluver.

Kernick, D.P. (2005). Facilitating resource decision making in public organizations drawing upon insights from complexity theory. *E:CO, 7*(1), 23-28.

Klein, J.T. (2004). Interdisciplinarity and complexity: an evolving relationship. *E:CO, 6*(1-2), 2-10.

Levy, D. (1994). Chaos theory and strategy: Theory, application and managerial implications. *Strategic Management Journal, 15*, 167-178.

Locke, K. (2001). *Grounded theory in management research*. London: Sage.

Martin, A.W. (2006). Large-group process as action research. In P. Reason & H. Bradbury (Eds.), *Handbook of action research* (Concise paperback ed., pp. 166-175). London: Sage.

Matthews, M.K., White, M.C., & Long, R.G. (1999). Why study the complexity sciences in the social sciences? *Human Relations, 52*(4).

McKelvey, B. (2004). Complexity science as order-creation science: New theory, new method. *E:CO, 6*(4), 2-27.

Mills, J., Bonner, A., & Francis, K. (2006). Adopting a constructivist approach to grounded theory: Implications for research design. *International Journal of Nursing Practice, 12*, 8-13.

Nickerson, J.A., & Zenger, T.R. (2004). A knowledge-based theory of the firm: The problem solving perspective. *Organization Science, 15*(6), 617-632.

Peltoniemie, M. (2006). Preliminary theoretical framework for the study of business ecosystems. *E:CO, 8*(1), 10-19.

Pidd, M. (2003). *Tools for thinking: Modelling in management science* (2nd ed.). Chichester: Wiley.

Rhodes, M.L., & MacKechnie, G. (2003). Understanding public service systems: Is there a role for complex adaptive systems theory? *Emergence, 5*(4), 57-85.

Simon, H.A. (1991). Bounded rationality and organizational learning. *Organization Science, 2*(1), 125-134.

Snowden, D., & Stanbridge, P. (2004). The landscape of management: Creating the context for understanding social complexity. *E:CO, 6*(1-2), 140-148.

Stengers, I. (2004). The challenge of complexity: Unfolding the ethics of science: In memorium Ilya Prigogine. *E:CO, 6*(1-2), 92-99.

Suddaby, R. (2006). From the editors: What grounded theory is not. *Academy of Management Journal, 49*(4), 633-642.

Walker, D., & Myrick, F. (2006). Grounded theory: An exploration of process and procedure. *Qualitative Health Research, 16*(4), 547-559.

Walsh, J.P. (1995). Managerial and organizational cognition: Notes from a trip down memory lane. *Organization Science, 6*(3), 280-321.

Walt, v. d. (2006). A framework for knowledge innovation. *E:CO, 8*(1), 21-29.

Warren, K. (2002). *Competitive strategy dynamics*. Chichester, UK: Wiley.

Warren, K. (2004). Why has feedback systems thinking struggled to influence strategy and policy formulation? Suggestive evidence, explanations and solutions. *Systems Research and Behavioral Science, 21*, 331-347.

Webb, C., Lettice, F., & Lemon, M. (2006). Facilitating learning and innovation in organizations using complexity science principles. *E:CO, 8*(1), 30-41.

Weick, K.E. (1991). The nontraditional quality of organizational learning. *Organization Science, 2*(1), 116-124.

Whitney, D., & Trosten-Bloom, A. (2003). *The power of appreciative inquiry*. San Francisco: Berret-Koehler.

Chapter II
Does Knowledge Management Improve Firm Performance?
The Effect of Knowledge Distinctive Competences

César Camisón Zornoza
Universitat Jaume I, Spain

Daniel Palacios Marqués
Universitat Jaume I, Spain

Fernando José Garrigós Simón
Universitat Jaume I, Spain

ABSTRACT

In the resource-based view (RBV) approach, the knowledge border rests on the understanding of the distinctive competences creation and recreation process. Moreover, in spite of the importance of knowledge assets, how knowledge is generated in organizations is still an unknown factor. This research studies the effect of introducing knowledge management programs in the development of knowledge distinctive competences, as well as their capability to create economic rents. In addition, we established a conceptual delimitation of knowledge management as a directive system through a set of principles and practices, which is a theoretical innovation in this research line. The theoretical relationships we propose are tested in an empirical study carried out in 222 firms from the Spanish biotechnology and telecommunication sectors.

INTRODUCTION

The study of the process of generation and re-generation of distinctive competences in the firm constitutes a relevant problem. Knowledge on organizational actions and decisions that allow for the development and renewal of the strategic assets portfolio in an organization still lacks a satisfactory structure (Zollo & Winter, 2002). While certain authors refer to the "knowledge-based economy", there is a gap in the knowledge about how knowledge is generated (Nonaka & Takeuchi, 1995). The aim of this research is to analyze how the introduction of knowledge management (KM) systems allows for the generation of distinctive competences based on knowledge assets, in order to create lasting abnormal results. Our interest lies in how KM might influence the acquisition and generation of competences and how it leads to economic rents being obtained. This problem is more closely related with the dynamic approaches of resource-based view (RBV) (Teece, Pisano & Shuen, 1997), which focuses on explaining how distinctive competences are created, developed, and accumulated.

In recent years, KM has aroused much interest in the field of management (Barnes, 2002; Davenport & Prusak, 2000; Mertins, Heisig, & Vorbeck, 2001; Mu-Yen & An-Pin, 2006; Nonaka & Takeuchi, 1995). Although knowledge is not a new concept, the increasing spread of theoretical works on KM is due to its significance to business, as well as to the development of the knowledge-based approach (KBA) (Grant, 1996a; Kogut & Zander, 1992; Nonaka, 1994; Nonaka & Takeuchi, 1995). KM has gained popularity as a consequence of the emergent need to incorporate the dynamics of changes to the information architecture and the business model, as well as to develop and encourage the growth of systems that are useful in adapting to a turbulent environment inherent to a knowledge-based economy (OCDE, 1996).

However, research into the possible effects of KM introduction on firm performance has been scarce and has many shortcomings (Davenport, 1999; DeCarolis & Deeds, 1999). Studies into KM and its effects have been mainly theoretical with little empirical evidence. The establishment of a direct causal relationship between KM and firm performance has a weak theoretical and empirical background (Alavi & Leidner, 2002; Real, Leal, & Roldan, 2006). As McEvily and Chakravarthy (2002) and Davenport (1999) point out, there is a lack of relevant contributions in the literature to justify the causal relationship between KM and firm performance and whether or not that relationship is mediated by other intermediate latent variables. Three specific problems make progress in the topic particularly difficult.

First, it is necessary to conceptualize KM as a base for the design of a measurement tool that includes all the essential dimensions needed to analyze the extent to which KM is implemented in the firm. To claim that knowledge competences are a result of the effective application of a KM system also seems a tautology. To avoid this risk, a suitable conceptualization of the two constructs involved in the relation, knowledge distinctive competences and KM, must be put forward. The recent literature (Alavi & Leidner, 2002; McEvily & Chakravarthy, 2002) recognizes the vulnerability of measurement indices and that it is essential to develop a metric to evaluate the benefits of KM systems. Alavi and Leidner (2002) show how none of the 109 leader organizations included in their research had introduced a formal cost-benefit analysis in their KM systems. We conceptualize KM as a management tool characterized by a set of principles and practices, whose aim is to create, disseminate, and benefit from knowledge.

A second question is the causal justification of the theoretical relationship between KM and firm performance. Dyer and McDonough (2001) conclude that four fundamental reasons exist for introducing KM in organizations: to capture and share best practices (77.7%), for training and learning (62.4%), to manage customer relations so as to improve customer satisfaction (58%), and to develop competitive intelligence (55.7%). Therefore, linking directly KM and firm performance may be erroneous, since KM activities do not necessarily imply direct improvements in firm performance. Consequently, we assume the existence of certain variables that mediate the relationship (Davenport, 1999; McEvily & Chakravarthy, 2002). Activities related to KM initiatives could include employees' capacities in tasks connected to knowledge, firm innovative competences, information technologies management systems, or organizational mechanisms to capture, deal with, store, and spread information and knowledge between all the members.

Since we have taken KBA and RBV as our theoretical background, we propose knowledge distinctive competences as the mediating variable, which constitute the foundation of the firm innovation capacity (Nonaka & Takeuchi, 1995; Teece et al., 1997). Research must be carried out into how the introduction of KM in an organization is able to create or improve the stock of knowledge-based distinctive competences. Particularly, we aim to clarify the relationship between KM and competences for the regeneration of strategic assets stock or innovation competences (Nonaka & Takeuchi, 1995; Teece et al., 1997). This problem requires an analysis of those theoretical frameworks to determine the characteristics and processes through which knowledge-based distinctive competences and economic rents are created. We conceptualize these competences as a set of abilities, skills, and cognitive features that the firm owns, and we enable research and development (R&D) management and the development of KM programs that distinguish the firm from its competitors.

An appropriate context in which to examine the effect of KM on the stock of organizational knowledge and its relationship with firm performance is presented by dynamic industries, where knowledge and technological innovation have become successful key factors. For this reason, we have used Spanish biotechnology and telecommunications industries for the empirical work.

This chapter is structured in three sections. The first section studies the three key problems mentioned above. We then explain the empirical design used in this research. Finally, we present our results and discuss their relevance to the knowledge accumulated.

THEORY AND HYPOTHESES

Knowledge-Based Distinctive Competences and Performance

In its initial phase, RBV developed a static analysis of the conditions of strategic assets (Barney, 1991). Models of imperfect factors markets that explain the equilibrium conditions ignore Schumpeterian competence and efforts by competitors to continuously improve, which erode the value of firm strategic assets. In this sense, this phase does not explain how competences are created, recreated, and accumulated. The second phase saw the development of dynamic approaches of RBV (Teece et al., 1997). The core idea of this approach is the interpretation of sustained competitive advantage from a competitive model based on disequilibrium. In this sense, the significant role of knowledge-based competences, able to create Schumpeterian shocks, is emphasized. These dynamic approaches focus more on processes than on assets, and specifically on the development process of new competences that allow competitive advantage to be renewed.

According to KBA, firms are heterogeneous organizations characterized by a unique knowledge base. Knowledge is generated, stored, and integrated in firms (Grant, 1996a; Kogut & Zander, 1992; McEvily & Chakravarthy, 2002; Nonaka & Takeuchi, 1995). A key postulate of KBA holds that the sustainable competitive advantage emanates from the possession of knowledge assets and the ability to combine them with other assets (DeCarolis & Deeds, 1999; Drucker, 1993; Grant, 1996a, b; Lei, Hitt & Bettis, 1996; Nonaka, 1994; Teece et al., 1997). In this sense, authors such as

Bollinger and Smith (2001), Teece et al. (1997), and Dierickx and Cool (1989) have suggested that the knowledge incrusted in the firm and the abilities and skills of its employees could be a distinctive competence for the firm, a source of sustained differentiation, and constitute the main source of competitiveness. The importance of knowledge as a key factor in creating competitive advantages is strengthened in knowledge intensive industries, where innovations are continuously developed (Alvensson, 2000; DeCarolis & Deeds, 1999).

Knowledge is not directly observable or measurable. When referring to this construct, we must therefore take into account its inferred capacities, which are observable. Knowledge is a rare and relevant intangible asset for the organization (Grant, 1996a, 1997). Furthermore, it is more inimitable when it is maintained tacit in the organization, and when it is developed by interacting with other organizational assets, thus acquiring social complexity (Nonaka, 1994; Zander & Kogut, 1995) and causal ambiguity (Dierickx & Cool, 1989). Knowledge distinctive competences are a key factor for long term heterogeneity in firms, due to their capacity to develop continuously new competences. Therefore, we can formulate the following hypothesis:

Hypothesis 1. There is a direct and positive relationship between knowledge-based distinctive competences and firm performance.

KNOWLEDGE MANAGEMENT AND KNOWLEDGE-BASED DISTINCTIVE COMPETENCES

Curiously, in spite of the theoretical importance of knowledge, it has been considered invisible (Zack, 1999). Its explicit management has not been considered. The recent literature and particularly KBA, argue that for knowledge to become a relevant strategic asset, the capacity to manage it must be stimulated (Grant, 1997, 1996a; Zack,

1999). KBA focuses on the usefulness of the KM systems for the creation, development, and application of knowledge that can have the conditions of strategic asset (Grant, 1996b; Nonaka, 1991, 1994; Nonaka & Takeuchi, 1995).

KM is more than just a set of management tools used sporadically and in isolation, since as Dibella and Nevis (1998) state, KM is based on a holistic approach. The literature has particularly criticized approaches that only focus on information technologies. Although KM is related to database management technology and it has been defined as technology-based management, it cannot be considered as simply a technology. In this line, Gurteen (1999) understands KM as "a business philosophy that includes a set of principles, processes, organizational structures, and technology applications that help people share and leverage their knowledge to meet their business objectives." Davenport (1997) identifies the following KM elements: culture (values and beliefs in the organization concerning information and knowledge), behavior and work processes (how people use information and knowledge), policies (problems of sharing information and knowledge), and technology (the information systems installed). Therefore, a KM system has to incorporate some principles as drivers for the generation and application of knowledge or features of the learning organization and appropriate practice groups to introduce beliefs and values.

Through a literature review (Bhatt, 2001; Davenport & Prusak, 2000; Nonaka, 1991, 1994; Nonaka & Takeuchi, 1995; Rastogi, 2000), we can assume the existence of six basic principles in the organizations that focus on KM.

First, we assume an orientation towards the development, transfer, and protection of knowledge (Nonaka & Takeuchi, 1995) and towards the management of knowledge stocks and flows (Fahey & Prusak, 1998). Second, we assume continuous learning in the organization (Hamel & Prahalad, 1994; Senge, 1990). Third, we assume an understanding of the organization as a global system

(Dibella & Nevis, 1998), with the goal to facilitate the fit between the corporate objectives and the organizational member objectives for reaching their commitment in the development and share of knowledge inside the organization through a process known as "knowledge management socialization". Fourth, we assume the development of an innovative culture that encourages R&D projects (Nonaka & Takeuchi, 1995). Fifth, we assume an approach based on people (Davenport, 1999). Sixth, we assume competences development and management based on competences, as a basis to establish programs that guide the internal development of technological competences, taking into account innovation competences referring to the key technologies (Hamel & Prahalad, 1994; Prahalad & Hamel, 1990).

A set of practices related to KM must be developed to introduce these principles. Many practices exist that enable the development, transference, and protection of knowledge (Davenport & Prusak, 2000; Dibella & Nevis, 1998; Liebowitz & Wilcox, 1997; Mertins et al., 2001; Nonaka, 1994). The efficiency of internal knowledge flow can be improved by means of several techniques such as dialogue and debate (distribution of written reports, meetings, forums, etc.). The procedures of internal benchmarking and the introduction of information technologies (Internet, teleworking, etc.) also can be useful to encourage the sharing of best practices between departments and employees (Frappaolo & Capshaw, 1999). Nonaka (1994, pp. 27-29) highlights the importance of purpose, autonomy, redundancy, and variety of tasks together with two organizational models that encourage collective knowledge: middle-up-down management, related to management style, and hypertext organization, connected to organizational design.

The promotion of continuous learning takes advantage of practices such as career and training plans or continuous improvement systems (Rastogi, 2000). The understanding of the organization as a global system, where all the members interact,

is positively affected by establishing enterprise resource planning systems, interdepartmental projects, and the introduction of incentive mechanisms based on group aims (Rastogi, 2000), as soon as the availability of systems and resources to gather relevant information about suppliers, customers, financial markets, laws, and so forth are present (Carlile, 2002). The development of an innovative culture that encourages knowledge generation projects requires a change in management style, active leadership policies, training actions, and suitable management models to develop innovations.

The firm can train its employees to become involved in the KM strategy through programs that identify resource and information needs, through procedures to find out their degree of satisfaction, with teamwork systems to incite sharing knowledge, and with communication and compensation systems to reward generating and sharing knowledge (Dibella & Nevis, 1998; Rastogi, 2000). Finally, competences development and management based on competences can be achieved with practices that provide the necessary tools to develop employee competences as formation programs, with remuneration and promotion systems linked to the generation of ideas, task rotation, multidisciplinary teamwork, encouraging diversity in research lines, and benchmarking.

KM adoption has a positive effect on the organizational processes that create, store, distribute, and interpret knowledge, as well as the recruitment, retention, and active involvement of talented employees. Lei et al. (1996) conceive KM as a process by which an organization creates value through its intellectual assets or knowledge base.

In this line, Zollo and Winter (2002, p. 339) state that the organization develops dynamic competences when three mechanisms coexist: the accumulation of experience, the articulation of knowledge, and its codification. A KM system includes these elements. Continuous learning and an innovative culture, together as a system focused on development of new knowledge and competences, have a positive effect on the firm skill to manage R&D projects, to leverage the internal capability for knowledge acquisition, and to increase and to regenerate the knowledge stock (Dibella & Nevis, 1998). A systemic view of the organization can multiply the access to new knowledge, because it involves the development of systems that include all agents connected to the organization and scanner the environment.

Firm competence to internally generate valuable ideas or to absorb them from other organizations is supported by the effective exploitation and use of relevant and updated information systems, and the intelligence to transform this information into valuable knowledge as product, process, or organizational innovations that enable a more rapid competitive response than firm competitors. The development of an organizational culture that encourages the sharing of knowledge promotes dialogue about work and the mistakes that have been made.

A focus on individuals allows human capital fast and free access to knowledge to develop usual tasks. An organizational and cultural context like this can attract talented people, thereby increasing human capital with relevant tacit knowledge. An organization focused on the development and transference of knowledge provides its human capital with rapid access to requested knowledge and technologies. Internal knowledge transference occurs when knowledge-based assets are acquired and used. The organization of human and technical means to spread organizational memory promotes the capacity to apply technologies and innovations, to throw out obsolete knowledge, and to try alternative ideas. The codification of the tacit knowledge gathered by the members of an organization (for example, in databases or expert directories) enables knowledge diffusion to take place (Nonaka, 1994; Zander & Kogut, 1995).

The introduction of KM can strengthen the sustainability of the competitive advantages generated, enabling the development of distinctive competences. Lei et al. (1996) go so far as to consider KM as the main drive behind the set of competences in an organization. The way KM is configured in an organization is unique, since the principles and practices used depend on its social and technological context in the firm. The possibility a firm has of appropriating the rents generated by its resources depends on the existence of perfectly defined property rights. The rents generated are the result of a complex network of relationships, and are not attributed to determined production factors. We consider that KM enables firm rents to be appropriated since it promotes group work, and encourages the sharing of knowledge and the breaking down of interdepartmental barriers. In fact, the more the individuals' knowledge is inserted into organizational routines, the greater the possibility of the firm appropriating the results (Grant, 1996a).

In particular, KM implantation has a positive effect on the creation, renovation, and application of knowledge-based distinctive competences. The firm ability to create, share, and use tacit and shared knowledge can be defined as a knowledge-based distinctive competence that is a source of sustained competitive advantage. Some authors go so far as to state that in the near future, the sole source of sustained competitive advantage will be the creation of organizational knowledge and its efficient management (Drucker, 1993; Grant, 1996b, 1997; Nonaka, 1994).

This theoretical reasoning implies defining KM as an antecedent variable of knowledge distinctive competences, or alternatively, defines knowledge distinctive competences as a mediating variable between KM and firm performance. The argumentation of the positive effects of KM on the generation or regeneration of knowledge distinctive competences, by highlighting its strategic relevance, permits us to formulate the following hypothesis:

Figure 1. Theoretical framework of relationships between KM, knowledge distinctive competences and firm performance

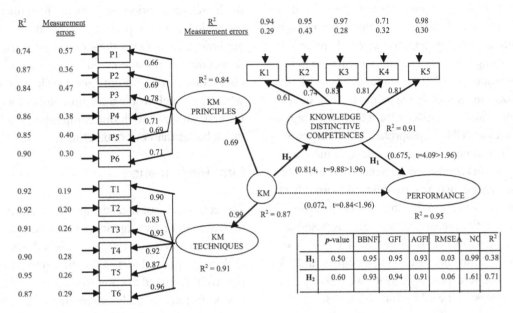

P/T1 = Orientation towards the development, transfer and protection of knowledge
P/T2 = Continuous learning in the organisation
P/T3 = An understanding of the organisation as a global system
P/T4 = Development of an innovative culture that encourages R&D project
P/T5 = Approach based on individuals
P/T6 = Competences development and management based on competences

K1 = KM System
K2= Internal acquisition of knowledge
K3= Internal Knowledge transfer
K4= Internal Knowledge interpretation and application
K5= Organizational memory

Hypothesis 2. The degree to which KM principles and practices are adopted is an antecedent of the knowledge distinctive competences stock, which indirectly conditions firm performance.

The theoretical model we develop with the three key constructs is shown in Figure 1.

METHODS

Variable Definition

Knowledge Management (KM)

In spite of the growing recognition of its importance and wide use in firms, there is no widely accepted definition of the construct "knowledge management" both among managers (AMA, 1999) and by the scientific community. Our conception of KM consists of a management system characterized by a set of principles and practices, whose aim is to create, store, convert, transfer, disseminate, and apply the knowledge of the firm. This definition allows us to verify whether a management system functions on the basis of the beliefs and values embodied in KM principles. Equally important is the analysis of whether these principles materialize in a set of practices and techniques in the routine behavior of the firm that permits organizational knowledge to be created, converted, spread, and used.

Thus, we define KM as a third-order level latent construct with two dimensions: principles and practices. Every dimension is a second-order level latent construct with six elements that are the basic principles and practices that the organization uses to introduce these principles: orientation towards the development, transfer and protection of knowledge (P1/T1), continuous learning in the organization (P2/T2), an understanding of the organization as a global system (P3/T3), development of an innovative culture that encourages R&D projects (P4/T4), approach based on people (P5/T5), and new competence development and management based on competences (P6/T6). The 12 first-order constructs are inferred thorough its indicators, which are the observable variables.

We use the measurement scale proposed by Palacios and Garrigós (2004) that consists of 49 items, 26 to measure KM principles and 23 to measure KM practices. Both were five-point Likert scales: in the KM principles measurement scale, the degree of importance attributed by the firm to the corresponding item is measured, while the KM practices measurement scale measures the degree to which the technique is used.

Knowledge Distinctive Competences

Although KBA highlights how crucial knowledge is to success, efforts made to measure firm knowledge-based competences it are still limited (King & Zeithaml, 2003). Following these authors, we adopted a perceptual approach to measure this construct. Specifically, we measured knowledge distinctive competences by the scale proposed by Camisón (2002). This scale defines knowledge distinctive competences as a second-order level latent factor with five dimensions: skill for management of knowledge investments and flows (K1), internal acquisition (internal capability of the stock growth) of knowledge (K2), internal knowledge transfer (K3), internal knowledge interpretation and application (K4), and organizational memory (K5). The first-order level latent factors are measured through a set of 37 indicators which represent the observable

variables. The scale measures distinctive competences with a subjective semantic scale, based on the self-evaluation made by the firm manager in relation to its competitors. Respondents evaluate how they perceive the stock of firm distinctive competences in comparison to that of their competitors. A five-point Likert scale was used, where 1 = much worse than our competitors, 3 = normal, on a par with our competitors, and 5 = much better than our competitors.

Firm Performance

The complexity of measuring firm performance increases in knowledge intensive industries. Liebowitz and Wilcox (1997) highlight the poverty in the metrics used to measure firm performance in activities related to knowledge. Knowledge intensive firms are usually entrepreneurial, with few products in the market and consequently with a reduced sales path. They have high capital intensity, accumulate a great deal of intangible assets, and suffer losses at the beginning (DeCarolis & Deeds, 1999, p. 960). The traditional measures of firm performance, such as capital profitability indices, sales growth, or market share are inadequate as only indicators in these contexts. DeCarolis and Deeds (1999, p. 960) use the market value of the firm to measure future firm performance, since these firms frequently use an initial public offering to raise the necessary capital. This criterion assumes the hypothesis of the efficient market, where the firm market value captures all the relevant information, including the capacity to generate rents in the future, its intangible assets, and knowledge potential. However, market measures of firm performance are biased by the economic cycle and the situation of the stock market. The problem of obtaining information also presents a hurdle. These measures can only be applied to firms quoted on the stock market, and their value for fragmented industries and many family firms decreases sharply.

In this research, we use the scale designed and validated by Camisón (2004). This instrument measures firm performance with a five-point Likert-type scale, constructed from the self-classification by management of their company in relation to their competitors. This scale consists of 25 variables that evaluate the classic economic and financial indicators, the position in the market and the firm future potential, and the objectives of the different stakeholders in the organization. An additional advantage of this scale is that it covers the effects of intangible or knowledge-based assets, which constitute the most valuable assets in the population studied (DeCarolis & Deeds, 1999). Overall organizational performance was evaluated by taking an average of the items forming the scale.

Statistical Methods

The validation of the measurement tools and the testing of the hypotheses are carried out through structural equation models in two stages (Anderson & Gerbing, 1988), using the EQS 5.7b software program. These stages consist of a measurement analysis of the latent variables and their link to a structural model. These models allow us to establish a set of simultaneous causal relationships between the variables of the model. Through this multiple causal analysis, as well as estimating direct structural effects, we can also estimate indirect effects. As the sample does not fulfill the multivariate normality assumption and it uses noncontinuous variables, the parameter estimation used the ML procedure with robust standard estimators (Satorra & Bentler, 2001).

Data and Sample

The information on the variables was collected in a primary study, carried out by mail questionnaire. The questionnaire uses the scale to measure KM principles (26 items) and KM practices (23 items) designed by Palacios and Garrigós (2004),

the knowledge distinctive competences scale designed by Camisón (2002) (37 items), and the firm performance scale by Camisón (2004) (25 items). The questionnaire respondent was the manager of the firm, since he or she has the necessary global perspective to answer all the questions. The measuring instrument was pretested in 20 firms, 10 from the biotechnology and 10 from the telecommunications industries. The fieldwork was undertaken between December 2001 and March 2002.

We considered knowledge or high technology intensive industries (Blackler, 1995, p. 1021) to be the most suitable population on which to carry out the empirical study. The biotechnology and telecommunications industries were chosen for the research because the management of intangibles is more clearly appreciated than in other types of industry. Knowledge is not a simple asset, but rather it focuses the other assets. To be successful, firms must be able to learn continually and apply their knowledge, by anticipating market changes (Alvesson, 2000; DeCarolis & Deeds, 1999). These firms offer high technology products and services, using knowledge as the main resource. They are dynamic industries characterized by technological discontinuity, where innovation (usually radical) is a fundamental aim (Elmes & Kasouf, 1995) and the R&D effort is very high (DeCarolis & Deeds, 1999). Thus, the generation of new knowledge is continuous and fast. Consequently, we can appreciate KM functions since the firms continuously receive knowledge flows (internal and external) and accumulate knowledge stock (DeCarolis & Deeds, 1999, p. 955). In this context, firm performance in knowledge intensive industries should depend on the knowledge assets stock and their skill in organizing knowledge flows with KM systems.

Within the knowledge intensive industries, the universe selected was the Spanish population of biotechnology and telecommunications industries. This decision has precedents in both the biotechnology field (i.e., DeCarolis & Deeds,

Table 1. Descriptive statistics and correlation coefficients

		Mean	s.d.	1	2
1	Global organizational performance	3.07	0.22		
2	Knowledge distinctive competences	3.71	0.35	0.43***	
3	Knowledge management	3.78	0.37	0.10**	0.11***

*** $p < 0.001$; ** $p < 0.01$

1999) and the information technologies field. From the ASEBIO (Spanish Association of Biotechnology firms) Report (2002), the number of firms in this industry was 226 in 2001. According to the Spanish National Statistical Institute, the telecommunications industry had 846 firms in the same year.

The questionnaire was sent to all the firms making up the population. A total of 257 questionnaire responses were obtained. The statistical debugging of the questionnaires forced us to eliminate 35 of them for various reasons (existence of items without any answer, doubts about the reliability of the responses, etc.). The sample finally included 222 firms (102 from the biotechnology industry and 120 from the telecommunications industry), thus giving a response rate of 45.1% and 14.2% respectively, and 20.72% as a combined response rate. This final sample has a statistical margin of error of ± 5.7% with a 95.5% confidence interval (for the worst case scenario).

The correlation matrix and the mean and standard deviation for each variable are reported in Table 1.

RESULTS

Validation of the Scales

The first phase consists of the development of a measurement model through the specification of factorial models. Following Bagozzi (1981), we carried out an analysis of the dimensionality, reliability, and validity of all the scales through confirmatory factorial analysis.

Validation of the Knowledge Management Measurement Scale

As a previous step to the confirmatory factorial analysis, we studied the quality of fit of the estimated factorial models. The analysis of the models goodness of fit was based on the estimation of different tests proposed by Hair, Anderson, Tatham, and Black (1998). The results (Table 2), where we show the first-order, second-order, and third-order factorial models, corroborate the goodnesses of fit. The only exceptions are the models corresponding to factors T2 and T6, which are saturated and with a perfect fit, since there are three measurement indicators and zero degrees of freedom. With the aim of validating both factors, we established a global model (T2+T6), which provided the result that both dimensions are separated but correlated. The rest of the models have a positive number of degrees of freedom. The quality of the absolute fit (GFI ≥ 0.90 and Satorra-Bentler χ^2 p value ≥ 0.05), incremental fit (AGFI, BBNFI, and IFI ≥ 0.90) and parsimonious fit (PGFI ≥ 0.90 and NC ≤ 2) are shown. In all the cases, the fit indices are greater than the recommended minimum value.

The dimensionality analysis attempts to corroborate the KM structure as a third-order latent bidimensional construct, characterized by a set of principles and practices. Principles and practices are considered second-order latent constructs with six dimensions. The goodness of fit of the first-order factorial models validates the one-dimensionality of the individual dimensions for each principle and practice. The observed individual indicators for each first-order factor represent the same theoretical concept. The indicators were estimated according to their factorial loadings through the LMTEST (Lagrange Multiplier Test), one function of the EQS program with the ability to report new improvements to be incorporated in the models. Following these recommendations, indicators M6 and M24 from the KM principles

Table 2. Fit indices for the initial factorial models for the KM and knowledge distinctive competences constructs

	Satorra-Bentler χ^2	d.g.	p-value	BBN-FI	IFI	GFI	AGFI	PGFI	NC
KM principles (first-order factorial individual models)									
P1	0.0663	2	0.5126	0.9522	0.9621	0.9786	0.9532	0.9485	1.22
P2	0.0811	1	0.2956	0.9424	0.9486	0.9471	0.9198	0.9365	1.42
P3	0.0556	2	0.7352	0.9901	0.9935	0.9878	0.9656	0.9877	1.02
P4	0.0693	2	0.5121	0.9579	0.9541	09539	0.9371	0.9512	1.28
P5	0.0597	2	0.5365	0.9852	0.9804	0.9847	0.9601	0.9742	1.36
P6	0.0726	1	0.3125	0.9421	0.9477	0.9224	0.9103	0.9289	1.41
KM practices (first-order factorial individual models)									
T1	0.0289	2	0.8595	0.9972	0.9991	0.9952	0.9762	0.9856	0.91
T3	0.8565	2	0.6523	0.9740	0.9795	0.9625	0.9478	0.9785	1.73
T4	0.9651	2	0.5263	0.9553	0.9584	0.9377	0.9101	0.9562	1.39
T5	0.0365	2	0.8462	0.9947	0.9976	0.9917	0.9744	0.9832	0.95
T2+T6	7.9819	5	0.4356	0.9425	0.9452	0.9536	0.9296	0.9523	1.41
KM (second-order factorial models)									
KM principles	28.1856	23	0.5034	0.9562	0.9568	0.9591	0.9381	0.9602	0.99
KM practices	24.0257	21	0.1629	0.9884	0.9891	0.9834	0.9551	0.9899	1.46
KM (third-order factorial model)									
KM	372.2563	322	0.6526	0.9252	0.9356	0.9125	0.8901	0.9415	1.16
Knowledge distinctive competences (first-order factorial individual models)									
K1	18.8596	12	0.8523	0.9245	0.9276	0.9245	0.9051	0.8952	0.89
K2	23.4187	17	0.6093	0.9326	0.9342	0.9327	0.9015	0.9215	1.98
K3	20.0582	14	0.5247	0.9654	0.9659	0.9654	0.9245	0.9526	1.12
K4	0.3694	2	0.5481	0.9102	0.9103	0.9103	0.8923	0.9123	1.36
K5	31.3641	26	0.1502	0.9087	0.9089	0.9687	0.9162	0.8958	1.59
Knowledge distinctive competences (second-order factorial individual model)									
Knowledge distinctive competences	85.2368	81	0.3433	0.9557	0.9578	0.9651	0.9442	0.9689	1.07

scale were eliminated, together with M30 and M36 from the KM practices scale. The goodness of fit for the second-order factorial models shows that these factors (KM principles and KM practices) are multidimensional constructs, with their dimensions representing the same theoretical concept. Finally, the quality of the third-order factorial model confirms KM as a multidimensional construct with the theoretical structure we had assumed. Standardized factorial loadings

have values greater than 0.6. Furthermore, all the estimated parameters are statistically significant at 95%.

Following Sharma (1996), we estimated the individual reliability of the indicators using the square of the multiple correlation coefficient (R^2). It can be observed how this index exceeds the minimum value (0.5) in almost all the indicators on the KM principles scale. We retained the items M1, M3, M4, M8, M11, M13, and M20, since they are close to the minimum, and so as not to change the definition of the construct domain. The reliability of the dimensions was evaluated through compound reliability. The compound reliability for the second-order and third-order latent factors is also greater than the minimum value 0.70 in all the cases.

The validity analysis of a measurement refers to the degree to which the measuring process is free from both systematic and random error. Internal or convergent validity indicates that the different items used to measure the concept are correlated. This type of validity can be assured in three ways: first, through the fit of the models, particularly with the goodness of the incremental fit measures (AGFI or BBNFI); second, by factorial loadings greater than or close to the minimum (Hair et al., 1998); and third, in accordance with Anderson and Gerbing (1988), internal validity is assured by the statistical significance of all the loadings (t ≥ 1.96, $\alpha = 0.05$). Discriminant validity indicates to what extent two measures developed for similar but conceptually different constructs are related. To evaluate this, we use the χ^2 differences test recommended by Jöreskog (1971). For all the dimensions (6 principles + 6 practices), we carried out 66 chi-square tests, obtaining in all cases statistically significant differences (p < 0.05). All the dimensions represent different concepts, thus revealing the existence of discriminant validity.

Validation of the Knowledge Distinctive Competences Measurement Scale

The results show the goodness of fit for the first-order and second-order factorial models. All the models have a positive number of degrees of freedom. The absolute fit indices (GFI ≥ 0.90 and Satorra-Bentler χ^2 p value ≥ 0.05), the incremental fit indices (AGFI, BBNFI, IFI, and PGFI ≥ 0.90), and the parsimonious fit index (NC ≤ 5) all have statistically significant values (Hair et al., 1998) (Table 2).

The dimensionality analysis seeks to corroborate the structure of the knowledge distinctive competences as a second-order latent construct, composed of five dimensions defined as a first-order latent construct. The confirmatory factorial analysis shows this dimensionalization, without having to modify the initially proposed models. Standardized factorial loadings have values greater than 0.6. Moreover, all the estimated parameters are statistically significant at 95%.

If we analyze the R^2 values, we can deduce that the reliability of the scale is acceptable. This index is greater than 0.5, except in some items where this value is very close and they were therefore not eliminated so as not to change the definition of the construct domain. Furthermore, the compound reliability for the first-order and second-order latent factors is statistically significant; in all the cases, it is greater than 0.70.

The internal validity of the scale has been assured, first by the fit of the models and, in particular, by the goodness of the incremental fit measures, and, second, by the magnitude of the factorial loadings, with values greater than 0.40. Third, following Anderson and Gerbing (1982), internal validity is assured by the statistical significance of all the loadings (t ≥ 1.96, $\alpha = 0.05$). Discriminant validity is shown with the χ^2 test. We carried out 36 χ^2 tests for the five dimensions, obtaining statistically significant differences in all cases (p < 0.01). Therefore, all the dimensions represent different concepts, showing the existence of discriminant validity.

Validation of the Firm Performance Measurement Scale

To evaluate the Camisón (2004) measurement scale, we assume that all the items make up the same scale, since we calculate the mean of them all. The compound reliability of the scale (0.954) is greater than the recommended minimum value. All the indicators have positive factorial loadings and are statistically significant ($p < 0.05$). The convergent validity, together with the quality of the incremental fit tests (BBNFI = 0.9522 > 0.90), supports this fact.

EMPIRICAL TESTING OF THE HYPOTHESIS

Once we have confirmed the measurement model, we proceed to analyze the causal relationships between the variables. We followed the typical phases of specification, identification, estimation, and interpretation.

The specification phase consists of establishing dependence relations between variables according to theoretical reasoning, in other words, to convert the theoretical hypothesis in an equation system. This research considers the implantation of a KM system as an exogenous latent variable. There are two endogenous variables: knowledge distinctive competences and firm performance. We developed two structural models to test the hypothesis. The complete causal model is shown in Figure 1.

We previously checked the goodness of the measurement models for all the variables. However, the inclusion of all the observable individual indicators in a complete structural model requires a large sample. In order to solve this problem, compound variables are normally used, which use aggregates of the measurement indicators for the structural modelization. In this way, in order to measure individual dimensions of KM and knowledge distinctive competences constructs (first-order factors P1-T1/P6-T6 and K1-K5, respectively), one single indicator was considered: the mean of all its observable items, using its aggregation as an estimation of these latent variables.

The identification implies that the parameters of the model can be derived from the variance and covariance between the observable variables, in order to estimate the model. The necessary condi-

tion that requires the number of equations to be greater than the parameters necessary to estimate the model is ensured, since both models are over-identified (d.f. = 76 and 98, respectively).

Once we have ensured the suppositions of the structural model, we can estimate the results, as well as the significance level of the estimated parameters and the reliability of the structural equations.

Relationship Between Knowledge Distinctive Competences and Firm Performance (H1)

First, we analyze the fit of the measurement model, in order to test whether the estimated parameters are significant in the causal model. In the structural equation of the first causal model, we obtain a positive coefficient in the equation ($\alpha = 0.64$), greater than the recommended minimum value 0.40 (Hair et al., 1998) and statistically significant ($p < 0.001$). The rest of the estimated parameters (K1 = 0.649, K2 = 0.747; K3 = 0.873; K4 = 0.891; K5 = 0.657) are also significant.

With regard to the reliability of the knowledge distinctive competences construct, all the indicators have R^2 values greater than 0.50 (K1 = 0.804, K2 = 0.851; K3 = 0.904; K4 = 0.919; K5 = 0.814). Furthermore, the compound reliability of the construct (0.858) is clearly superior to 0.70. Thus, the measurement model fits the data, with reliable and valid measurement indicators.

The estimation of the structural model for hypothesis H1 obtains adequate indices of global fit. Absolute fit measures (GFI = 0.9584; RMSEA = 0.0347; chi-square value p = 0.5012), incremental fit measures (AGFI = 0.9306; BBNFI = 0.9591) and the parsimonious fit measure (NC = 0.99) meet the recommended minimum values.

The reliability of the structural model is high ($R^2 = 0.381$). The empirical evidence confirms H1, proving the high explanatory capacity of firm performance attributable to the knowledge distinctive competences. Although all the dimensions are important in explaining the direct effect of knowledge distinctive competences on firm performance, the ability of the firm to distribute, interpret, and apply the knowledge stock has a more significant weight. However, the magnitude of the estimated parameter and the reliability of the structural model indicate that there are other hidden variables that should be taken into account when considering the relationship between both constructs.

Relationship Between KM, Knowledge Distinctive Competences and Firm Performance (H2)

As refers to the fit of the measurement model, in order to test whether the estimated parameters are significant in the causal model, factorial loadings are greater than 0.40 and statistically significant (p < 0.001). Thus, all the indicators have an important weight on the theoretical constructs.

The structural model has a high reliability (R^2 = 0.713), greater than that obtained for hypothesis H1. This means that knowledge distinctive competences and the degree of KM implantation jointly better explain the variation of the firm performance than when only the first variable is considered. Furthermore, by observing the coefficients of the structural equations, the direct effect of knowledge distinctive competences on firm performance is practically the same (0.675, p < 0.001) as that estimated for hypothesis H1. The degree of KM introduction has a strong effect on the accumulation of knowledge distinctive competences (0.814, p < 0.001), and indirectly on firm performance (0.549, p < 0.001). Collaterally, the degree of KM implantation has no significant statistical effect on firm performance. Hence, the empirical evidence confirms H2.

All the dimensions of the knowledge distinctive competences construct are important and statistically significant (p < 0.05) in explaining their direct effect on firm performance. However, as we concluded in H1, the ability of the firm to

distribute, interpret, and apply the knowledge stock has a more significant weight.

The model developed for the second hypothesis introduces knowledge distinctive competences as a mediating variable between KM and firm performance. This structural model considers KM as a third-order exogenous latent variable. KM principles and practices are considered a second-order exogenous latent variable. Their 12 dimensions (P1-T1/P6-T6) are considered as exogenous observable variables. Knowledge distinctive competences are viewed as a second-order endogenous latent variable, with their dimensions (K1-K5) as endogenous observable variables. Finally, firm performance is considered an endogenous observable variable (Figure 1).

The estimation of the structural model for hypothesis H2 shows excellent global fit indices. Absolute fit measures (GFI = 0.9488; RMSEA = 0.0682; chi-square value p = 0.6049), incremental fit measures (AGFI = 0.9108 BBNFI = 0.9336), and parsimonious fit index (NC = 1.61) are greater than the recommended minimum values.

The effect of KM on the accumulation of knowledge distinctive competences, and indirectly on firm performance, is explained by the utilization of practices (0.99, p < 0.001) more than by the acceptance of the principles (0.69, p < 0.001), taking into account that both weights are positive and statistically significant (p < 0.001). Furthermore, all the KM principles and practices are positive and with significant factorial loadings (p < 0.05), which highlights their importance in increasing the stock of knowledge assets.

CONCLUSION

From the theoretical model developed and subsequently validated through the empirical data, we can draw the following conclusions:

1. There is a positive causal relationship between KM (principles and practices) and

knowledge distinctive competences. Introducing a KM program in the organization has a positive effect on the generation of knowledge-based distinctive competences. The abilities that KM contributes to develop are skills in investment and knowledge flow management, the acquisition of internal knowledge, transfer, dissemination and internal application of the accumulated knowledge, and an increase in the variety of the organizational memory. In this sense, KM should be understood as an institutional mechanism able to stimulate the coordination of explicit and tacit knowledge which is disseminated through the organization and its environment. Therefore, KM is strongly connected to the innovation capacity of the firm (Nonaka & Takeuchi, 1995; Teece et al., 1997). This empirical evidence allows us to further the knowledge on organizational actions that enable development and renewal of the strategic assets portfolio, proclaimed by the dynamic approaches of RBV (Zollo & Winter, 2002).

2. Knowledge distinctive competences have a strong direct effect on firm performance. This empirical evidence confirms the KBA basic postulation (Grant, 1996a; Nonaka, 1994), which considers knowledge assets a basic source of economic rents. However, although the magnitude of the causal relationship is maintained, the explanatory power of firm performance is greater in the structural model for H2 than in H1. We conclude that an analysis of the causal relationships between these complex variables requires the introduction of all the hidden variables that can mediate or determine the direct effects. A second conclusion indicates that the full implications and sustainability of the economic rents is determined, not only by the present volume of knowledge assets, but also by the power to create Schumpet-

erian competences in the organization. In this sense, KM is a useful tool.

3. This work is an interesting contribution to the literature (Davenport, 1999; McEvily & Chakravarthy, 2002) in that it exacts a knowledge of the causal relationship between KM and firm performance and the variables that mediate both constructs. The implantation of a KM system is not able to directly improve firm performance, but it exerts an indirect influence by developing knowledge distinctive competences. Thus, consultant and software firm advertising that considers KM as a panacea to improve organizational competitiveness is shown to have no basis. A firm will successfully introduce KM programs if it is able to imbue KM principles and practices with processes, routines, and individuals, in order to increase its organizational memory and its ability to obtain, transfer, and apply knowledge.

4. The effect of KM introduction on the accumulation of knowledge distinctive competences and firm performance is due to the utilization of practices, more than to the acceptance of a set of principles. This supports the work of Drucker (1993), who predicted that an important challenge to organizations in the knowledge society would be the systematic construction of practices to manage their own auto-transformation. This empirical study reveals that it is more important to put KM principles into practice, than the existence of a commitment towards the KM approach, but this does not articulate across practices. In the present business context, this result indicates that it is not possible to develop principles to manage and develop knowledge without the support of technological and organizational practices. KM stimulates the raising, dissemination, and application of knowledge through the organization by means of techniques and

practices that promote continuous learning, development, and management of employees' cognitive competences, as soon as people develop skill and disposition to identify and share knowledge, removing technological, cultural, and organizational barriers.

Another aim of this study, to conceptualize and to measure rigorously the construct "knowledge management", has been successfully achieved. The instrument used constitutes a significant methodological contribution to the state of the art characterized by the lack of reliable metrics (Alavi & Leidner, 2002; McEvily & Chakravarthy, 2002). The construct suggests the existence of two dimensions: principles and practices. Principles, referring to a higher level of research which is more abstract or related to ideas, are carried out through a set of techniques that add the necessary tools to guarantee that KM is adequately implemented in the organization. Therefore, we understand that the degree to which a KM system is adopted requires principles and practices to be introduced that focus on the orientation towards the development, transfer, and protection of knowledge, continuous learning in the organization, an understanding of the organization as a global system, the development of an innovative culture that encourages R&D projects, an approach based on individuals and competence development, and management based on competences. The reductionist perspective, which focuses on the role of information technologies in KM (Frappaolo & Capshaw, 1999), is surpassed by the holistic approach which stresses the importance of combining principles and practices.

FUTURE RESEARCH DIRECTIONS

Future research should extend the scope of the study by introducing new elements, as well as incorporating the breakthroughs in the field.

A first line of study lies in the methodological field. Although the KM measurement scale has been successfully validated, it is an exploratory contribution that requires new empirical works to test and improve it. A second line of research should introduce longitudinal works that include knowledge stocks and flows. For organizations, it would be especially interesting to determine the knowledge flows that allow for the improvement of a determined type of competences, recombining their resources to prioritize some flow variables.

A longitudinal approach would enable us to theoretically reflect the existence of a temporal gap between the beginning of a KM program and the generation of results. Besides, these types of studies allow the inference of causality between variables with more statistical consistency. In addition, the necessary time could be calibrated to widen the stock of knowledge distinctive competences and its effect on firm performance. At a theoretical level, it would be of interest to study KM effects on all types of distinctive competences. Adding cohesion and functional competences could incorporate new knowledge about the way in which the introduction of a KM system may improve functional activities, as well as the combination of resources and capacities that adjust better to the market.

REFERENCES

Alavi, M., & Leidner, D.E. (2002). Experiences into the practice of knowledge management systems. In S. Barnes (Ed.), *Knowledge management systems: Theory and practice* (pp. 17-40). New York: Thomson Learning.

Alvesson, M. (2000). Social identity and the problem of loyalty in knowledge-intensive companies. *Journal of Management Studies, 37*, 1101-1111.

American Management Association (AMA). (1999). *Knowledge management* (Research Report). New York: Author.

Anderson, J., & Gerbing, D.W. (1988). Structural equation modelling in practice: A review and recommended two step approach. *Psychological Bulletin, 103*, 411-423.

Asociación Española de Bioempresas (ASEBIO). (2002). *Informe Asebio 2001.* Madrid: Author.

Bagozzi, R.P. (1981). Evaluating structural equations models with unobservable variables and measurement error: A comment. *Journal of Marketing Research, 18*, 375-381.

Barnes, S. (Ed.). (2002). *Knowledge management systems: Theory and practice.* New York: Thomson Learning.

Barney, J.B. (1991). Firm resources and sustained competitive advantage. *Journal of Management, 17*, 99-120.

Bhatt, G.D. (2001). Knowledge management in organizations: Examining the interaction between technologies, techniques and people. *Journal of Knowledge Management, 5*(1), 68-75.

Blackler, F. (1995). Knowledge, knowledge work and organizations: An overview and interpretation. *Organization Studies, 16*, 1021-1046.

Bollinger, A.S., & Smith, R.D. (2001). Managing organizational knowledge as a strategic asset. *Journal of Knowledge Management, 5*(1), 8-18.

Camisón, C. (2002). *A proposal of conceptualization for organization distinctive competences stock* (Working Paper No. 3-02). Castellón: University Jaume I, Research Group on Strategy, Knowledge Management and Organizational Learning.

Camisón, C. (2004). Shared, competitive, and comparative advantages: A competence-based view of industrial-district competitiveness. *Environment and Planning A, 36*, 2227-2256.

Carlile, R. (2002). A pragmatic view of knowledge and boundaries: Boundary objects in new product development. *Organization Science, 13*, 442-455.

Davenport, T.H. (1997). *Secrets of successful knowledge management.* Austin, TX: Quantum.

Davenport, T.H. (1999). Knowledge management and the broader firm: Strategy, advantage, and performance. In J. Liebowitz (Ed.), *Knowledge management handbook* (pp. 1-11). Boca Raton, FL: CRC Press.

Davenport, T.H., & Prusak, L. (2000). *Working knowledge: How organisations manage what they know.* New York: McGraw-Hill.

DeCarolis, D.M., & Deeds, D.L. (1999). The impact of stocks and flows of organizational knowledge on firm performance: An empirical investigation of the biotechnology industry. *Strategic Management Journal, 20*, 953-968.

Dibella, A., & Nevis, E. (1998). *How organizations learn: An integrated strategy for building learning capacity.* San Francisco: Jossey-Bass.

Dierickx, I., & Cool, K. (1989). Asset stock accumulation and sustainability of competitive advantage. *Management Science, 35*, 1504-1513.

Drucker, P.F. (1993). *Post-capitalism society.* Oxford: Butterworth Heinemann.

Dyer, G., & McDonough, B. (2001, May). The state of KM. Communicator eNewsletter. Retrieved May 16, 2007, from http://http://www.destinationcrm.com/km/

Elmes, M.B., & Kasouf, C.J. (1995). Knowledge workers and organizational learning: Narratives from biotechnology. *Management Learning, 26*, 403-422.

Fahey, L., & Prusak, L. (1998). The eleven deadliest sins of knowledge management. *California Management Review, 40*(3), 265-275.

Frappaolo, C., & Capshaw, C. (1999). Knowledge management software: Capturing the essence of know-how and innovation. *Information Management Journal, 33*(3), 44-48.

Grant, R.M. (1996a). Toward a knowledge-based theory of the firm. *Strategic Management Journal, 17*(winter special issue), 109-122.

Grant, R.M. (1996b). Prospering in dynamically-competitive environments: Organizational capability as knowledge integration. *Organizational Science, 7*, 375-388.

Grant, R.M. (1997). The knowledge-based view of the firm: Implications for management practice. *Long Range Planning, 30*, 450-454.

Gurteen, D. (1999). Creating a knowledge sharing culture. *Knowledge Management Magazine, 2*(5). Retrieved May 16, 2007, from http://www.kmmagazine.com

Hair, H.F., Anderson R.E., Tatham, R.L., & Black, W.C. (1999). *Multivariate analysis*. New York: Prentice Hall.

Hamel, G., & Prahalad, C.K. (1994). *Competing for the future*. Boston: Harvard Business School Press.

Jöreskog, K.G. (1971). Simultaneous factor analysis in several populations. *Psychometrica, 57*, 409-426.

King, A.W., & Zeithaml, C.P. (2003). Measuring organizational knowledge: A conceptual and methodological framework. *Strategic Management Journal, 24*, 763-772.

Lei, D., Hitt, M.A., & Bettis, R. (1996). Dynamic core competences through meta-learning and strategic context. *Journal of Management, 22*, 549-569.

Liebowitz, J., & Wilcox, L.C. (Eds.). (1997). *Knowledge management and its integrative elements*. Boca Raton, FL: CRC Press.

McEvily, S., & Chakravarthy, B. (2002). The persistence of knowledge-based advantage: An empirical test for product performance and technological knowledge. *Strategic Management Journal, 23*, 285-305.

Mertins, K., Heisig, P., & Vorbeck, J. (Eds.). (2001). *Knowledge management: Best practices in Europe*. Berlin: Springer-Verlag.

Mu-Yen, Ch., & An-Pin, Ch. (2006). Knowledge management performance evaluation: A decade review from 1995 to 2004. *Journal of Information Science, 32*(1), 17-38.

Nonaka, I. (1991). The knowledge-creating company. *Harvard Business Review, 69*(6), 96-104.

Nonaka, I. (1994). A dynamic theory of organizational knowledge creation. *Organization Science, 5*, 14-37.

Nonaka, I., & Takeuchi, H. (1995). *The knowledge creating company*. Oxford: Oxford University Press.

OCDE. (1996). *The knowledge-based economy*. Paris: Author.

Palacios, D., & Garrigós, F. (2005). A measurement scale for knowledge management in the biotechnology and telecommunications industries. *International Journal of Technology Management, 31*(3/4), 358-374.

Prahalad, C.K., & Hamel, G. (1990). The core competence of the corporation. *Harvard Business Review, 90*(3), 79-91.

Rastogi, P.N. (2000). Knowledge management and intellectual capital: The new virtuous reality of competitiveness. *Human Systems Management, 19*, 19-26.

Real, J., Leal, A., & Roldan, J. (2006). Determinants of organisational learning in the generation of technological distinctive competencies. *International Journal of Technology Management, 35*(1-4), 284-307.

Satorra, A., & Bentler, P.M. (2001). A scaled difference chi-square test statistic for moment structure analysis. *Psychometrika, 66*, 507-514.

Senge, P.M. (1990). *The fifth discipline: The age and practice of the learning organization.* London: Century Business.

Sharma, S. (1996). *Applied multivariate techniques.* New York: John Wiley & Sons.

Teece, D.J., Pisano, G., & Shuen, A. (1997). Dynamic capabilities and strategic management. *Strategic Management Journal, 18*, 509-533.

Zack, M.H. (1999). Managing codified knowledge. *Sloan Management Review, 40*(4), 45-58.

Zander, U., & Kogut, B. (1995). Knowledge and the speed of the transfer and imitation of organizational capabilities: An empirical test. *Organization Science, 6*, 76-92.

Zollo, M., & Winter, S. (2002). Deliberate learning and the evolution of dynamic capabilities. *Organization Science, 13*, 339-351.

Additional Reading

Albert, S. (1998, September 7). Knowledge management: Living up to the hype? *Midrange Systems, 11*(13), 52.

Barlett, C. (1996). *Mckinsey & Co.: Managing knowledge and learning* (Case 9-396-357). Boston: Harvard Business School.

Bruce, M., Cooper, R., Morris, B., & Wootten, A. (1999, April). Managing requirements capture within a global telecommunications company. *R&D Management, 29*(2), 107-119.

Butler, J.G. (1997). *Information technology: Converging strategies and trends for the 21st century.*

Chou, S.W., & Tsai, Y.H. (2004). Knowledge creation: Individual and organizational perspectives. *Journal of Information Science, 30*(3), 205-218.

Chou, S.W., & He, M.Y. (2004). Knowledge management: The distinctive roles of knowledge assets in facilitating knowledge creation. *Journal of Information Science, 30*(2), 146-164.

Collins, D. (1998, March). Knowledge work or working knowledge? Ambiguity and confusion in the analysis of the knowledge age. *Journal of Systemic Knowledge Management.*

Copeland, L. (1998, August 7). Lotus takes integration route to knowledge management. *Computer Reseller News, 803*, 69-70.

Cunningham, C., & Trott, B. (1998, November 23). Microsoft looks for knowledge. *Infoworld, 20*(47), 10.

Cushman, A., Fleming, M., Harris, K., Hunter, R., & Rosser, B. (1999, March). The knowledge management scenario: Trends and directions for 1998-2003 (Gartner's Group Strategic Analysis Report R-07-7706, p. 38).

Cutcher-Gershenfeld, J. (1998). *Knowledge-driven work: Unexpected lessons from Japanese and United States work practices.*

Davis, M. (1998). Knowledge management, information strategy. *The Executive's Journal*, pp. 11-22.

Doyle, D., & Dutoit, A. (1998, January). Knowledge management in a law firm. *ASLIB Proceedings, Vol. 50*(1), pp. 3-8.

Gertler, M.S., & Wolfe, D.A. (2004). Local social knowledge management: Community actors, institutions and multilevel governance in regional foresight exercises. *Futures, 36*(1), 45-65.

Hafstad, S. (1997, September). The knowledge management process in a business school environment. *Business Information Review, 14*(3), 135-140.

Heisig, P. (1998). *Knowledge management improvements survey*. Berlin: Fraunhofer Institute.

KMPG. (1998). *Knowledge management research report* (+44 171 311 1000).

McKenna, B. (1999, May). All together now! Creating an assembly of knowledge workers. *Knowledge Management*.

Moore, C. (1998, November 15). Knowledge management: A case study (Section 1). *CIO, 12*(4), 66.

Mullin, R., & Newlin, S. (1999, March 31). Knowledge management: Field-smart Nalco forges ahead. *Chemical Week, 161*(12), 41.

Pemberton, J.M. (1997, April). Chief knowledge officer: The climax to your career? *Records Management Quarterly, 31*(2), 66-69.

Petrash, G. (1996). Dow's journey to a knowledge value management culture. *European Management Journal, 14*(4), 365-373.

Pinelli, T.E., & Barclay, R.O. (1998). Maximizing the results of federally-funded research and development through knowledge management: A strategic imperative for improving US competitiveness. *Government Information Quarterly, 15*(2), 157-172.

Raitt, D., Loekken, S., Scholz, J., Steiner, H., & Secchi, P. (1997, November). Corporate knowledge management and related initiatives at ESA. *ESA Bulletin-European Space Agency, 92*, 112-118.

Rollett, H. (2003). *Knowledge management: Processes and technologies*. Boston: Kluwer Academic Publishers.

Rowland, H. (1998). Building a knowledge-based health service: R&D gap. *KM Review, 3*(17).

Schwabe, G. (1999). Understanding and supporting knowledge management and organizational memory in a city council. *Proceedings of the Hawaii International Conference on System Sciences* (p. 47). Los Alamitos, CA: IEEE Computer Society.

Chapter III
Knowledge Management Leaders' Top Issues

Anne-Marie Croteau
Concordia University, Canada

Marc Dfouni
Concordia University, Canada

ABSTRACT

This chapter presents the results obtained after reaching a consensus among 100 knowledge leaders on their critical issues. These issues include the perceived knowledge management benefits and obstacles, the knowledge leaders' roles and skills, as well as the technologies they used for implementing knowledge management initiatives. Using a Web-based Delphi method, the results indicate that an increase in internal knowledge sharing is judged to be the most significant of all perceived knowledge management benefits. Their most important role is to foster a knowledge sharing culture in their organization in order to overcome the most important obstacle: organizational culture. They also suggest that the key abilities they should possess are those of strong interpersonal and leadership skills. Finally, portals and information retrieval engines are found to be the most widely used technologies to develop and/or implement knowledge management initiatives.

INTRODUCTION

Knowledge leaders are hired by organizations to create and maintain knowledge management (KM) environments supported by various technologies, which bring their potential of difficulties and technological issues. However, these individuals' perceptions of KM top issues appear to be imprecise and ambiguous when referring to the literature. As the need for organizations to manage and extract knowledge increases, so does the demand for identifying KM leaders' top issues that they deal with on a regular basis.

Using a Web-based Delphi method, this chapter presents the result of a worldwide consensus found among KM leaders regarding their top issues. These issues include KM leaders' perception of KM benefits and obstacles, their roles and skills, as well as the technologies they used for implementing KM initiatives. These issues were first retrieved from existing KM literature and then presented to KM experts in order to be validated. A stable level of agreement among 100 KM leaders was reached on these issues, which are discussed below. These results put together a baseline allowing KM leaders to better understand, plan, and execute future KM initiatives. It provides a comprehensive view of the reality of KM leaders by addressing those five critical issues at the same time and by the same respondents.

The next section offers a description of what was found in the literature. The methodology used to find a stable understanding of the top issues for knowledge leaders is then explained. Next, the findings are depicted and discussed. Finally, the last section provides conclusions along with implications of this study.

LITERATURE REVIEW

Knowledge management's recent emergence is mainly due to the nomadic working lifestyle of today's employees. It has been asserted that employees change their jobs once every two years, carrying with them the knowledge they have acquired through years of experience. To alleviate this problem, KM's main objective is to maximize organizational knowledge sharing, while minimizing knowledge loss. In order to initiate KM, organizations need individuals to undertake the responsibility of developing and maintaining a KM environment. Accordingly, organizations need knowledge leaders. Unfortunately, the amount of academic literature that

has researched and analyzed knowledge leaders at this point in time is very limited, although the frequency of KM research is increasing expeditiously. The following subsections provide a definition of knowledge leaders, the benefits and obstacles they encounter when they implement KM initiatives, the roles and skills that they need to be successful in such an endeavor, and the most important technologies that they used to foster the use of KM.

Knowledge Leader Definition

Chief knowledge officers (CKOs) are defined in general terms as "the leaders of their organizations' knowledge management initiatives" (Bonner, 2000, p. 36; Rasmus, 2000; p. 5), and as "senior executives responsible for ensuring that an organization maximizes the value it achieves through one of its most important assets — knowledge" (Skyrme, 1997). More specifically, a CKO is "the catalyst for a knowledge-sharing culture, owner of the infrastructure specifications that facilitate knowledge transfer and storage, and maintainer of the closed-loop learning system" (Rasmus, 2000, p. 3). CKO is also recognized for setting "strategic policy for an organization's acquisition and distribution of knowledge and learning, based on the premise that increasing people's capacity to take action will enable them to respond more effectively and efficiently to their customers" (Barclay, 1997, p. 8).

Various job titles were retrieved from the KM literature including chief knowledge officer, chief learning officer, knowledge manager, knowledge facilitator, and so forth. To simplify these various definitions, this study uses the term "knowledge leader" (KL), reflecting the philosophy that CKOs have to show leadership when implementing KM initiatives. Therefore, a KL is an individual responsible for creating and/or maintaining a KM environment.

Knowledge Management Benefits

In the context of this study, a benefit is the positive effect or support yielded from implementing KM. It can be understood as advantages, gains, as well as usefulness. As described by Skyrme (1997), major organizations have been benefiting from the implementation of KM initiatives. British Petroleum has accelerated its solution of critical operation problems by implementing virtual teamworking using videoconferencing. Hoffman La Roche has reduced cost and time in accomplishing regulatory approvals for new drugs by implementing the "Right First Time" program. Dow Chemical was able to generate over US$125 million in revenues from licensing by exploiting its intangible assets. Texas Instruments has saved the equivalent of investing in a new plant through the sharing of best practices between their semiconductor fabrication plants. Skandia Assurance has increased their revenues quicker than their industry average through the development of new measures of intellectual capital. And Hewlett-Packard was able to bring new products to market quicker than in the past by sharing existing company expertise.

Some of the most important organizational benefits gained by KM initiatives are better decision-making, increased responsiveness to customers, and improved efficiency of people and operations (Charney & Jordan, 2000; Chase, 1997; KPMG, 2000). Innovation and growth, organizational responsiveness, customer focus, supply network, and internal quality are also seen as KM benefits (Breu et al., 2000). In addition to these benefits, a recent report has summarized various benefits of implementing KM initiatives gathered from various other articles and studies (Waruszynski, 2000). All these benefits served for the first-round of the Web-based Delphi survey (see Appendix A).

Knowledge Management Obstacles

In the context of this study, a KM obstacle is a tangible or intangible barrier that could prevent or impede the implementation of KM in an organization. It can be understood as an obstruction, impediment, difficulty, hindrance, and/or barrier.

Although some studies observe that organizational culture is the most important obstacle to KM (Chase, 1997; McKeen & Staples, 2001; Miles et al., 1998; Waruszynski, 2000), they add that other issues such as lack of ownership of the problem, lack of time, and information/communication technology can also create barriers to developing and implementing KM initiatives. A compilation of the 10 most recurrent obstacles and the studies where they can be found was prepared (see Appendix A). These obstacles were also part of the first-round questionnaire of the Web-based Delphi survey.

Knowledge Leaders' Roles

A role is defined as a set of systematically interrelated and observable behaviors that belong to an identifiable job or position (Mintzberg, 1975). In the context of this study, a role is the duty that KLs are expected to perform to develop and/or implement a KM environment in their organization.

Previous research has examined the responsibilities of 20 KLs in North America and Europe to understand their roles and gain insight on evolving KM practices (Earl & Scott, 1999). It was shown that the mandates and overall mission of a KL were unclear. A recent study emphasized this lack of consensus regarding the competencies needed by individuals charged with leading KM initiatives (Neilson, 2000). In another study, 18 KLs representing various industries from large private and public organizations described themselves as first generation incumbents who started their jobs less than three years ago without a clear definition of their roles, responsibilities, and daily activities (Bonner, 2000).

It is not surprising that KLs do not have clearly defined roles. Since KM is an emerging field, the only available resources for these individuals are books, conferences, the Internet, and input from a limited number of consulting firms. Knowledge leaders do not have predecessors from whom they can seek guidance. Nevertheless, a compilation of the five most recurrent roles was done from the literature. These roles were part of the first-round questionnaire (see Appendix A).

Knowledge Leaders' Skills

A knowledge leaders' skill is a special ability or competency that this individual possesses to accomplish assigned roles. A review of seven KM case studies reports that "CKOs need to view organizations holistically and possess a mix of hard and soft skills characteristic of a leader of a strategic change management program" (Abell & Oxbrow, 1999 in Neilson 2000, p. 6). In addition, the authors divided the CKOs skills into two main categories: (1) skills to develop the KM vision and (2) skills to plan the KM program. A compilation of the five most recurrent skills was done from the literature and were part of the first-round questionnaire (see Appendix A).

Knowledge Management Technologies

Spending on KM software reached $330 million in 1999 and should account for approximately $1.8 billion in 2003 (PriceWaterHouseCoopers, 2000). KM technologies have been assisting KLs to develop and implement KM programs for several years (Alavi & Leidner, 1999; Chase, 1997; Duffy, 2001; KPMG, 2000; Offsey, 1997; TechWeb, 1999; Wensley & O'Sullivan, 2000).

While one study cites that the most effective technologies include e-mail, Intranet, Internet, firm yellow pages, and groupware (Chase, 1997), another study reports that Intranet and data warehousing are the most effective and that Internet is the least effective technology (KPMG, 2000). Contradictions among these articles are common.

Therefore, this study will attempt to reach an acceptable degree of agreement among KLs on the technologies they are using to develop and implement KM in their organization. A compilation of the 10 most recurrent technologies was prepared and was part of the first-round questionnaire (see Appendix A).

METHODOLOGY

A Web-based Delphi method was used to reach a worldwide consensus on major issues concerning today's KLs. Although various issues were retrieved from existing KM literature and presented to KM experts in order to be rated, this method also required experts to suggest missing issues.

The five objectives of this study are to identify the KM benefits and obstacles, knowledge leaders' roles and skills, as well as the technologies used to implement and/or maintain a KM environment. These issues were combined for the first time within the same study. Thus, the following research questions aimed at identifying these five major issues:

What are knowledge leaders' current most important perceived benefits and obstacles in implementing knowledge management initiatives?

What are knowledge leaders' most important roles and skills?

What are knowledge leaders' perceptions of the most important technologies for knowledge management initiatives?

Table 1. Summary of different alternatives to evaluate the level of agreement and stabilization of the results

Alternatives to evaluate consensus	Ranking evaluation method	Rating evaluation method	Movement towards a consensus if the ...
Mean	Yes	Yes	Mean increases for most important items Mean decreases for least important items
Standard deviation	No	Yes	Standard deviation decreases
Median	Yes	Yes	Median increases
Interquartile range	Yes	Yes	IQR decreases
Percent top issues	Yes	Yes	Percent top issues increases
Kendall coefficient of concordance W	Yes	Yes	Kendall's W increases

Delphi Method

The Delphi method is defined as a procedure to "obtain the most reliable consensus of opinion of a group of experts ... by a series of intensive questionnaires interspersed with controlled opinion feedback" (Dalkey & Helmer, 1963, p. 458). The process stops when an acceptable or stable level of consensus is reached. This method allows anonymity, eliminates confrontation, group domination, and geographical barrier, but, most importantly, it allows researchers to measure the level of agreement on the issues studied.

In this study, "experts" are defined as individual panelists who possess more knowledge about the subject matter than most people or possess certain KM experience (Hill & Fowles, 1975; Whitman, 1990). In order to control the level of expertise, potential respondents were asked if they associated themselves with the previously proposed KL definition before filling out the questionnaire. This precaution was useful since some potential respondents declined to participate to the study because their experience did not correspond to the KL definition.

Level of Consensus

In order to determine the level of consensus on the items studied, various analyses were performed, including mean ratings, standard deviations, medians, inter-quartile range (IQR), percent top issues, and Kendall's coefficient of concordance (Brancheau, Janz & Wetherbe, 1996; Brancheau & Wetherbe, 1987; Couger, 1988; Dexter, Janson, Kiudorf & Laast-Laas, 1993; Dickson, Leitheiser & Brancheau, 1984; Doke & Swanson, 1995; Green & Price, 2000; Niederman, Brancheau & Wetherbe, 1991; Schmidt et al., 2001; Siegel, 1956; Watson, 1989). Hence, a fourth round would not have had an impact on the results. Table 1 summarizes the different alternatives listed above to determine the level of agreement and stabilization of the results, depending on the evaluation method used (ranking or rating).

Web-Based Survey

A Web-based survey was chosen to collect the data required. Web-based surveys offer the advantage of a faster response speed than other means of surveying. The average response time between Web-based surveys and other types of surveying lies between 1.2 days and 18.5 days (Dommeyer & Moriart, 2000). Moreover, undeliverable e-mails can be instantly identified (Oppermann, 1995), allowing the researcher to immediately substitute returned e-mails with new potential respondents. Due to the international characteristic of this study, a Web-based survey avoids the costs associated with printing, postage, paper, envelopes, collating, and envelop stuffing. Studies that have analyzed

Web-based surveys found that they produced high response quality. Higher response quality means fewer item omissions and fewer mistakes (Kiesler & Sproull, 1986; Schaefer & Dillman 1998), as well as a greater response to open-ended questions (Mehta & Sivadas, 1995; Schaefer & Dillman, 1998). The latter characteristic are of particular interest for the present study since questions in the first round questionnaire were open-ended.

In addition to the above-mentioned advantages, researchers who compared Web-based and mail respondents on demographic and/or attitudinal data have concluded that there are no significant response biases between the two methods (Mehta & Sivadas, 1995; Tse, 1998). Furthermore, it was found that a Web-based survey is no more likely than a mail survey to produce "extreme responses" (Kiesler & Sproull, 1986).

Nevertheless, the majority of studies comparing multiple means of surveying have indicated a lower response rate for e-mail solicited surveys, a fact that warrants attention (Kiesler & Sproull, 1986; Tse, 1998). Other precaution measures that researchers should take into consideration when conducting a Web-based survey include assuring respondents that their identity will not be revealed because the lack of anonymity potentially prevented certain individuals from responding (Dommeyer & Moriart, 2000); building a questionnaire that is respondent-friendly, easy to fill out, appealing, and that avoids confusion (Dillman, Sinclair & Clark, 1993); and taking into account that an e-mail is very easy to dispose of and/or ignore. This method consists of inviting potential respondents to go to a Web address in order to complete the questionnaire (Dommeyer & Moriart, 2000).

Data Collection

The first source of respondents consisted of a list of 150 KLs compiled from past literature. The second source involved contacting international KM associations and requesting that they publish a short summary of the study's objectives on their Web site and/or newsletter. A last source for finding KLs consisted of posting a message on various international KM online discussion groups. It is important to note that potential respondents from KM associations and online discussion groups were not directly contacted; therefore, it is not relevant in this case to use the term "response rate" *per se*.

Three rounds of questionnaires were employed by this study to reach a stable level of consensus among KM experts. Each questionnaire was pretested with academics and graduate students; they all contained a cover letter, general instructions with a definition of KL, and a thank you page.

Round One. The first questionnaire respectively and randomly listed the most cited 10 benefits, 10 obstacles, 5 skills, 5 roles, and 10 technologies. Respondents were asked to rate the provided issues using a five-point Likert-type scale. This scale ranged from 1-Highly not important to 5-Highly important. An additional choice "6-Not applicable" was provided as well. Respondents were also encouraged to add and briefly explain as many as five issues per area. Usable responses were received from 117 worldwide KLs.

Round Two. Potential respondents for the second round included those who had answered the first questionnaire. Since the analysis was to include only respondents that had filled out the three questionnaires, as well as those who had completed the second and third round questionnaires, the authors of this study opted to follow various studies by recontacting online KM associations and forums to compensate for the possible attrition of the first round participants (Brancheau et al, 1996; Green & Price, 2000; Keller, 2001; Niederman et al, 1990; Watson, 1989).

The first questionnaire yielded new items for the second questionnaire which also included the most recurrent ones from the first round. Respondents were asked to rate the following most important and recurrent issues: 17 benefits, 17 obstacles, 11 skills, 15 roles, as well as 16 KM technologies. The issues were randomly ordered and the respondents were provided with the same scale as the one used in the first round. Usable responses were received from 142 worldwide KLs.

Round Three. The third round questionnaire was sent to respondents who had participated in the first and second rounds, or only to the second round. Knowledge leaders rated the most cited 10 KM benefits and 10 obstacles, 10 KM leaders' roles and 5 skills, and 10 technologies that were retrieved from round two. They were randomly ordered and placed in the appropriate sections in the third round questionnaire. Similarly to the second round, all of the questions in the third round questionnaire were closed, requiring the respondents to rate the items using the same scale as the one used in previous rounds. Usable responses were received from 100 worldwide KLs.

RESULTS

Respondents originated from five continents: 35% from North America, 22% from Australia, 19% from Europe, 17% from Asia, and the remaining 7% from South America and Africa. A total of 30% of the respondents' companies were in business services, 20% in the educational/governmental sector, 17% in IT services, 9% in finance, insurance, and real-estate, and the remaining in other industries.

As previously stated, the Delphi method requires experts as participants. The respondents' level of KM expertise for this study was judged to be high, given the fact that 56% of the respondents worked in KM related jobs and 13% in IT/IS related jobs, and that 69% of the respondents had more than three years of KM experience.

In order to measure the level of consensus on the perceived importance of KM benefits rated in the third round, all of the six previously discussed methods were used (see Delphi Criteria section). A comparison between round two and round three's results using each method determined the level of consensus for each item (see Appendix B).

Kendall's Coefficients of Concordance W for rounds three and two, as well as the difference between these two values, are presented in Appendix C. Due to the high number of respondents, it was more difficult to obtain a strong agreement on the rated importance of the roles. For panels consisting of more than 10 experts, even very small values of W can be significant (Schmidt, 1997). An exact interpretation of W for large size panels could not be found in the literature. However, by using the differences of W between rounds three and two, which are negligible, it can be asserted that the experts are essentially applying the same standards in rating the items for each section.

DISCUSSION

This section discusses the results obtained from this survey illustrated in Figure 1. The top KM benefits as perceived by KM leaders are first discussed followed by the obstacles they encountered. To overcome them and attain the discussed benefits, respondents agreed on five most important roles played by KM leaders and what the most important skills are. Finally, technologies used to implement KM initiatives are presented.

Top Five Knowledge Management Benefits

The most critical KM benefits perceived by KM leaders are listed in Figure 1. Each benefit is discussed below.

Increase Internal Knowledge Sharing

The most important perceived benefit that organizations realize through KM is an internal increase in knowledge sharing. The high value of this benefit is not surprising since a major goal of KM is to increase knowledge sharing (Capshaw, 1999). By cultivating a knowledge sharing culture, communication barriers tend to disappear, thus allowing employees to more effectively and efficiently communicate and share knowledge.

Deliver Higher Quality Products and Services

This benefit has been supported by Neilson (2000), who correctly affirms that "explicit and tacit (implicit) knowledge about a product or service are as important as the product or service itself because it serves as a basis to improve or develop new products or services" (p. 2). Companies are capturing and using organization-wide knowledge to market, sell, and service customers more efficiently and effectively (APQC, 2001). Effectively using market and customer information to

guide the development of products and services can substantially reduce the risk of new product development. For example, Hewlett Packard maintains a large database of customer comments about products. When an HP employee receives a customer complaint, comment, or suggestion for improvement of any kind about an HP product or service, the employee can input it into a knowledge base. The development engineers and product managers can use that information to help plan future products.

Avoid Re-Inventing the Wheel

The re-use of existing knowledge elements prevents recurring costs related to repeated research

Figure 1. Knowledge leaders' top issues

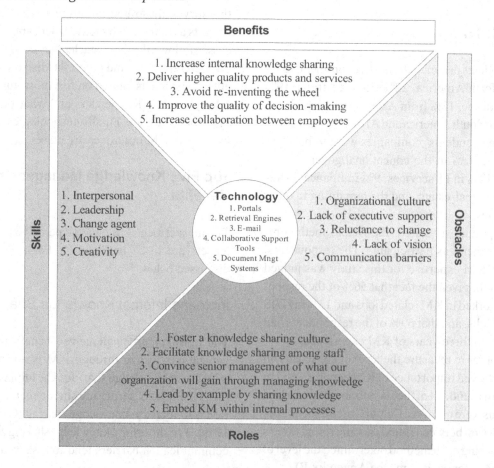

of the same topics, and repeated formulation of the same solutions.

Improve the Quality of Decision-Making

Making an informed decision requires the availability of sound knowledge. A well-run and well-organized knowledge system is critical in making a quality decision. A useful KM initiative ensures that employees have the necessary access to required knowledge in a form that is advantageous to their decision-making process.

Increase Collaboration Between Employees

By building communities of practice and encouraging informal social interactions, collaboration between employees is believed to increase.

Top Five Knowledge Management Obstacles

Although the most studied KM obstacle in the academic literature is organizational culture, four other important obstacles have emerged in this study and are discussed below.

Organizational Culture

As stated earlier, the most crucial role of a KM leader is to foster a knowledge sharing culture. Its importance makes perfect sense when related to the fact that organizational culture was named as the most important obstacle to overcome. A healthy corporate culture is a necessity for successful KM initiatives (Liebowitz, 2000). Differing cultures within an organization could hinder successful KM initiatives. These cultures can arise from diverse educational backgrounds and expectations (De Long & Fahey, 2000) and are often firmly rooted in the varying functions of departments in an organization. Effective knowledge creation depends on the physical, virtual,

and emotional context of an organization (Von Krogh, Ichijo, & Nonaka, 2000). The authors suggest that organizations must actively pursue the work context as a learning organization where the individuals become responsive to learning new things. Bureaucratic cultures suffer from a lack of trust and a failure to reward and promote cooperation and collaboration (Zand, 1997). The lack of a trusting and properly motivated workforce could result in rarely shared or applied knowledge, ceasing innovation and risk-taking, and non-existent organizational cooperation and alignment.

Lack of Senior Management Support

Due to the importance of this obstacle, it can be asserted that the role of convincing senior management of what the organization will gain through managing knowledge has been justly rated as being third in importance. Difficulties encountered in trying to change years of knowledge hoarding are multiplied when employees are not fully convinced that the highest levels of the organization support the change in behavior.

Reluctance to Change

To tap a company's knowledge, some substantial changes must occur, which are not just organizational or structural, but personal as well. Unless change occurs at the level of attitude or behavior, an organization cannot fully mine the gold of its people. Reluctance to change is directly related to human nature, which leads individuals to resist change. The change management field has done and is still doing extensive research on how to facilitate the implementation of a change program by minimizing the individuals' resistance.

Lack of Vision

KM leaders, along with top management, should create a knowledge vision that defines the world in which they are living and the general direction of knowledge they ought to discover and create. The knowledge vision should cultivate personal commitment of the organization's staff by providing meaning to their daily tasks. Yogesh Malhotra, a KM guru, believes that a knowledge vision should allow diversity of multiple personal perspectives by being decisively vague and open-ended (Srikantaiah & Koenig, 2000). Without a clearly defined vision, KM tends not to be understood, which results into lost opportunities.

Communication Barriers

Communication barriers needed to generate and share knowledge could be caused by obstacles depicted in this paper. In addition, other factors such as the physical and time distance can also hinder effective communication. Although technology may offer a partial solution, much knowledge is generated and transferred through body language or the physical demonstration of skills. Furthermore, a certain level of intimacy may be necessary to establish comfortable communication of knowledge. Internet-based friendships suggest that intimacy does not depend solely on physical co-location, but it remains to be seen whether such friendships are based enough in reality to mimic the mutual understanding born of face-to-face encounters (Leonard & Sensiper, 1998).

Top Five Knowledge Management Leaders' Roles

The top five critical knowledge leaders' roles are listed in Figure 1. Each role will be briefly discussed below.

Foster a Knowledge Sharing Culture

The role of fostering a knowledge sharing culture ranked first in importance. An organizational culture is best defined as a pattern of basic assumptions that has worked well enough to be trusted by the organization's staff (Schein, 1985). The confusion around creating the right culture for KM assumes that the KM leader knows what the current culture is and how it relates to KM. This implies understanding how knowledge contributes to value within the organization, how culture around knowledge operates in the organization, how it arose and is maintained in its current state, and what might be done to encourage it to move in the desired direction. The KM leader will not single-handedly change a culture, but the KM leader should be the driver for cultural change as it relates to knowledge sharing. Hence, the KM leader helps shape the human factors toward a knowledge-sharing culture while simultaneously designing the systems and spaces that will support knowledge transfer among people.

Facilitate Knowledge Sharing Among Staff

Although the role of facilitating knowledge sharing among staff ranked second in importance, its mean rating difference with the previous role is very small, suggesting that the level of importance of both roles is very similar. An explanation for this observation is that accomplishing this role poses an enormous challenge if a knowledge sharing culture is non-existent. To facilitate knowledge sharing in their organization, various researchers suggest that KM leaders should identify the obstacles of effective knowledge sharing (Sears, 2001), encourage informal social interactions and build communities of practice (Earl & Scott, 1999), as well as develop corporate or in-house universities and labs (Bonner, 2000).

Convince Senior Management of KM Benefits

KM leaders should communicate and sell this new KM concept to executives (Corcoran & Jones, 1997). Knowledge merits an increased attention of top managers as a company increases their use of knowledge at a competition level (Foote, Matson & Rudd, 2001). Hence, as with any other major organizational projects (CRM, TQM, etc.), senior management should agree on what it hopes to gain from managing knowledge explicitly to better support a learning environment (Bonner, 2000; Flash, 2001; Guns, 1998; Liebowitz, 1999).

Lead by Example by Sharing Knowledge

Although this role was not advocated in the reviewed literature, it stands among the most important ones generated from the first questionnaire. The ability to share knowledge fosters a cooperative and collaborative environment. Respondents suggested that KM leaders should be role models in terms of sharing knowledge. One respondent stated that he or she "sets an example to others in sharing what [he or she] knows." Another respondent stated that KM leaders should be "KM crusaders", leading the way to knowledge sharing.

Embed KM within the Organization's Internal Processes

Likewise to the previous one, this role was proposed by respondents in the first questionnaire. The respondents' comments varied from "identifying business processes that create new knowledge" to "embedding knowledge processing capabilities by leading process redesign initiatives". A knowledge vision and culture could potentially help the company to rearrange knowledge in novel ways, as well as help the organization understand its history with the aim of managing knowledge differently. However, and more importantly, in order to properly embed KM within the organization's internal procedures, a KM leader should identify "where the company needs to change how [managing knowledge] gets done" (Von Krogh et al., 2000, p. 107).

Top Five Knowledge Management Leaders' Skills

Interpersonal and Leadership Skills

Due to the very small difference between the interpersonal and leadership skills' mean ratings, it can be asserted that both interpersonal and leadership skills are equally important. In order to surmount the fourth most important KM obstacle (lack of vision), KM leaders need to possess strong visionary leadership skills. The learning organization should be used as a model for crafting their vision and how KM can benefit their organization. Guns (1998, p. 317) accurately adds that they also "need a clear idea of what the corporation would look like once the vision had been realized". Today's KM leaders actively participate in senior executive decision-making (part of the third most important role). They must provide integrative insight and analysis based on what matters to the business, and recommend ways KM can contribute to the organizational success. Often, this will involve integration of complex strategic initiatives of the various enterprise lines of business. In these executive forums, the KM leader must know how to treat knowledge as an asset, and KM as a corporate function and a component of the enterprise, not as a separate entity. Knowledge leaders must use these sessions to present new ways KM investments can contribute to the business strategy. In addition, KM leaders can help business executives determine what business success can and should look like, and how KM adds value to the organization. All the above mentioned activities require KM leaders to possess exceptional interpersonal and leadership skills. Included in the interpersonal skills are people and communication skills. Since KM is a relatively new discipline, KM leaders are still trying to convince and create awareness on how KM can be beneficial to their organization. These skills can also assist the overall education of the executive team and organizational staff in its understanding of the value of leveraging knowledge, along with gaining the trust and confidence of all employees. Foote et al. (2001) rightly assert that KM leaders "stand or fall by their power to influence". Good people and communication skills have the power to assist in conveying proper understanding and application of KM to all levels of the organization. Thus, these skills will still be needed, long after the KM leader has proven herself or himself on the job.

Change Agent Skills

Knowledge leaders should be champions of change, bringing change into their organizations' daily business activities and how these are viewed. Consequently, KM leaders serve as agents of change for their organizations. They should be in the forefront of providing business process re-engineering and process improvement efforts. However, as one respondent noted: "Knowledge leaders don't lead change, they assist with it", thus they would not lead business process re-engineering efforts in the organization, but would assist those process improvement specialists with the appropriate KM support for the desired improvements. Moreover, with their most important role being to foster a knowledge sharing culture in the organization, KM leaders require change agent skills in order to recondition corporate cultures into becoming knowledge sharing cultures.

Motivational Skills

The motivational skills that should be possessed by KM leaders help them to achieve various tasks. Knowledge leaders should motivate the organization's staff to understand, value, and participate in knowledge sharing. As stated earlier, one method for doing so is to develop incentive or reward programs. However, this is only a tool used to help KM leaders motivate their staff. They still require motivational skills to propel the use of these programs and, even more importantly, to be use them effectively.

Creativity Skills

Knowledge leaders, like any business professional, tacitly rely upon basic metaphors or images. Since the methods of KM are based upon readily changing technologies, KM is a field that requires imaginative professionals to discern the significance of pertinent technological developments as well as knowledge paths. For example, KM leaders could take the role of cartographers, mapping the passages through which knowledge can travel. Knowledge, in order to be methodically categorized and trustworthy, should be imagined as something like the movement of traffic on roads, where there will be a perceived need for reliable roadmaps, consistent rules of the road and traffic regulations.

Top Five Knowledge Management Technologies

A growing number of organizations employ technologies to support their KM initiatives (Zyngier, 2001). The most critical KM technologies perceived by KM leaders are briefly discussed below.

Portals (Internet/Intranet/Extranet)

Portals ranked first in importance with a mean rating of 4.49. One of the Internet's greatest assets is that it is interactive and, thus, has the potential reciprocity to foster knowledge sharing and learning. It allows those who are seeking knowledge to access millions of Web pages.

Information Retrieval Engines

Information retrieval engines, the center of information businesses, mainly include searching printed reference sources, online sources, CD-ROMs, hypermedia, and Internet databases. To maintain high-quality control in information production and services in the highly competitive information business world, the speed of retrieval, the accuracy of retrieved information, and the cost of searching an enormous scale of information field must be strategically planned and tactically coordinated.

E-Mail

E-mail enables a community of practice to share knowledge asynchronously across the world. Although e-mail can be very effective, it may become too impersonal if there are few occasions for individuals in the community to get to know one another.

Collaborative Support Tools

These technologies allow formal and ad hoc conversations when the participants cannot communicate in real time, therefore enhancing the exchange of knowledge.

Document Management Systems

Explicit knowledge—knowledge that has been codified and is available to the seeker—can be easily captured and distributed through systems. In many organizations, knowledge has and still is being embedded in documents, hence the need for a document management system that "supports the unstructured data management requirements of KM initiatives through a process that involves capture, storage, access, selection, and document publication" (Duffy, 2001, p. 65).

CONCLUSION

Using a three-round Delphi procedure, this research reached an acceptable and stable level of agreement as well as a deeper understanding of the most important issues of today's KM leaders internationally. These issues included perceived KM benefits and obstacles, KM leaders' current roles and skills, as well as technologies used to develop and/or implement KM initiatives in their organizations.

An intense pace of competition, global markets, informed customers, and technological innovations has made the marketplace an increasingly level playing field. This study found that an organization needs to develop and implement KM initiatives not just to increase internal knowledge sharing, but to deliver higher quality products and services, avoid re-inventing the wheel, improve the quality of decision-making, as well as increase employees' collaboration.

The findings suggest that although specific approaches to KM vary from firm to firm, key themes and common concerns emerge. The most important KM leaders' roles are to foster a knowledge sharing culture, facilitate knowledge sharing among staff, and convince senior management of KM's benefits. In order to accomplish these duties, KM leaders need a wide range of skills. More precisely, they need to possess interpersonal, leadership, change agent, motivational, and creativity skills.

This study finds that the most important technologies are portals (Internet, Intranet, and Extranet), information retrieval engines, e-mail, collaborative work support tools, as well as document management systems. Other important technologies include corporate yellow pages of skills and expertise, knowledge maps, discussion boards, e-learning technologies, and data mining.

Results presented in this chapter can be summarized by saying that KM initiatives are successfully implemented as long as the right people, in this case KM leaders, have the right skills and are supported by the proper processes. This can be realized when the structure and culture are properly fostered to facilitate KM activities. These findings are aligned with previous recommendations made in the theory of collaboration where people, process, and structure are key elements to leadership activities (Huxham & Vangen, 2000; Winkler, 2006).

Our results also support the conclusion made by Hitt and Ireland (2002) where they clearly indicate that "strategic leaders must continuously evaluate, change, configure and leverage human capital and social capital" (p. 11). They must be able to identify the implicit knowledge needed by employees, evaluate and foster their tacit capabilities, and develop and maintain a culture of collaboration and trust between employees. These activities, which are unique to the company, are key elements to create a strategic advantage.

IMPLICATIONS FOR PRACTITIONERS AND RESEARCHERS

As stated by Whitley (1996, p. 23), one of the criteria in assessing the usefulness of a research theory is that it "should be applicable to the real world, helping us understand the processes involved in people's everyday lives". In other words, practitioners as well as academics should be able to benefit from research. Increasing this research's applicability to the real world is achieved first by providing future researchers with critical issues and perceived KM benefits and obstacles, as suggested by today's KM leaders. Researchers will be able to focus their studies on the most critical issues in order to help KM leaders make well-informed decisions. Researchers and practitioners will additionally be able to concentrate on finding new ways to help KM leaders attain KM benefits, as well as to overcome existing obstacles. Furthermore, by knowing about these benefits, KM leaders will be able to answer questions such as: "Why should I implement KM?", "How can KM benefit my company?", and so forth, questions that have now reached consensus among KM practitioners.

Second, the results of this research are aimed at academic program developers and people responsible for appointing KM leaders (Human Resources, CEOs, etc.). Academic KM programs

are beginning to emerge. Herschel and Nemati (1999) enumerate the School of Information Management and Systems at the University of California, Berkeley, the Fielding Institute, and the RMIT University in Melbourne, Australia as some of the few academic institutions currently offering a KM program. Hence, the need to know about KM leaders' roles and skills is becoming increasingly important. By providing these individuals with current KM leaders' roles and skills, the study allows academic developers to accurately craft graduate KM programs and properly educate their students on the roles played by KM leaders, as well as to build their students' skills and help them become KM leaders. The results of this study also guide Human Resources by enabling them to hire KM leaders that have the required skills, educational and professional backgrounds, and assign them the critical roles already played by current KM leaders.

Third, this KM study utilized the Delphi method in a Web-based environment. Findings suggest that when conducting a Delphi study, researchers should carefully consider certain criteria: the selection of experts, the level of agreement, the presence/absence and nature of the feedback provided to respondents, and the number of rounds. Applying the Delphi method in a Web-based environment was very convenient. The traditional Delphi procedure is time-consuming and costly, with a risk of high sample attrition between rounds. These drawbacks were easily controllable with a Web procedure, which resulted in faster response rates, lower costs, higher quality replies, and had the potential to reach an international audience.

Finally, but nonetheless importantly, the findings are also aimed at system and software developers. With a list of the most important technologies used for developing and implementing KM programs and initiatives, software and system developers will be able to understand and direct their efforts and resources in developing and/or enhancing the proper technologies, and in turn, will help ease the work of KM leaders dealing with KM current critical issues and obstacles, as well as to facilitate reaching KM benefits.

RESEARCH DIRECTIONS

Another criterion in assessing the usefulness of a research theory is that it "should stimulate research, not only basic research to test the theory, but also applied research to put the theory into use, and should inspire new discoveries" (Whitley, 1996, p. 23). This is similar to the first study conducted by Dickson et al. (1984), this study could stimulate research and be replicated after a period of time (i.e., four to five years) in order to update the results found as this "continuity of method and issue framework facilitate[s] longitudinal comparison of data" (Brancheau et al., 1996, p. 227). It can also be replicated in order to collect data that would enable results comparison.

REFERENCES

Abell, A., & Oxbrow, N. (1999). *Skills for knowledge management*. London: TFPL Ltd.

Alavi, M., & Leidner, D. (1999). Knowledge management systems: Emerging view and practices from the field. In *32nd Proceedings of the Hawaii International Conference on System Science*. January 5-9, Maui.

APQC. (2001). *Embedding KM: Creating a value proposition*. TX: Author.

Barclay, R.O. (1997). *The CKO: Vision, strategy, ambassadorial skills, and a certain je ne sais quoi*. Retrieved May 17, 2007, from *http://www.ktic.com/*

Bonner, D. (2000). Enter the chief knowledge officer. *Training & Development, 54*(2), 36-41.

Brancheau, J.C., Janz, B.D., & Wetherbe, J.C. (1996). Key issues in information systems management: 1994-95 SIM Delphi results. *MIS Quarterly, 20*(2), 225-242.

Brancheau, J.C., & Wetherbe, J.C. (1987). Key issues in information systems management. *MIS Quarterly, 11*(1), 22-45.

Breu, K., Grimshaw, D., Myers, A. (2000). *Releasing the value of knowledge: A survey of UK industry*. Cranfield School of Management.

Capshaw, S. (1999, July). Spotlight on knowledge leadership, where's the CKO? *Inform*, pp. 20-21.

Charney, M., & Jordan, J. (2000). The strategic benefits of knowledge management. Serviceware Technologies.

Chase, L. R. (1997). The knowledge-based organization: An international survey. *Journal of Knowledge Management, 1*(1), 38-49

Corcoran, M., & Jones, R. (1997). Chief knowledge officer? Perceptions, pitfalls, & potential. *Information Outlook, 1*(6), 30-36.

Couger, D.J. (1988). Key human resource issues in IS in the 1990s: Views of IS executives versus human resource executives. *Information & Management, 14*(4), 161-174.

Dalkey, N.C., & Helmer, O. (1963). An experimental application of the Delphi method to the use of experts. *Management Science, 9*(3), 458-467.

De Long, D. W., Fahey, L. (2000). Diagnosing cultural barriers to knowledge management. *Academy of management executive, 14*(4), 113-127.

Dexter, S.A., Janson, A.M., Kiudorf, E., & Laast-Laas, J. (1993). Key information technology issues in Estonia. *International Journal of Information Management, 2*(2), 139-153.

Dickson, G.W., Leitheiser, R.L., & Brancheau, C.J. (1984). Key information systems issues for the 1980's. *MIS Quarterly, 8*(3), 135-159.

Dillman, D.A., Sinclair, M.D., & Clark, J.R. (1993). Effects of questionnaire length, respondent-friendly design, and a difficult question on response rates for occupant-addressed census mail surveys. *Public Opinion Quarterly, 57*(3), 289-304.

Doke, E.R., & Swanson, N.E. (1995). Decision variables for selecting prototyping in information systems development: A Delphi study of MIS managers. *Information & Management, 29*(4), 173-182.

Dommeyer, C.J., & Moriart, E. (2000). Comparing two forms of an e-mail survey: Embedded vs. attached. *International Journal of Market Research, 42*(1), 39-50.

Duffy, J. (2001). The tools and technologies needed for knowledge management. *The Information Management Journal, 35*(1), 64-67.

Earl, M.J., & Scott, I.A. (1999). What is a chief knowledge officer? *Sloan Management Review, 40*(2), 29-38.

Flash, C. (2001, May). Who is the CKO? *Knowledge Management Magazine*. Freedom Technology Media Group. Retrieved August 31, 2007 from http://www.destinationkm.com/articles/default.asp?ArticleID=232

Foote, N.W., Matson, E., & Rudd, N. (2001). Managing the knowledge manager. *The McKinsey Quarterly, 3*, 120-129.

Green, A., & Price I. (2000). Whither FM? A Delphi study of the profession and the industry. *Facilities, 18*(7/8), 281-292.

Guns, B. (1998). The chief knowledge officer's role: Challenges and competencies. *Journal of Knowledge Management, 1*(4), 315-319.

Herschel, T.R., & Nemati, R.H. (1999). CKOs and knowledge management: Exploring opportunities for using information exchange protocols. *Proceedings of the 1999 ACM SIGCPR conference on Computer personnel research* (pp. 42-50).

Hill, Q.K., & Fowles, J. (1975). The methodological worth of the Delphi forecasting technique. *Technological Forecasting and Social Change, 7*(2), 179-192.

Hitt, M.A., & Ireland, R.D. (2002). The essence of strategic leadership: Managing human and social capital. *The Journal of Leadership and Organizational Studies, 9*(1), 3-14.

Huxham, C., & Vangen, S. (2000). Leadership in the shaping and implementation of collaboration agendas: How things happen in a (not quite) joined-up world. *Academy of Management Journal, 43*(6), 1159-1175.

Keller, A. (2001). Future development of electronic journals: A Delphi survey. *The Electronic Library, 19*(6), 383-396.

Kiesler, S., & Sproull, L.S. (1986). Response effects in the electronic survey. *Public Opinion Quarterly, 50*(3), 402-413.

KPMG (2000). *Knowledge management research report 2000*. London.

Leonard, D., & Sensiper, S. (1998). The role of tacit knowledge in group innovation. *California Management Review, 40*(3), 112-131.

Liebowitz, J. (1999). The new star in organizations: The chief knowledge officer and the knowledge audit function. *Proceedings of the 1999 ACM SIGCPR conference on Computer personnel research* (pp. 11-13).

Liebowitz, J. (Ed.). (2000). *Knowledge management handbook*. Boca Raton, FL: CRC Press.

McKeen, D. J., & Staples, D.S. (2001). *Knowledge managers: Who they are and what they do* (pp. 1-17). Kingston: Queen's School of Business.

Mehta, R., & Sivadas, E. (1995). Comparing response rates and response content in mail versus electronic mail surveys. *Journal of the Market Research Society, 37*(4), 429-439.

Miles, G., R. E., Perrone, V., & Edvinsson, L. (1998). Some conceptual and research barriers to the utilization of knowledge. *California Management Review 40*(3), 281-292.

Mintzberg, H. (1975, July-August). The manager's job, folklore and fact. *Harvard Business Review, 53*, 49-61

Neilson, R.E. (2000). Knowledge management and the role of the chief knowledge officer. Retrieved May 17, 2007, from *http://www.ndu.edu/ndu/irmc/km-cio_role/km-cio-role.htm*

Niederman, F., Brancheau, J.C., & Wetherbe, J.C. (1991). Information systems management issues for the 1990s. *MIS Quarterly, 15*(4), 474-500.

Offsey, S. (1997). knowledge management: Linking people to knowledge for bottom line results. *Journal of Knowledge Management, 1*(2), 113-122.

Oppermann, M. (1995). E-mail surveys: Potentials and pitfalls. *Marketing Research, 7*(3), 28-33.

PriceWaterHouseCoopers. (2000). *Technology forecast: 2000.* Menlo Park, CA: Author.

Rasmus, D. (2000). How to make the chief knowledge officer (role) work. *Giga* (p. 6).

Schaefer D.R., & Dillman, D.A. (1998). Development of a standard e-mail methodology: Results of an experiment. *Public Opinion Quarterly, 62*(3), 378-397.

Schein, E.H. (1985). *Organizational culture and leadership.* San Francisco: Jossey-Bass.

Schmidt, R.C. (1997). Managing Delphi surveys using nonparametric statistical techniques. *Decision Sciences, 28*(3), 763-774.

Schmidt, R., Lyytinen, K., Keil, M., & Cule, P. (2001). Identifying software project risks: An international Delphi study. *Journal of Management Information Systems, 17*(4), 5-36

Sears, R. (2001). Managing the knowledge asset manager. *Knowledge Management Asia-Pacific, 1*(2), 8-10.

Siegel, S. (1956). *Nonparametric statistics for the behavioral sciences.* New York: McGraw-Hill.

Skyrme, D.J. (1997). Knowledge management: Making sense of an oxymoron. Retrieved May 17, 2007, from *http://skyrme.com/insights/22km.htm*

Srikantaiah, K.T., & Koenig, E.D.M. (Eds.). (2000). *Knowledge management for the information professional.* Medford, NJ: Information Today, Inc.

TechWeb (1999). *Sharing knowledge isn't easy yet.* Retrieved August 31, 2007 from http://www.informationweek.com/bizint/biz748/48bzshr.htm

Tse, A.C.B. (1998). Comparing the response rate, response speed, and response quality of two methods of sending questionnaires: E-mail vs. mail. *Journal of the Market Research Society, 40*(4), 354-361.

Von Krogh, G., Ichijo, K., & Nonaka, I. (2000). *Enabling knowledge creation.* New York: Oxford University Press.

Waruszynski, T.B. (2000). *The knowledge revolution: A literature review.* Ottawa: Defence R&D Canada.

Watson, T.R. (1989). Key issues in information systems management: An Australian perspective. *The Australian Computer Journal, 21*(2), 118-129.

Wensley, K. P. A., & O'Sullivan, A. V. (2000). *Tools for knowledge management.* Retrieved August 30, 2007 from http://www.icasit.org/km/toolsforkm.htm

Whitley, B. (1996). *Principles of research in behavioral science.* Mountain View, CA: Mayfield Publishing Company.

Whitman, I.N. (1990). The Delphi technique as an alternative for committee meetings. *Journal of Nursing Education, 29*(8), 377-379.

Winkler, I. (2006). Network governance between individual and collective goals: Qualitative evidence from six networks. *Journal of Leadership and Organizational Studies, 12*(3), 119-133.

Zand, D. (1997). *The leadership triad: Knowledge, trust, and power.* Oxford: Oxford University Press.

Zyngier, M. S. (2001). *Knowledge management strategies in Australia.* Caulfield East, AU: Monash University.

Additional Reading on Knowledge Management

Abell, A., & Oxbrow, N. (1999). *Skills for knowledge management.* London: TFPL Ltd.

Baek, S., Liebowitz, J., Prasad, S.Y., & Granger, M. (2000). Intelligent agents for knowledge management: Toward intelligent Web-based collaboration within virtual teams. In J. Liebowitz (Ed.), *Knowledge management handbook* (p. 169).

Bair, J., & O'Connor, E. (1998). The state of the product in knowledge management. *Journal of Knowledge Management, 2*(2), 20-27.

Berry, M.J.A., & Linoff, G.S. (2000). *Mastering data mining.* New York: Robert Ipsen.

Blaylock, K.B., & Rees, P.L. (1984). Cognitive style and the usefulness of information. *Decision Sciences, 15*(1), 74-91.

Bontis, N. (2000). CKO wanted: Evangelical skills necessary: A review of the chief knowledge officer position. *Knowledge and Process Management, 8*(1), 29-38.

Charney, M., & Jordan, J. (2000). The strategic benefits of knowledge management.

Davenport, T. (1994). Coming soon: The CKO. Retrieved May 17, 2007, from *http://www.informationweek.com/509/cko.htm*

Davenport, T. (2000). Knowledge management and the broader firm: Strategy, advantage, and performance. *Knowledge Management Handbook.* In J. Liebowitz (Ed.), *Knowledge management handbook* (pp. 32-41).

Despres, C., & Chauvel, D. (1999). Knowledge management(s). *Journal of Knowledge Management, 3*(2), 110-120.

Duffy, J. (2000). The KM technology infrastructure. *Information Management Journal, 34*(2), 62-66.

Han, J., & Kamber, M. (2001). *Data mining concepts and techniques.* Morgan Kaufmann.

Hansen, M.T., Nohria, N., & Tierney, T. (1999, March/April). What's your strategy for managing knowledge. *Harvard Business Review*, pp. 106-116.

KPMG. (2000). *Knowledge management research report 2000.* London.

Lee, C.C., & Yang, J. (2000). Knowledge value chain. *The Journal of Management Development, 19*(9), 783-794.

Manasco, B. (1997, July). Should your company appoint a chief knowledge officer. Retrieved May 17, 2007, from *http://www.Webcom.com/quantera/Empires0797.html*

Nissen, M., Kamel, M., & Sengupta, K. (2000). Integrated analysis and design of knowledge systems and processes. In Y. Malhotra (Ed.), *Knowledge management and virtual organizations* (pp. 214-242). Hershey, PA: Idea Group Publishing.

Nonaka, I., & Takeuchi, H. (1995). *The knowledge creating company: How Japanese companies cre-*

ate the dynamics of innovation. Oxford: Oxford University Press.

Offsey, S. (1997). Knowledge management: Linking people to knowledge for bottom line results. *Journal of Knowledge Management, 1*(2), 113-122.

Paquette, P. (1998). CKO: Trendiest job in business. *High Technology Careers Magazine.* Retrieved May 17, 2007, from *http://www.hightechcareers. com/doc498e/trendiest498e.html*

Parks, M.R., & Floyd, K. (1996). Making friends in cyberspace. *Journal of Communication, 46,* 80-97.

Rosser, B. (1999). *Knowledge mapping: Automated or manual?* Gartner Group.

Sproull, L.S. (1986). Using electronic data collection in organizational research. *Academy of Management Journal, 29*(1), 159-169.

Thomsen, S.R. (1996). @ work in cyberspace: Exploring practitioner use of the PR Forum. *Public Relations Review, 22,* 115-131.

Venzin, M. (1997). Crafting the future: Strategic conversations in the knowledge economy. *Business & Administration.* University of St. Gallen.

Williams, J. (2002, January/February). Practical issues in knowledge management. *IT Professional*, pp. 35-39.

Zelwietro, J. (1998). The politicization of environmental organizations through the Internet. *The Information Society, 14,* 45-56.

Additional Reading on the Delphi Method

Benaire, M. (1988). Delphi and Delphi like approaches with special regard to environmental standard. *Technological Forecasting and Social Change, 33,* 149-158.

Birdir, K., & Pearson, E.T. (2000). Research chefs' competencies: A Delphi approach. *International Journal of Contemporary Hospitality Management, 12*(3), 205-209.

Chakravarti, K.A., Vasanta, B., Krishnan, A., & Dubash, R. (1998). Modified Delphi methodology for technology forecasting. *Technological Forecasting and Social Change, 58,* 155-165.

Dekleva, S., & Zupancic, J. (1996). Key issues in information systems management: A Delphi study in Slovania. *Information & Management, 31,* 1-11.

Delbecq, A.L., Van de Ven, A.H., & Gustafson, D.H. (1975). *Group techniques for program planning: A guide to nominal group and Delphi processes.* Glenview, IL: Scott-Foresman.

Erffmeyer, R.C., Erffmeyer, E.S., & Lane, I.M. (1986). The Delphi technique: An empirical evaluation of the optimal number of rounds. *Group & Organization Studies, 11*(2), 120-128.

Fowles, J. (1978). *Handbook of futures research.* Westport, CT: Greenwood Press.

Gray, P., & Nilles, J.M. (1983). Evaluating a Delphi forecast on personal computers. *IEEE Transactions on Systems, Man, and Cybernetics, 13*(2), 222-224.

Gupta, U.M., & Clarke, E.R. (1996). Theory and applications of the Delphi technique: A bibliography (1975-1994). *Technological Forecasting and Social Change, 53,* 185-211.

Haan, J., & Peters, R. (1993). Technology: Toys or tools? Results of a Dutch Delphi study. *Information & Management, 25,* 283-289.

Jeffery, D., Ley, A., Bennun, I., & McLaren, S. (2000). Delphi survey of opinion on interventions, service principles and service organisation for severe mental illness and substance misuse problems. *Journal of Mental Health, 9*(4), 373-384.

APPENDIX A: TOP ISSUES AND THEIR MAIN SOURCES

Top Issues	Sources
Knowledge Management Benefits	
Increase the effective utilization of knowledge resources	Breu et al., 2000
Avoid re-inventing the wheel	Waruszynski, 2000
Improve the quality of decision-making	Chase, 1997; Charney & Jordan, 2000
Deliver higher quality products and services	Waruszynski, 2000
Decrease learning/training time	Breu et al., 2000; Waruszynski, 2000
Increase internal knowledge sharing	Breu et al., 2000; Waruszynski, 2000
Increase external knowledge sharing	Breu et al., 2000; Waruszynski, 2000
Help identifying new business opportunities	Chase, 1997; Charney & Jordan, 2000; KPMG, 2000
Increase employee satisfaction	Breu et al., 2000; Waruszynski, 2000
Increase innovation	Waruszynski, 2000
Knowledge Management Obstacles	
Organizational culture	Chase, 1997; Waruszynski, 2000; McKeen & Staples, 2001
Lack of time	Chase, 1997; Waruszynski, 2000
Information/communication technology	Chase, 1997; McKeen and Staples, 2001
Lack of incentive (reward) system	Chase, 1997; Waruszynski, 2000
Lack of senior management support	Chase, 1997; Waruszynski, 2000
Organizational structure	Chase, 1997
Staff turnover	Chase, 1997; Waruszynski, 2000; McKeen & Staples, 2001
Physical layout of work spaces	Chase, 1997
Nonstandardized processes	Chase, 1997; McKeen & Staples, 2001
Emphasis on individual rather than team	Chase, 1997; Waruszynski, 2000
Knowledge Leaders' Roles	
Foster a knowledge sharing culture in my organization	Davenport, 1994; Corcoran & Jones, 1997; Guns, 1998, Earl & Scott, 1999; Herschel & Nemati, 1999; Bonner, 2000; Flash, 2001; Sears, 2001
Develop my organization's knowledge resources	Davenport, 1994; Skyrme, 1997; Guns, 1998; Paquette, 1998; Herschel & Nemati, 1999; Liebowitz, 1999; Bonner, 2000; Lee & Yang, 2000
Convince senior management of what our organization will gain through managing knowledge	Corcoran & Jones, 1997; Guns, 1998; Liebowitz, 1999; Bonner, 2000; Flash, 2001; Foote et al., 2001
Drive initiatives to measure KM benefits in my organization	Davenport, 1994; Guns, 1998; Earl & Scott, 1999; Herschel & Nemati, 1999; Flash, 2001
Select and provide support for technologies that contribute to implement KM activities in my organization	Guns, 1998; Earl & Scott, 1999; Bonner, 2000; Lee & Yang, 2000
Knowledge Leaders' Skills	
Project management skills	Abell & Oxbrow, 1999; Barclay, 1997; Bonner, 2000; Brown, 1999; Corcoran & Jones, 1997; Earl & Scott, 1999; Flash, 2001; Guns, 1998; Herschel & Nemati, 1999; Lee & Yank, 2000; Manasco, 1997; Rasmus, 2000; Schelin, 2001; Weinstein, 1998
Technological skills	Barclay, 1997; Corcoran & Jones, 1997; Davenport, 1994; Flash, 2001; Herschel & Nemati, 1999; Liebowitz, 1999; Paquette, 1998; Rasmus, 2000; Schelin, 2001; Weinstein, 1998

continued on following page

APPENDIX A: CONTINUED

Interpersonal skills	Abell & Oxbrow, 1999; Bonner, 2000; Corcoran & Jones, 1997; Earl & Scott, 1999; Flash, 2001; Guns, 1998; Neilson, 2000; Rasmus, 2000; Schelin, 2001; Skyrme, 1997
Leadership skills	Abell & Oxbrow, 1999; Bonner, 2000; Corcoran & Jones, 1997; Flash, 2001; Foote et al., 2001; Herschel & Nemati, 1999; Neilson, 2000; Rasmus, 2000; Skyrme, 1997
Change agent skills	Abell & Oxbrow, 1999; Bonner, 2000; Flash, 2001; Guns, 1998; Rasmus, 2000; Skyrme, 1997
Knowledge Management Technologies	
Portals (Internet/intranet/extranet)	Offsey, 1997; Chase, 1997; TechWeb, 1999
E-mail	Chase, 1997; Duffy, 2001; Bontis, 2000
Information retrieval engines	Offsey, 1997; Bair & O'Connor, 1998
Collaborative work support tools	Chase, 1997; Offsey, 1997; Bair & O'Connor, 1998; TechWeb, 1999; APQC, 2001; Duffy, 2001
Corporate yellow pages of skills and expertise	Chase, 1997; TechWeb, 1999
Videoconference	Chase, 1997
Audio-conference	Chase, 1997
Document management systems	Offsey, 1997; Bair & O'Connor, 1998; TechWeb, 1999; Duffy, 2001
Data mining	Chase, 1997; Offsey, 1997; TechWeb, 1999; Duffy, 2001
Help-desk applications	Offsey, 1997

APPENDIX B: COMPARISONS BETWEEN RESULTS OF THE FINAL AND PREVIOUS ROUNDS

	R3 Mean	R3 SD	Difference between Round 3 and Round 2 (R3 –R2)						
			Mean	SD	Median	Mode	IQR	%rate >=4	Rank
Benefits									
1. Increase internal knowledge sharing	4.57	0.57	0.01	0.01	0	0	0	-0.03	-1
2. Deliver higher quality products and services	4.48	0.64	0.12	-0.15	1	0	0	0.02	-7
3. Avoid re-inventing the wheel	4.47	0.75	-0.14	0.08	0	0	0	0.00	2
4. Improve the quality of decision-making	4.42	0.69	-0.10	0.09	0	0	0	-0.04	1
5. Increase collaboration between employees	4.39	0.59	-0.06	-0.04	-1	-1	0	0.02	0
Obstacles									
1. Organizational culture	4.58	0.66	-0.06	0.06	0	0	0	-0.01	0
2. Lack of senior management support	4.43	0.75	-0.05	0.02	0	0	0	-0.02	0
3. Reluctance to change	4.16	0.70	-0.08	-0.09	0	0	0	0.01	0
4. Lack of vision	4.09	0.89	-0.15	0.16	0	0	0	-0.08	0
5. Communication barriers	4.00	0.77	0.00	-0.03	0	0	0	0.00	0

continued on following page

APPENDIX B: CONTINUED

Roles									
1. Foster a knowledge sharing culture in my organization	4.59	0.64	-0.19	0.12	0	0	1	-0.03	0
2. Facilitate knowledge sharing among staff	4.56	0.61	0.23	-0.01	1	1	0	0.04	-3
3. Convince senior management of what our organization will gain through managing knowledge	4.49	0.67	-0.01	0.04	0	0	0	-0.03	0
4. Lead by example by sharing knowledge	4.48	0.72	-0.06	0.08	0	0	0	-0.01	2
5. Embed KM within internal processes	4.37	0.66	0.05	-0.01	0	1	0	-0.03	-2
Skills									
1. Interpersonal skills	4.54	0.61	-0.10	0.05	0	0	0	-0.02	0
2. Leadership skills	4.53	0.54	-0.02	-0.02	0	0	0	0.01	0
3. Change agent skills	4.43	0.73	0.06	-0.04	0	0	0	0.02	-1
4. Motivational skills	4.40	0.65	-0.09	0.02	-1	0	0	0.00	1
5. Creativity skills	4.12	0.77	-0.04	0.07	0	0	0	-0.07	0
Technologies									
1. Portals	4.49	0.70	0.05	0.04	0	0	0	0.03	0
2. Information Retrieval Engine	4.28	0.66	0.08	-0.09	0	0	0	0.02	-1
3. E-mail	4.24	0.90	-0.10	0.18	1	0	0	-0.11	1
4. Collaborative Work Support	4.04	0.82	-0.04	0.05	0	0	0	-0.04	0
5. Document Management Systems	4.03	0.73	-0.05	-0.01	0	0	-1	0.01	1

APPENDIX C: KENDALL'S COEFFICIENT OF CONCORDANCE W IN ROUNDS TWO AND THREE

Jenkins, D.A., & Smith, T.E. (1994). Applying Delphi methodology in family therapy research. *Contemporary Family Therapy, 15*, 205-208.

Jones, T. (1980). *Options for the future: A comparative analysis of policy oriented forecasts.* New York: Praeger Publishers.

Linstone, H.A., & Turoff, M. (1975). *The Delphi method: Techniques and applications.* Addison-Wesley Publishing Company.

Lynn, M.R., Layman, E.L., & Englebardt, S.P. (1998). Nursing administration research properties: A national Delphi study. *Journal of Nursing Administration, 28*(5), 7-11.

Masser, I., & Foley, P. (1987). Delphi revisited: Expert opinion in urban analysis. *Urban Studies, 24*(3), 217-224.

Murry, W.J.J., & Hammons, O.J. (1995). Delphi: A versatile methodology for conducting qualitative research. *The Review of Higher Education, 18*(4), 423-436.

Section II
Knowledge Management (KM) Strategies

Chapter IV
External Knowledge Search Strategy as an Essential Element of a Knowledge Management Strategy

Fergal McGrath
University of Limerick, Ireland

Rebecca Purcell
University of Limerick, Ireland

ABSTRACT

This chapter introduces external knowledge search strategy as a central element of an organizations overall knowledge management strategy. The argument cites how knowledge management has developed around a myopic internal focus and has thus far failed to take full account of the many sources of knowledge external to the organization. The chapter offers external knowledge search strategy as a means of integrating this external focus into knowledge management understanding, by providing a conceptual framework for organizations involved in the external knowledge management activity of external knowledge search. The framework identifies 10 search paths organizations may follow into the search space, four of which relate exclusively to external knowledge search. The authors hope that establishing an external element within knowledge management strategy will inform knowledge management's recognition of the value of the extended enterprise.

FILLING KNOWLEDGE GAPS

Knowledge management research and practice predominantly focuses on the internal knowledge possessed by organizations and the issues that surround the management and coordination of this knowledge. This internal focus has lead to knowledge management's obsession with identifying, measuring, manipulating, and codifying knowledge that is held internal to the organization. An alternative way to look at knowledge management is to regard it in terms of "the knowledge we don't have", also referred to as knowledge absences (Spender, 2006) and knowledge gaps (Zack, 1999, 2005). If this alternative stance is adopted, the purpose of knowledge management becomes twofold: first, to identify the knowledge spaces to be filled within the organization and, second, to coordinate the activities that will lead to this space being filled. The focus of this chapter is on the second activity, and how in order to fill knowledge absences and gaps organizations must engage in search activity across the external search space, thus making external knowledge search an important knowledge management activity.

General business strategy takes into account the importance of a balance between internal and external strategic activities. This balanced focus is lacking in knowledge management strategy, however. The appropriateness of an organization's overall strategy is related to its resources, environmental circumstances, and core objectives. This is represented by a balanced approach to SWOT analysis, whereby organizations focus on both the internal elements of strengths and weaknesses and the external elements of opportunities and threats (Zack, 1999). Knowledge management strategy, however, remains overly focused on the internal elements of strengths and weaknesses. This leads to organizations being blind-sided by missed opportunities and potential threats from the external environment (Christensen, 1997). Contemporary organizational understanding should take into account the many metaphors of knowledge at work

in and around organizations, including knowledge as power, knowledge as meaning, and knowledge as asset. A balanced approach to knowledge management strategy should therefore draw on all of these understandings of knowledge to identify, refine, and solve market-based problems through creative decision-making, which in turn results in the development of new knowledge from both internal and external sources. Any organization's value creation is based on a combination of the effective management of its knowledge base (Spender, 1996) both actual (internal) and potential (external). To this end, knowledge search is one of the main activities through which organizations develop their knowledge bases through the alignment of internal and external knowledge strategies (Levinthal & March, 1993).

Bounded rationality perspectives on management lead us to assume that a manager's decision-making ability is constrained by limitations of knowledge (Cyert & March, 1963); the same is true of organizations themselves. While an organizations existence is a consistent attempt to achieve higher levels of knowledge generation and integration than the market (Spender, 1996), they endeavor to do this under conditions of knowledge limitations. Thus, organizations cannot internally possess or control all of the diverse knowledge relevant to their existing or potential innovative processes. These internal knowledge limitations lead many innovative organizations to search for and acquire knowledge from external sources.

Literatures, including externalities and spillovers (Breschi & Lissoni, 2001; Powell, Koput & Smith-Doerr, 1996; Tallman, Jenkins, Henry, & Pinch, 2004), learning regions (Florida, 1995; Morgan, 1997), and absorptive capacity (Cohen & Levinthal, 1990; Zahra & George, 2002) suggest that the ability of the firm to access and use knowledge from outside its confines is important to overall performance. External knowledge is important to organizations because it allows firms to create new knowledge and grow (Arrow, 1962; Bierly & Chakrabarti, 1996) and to avoid the risk of an over-reliance on internal knowledge and thus learning traps (Ahuja & Lampert, 2001; Levinthal & March, 1993). As argued by Leonard-Barton (1995), companies need to import outside knowledge in order to build core capabilities. It can be argued therefore that the continued success of innovative performance is at least somewhat dependent on externally sourced knowledge and know-how (Camagni, 1991; Keeble, Lawson & Wilkinson, 1999).

Organizations pursue external knowledge through external knowledge search. External knowledge search is the active process of searching for organizational knowledge outside the boundaries of the searching organization in the external knowledge search space or landscape. This knowledge search space is defined here in terms of technological, geographic, and social elements. External knowledge search is distinct from the passive permeation of knowledge spillovers, as it is manifested as a definitive action at the organizational, group, community, or individual network level. External knowledge search is also a central part of problem solving, decision-making, and thus innovative activity. Search targets external to the organization include subsidiary and parent firms, customers, competitors, suppliers, joint venture partners, government agencies, industry and trade associations, and universities at the organizational level and personal business contacts at the individual level (Audretsch & Stephan, 1996; Baden-Fuller & Grant, 2004; Cohen, Nelson & Walsh, 2002; Neely, Filippini, Forza, Vinelli & Hii, 2000; Powell et al., 1996; Prahalad & Ramaswamy, 2000; Pyke, Beccattini, & Sengenberger, 1990).

The purpose of this chapter is to provide a conceptual framework for organizations involved in the external knowledge management activity of external knowledge search. The framework identifies 10 search paths organizations may follow into the search space, four of which relate exclusively to external knowledge search. The remainder of the chapter is structured as follows.

First, key insights from the extant knowledge search literature are highlighted and the existing technology based view of search activity and the search space is reviewed. Second, novel propositions from the knowledge management literature on the nature of knowledge lead to a reconceptualization of knowledge based search activity. Thus geographical and social dimensions are added as central phenomena to the search action and search space. Third, knowledge search is linked to knowledge strategy through the identification of internal and external search paths based on the three dimensions that define the search space. Following these search paths enables organizations to engage in a balanced approach to internal and external knowledge management strategy. Future trends and conclusions follow in the final sections.

BACKGROUND: CONDITIONS OF KNOWLEDGE SEARCH

Search has always been recognized as an important organizational activity, and the conditions under which organizations engage in search activity are a central discussion in organizational theory's main fields. These include the behavioral theory of the firm (Cyert & March, 1963) which describes search in problemistic terms; that is, organizations search in order to problem solve and stop when a solution is found or the cost of further search outweighs the benefits of potential returns from continued search action. Problemistic search is also linked to the idea of satisficing- or failure-induced search, whereby "search is stimulated if the most preferred known alternative is below the target" (March, 1991, p. 72). The evolutionary theory of the firm (Nelson & Winter, 1982) also regards search as a central mechanism by which organizations evolve over time, going as far as to cite variations in search activity and search capability as conferring an organizational advantage. As well as echoing behavioral theories of the firm by emphasizing the satisficing nature of search, evolutionary theory also points to the "localness" of search activity, or the probability that organizations will focus search activity on knowledge and technologies that are similar to the searching organizations own core knowledge, resulting in path-dependent organizational evolution. March (1991) later refers to this path-dependent search activity as exploitation.

Finally, organizational learning theorists also emphasize the importance of search as a driver of organizational learning cycles and organizational learning processes (Levitt & March, 1988). Knowledge search is cited as being one of the activities leading to change in organizational rules, routines, and beliefs, and thus leading to organizational learning. Organizational learning views searching organizations as biased toward exploitation-based search and learning by doing and thus the re-use and recombination of routines already known to the organization (Baum, Xiao-Li, & Usher, 2000). Early works on organizational learning regarded new search activity as beginning from the last prior choice made (Levitt & March, 1988). More recently, writings in the area by the same authors have warned of the "myopia of learning" and learning and competency traps, stating that "learning is constrained by the same limits as rationality i.e. experience is a poor teacher" (Levinthal & March, 1993, p. 96).

Representing extant discussions on search conditions into a single model proves taxing; however, Levinthal and March's (1981) stochastic model of adaptive organizational search, presented in Figure 1, embodies both previous and subsequent discussions on search from various literatures. In the model, search activity is stimulated under various conditions, including a need to problem solve or the perceived success or failure of the organization in a given period. Success or failure is shown to lead to an increase or decrease in aspiration levels. These aspiration levels in turn impact the setting of organizational performance related goals, which determine the allocation of resources to search activity. Levinthal and March's (1981) model views knowledge search as conducted along a technological trajectory or orientation; thus they regard the knowledge search space as defined solely by the technological knowledge being searched for; organizations tend towards a focus of search activity within the innovation knowledge pool in times of success, while organizations deemed to have failed relative to goals in a given period search predominantly in the refinement pool of knowledge. The searching organization subsequently selects the highest value technology from the knowledge pool searched. The chosen technology positively or negatively impacts performance levels and determines success or failure for that period, and thus the cycle

Figure 1. An adaptive model of organizational search

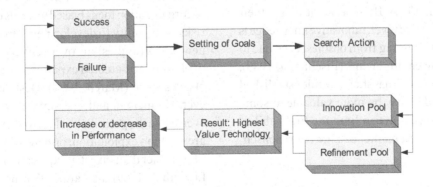

begins again. An interpretation of this model is presented in Figure 1.

Success, as determined by an achieving or surpassing of organizational goals, leads to increases in spending on search in the innovative pool and thus an increased propensity to innovate. Success also leads to increasing levels of slack or stocks of knowledge within the organization that act as a buffer against periods of failure. Failure on the other hand leads organizations to increase spending on refinement and thus increases an organizations propensity toward path-dependence. Throughout the search activity, the model proposes that organizational search experience is continually improving and developing based on learning by doing.

Technology: The Existing Dimension of Knowledge Search

Both traditional and contemporary discussions on organizational search propose that search is conducted along a single technological search orientation, thus the search space is defined solely in terms of the technological knowledge organizations search. Levinthal and March (1981) refer to this as a focusing of search activity on the refinement or innovative pools of knowledge. March (1991) later adapts this technology construct under the terms exploitation, referring to refinement, and exploration, referring to innovation. Organizations face a choice of dividing attention and resources between theses two alternatives (March, 1991, 1994). Both strategies have their own limitations; however, innovative knowledge is often cited as suffering from obsolescence due to ever-changing environments (Eisenhardt, 1989). Conversely, research has shown, while established older knowledge may be more valuable to some innovative process, it can limit the firms ability to react quickly to market change (Christensen, 1997).

Exploitation Dimension of Knowledge Search

Exploitation or refinement refers to a concentration of search activity on technologies similar to the organization's own core technologies and includes the re-use of technology internal to the organization, through experiential refinement and the selection of existing routines, incremental organizational change, mergers and acquisitions, and strategic alliances with similar organizations (Ginsberg & Baum, 1994; Gulati & Gargiulo, 1999; Kelly & Amburgey, 1991; Simonin, 1997; Stuart & Podolny, 1996). Exploitation facilitates competence building through its recurrent concentration on areas of established organizational competence (Baum et al., 2000). As a search activity, it also benefits from increasing returns to scale, in that exploitation in one area renders all other exploitation in that area more efficient (Levinthal & March, 1981), and relative certainty, in that inventors learn from past mistakes (Fleming, 2001) and is seen to lead to the development of absorptive capacity (Cohen & Levinthal, 1990). From the resource perspective, the exploitation of internal technologies can in many cases lead to competitive advantage due to the fact that these internal technologies are not widely accessible to other firms. Exploitation is a necessary activity due to time lags that exist in the development of knowledge and markets (Garud & Nayyar, 2004). The result of exploitation is in the main incremental innovation (Nelson & Winter, 1982). An organization focus biased towards exploitation risks an inability to develop new capabilities and new opportunities, an over-reliance on subjectively framed outdated experience, and therefore obsolescence (March, 1994). Despite this, however, Kahneman and Tversky (1979) found that even when the perceived value from exploration is greater than exploitation, organizations may take a loss rather than invest in exploration. Cohen and Levinthal (1989) also argue that positive R&D

Figure 2. The technological dimension of knowledge search

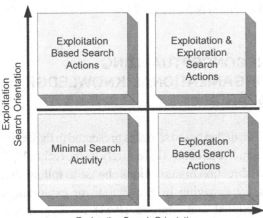

results are greater the closer the R&D activity is to the organizations existing competencies. However a knowledge strategy focused on the exploitation of knowledge repositories requires knowledge transfer to occur across time, which in turn requires organizations to develop the ability to retrieve and re-use knowledge held over time in the organization (Garud & Nayyar, 2004). Figure 2 presents the four search positions an organization can hold in relation to the technological direction of their search activity. Organizations biased towards following an exploitation based search trajectory are represented in the upper left quadrant of Figure 2. Added to the exploitation search domain is the dimension of search depth (Katila & Ahuja, 2002), which refers to how deeply a firm re-uses its existing knowledge.

Exploration Dimension of Knowledge Search

Exploration is a search conducted in technological domains far removed from the organizations own core technologies (Baum et al., 2000; March, 1991; March & Levitt, 1988; Katila & Ahuja, 2002; Rosenkopf & Nerker, 2001). Examples of exploration based activity include partnerships with universities, government agencies, and independent inventors (Katila, 2002; Laursen & Salter, 2003). Exploration implies increased risk-taking and time and cost requirements on the part of the organization; however, this also implies the possibility of increased rewards (March, 1994). Exploration is the main driver of first mover advantage (Levinthal & March, 1993) and has been shown to aid in the creation of architectural competence (Henderson & Cockburn, 1994), dynamic capability (Teece, Pisano, & Shuen, 1997), and a positive influence on learning, knowledge generation, innovation, and performance (Sidhu, Volberda & Commandeur, 2004). Exploration or path creating search results from idiosyncratic situations faced by firms engaged in local or exploitative search, external boundary spanning activities and networking (Ahuja & Katila, 2004). Successful exploration results predominantly in radical innovation (Ettlie, Bridges & O'Keefe, 1984). An organization focus biased towards exploration, however, incurs many of the costs associated with search and experimentation without gaining proportionate benefits (March, 1994). Levinthal and March (1993) recommend a strategy whereby organizations explore the successful explorations of others; Katila (2002) also found that the optimal time to engage in explorative activity is when the technological knowledge in question is not "new" allowing time for articulation and diffusion across the industry. However, as exploration is a systemwide phenomenon such a strategy would ultimately result in a decrease in the technologies available for exploration (Levinthal & March, 1993). To avoid this, industry sectors and individual organizations can reward individuals and firms for engaging in explorative activity, that is, through patenting (Levinthal & March, 1993); to this end, Henderson and Cockburn (1994) demonstrate that firms who look beyond their core competence and place more emphasis on being part of a larger scientific community generate more patents. Consistent levels of exploration have also been shown to achieve better results than internal exploitation (Rosenkopf & Nerker, 2001).

Daft, Sormunen, and Parks (1988) also suggest the importance of the proactive approach, finding that high performing firms searched more often and broadly under conditions of strategic uncertainty or exploration. Organizations following an exclusively exploration based search path are represented in the lower right quadrant of Figure 2. Added to exploration search space is the extra dimension of search scope, which refers to how widely an organization searches the exploration landscape (Katila & Ahuja, 2002).

Balancing Exploitation and Exploration Based Knowledge Search

Compared to exploration, the returns from exploitation exist in the short term and to ensure continued value creation both strategies need to be employed to some degree[1]; therefore, it is necessary to strike a balance between the two to maximize the returns from search activity (March, 1991; Levinthal & March, 1993). This balance results in trade-offs over time, people and knowledge. In effect the majority of organizational processes, including learning, imitation, technical change, and regeneration, all involve a trade-off between exploration and exploitation (March, 1991). To achieve a balance of both activities, exploitation and exploration can be separated departmentally; this strategy relies on a well-developed internal transfer capability (Zack, 1999). Organizations can also adapt to an ambidextrous form, allowing for centralization and decentralization to occur at different departmental levels (Tushman, 2003). In Figure 2 organizations that have achieved a balance in their exploitation and exploration activities are represented in the upper right quadrant, while those organizations engaging in minimal knowledge search activity are portrayed in the lower left quadrant. Organizations can change the technological focus of their search activity over time, to move between all four quadrants, with the desired technologi-

cally based search position being a balance of exploitation and exploration based search activity (Levinthal & March, 1993).

RECONCEPTUALIZING ORGANIZATIONAL KNOWLEDGE SEARCH

Knowledge based search is presented in the extant literature as controlled entirely by the technological direction organizations choose to follow, that is, by engaging in exploitation or exploration. Levinthal and March's (1981) existing model of adaptive search is also linear and sequential, taking an informational rather than knowledge based view of search activity. However knowledge management's recent investigations into the nature of knowledge, knowing, and knowledge based activities have taught us that knowledge and knowing are inherently complex and dynamic (Cook & Brown, 1999; Hargadon & Fanelli, 2002; Orlikowski, 2002), often chaotic (Schultze & Stabell, 2004; Tsoukas, 2001), routed in informal interactions (Pfeffer & Sutton, 1999; Wenger & Snyder, 2000) and communities, (Sawhney & Prandelli, 2004) and show little respect for the boundaries of the organization (Baden-Fuller & Grant, 2004). Added to this are enhanced understandings on the characteristics of knowledge search from the contemporary search literature, such as search's irreversibility, dependency on existing pools of knowledge, uncertainty of process, dynamism and chaos (Koput, 1997; March, 1994; Nelson & Winter, 1982), as well as the view that the search space or landscape is not defined solely in terms of a technology dimension. To fully incorporate the specific characteristics of organizational knowledge and the impact these characteristics have on the search process, two additional search trajectories or orientations are proposed in addition to the technological orientation, a geographic search orientation and a social search orientation.

The Geographical Dimension of Knowledge Search

Organizations choose a geographic search orientation by focusing their search activity on knowledge sources that are either internal or external to the organization's boundaries. This internal and external knowledge can take any technological form (Garud & Nayyer, 2004) and also adds a geographic dimension to the knowledge search space.

Internal Geographical Dimension of Knowledge Search

The importance of internal knowledge to the organization has been the stalwart of management thought since its inception (Arrow, 1962; Barney, 1991; Drucker, 1959; Grant & Spender, 1996; Penrose, 1959). The importance attributed in the literature to internal technologies can be viewed as an outgrowth of the resource-based view of the firm, which points to the futility of solely exploiting external technologies as a competitive strategy (Barney, 1991); according to Grant (1996), the problems of community-wide accessibility attributed to internal technologies result in them, forming the basis of sustainable advantage. Conversely, external technologies are viewed as available to all firms. The perceived importance of internal knowledge to the organization has also been demonstrated at length through knowledge management's focus on, among other things, the knowledge based view of the firm (Grant, 1996), knowledge based organizational forms (Hedlund, 1994), internal knowledge strategies (Hansen, Nohria, & Tierney, 1999), internal knowledge creation (Nonaka & Takeuchi, 1995), and internal knowledge transfer (Szulanski, 2003). Figure 3 presents the four search positions an organization can hold in relation to the geographical direction of their search activity. Organizations with a predominantly internal focus to their search activity are represented in the upper left quadrant of Figure 3.

Figure 3. The geographical dimension of knowledge search

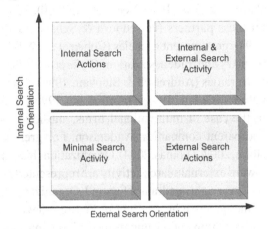

External Geographical Dimension of Knowledge Search

Research concerning the importance of external knowledge to organizations has been somewhat less prevalent, but is of ever-growing importance (Leonard-Barton, 1995). As innovative activity predominantly results from organizational and industrial level adaptation (Frishammar & Horte, 2005), being in touch with one's organizational environment is important to the organization's knowledge creation processes, such that a key element when evaluating innovative potential is a measure of "openness" to the external environment (Caloghirou, Aimilia, Yiannis, & Lefteris, 2004; Laursen & Salter, 2006). Added to this are the findings of absorptive capacity, which cite the organization's ability to "recognize the value of new external knowledge, assimilate it, and apply it to commercial ends" (Cohen & Levinthal, 1990, p. 128) as leading to the development of dynamic capabilities (Zahra & George, 2002). Breschi and Lissoni (2001) have gone as far as to cite the social network within which an innovating firm exists as the main driver of innovation, rather than the organization itself. Sources of external knowledge for organizations and their members include friends (Ben-Porath, 1980; Uzzi, 1996), customers (Prahalad & Ramaswamy, 2000; Von Hippel, 1977, 1978, 1988), suppliers (Kogut, Walker & Shan, 1994; Neely et al., 2000), other business partners (Hagedoorn & Schakenraad, 1994), government agencies (Cohen et al., 2002), industry and trade associations (Pyke et al., 1990), universities (Audretsch & Stephan, 1996), competitors (Gulati, 1995; Powell et al., 1996), and in the case of multinational firms, subsidiaries and parent companies (Andersson, Forsgren & Holm, 2002; Thomas, 2004). Organizations biased toward external search activity are represented in the lower right quadrant of Figure 3. Organizations in the upper right quadrant of Figure 3 have an understanding of the importance of both internal and external knowledge sources; subsequently, these organizations divide search activity between both geographic search spaces. As with technological search positions, organizations positioned in the lower left quadrant of Figure 3 engage in minimal knowledge search activity. Organizations can change the geographical focus of their search activity over time in accordance with where along the geographical search trajectory they view the most appropriate knowledge residing.

The Social Dimension of Knowledge Search

The social domain of knowledge search refers to the social mechanisms used by organizations, groups, communities, and individuals to interact with each other and their environment to search for and acquire knowledge from internal and external sources. These interactions can appear as formal organizational and group level processes or informal community and individual level processes (Keeble & Wilkinson, 1999). Adding a social search orientation to knowledge search activity also emphasizes the importance of informal and formal search mechanisms in defining the knowledge search space.

Informal Social Dimension of Knowledge Search

Informal search methods aimed at the capture of external knowledge are those interactions without prior authorization from the organizations decision making unit; they are continually occurring in the day to day activities of communities and individuals within the organization. These interactions exist through friendships (Ingram & Roberts, 2000), informal networks (Reagans & Zuckerman, 2001), and boundary spanning communities of practice (Wenger & Snyder, 2000). Ingram and Robert's (2000) study on friendship in the context of the Sydney hotel industry shows how cohesive networks of competing managers have a positive effect on overall hotel performance. Informal friendships among competitors benefit organizations through collaboration, the mitigation of competition, increased information exchange (Uzzi, 1996), and the encouragement of a level of conformity to group norms and central tendencies (Geletkanycz & Hambrick, 1997). Informal friendship networks appear most effective when cohesive in nature (Ingram & Roberts, 2000) as opposed to the higher performing nonredundant networks as put forward in Granovetter's (1985) "strength of weak ties" theory. Knowledge also flows informally to and from organizations through boundary spanning communities of practice (Wenger & Snyder, 2000). Wenger and Snyder (2002) note the tendency of engineers working for buyers and suppliers in the hard drive industry to form boundary spanning communities of practice to make full use of the knowledge held in the extended enterprise. Informal mechanisms of knowledge search and exchange often lack the contractual legalities that accompany the majority of formal external search and capture techniques, which can have both positive and negative impacts on the knowledge sharing process. Figure 4 presents the four search

Figure 4. The social dimension of knowledge search

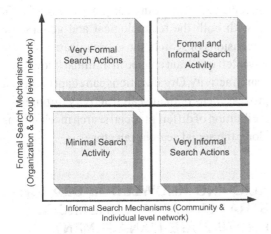

positions an organization can hold in relation to the social mechanisms used to direct their search activity. Organizations focused toward the facilitation of informal search activity and exhibiting recognition of its importance to organizational performance are represented in the lower right quadrant of Figure 4.

Formal Social Dimension of Knowledge Search

Formal search methods are those activities with full authorization from the organization's decision-making unit; these actions occur at the organizational and group level network. They include formal networking (Powell et al., 1996), environmental scanning techniques, such as market research (Frishammar & Horte, 2005), and competitor analysis (Porter, 1980), alliances (Baden-Fuller & Grant, 2004), mergers and acquisitions, equity investments (Dushnitsky & Lenox, 2005), membership of boundary spanning teams (Ancona & Caldwell, 1992) and knowledge clusters (Asheim & Coenen, 2005), and finally collaborative projects both real world (Appleyard, 2003) and virtual (Sawhney, 2002).

Reagans and Zuckerman (2001) find that scientists' membership of nonredundant formal networks outside of their work team leads to an increase in overall productivity for the organization, while organizations that permit their scientists to participate in external knowledge networks have a decreased staff turnover and increased success when attracting new staff (Deutschman, 1994). Liebeskind (1996) cite external networks as allowing the organization to comparatively evaluate their own knowledge base with that of others. This in turn can lead to increased efficiency through a focus on higher performing capabilities. The success of knowledge networks and clusters are likely to be due in part to the enhanced absorptive capacity attributed to collaborating entities with similar knowledge bases (Cohen & Levinthal, 1990), the perceived ease of mobility ascribed to knowledge flowing within cohesive and nonredundant networks (Maskell, 2001), as well as a reduction in the ability to imitate knowledge resources due to the idiosyncratic nature of network creation and development (Andersson et al., 2002).

Organizations also search and scan their environment gain knowledge of and ascertain the knowledge levels of customers, through market research (Frishammar & Horte, 2005) and competitors, through competitor intelligence gathering systems (Porter, 1980). Environmental scanning can also include scanning non-organizational sources, such as patent citations, journals, conferences, and the Internet (Caloghirou et al., 2004). It is not unusual among high-ranking knowledge intensive organizations, in industries such as pharmaceuticals, biotechnology, and computing equipment, to find director level roles specifically focused on external scanning activity. Organizations such as Novartis, Mead Johnson, Bristol-Meyers Squibb, and Procter and Gamble all carry director of external development roles or their equivalent. Organizations also seek to overcome their internal knowledge limitations through the purchasing of external knowledge, outsourcing, merger and acquisition activity, and equity investment activity in new ventures (Dushnitsky & Lenox, 2005).

As organizational knowledge itself is both emergent and contextually dependent, many organizations have chosen to supplement static one-sided scanning techniques with increasingly dynamic knowledge gathering and creation techniques. Collaboration through both alliances and one-off projects is one such technique (Inkpen, 1996); organizations have been shown to collaborate with customers, competitors, universities, and suppliers, among others. Customers' own knowledge is often the main determinant of increased value for the customer (Novo, 2001). Customers are also involved in idea generation through end user innovation (Neely et al., 2000; Shah, 2005; Von Hippel, 1989), which has resulted in innovative products and services in the open-source software (Von Krogh & Von Hippel, 2003) and sports equipment (Shah, 2005) fields, among others. Customer collaboration has also moved to the online world (Rowley & Slack, 2001), with specific cases representing the financial services sector (Barnatt, 1998). While Segrestin (2005) refers to Renault and Nissan's collaborative alliance as an example of competitor collaboration. Universities also represent a mainstay of innovation based collaborative alliances (Autant-Bernard, 2001). Alliances, particularly in the high technology sector, have been shown to contribute to accelerated growth rates (Powell et al., 1996), increased organizational life span (Mitchell & Singh, 1996), improved organizational adaptation (Uzzi, 1996), and improved share price (McConnell & Nantell, 1985). The potential of capturing know-how through contract-protected channels drives alliance foundation in knowledge intensive industries, which demonstrate a high degree of alliance intensity (Hagedoorn, 1993); this is reflected upon further by Dyer and Singh (1998) who correlate the effective governance of inter-organizational relationships with increased exchange efficiency. Organizations biased toward the facilitation of formal search activity are represented in the upper left quadrant of Figure 4. Those organizations who recognize the role played by both formal and informal search mechanisms and provide adequate support to both activities are represented in the upper right quadrant. Again as with both the technological and geographic dimensions of search, those organizations in the lower left quadrant engage in minimal knowledge search activity. Organizations can adapt the social process focus of their search activity through the facilitation of different social search mechanisms along the social search trajectory.

ALIGNING KNOWLEDGE SEARCH STRATEGY WITH A BALANCED KNOWLEDGE MANAGEMENT STRATEGY

In addition to the existing technological dimension of knowledge search, the current authors have presented two additional dimensions to the knowledge search space, the geographic and social dimensions. Thus, the knowledge search space is defined in terms of three dimensions, the technological direction of search activity, the geographic direction of search activity, and the social mechanisms employed by organizations engaged in search activity. These three dimensions, when considered together, offer organizations 10 alternative knowledge search paths, along which they can engage in knowledge search and capture; nine search paths relate to combinations of technological, geographical, and social orientation alternatives, and the tenth search path derives from the option of minimal search activity open to all organizations, groups, communities, and individuals. Table 1 lists these 10 possible search paths based on the search trajectories developed earlier in this chapter.

As discussed at the beginning of this chapter, to ensure a balance to knowledge management activity, organizations should be continually involved in two types of knowledge management strategy, as illustrated in Figure 5. First, organizations should focus on knowledge held internally,

Table 1. Internal and external knowledge search paths

Search Path 1	Organizations engage in Internal and External, informal and formal, exploitation and exploration
Search Path 2	Organizations engage in Internal, informal, exploitation
Search Path 3	Organizations engage in Internal, informal, exploration
Search Path 4	Organizations engage in Internal, formal, exploitation
Search Path 5	Organizations engage in Internal, formal, exploration
Search Path 6	Organizations engage in External, formal, exploitation
Search Path 7	Organizations engage in External, informal, exploitation
Search Path 8	Organizations engage in External, formal, exploration
Search Path 9	Organizations engage in External, informal, exploration
Search Path 10	Organizations engage in Minimal Search Activity

Figure 5. Knowledge search activity as an essential element of a balanced knowledge management strategy

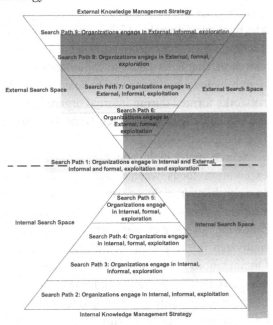

referred to as internal knowledge management, while, second, organizations should focus on potential knowledge which exists externally, referred to as external knowledge management. The first arm of a balanced knowledge management strategy focuses on making better use of the knowledge that already exists in the firm. To this end, organizations focus on searching within the internal search space by following knowledge search paths one to five presented in Table 1 and Figure 5. This internal focus is achieved through the facilitation of internal knowledge transfer mechanisms, such as intranets and the encouragement of internal networking between groups and communities; knowledge management audit techniques also allow organizations to take stock of the internal levels of codified knowledge. Knowledge search path one represents a combined internal and external focus to search activity, and thus traverses both the internal and external search space. Search paths two to five, as shown in Figure 5, are focused on the internal search space as illustrated.

The second arm of a balanced approach to knowledge management strategy should see organizations engage in the creation and recombination of new knowledge from external sources. When engaging in the creation and recombination of external knowledge, and thus searching in the

external search space, organizations follow knowledge search paths one and six to nine in Table 1 and Figure 5. Following these externally focused search paths allows organizations to access knowledge from outside their boundaries. Once again, search path one is used by organizations engaged in a combination of both internal and externally focused knowledge strategies.

Knowledge search paths six to nine represent the alternatives for engaging in external knowledge search. Thus, they represent the main focus of this chapter which centers on external knowledge search as an essential element of knowledge management strategy. Organizations following *search path six* engage in *external, formal exploitation* and are motivated primarily by incremental process and product innovations. Organizations thus search for knowledge similar to their own core knowledge base using formal search mechanisms. These include competitor alliance formation, market research among existing customers, and collaborative projects with supply chain members. Followers of *search path seven* engage in *external, informal exploitation*. Once again due to the exploitation based focus, these communities and individuals are searching along a technological domain which is within their organization's own area of core knowledge. Informal search mechanisms suited to exploitation based search include conference attendance, informal networks formed during internal organizational training, and educational exercises and work based friendship networks.

Search paths eight and nine both have an exploration focus when searching externally. In *search path eight* organizations engage in *external, formal exploration*. Organizations following search path eight are predominantly motivated in the pursuit of radical innovation. Organizations thus search for knowledge that is very different from their core knowledge base, using formal search mechanisms, such as alliances and collaborative projects with organizations and groups from different industries, environmental scanning of noncompeting products, and formal networking across industries. The organizational and group level decision to engage in formal search mechanisms may also point to the need to control the search action; organizational and group level control is relinquished somewhat when searching through informal mechanisms. Finally, communities and individuals following *search path nine* engage in *external, informal exploration*. Organizations facilitate communities and individuals to follow search path nine with a radical innovation view, due to an exploration based focus on knowledge radically different from the searcher's core knowledge base. Boundary spanning communities of practice are one such informal search mechanism. These communities are suited to exploration-based activity due to the many diverse worlds within which members operate. Friendship networks work along these same principles.

When knowledge management is considered in terms of the knowledge we do not have, external

knowledge management strategy becomes central to closing knowledge absences and knowledge gaps. Once internal and external knowledge gaps are identified, organizations must choose the most appropriate search path or combination of search paths to retrieve the knowledge necessary to fill these knowledge gaps. Knowledge search is a significantly important organizational activity, which leads to increased levels of organizational learning (Levinthal & March, 1993), the development of absorptive capacity (Cohen & Levinthal, 1990), a reduction in uncertainty (March, 1994), increased levels of knowledge slack (March, 1999), and an increased buffer against disruptive technologies (Christensen, 1997).

FUTURE RESEARCH DIRECTIONS

Three distinct research directions can be identified. First, much of the current writing on knowledge search and its importance as an organizational activity has yet to enter the sphere of knowledge management study. Yet this in itself offers an opportunity for knowledge management researchers to integrate a rigorous and well-founded research topic. Added to this are opportunities to add to further investigation through empirical research in the area of knowledge search. Questions to be posed include: are specific types of knowledge or technologies better suited to particular search paths? How can organizations effectively facilitate informal knowledge search activity without formalizing the search process? Can organizations engage in blind search and search for knowledge they do not know they need?

Second, the idea of externally focused knowledge management activity has received scant attention compared to the dominant discussions on internal knowledge management. If knowledge management is to fully embrace the informal and complex nature of knowledge, it must recognize the need to move understanding outside the boundaries of the organization. As with most areas of knowledge management research, external knowledge management will most likely benefit from investigation into appropriate research methods and measures. Most needed are better measures and research designs to answer the many questions that arise from a conceptual study such as this. Questions to be put forward include: how can external search activity be linked to internal knowledge management activities? What does a focus on external knowledge management add to existing knowledge management models? What implications does external knowledge management have for knowledge management practitioners?

Finally, as value and innovation systems continue to move outward from the organization (from traditional closed models of innovation, to open models, to entirely external models in the form of open source communities and end user models of creation) the importance of external knowledge to organizational development is reinforced. A final research direction must address practitioner requirements in learning, to adapt from an internal focus to an external orientation. External knowledge search is one process by which managers can learn to re-orientate their organizations outward. Other activities at the interface of internal organization systems and external knowledge environments will provide ample research opportunity, and maximum practitioner value going forward.

CONCLUSION

The intent in this chapter has been to outline the dynamics of knowledge based search, particularly knowledge search with an external focus. Three dimensions of knowledge search, one existing and two new, have been investigated and presented; also four organizational positions in relation to each dimension or search trajectory have been offered. This has culminated in the defining of the knowledge search space in terms of the three

dimensions of search identified here, the technological, geographical, and social. Once mapped, the knowledge search space offers organizations 10 alternative search paths, through which they may pursue knowledge aimed at closing their knowledge gaps (Zack, 1999) and absences (Spender, 2006). Thus choosing the appropriate search path(s) becomes a central strategic activity of external knowledge management. And in turn external knowledge management becomes central to a balanced approach to knowledge management in general.

Organizational theorists have described the significant role external knowledge plays in organizational performance; this element of organizational literature remains somewhat distant from current knowledge management research, however. This discussion not only presents a way for knowledge management to integrate an external perspective when identifying knowledge absences or problems, but also offers alternative paths along which organizations may seek solutions to these problems.

The external dimension of knowledge management remains understudied and knowledge search as an element of external knowledge management suffers the same fate. Both qualitative and quantitative work on this facet of knowledge management offers many opportunities for further investigation.

REFERENCES

Ahuja, A., & Katila, R. (2004). Where do resources come from? The role of idiosyncratic situations. *Strategic Management Journal, 25*(8/9), 887-907.

Ahuja, G., & Lampert, C.M. (2001). Entrepreneurship in the large corporation: A longitudinal study of how established firms create breakthrough inventions. *Strategic Management Journal, 22*(6/7), 521-543.

Ancona, D., & Caldwell, D. (1992). Bridging the boundary: External activity and performance in organizational teams. *Administrative Science Quarterly, 37*(4), 634-665.

Andersson, U., Forsgren, M., & Holm, U. (2002). The strategic impact of external networks: Subsidiary performance and competence development in the multinational corporation. *Strategic Management Journal, 23*(11), 979-996.

Appleyard, M. (2003). The influence of knowledge accumulation on buyer-supplier co-development projects. *The Journal of Product Innovation Management, 20*(5), 356-373.

Arrow, K. (1962). The economic implications of learning by doing. *Review of Economic Studies, 29*(3), 155-173.

Ashiem, B.T., & Coenen, L. (2005). Knowledge bases and regional innovation systems: Comparing Nordic clusters. *Research Policy, 34*(8), 1173-1190.

Audretsch, D.B., & Stephan, P.E. (1996). Company-scientist locational links: The case of biotechnology. *American Economic Review, 86*(3), 641-652.

Autant-Bernard, C. (2001). Science and knowledge flows: Evidence from the French case. *Research Policy, 30*(7), 1069-1078.

Baden-Fuller, C., & R, G. (2004). A knowledge accessing theory of strategic alliances. *Journal of Management Studies, 41*(1), 61-84.

Barnatt, C. (1998). Virtual communities and financial services: On-line business potentials and strategic choice. *International journal of Bank Marketing, 16*(4), 161-169.

Barney, J. (1991). Firm resources and sustained competitive advantage. *Journal of Management, 17*(1), 99-120.

Baum, J., Xiao-Li, S., & Usher, J. (2000). Making the next move: How experiential and vicarious learning shape the locations of chains acquisitions. *Administrative Science Quarterly, 45*(4), 766-801.

Ben-Porath, Y. (1980). The f-connection: Families, friends, and firms and the organization of exchange. *Population and Development Review, 6*(1), 1-30.

Bierly, P., & Chakrabarti, A. (1996). Generic knowledge strategies in the US pharmaceutical industry. *Strategic Management Journal, 17*(Winter), 123-135.

Breschi, S., & Lissoni, F. (2001). Localised knowledge spillovers vs. innovative milieux: Knowledge "tacitness" reconsidered. *Papers in Regional Science, 80*(3), 255-273.

Caloghirou, Y., Aimilia, P., Yiannis, S., & Lefteris, P. (2004). Industry versus firm-specific effects on performance: Contrasting SMEs and large-sized firms. *European Management Journal, 22*(2), 231-243.

Camagni, R. (1991). *Innovation networks: Spatial perspectives*. London: Belhaven Press.

Christensen, C.M. (1997). *The innovator's dilemma: When new technologies cause great firms to fail*. Boston: Harvard University Press.

Cohen, W., & Levinthal, D. (1989). Innovation and learning: The two faces of R&D. *Economic Journal, 99*(397), 569-586.

Cohen, W., & Levinthal, D. (1990). Absorptive capacity: A new perspective on learning and innovation. *Administrative Science Quarterly, 35*(1), 128-152.

Cohen, W., Nelson, R., & Walsh, J. (2002). Links and impacts: The influence of public research on industrial R&D. *Management Science, 48*(1), 1-23.

Cook, S., & Brown, J. (1999). Bridging epistemologies: The generative dance between organizational knowledge and organizational knowing. *Organization Science, 10*(4), 381-400.

Cyert, R., & March , J. (1963). *A behavioural theory of the firm.* Englewood Cliffs, NJ: Prentice Hall.

Daft, R.L., Sormunen, L., & Parks, D. (1988). Chief executive scanning, environmental characteristics, and company performance: An empirical study. *Strategic Management Journal, 9*(2), 123-139.

Deutschman, A. (1994, October). The managing wisdom of high tech superstars. *Fortune, 17,* 197-206.

Drucker, P. (1959). *Landmarks of tomorrow.* New York: Harper.

Dushnitsky, G., & Lenox, M. (2005). When do firms undertake R&D by investing in new ventures? *Strategic Management Journal, 26*(10), 947-965.

Dyer, J., & Singh, H. (1998). The relational view: Cooperative strategy and sources of

interorganizational competitive strategy. *Academy of Management Review, 23*(4), 660-679.

Eisenhardt, K. (1989). Making fast strategic decisions in high velocity environments. *Academy of Management Journal, 32*(3), 543-576.

Ettlie, J., Bridges, W., & O'Keefe, R. (1984). Organizational strategy and structural differences for radical vs. incremental innovation. *Management Science, 30*(6), 682- 695.

Fleming, L. (2001). Recombinant uncertainty in technological search. *Management Science, 47*(1), 117-132.

Florida, R. (1995). Toward the learning region. *Futures, 27*(5), 527-536.

Frishammar, J., & Horte, S. (2005). Managing external information in manufacturing firms: The impact on innovation performance. *Journal of Product Innovation Management, 22*(3), 251–266.

Garud, R., & Nayyer, R. (2004). Transformative capacity: Continual structuring by intertemporal technology transfer. In K. Starkey, S. Tempest & A. McKinlay (Eds.), *How organizations learn* (pp. 137-165). London: Thompson.

Geletkanycz, M.A., & Hambrick, D.C. (1997). The external ties of top executives: Implications for strategic choice and performance. *Administrative Science Quarterly, 42*(4), 654-681.

Ginsberg, A., & Baum, J.C. (1994). Evolutionary processes and patterns of core business change. In J.C. Baum & J. Singh (Eds.), *Evolutionary dynamics of organizations* (pp. 127-151). New York: Oxford University Press.

Granovetter, M. (1985). Economic action and social structure: The problem of embeddedness. *The American Journal of Sociology, 91*(3), 481-510.

Grant, R.M., & Spender, J.C. (1996). Knowledge and the firm: Overview. *Strategic Management Journal, 17*(Winter Special Issue), 5-9.

Gulati, R., & Gargiulo, M. (1999). Where do inter organizational networks come from? *American Journal of Sociology, 104*(3), 1439-1493.

Hagedoorn, J. (1993). Understanding the rationale of strategic technology partnering: Inter-organizational modes of cooperation and sectoral differences. *Strategic Management Journal, 14*(5), 371-385.

Hagedoorn, J., & Schakenraad, J. (1994). The effect of strategic technology alliances on company performance. *Strategic Management Journal, 15*(5), 291-309.

Hansen, M.T., Nohria, N., & Tierney, T. (1999). What's your strategy for managing knowledge? *Harvard Business Review, 77*(2), 106-116.

Hargadon, A., & Fanelli, A. (2002). Action and possibility: Reconciling dual perspectives of knowledge in organizations. *Organization Science, 13*(3), 290-302.

Hedlund, G. (1994). A model of knowledge management and the N-form corporation. *Strategic Management Journal, 15*(Special Issue), 73-90.

Henderson, R., & Cockburn, I. (1994). Measuring competence? Exploring effects in pharmaceutical research. *Strategic Management Journal, 15*(Winter Special Issue), 63-84.

Ingram, P., & Roberts, P. (2000). Friendships with competitors in the Sydney hotel industry. *American Journal of Sociology, 106*(2), 387-423.

Inkpen, A. (1996). Creating knowledge through collaboration. *California Management Review, 39*(1), 123-140.

Kahneman, D., & Tversky, A. (1979). Prospect theory: An analysis of decision under risk. *Econometrica, 47*(2), 263-291.

Katila, R. (2002). New product search over time: Past ideas in their prime? *Academy of Management Journal, 45*(5), 995-1010.

Katila, R., & Ahuja, G. (2002). Something old, something new: A longitudinal study of search behaviour and new product introduction. *Academy of Management Journal, 45*(6), 1183-1194.

Keeble, D., Lawson, C.B.M., & Wilkinson, F. (1999). Collective learning processes, networking and "institutional thickness" in the Cambridge region. *Regional Studies, 33*(4), 319-332.

Keeble, D., & Wilkinson, F. (1999). Regional networking, collective learning and innovation in high-technology SMEs in Europe. *Regional Studies, 3*(4), 295-400.

Kelly, D., & Amburgey, T.L. (1991). Organizational inertia and momentum: A dynamic model of strategic change. *Academy of Management Journal, 34*(3), 591-612.

Koput, K. (1997). A chaotic model of innovative search: Some answers, many questions. *Organization Science, 8*(5), 528-542.

Kogut, B., Walker, G., & Shan, W. (1994). Inter-firm cooperation and startup innovation in the biotechnology industry. *Strategic Management Journal, 15*(5), 387-394.

Laursen, K., & Salter, A. (2003). Searching low and high: What types of firms use Universities as a source of innovation? (Working Paper Series). Danish Research Unit for Industrial Dynamics (DRUID).

Laursen, K., & Salter, A. (2006). Open for innovation: The role of openness in explaining innovation performance among UK manufacturing firms. *Strategic Management Journal, 27*(2), 131-150.

Leonard-Barton, D. (1995). Core capabilities and core rigidities: A paradox in managing new product development. *Strategic Management Journal, 13*(2), 111-126.

Levinthal, D., & March, J. (1981). A model of adaptive organizational search. *Journal of Economic Behaviour and Organization, 2*, 307-333.

Levinthal, D., & March, J. (1993). The myopia of learning. *Strategic Management Journal, 14*(2), 95-112.

Levitt, B., & J, M. (1988). Organizational learning. *Annual Review of Sociology, 14*(1), 319- 340.

Liebeskind, J. (1996). Knowledge, strategy, and the theory of the firm. *Strategic Management Journal, 17*(Winter Special Issue), 93-107.

March, J. (1991). Exploration and exploitation in organizational learning. *Organization Science, 2*(1), 71-87.

March, J. (1994). *A primer on decision making.* New York: The Free Press.

March, J. (1999). *The pursuit of organizational intelligence.* Malden, MA: Blackwell Publishers.

Maskell, P. (2001). Knowledge creation and diffusion in geographic clusters. *International Journal of Innovation Management (Special Issue), 5*(2), 213-238.

McConnell, J., & Nantell, T. (1985). Corporate combinations and common stock returns: The case of joint ventures. *Journal of Finance, 40*(2), 519-536.

Mitchell, W., & Singh, H. (1996). Precarious collaboration: Business survival after partners shut down or form new partnerships. *Strategic Management Journal, 17*(2), 99-115.

Morgan, K. (1997). The learning region: Institutions, innovation and regional renewal. *Regional Studies, 31*(5), 491-503.

Neely, A., Filippini, R., Forza, C., Vinelli, A., & Hii, J. (2000). A framework for analyzing business performance, firm innovation and related contextual factors: Perceptions of managers and policy makers in two European regions. *Integrated Manufacturing Systems, 12*(2), 114–124.

Nelson, R., & Winter, S. (1982). *An evolutionary theory of economic change.* Cambridge, MA: Harvard University Press.

Nonaka, I., & Takeuchi, T. (1995). *The knowledge-creating company: How Japanese companies create the dynamics of innovation.* New York: Oxford University Press.

Novo, J. (2001). The source of customer value: Customer knowledge. Retrieved May 19, 2007, from http://www.ckm-forum.com

Orlikowski, W. (2002). Knowing in practice: Enacting a collective capability in distributed organizing. *Organization Science, 13*(3), 249-273.

Penrose, E. (1959). *The theory of the growth of the firm.* New York: John Wiley.

Pfeffer, J., & Sutton, R., (1999). Knowing what to do is not enough: Turning knowledge into action, *California Management Review, 42*(1), 83-108.

Porter, M. (1980). *Competitive strategy.* New York: The Free Press.

Powell, W. W., Koput, K. W., & Smith-Doerr, L. (1996). Interorganizational collaboration and the locus of innovation: Networks of learning in biotechnology. *Administrative Science Quarterly, 41*(1), 116-145.

Prahalad, C., & V., R. (2000). Co-opting customer competence. *Harvard Business Review, 78*(1), 9.

Pyke, F., G, B., & W, S. (1990). *Industrial districts and inter-firm cooperation in Italy.* Geneva: International Institute for Labour Studies.

Reagans, R., & Zuckerman, E. (2001). Networks, diversity, and performance: The social capital of corporate R&D units. *Organization Science, 12*(4), 502-517.

Rosenkopf, L., & Nerker, A. (2001). Beyond local search: Boundary-spanning, exploration and impact in the optical disk industry. *Strategic Management Journal, 22*(4), 287- 306.

Rowley, J., & Slack, F. (2001). Leveraging customer knowledge: Profiling and personalisation in e-business. *International journal of Retail and Distribution Management, 29*(8/9), 407-415.

Sawhney, M. (2002). Don't just relate: Collaborate. *MIT Sloan Management Review, 43*(Spring), 96.

Sawhney, M., & Prandelli, E. (2004). Communities of creation: Managing distributed innovation in turbulent markets. In K. Starkey, S. Tempest & A. McKinlay (Eds.), *How organizations learn* (pp. 271-301. London: Thompson.

Schultze, U., & Stabell, C. (2004). Knowing what you don't know? Discourses and contradictions in knowledge management research. *Journal of Management Studies, 41*(4), 549-573.

Segrestin, B. (2005). Partnering to explore: The Renault-Nissan Alliance as a forerunner of new cooperative patterns. *Research Policy, 34*(5), 657-672.

Shah, S. (2005). Open beyond software. In C. Dibona, D. Cooper and M. Stone (Eds.), *Open Sources 2* (pp. 339-360). Sebastopol, CA: O'Reilly Media.

Sidhu, J., Volberda, H., & Commandeur, H. (2004). Exploring exploration orientation and its determinants: Some empirical evidence. *Journal of Managment Studies, 41*(6), 913- 932.

Simonin, B. (1997). The importance of collaborative know-how: An empirical test of the learning organization. *Academy of Management Journal, 40*(5), 1150-1174.

Spender, J.C. (1996). Making knowledge the basis of a dynamic theory of the firm. *Strategic Management Journal, 17*(2), 45-62.

Spender, J.C. (2006). Managerial practice: Shaping the reasoning and imagining of others (CIKM 2006 Working Paper Series). Retrieved May 19, 2007, from *http://www.cikm.ul.ie*

Stuart, T., & Podolny, J. (1996). Local search and the evolution of technological capabilities. *Strategic Management Journal, 17*(1), 21-38.

Szulanski, G. (2003). *Sticky knowledge: Barriers to knowing in the firm.* London: Sage Publications.

Tallman, S., Jenkins, M., Henry, N., & Pinch, S. (2004). Knowledge, clusters and competitive advantage. *Academy of Management Review, 29*(2), 258-271.

Teece, D., Pisano, G., & Shuen, A. (1997). Dynamic capabilities and strategic management. *Strategic Management Journal, 18*(7), 509-533.

Thomas, L.G. (2004). Are we all global now? Local vs. foreign sources of corporate competence: The case of the Japanese pharmaceutical industry. *Strategic Management Journal, 25*(8/9), 865-886.

Tsoukas, H., & Vladimirou, E. (2001). What is organizational knowledge? *Journal of Management Studies, 38*(7), 973-993.

Tushman, M. (2003). Exploitation, exploration and process management: The productivity dilemma revisited. *Academy of management review, 28*(2), 238-256.

Uzzi, B. (1996). The sources and consequences of embeddedness for the economic performance of organizations: The network effect. *American Sociological Review, 61*(4), 674-698.

Von Hippel, E. (1978). Successful industrial products from customer ideas. *Journal of Marketing, 42*(1), 39-49.

Von Hippel, E. (1988). *Sources of innovation.* New York: Oxford University Press.

Von Hippel, E. (1989). New product ideas from "Lead Users". *Research Management, 32*(3), 24-27.

Von Krogh, G., & Von Hippel, E, (2003). Open source software: Introduction to a special issue of research policy. *Research Policy, 32*(7),1149-57.

Wenger, E., & Snyder, W.M. (2000). Communities of practice: The organizational frontier. *Harvard Business Review, 78*(1), 139-146.

Zack, M. (1999). Developing a knowledge strategy. *California Management Review, 41*(3), 125-145.

Zack, M.H. (2005). The strategic advantage of knowledge and learning. *International Journal of Intellectual Capital and Learning, 2*(1), 1-20.

Zahra, S., & George, G. (2002). Absorptive capacity: A review, reconceptualisation and extension. *Academy of Management Review, 27*(2), 185-203.

Additional Reading

Allen, T. (1977). *Managing the flow of technology.* Cambridge, MA: The MIT Press.

Argote, L., & Ingram, P. (2000). Knowledge transfer: A basis for competitive advantage in firms.

Organizational Behavior and Human Decision Processes, 82(1), 150-169.

Boisot, M. (1998). Knowledge *assets: Securing competitive advantage in the information economy.* Oxford: Oxford University Press.

Chesbrough, H. (2006). *Open business models: How to thrive in the new innovation landscape.* Boston: Harvard Business School Press.

Chesbrough, H., & Schwartz, K. (2007). Innovating business models with co-development partnerships. *Research Technology Management, 50*(1), 55-59.

Christensen, C., Suarez, F., & Utterbank, J. (1998). Strategies for survival in fast changing industries. *Mangement Science, 44*(12), 207-220.

Cross, R., & Parker, A. (2004). *The hidden power of social networks.* Boston: Harvard Business School Press.

Dixon, N.M. (2002). *Common knowledge: How companies thrive by sharing what they know.* Boston: Harvard Business School Press.

Easterby-Smith, M., & Lyles, M.A. (2003). *The Blackwell handbook of organizational learning and knowledge management.* Oxford: Blackwell Publishing.

Ford, R. (2006). Organizational learning, change & power: Toward a practice-theory framework. *The Learning Organization, 13*(5), 495-524.

Hildreth, P., & Kimble, C. (2004). *Knowledge networks: Innovation through communities of practice.* London/Hershey, PA: Idea Group.

Huston, L., & Sakkab, N. (2006). Connect and develop: Inside Procter and Gamble's new model for innovation. *Harvard Business Review, 84*(3), 58-66.

March, J. (1996). Continuity and change in theories of organizational action. *Administrative Science Quaterly, 41*(2), 278-287.

Mezias, S., & Glynn, M. (1993). The three faces of organizational renewal: Institution, revolution and evolution. *Strategic Management Journal, 14*, 79-101.

Miller, K., Zhao, M., & Calantone, R. (2006). Adding interpersonal learning and tacit knowledge to March's exploration: Exploitation model. *Academy of Management Journal, 40*(4), 709-722.

Perretti, F., & Negro, G. (2006). Filling empty seats: How status and organizational hierarchies affect exploration versus exploitation in team design. *Academy of Management Journal, 49*(4), 759-777.

Polanyi, M. (1967). *The tacit dimension.* Garden City, NY: Doubleday.

Saxenian, A. (1994). *Regional advantage.* Cambridge, MA: Harvard University Press.

Snowden, D.J. (2002). Complex acts of knowing: Paradox and descriptive self-awareness. *Journal of Knowledge Management, 6*(2), 100-111.

Starkey, K., Tempest, S., & McKinlay, A. (2004). *How organizations learn: Managing the search for knowledge.* London: Thompson Learning.

Sveiby, K.E. (1997). *The new organizational wealth: Managing & measuring knowledge-based assets.* San Franciso: Berrett-Koehler Publishers.

Warsh, D. (2006). *Knowledge and the wealth of nations: A story of economic discovery.* New York: W.W. Norton & Co Inc.

Watts, D. (2003). *Six degrees: The science of a conected age.* London: Vintage Publishers.

ENDNOTES

[1] Exploration is required to establish a leading position in the marketplace, and exploitation can be used in the short term to maintain the position, however a return to exploration is eventually required to avoid obsolescence.

Chapter V
Knowledge Transfer Strategy:
An Emerging
Classification System

Robert Parent
University of Sherbrooke, Canada

Denis St-Jaques
University of Sherbrooke, Canada

Julie Bélievau
University of Sherbrooke, Canada

Creating a new theory is not like destroying an old barn and erecting a skyscraper in its place. It is rather like climbing a mountain, gaining new and wider views, discovering unexpected connections between our starting point and its rich environment.

—Albert Einstein

ABSTRACT

This chapter reviews recent literature on knowledge and knowledge transfer (KT) and proposes the emergence of a classification system of the core KT concepts, models, and contexts that helps address issues of a strategic nature. The two paradigms that inform most of the KT literature, the positivist and social construction paradigms, and their implications on strategy formulation, are discussed. The positivist paradigm views knowledge as an object that can be passed on mechanistically from the creator to a translator who then adapts and transmits it to the user. The social construction paradigm views knowledge as the dynamic by-product of interactions between human actors who are trying to understand, name, and act on reality. In keeping with this dual paradigm logic, the literature on KT can be categorized as originating either from an information technology paradigm or an organic paradigm. The chapter discusses how most of the past strategy-related KT issues focused on the transfer of explicit knowledge and indicates that the future direction implies a shift in attention towards more tacit knowledge transfer considerations.

INTRODUCTION

The objectives of this chapter are to:

- Review the recent literature on knowledge, KT, and KT strategy;
- Propose the emergence of a classification system of the core concepts, models, and contexts evident in the KT literature related to strategy;
- Consider the implications of this classification system for organizational strategy formulation;
- Compare the two paradigms that inform most of the KT literature, the positivist and social construction paradigms;
- Demonstrate that the literature on knowledge transfer can be categorized as originating either from an information technology paradigm or an organic or humanist paradigm; and
- Identify and discuss the trend towards a holistic approach to knowledge transfer.

The primary purpose of this chapter is to guide researchers and practitioners in initiating KT projects and strategies that are informed by the existing body of knowledge, and in generating propositions for further study.

BACKGROUND

Knowledge, and how it gets managed and transferred, is one of the fastest-growing and more complex areas of strategic interest emerging from the global economy. In recent years, many research studies, including Nelson and Winter's (1982) treatise on organizational routines; Teece's (1982) and Teece, Pisano, and Shuen's (1997) analyses of technology transfer and proprietary knowledge; Nonaka's (1990, 1994) work on knowledge-creating companies; Prusak's (1997) work on knowledge in organizations; Davenport

and Prusak's (1998) study of how organizations manage what they know; Serban and Luan's (2002) overview of knowledge management; and Diakoulakis, Georgopoulos, Koulouriotis, and Emiris' (2004) "Towards a Holistic Knowledge Management Model", all reinforce the idea that more and more organizational scientists and practitioners are turning their attention towards—knowledge management to increase the competitive advantage of companies. In a survey conducted by Simmonds, Dawley, Ritchie, and Anthony (2001), management practitioners cited knowledge transfer (knowledge transfer/information flows) as the most familiar and useful idea among nine key concepts in strategic management.

Many researchers have focused on the importance of knowledge transfer to an organization's competitive advantage (Cavusgil, Calantone & Zhao, 2003; Dayasindhu, 2002; Lynn, Skov & Abel, 1999; Szulanski, 1996). For Nielson (2005), researchers and practitioners argue that competitive advantage comes from knowledge based resources, especially if they are not easily imitated. Thomas, Sussman, and Henderson (2001) suggest that much of the dialogue in strategic management lately comes from differences in knowledge uses in different organizations. Still other researchers provide numerous examples of organizations that have significantly improved their performance by instituting knowledge transfer programs (Büchel & Raub, 2002; Buckman, 1998; O'Dell & Grayson, 1999). Hoopes and Posterel (1999) take a different tack by demonstrating instances when the lack of information sharing by employees has increased production costs significantly. Blumentritt and Johnston (1999) suggest, on a more macrolevel, that "the ability to identify, locate and deliver information and knowledge to a point of valuable application is transforming existing industries, and facilitating the emergence of entirely new industries" (p. 287).

But the task of transferring knowledge successfully is far from straightforward. There are countless examples of sound academic research never making it to the practice community, and of organizations in need of solutions ignoring academic research findings in developing management strategies and practices (Rynes, Bartunek & Daft, 2001). O'Dell and Grayson (1999) report on research suggesting that the transfer of "best practices" between two divisions of the same organization takes, on average, 27 months to complete. Both Argote (1999) and Szulanski (1996) determined that the effectiveness of knowledge transfer initiatives varies significantly among organizations, and Argote and Ingram (2000) note that knowledge transfer initiatives often fall far short of delivering on all the sought-after results. So, while knowledge transfer is generally recognized as good common sense, it is a long way from being good common practice.

Because KT is a relatively new and complex area of practitioner and research interest, it is still somewhat difficult to structure and conceptualize. Researchers and practitioners alike agree that knowledge is important, but often struggle to understand, name, and act on the various concepts. Some of these difficulties result from the problem researchers have had defining the term "knowledge". Holtshouse (1998) may have said it best when he suggested that the very nature of knowledge makes it "fuzzy and intangible" (p. 277). Fahey and Prusak (1998) suggest that the lack of clarity around the concept of knowledge is one of the primary causes for the difficulties faced by organizations trying to implement knowledge management programs.

CORE CONCEPTS IN THE KT LITERATURE

If one tries to conduct a literature review of knowledge transfer, one of the first things that needs to be investigated is what researchers mean by the term "knowledge". Such a review reveals that relatively few authors have actually attempted to describe knowledge, and those that have present different and conflicting descriptions of the term (Bender & Fish, 2000; Blumentritt & Johnston, 1999; Brown & Duguid, 2001; Chiva & Alegre, 2005; Cook & Brown, 1999; du Toit, 2003; Gherardi & Nicolini, 2000; Nonaka & Konno, 1998; Roy, Guindon & Fortier, 1995; Spender, 1996).

There are a multitude of concepts generally associated with knowledge and its transfer in the literature. These include knowledge; knowledge management; knowledge transfer; knowledge translation, knowledge exchange, knowledge utilization, ontology, epistemology, and typology; paradigms (including related concepts such as information technology, databases/knowledge repositories, social capital, intellectual capital, networks, communities of practice, etc.); schools of thought; measures of the value of knowledge and knowledge transfer; and finally research utilization, implementation, diffusion, and dissemination. Among the major contributions to this body of literature are Chiva and Alegre (2005), Hazlett, McAdam, and Gallagher (2005), Assudani (2005), Cummings and Teng (2003), Earl (2001), Wenger and Snyder (2000), Cook and Brown (1999), Davenport, De Long, and Beers (1998), Lave and Wenger (1991), Brown and Duguid (1991), Landry, Amara, and Lamari (2001), Lavis, Toss, Hurley, Hohenadel, Stoddart, Woodward, and Abelson (2002), and Lomas (2000).

There does appear to be some general consensus that there are at least two kinds of knowledge, explicit and tacit (Goh, 2002; Havens & Knapp, 1999; Kidwell, Vander Linde & Johnson, 2000; Nonaka & Takeuchi, 1995). For Goh (2002), "tacit knowledge is personal; it is hard to formalize and communicate to others. It is also generally more complex, existing in the mental models and expertise gained over time and through personal insights" (p. 27). Explicit knowledge, on the other hand, is "what is written or recorded in manuals, patents, reports, documents, assessments and databases, and can be readily codified, articulated, and captured" (Goh, 2002, p. 27). In the past, the tendency has been to focus on the "explicit knowledge as object" perspective of KT and to neglect the more human, tacit characteristics of knowledge.

Many KT researchers tend to compare different types of knowledge, such as individual knowledge vs. organizational knowledge (Bhatt, 2002; Fairlough, 1982; Kogut & Zander, 1995; Reix, 1995), or explicit vs. tacit knowledge (Andreu & Sieber, 2005; Augier & Vendelo, 1999; Castillo, 2002; Fernandes & Raja, 2002; Goh, 2002; Jasimuddin, Klein & Connell, 2005; Leonard & Sensiper, 1998; Li & Gao, 2003; Smith, 2001). However, this does not help us answer the question of what is, or is not, knowledge. By comparing different types of knowledge, we have come to view knowledge management and knowledge transfer as an "either/or" approach to knowledge. Either we are managing or transferring explicit knowledge with specific tools and techniques, or we are managing or transferring tacit knowledge with different and equally specific tools or techniques.

Developing a better understanding of what knowledge is can obviously help us address the questions: "What is it that we want to transfer?" and "What is really transferable?" In an organizational context, we can be even more precise by asking, "What knowledge can be transferred to improve the organization's performance?" The operational distinction suggested by Blumentritt and Johnston (1999) between data, information, knowledge, and wisdom helps clarify some of the thinking about what knowledge is:

Data are unstructured "facts" without meaning, information is "data endowed with relevance and purpose," knowledge embodies cognition, insight, erudition and scholarship and wisdom is a consequence of the fusing of knowledge with values and experience. (p. 291)

O'Dell and Grayson (1998) consider that "knowledge is information in action" (p. 5). Others distinguish between information and knowledge, pointing out that "information becomes knowledge when introduced into one's mental model. When transferred to another, this knowledge reverts to information, and so on" (Blumentritt & Johnson, 1999, p. 293). Other researchers break down knowledge into different categories, but the general consensus places knowledge on a continuum from explicit, which is simple to codify and relatively easier to transfer, to tacit, which is complex and relatively more difficult to transfer.

Overall, the management and transfer of data and information is well developed because of recent advances in information technology. Knowledge, on the other hand, since it is created quietly within a person's mind, is considerably more difficult to capture and transfer. While data and information are transferred through increasingly sophisticated electronic means, knowledge transfer needs human networks. This is significant when viewed in the context of a knowledge society in which knowledge is the most important organizational asset. As Davenport et al. (1998) have stated:

Unlike data, knowledge is created invisibly in the human brain, and only the right organizational climate can persuade people to create, reveal, share and use knowledge. ... Data and information are constantly transferred electronically but knowledge travels most felicitously through a human network. (p. 56)

Davenport et al. (1998) argue that one must be able to demonstrate that the new knowledge has been used in order to prove that the knowledge has actually been transferred. Knowledge transfer involves two actions: transmission (sending or presenting knowledge to a potential recipient) and absorption by that person or group. If knowledge is not absorbed, it has not been transferred. Merely making knowledge available is not transfer. Access is necessary but by no means sufficient to ensure that knowledge will be used. The goal of knowledge transfer is to improve an organization's ability to do things, and therefore increase its value. Even transmission and absorption together have no useful value if the new knowledge does not lead to some change in behaviour, or the development of some new idea that leads to new behaviour. The following definitions illustrate the multiplicity of perspectives from which knowledge transfer has been viewed recently.

Knowledge Transfer from a Process Perspective

Szulanski (2000): "Knowledge transfer is seen as a process in which an organization recreates and maintains a complex, causally ambiguous set of routines in a new setting" (p. 10).

Argote and Ingram (2000): "Knowledge transfer in organizations is the process through which one unit (e.g., group, department, or division) is affected by the experience of another. This definition is similar to definitions of transfer at the individual level of analysis in cognitive psychology" (p. 151).

Darr and Kurtzberg (2000): "Knowledge transfer is conceived as an event through which one organization learns from the experience of another" (p. 29).

Kalling (2003): "Knowledge transfer within an organization may be thought of as the process by which an organization makes available knowledge about routines to its members, and is a common phenomenon that can be an effective way for organizations to extend knowledge bases and leverage unique skills in a relatively cost-effective manner" (p. 115).

From an Objective of KT Perspective

Cummings and Teng (2003): "Regardless of the setting, the objective of any knowledge transfer project is to transfer source knowledge successfully to a recipient. Researchers have used four different approaches to define transfer success as a dependent variable" (p. 41).

From the Technology Transfer Perspective

Kotabe, Martin, and Domoto (2002): "Technology transfer, as we label it in short, refers to concerted projects that allow one partner to access or replicate complete technological capabilities of the other partner" (p. 298).

Knowledge Transfer and Learning

Goh (2002): "A critical factor in knowledge management, the ability of the organization to transfer knowledge. Knowledge transfer is also a key dimension of learning organization. Learning occurs when knowledge in one part on an organization is transferred effectively to other parts and used to solve problems there or to provide new and creative insights" (p. 23).

Lord and Ranft (2000): "The effective internal transfer of knowledge—the dissemination of knowledge from one division to another division within the same firm—is not likely to be easy or automatic" (p. 574).

As the literature on knowledge transfer grows, there appears to be significant overlap between various categories of knowledge, as well as between the various tools available to transfer knowledge. In fact, knowledge management and knowledge transfer have become so pervasive that in some disciplines, they appear to have taken on an almost mythical stature. Some go so far as to lend them the title of unified-field theories of everything. For some, it has become the Holy Grail of the knowledge economy. It should not be surprising to note that knowledge is a very complex body of knowledge that transcends any one discipline that to be understood likely requires several lifetimes and PhDs in a variety of subjects including sociology, psychology, philosophy, anthropology, information technology, complex adaptive systems, library science, statistics, computer programming, and communications. Knowledge transfer implies the use of both the electronic and human networks within which data, information, and knowledge transfer gets accomplished. There does appear to be a holistic approach to knowledge transfer beginning to emerge in which approaches from both explicit and tacit knowledge transfer are beginning to coalesce, adding value to the knowledge transfer landscape.

Perhaps a good way of looking at knowledge is to take a page from the book of ontology or understanding of human nature. Ultimately, knowledge is really just a way of looking at the world of systems. It is a realization that who and what the system knows are assets to be managed for the greatest possible return on investment. As such, we define knowledge transfer as the effective and sustained exchange between a system's stakeholders (researchers, government, practitioners, etc.); exchanges characterized by significant interactions resulting in the appropriate use of the most recent successful practices and discoveries in the decision making process. Such a definition implies a dramatic change in how knowledge is being viewed in organizations, as explained in the following section.

VARIOUS CONTEXTS FOR KNOWLEDGE TRANSFER

Early research activities around organizational knowledge transfer cluster mainly around inter-organizational transfer, which is understandable given the complexity and problems associated with transferring knowledge between organizations (Bhagat, Kedia, Harveston & Triandis, 2002; Bresman, Birkinshaw & Nobel, 1999; Cummings & Teng, 2003; Daghfous, 2003; Inkpen & Tsang, 2005; Kostova, 1998, 1999). For example, the early industrial organization (IO) view of organizational

strategy, popularized by Porter (1979), focused its attention on understanding how the external environment was developing and how to transfer knowledge from that environment to the organization to develop a competitive advantage. Lately, the "resource-based" view of the firm, popularized by Barney (1991) and Wernerfelt (1984), focuses attention on the inimitable resources of the firm as the ultimate source of competitive advantage. This has led to the "knowledge-based" view of the firm that argues knowledge is the most important resource the organization has (Conner & Prahalad, 1996; Grant, 1997; Kogut & Zander, 1992; Spender, 1996).

Finally, networks are at the heart of the new global economy. Castells (2000) defines the networked society as a social structure characteristic of the "information age." Although networks have existed for quite some time, they are being re-energized by information technology (Bunnell, 2000; Castells, 1996, 2000; Schiller, 1999; Shapiro & Varian, 1999).

MODELS TO HELP US LEARN ABOUT KNOWLEDGE TRANSFER

Even though the field of knowledge transfer is relatively young, it has its share of models that attempt to explain how knowledge transfer occurs or what is required for knowledge transfer to occur. This literature reflects contributions from the practice, theory, and research communities.

Models Generated by Practice: Praxis

In the area of practice, we generally find works by consultants and organizations trying to name and act on knowledge transfer. These include Buckman Laboratories, Ford, General Electric, General Motors, KPMG, Monsanto, Northrop Grumman, PriceWaterhouseCoopers, Skandia, Toyota, United States Army/United States Air

Force, Chevron, BP, and so forth. The major contributions to this literature include Sveiby (2001), Earl (2001), Dyer and Nobeoka (2000), Lahti and Beyerlein (2000), Pan and Scarbrough (1998), Buckman (1998), Davenport (1997). These models tend to be more prescriptive in nature.

Models Generated by Theory and Reflection

This category of models refers to those resulting from reflection and theorizing and include such works as Inkpen and Tsang (2005), Guzman and Wilson (2005), Cummings and Teng (2003), Ipe (2003), Garavelli, Gorgoglione, and Scozzi (2002), Goh (2002), Fernandes and Raja (2002), and Argote and Ingram (2000).

Models Generated by Research

The research community has contributed substantially to the literature on knowledge transfer, primarily in attempts to describe what successful knowledge transfer looks like. Within this category, we find surveys, case studies, grounded theory, narratives, discussion groups, observation, participation, comparative studies, and quantitative and qualitative analysis. A variety of different terminologies are used, including knowledge exchange, knowledge application, knowledge utilization, knowledge translation, and knowledge uptake. Some of the most often cited literature in this category includes Argote and Ingram (2000), Szulanski (1996, 2000), Cohen and Levinthal (1990), Tsai (2001), Dyer and Nobeoka (2000), Bresman et al. (1999), Landry et al. (2001), Lavis et al. (2002), and Lomas (2000). All of these different models look at KT from either a prescriptive or descriptive logic.

PARADIGMS THAT INFORM THE KT LITERATURE

A paradigm shift in the ownership of knowledge is beginning to take hold in business, in particular, and society, in general. This shift suggests that knowledge is no longer the exclusive domain of a few experts, researchers, or senior managers, but needs to be distributed throughout the entire business community. In some of the organizations mentioned elsewhere in this chapter and book, we are beginning to see the early steps of a movement away from "knowledge is power" (which implies that to increase my power, I need to keep it to myself), in favour of a paradigm in which "knowledge transfer/exchange is power" (so I need to ensure that knowledge gets shared and transferred throughout our entire system to increase our system's power). For example, a recent Booz Allen resilience report titled "The Megacommunity Manifesto" by Gerencser, Napolitano, and Van Lee (2006), suggests that:

The root cause of the challenges confronting leaders [today] is complexity: the growing density of linkages among people, organizations, and issues all across the world. Because people communicate so easily across national and organizational boundaries, the conventional managerial decision-making style—in which a boss exercises decision making rights or delegates them to subordinates—is no longer adequate. Solutions require multi organizational systems that are larger and more oriented to multilateral action than conventional cross-sector approaches are. In such systems, the most successful leaders are not those with the best technical solution, the most compelling vision, or the most commanding and charismatic style. The "winners" are those who understand how to intervene and influence others in a larger system that they do not control. (p. 1)

Both the research and practice communities interested in knowledge transfer rely on certain assumptions about knowledge and the best ways of managing its transfer. We can group these assumptions into two broad categories or paradigms: the positivist and the social construction paradigms. The positivist paradigm supports the view of knowledge as an object, capable of being codified, and general enough to apply to a variety of contexts. The social construction paradigm supports the view that knowledge is a product of a social construction process that cannot be separated from its context.

In the field of management, these two paradigms have been accepted, but tagged with management names. Hazlett et al. (2005) refer to the computational and organic paradigms; Gloet and Berrell (2003) discuss the technology and information paradigm vs. the humanist paradigm; and Earl (2001) talks about seven schools of knowledge management thought regrouped into three large categories, namely, technocratic, commercial-economic, and behaviourists. Earl's first category refers to information technology and the last to the human aspects of organizations.

For Hazlett et al. (2005, p. 7), the principal characteristics that differentiate these two paradigms are outlined in Table 1.

We find similar differences among the authors mentioned earlier. The two different visions of knowledge inspire not only different models of knowledge creation, diffusion, and use, but

Table 1.

Positivist Paradigm	Social Construction Paradigm
Technological	Socio-organizational
Systems/Techno-centric	People-centric
Linear (mechanistic)	Nonlinear (discontinuous)
Explicit only	Tacit and explicit knowledge
Acontextual	Highly contextual
Static (non-wicked environment)	Dynamic (wicked environment)
MAX (optimization)	MAX (adaptation)

also different interpretations of the principal challenges faced by organizations. For example, what type of knowledge does the organization need? How should they generate and import it? How do they ensure that it gets used in the right way? Or, put differently, what is an organization's knowledge transfer strategy?

Advances in information technology have resulted in the development of powerful tools to stock and treat information (databases, knowledge repositories, data warehouses, data mining, expertise profiling, metadata tagging, archiving, etc.). They have also made new communications tools available, including e-mail, forums, chat rooms, shareware, instant messaging, groupware, wikis, intranets, extranets, portals, and so forth, which provide quick and relatively easy access to a variety of information. All of this new technology has generated new challenges for the positivist culture of inquiry, including the efficient management and storing of information, its accessibility (by the right person at the right time), and the assurance that the right knowledge will be used in the right circumstances.

PRESCRIPTIVE LITERATURE: WHAT NEEDS TO BE DONE FOR KNOWLEDGE TRANSFER TO SUCCEED?

The focus here is on practice and prescribing what needs to be done for knowledge transfer to succeed. It includes the process of knowledge transfer, methodology, tools, and methods for knowledge transfer to take place, and strategies and best practices for knowledge transfer. Some of the more popular models to come out of this literature include the linear, push, pull, and exchange models of knowledge transfer. Most of the attention on knowledge transfer has focused on it as a process. The most significant literature in this category includes Szulanski (1996), Kodama (2005), Daghfous (2003, 2004), Jones, Herschel, and Moesel (2003), Stenfors (2003), MacNeil (2003), Darroch (2003), Buchel and Raub (2002), Dyer and Nobeoka (2000), O'Dell and Grayson (1998), Leonard and Sensiper (1998), Landry et al. (2001), Lavis et al (2002), and Lomas (2000).

DESCRIPTIVE LITERATURE: WHAT IS REQUIRED FOR KNOWLEDGE TRANSFER TO OCCUR?

The focus here is on describing the factors and conditions for knowledge transfer to take place and the capacities required. Included in this body of literature are the articles that deal with the difficulties encountered in attempts to transfer knowledge. For example, Cummings et al. (2003) remind us of the difficulties experienced by General Motors when they attempted to transfer best practices from one Saturn division to another.

When General Motors (GM) found success in its Saturn division, it did not hesitate to seek to transfer some of the insights and best practices learned to its other divisions. Unfortunately, as Kerwin and Woodruff (1992) found, knowledge sharing at GM proved to be like in many organizations, more difficult than expected. (Gupta & Govindarajan, 1991, p. 39)

Szulanski and Capetta (2003) go even further by suggesting that difficulties associated with knowledge transfer are not only possible but commonplace, so much so that they should be considered the norm rather than the exception.

The idea that sticky transfers might actually be the norm rather than the exception when it comes to transfer knowledge within organizations is beginning to be accepted by scholars and practitioners interested in knowledge management and organizational learning. That is because, so far, efforts to transfer knowledge have had a distinctly modest record of success. Ruggles (1998) finds that only 12 percent are happy with how their organizations transfer knowledge. Tom Stewart (2001) reports that seven out of eight knowledge

management projects fail to include return on investment considerations and that CKOs and CIOs come and go. Galbraith (1990) reports that transfers are invariably found more difficult than anticipated. Gupta and Govindarajan (2000) report that expectations vastly outperform reality when it comes to knowledge transfer. Rather than automatic, transfers of knowledge appear fraught with difficulty. (p. 514)

Kalling (2003) suggests that the most important factors in successful knowledge transfer are the motivation of the recipient to change behaviour.

In knowledge transfer theory, cognitive factors such as the nature of knowledge and the absorptive capacity of recipients are key "knowledge barriers" (von Hippel, 1994; Szulanski, 1996; Simonin, 1999). This study implies that cognitive factors, such as causal ambiguity and tacitness, and absorptive and retentive capacity, are affected by motivation. The stronger the motivation to learn, the more likely it is that individuals will work harder on trying to learn and pick up new knowledge. Trying to make explicit what might be seen as tacit, at least partly, may improve learning. Here, motivation is absolutely central; what else will trigger learning, if we assume that local knowledge and abilities are naturally inflexible? Thus we propose that motivation may be a factor behind cognition in the first place.

Furthermore, the differences in motivation, in the reported cases, are also evident in local perceptions of transfer programmes, by the local aspirations and strategic ambitions, by the view on internal competition and partly in the internal communication. Those who perceive the programme as an opportunity to learn, rather than as a "stick", succeed. Those who see a direct fit with the existing local strategy and those who aspire to improve their performance, are likely to be more keen on using the transferred knowledge. (p. 121)

Szulanski (1996) empirically investigated both the context of transfer and the characteristics of the knowledge being transferred. He concentrated his attention on what he referred to as the "stickiness" of knowledge to characterize the challenges involved in the transfer and found that most of the difficulties with knowledge transfer emanated primarily from the receiving unit. Our experience in a broad variety of organizational settings, ranging from highly creative research organizations to more practical manufacturing settings, supports Szulanski's view of the importance of context. However, in addition to context, our current research also indicates that knowledge transfer capacity within the entire social system can pose significant challenges to effective knowledge transfer.

The literature focused on here includes works by Abou-Zeid (2002), Inkpen and Tsang (2005), Syed-Ikhsan and Rowland (2004), Caloghirou, Kastelli, and Tsakanikas (2004), Cummings and Teng (2003), Kalling (2003), Szulanski and Capetta (2005), Szulanski (1996), Zellner and Fornahl (2002), Goh (2002), Rogers, Takegami, and Yin (2001), Ipe (2003), and Cohen and Levinthal (1990).

LIMITATIONS

Until recently, most of the attention on knowledge and knowledge transfer focused on knowledge as an object (explicit knowledge) and knowledge transfer as a process supported significantly by information technology. The trends presented in this chapter point to knowledge increasingly being viewed less as an object and more as a social construction (tacit knowledge) and, as such, knowledge transfer is more about the capacities required by a system to transfer knowledge successfully. Organizations in general are in the very early stages of this shift as is the literature contained in this review. As the body of knowledge grows and researchers increase their investigations, the categorization system will likely experience severe modifications. A better understanding of the capacities required for knowledge transfer to

occur will no doubt contribute to the robustness of a knowledge transfer classification system.

CONCLUSION

This emerging classification system is useful for anyone wishing to begin to navigate the uncharted waters of knowledge transfer. It represents the variety of perspectives from which the subject has been viewed and provides a starting point which we hope others will use to critique, dismantle, improve, or otherwise advance our collective understanding of knowledge transfer. A holistic view of the main concepts, models, and applications of KT makes it possible for newcomers to the field to quickly situate the different literature, contextualize it, and appreciate its implications. By distinguishing between the prescriptive and descriptive categories of KT literature and the contexts of their application, it can also help regroup existing literature based on the objectives of the investigation.

This classification system builds a roadmap to help track and categorize new literature on the subject of KT. As more attention becomes focused on the science and practice of KT, it will need to be adapted and renewed to track and capture significant developments in the field.

From a strategy perspective, this classification system helps reinforce the argument that organizations looking for competitive advantage need to rely not only on an explicit (information technology) knowledge transfer logic, which all agree represents only a part of the knowledge in organizations, and pay increasing attention to a more tacit knowledge transfer logic representing the majority of the knowledge residing in organizations. So while information technology contributes significantly to developing a competitive advantage, it represents a part, and a small part at that, of the knowledge transfer needs of the organization. For knowledge transfer to be truly strategic, it must assume a holistic approach to knowledge transfer and also address the realm of knowledge commonly referred to as tacit knowledge.

FUTURE RESEARCH DIRECTIONS

The systems thinking and complex adaptive systems implications of this chapter clearly point to social system-related research to more fully understand knowledge transfer. More specifically, the future of knowledge transfer research appears to rest in the areas of tacit knowledge transfer and social system capacity building. As we learn to view knowledge less as an object and more as a social construction (tacit knowledge), we will experience a shift in research attention away from knowledge as object in favor of knowledge as social process and social system capacity building. Some questions resulting from this shift in focus towards tacit knowledge would include: What capacities does a system need to successfully transfer knowledge? What are the best practices for tacit knowledge transfer? What do organizations need to do to capitalize on this new shift in knowledge as social construction? How does tacit knowledge transfer affect competitive advantage?

Bodies of knowledge that can realistically be expected to produce interesting research settings for the next level of knowledge transfer research would include social network analysis, stakeholder theory, learning histories, learning organizations, communities of practice, and collaboration and trust, among multidisciplinary networks. From a strategic perspective, the resource based view with a focus on knowledge transfer capacity can be expected to generate considerable research attention in the immediate future. From a purely systems perspective, research on systems thinking and complex adaptive systems can be counted on to point researchers in new and interesting directions, as will research on the new science and chaos and complexity theory.

Research on knowledge transfer is in the process of shifting gears and the authors foresee that giant leaps in mankind's understanding of how knowledge gets transferred through social systems and capacity building are about to be made that will contribute significantly to changing our understanding of how organizations transfer and manage knowledge.

REFERENCES

Abou-Zeid, E.-S. (2002). An ontology-based approach to inter-organizational knowledge transfer. *Journal of Global Information Technology Management, 5*(3), 32-47.

Andreu, R., & Sieber, S. (2005). Knowledge integration across organizations: How different types of knowledge suggest different "integration trajectories". *Knowledge and Process Management, 12*(3), 153-160.

Argote, L. (1999). *Organizational learning: Creating, retaining, and transferring knowledge.* Norwell, MA: Kluwer.

Argote, L., & Ingram, P. (2000). Knowledge transfer: A basis for competitive advantage in firms. *Organizational Behaviour and Human Decision Processes, 82*(1), 150-169.

Assudani, R.H. (2005). Catching the chameleon: Understanding the elusive term "knowledge". *Journal of Knowledge Management, 9*(2), 31-44.

Augier, M., & Vendelo, M.T. (1999). Networks, cognition and management of tacit knowledge. *Journal of Knowledge Management, 3*(4), 252-261.

Barney, J.B. (1991). Firm resources and sustainable competitive advantage. *Journal of Management, 17*(1), 99-120.

Bender, S., & Fish, A. (2000). The transfer of knowledge and the retention of expertise: The continuing need for global assignments. *Journal of Knowledge Management, 4*(2), 125-137.

Bhagat, R.S., Kedia, B.L., Harveston, P.D., & Triandis, H.C. (2002). Cultural variations in the cross-border transfer of organizational knowledge: An integrative framework. *Academy of Management Review, 27*(2), 204-221.

Bhatt, G.D. (2002). Management strategies for individual knowledge and organizational knowledge. *Journal of Knowledge Management, 6*(1), 31-39.

Blumentritt, R., & Johnston, R. (1999). Towards a strategy for knowledge management. *Technology Analysis & Strategic Management, 11*(3), 287-300.

Bresman, H., Birkinshaw, J., & Nobel, R. (1999). Knowledge transfer in international acquisitions. *Journal of International Business Studies, 30*(3), 439-462.

Brown, J.S., & Duguid, P. (1991). Organizational learning and communities-of-practices: Toward a unified view of working, learning, and innovation. *Organization Science, 2*(1), 40-57.

Brown, J.S., & Duguid, P. (2001). Knowledge and organization: A social-practice perspective. *Organization Science, 12*(2), 198-213.

Büchel, B., & Raub, S. (2002). Building knowledge-creating value networks. *European Management Journal, 20*(6), 587-596.

Buckman, R.H. (1998). Knowledge sharing at Buckman Labs. *The Journal of Business Strategy, 19*(1), 11-15.

Bunnell, D. (2000). *Making the Cisco connection: The story behind the real Internet superpower.* New York: John Wiley.

Caloghirou, Y., Kastelli, I., & Tsakanikas, A. (2004). Internal capabilities and external knowledge sources: complements or substitutes for

innovative performance? *Technovation, 24*(1), 29-39.

Castells, M. (1996). *The Rise of the Network Society.* Oxford: Blackwell.

Castells, M. (2000). Materials for an exploratory theory of the network society. *British Journal of Sociology, 51*(1), 5-24.

Castillo, J. (2002). A note on the concept of tacit knowledge. *Journal of Management Inquiry, 11*(1), 46-57.

Cavusgil, S.T, Calantone, R.J., & Zhao, Y. (2003). Tacit knowledge transfer and firm innovation capability. *The Journal of Business & Industrial Marketing, 18*(1), 6-22.

Chiva, R., & Alegre, J. (2005). Organizational learning and organizational knowledge: Towards the integration of two approaches. *Management Learning, 36*(1), 49-68.

Cohen, W.M., & Levinthal, D.A. (1990). Absorptive capacity: A new perspective on learning and innovation. *Administrative Science Quarterly, 35*(1), 128-152.

Conner, K.R., & Prahalad, C.K. (1996). A resource-based theory of the firm: Knowledge versus opportunism. *Organization Science, 7*(5), 477–501.

Cook, S.D.N., & Brown, J.S. (1999). Bridging epistemologies: The generative dance between organizational knowledge and organizational knowing. *Organization Science, 10*(4), 381-400.

Cummings, J.L., & Teng, B.-S. (2003). Transferring R&D knowledge: The key factors affecting knowledge transfer success. *Journal of Engineering and Technology Management, 20*(1/2), 39-68.

Daghfous, A. (2003). Uncertainty and learning in university-industry knowledge transfer projects. *Journal of American Academy of Business, 3*(1/2), 145-151.

Daghfous, A. (2004). Organizational learning, knowledge and technology transfer: A case study. *The Learning Organization, 11*(1), 67-83.

Darr, E.D., & Kurtzberg, T.R. (2000). An investigation of partner similarity dimensions on knowledge transfer. *Organizational Behaviour and Human Decision Processes, 82*(1), 28-44.

Darroch, J. (2003). Developing a measure of knowledge management behaviours and practices. *Journal of Knowledge Management, 7*(5), 41-54.

Dayasindhu, N. (2002). Embeddedness, knowledge transfer, industry cluster and global competitiveness: A case study of the indian software industry. *Technovation, 22*(9), 551-560.

Davenport, T.H. (1997). Ten principles of knowledge management and four case studies. *Knowledge and Process Management, 4*(3), 187-208.

Davenport, T.H., De Long, D.W., & Beers, M.C. (1998). Successful knowledge management projects. *Sloan Management Review, 39*(2), 43-57.

Davenport, T.H., & Prusak, L. (1998). *Working knowledge: How organisations manage what they know*. Cambridge, MA: Harvard Business School Press.

Diakoulakis, I.E., Georgopoulos, N.B., Koulouriotis, D.E., & Emiris, D.M. (2004). Towards a holistic knowledge management model. *Journal of Knowledge Management, 8*(1), 32-46.

du Toit, A. (2003). Knowledge: A sense making process shared through narrative. *Journal of Knowledge Management, 7*(3), 27-37.

Dyer, J.H., & Nobeoka, K. (2000). Creating and managing a high-performance knowledge-sharing network: The Toyota case. *Strategic Management Journal, 21*(3), 345-367.

Earl, M. (2001). Knowledge management strategies: Toward a taxonomy. *Journal of Management Information Systems, 18*(1), 215-233.

Fahey, L., & Prusak, L. (1998). The eleven deadliest sins of knowledge management. *California Management Review, 40*(3), 265-276.

Fairlough, G. (1982). A note on the use of Weltanschauung in Checkland's systems thinking, systems practices. *Journal of Applied Systems Analysis, 9*, 131-132.

Fernandes, K.J., & Raja, V. (2002). A practical knowledge transfer system: A case study. *Work Study, 51*(2/3), 140-148.

Garavelli, C.A., Gorgoglione, M., & Scozzi, B. (2002). Managing knowledge transfer by knowledge technologies. *Technovation, 22*(5), 269-279.

Gerencser, M., Napolitano, F., & Van Lee, R. (2006). The megacommunity manifesto. Retrieved May 20, 2007, from http://www.strategy-business.com/resiliencereport/resilience/rr00035

Gherardi, S., & Nicolini, D. (2000). To transfer is to transform: The circulation of safety knowledge. *Organization, 7*(2), 329-348.

Gloet, M., & Berrell, M. (2003). The dual paradigm nature of knowledge management: Implications of achieving quality outcomes in human resource management. *Journal of Knowledge Management, 7*(1), 78-89.

Goh, S. C. (2002). Managing effective knowledge transfer: An integrative framework and some practice implications. *Journal of Knowledge Management, 6*(1), 23-30.

Grant, R. G. (1997). The knowledge-based view of the firm: Implications for management practice. *Long Range Planning, 30*(3), 450-454.

Gupta, A.K., & Govindarajan, V. (1991a). Knowledge flows and the structure of control within multinational corporations. *Academy of Management Review, 16*(4), 768-792.

Guzman, G.A.C., & Wilson, J. (2005). The "soft" dimension of organizational knowledge transfer. *Journal of Knowledge Management,* *9*(2), 59-74.

Havens, C., & Knapp, E. (1999). Easing into knowledge management. *Strategy Leadership,* *27*(2), 4-9.

Hazlett, S.-A., McAdam, R., & Gallagher, S. (2005). Theory building in knowledge management: In search of paradigms. *Journal of Management Inquiry, 14*(1), 31-42.

Holtshouse, D. (1998). Knowledge research issues. *California Management Review, 40*(3), 277-280.

Hoopes, D.G., & Postrel, S. (1999). Shared knowledge, "glitches", and product development performance. *Strategic Management Journal, 20* (9), 837-865.

Inkpen, A.C., & Tsang, E.W.K. (2005). Social capital, networks, and knowledge transfer. *Academy of Management Review, 30*(1), 146-165.

Ipe, M. (2003). Knowledge sharing on organizations: A conceptual framework. *Human Resource Development Review, 2*(4), 337-359.

Jasimuddin, S.M., Klein, J.H., & Connell, C. (2005). The paradox of using tacit and explicit knowledge: Strategies to face dilemmas. *Management Decision, 43*(1), 102-112.

Jones, N.B., Herschel, R.T., & Moesel, D.D. (2003). Using "knowledge champions" to facilitate knowledge management. *Journal of Knowledge Management, 7*(1), 49-63.

Kalling, T. (2003). Organization-internal transfer of knowledge and the role of motivation: A qualitative case study. *Knowledge and Process Management, 10*(2), 115-126.

Kidwell, J.J., Vander Linde, K.M., & Johnson, S.L. (2000). Applying corporate knowledge management practices in higher education. *Educause Quarterly, 4*, 28-33.

Kodama, M. (2005). Knowledge creation through networked strategic communities: Case studies on new product development in Japanese companies. *Long Range Planning, 38*(1), 27-49.

Kogut, B.M., & Zander, U. (1992). Knowledge of the firm, combinative capabilities, and the replication of technology. *Organization Science, 3*(3), 383-397.

Kogut, B.M., & Zander, U. (1995). Knowledge and the speed of the transfer and imitation of organizational capabilities: An empirical test. *Organization Science, 6*(1), 76-92.

Kostova, T. (1998). *Success of the transnational transfer of organizational practices within multinational companies* (Working Paper No. 98-4). Carnegie Bosch Institute.

Kostova, T. (1999). Transnational transfer of strategic organizational practices: A contextual perspective. *Academy of Management Review, 24*(2), 308-324.

Kotabe, M., Martin, X., & Domoto, H. (2003). Gaining from vertical partnerships: Knowledge transfer, relationship duration, and supplier performance improvement in the U.S. and Japanese automotive industries. *Strategic Management Journal, 24*(4), 293-316.

Lahti, R.K., & Beyerlein, M.M. (2000). Knowledge transfer and management consulting: A look at "the firm". *Business Horizons, 43*(1), 65-74.

Landry, R., Amara, N., & Lamari, M. (2001). Utilization of social science research knowledge in Canada. *Research Policy, 30*(2), 333-349.

Lave, J.C., & Wenger, E. (1991). *Situated learning: Legitimate peripheral participation.* New York: Cambridge University Press.

Lavis, J.N., Toss, S.E., Hurley, J.E., Hohenadel, J.M., Stoddart, G.L., Woodward, C.A., & Abelson, J. (2002). Examining the role of health services research in public policymaking. *The Milbank Quarterly, 80*(1), 125-154.

Leonard, D., & Sensiper, S. (1998). The role of tacit knowledge in group innovation. *California Management Review, 40*(3), 112-132.

Li, M., & Gao, F. (2003). Why Nonaka highlights tacit knowledge: A critical review. *Journal of Knowledge Management, 7*(4), 6-14.

Lomas, J. (2000). Using linkage and exchange to move research into policy at a canadian foundation. *Health Affairs, 19*(3), 236-240.

Lord, M.D., & Ranft, A.L. (2000). Organizational learning about new international markets: Exploring the internal transfer of local market knowledge. *Journal of International Business Studies, 31*(4), 573-589.

Lynn, G.S., Skov, R.B., & Abel, K.D. (1999). Practices that support team learning and their impact on speed to market and new product success. *The Journal of Product Innovation Management, 16*(5), 439-454.

MacNeil, C.M. (2003). Line managers: Facilitators of knowledge sharing in teams. *Employee Relations, 25*(3), 294-307.

Nelson, R.R., & Winter, S.G. (1982). *An evolutionary theory of economic change.* Cambridge, MA: Belknap Press.

Nielson, B.B. (2005). Strategic knowledge management research: Tracing the co-evolution of strategic management and knowledge management perspectives. *Competitiveness Review, 15*(1), 1-13.

Nonaka, I. (1990). Redundant overlapping organization: A japanese approach to managing the innovation process. *California Management Review, 32*(3), 27-39.

Nonaka, I. (1994). A dynamic theory of organizational knowledge creation. *Organization Science, 5*(1), 14-38.

Nonaka, I., & Konno, N. (1998). The concept of "ba": Building a foundation for knowledge creation. *California Management Review, 40*(3), 40-54.

Nonaka, I., & Takeuchi, H. (1995). *The knowledge creating company: How japanese companies create the dynamics of innovation.* New York: Oxford University Press.

O'Dell, C., & Grayson, C.J. (1998). If only we knew what we know: Identification and transfer of internal best practices. *California Management Review, 40*(3), 154-174.

O'Dell, C., & Grayson, C.J., Jr. (1999). Knowledge transfer: Discover your value proposition. *Strategy & Leadership, 27*(2), 10-15.

Pan, S.L., & Scarbrough, H. (1998). A socio-technical view of knowledge-sharing at Buckman Laboratories. *Journal of Knowledge Management, 2*(1), 55-66.

Porter, M. (1979, March/April). How competitive forces shape strategy. *Harvard Business Review, 57*(2), 137-144.

Prusak, L. (1997). *Knowledge in organizations.* Boston: Butterworth-Heinemann.

Reix, R. (1995, September/October). Savoir tacite et savoir formalisé dans l'entreprise. *Revue Française de Gestion,* 105, 17-28.

Rogers, E.M., Takegami, S., & Yin, J. (2001). Lessons learned about technology transfer. *Technovation, 21*(4), 253-261.

Roy, M., Guindon, J.C., & Fortier, L. (1995). *Transfert de connaissances: Revue de littérature et proposition d'un modèle* (Rapport R-099). Montréal: IRSST.

Rynes, S.L., Bartunek, J.M., & Daft, R.L. (2001). Special research forum: Knowledge transfer between academics and practitioners. *The Academy of Management Journal, 44*(2), 340-355.

Schiller, D. (1999). *Digital capitalism: Networking the global market system.* Cambridge, MA: MIT Press.

Serban, A., & Luan, J. (2002). Overview of knowledge management. *New Directions for Institutional Research*, 113, 5-16.

Shapiro, C., & Varian, H. R. (1999). *Information rules: A strategic guide to the network economy.* Boston: Harvard Business School Press.

Simmonds, P.G., Dawley, D., Ritchie, W., & Anthony, W. (2001). An exploratory examination of the knowledge transfer of strategic management concepts from the academic environment to practicing managers. *Journal of Managerial Issues, 13*(3), 360-376.

Smith, E.A. (2001). The role of tacit and explicit knowledge in the workplace. *Journal of Knowledge Management, 5*(4), 311-321.

Spender, J.C. (1996). Making knowledge the basis of a dynamic theory of the firm. *Strategic Management Journal, 17*, 45-62.

Stenfors, T. (2003). Narrated knowledge: How to use stories for knowledge dissemination. In F. McGrath & D. Remenyi (Eds.), *Fourth European Conference on Knowledge Management* (pp. 853-860).

Sveiby, K.E. (2001). Knowledge management: Lessons from the pioneers. Retrieved May 20, 2007, from http://www.sveiby.com/Portals/0/articles/KM-lessons.doc

Syed-Ikhsan, S.O.S., & Rowland, F. (2004). Knowledge management in a public organization: A study on the relationship between organizational elements and the performance of knowledge transfer. *Journal of Knowledge Management, 8*(2), 95-111.

Szulanski, G. (1996). Exploring internal stickness: Impediments to the transfer of best practice within the firm. *Strategic Management Journal, 17*(1), 27-43.

Szulanski, G. (2000). The process of knowledge transfer: A diachronic analysis of stickiness. *Organizational Behaviour and Human Decision Processes, 82*(1), 9-27.

Szulanski, G., & Capetta, R. (2005). Stickiness: Conceptualizing, measuring, and predicting difficulties in the transfer of knowledge within organizations. In M. Easterby-Smith & M.A. Lyles (Eds.), *Handbook of organizational learning and knowledge management* (pp. 513-534). Malden, MA: Blackwell Publishing.

Teece, D.J. (1982). Towards an economic theory of the firm. *Journal of Economic Behaviour and Organization, 3*(1), 39-63.

Teece, D., Pisano, G., & Shuen, A. (1997). Dynamic capabilities and strategic management. *Strategic Management Journal, 18*(7), 509-533.

Thomas, J.B., Sussman, S.W., & Henderson, J.C. (2004). Understanding "strategic learning": Linking organizational learning, knowledge management and sensemaking. *Organization Science, 12*(3), 331-345.

Tsai, W. (2001). Knowledge transfer in intraorganizational networks: Effects of network position and absorptive capacity on business unit innovation and performance. *Academy of Management Journal, 44*(5), 996-1004.

Wenger, E.C., & Snyder, W.M. (2000). Communities of practice: The organizational frontier. *Harvard Business Review, 78*(1), 139-145.

Wernerfelt, B. (1984). A resource-based view of the firm. *Strategic Management Journal, 5*(2), 171-180.

Zellner, C., & Fornahl, D. (2002). Scientific knowledge and implications for its diffusion. *Journal of Knowledge Management, 6*(2), 190-198.

Additional Reading

Argote, L. (2005). Reflections on two views of managing learning and knowledge in organizations. *Journal of Management Inquiry, 14*(1), 43-48.

Bou-Llusar, J.C., & Segarra-Ciprés, M. (2006). Strategic knowledge transfer and its implications for competitive advantage: An integrative conceptual framework. *Journal of Knowledge Management, 10*(4), 100-112.

Chen, M.-Y., & Chen, A.-P. (2006). Knowledge management performance evaluation: A decade review from 1995 to 2004. *Journal of Information Science, 32*(1), 17-38.

Chou, S.-W. (2005). Knowledge creation: Absorptive capacity, organizational mechanisms, and knowledge storage/retrieval capabilities. *Journal of Information Science, 31*(6), 453-465.

Denis, J.-L., Lehoux, P., Hivon, M., & Champagne, F. (2003). Creating a new articulation between research and practice through policy? The views and experiences of researchers and practitioners. *Journal of Health Services Research and Policy, 8*(4), Suppl. 2, 44-50.

Dyer, J.H., & Hatch, N.W. (2006). Relation-specific capabilities and barriers to knowledge transfers: Creating advantage through network relationships. *Strategic Management Journal, 27*(8), 701-719.

Erhardt, L.R. (2005). Barriers to effective implementation of guideline recommendations. *American Journal of Medicine, 118,* Suppl. 12A, 36-41.

Estabrooks, C.A., Floyd, J.A., Scott-Findlay, S., O'Leary, K.A., & Gushta, M. (2003). Individual determinants of research utilization: A systematic review. *Journal of Advanced Nursing, 43*(5), 506-520.

Friedman, V.J., Lipshitz, R., & Popper, M. (2005). The mystification of organizational learning. *Journal of Management Inquiry, 14*(1), 19-30.

Graham, I.D., Logan, J., Harrisson, M., Straus, S.E., Tetroe, J., Caswell, W., & Robinson, N. (2006). Lost in knowledge translation: Time for a map? *The Journal of Continuing Education in the Health Professions, 26*(1), 13-24.

Hewitt-Dundas, N., Andréosso-O'Callaghan, B., Crone, M., & Roper, S. (2005). Knowledge transfers from multinational plants in Ireland: A cross-border comparison of supply-chain linkages. *European Urban and Regional Studies, 12*(1), 23-43.

Jackson-Bowers, E., Kalucy, L., & McIntyre, E. (2006). Knowledge brokering. *FOCUS on..., 4,* 1-16. Retrieved May 20, 2007, from http://www.phcris.org.au/phplib/filedownload.php?file=/elib/lib/downloaded_files/publications/pdfs/phcris_pub_3238.pdf

Jacobson, N., Butterill, D., & Goering, P. (2005). Consulting as a strategy for knowledge transfer. *The Milbank Quarterly, 83*(2), 299-321.

Kramer, D.M., & Wells, R.P. (2005). Achieving buy-in: Building networks to facilitate knowledge transfer. *Science Communication, 26*(4), 428-444.

Kwan, M., & Cheung, P.-K. (2006). The knowledge transfer process: From field studies to technology development. *Journal of Database Management, 17*(1), 16-32.

Laihonen, H. (2006). Knowledge flows in self-organizing processes. *Journal of Knowledge Management, 10*(4), 127-135.

Lane, P.J., Balaji, R.K., & Seemantini, P. (2006). The reification of absorptive capacity: A critical review and rejuvenation of the construct. *Academy of Management Review, 31*(4), 833-863.

Lavis, J.N., Robertson, D., Woodside, J.M., McLeod, C.B., Abelson, J., & the Knowledge Transfer Study Group. (2003). How can research organizations more effectively transfer research knowledge to decision makers? *The Milbank Quarterly, 81*(2), 221-248.

Lucas, L.M. (2005). The impact of trust and reputation on the transfer of best practices. *Journal of Knowledge Management, 9*(4), 87-101.

Lucas, L.M. (2006). The role of culture on knowledge transfer: The case of the multinational corporation. *The Learning Organization, 13*(3), 257-275.

Muthusamy, S.K., & White, M.A. (2005). Learning and knowledge transfer in strategic alliances: A social exchange view. *Organization Studies, 26*(3), 415-441.

Richens, Y., Rycroft-Malone, J., & Morrell, C. (2004). Getting guidelines into practice: A literature review. *Nursing Standard, 18*(50), 33-40.

Sherif, K. (2006). An adaptive strategy for managing knowledge in organizations. *Journal of Knowledge Management, 10*(4), 72-80.

Stiekema, E.I. (2005). Innovation in the Netherlands: Toward guidelines for knowledge transfer. *Higher Education Management and Policy, 17*(1), 1-10.

Strach, P., & Everett, A.M. (2006). Knowledge transfer within Japanese multinationals: Building a theory. *Journal of Knowledge Management, 10*(1), 55-68.

Szulanski, G., & Jensen, R.J. (2004). Overcoming stickiness: An empirical investigation of the role of the template in the replication of organizational routines. *Managerial and Decision Economics, 25*(6-7), 347-363.

Szulanski, G., & Jensen, R.J. (2006). Presumptive adaptation and the effectiveness of knowledge transfer. *Strategic Management Journal, 27*(10), 937-957.

Trottier, L.-H., & Champagne, F. (2006). *L'utilisation des connaissances scientifiques: Au cœur des relations de coopération entre les acteurs.* (R06-05). Montréal, Canada: Université de Montréal, Groupe de recherche interdisciplinaire en santé.

Tseng, Y.M. (2006). International strategies and knowledge transfer experiences of MNCs' Taiwanese subsidiaries. *Journal of American Academy of Business, 8*(2), 120-125.

van den Bosch, F.A.J., van Wijk, R., & Volberda, H.W. (2005). Absorptive capacity: Antecedents, models and outcomes. In M. Easterby-Smith & M. Lyles (Eds.), *Handbook of organizational learning and knowledge management* (pp. 278-301). Oxford: Blackwell Publishing Ltd.

Willem, A., & Scarbrough, H. (2006). Social capital and political bias in knowledge sharing: An exploratory study. *Human Relations, 59*(10), 1343-1370.

Yih-Tong Sun, P., & Scott, J.L. (2005). An investigation of barriers to knowledge transfer. *Journal of Knowledge Management, 9*(2), 75-90.

Chapter VI
Modular Organizations and Strategic Flexiblity:
The Mediating Role of Knowledge Management Strategy

Emmanuel D. Adamides
University of Patras, Greece

Nikolaos Pomonis
University of Patras, Greece

ABSTRACT

This chapter addresses the question of whether a modular organizational structure cultivates long-term proactive strategic flexibility. With the help of system dynamics modeling, our analysis suggests that a consistent organizational-learning supporting, personalization-oriented knowledge management strategy that encourages the creation of new knowledge through richer exchanges can be the enabler of strategic flexibility in modular organizations. The chapter emphasizes the mediating role of such a knowledge strategy and discusses three of its core elements, namely, boundary spanners and boundary objects, collaboration-supporting systems, and participative scenario planning, as practices and systems, which under a common umbrella, can contribute towards achieving real strategic flexibility in modular organizations.

INTRODUCTION

Although the relationship between organizational modularity, the flexibility of the product development process, and the resulting simplified knowledge management and decision-making processes has been investigated quite extensively (Hayes & Pisano, 1994; Sanchez, 2002; Sanchez & Collins, 2001; Sanchez & Mahoney, 1996; Simon, 2003; Slack, 1983), the relation of organizational modularity to corporate-level strategic flexibility and the mediating role of learning and knowledge management strategy have not been discussed under a holistic, consistent, and dynamic perspective. This chapter aims at doing so by investigating whether, and under which conditions, modularity can contribute to gaining sustainable competitive advantage in turbulent environments through strategic flexibility. Based on insights from cognitive science and the theory of the learning organization, we argue that the strategic benefits of modularity with respect to strategic flexibility can be seized repeatedly only when there are appropriate long-term cross-module learning and knowledge management practices and systems in place.

So far, many authors (e.g., Nadler & Tushman, 1999; Sanchez & Heene, 2004; Worren, Moore ,& Cardona, 2002) have stressed the position that product and organization modularity result in augmenting the strategic flexibility of organizations and their chances of sustaining their competitive advantage. According to this stream of logic, modular products lead to modular organizations (Sanchez & Mahoney, 1996) as the different organizational units involved in the design process of products with interchangeable components are loosely coupled, operate autonomously, and can be easily reconfigured to provide rapidly changing technologies and products that markets want. Furthermore, generalizing the product development process to all organizational activities, it is argued that loosely coupled organizational forms allow organizational components, such as a contract

manufacturer, an ally firm, or a new department, and their corresponding resources to be flexibly integrated and/or recombined for forming a wide range of different configurations (Helfat & Eisenhardt, 2004; Karim, 2006; Schilling & Steensma, 2001). As a consequence, strategic flexibility is being increased as organizational knowledge is managed in a way that facilitates specific forms of "coordinated self-organizing processes" (Sanchez & Mahoney, 1996). This means that in modular organizations, coordination tasks are delegated to individual modules (functions, teams, etc.) and organizational coherence and strategic alignment are easily achieved through fully specified interfaces and standardized reconfiguration procedures, which are the result of the codification of the specific knowledge that exists inside and across modules (Sanchez, 2002). In addition to reducing managerial complexity and simplifying the flows of knowledge and information, this structural, hierarchical function-based decomposition results in the localization of the impacts of environmental disturbances within specific modules, thereby increasing the immunity and adaptability of the organization (Sanchez & Mahoney, 1996; Schilling, 2000).

Nevertheless, a fundamental question that arises from the operational characteristics of modular organizations with respect to the sustainability of competitive advantage is whether this organizational form can be self-sustained by internally fostering forces that catalyze the generating core of strategic flexibility, that is, whether this particular organizational structure breeds mechanisms that proactively cultivate strategic—not operational—flexibility. In the rest of this chapter, we examine this question from the perspective of the cognitive and learning schools of strategic management. With the aid of system dynamics modeling and simulation, we explore the long-term dynamics of the relationship between modularity and strategic flexibility, and examine the mediating role of knowledge strategy. Based on the assumption that in the cognitive perspective, strategies are mental constructs, the specific research questions to be addressed become: Do modular organizations encourage organizational learning processes that augment the capability to generate more strategic options and, thus, increase strategic flexibility? Is organizational modularity a (suboptimal) necessary and sufficient condition for achieving strategic flexibility, or do the resulting "fragmented" codification-based knowledge and learning practices (Hansen, Nohria & Tierney, 1999) constitute an undermined mechanism that gradually results in strategic rigidity? What are those knowledge management practices and systems which can compensate for the erosive (if they are so) effects of modularity and guarantee strategic flexibility? In addition to trying to answering these questions, this chapter aims at contributing methodologically to the growing stream of research that employs the cognitive perspective for understanding the conditions for the achievement of competitive advantage through strategic flexibility (e.g., Combe & Greenley, 2004; Shimizu & Hitt, 2004) by adding a systemic and dynamic perspective. It should be noted that in the discussion that follows organizational learning and the related terms are used with their late, richer meaning which is close to knowledge creation, rather than to the ability of a "memoryless" organization to adapt by simply responding to external environmental changes (see later discussion and Nonaka & Takeuchi, 1995; McElroy, 2000; and Amin & Cohendet, 2004).

In the rest of this chapter, first, we review and analyze the notion of strategic flexibility as a requirement for both strategy innovation and effective change management. We then discuss organizational modularity and its supposed links to strategic and organizational flexibility. In the section that follows, we visit organizational learning and examine it as the mediating link between organizational architecture and strategic performance. Organizational learning and knowledge creation are viewed from their cognitive base (Gamble & Blackwell, 2001; Nahapiet & Ghosal,

1998). Their attributes concerning the strategy development process and its effectiveness in fast changing environments are discussed in more detail. A conceptual model that relates the building and use of strategic flexibility through cognition is developed. Then, after adding the parameter of modularity, this model is translated into a system dynamics simulation model for examining the dynamics of learning in the strategic management of organizations with varying degrees of modularity. With the aid of this model, we investigate the dynamic relationship between organizational modularity, organizational learning, and strategic flexibility. We identify the long-term pitfalls of modular organizations with respect to strategic flexibility, and we show how they are reinforced by the elsewhere suggested codification-based "fragmented" knowledge management strategies. We outline sources of compensating actions. Finally, we stress the need for specific organizational-learning-supporting knowledge management strategies, and we present in more detail the knowledge management practices and systems which may form the core constituent parts of such strategies. We conclude the chapter by outlining future research directions.

CHANGE, INNOVATION, AND THE OBJECTIVE OF STRATEGIC FLEXIBILITY

Strategic flexibility is one dimension of organizational flexibility (Schilling & Steensma, 2001) that has been defined as the capability of a firm to proact or respond quickly to changing competitive conditions for sustaining its competitive advantage (Hitt, Hoskisson & Harrison, 1991; Sanchez, 1995). In practice, strategic flexibility is an organizational capability expressed in the fast identification of major changes in the external environment (e.g., a disruptive technology), in the realization that value exists in a different market position and the consequent rapid commitment of resources to new courses of action is required, or in the on-time identification of the appropriate moment for halting, or changing, resource commitment in the presence of problems and/or poor results, that is, the realization of strategic mistakes.

This means that strategic flexibility has to be thought of in the framework of dual strategies (Abell, 1993): a strategy for today that incorporates the elements of a strategy for the future, and vice versa. Although strategic flexibility concerns the ability of the organization to respond promptly at some point in time in the future, it is primarily determined at a previous stage, when the type and range of external environmental uncertainties have to be somehow anticipated. Strategic flexibility has to be built before it can be used. As a result, it can be thought of as a property extending along two inter-related dimensions: on the one dimension, it concerns the variation and diversity of planned strategies, while, on the other, it refers to the degree at which firms can rapidly shift from one strategy to another (Nadkarni & Narayanan, 2004; Slack, 1983). In a more operational perspective, Sanchez and Heene (2004) argue that strategic flexibility is a function of the firm's resources' flexibility, defined as the number of different uses to which the resources can be applied, of the cost and time required to switch the resources to different uses, as well as of the managerial capabilities required to achieve coordination flexibility. In addition, coordination capability, on which the sustainability of resource flexibility indirectly depends, is contingent on the ability of management to envision and generate strategic options with respect to resource endowment and dynamics, for example, to envision and implement the type and range of flexibility required in its products, as well as in its production and delivery processes.

The underlying assumption in all the facets and meanings of strategic flexibility is that managers and employees have the ability to foresee the possible future turns of the external environ-ment and build the appropriate flexibility in the organization's resources and systems on time. An organization cannot have strategic flexibility if it has not anticipated, directly or indirectly, the range of the external variables, if it has not assessed the risks involved in possible moves. The better the ability to understand the external environment, the organization, and their dynamics, the more likely it is to build strategic flexibility by considering more options. The first question that comes to the surface is how can one do this and be able to build more strategic options in the development of organizational assets and processes for accomplishing strategy innovation. In a following section, we argue that the answer to this question has to do with the way organizations manage their intellectual capital. Understanding the environmental and the organizational dynamics is a function of managers' (in general, employees') cognitive abilities, which, in turn, depend on the way the firm manages organizational learning and knowledge stocks, under specific divisions of labor imposed by formal and informal organizational structures. However, before moving to this issue, we focus on the idea of organizational modularity and its apparent consequences on strategic flexibility.

MODULAR PRODUCTS, MODULAR ORGANIZATIONS, AND STRATEGIC FLEXIBILITY

In the field of management, initially, modularity has been associated to product design and has been studied as a driver and enabler of mass-customization (Meyer & Lehnerd, 1997; Pine, 1993; Sanchez, 1995). Inevitably, the idea of modularity has been extended to embrace process architecture (Sanchez, 2002), leading the way to the introduction of the concept of modular organization, although recently reservations have been expressed towards this direct modular-product-modular-organization analogy (Hoetker, 2006). Organizational modularity means that key company activities are decomposed into specific routines and interfaces, so that they can easily be reconfigured (Meyer & Lehnerd, 1997; Worren et al., 2002). Modular organizations are formed from functions/modules in which resources and activities are module-specific and have well-defined, sometimes standardized, interfaces with other functions/modules, resources, and activities. In other words, in these organizational forms, activities and processes, where coordination needs are most intense, are organized into modules (Grant, 2003). Modularity has been, explicitly or implicitly, assumed to be a desirable organizational characteristic because it augments the responsiveness of the firm to the environmental signals. Market signals are better understood by the specialized units/modules (Sanchez & Mahoney, 1996), and loose coupling permits easier, faster, and more extensive organizational reconfiguration.

However, although organizational modularity is a recurrent theme in the literature of change management, and has been advocated as a necessary condition for surviving the current turbulent competitive environment (Grant, 2003; Helfat & Eisenhardt, 2004; Nadler & Tushman, 1999; Schilling & Steensma, 2001), most of the empirically-determined conclusive results concern the modularity of products and their, somehow arbitrary or very context-specific, associations with modular organizations (Baldwin & Clark, 2000; Cusumano & Nobeoka, 1997; Meyer & Seliger, 1998; Sanchez & Collins, 2001; Sanderson & Uzumeri, 1997; Worren et al., 2002). Concrete examples of organizational modularity have been limited to contract manufacturing (outsourcing, in general), the so-called alternative (flexible) work arrangements, and the use of alliances (Schilling & Steensma, 2001). Modular-product-related organizational forms include the modularization of the innovation and product development function in direct correspondence to the modular product architecture (Sanchez & Collins, 2001; Sanchez & Mahoney, 1996), the use of "patching" (Eisenhardt & Brown, 1999; Helfat & Eisenhardt,

2004), and the concept of platform organization (Ciborra, 1996).

A firm may exploit modularization and organizational flexibility at different levels. At the pure operations level, a change may be synonymous with the introduction of a new process for a novel product. Modular processes and standardized software and hardware interfaces would allow the fast incorporation of the new process in existing facilities, as well as the inclusion of the new product requirements in the existing production planning and control systems. At a higher level, change may concern operations strategy, and may be expressed as a shift from a focus on low-cost production to increasing flexibility. Such a move may imply the substitution of a high-volume specialized contract manufacturer with a flexible jobshop-like one. At the strategic level, as it was already stated, change may have a passive or active imperative. It may concern the development and/or acquisition of resources and capabilities for addressing new markets and/or new market segments. It may be the positioning and/or repositioning of existing products, or the development of innovative technologies and/or products to cover foresighted markets.

Structurally, a change of strategy, at any level, may imply changes in organizational modules at three levels: the *interior* of an organizational module/unit, for example, the development of a new technology by acquiring new module-specific resources; the *exterior* of an organizational module/unit, for example, the addition or deletion of a module or the movement of a module in the organizational architecture; and the *architectural* level, that is, new modularization by mixing modules and/or moving resources from one module to another, for example, the merging of two product specific development teams (for instance, conventional and synthetic materials groups). Strategic flexibility is the organization's ability to accomplish these changes fast and without great difficulty. As it was already mentioned, focusing on the first two levels, the proponents of organizational modularity argue that modular organizations are in a position to do that. However, what has to be kept in mind is that the degrees of freedom and, consequently, the extent of strategic flexibility concerns the third level and is predetermined before the decision to change or adapt is made. Both this capability to predetermine the strategic space, as well as the capability to scan and understand the dynamics of the current environment, and subsequently trigger change depend on organizational learning and its supporting knowledge management practices, that is, on the ability of the organization to learn faster and better than its competitors, to create new knowledge, and to embed it in its strategic processes (Zack, 2002).

COGNITION, ORGANIZATIONAL STRUCTURE, AND ORGANIZATIONAL LEARNING

Henry Mintzberg and his colleagues are well known for their review, analysis, critique, and eventual synthesis of the different schools of the strategy formulation process (Mintzberg, Ahlstrand & Lampel, 1998; Mintzberg & Lampel, 1999). For them, schools are rather stages in a more integrative and pragmatic process, in the center of which sits the mind(s) of the strategist(s) (the premise of the cognitive school). In other words, strategy formulation "is judgmental designing, intuitive visioning, and emergent learning; it is about transformation as well as perpetuation; it must involve individual cognition and social interaction, cooperative as well as conflictive; it has to include analyzing before and programming after as well as negotiating during" (Mintzberg & Lampel, 1999, p. 27). Hence, the concept of managerial cognition is central to integrative approaches to strategic management, such as the competence (Sanchez & Heene, 2004) and *JOURNEY* (Eden & Ackermann, 1998) ones.

The term cognition refers to the way individuals perceive, filter, and conceptualize information (Weick, 1990) and can be thought of as a term describing the process of *knowing* (Hilgard, 1980). Perceptions become cognitive schemata that take the form of frames (Goffman, 1974), mental models (Senge 1990), or cognitive maps (Axelrod, 1976) (and many other names), and indicate the way individuals associate various concepts and use them as the foundation for their decisions and actions. The impact of executive cognition on the strategy formulation processes and their outcomes has been a subject of great interest in the strategic management literature, especially for the learning-inclining, nonprescriptive schools. According to upper echelons (Hambrick & Mason, 1984) and other related agency theories, the organization is a reflection of its managers whose beliefs have a decisive impact on the majority of the strategy attributes (innovation, diversification, quality management, risk-taking, etc.) (Adamides & Karacapilidis, 2005). The factors and processes that shape executives' beliefs and cognition include knowledge-constituting attributes such as executive demographics, functional position and professional background, peer-assigned roles and performance metrics (Schwarz, 2003), organization's size, structure, strategy, and recent financial success (Barr & Huff, 1997; Schwarz, 2003). While cognitive schemata, such as frames, originate from the cognitive psychology of the individual, management scholars have found it useful to conceptualize them as a property of larger organizational entities such as groups and firms (Prahalad & Bettis, 1986; Reger & Huff, 1993). Cognitive schemata at the level of module are the result of organizational learning, which, in turn, may be thought of as a process of change in the states of individual and collective cognitive schemata (knowledge structures). These changes are the result of the interplay of individual cognition with social processes taking place at the organization level (Nahapiet & Ghosal,

1998; Akgün, Lynn & Byrne, 2003). The strategy development process, which and how individual mental models converge (or are "accommodated") towards a coherent list of actions, plays a decisive role in the justification of this assumption. The strategy process may be formal and restricted in time and place (executive strategy-making sessions in appropriately arranged rooms with shared screens, etc.), or can take place in a continuous *ad hoc* manner, involving problem-related formal and/or informal meetings, informal discussions, memo circulations, and so forth.

In the majority of modern organizations comprised of flat structures, project-based work, and so forth, organizational learning takes place by means of two processes: *learning-by-absorption* and *learning-by-reflection* (Scarbrough, Bresnen, Edelman, Laurent, Newell & Swan, 2004). Central to the former is the notion of absorptive capacity, whereas the latter relies on the development of reflective practices. In fact, learning-by-reflection is the process by which organization members and units make their prior and implicit knowledge more explicit to themselves (*surfacing*) and to other group members through activities based on review and self-diagnosis. The results of reflective practices *per se*, as well as their significance to overall learning, depend on the relative diversity of the individuals involved and their associated cognitive entities (Adamides & Karacapilidis, 2006), as well as on time boundaries (Lindkvist, Soderlund & Tell, 1998).

Regarding absorptive learning, *absorptive capacity* is a term introduced by Cohen and Levinthal (1990) to describe an organization's capability to recognize the value of new external information, assimilate it, and apply it to commercial ends. It depends on the prior knowledge of the organization and is vital for its innovative capacity. More recent research (Jones, 2006; Zahra & George, 2002) associates absorptive capacity to the dynamic capabilities framework and stresses its importance as a degrees-of-freedom provider towards strategic flexibility. As in

the case of reflective learning, absorptive capacity is a function of the richness/diversity of the pre-existing knowledge structure, personalized (tacit) and impersonalized (codified). Adopting a cognitive-science perspective, Cohen and Levinthal (1990) state:

In a setting in which there is uncertainty about the knowledge domains from which potentially useful information may emerge, a diverse background provides a more robust basis for learning because it increases the prospect that incoming information will relate to what is already known. In addition to strengthening assimilative powers, knowledge diversity also facilitates the innovative process by enabling the individual to make novel associations and linkages. (p. 131)

The importance of the diversity of prior knowledge in both types of learning can be better understood by considering two key attributes of mental models (in the rest of the chapter, we will use the term "mental model" to denote networks of cause-effect relationships—causal maps—between concept nodes that include the characteristics of all similar cognitive schemata) that are of particular importance to strategic flexibility: *complexity* and *centrality* (Nadkarni & Narayanan, 2004, 2005). Complexity is the result of the degree of differentiation (the range/diversity of internal and external organizational concepts included in the model) and integration (degree of connectedness among concepts) of the model. Complex strategy-, change-, and innovation-related mental models embrace a wide range of strategic logics and a diverse set of alternative strategic solutions. Clearly, at the organizational level, such models allow firms to notice and respond to a larger number of different stimuli, thus increasing their adaptability (Lyles & Schwenk, 1992). Complex mental models contribute to the reduction of *discounting* (the phenomenon of focusing in specific—more familiar—events ignoring other objectively considered as more important) and *cognitive inertia* (the search for specific events and causes to strengthen the dominant logic(s) of the model). They allow managers to scan the environment and respond to stimuli coming from it more effectively by associating environmental events with elements of the existing organizational knowledge base.

Centrality, on the other hand, refers to the focus and hierarchy of mental models. A centralized model is focused around a limited number of core concepts. The continuous long-term involvement with a limited number of concepts, as well as people with similar jobs, interests, and organizational tasks, breeds centrality of mental models (Carley & Palmquist, 1992) and, as a result, amplifies a limited number of dominant logics (frequently a single one). Centralized mental models lead to cognitive inertia since firms always refer to their past key successes instead of looking at how to absorb new knowledge and create novel strategic options (Adamides, Stamboulis, & Kanellopoulos, 2003; Reger & Palmer, 1996). In addition, centrality slows down participative decision processes and makes the convergence of different views expressed in them more difficult.

Obviously, complex mental models are responsible for increased absorptive and reflective learning capacity, making the organization more responsive to the requirements of strategic flexibility. Their diversity allows for the consideration, creation, and eventual implementation of a wider and wiser set of strategic options, as well as for more effective scanning and understanding of environmental signals. The former contributes to the development of flexible resources and processes, limiting excessive scope and capacity, whereas the latter triggers fast response to change by fast resource and process reconfiguration. As far as reflective learning is concerned, mental model complexity contributes to the development of a richer language for representing, communicating, and understanding a broader set of concepts.

Vickers explained the formation and dynamics of individual and shared/group mental models

through the concept of "appreciative systems" (Vickers, 1983). He distinguished human systems from natural and man-made systems by identifying judgment as the additional aspect of the former (Vickers, 1984). Judgment is an inherent attribute of decision making's three principal functions: noticing things about the situation (receiving information), evaluating the information (comparing to a "standard"), and acting on the interpretation (selecting a response). This was termed by Vickers an *appreciative system* and the mental activity and social process of attaching meaning to perceived signals as appreciation. The appreciative system determines what facts to select from those related to the situation, the meaning that is given and the means that are used to fill the gap between existing and desired situations. The standards or criteria by which actions to be followed are judged are not given from outside. They are generated by the previous history of the system and its interaction with the environment (cultural context).

This implies that in strategy development processes, managers set standards or norms subjectively, rather than objective measurable goals of Simon's rationalistic tradition (Checkland & Holwell, 1998), and they focus on managing relationships according to standards generated by their own culture, history, and power status, and maintained through their self-reference attribute. The discussion and debate which leads to action is the one in which those taking part make judgments about both "what is the case" (reality judgments) and about its evaluation as "good" or "bad", "satisfactory" or "unsatisfactory" (appreciative judgments). Under this prism, strategy-making can be thought of as social action, based upon personal and collective *sense making* rather than a one-off task performed on the basis of objective scientific foundations. Consequently, in the long term, strategic processes *per se* influence executive beliefs and mental models in the same way their outcome is influenced by them (Chattopadhyay, Glick, Miller, & Huber, 1999;

Figure 1. Appreciative systems, learning capacity, and strategic flexibility

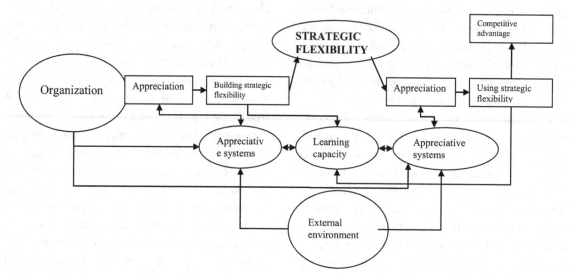

Weick, 1995). In knowledge management terms, different perceptions/beliefs are the result of managers' association with different sources of principally tacit, cultural and, to a lesser extent, codified knowledge.

Naturally, as the above discussion suggests, strategic processes are contingent on organizational forms and operational structures. Hence, strategic flexibility and managerial mental models are not inter-related only through external environmental attributes, such as industry clockspeed (Nadkarni & Narayanan, 2004), but also through internal (organizational) ones (Figure 1). Appreciation of both the internal and external environment through managers' appreciative systems drives the building of strategic flexibility, while appreciative systems are influenced by, as much as they influence, learning capacity. In addition, appreciative systems are responsible for the way the environment is scanned and strategic flexibility is used. Narrow strategic processes with limited participation and interaction due to immature relationships, which are simplified through well-defined interaction rules/interfaces, lead to managerial mental models of limited complexity,

as managers have to focus on a limited number of concepts (a specific technology, a specific product, or specific functional elements of a product range) and communicate them through the established interfaces. In a static and short-term view, this seems logical and is the main advantage of the modular organization. A different, more dynamic and longitudinal stance, however, suggests that modular organizational architectures enhance the centrality of managers' mental models at the expense of complexity. As a consequence, the ability of managers to envision and create strategic options (i.e., novel systems of activities and resources) is reduced, and the firm's strategic flexibility does not increase. On the other hand, strategy development and implementation processes that include managers with wide mental horizons, who can actively contribute to them, do not only result in more diverse and innovative strategies, but also themselves further widen the mental models of the participants (De Geus, 1997). Under these assumptions, and based on the discussion so far, to explore the dynamics of mental model characteristics with respect to organizational modularity and strategic flexibility and in order to determine appropriate interventions at the strategic level, we have built the system dynamics model presented in the following section.

THE DYNAMICS OF LEARNING AND STRATEGY-MAKING IN MODULAR AND STRATEGICALLY FLEXIBLE ORGANIZATIONS

Based on the conceptual model of the previous section, the system dynamics model of Figure 2 links the concepts of modularity, learning, and strategic flexibility through the properties of cognitive representation (mental models—causal maps) and learning capacity. In addition, it provides guidelines for the development of knowledge management processes to compensate the undesired effects of modularity while exploring its advantages. System dynamics is a systems modeling approach which focuses on feedback loops that contain stocks (levels, represented as rectangular boxes) and flows (rates, represented as taps). Stocks represent the state of a system variable, whereas flows the rate of its change. This stock-flow language provides a clear distinction in the modeling of management processes (flows) and the results of these processes (stocks). Moreover, system dynamics modeling is a very useful tool for exploring knowledge and information management phenomena when adopting, as in our case, a functionalist (or neofunctionalist) perspective (Markus, 2004). Nevertheless, in contrast to first-order models that are used for theory testing, the model of Figure 2 can be considered as a second-order one. That is, based on a plausible reconstruction/integration of an underlying theoretical narrative (the discussion in the last three sections), the model is used as an aid to theory building (Larsen & Lomi, 2002). All variables of the model can refer to both individual managers or organizational entities.

Complexity and centrality, which are the two principal attributes of mental models relevant to strategic flexibility, are represented as stocks. The flow *build_new_nodes* represents the addition (horizontally, adding breath) of new nodes/concepts to managerial mental models which result in increasing their complexity (flow in the *COMPLEXITY* stock). The flow *nodes_not_used* represents the natural depletion of mental models' complexity as nodes that are not used become obsolete and are rejected because the limited capacity of the human brain replaces them with new ones. As far as *CENTRALITY* is concerned, the flow *strengthen_links* refers to the process of strengthening existing links between existing nodes (or adding depth to a specific node), whereas the opposite is represented by the flow *weaken_links*. The continuous consideration of the same, or similar, concepts strengthens the links of existing nodes while, on the other hand, increased focus on core concepts results in the loosening of some concepts in the periphery, which are then gradually driven out of the model. In addition, naturally, as no new events are noticed (or taken into account seriously) to confirm existing links, some facts are gradually disassociated.

The organization's absorptive and reflective learning capacity is represented by the stock *LEARNING_CAPACITY_absorptive_&_reflective*. The rate at which this stock is built (*building_learning_capacity*) is a function of the difference between *COMPLEXITY* and *CENTRALITY* (in fact, it is a function of the percentage value of *CENTRALITY* with respect to that of *COMPLEXITY*). This is a valid assumption as the rate of building learning capacity is positively correlated to complexity and negatively to centrality, and the two variables are not mutually exclusive in the short term. Since both are stock variables, for instance, an increase in *CENTRALITY* will only have a relative effect on learning as the level of *COMPLEXITY* will not be reduced in proportion. A fraction of the value of this difference is used for regulating the rate at which learning capacity is lost due to managers quitting, and so forth (*learning_capacity_depletion*).

Figure 2. The system dynamics model for exploring the dynamic relation between organizational learning, modularity, and strategic flexibility

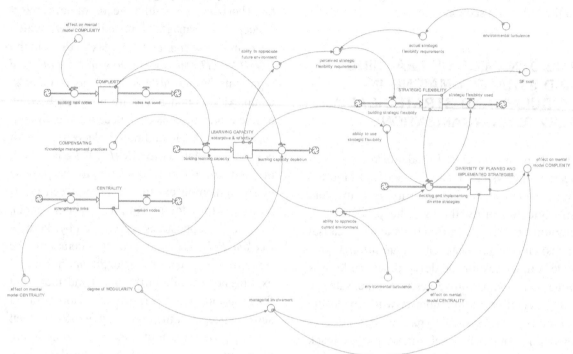

In the model, the stock *LEARNING_CAPAC-ITY_absorptive_&_reflective* plays a decisive role on both the building of strategic flexibility, as well as on the exploitation of strategic flexibility in the implementation of strategies, including change and innovation initiatives in response to environmental turbulence. As far as the planning and building of strategic flexibility is concerned (the flow *bulding_strategic_flexibility*), learning capacity, as a capability, contributes to the ability of management to appreciate the shape and the dynamics of the future competitive environment for developing the appropriate resources and mindsets (*ability_to_appeciate_future_environment*). The higher the level of this capability, the better the level of understanding the environmental signals, and the closer the perceived strategic flexibility requirements (*perceived_strategic_flexibility_requirements*) to the actual ones (*actual_strategic_flexibility_requirements*), the latter dictated by the dynamics of the environ-

ment (*environmental_turbulence*). Obviously, the higher the environmental turbulence, the more difficult to understand the environment and the higher the level of learning capacity required.

The stock *STRATEGIC_FLEXIBILITY* models the strategic flexibility of the organization available at any time period. It is a function of the difference between the rate at which strategic flexibility is built (*building_strategic_flexibility*) and the rate at which it is used (*strategic_flexibility_used*). The variable *SF_cost* represents the cost of the excessive (unused stock of) strategic flexibility.

In addition to building strategic flexibility, learning capacity also determines the ability to appreciate the current competitive environment (*ability_to_apprecite_current_environment*) and the ability to use strategic flexibility (*ability_to_use_strategic_flexibility*). Clearly, the latter is contingent on the degree of environmental turbulence too. On the other hand, the ability

Figure 3. Strategic flexibility as a function of organizational modularity

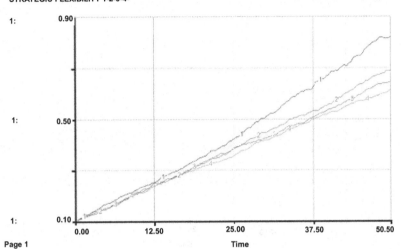

STRATEGIC FLEXIBILITY 1-2-3-4-

to use strategic flexibility and the ability to appreciate the current environment contribute to the rate at which diverse strategies, in response to environmental turbulence, are decided and implemented (flow *deciding_and_implementing_diverse_strategies*, stock *DIVERSITY_OF_PLANNED_AND_IMPLEMENTED_STRATEGIES*). In turn, the rate at which diverse strategies are decided and implemented determines the rate at which strategic flexibility from the available stock is used (*strategic_flexibility_used*). In addition, the stock of diverse strategies planned and implemented influences the degree of complexity and centrality of managers' mental models (*effect_on_mental_model_COMPLEXITY*, *effect_on_mental_model_CENTRALITY*) as the degree of managerial involvement in planning and executing does. Clearly, as the model indicates, and as it was previously discussed, the degree of managerial, direct or indirect, involvement (*managerial_involvement*) in diverse strategic issues plays a significant role on how planned and implemented strategies influence cognition. In turn, the degree of managerial involvement is highly dependent on the extent of organizational modularity (*degree_of_MODULARITY*).

After appropriately calibrating the model so that it exhibits the required sensitivity, and after running simulations with varying degrees of modularity, we initially observe that in all cases strategic flexibility increases with time as a result of increased learning (Figure 3). This is the result of the existence of a reinforcing loop between strategic flexibility, diversity of implemented strategies, and learning. However, the traces in the diagram indicate that as the degree of modularity increases (moving from trace 1 to trace 4), the relative value of strategic flexibility decreases (it should be noted that since the quantification of the model is somehow arbitrary, the results in the graphs should be interpreted only qualitatively). This is because the ability of managers to participate in diverse strategy planning and implementation projects is reduced, and the relationship between mental model complexity and centrality leans towards the latter, increasing the learning capacity of the organization at a slower rate. This, in turn, results in the building of a lower level stock of strategic flexibility, which, because of the reduced managerial involvement, further reduces the rate of building learning capacity, and so on.

Figure 4. The compensating role of increasing mental model complexity in learning

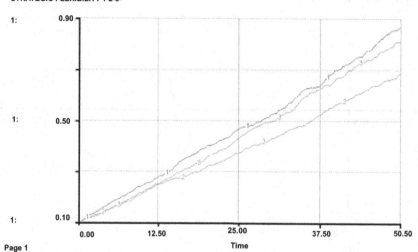

Clearly, this behavior signifies a structuration process where agency is influenced by the organizational structure, which, at the same time, is reproduced by the actions of organization's individual members. In line with this, as the concept of duality of technology (Orlikowski, 1992) suggests, information and knowledge management technology (use of technology to store and process codified, module-specific knowledge) structured to serve this organizational structure and functionality would only contribute to the continuation of the phenomenon (McDermott, 1999; Nardi & O'Day, 1999). As an antidote for breaking this vicious circle, many authors have insisted that information systems strategy (technology and use systems) should be part of organizational learning processes; that is, information and knowledge management systems should be shaped in a dynamic fashion as the organization learns in response to external and internal stimuli, including those coming from the use of information technology (Huysmann, Fischer & Heng, 1994; Walsham, 1993).

Returning to the model, in addition to building the logical consistency of the narrative so far, and exposing the long-term pitfalls of organizational modularity and strategic flexibility, it can be used

to determine whether some pre-assumed knowledge management interventions can increase the organization's performance with respect to flexibility. A point where management can intervene by deploying the appropriate modularity-compensating processes and systems is where individual mental models are influencing the accumulation of learning capacity. There, compensating knowledge management practices can be introduced so that the complexity of mental models is augmented independently of prior problem-specific managerial involvement in strategy planning and implementation.

In Figure 4, trace 2 corresponds to a situation where the degree of modularity has been doubled with respect to that corresponding to trace 1. As it was expected, the firm's strategic flexibility has been reduced. Nevertheless, trace 3 corresponds to the same situation with the additional assumption that a compensating program that widens mental models (*COMPENSATING_knowledge_management_practices* increases complexity by a specific factor) and increases learning capacity at a faster rate is in place. Obviously, the strategic flexibility of the organization has been augmented. Similar effects can be observed when managerial involvement is increased, or when additional knowledge and social processes are introduced for narrowing the gap between perceived and actual requirements of strategic flexibility. As mentioned, under the dialectic of structuration, information technology can support these interventions, which will, in turn, gradually result in a more effective use of the technology. Below, we concentrate on such leveraging knowledge management strategies, procedures, and technologies.

LEARNING AND KNOWLEDGE STRATEGIES FOR STRATEGIC FLEXIBILITY IN MODULAR ORGANIZATIONS

In the previous sections, we have discussed *which* individual or organizational cognitive characteristics influence organizational learning, and *why* organizational learning is a determinant of strategic flexibility. Previously, in our discussion we have emphasized that modular organizational structures promote specialization and localized planning and responsive actions resulting in fragmented learning processes which are unable to contribute to the principally systemic objective of strategic flexibility. In this section, we will discuss *how* organizational learning is accomplished and how modular organizations can leverage organizational learning and achieve strategic flexibility.

The simulations of the system dynamics model indicated that compensating actions can be implemented to overcome the drawbacks of modularity with respect to organizational learning. Three main areas of intervention have been identified: intervening on the way mental model characteristics influence the accumulation of learning capacity, improving managerial participation in the planning and deployment of strategies, and improving the processes, methods, and tools for assessing the future environment. All three activities can be thought of as part of a knowledge management strategy that organizes

social capital and technological artifacts in a way that organizational learning is augmented through increasing absorptive capacity and reflexive learning capability. Clearly, such a strategy lies on the personalization side of the personalization-codification spectrum of knowledge management strategic paradigms (Hansen et al., 1999; Scheepers, Venkitachalam & Gibbs, 2004). Below, in connection with the aforementioned interventions, we discuss the concepts of boundary spanners and boundary objects, collaborative decision-making, and scenario planning as the basic constituent parts of a consistent knowledge management strategy that enables strategic flexibility in modular organizations. However, before doing this, we discuss in more detail the notion of knowledge (management) strategy and its relation to organizational learning.

In the discussion so far, based on concepts of cognitive theory, we have argued that organizational learning is a capability that is crucial for augmenting the strategic flexibility of modular organizations. In fact, if organizational learning as a dynamic capability equivalent to double loop learning (Teece, Pisano & Schuen, 1997) exists in sufficient amount, the modular organization is capable of identifying value, and planning and executing different strategies in precise timings. Operationally, however, learning is a recombination/reconstruction process that takes some inputs, uses existing knowledge, and produces some outputs. The input of the learning process is information and knowledge in raw or in process form, and its output is again knowledge which may be codified, stored, and transmitted in paper, electronic, and other explicit forms, or alternatively, may be in tacit form "stored" in the minds and bodies of human actors. This output knowledge is capable of changing the range of the organization's possible behaviors (Huber, 1991). At the level of the organization, the execution of this process is facilitated by appropriate deliberate social process (collaboration in, participation in, coordination of work, etc.); that is, social capital facilitates the formation of intellectual capital (Nahapiet & Ghosal, 1998). In other words, in an all-inclusive conceptualization, "organizational learning is the way firms build, supplement and organize knowledge and routines around their activities and within their cultures and adapt and develop organizational efficiency by improving the use of broad skills of their workforces" (Dodgson, 1993, p. 377). Essentially, such a conceptualization of learning is closer to organizational knowledge creation than to simple adaptation. Hence, its process can become more efficient by either increasing the learning capability *per se*, or by improving the way information and knowledge is supplied to the process (thus requiring less capability to produce the same results), or both. The organization of the input (and output) knowledge of the learning process, which also directly influences the level of learning capability, is the object of knowledge management defined holistically as "the deliberate design of processes, tools, structures, etc. with the intent to increase, renew, share or improve the use of knowledge represented in any of the three elements (structural, human and social) of intellectual capital" (Seemann, De Long, Stucky & Guthrie, 2000, p. 82). In fact, it is the "social capital" embedded in individual relationships that under certain conditions can lead to significant increases in the knowledge base of "intellectual capital" of the organization (Nahapiet & Ghosal, 1998).

Hence, returning to our particular case, a knowledge management strategy that aims at the efficient and effective creation of knowledge from different organizational modules, as well as on augmenting learning capacity, should be primarily aiming at the development of social capital rather than on the installation of technology systems for the storage and distribution of codified knowledge. The objective of strategic flexibility, as the capability to survive in turbulent environments by shifting strategies, suggests a *personalization* rather than a *codification* knowledge management *meta*strategy (if we assume that the individual competitive strategies chosen have their own attributes leaning towards personalization or codification, accordingly) (Hansen et al., 1999; Scheepers et al., 2004), paying particular attention to identifying learning gaps, rather than knowledge ones (Zack, 2002). Nevertheless, this does not mean that there is no role for information and communication technology in this strategic choice. There is a wide range of technologies that can be used for communicating knowledge, for using existing knowledge, and for facilitating the building of relations among managers and other organizational actors (Andreu & Ciborra, 1996). Some of these technologies are mentioned in the following section in the framework of more systemic approaches of creating and using organizational knowledge.

CORE CONSTITUENT ELEMENTS OF A LEARNING-SUPPORTING KNOWLEDGE MANAGEMENT STRATEGY

The discussion so far suggests that a knowledge management strategy for the exploitation of organizational modularity to achieve strategic flexibility should be principally aiming at widening the mental models of the strategists through rich knowledge and information exchange among the modules. With the aid of the system dynamics simulations, three knowledge management practices were identified, which, with their associated processes and toolsets, are presented in more detail below.

Boundary Spanners and Boundary Objects

In modular organizations, more than in any other organizational form, there is an inherent dynamic tendency to localize and embed knowledge and learning practices within the boundaries of individual modules. Interfacing with other modules is by means of predefined, standardized interfaces. Clearly, this logic increases mental model centrality and fragments knowledge and knowing, and their creative interplay in strategic and operational processes (Amin & Cohendet, 2004). The result is an apparent loss of communication and reduced cooperation among modules, functions, and so forth, as language and meaning are *syntactically*, *semantically*, or *pragmatically* bound (Bourdieu, 1977; Carlile, 2002). The so-called pragmatic boundaries are the most intense and the related cross-boundary challenge is not just to facilitate communication, but principally to resolve the negative consequences of the attitudes of the individuals from each module against altering their own knowledge, as well as to leverage their capabilities of influencing or transforming the knowledge used by other modules/functions, that is, increasing mental model complexity and, consequently, learning capacity. Boundaries are not only important when the organization uses (static) knowledge in decision-making, but also when it develops knowing (learning) through decision-making (Amin & Cohendet, 2004; De Geus, 1997). In other words, knowledge boundaries limit not only the strategy development and deployment processes in response to environmental signals when changes at the interior, exterior, and architectural level of modules need to take place, but also the planning for the future one, when strategic flexibility is explored. Two inter-related concepts have been developed for overcoming the problems of knowledge boundaries and facilitating distributed coordination: *boundary spanners* and *boundary objects*.

Boundary spanners are organization members assigned the specific role to facilitate the collaboration of different organizations, or different organization modules. They coordinate activities across and on the edge of boundaries where they cross or overlap. They are representatives of the organization/module they formally belong to, facilitate information sharing back and forth

across the organizational boundaries, and help match needs and resources. Scanning, fluidity, and imaginativeness are associated with the roles of boundary spanners. The more sensitive boundary spanners are to significant information in the environment, the more active they are in their roles (Dollinger, 1984). Boundary spanners must be able to perceive and adjust to different settings. When they understand the different organizational languages and cultures, they are able to navigate and cross organizational boundaries as they work with others to address a problem domain.

The huge burden that the role of boundary spanner carries and the complex requirements that it imposes makes it very difficult to act as the "systemic glue" of module-specific knowledge and social processes. Boundary spanners can be complemented by boundary objects which are artifacts used to create shared context among different parties in cross-module activities (Star, 1989). Carlile (2002) adapted Star's boundary object classification scheme (repositories, platonic objects, terrains with coincident boundaries, and forms and labels) by essentially merging the last two to form a classification consisting of three classes: repositories; standardized forms and methods; and objects, models, and maps. This last category is the only one that directly supports the transformation of knowledge, in addition to representation and learning, and therefore is suitable for overcoming pragmatic knowledge boundaries.

The category of objects, models, and maps contains representations that can be observed and then used across different modules and/or functions. They can be module-specific emphasizing the idiosyncrasies and differences between modules, or boundary-specific concentrating on the relations and dependencies that exist between the modules. Boundary objects, such as process maps, strategy maps, process or system dynamics simulation models, as well as computer-based learning environments can trigger and support learning-by-adaptation processes (De Geus,

1997), eliminating, probably with the help of a boundary spanner, pragmatic knowledge boundaries. From a different perspective, they constitute "transitional objects" (Papert, 1980) for aligning, in the short term, and enlarging in the long term, mental models of individuals in different modules, thus increasing the organization's strategic flexibility.

Collaboration-Supporting Methods and Systems

Collaboration-supporting methods and systems, when used at a cross-functional level, can be considered a particular class of boundary objects that promote diverse participation and facilitate the activation of the micro-instantiation of the *organizational knowledge cycle* over particular cross-module issues and problems (Adamides & Karacapilidis, 2005). More specifically, these methods and artifacts structure the problem-solving process and the related dialoguing, and by the collaborative development and manipulation of structured models and the embedding of dialectic logic in the form of argumentation schemes in the collaboration processes (dialectic logic facilitates synthesis of perceptions), increase the organization's problem-solving and planning efficiency and effectiveness. Information and communication technologies (ICTs) are used to support the knowledge flows among the relevant actors and artifacts, in a way that enhances the creation of new knowledge (the process of *knowing*). These are the main tasks of a class of computer-based knowledge management systems (CKMS), which can be defined as systems intended at providing a corporate memory, that is, an explicit, disembodied persistent representation of the knowledge and information in an organization (a sort of knowledge base) and mechanisms that improve the sharing and dissemination of knowledge by facilitating interaction and collaboration (Taylor, 2004). Moreover, the provision of an associated ICT infrastructure that supports virtuality

(dispersed groups, asynchronous collaboration) attracts wider membership and hence increases the diversity and richness of knowledge, promotes active participation, and further increases the productivity of strategic issue resolution (Adamides & Karacapilidis, 2005).

The methods and systems developed over the last two decades for supporting collaboration include participative systems methodologies (such as soft systems methodology (SSM), Strategic options development and analysis (SODA), etc.), methodologies that rely on simulation modeling, methodologies that use collaborative information technology, and information systems supporting collaboration and argumentation (for a review, see Adamides & Karacapilidis, 2005, 2006).

Participative Scenario Planning

Scenario planning is the most frequently used tool of the "processualistic", or learning, school of strategic management. This school sits between the rational/analytic and the emerging strategy schools, and aims at overcoming the drawbacks and limitations of forecasting by providing a structured method to speculate about many possible futures (Schoemaker, 1995; Van der Heijden, 1996). As a consequence, the value of scenario planning does not stem from its outcomes, but rather from the *process* of scenario construction, which through the dynamic interaction between the organization and the environment stimulates learning by considering possible and "impossible" future events and their consequences (De Geus, 1988). Written scenarios, frequently complemented by computer simulations, are used to explore the concurrent impact of various uncertainties by changing multiple variables at a time and by speculating on their outcomes. In this way, the process of scenario construction stimulates and facilitates the sharing and recombination of personal knowledge to build a holistic understanding of the internal and external environment of the organization. Scenario planning makes explicit the implicit assumptions of individuals about the future—which are the results of their mental models expressed at the level of organization as learning capacity—stimulating strategic thinking and communication and hence improving the organization's flexibility of response to environmental uncertainty by closing the gap between the perceived requirements for strategic flexibility and the actual ones. In this way, the use of scenario planning reflects the proactive orientation of the organization (Codet, 2000), by discovering and comparing firm specific capabilities with future requirements.

Frequently, scenario planning is part of corporate-wide strategies for managing organizational knowledge and learning, and is executed at different levels within the organizational structure. Common areas of application include technology foresight, internationalization strategy, investment perspectives assessment, and so forth. In addition, scenario planning constitutes one of the most popular and effective exercises for knowledge creation and learning in knowledge management initiatives such as communities of practice (Wenger, 1998). Managers from different departments/modules participate in a typical scenario construction process, which is usually comprised of 10 distinct stages (Schoemaker, 1995): definition of the scope of scenario (products, markets, time frames, etc.); identification of major stakeholders; identification of the basic macro-environment trends; identification of key uncertainties; construction of initial scenario themes; checking for consistency and plausibility; development of learning scenarios (tools for research and study); identification of research needs; development of quantitative models; and development of decision scenarios. The scenario planning method has been developed and used extensively at Shell (De Geus, 1998). However, currently, a large number of public and private organizations use scenario in connection with advanced information systems (corporate data and knowledge bases, economic intelligence databases, GIS, technology databases, numerical projections tools, etc.) for mentally visiting the future in order to build the required flexibility in their tangible and intangible strategic resources.

CONCLUSION

In this chapter we have addressed the question of whether a modular organizational structure cultivates long-term proactive strategic flexibility. We examined this question from the perspectives of the cognitive and learning schools of strategic management using a system dynamics model to explore and demonstrate long-term dynamic effects. Our analysis and our model suggest that modular organizations do not necessarily encourage holistic organizational learning processes that promote strategic flexibility through knowledge codification and standardization of module interfaces. On the contrary, a consistent organizational-learning supporting personalization-oriented knowledge management strategy that encourages the creation of new knowledge through richer exchanges is the enabler of strategic flexibility in modular organizations. Towards this end, we have discussed three of its core elements: boundary spanners and boundary objects, collaboration-supporting systems, and participative scenario planning, as practices and systems, which under a common umbrella can contribute towards achieving real strategic flexibility in modular organizations.

FUTURE RESEARCH DIRECTIONS

The triangular relationship between organizational modularity, strategic flexibility, and knowledge management is a recurrent research theme over the last 10 years of turbulent competitive environments, flat and loose modular organizations, and highly "knowledge-based" firms. However, empirical research on this relation that provides concrete results and management guidelines is still very marginal, confined to a small number of case studies. The reason is probably the fluidity in the meaning of the terms involved. It is not yet commonly accepted what is exactly a modular organization, what we mean precisely by strategic flexibility, and which facet of "knowledge management" is the most appropriate and most related to the discussion of modularity and strategic flexibility. Nevertheless, empirical research will justify (or refute) theoretical results, and results of other more explorative methodologies, as the one used in this chapter, in addition to bringing forward new areas of investigation.

Independent of methodology, research needs to be conducted with respect to an area that has been identified since the early days of modularity and knowledge management (Grant, 2003). It concerns the definition and the development of the interfaces of organizational modules. Research on this area might be pursued at many different levels. Indicative areas, at different levels, include the standardized specification of process interfaces and the investigation of the role of information and communication technologies (databases, knowledge bases, data mining, case-based reasoning, human computer interaction (HCI), data representation standards, etc.).

Finally, an additional area of research, which is particularly related to the logic of this chapter, concerns the relation between knowledge management strategies associated with and aligned to specific competitive strategies and the modular organization architectural level metastrategy, that is, the knowledge management strategy for directly supporting strategic flexibility. As it was discussed in the main body of the chapter, this is a personalization-oriented strategy that cultivates specific cultures and attitudes. But, what happens if the chosen competitive strategy, at a particular time period, is at the opposite end (a codification-oriented strategy heavily supported by ICT)? And, what about changing this strategy in accordance with a new competitive strategy? How can path

dependence be overcome? Clearly, answering these questions necessitates the establishment of a new area of research concerned with *knowledge management strategic flexibility.*

REFERENCES

Abell, D.F. (1993). *Managing with dual strategies: Mastering the present, preempting the future.* New York: The Free Press.

Adamides, E., & Karacapilidis, N. (2005). Knowledge management and collaborative model building in the strategy development process. *Knowledge and Process Management, 12*(2), 77-88.

Adamides, E.D., & Karacapilidis, N. (2006). Information technology support for the knowledge and social processes of innovation management. *Technovation, 26,* 50-59.

Adamides, E.D., Stamboulis, Y., & Kanellopoulos, V. (2003). Economic integration and strategic change: The role of managers' mental models. *Strategic Change, 12,* 69-82.

Akgün, A.E., Lynn, G.S., & Byrne, J.C. (2003). Organizational learning: A socio-cognitive framework. *Human Relations, 56*(7), 839-868.

Amin, A., & Cohendet, P. (2004). *Architectures of knowledge: Firms, capabilities, and communities.* Oxford, UK: Oxford University Press.

Andreu, R., & Ciborra, C. (1996). Organisational learning and core capability development: The role of IT. *Journal of Strategic Information Systems, 5,* 111-127.

Axelrod, R.M. (1976). *Structure of decision: The cognitive maps of political elites.* Princeton, NJ: Princeton University Press.

Baldwin, C.Y., & Clark, K.B. (2000). *Design rules: The power of modularity (Vol. 1).* Cambridge, MA: MIT Press.

Barr, P.S., & Huff, A.S. (1997). Seeing isn't believing: Understanding diversity in the timing of strategic response. *Journal of Management Studies, 34*(3), 337-370.

Bourdieu, P. (1997). *Outline of a theory of practice.* Cambridge, UK: Cambridge University Press.

Carley, K., & Palmquist, M. (1992). Extracting, representing, and analyzing mental models. *Social Forces, 70*(3), 601-636.

Carlile, P.R. (2002). A pragmatic view of knowledge and boundaries: Boundary objects in new product development. *Organization Science, 13*(4), 442-445.

Chattopadhyay, P., Glick, W.H., Miller, C.C., & Huber, G.P. (1999). Determinants of executive beliefs: Comparing functional conditioning and social influence. *Strategic Management Journal, 20*, 763-789.

Checkland, P., & Holwell, S. (1998). *Information, systems and information systems.* Chichester, UK: Wiley.

Ciborra, C.U. (1996). The platform organization: Recombining strategies, structures and surprises. *Organization Science, 7*(2), 103-118.

Codet, M. (2000). The art of scenarios and strategic planning: Tools and pitfalls. *Technological Forecast and Social Change, 65*, 3-22.

Cohen, W.M., & Levinthal, D.A. (1990). Absorptive capacity: A new perspective on learning and innovation. *Administrative Science Quarterly, 35*, 128-152.

Combe, I.A., & Greenley, G.E. (2004). Capabilities for strategic flexibility: A cognitive content framework. *European Journal of Marketing, 38*(11/12), 1456-1480.

Cusumano, M., & Nobeoka, K. (1998). *Thinking beyond lean.* New York: The Free Press.

De Geus, A. (1988). Planning as learning. *Harvard Business Review, 66*(2), 70-74.

De Geus, A. (1997). *The living company: Habits for survival in a turbulent business environment.* Boston: Harvard Business Press.

Dodgson, M. (1993). Organizational learning: A review of some literatures. *Organization Studies, 14*(3), 375-394.

Dollinger, M.J. (1984). Environmental boundary-spanning and information processing effects on organizational performance. *Academy of Management Journal, 27*, 351-368.

Eden, C., & Ackermann, F. (1998). *Making strategy: The journey of strategic management.* London: Sage.

Eisenhardt, K.M., & Brown, S.L. (1999). Patching: Restitching business portfolios in dynamic markets. *Harvard Business Review, 77*(3), 72-82.

Gamble, P.R., & Blackwell, J. (2001). *Knowledge management: A state of the art guide.* London: Kogan Page.

Goffman, E. (1974). *Frame analysis: An essay on the organization of experience.* Boston: Northeastern University Press.

Grant, R.M. (2003). The knowledge-based view of the firm. In D.O. Faulkner & A. Campbell (Eds.), *The Oxford handbook of strategy* (pp. 203-229). Oxford, UK: Oxford University Press.

Hambrick, D.C., & Mason, P.A. (1984). Upper echelons: The organization as a reflection of its top managers. *Academy of Management Review, 9*, 193-206.

Hansen, M.T., Nohria, N., & Tierney, T. (1999). What's your strategy for managing knowledge? *Harvard Business Review, 77*(2), 106-116.

Hayes, R.H., & Pisano, G.P. (1994). Beyond world-class: The new manufacturing strategy. *Harvard Business Review, 72*(1), 77-86.

Helfat, C.E., & Eisenhardt, K.M. (2004). Intertemporal economies of scope, organizational modularity, and the dynamics of diversification. *Strategic Management Journal, 25*, 1217-1232.

Hilgard, E.R. (1980). Consciousness in contemporary psychology. *Annual Review of Psychology, 31*, 1-26.

Hitt, M.A., Hoskisson, R.E., & Harrison, J.S. (1991). Strategic competitiveness in the 1990s: Challenges and opportunities for U.S. executives. *Academy of Management Executive, 5*(2), 7-22.

Hoetker, G. (2006). Do modular products lead to modular organizations? *Strategic Management Journal, 27*, 501-518.

Huber, G.P. (1991). Organizational learning: The contributing processes and the literatures. *Organization Science, 2*(1), 88-115.

Huysman, M.H., Fischer, S.J., & Heng, M.S.H. (1994). An organizational learning perspective on information systems planning. *Journal of Strategic Information Systems, 3*(3), 165-177.

Jones, O. (2006). Developing absorptive capacity in mature organizations: The change agent's role. *Management Learning, 37*(3), 355-376.

Karim, S. (2006). Modularity in organizational structure: The reconfiguration of internally developed and acquired business units. *Strategic Management Journal, 27*, 799-823.

Larsen, E., & Lomi, A. (2002). Representing change: A system model of organizational inertia and capabilities as dynamic accumulation processes. *Simulation Modelling: Practice and Theory, 10*, 271-296.

Lindkvist, L., Soderlund, J., & Tell, F. (1998). Managing product development projects: On the significance of fountains and deadlines. *Organization Studies, 19*(6), 931-951.

Lyles, M., & Schwenk, C. (1992). Top management, strategy, and organizational knowledge structures. *Journal of Management Studies, 29*, 155-174.

Markus, M.L. (2004). Fit for function: Functionalism, neofunctionalism and information systems. In J. Mingers & L. Willcocks (Eds.), *Social thinking and philosophy for information systems* (pp. 29-55). Chichester, UK: Wiley.

McDermott, R. (1999). Why information technology inspired but cannot deliver KM. *California Management Review, 41*(4), 103-117.

McElroy, M.W. (2000). Integrating complexity theory, knowledge management and organizational learning. *Journal of Knowledge Management, 4*(3), 195-203.

Meyer, M., & Lehnerd, A. (1997). *The power of product platforms.* New York: The Free Press.

Meyer, M., & Seliger, R. (1998). Product platforms in software development. *Sloan Management Review, 40*(1), 61-74.

Mintzberg, H., Ahlstrand, B., & Lampel, J. (1998). *Strategy safari: A guided tour through the wilds of strategic management.* New York: The Free Press.

Mintzberg, H., & Lampel, J. (1999). Reflecting on the strategy process. *Sloan Management Review, 40*(3), 21-30.

Nadkarni, S., & Narayanan, V.K. (2004). *Strategy frames, strategic flexibility and firm performance: The moderating role of industry clockspeed* (Academy of Management Best Conference Paper 2004, BPS:U1-U9).

Nadkarni, S., & Narayanan, V.K. (2005). Validity of the structural properties of text-based causal maps: An empirical assessment. *Organizational Research Methods, 8*(1), 9-40.

Nadler, D., & Tushman, M. (1999). The organization of the future: Strategic imperatives and core competences for the 21st century. *Organizational Dynamics, 28*(1), 45-60.

Nahapiet, J., & Ghosal, S. (1998). Social capital, intellectual capital and organizational advantage. *Academy of Management Review, 23*(2), 223-229.

Nardi, B.A., & O'Day, V.L. (1999). *Information ecologies: Using technology with heart.* Cambridge, MA: MIT Press.

Nonaka, I., & Takeuchi, H. (1995). *The knowledge creating company: How Japanese companies create the dynamics of innovation.* Oxford, UK: Oxford University Press.

Orlikowski, W.J. (1992). The duality of technology: Rethinking the concept of technology in organizations. *Organization Science, 3*(3), 398-427.

Papert, S. (1980). *Mindstorms: Children, computers, and powerful ideas.* New York: Basic Books.

Pine, B.J. (1993). *Mass customization: The new frontier in business competition.* Boston: Harvard Business Press.

Prahalad, C.K., & Bettis, R.A. (1986). The dominant logic: A new linkage between diversity and performance. *Strategic Management Journal, 7*, 485-501.

Reger, R.K., & Huff, A.S. (1993). Strategic groups: A cognitive perspective. *Strategic Management Journal, 14*, 103-123.

Reger, R.K., & Palmer, T.B. (1996). Managerial categorization of competitors: Using old maps to navigate new environments. *Organization Science, 7*, 22-39.

Sanchez, R. (1995). Strategic flexibility in product competition. *Strategic Management Journal, 16*(5), 135-159.

Sanchez, R. (2002). Modular product and process architectures: Frameworks for strategic organizational learning. In C.W. Choo & N. Bontis (Eds.), *The strategic management of intellectual capital and organizational knowledge* (pp. 223-231). New York: Oxford University Press.

Sanchez, R., & Collins, R.P. (2001). Competing—and learning—in modular markets. *Long Range Planning, 34*, 645-667.

Sanchez, R., & Heene, A. (2004). *The new strategic management: Organization, competition and competence.* New York: Wiley.

Sanchez, R., & Mahoney, J.T. (1996). Modularity, flexibility, and knowledge management in product and organization design. *Strategic Management Journal, 17*(Winter Special Issue), 63-76.

Sanderson, S.W., & Uzumeri, M. (1997). *Managing product families.* New York: McGraw-Hill.

Scarbrough, H., Bresnen, M., Edelman, L., Laurent, S., Newell, S., & Swan, J. (2004). The process of project-based learning: An exploratory study. *Management Learning, 35*(4), 491-506.

Scheepers, R., Venkitachalam, K., & Gibbs, M.R. (2004). Knowledge strategy in organizations: Refining the model of Hansen, Nohria and Tierney. *Journal of Strategic Information Systems, 13*, 201-222.

Schilling, M.A. (2000). Toward a general modular systems theory and its application to interfirm product modularity. *Academy of Management Review, 25*(2), 312-334.

Schilling, M.A., & Steensma, H.K. (2001). The use of modular organizational forms: An industry level analysis. *Academy of Management Journal, 44*(6), 1149-1168.

Schoemaker, P.J.H. (1995). Scenario planning: A tool for strategic thinking. *Sloan Management Review, 36*(Winter), 25-40.

Schwarz, M. (2003). A multilevel analysis of the strategic decision process and the evolution of shared beliefs. In B. Chakravarthy, G. Mueller-Stewens, P. Loramge & C. Lechner (Eds.), *Strategy process: Shaping the contours of the field* (pp. 110-136). Oxford, UK: Blackwell Publishing.

Seemann, P., De Long, D., Stucky, S., & Guthrie, E. (2000). Building intangible assets: A strategic framework for investing in intellectual capital. In D. Morey, M. Maybury & B. Thuraisingham (Eds.), *Knowledge management: Classic and contemporary works* (pp. 81-98). Cambridge, MA: MIT Press.

Senge, P.M. (1990). *The fifth discipline: The art and practice of the learning organization.* New York: Currency/Doubleday.

Shimizu, K., & Hitt, M.A. (2004). Strategic flexibility: Organizational preparedness to reverse ineffective strategic decisions. *The Academy of Management Executive, 18*(4), 44-59.

Simon, H.A. (2003). The architecture of complexity. In R. Garud, A. Kumaraswamy & R.N. Langlois (Eds.), *Managing in the modular age: Architectures, networks, and organizations* (pp. 15-44). Oxford, UK: Blackwell Publishing.

Slack, N. (1983). Flexibility as a manufacturing objective. *International Journal of Operations and Production Management, 3*(3), 4-13.

Star, S.L. (1989). The structure of ill-structured solutions: Boundary objects and heterogeneous distributed problem solving. In L. Gasser & M.N. Huhns (Eds.), *Distributed artificial intelligence Vol. II* (pp. 37-54). London: Pitman Publishing.

Taylor, W.A. (2004). Computer-mediated knowledge sharing and individual user differences: An exploratory study. *European Journal of Information Systems, 13*, 52-64.

Teece, D.J., Pisano, G., & Schuen, A. (1997). Dynamic capabilities and strategic management. *Strategic Management Journal, 18*(7), 509-533.

Van der Heijden, K. (1996). *Scenarios: The art of strategic conversation.* Chichester, UK: Wiley.

Vickers, G. (1983). *The art of judgment.* London: Harper and Row.

Vickers, G. (1984). *Human systems are different.* London: Harper and Row.

Walsham, G. (1993). *Interpreting information systems in organizations.* Chichester, UK: Wiley.

Wenger, E. (1998). *Communities of practice: Learning, meaning and identity.* Cambridge, UK: Cambridge University Press.

Weick, K.E. (1990). Cartographic myths in organizations. In A.S. Huff (Ed.), *Mapping strategic thought* (pp. 1-11). Chichester, UK: Wiley.

Weick, K. (1995). *Sensemaking in organizations.* Thousand Oaks, CA: Sage.

Worren, N., Moore, K., & Cardona, P. (2002). Modularity, strategic flexibility, and firm performance: A study of the home appliance industry. *Strategic Management Journal, 23*, 1123-1140.

Zack, M.H. (2002). Developing a knowledge strategy. In C.W. Choo & N. Bontis (Eds.), *The strategic management of intellectual capital and organizational knowledge* (pp. 255-276). New York: Oxford University Press.

Zahra, S.A., & George, G. (2002). Absorptive capacity: A review, reconceptualization, and extension. *Academy of Management Review, 27*(2), 185-203.

Additional Reading

Baldwin, C.Y., & Clark, K.B. (1997). Managing in the age of modularity. *Harvard Business Review, 75*(5), 84-93.

Beyer, J., Chattopadhyay, P., George, E., Glick, W.H., Ogilvie, D., & Pugliese, D. (1997). The selective perception of managers revisited. *Academy of Management Journal, 40*, 716-737.

Boisot, M.H. (1998). *Knowledge assets: Securing competitive advantage in the information economy*. Oxford, UK: Oxford University Press.

Bolloju, N., Khalifa, M., & Turban, E. (2002). Integrating knowledge management into enterprise environments for the next generation decision support. *Decision Support Systems, 33*, 163-176.

Bose, R. (2003). Group support systems: Technologies and products selection. *Industrial Management and Data Systems, 103*(9), 649-656.

Carlson, S.A. (2003). Knowledge management and knowledge management systems in inter-organizational networks. *Knowledge and Process Management, 10*(3), 194-206.

Chesbrough, H.W., & Kusunoki, K. (2001). The modularity trap: Innovation, technology phase shifts and the resulting limits of virtual organizations. In I. Nonaka & D. Teece (Eds.), *Managing industrial knowledge: Creation, transfer and utilization* (pp. 202-230). London: Sage.

Choo, C.W. (2001). The knowing organization as learning organization. *Education and Training, 43*(4/5), 197-205.

Cohen, D., & Prusak, L. (2001). *In good company: How social capital makes organizations work*. Boston: Harvard Business School Press.

Conklin, J. (2006). *Dialogue mapping: Building shared understanding of wicked problems*. Chchester, UK: Wiley.

Coombs, R., & Hull, R. (1998). "Knowledge management practices" and path-dependency in innovation. *Research Policy, 27*, 237-253.

Davenport, T., & Prusak, L. (1998). *Working knowledge: How organizations manage what they know*. Boston: Harvard Business School Press.

Dierickx, I., & Cool, K. (1989). Asset stock accumulation and the sustainability of competitive advantage. *Management Science, 35*, 1504-1511.

Evangelou, C., & Karacapilidis N. (2005). On the interaction between humans and knowledge management systems: A framework of knowledge sharing catalysts. *Knowledge Management Research and Practice, 3*(4), 253-261.

Evans, J.S. (1991). Strategic flexibility for high-technology manoeuvres: A conceptual framework. *Journal of Management Studies, 28*(1), 69-89.

Foss, N.J. (2005). *Strategy, economic organization, and the knowledge economy: The coordination of firms and resources*. Oxford, UK: Oxford University Press.

Garavelli, C., Gorgoglione, M., & Scozzi, B. (2004). Knowledge management strategy and organization: A perspective of analysis. *Knowledge and Process Management, 11*(4), 273-282.

Hamel, G. (1998). Strategy innovation and the quest for value. *Sloan Management Review, 39*(2), 7-14.

Kim, D.H. (1993). The link between individual and organizational learning. *Sloan Management Review, 35*(1), 37-50.

Kogut, B., & Zander, U. (1992). Knowledge of the firm, combinative capabilities, and the replication of technology. *Organization Science, 3*, 383-397.

Leonard, D., & Sensiper, S. (2003). The role of tacit knowledge in group innovation. In C.W. Choo & N. Bontis (Eds.), *The strategic management of intellectual capital and organizational knowledge* (pp. 485-499). Oxford, UK: Oxford University Press.

Lilley, S., Lightfoot, G., & Anaral, M.N.P. (2004). *Representing organization: Knowledge, management, and the information age*. Oxford, UK: Oxford University Press.

Nonaka, I. (1994). A dynamic theory of organizational knowledge creation. *Organization Science, 5*(1), 14-37.

Pemberton, J., & Stonehouse, G. (2000). Organizational learning and knowledge assets. An essential partnership. *The Learning Organization, 7*(4), 184-194.

Petty, R., & Guthrie, J. (2000). Intellectual capital literature review: Measurement, reporting and management. *Journal of Intellectual Capital, 1*(2), 155-176.

Schwenk, C.R. (1984). Cognitive simplification processes in strategic decision-making. *Strategic Management Journal, 5*(2), 111-128.

Teece, D.J. (2000). *Managing intellectual capital.* Oxford, UK: Oxford University Press.

Tsoukas, H. (1996). The firm as a distributed knowledge system: A constructionist approach. *Strategic Management Journal, 17*(special winter issue), 11-25.

Volberda, H.W. (2003). Strategic flexibility: Creating dynamic competitive advantages. In D.O. Faulker & A. Campbell (Eds.), *The Oxford handbook of strategy, Vol. II: Corporate strategy* (pp. 447-506). Oxford, UK: Oxford University Press.

Zuboff, S. (1988). *In the age of the smart machine: The future of work and power.* New York: Basic Books.

Chapter VII
Socializing a Knowledge Strategy

Peter H. Jones
Redesign Research, USA

ABSTRACT

Proponents of the resource-based view of strategic management have argued for processes that align organizational knowledge resources to business strategy. In this view, a unique competitive advantage accrues from accelerating organizational learning and non-appropriable knowledge. An empirical approach known as socialization counters theories of both institutionalization and "strategic alignment." Socialization diffuses an organization's knowledge strategy through values leadership and practice-led process redesign. Consistent with structuration theory (interaction of agency and structure), socialization creates enduring, flexible process structures co-constructed by leaders and participants in a domain of practice. Socialization results in durable, accessible processes, uniquely configured to business strategy, and more resilient than acquired process structures. Values leadership orients participants toward the goals, meaning, and value of organizational knowledge inherent in indigenous processes. Socialized business processes are driven by strategic intent, are non-appropriable by competitors, and are oriented to enduring organizational values that protect process integrity. A socialization approach integrates practice-level internal knowledge networks to support business processes and strategy, leveraging and exchanging knowledge more effectively than authoritative ("top-down") institutionalization.

INTRODUCTION

Since Nonaka's (1991) concept of the knowledge-creating company, businesses have attempted to organize knowledge as a resource or asset of the firm, with the purpose of creating competitive advantage based on knowledge. Recent surveys and industry trends show that, after a decade of development of knowledge management (KM) as a technology enabler for organizational learning and knowing, few of KM's original propositions have been fulfilled. Contemporary firms have found Nonaka's model of the knowledge-creating company untenable in practice, for reasons ranging from cultural differences to the changing business climate. The originally envisioned promises of information technology have failed to harness tacit knowledge in any meaningful way, and "knowledge sharing" applications have largely reverted to document exchange within the current deployments of organizational portals. But regardless of KM technology over-reach, the significant opportunities for competitive advantage envisioned by *knowledge strategy* have been overlooked by modern organizations. Since the advantages of knowledge strategy are not associated with recognized methods for quantifying internal rates of return, consulting practice has also bypassed this opportunity. We find in knowledge strategy a strong theoretical basis with few empirical applications.

Knowledge strategy was proposed by Zack (1999) and others during the period of rapid KM technology diffusion, and remains overlooked by many strategy thinkers. Most research following Zack focuses on strategies for knowledge management, and not knowledge-based strategy. This discussion builds upon Zack's proposition and explicates the relationship of knowledge resources and processes to competitive *business strategy*. The relationship of organizational knowledge to competitive advantage is often noted, but poorly operationalized in research and practice. The following discussion presents a model for strategic management based on an organization's knowledge, processes, and values. An empirical approach known as *socialization* counters the popular theory of "strategic alignment." Instead, this treatment develops a model of enabling knowledge strategy through values leadership and practice-level socialization.

Recent research revises Nonaka's and Zack's models and suggests strategic applications of the basic theories behind knowledge management.

This body of work draws together theory and observation in applications to business strategy. Penrose's (1959) theory of strategic growth underpins the notion that superior knowledge resources enhance the firm's competitive position. A well-established line of thinking and research extends from Penrose through Nelson and Winter's (1982) evolutionary economics theory to current strategy research (Grant, 1996; Venkatraman & Tanriverdi, 2005; Zack, 1999). This school of thought views the firm as a collection of dynamic capabilities that create and integrate knowledge as a necessary resource for competition. A major goal of business strategy drawing from this *internal* perspective is to develop dynamic capabilities that effectively respond to changing, *external* market trends and competitive conditions.

While management research has explicated a meaningful association between strategic growth theory and knowledge practices, a daunting gulf of execution is found in management practices. Theoretically sound research does not necessarily inspire leadership action. The linkages between knowledge strategy and organizational leadership are rarely described empirically, with some notable exceptions (Winter, 1987). While Nonaka's (1991) research presents extraordinary observations from Japanese business culture, there are cultural determinations and organizational barriers in the application of such models in different business climates and organizational cultures.

Rescuing Strategy from Knowledge Management

Knowledge management (KM) developed within industry from the converging trends of management theories of organizational knowledge and the rapid diffusion of cost-effective information technology (IT). The influential convergence of technology overshadowed the management theories, which remain under-appreciated in firms that deployed KM, expecting to build knowledge-creating organizations. We find almost no current research or even case studies reporting the effectiveness of organizational knowledge strategies sans IT. Yet research from a sociology of knowledge perspective shows the static models of knowledge adopted by most technology frameworks are inadequate at best (Orlikowski, 2002), and may be ill-conceived for the purposes of dynamic organizations.

Failed knowledge management initiatives are common, if not legendary. Obviously failures are not as widely publicized by firms as "successes," which often are merely those projects succeeding by fact of their completion. From the very start, KM technology suffered difficulties with organizational adoption and business purpose. Chae and Bloodgood (2006) report a meta-analysis of KM-related initiatives (including IT and organizational change initiatives), finding more reports of KM failures than success. Also citing Malhotra (2004) and Mertins, Heisig, and Vorbeck (2001), they report a study across more than 1,200 European firms that fewer than 10% were satisfied with their KM initiatives.

Some critics in information science consider the appropriated concept of knowledge in KM as a meaningless glorification of "information." Wilson (2002) exhausts the published literature in a critical meta-analysis deconstructing the value and meaning of "knowledge" as found in peer-reviewed KM articles. He finds no relationship between Polanyi's (1967) concept of *tacit knowing* and the framing of *knowledge* across the business and information systems literatures. If Wilson is at least partially correct in his analysis, the emphasis on knowledge as a stock/resource may be misleading and widely misinterpreted. He places blame on its highly-visible adoption by management consultancies and the original Nonaka research itself (for misconstruing Polanyi). However, Wilson and other critics also miss the context within which Nonaka's work is presented. While Nonaka correctly cites and interprets Polanyi's tacit knowing, the knowledge-creation cycle has been lifted from context and

widely used as a general purpose model of organizational knowledge *management*. Knowledge creation is not a general process applicable to all organizational functions.

Simple explanations readily appear for the "failure" of KM to take hold. Our management theories of knowledge may be wrong, from Nonaka (1991) to Chae and Bloodgood (2006), untenable and untested. The focus on KM technology may misdirect valuable organizational attention, preventing organizations from implementing valuable knowledge management theory. Or, organizations generally lack the thoughtful leadership necessary to deploy *organizationally-centered* knowledge management, a critique that emerges between the lines in Nonaka's own explanations of the cross-cultural differences between KM as found in Japan and the U.S.

Knowledge management *as technology* cannot resolve or address the paradox of knowledge strategy. In the concept of knowledge strategy, managers recognize the competitive advantage of organizational knowing and learning, guided by strategic goals and constituted in effective internal processes. The paradox emerges when executives envision the strategic value of developing knowledge as a resource of the firm, but have no control, accounting, or valuation of knowledge as an actual asset. The top-down vantage point of (traditional) strategy is unable to generate knowledge exchange within an organization, unlike the control of other assets. Simply put, knowledge does not function as a strategic *asset* (Venkatraman & Tanriverdi, 2005); it cannot be sold or exchanged like a building or plant. Strategically, firms following this model may operate from an unworkable theory.

Another explanation accounts for these and also suggests a resolution. The development of "strategic knowing," or knowledge contributing to organizational competitiveness, is not a matter of cultivating and cataloguing knowledge assets. It is based on the dynamic capabilities orientation (Grant, 1996; Teece, Pisano & Schuen,

1997), rather than the stock assets view inherent in knowledge management. Strategic knowing is a process of organizational socialization that occurs over time, under the guidance of values-oriented leadership. (While this is not Nonaka's "socialization" as the function of transferring tacit-to-tacit knowledge, it is consistent with the notion of organizational knowledge exchange within processes.)

Reframing the Strategic Context of Knowledge

The argument for organizational investment in knowledge management is based on business strategic need, competitiveness based on innovation or market growth. But the essential promises of knowledge management have not been widely fulfilled since the widespread emergence of Nonaka's formative definitions. Management theory appropriated knowledge management as a way to implement Nonaka's theory, but only to invest in popular technological panaceas that eventually disappointed. IT deployments, KM among them, can delay the difficult changes necessary to accomplish organizational knowledge integration as people focus on the new functions routinized by information systems.

Recent research (King & Zeithaml, 2003) finds the value and leverage of knowledge resources highly variable by industry and organization, and a generic set of knowledge resources will not be competitive across industries. Competitive *specific* knowledge, non-appropriable processes and capabilities, are not amenable to development using a common method across firms. Therefore, deployment of similar technological (IT) enablers across firms also results in no competitive advantage to any one firm solely due to the change. Venkatraman and Tanriverdi (2005) note that while IT investments have been shown to improve intrafirm performance, IT fails to satisfy the competitive requirements of "rareness, inimitability, nonsubstitutability." It nearly goes without saying

that the best possible outcome with even advanced technology would be a more advanced, but still commonly available, baseline of technological infrastructure. Improving productivity does not necessarily improve competitive position and at best supports operational effectiveness and to some extent growth. They argue that knowledge resources may not be accessible using quantitative "content-free" approaches such as research and development (R&D) expenditures, patent data, or research surveys that presuppose managers' assumptions about organizational knowledge.

We should therefore concede that technology-based knowledge management made promises that were impossible to fulfill, whether due to technology or inappropriate models of knowledge. But the inability to develop a strategic approach to leveraging a firm's knowledge may have more to do with its priorities, routinized processes, and organizational values. In most firms, except the start-up and small, a vast organizational gap stretches between strategic management and knowledge-based practices. The applications of "knowledge" are very different between these organizational domains. In strategic practice, the fundamental definitions and understanding of knowledge, whether possessed by individuals or organization, relate to knowledge as *owned by the firm* as a competitive resource. At the level of *practice*, knowledge remains deeply embedded in individual expertise, localized communities of practice, and unique work processes developed in the course of everyday problem solving. How do we resolve these two differently-scaled organizational knowledge resources?

Observations of product development organizations characterized by continuous knowledge work reveal knowledge functions as an *activity*, not as an asset or collection of identifiable resources. Even the commonly-held notions of tacit and explicit *knowledge* betray this objectification of knowledge. As Orlikowski (2002) points out, Polanyi's (1967) original conception of *tacit knowing* was based in the performance of practice, of know-*how*, not know-*what*, as she claims "enacted—every day and over time—in people's practices" (p. 250). Choo (1998) also promotes the notion of the "knowing organization," based on Weick's (1995) organizational sense-making and organizational learning (Argyris & Schön, 1978). Nonaka (1991, 1996) also speaks of *knowing*, but his core model of the knowledge creation process encouraged a turn toward objectification, which neatly corresponded to the extraordinary diffusion of information technology within the same decade. While this "resource view of knowledge" may have led to the innovations known as knowledge management systems, its impact on competitive business strategy was disappointing. In recent work and interviews, Nonaka clarifies his stance toward the vision for management action as Venkatraman and Tanriverdi (2005) state in their conclusion:

The current state of clarity in this area is woefully inadequate if this is to emerge as an important anchor for new perspectives of strategic management. Time is right for making important strides in this area so that we can better understand drivers of organizational success that go beyond tangible assets. (2005, p. 59)

It is no wonder that the promise of "competing on knowledge" has proven confusing in practice. From a strategy perspective (rather than knowledge practices), it appears there are no *objects* called knowledge to manage, no levers to move "knowledge" in this way. However, adapting to the distinctions developed in the concept of "knowing" rather than knowledge fundamentally revises the strategic notion of "competing on knowledge." These are not subtle differences, but instead significant variations that should update our mental models about knowledge management, knowledge strategy, and even "knowledge work."

STRATEGY AND ORGANIZATIONAL KNOWLEDGE RESOURCES

Knowledge strategy is an application of a resource-based, internal strategy directed toward improving competitive performance, as opposed to a school or theory of strategic thought (Mintzberg, 1990, 1994). Essentially this means "competing on knowledge," as opposed to competing by position, growth, customer intimacy, or other relationships to the market that improve or maintain competitive leverage. Knowledge strategy has often been reduced to innovation strategy, under the assumption that innovation is the most knowledge-intensive process in most firms. Some accounts of knowledge strategy develop "strategies of managing knowledge" (Tierney, 1999) which, as explained, result in IT deployment for "knowledge sharing" as document management, and coordinating and cataloguing intellectual property. My account of knowledge strategy is based on the Zack (1999) definition of coordinating intangible resources (referred to as knowledge) toward a planned, sustainable competitive advantage.

But unlike most approaches to competitive strategy, knowledge (or "knowing") is exclusively a resource of the firm, and does not necessarily correspond to industry or market structures. Knowledge, as informed capability, constitutes the core of all competencies. To a great extent, knowledge strategy is a model of competency development. Organizational knowing may be the most *significant* enabler of firm capabilities and non-appropriable processes, but does any firm compete solely on its "knowledge" as a competitive strategy? Most published perspectives of knowledge strategy affirm its enabling relationship to *business strategy*.

The notion of distinguishing a knowledge strategy from business strategy suggests an inherent difficulty of mobilizing knowledge as a business resource. After all, we do not speak of human resources as a competitive strategy. But knowledge has been adopted as such, at least by innovation strategists, if not growth and market/industry strategists. While human and organizational knowledge may be core competitive resources, few firms maintain an active knowledge-based strategy as a practice in strategic management. This suggests one, or a mix of, the following situations in strategic management:

- Knowledge strategy remains insufficiently developed in theory and practice to deploy in competitive business strategy,
- Knowledge has been fully adopted as an internally managed resource and requires no exclusive attention by strategy, or
- Managers largely ignore knowledge resources in strategic thinking and typically focus on competitors, industry structures, and other externalities.

As with most applications to organizational knowledge management, Zack's (1999) approach distinguishes the value of developing tacit and explicit knowledge resources. The central contribution of this approach shows in reciprocal relationship of coordinating KM with business strategy, and aligning and developing knowledge resources as an organizational strategy. Organizational knowledge therefore follows a firm's competitive demands, as the strategic *internal* complement to an externally-facing competitive strategy.

Internally-focused approaches to business strategy (e.g., cultural, learning, organizational) adopt a resource-based view (RBV) of the firm (Barney, 1986; Penrose, 1959) as a theory of growth. Zack (1999), taking this view of "Penrose rents," expresses knowledge strategy as an *alignment* of an organization's knowledge resources to its competitive business strategy, with the aim of leveraging internal resources in the context of external competitive demands. Alignment is

viewed as a strategic selection process: "How should an organization determine which efforts are appropriate, or which knowledge should be managed and developed?" The development of the knowledge strategy approach draws from this guideline, suggesting "the most important context for guiding knowledge management is the firm's strategy," and this link, "while often talked about, has been widely ignored in practice" (Zack, 1999, p. 125).

Such a link may seem obvious to business thinkers. But the links between business strategy and knowledge are by no means direct. Business strategy is a complexity management exercise, with its focus on markets, risk, and uncertainty, growth of market share and profit, product portfolios, customer retention, alliancing, and competitor growth. Organizational knowledge represents complex human issues and practices, such as individual and team knowledge integration, organizational learning, unique and embedded routines and management processes, intellectual property and intangible capital, and incentives and benefits for knowledge sharing. Given these differential goals and drivers, knowledge strategy decision makers inhabit different organizational worlds from those setting business direction. How should decision makers identify and select investments in knowledge and organizational change with strategic goals set by executives in a completely dissociated context?

Knowledge is viewed as "the fundamental basis of competition" (Zack, 1999, p.145). But knowledge does not arise as a freely available resource; it emerges from within and makes sense within a particular organizational culture, is directed toward organizational goals, and constrained within contexts of organizational processes and values. Organizational knowledge and values represent competitive resources, since these enable cooperative behavior toward economic development, and resist appropriation or replication by competitors. Therefore, even individual knowledge ties deeply to the organizational context, and may be significantly nontransferable outside that context (Barney, 1986). To some extent, individual experts (and their knowing) are not readily transferable to other firms due to their unique expertise drawing from a co-emergence of their learning and knowledge within the organizational context of its development.

Another paradox emerges from the question of where organizational knowledge actually lives. Do we find "organizational knowing" within the person (organizational *agent*), or the organizational *structures* that motivate and generate the knowledge-producing activity of the person? This question is important from a strategic management perspective, since leadership must select the highest-leverage internal investments in an internal strategy. This account proposes a resolution of the paradox in both theoretical and pragmatic terms. The structures of organizational knowing are located in the firm's processes and related community practices. Individual know-how is deeply integrated within these processes, and is also subject to and motivated by individual and institutional *values*. We propose the link between values and processes as a significant, yet missing function in strategic management.

Organizational Functions of Knowledge Strategy

The first decade of knowledge management (1991-2000) started with observations of knowledge used as flow, as knowledge creation (Nonaka, 1991), then recognized as exchange or transfer (Zander & Kogut, 1995). The eventual reliance on IT enablers that popularized the field largely focused on knowledge as an *asset* of organizations (Hall, 1993), an approach which (by definition of asset) converts knowledge into a target of management, subject to budgeting, controls, and procedure. In practice, organizations found knowledge *as assets* to be intangible, unmanageable by classic means of control, and difficult to transfer and apply to concrete situations requiring expertise or innova-

tion. The mistakes made in KM applications were, predictably, those of applying then-current information technologies to the emerging knowledge problems. Technology claims were often based on operationalizing subtle cognitive concepts, such as the "conversion of tacit to explicit knowledge." Other claims, such as searching for unrealized knowledge through data mining, were based on emerging IT capabilities, but were unsupported by empirical research or the original theories leading to such operationalized approaches. This divergence of KM technology from its originating theory eventuated in significant disconnects between claim and operational system.

A more critical perspective of the knowledge management literature reveals knowledge treated as a property contained within individuals, and as a manageable resource expressed in similar terms as information. The common dichotomy of tacit and explicit knowledge as referring to "types" signifies this model in use. The knowledge *creation* cycle (Nonaka, 1991) has been detached to refer to taxonomic types of knowledge, which was not the intent of its originating context (even if Nonaka does describe knowledge creation as "stock"). Once defined as *types*, categories became appropriated as ostensible resources in information technology and asset management approaches. It remains common in practice to hear of projects attempting to encode tacit knowledge into explicit forms for organizational reuse (Drew, 1999; Tierney, 1999), implicitly referring to knowledge as a stock (Venkatraman & Tanriverdi, 2005).

Venkatraman and Tanriverdi (2005) identify three schools of thought of knowledge adoption in strategic use: as stock, as flow, and as driver of an organizational capability. While all three perspectives offer value as strategic drivers for knowledge, they attest to similar criticisms with the stocks and flow perspectives as cited here. Essentially, the value of knowledge as a strategic asset or stock (from the RBV perspective) is that strategic knowledge stock (per Penrose) are nontradable, non-imitable and nonsubstitutable

(Teece, 1998). This is often reflected by firms in measures such as research and development spending, which reflects consideration as a cumulative asset base.

From a strategic perspective, knowledge resources are better viewed as an organizational capability, as dynamic practices that create and integrate knowledge (Grant, 1996; Teece et al., 1997; Zack, 1999) and not as ostensible assets (stocks). Theoretical support for this approach draws from Penrose's (1959) resource-based view of the firm in which sustainable competitive advantages accrue to firms that leverage internal knowledge to develop unique, nonreplicable routines and processes (Grant, 1996; Spender, 1994). Here the focus is on continuous, dynamic learning practices, as embedded in routines or processes. While strategy cannot quantify the asset value of knowledge as stock, strategy should specifically select knowledge processes to be adopted or enhanced for competitive advantage. This involves the identification of missing or subperforming capabilities and selection of processes and practices that will reliably produce the required performance.

There are few good examples of firms effectively adopting knowledge strategy as business guidance. Knowledge management theories may have launched numerous experimental IT implementations, but managers may not find KM sufficiently motivating to dramatically reconfigure a firm's approach to strategy, planning, and human resources. Organizations are more likely to take incremental steps toward a knowledge-based business strategy, an approach which treats valuable human-centered knowledge as one of many "intangible" resources. Since Porter's (1980, 1998) ideas remain influential in corporate strategy, we might also expect to find a continuing reception of resource-based strategy as a complementary or supplemental approach.

In many Western firms, adapting resources and initiatives to an emergent or learning-oriented strategic models may incur significant

risks in operations and management disruption. There are several reasons for this assertion, ranging from the difficulty most organizations have in designing competitive strategies, to the disruptive shift caused by significant changes in strategic goals, to the need to re-educate or replace management to accomplish and execute a knowledge-based strategy. Investment in enhancing the dynamic capability of processes (and the people participating in those processes) can be incompatible with cost drivers (as found in most process re-engineering). Although process re-engineering (Davenport, Thomas, & Short, 1990; Hammer & Champy, 1993) has been widely misapplied since its inception, cost-based process redesign continues as a common business response, arguing against a process-oriented knowledge strategy. Reviewing the originating claims of business process re-engineering (BPR), its model suggests substantial value as a type of process-based knowledge strategy. This view has been supported by current research into process redesign as strategy (Wu, 2002) and has matured to embrace knowledge-enabled BPR applications (Heusinkveld & Benders, 2001).

As with other trends in popular management, or "management fads," the originating theories and unique real-world applications of those theories had significant merit. However, general applications of such theories may often fail in practice, essentially proving the strategic knowledge claim of nontransferable processes and inimitability. Even a cursory review of the successful implementations of knowledge creation (Nonaka, 1991, 1996) and BPR reveals potential conjoint factors influencing the successful cases, such as national and organizational culture, organizational need and commitment, the fortunate coordination of such initiatives to compatible business strategy, supportive organizational values, and so on. Organizations are laboratories of social complexity, but published accounts typically distill theoretical claims beyond the pragmatic applications that proved the original claim. The real-world applications in actual firms show mixed results.

Research indicates that competitive advantages are created by the very uniqueness and embeddedness of firm-specific processes that generate market growth and are difficult to transfer. We should not expect business or knowledge strategy to be any more transferable than successful processes. In fact, strategic management is a type of knowledge-based process, subject to the same factors of uniqueness to firm leverage of specialized internal resources, uniquely motivating values and significant inimitability. Strategy is always a "custom solution" to a business problem.

Yet the purpose of research is to learn from observations and develop reliable accounts to enable further learning. We must make generalizations from particular cases that correspond closely enough to theoretical models to suggest general working theories of pragmatic strategic practice. We find, from the history of these theoretically-driven approaches to management strategy, two strategic knowledge functions of every organization: processes and values. Many organizations modify their processes to adapt to changing market drivers or strategic intent, and it may be the most common lever employed in implementation. Top-down process change, while necessary, is insufficient.

Processes carry the organizational values and expectations for the internal customer served by the process, as well as individual and practice values of process participants. Therefore, all constituents of an integrated, interconnected process are affected when the practices and routines used in that process change. But the most significant overlooked factor may be the difficulty in changing embedded organizational values within processes, which tend to maintain an operational status quo (Jones, 2000) regardless of the process mechanics. Organizational values determine the priorities upon which decisions are made (Christensen, 1997; Dose & Klimoski, 1999; Oliver, 1999), implicitly constraining the range of practices and filtering the opportunities available in new practices.

Resource-Based Strategic Perspective

Before the rise of two knowledge-based trends in business (innovation and knowledge management), popular approaches to strategic planning adapted Porter (1980) Five Forces model of strategy. Porter's model was based on competitive positioning within an industry structure to generate monopoly rents. Firms defined strategy based on five positions within their markets, based substantially on a stable, knowable field of competition.

While a resource view strongly implies a coherent internal knowledge strategy, observations and popular articles show most firms operate from and within an industry-facing, Porter's (1980, 1998) perspective based on industry structure, positioning, and external competition. The extraordinary rise of mergers and leveraged financing of global and large national firms in the first years of the twenty-first century show the Porter model is alive and well. The Five Forces perspective continues to dominate popular business thinking and, more importantly, in the guidance of execution. If we evaluate the models of knowledge strategy in the context of contemporary business conditions and even cultures, these two approaches appear to be incompatible in theory and practice.

Nelson and Winter (1982) and Teece (1984) were early critics of Porter's external "industry" view, holding to a model of strategy based on internal resources of the firm, of which knowledge can be considered among the most significant. More recently, Spender (1994), Kogut and Zander (1996), Grant (1996), and Zack (1999) further developed theories and dynamics of knowledge-based resource strategy, drawing from Penrose's (1959) theory of the growth of the firm. Penrose's observations were significant contributions to strategies of economic value, from empirical explanations of growth dynamics based on leveraging internally-managed resources. Adherents to Penrose promote a view of knowledge and learning as developing unique, non-appropriable routines from practices in the firm that lead to growth, and are sustained due to their effective adaptation to markets.

An essential Penrose notion is that a firm's only competitive advantage rests in its superior adaptation to business conditions by effectively coordinating its internal resources. Most of these resources are considered intangibles, such as competencies, employee knowledge, unique organizational routines, and ability to learn. Penrose rents (the power to extract revenues from markets) were based on the notion that a firm's unique knowledge-based capabilities were economically unfeasible to replicate. Growth is based on coordination of resources (and *learning within routines*) to develop "excess resources" that could be deployed to the market at zero marginal cost, an incentive for innovation and continued growth.

Nelson and Winter's (1982, p. 134) early proposition held that a firm's strategic knowledge capabilities are developed in collective practice, "embedded in the form of routines and operating procedures, allowed for the possibility that the collective had knowledge which is unknown to any of its members." Spender (1994) identifies how both explicit and implicit knowledge show up socially and individually, focusing on the competitive value of social collective knowledge. Collective knowledge in organizational routines can be viewed as emerging from coordination among resources, a highly context-specific property of the firm's practices, contextually embedded in practices; it cannot be appropriated by competitors or even individuals that leave the firm.

For example, Microsoft has developed unique practices in its forms of software engineering that have been described and copied by competitors. However, the coordination of resources between product lines, staff roles, and deep knowledge of product code, the operating system code, and their internal processes cannot be replicated within a competitive timeframe. To the extent that their product lines remain dominant in the marketplace, Microsoft's knowledge-based collective operations establish a powerful beachhead against competition. Both efficient and "dynamic," refreshed by research, their processes sustain advanced product lines and frustrate competitors through sheer scale of output.

As firms adapt to their markets and customers during growth periods, the predominant organizational values change, leading process changes that tend to follow. A large firm identified as Autoline (referenced as a case study in prior research (Jones, 2002a)) gained and held the dominant position in its market for two decades, through the widespread adoption of its retail management systems. What began as an external business strategy for Autoline became internally focused as the dominant product line sustained its competitive position. For two decades, Autoline's strategic perspective was oriented toward growth of its dominant product line beachhead, and its organizational values reflected that orientation. Internal resources were focused on supporting growth of the product portfolio, but not new knowledge-based practices. During the growth period, the firm reduced research and development, market research, and new product design capability, even while expanding product lines to meet the growing market.

As the market changed over time, the values espoused by executives also reverted from industry-facing positions to a customer-focused, "intimacy" perspective. This shift in strategic outlook demanded the coordination of internal responses to the strategy. New executive leadership initiated a clear position of values leadership, focused on customer needs and a radical change to product portfolio targets. This resulted in an intentional shift of values (toward a clearly-defined customer-centered values system) and processes (creating new design, sensing, and feedback practices), all as internally-developed resources of the firm.

KNOWLEDGE STRATEGY IN PRACTICE

We turn to practice to consider the feasibility of such a competitive knowledge strategy, aside from theoretical considerations. Competitive business strategy in practice answers the strategic question: "how do we compete?" In popular management thinking, one of three broad orientations toward market competition are employed, growth (or market value), operational effectiveness (or cost reduction), and customer intimacy (or market share). Market growth or overall value through products and services drives innovation; effectiveness drives internal knowledge sharing and management, to leverage use of knowledge to avoid costly reinvention and churn. Customer capture/intimacy drives innovating services for customers, leveraging internal knowledge of customer behavior, and sustaining revenues through customer retention.

Consider the interactions and possible decisions manifested by the directions of both business and knowledge strategy. If business strategy is to be used as guidance for knowledge initiatives, then which strategic goals are best supported by knowledge? What knowledge resources are best driven by business goals? An illustration of these relationships shows in Table 1, where both strategic orientations are mapped to these three fields of competition.

Table 1 portrays processes (associated with drivers or needs) for the two strategic vectors. The relationships between business and knowledge drivers are simply represented, with explicit orientation to external and internal management processes. The chart is illustrative of the difference in focus and management between knowledge and business strategies. These differences are oversimplified in the table and discussion to clarify the relationship of strategic management to process. In strategic practice, the drivers may be similar but strategies will integrate as many drivers as necessary to respond to competitive demands.

For example, *product innovation* suggests an internal converse of the external business drivers of product sales and customer needs. Knowledge creation may be a necessary internal driver associated with patent leverage or pricing strategy. An organizational learning culture (and *process innovation* in its many forms) may be cultivated to respond to the internal drivers for operational effectiveness. Because process innovation (improvement of internal routine effectiveness) is typically deployed in strategies for improving operational performance, it is more suited as a response to the cost/performance drivers underlying the selection of operational effectiveness strategy than a response to growth demands. In large, complex organizations multiple strategies are integrated as a whole. The table is meant to

Table 1. Business and knowledge strategy processes

	Growth	Operational Effectiveness	Customer Capture
Knowledge Strategy	Product Innovation Knowledge Creation Intellectual Capital	Process Innovation Developing Learning Culture Knowledge Sharing	Product Innovation Customer Knowledge Integration Branding Knowledge
Business Strategy	Product Sales Time to Market Distribution Networks Pricing Strategy Patent Leverage	Process Streamlining Supply Chain Management Financing Processes	Customer Retention Customer Product Needs Revenue Growth Alliance Strategies

distinguish the selections afforded each major driver, a simplified model of the common competitive orientations.

In a rapidly changing and globalized business environment, traditional strategic practices (planners and boards) have been jettisoned in large firms, and in many cases these roles have not been realigned to contemporary thinking or research. Reductive (if exhaustive) SWOT analyses and hybrid strategies (product innovation and cost reduction) have sufficed as practice in many organizations. We should not expect knowledge strategy to find widespread converts across boardrooms, even if justified as competitive. The traditional roles of strategy *advocacy* have been largely taken up by management consultants, who rely on quantifiable external or internal strategies, since they cannot efficiently learn and analyze internal knowledge networks.

Some strategy thinkers (Beinhocker, 1999; Collins & Porras, 1996) advocate adaptive strategies, ensuring the organization has a repertoire of action options available to it as a population of strategies. Internally-oriented knowledge strategy meets the criteria for an adaptive strategic repertoire, providing as it does a sustainable, organizationally embedded role for deploying business strategy.

For internal knowledge strategies, substantial organizational investment must be made, and new programs require time and learning of organizational members. Clearly, it is more difficult to implement programs considered as potentially "overhead" when external conditions suggest a focus on production. So how do decision makers identify the internal strategic "alignments" to processes that have the highest leverage or influence on the others? What path dependencies might be coordinated among knowledge processes, where one "informed capability" accelerates the performance of other activities in internal value chains? How do the values of decision makers determine the investment in knowledge-based processes?

Strategic Knowledge Integration

Grant (1996) identifies the goal for a knowledge-based strategy as to develop the dynamic capabilities of the firm, to establish organizational responsiveness to changing markets and competitive situations. According to Teece (1998), dynamic capabilities are "the ability to sense and then to seize new opportunities, and to reconfigure and protect knowledge assets, competencies, and complementary assets and technologies to achieve sustainable competitive advantage." Dynamic capabilities turn on *knowledge integration*, in Grant's (1996) view the core function of the firm itself. Knowledge integration is a function of incorporating the experience of knowing and learning into the processes of complex work. A core notion in this approach is the competitive effectiveness of nonreplicable routines, which Grant (1991) asserts, as scarce, idiosyncratic, nontransferable resources created and sustained largely by tacit knowledge in the context of production work. Whether by improving routines or complex processes, integration serves the firm by constructing repeatable practices that embody the learning of multiple experts and practitioners. Repeatable, yet often implicitly learned practices minimize the organizational burden of reproducing effective results in innovation or production.

The purpose of knowledge integration is defined as the achievement of flexible integration across multiple knowledge processes. The perspective on knowledge used in strategic assessment now becomes a critical choice. If knowledge is viewed as asset stock (as the KM view typically adopted), integration of stock knowledge leads to IT implementation, knowledge portals, and document management. If knowledge is viewed as flow and exchange, integration should lead to new and effective practices and accelerated organizational learning. Following the dynamic capability view, integration leads to coordinating knowledge flows within the practices of currently effective, adaptive routines that produce value for the firm.

Embedding knowledge in organizational routines is made more challenging when the critical knowledge changes rapidly, as in technology industries. Supporting dynamic capabilities requires a flexible organizational strategy, enabling responsive adaptation to market change, while furthering the development of competitive capabilities. The ability to shift the organization when market dynamics change is considered highly dependent on the firm's ability to adapt its knowledge to emerging situations, and to learn collectively.

But knowledge strategy research has not been oriented toward management guidance and practice. While a sound theoretical basis for knowledge strategy has been developed, there are few published applications, perhaps also due to the confidentiality of meaningful strategy. A significant gap remains between theories of dynamic capabilities of the firm and the decisions necessary to energize dynamic capabilities, and to motivate knowledge integration. At some point, managers require guidance for using a framework to improve knowledge-based processes and firm performance based on the theory and empirical observations developed in this field.

To further anchor knowledge strategy to practical management, guidance is required to identify the best leverage points (factors that have maximum influence with least relative effort) and dependent relationships between these variables. These can be simplified as two working models for these purposes:

1. A working model of dynamic organizational capabilities.
   A simplified model that describes the fit of organizational resources, routines, and actions to the firm's goals of knowledge integration.
2. A description of organizational interaction within this model.

A model of the functions or variables within the organizational processes that guide process decisions and practice development.

RPV: A Resource-Based Dynamic Capabilities Model

Zack (1999) outlines a framework for operationalizing knowledge strategy, but few other published examples are found, leading necessarily to question whether any published examples exist of successful deployment. The Resources-Processes-Values framework developed by Christensen (1997) to guide innovation strategy serves the same purposes of competitive knowledge strategy (within which *innovation* is a candidate strategic process). The RPV model represents a resource-based strategy framework, based on empirical research and application (with theoretical support). RPV enjoys operational credibility due to its development over numerous applications in innovation consulting with large product firms. Because management theory remains inadequate if not successfully applied, this leading *empirical* framework is offered for critical examination and "reverse engineered" back to theoretical foundations to promote a proven innovation model to knowledge strategy applications. This approach is consistent with Mahoney and Sanchez (2004), who suggest a pragmatic turn in management theory, wherein meaning and value are realized from the outcome of actions taken from the strategy. They describe the pragmatic, contextual orientation to strategy development as resolving the dissociation between strategy formulation and implementation. RPV, having been developed empirically as a response to innovation cycles found across many industries, meets the test of a pragmatic, competence-based theory, as specified by Mahoney and Sanchez (2004). Based on this "test," RPV serves as an example of strategic theory building that enables both "inquiry from the inside" as a pragmatic model based on learning from management action, *and* "inquiry from the outside" as a deductive-theoretical model applied to specific competitive contexts studied with actual firms.

Table 2 illustrates the RPV framework, identifying types in each of the three dimensions. Resources (consistent with Penrose) are assets, materials, and business instruments recognized by the firm as valuable. Resources are typically things and assets, identified and managed by common accounting practices, and can be obtained, transferred, and sold. Resources are considered fungible, and are readily obtained and transferred, as opposed to processes and values, which are embedded, nontransferable, and unique. Christensen's model does not explicitly resolve knowledge as a resource, but relies on conventional definitions.

Christensen's model provides reference to a published empirical strategy, to support two arguments: (1) the saliency of values in strategic management and (2) the relationship of processes and values to practice and leadership.

Processes encapsulate knowing and doing, both in explicit representations and tacit "tribal knowledge" of procedural knowledge within the organization. Processes constitute all the types of business, production, and knowledge work practices that are defined methods for coordinating multiple inputs, resources, and labor into internal value and products and goods for sale. They range in scale from those formal, institutionalized business processes to intermediate added-knowledge

processes such as product design and development, to informal practices that have been routinized through continual use and learning. Christensen notes that processes, as dynamic organizational capabilities, reveal choices of *practices* that necessarily exclude other possible choices. The RPV process model suggests that a productive capability represents an organizational investment in a way of performing knowledge work. The development of processes represents a cumulative, expensive set of skills learned over time, which become repeatable, embedded routines, as the "mechanisms through which organizations create value are intrinsically inimical to change" (Christensen, 1997, p. 164).

RPV explicitly describes the function of values, a unique aspect of RPV compared to other models of process or knowledge management. These organizational values are not the motivational platitudes displayed on the walls in headquarters. Values are a significant type of knowledge "asset," as a valuable function for coordinating resources within the firm. Values include organizational knowledge ("how we do things"), individual knowing, community and team-level norms, and govern the details of how processes are performed. As enduring constructs, they define a firm's identity and its style of work life. Over time, values build a significant organizational competency and shared outlook toward strategy.

An organization's values are complex and often contradictory formations of collective knowledge

Table 2. Resources, processes, and values (Adapted from Christensen, 1997)

RESOURCES	PROCESSES	VALUES
Assets, materials that can be bought, sold, transferred.	Routines, practices that transform resource inputs into value.	Organizational criteria that underlie priorities and decisions.
People	Personnel hiring	Cost structure
Technologies	Training, organizational development	Corporate reports
Product lines	Product development	Customer interaction
Facilities & equipment	Project management	Opportunity scale & scope
Information	Manufacturing	Organizational culture
Cash & investments	Accounting, budgeting	Espoused corporate values
Brand & corporate identity	Market & customer research	Values in use, as practices
Distribution channels	Product design & testing	Ethical actions & statements

and organizational priorities, and can be described as "values systems" in the organization. They are a type of tacit knowledge (Jones, 2002a) and demonstrate individual action (Argyris, 1992) in the organization as *values in-use*. Being largely tacit and contextually embedded, values are difficult to self-disclose as explicit issues or as knowledge, but they influence processes, products, and technologies, and are observable in use (Johnson, 1997; Jones, 2002a). Values systems differ from "value systems," which are defined as networks of value-producing services in a production supply chain network (Normann & Ramirez, 1993).

Values perform significant, if overlooked, functions in growth, innovation, and strategy. There are several categories of values found in operation in organizational contexts (Jones, 2002a), but there are consistent *functions* of values that operate regardless of type and level. Values generally constrain and often define *how* people work within a process. For example, professional services firms support sophisticated processes, such as client development, that incorporate long-standing and tacit values that cultivate a desired type of client relationship, as well as more overt requirements relating to communication, billing, and sales. They influence the priorities of work practice and determine the style and presentation of internal deliverables and production outputs.

Values establish priorities, which are often in conflict with each other in organizational life. In everyday work, individual and organizational values may be widely inconsistent, and values systems may be internally inconsistent. They are not always productive and positive; they may be hidden and antiproductive. People value knowledge sharing in general, for example, but also value career advancement, and may "hoard knowledge" where it enables gain. Values also embed (and thereby both hide and sustain) counterproductive priorities within organizations, showing up in dynamics such as internal competition.

Many organizations can identify historically established values, such as cooperation and re-

specting peers, that persist as inviolable, similar to an individual's ethical values. Since the assessment of performance according to values is determined intersubjectively, rating values performance is notoriously relative. As with other forms of tacit knowledge, *explicated* values may find only tenuous connection to a strategic context; an individual's action is inseparable from tacit knowing or their values. The real priorities of values (*in use* as opposed to espoused) often show up in operational conflicts, and not in explicit discussion.

Christensen identifies values as the source of all prioritization decisions, which may be generalized to all decisions. From a strategic perspective, values influence cost structures, which reflect values and priorities. Markets and projects are identified and selected or disregarded, rapidly and strategically, based on the filter mechanism of organizational values. Theoretically, if an organization could renew and determine its values in practice, these values would redefine the business, its priorities, processes, and interactions with customers. If managers could direct organizational and individual values to adapt to strategy, the ideal of "alignment" could be realized. But instead, the problem of deeply embedded values prevents the very possibility of this rationalized approach to organizational dynamics.

THE STRATEGIC FUNCTION OF ORGANIZATIONAL VALUES

The concept of "values" has been used cautiously in research. Consistent with values, the closely related concept of *norms* (Giddens, 1984) is found in social research, or *principles* in leadership research, with slightly different meanings in those contexts. A value is held by an individual as a meaningful principle from which one responds with action or concern, or a strong preference for a type of behavior. Organizational values are principles and preferences explicitly communicated or espoused, while values *in use* (as theories in use, Argyris & Schön, 1978) are preferences which drive responses and action, but remain implicit.

As a strategic function, values are highly leveraged, since they have some influence on all decisions. Values direct an organization's knowing and doing, which affords them an extraordinary (and underemployed) leverage in strategy. Values constitute the underlying beliefs and core principles and priorities by which organizational and individual decisions are made. Values are the least transferable of resources, due to their embeddedness in nontransferable processes, informal practices, social/occupational networks, and history. In RPV, values are the longest duration variable and the slowest factor to change. As with individual values, organizational values are also "important to the individual, have effects in a variety of situations, and are comparatively difficult to change" (Dose & Klimoski, 1999).

Values and values systems show a bidirectional valence pattern with respect to strategic management. They *follow* strategic changes over time, as strategies based on significant business realities also change the values systems within the firm. But in immediate situations they *lead* decisions, by influencing and constraining the range of options available to business strategy. Therefore, firms rarely execute strategic decisions in conflict with their current organizational values. In both directions, the change of values systems lags other business changes, since their embeddedness ensures they are perhaps the last organizational function to release from a former enculturated pattern. But the persistence of values ensures they also lead new strategic efforts due to their pervasive influence within current thinking as change decisions are contemplated.

Values (in-use) are resistant to change, due to their social embeddedness within the historical memory and social practices of the organization. They are difficult to change because the tacit agreement necessary to propagate new values requires a structural change not just in normative behaviors,

but in meaning, power, and legitimation. Values are too embedded to be managed as organizational tools; *meaningful* changes to espoused, explicit values systems cannot be changed by a committee and just posted to the wall.

Values systems are collections of values within a process or organizational unit that exhibit dependencies or collective relationships. Independent values identified in use may regularly co-occur with similar values or specifically dependent values. When occurring as a values system, the independent priorities or principles may not be easily separable. Consider the values system of "innovativeness," nearly always an aggregate values system. The related values of innovative thinking, creativity, individual excellence, and competitiveness may co-occur in an organizational setting, and recur due to social reinforcement of their performance. Competitive strategy may require transformative change within an organization, and while process changes are often planned, the impact of historical organizational values is not typically foreseen at the level of strategic decision making. Values enable or constrain all other priorities by virtue of history and organizational culture. Values are not functions that can be changed by command.

Values also become anchored within organizational processes throughout everyday performance and enhancement cycles. In processes, the selection of specific operational routines is usually based on organizational priorities and individual work/professional values. These values systems accrue within processes to become inherent values of the process. Innovation management (product design, development, and marketing) is especially sensitive to organizationally embedded values. Barriers to radical innovation in large organizations are found in both overdeveloped product development processes and the associated values systems inherent in successful and long-standing practices. In large organizations, the risks of "creative destruction" of processes and values systems must be weighed against the foreseeable or strategic value of radical innovation. Christensen (1997) and Jones (2002b) empirically demonstrate that large product firms may be structurally unable to radically innovate, partly due to the function of inherited values systems within the current innovation practices.

Christensen (1997) describes the macrodynamics of values in innovation:

One of the bittersweet rewards of success is, in fact, that as companies become large, they literally lose the capability to enter small emerging markets. Their disability is not because of a change in the resources within the companies—their resources typically are vast. Rather, it is because their values change. (p. 190)

Organizational values both reflect and precede the changing approach to competition, shifting preferences from innovation and other knowledge-based strategies to exploiting the growing market. The organizational locus of power shifts from product managers and designers to marketing, sales, and even accounting, champions of the new values that define "success." A recent trend of "high design" in the stable and slow-growing consumer products sector (e.g., Procter and Gamble) does little to dispel this assessment, since design managers are elevated to newly created leadership positions to reflect the strategy. But it remains a continuation of an "exploitation" growth strategy, not an exploration (or radical innovation) strategy. Furthermore, while industrial design adds considerable value as an innovative knowledge *practice*, its recent contribution to corporate brands has served to raise American market design values closer to the traditionally more advanced European high design standard. The branded design strategy (while often linked with the language of innovation) largely remains a market-facing instrument of a market exploitation strategy. This current trend should engender more "positive" organizational values than found in examples of other firms deploying customer base exploitation strategies, *leading* future innovations and organizational change due to a larger scale values change.

As strategic choices and associated values spread through the firm during growth, the organization also forms large social networks. As the successful firm embraces more conservative business values over time, they embed into management processes, from market research to human resources, from R&D to sales. As both customer intimacy and margin-oriented values unify with everyday project and product management practice, these values become implicit and more resistant to change. The same values that create team loyalty, organizational purpose, and a shared sense of identity also implicitly limit types of work practices, investments, and customers. Values are considered the ultimate source of decisions (Christensen, 1997; Maslow, 1965; Oliver, 1999). However, being tacit in everyday use, managers cannot easily see these constraints, let alone question their impact.

Integrated Model of Organizational Values

The organizational researcher has multiple classifications of values from which to draw in developing workable models for strategic consideration. We do not suggest one class will produce superior strategic insights over another, since so many social and pragmatic business variables will always intervene with analysis or comparison. The selection of a valid values framework may be considered a lens for magnification of desired aspects and minimization of others. Several models have been developed in support of studying individual values, moral decisions, and orientation to work practice. For example, a human resources strategy might select the frequently-cited Rokeach (1973), or managers might review Dose's work values models (Dose, 1997; Dose & Klimoski, 1999) for guidance on productive team composition.

A small set of values models are widely-referenced across the organizational literatures (e.g., Dose, 1997; Rokeach, 1973) indicating their acceptance and applicability to continuing research. Many researchers adopt Rokeach's definition, and have developed upon this well-accepted model of human values (Braithwaite & Law, 1985; George & Jones, 1997; Rokeach, 1973; Schwartz, 1994). Some researchers have used this prior work as a basis for studying or developing "universal" approaches to human values (Ellis & Hall, 1994; Schwartz, 1994). As defined by Rokeach (1973), values are "an enduring organization of beliefs that are "general plans employed to resolve conflicts and to make decisions." Rokeach's values model shows personal choice based on appropriate behaviors (*instrumental*) or end states (*terminal*), both of which support personal or socially directed values. Instrumental values generally correspond to the values involved in organizational action, and terminal values to those inviolable or "protected" values (Baron & Spranca, 1997) which hold across transactions and display resistance to trade-offs.

Maslow's (1965, 1971) values model developed from the psychological model of the hierarchy of needs. Maslow distinguishes between "deficiency" values and the terminal values of being, B-values, which motivate individuals beyond merely personal value. Many of the B-values refer to almost Platonic ideal states, while many others represent noncontroversial human and social values such as honesty, justice, and autonomy. Maslow's work extended the notion of values to embrace a "fusion of facts and values," and left a legacy of research questions and testable propositions that even today remain unaddressed.

Nonaka (1996, 2001) has also written of the "foundation of knowledge" as the ideals of truth, goodness, and beauty (Kalthoff, Nonaka & Nueno, 2001). These represent the terminal ideal values, and correspond to Maslow's "values of being," which he asserted were experienced by people as a single fusion of all higher values. Like Maslow, Nonaka's claims represent an ideal that motivates the expression and exchange of knowledge.

In organizational values research, Jones (2000, 2002a) developed a composite model for use in data collection and analysis, including four families of composites. The composites were constructed both inductively and synthetically from empirical research rather than deductive models based on moral theory. The four families of values systems specified both *individual* (humanistic and design) and *institutional* (organizational and technical) values systems.

Individual Values

- **Design values:** Drawn from Friedman (1997), Kling (1996), Kumar and Bjorn-Andersen (1990), and several design studies. Situated in design research, this composite drew from models affecting the design of systems and products, not human values.
- **Humanistic values:** Humanistic values integrated the human values of Rokeach (1973) and incorporated Maslow's (1971) values framework.

Institutional Values

- **Organizational values:** Organizational values constructs were drawn from empirical case studies (e.g., Walsham & Waema, 1994) and mapped to well-supported values models (Crosby, Bitner & Gill, 1990).
- **Technical/engineering values:** Drawn from Kumar and Bjorn-Andersen (1990) and Banathy (1996), these values apply to systems engineering and development practice, the processes of focus in the research.

The organizational values family is of most interest to the strategic function, although the technical values have bearing on embedded values in specific organizational processes. The composition and range of the organizational values are displayed in Table 3.

Table 3. Institutional values framework: Organizational values (from Jones, 2000)

Organizational values	Range of Attributes	
1. Economic	Profit driven	Socially driven
2. Information as symbolic	Policy focus	Communicative
3. Control/power	Centralized	Distributed
4. Management style	Participative	Autocratic
5. Locus of decision making	Decentralized	Centralized
6. Leadership style	Informality	Formality
7. Communication style	Open	Closed
8. Organizational processes	Structured	Flexible
9. Task coordination	Single way	Multiple alternatives
10. Impact on work	Job enrichment	Isolation
11. Focus of work	Customer focus	Internal focus
12. Social nature of work	Participatory	Nonparticipatory
13. Team behavior	Cooperative	Competitive

Most of these values are easily identified within organizations, and are testable by self-selection within the range of attributes, and by case study and observational research. As values systems, clusters of similar value attributes often occur together within a focus organization, such as "open communication, flexible process, participative management." The attempt to produce a generalizable model negates the variety and range of values that might also be incorporated. The strategic function of values, again, should be to enhance the unique values systems that complement both strategy and organizational culture. A specific values model such as the example in Table 3 may be used to evaluate change from a baseline, or to take measure of specific processes in question as an organizational strategy progresses.

While many researchers extol the virtue of values as positive motivating drivers in organizations, unexamined values may have a significantly negative influence on strategic change. Christensen's (1997) RPV model complements Jones' (2000, 2002a) findings of embedded values in processes mediating new practices toward the form of existing values. Jones (2000) found values function as barriers to innovation due to the resistance of either strongly-held personal values or embedded process values to adapt to organizational demands. Both models are proposed as compatible organizational perspectives on developing knowledge resources and managing innovation. Both assert, from empirical observations, that values underpin organizational decisions and processes, and strategy is guided by and depends on values espoused in decisions and statements of priority. As values are embedded in processes (and in turn are embedded in communities and social networks), *processes* are the knowledge structures affording individuals opportunity for agency and action.

But effective process change requires knowledgeable intervention and conservation of values consistent with the process participants. Processes must therefore be adapted by the organizational communities whose values are at stake in the organizational commitments and everyday operation of the process. Consistent with Nonaka's (1991) "middle-up-down" approach to management of knowledge practices, a *socialization* methodology coordinates knowledgeable participants and conserves the adaptation of their values. The socialization approach requires understanding and assent from organizational members to fully engage with and adapt the business strategy (to associate the new values inherent in the strategic intent). Socialization generates lateral relationships that support social networks for knowledge creation and maintenance. The virtuous cycle of socialization between process and values recommends a complementary function to strategic management.

SOCIALIZATION OF PROCESSES AND VALUES

How do managers effect changes to organizational functions based on this strategic perspective? We are interested in guiding the diffusion of selected values systems within the organization and within key, leveraged processes. A socialization approach asserts the necessity of process leaders and participants in defining new processes, performance metrics, and deliverables. Socialization also recognizes the need to negotiate changes to embedded values to minimize unproductive (but not necessarily *creative*) conflict. Socialization gains validity from its understood function in other organizational contexts, but also counters the passivity implied in the popular opposing construct, the notion of *strategic alignment*.

An Argument Against Strategic Alignment

A central organizing function of traditional strategic management is the alignment of organizational resources and processes to a defined strategic agenda and competitive posture. As strategic research continues to develop theoretically and empirically, the assumptions underpinning alignment break down. Two assumptions are briefly addressed:

1. That some agents in the organization perform work toward a state of *alignment* with

strategic intent, based on organizational communications and leadership direction.
2. The notion that competitive strategy represents a fixed agenda to which decisions and resources can be aligned throughout the organization.

Alignment suggests that organizational structures and participants are capable of intentionally adapting to direction and to initiate activities consistent with a selected executive vision and agenda. It also assumes a top-down hierarchical diffusion of strategy toward which passive actors are expected to metaphorically "align."

Few commentators have challenged this received notion. Without belaboring the implied hierarchical, even military "command and control" model implied in the concept, observations about the function of alignment find no ability to coordinate resources "by alignment" within an established firm. The notion of "alignment to strategy" appears to have entered the vernacular as a rationalization developed from management consulting, not from business research. Consistent with both adaptive and learning strategy models, Ciborra (1998), calling for a return to empirical investigations of actual practice, finds the alignment concept "bankrupt" as a basis for research.

The Socialization of Processes to Strategy

To enable the organizational dynamics of the described virtuous cycle, we find a function that coordinates knowledge strategy through values leadership (top-down) and process adaptation (bottom-up). The notion of "socialization" displaces strategic alignment as a functional mechanism for such a resource strategy. "Strategic alignment of knowledge" fails in both practice and theory. The ideals and abstractions of strategic intent do not match the concrete demands and pragmatic motivations of organizational practice, of people working within teams and occupational communities. Concurrently, new knowledge in the organization is developed at the level of practice, in projects and production. Top-down strategy has very limited access to the contextual knowledge within processes.

Socialization as used here in the context of process agrees with the operational definition cited in most studies (Kraimer, 1997; Louis, 1980), except that typically socialization is considered a time-limited cycle of initiation or indoctrination into an organization. We extend the process of socialization to a dynamic organizational context, wherein processes and values are created and led by strategic change. The definition of Louis (1980) holds in this context: "A process by which an individual comes to appreciate the values, abilities, expected behaviors, and social knowledge essential for assuming an organizational role and for participating as an organization member" (p. 229).

Socialization of values, capabilities, and behaviors is repurposed toward modifying the routines of on-going practices, to adapt or create new processes within the organizational community that owns the process. Whereas indoctrination (e.g., of the newcomer) assumes socialization occurs at the organizational level, adaptation of work practices assumes a socialization among existing participants, each of which may display variances among expected values systems. Indoctrinating socialization involves substantial tacit knowing and tacit agreement. The social networking mechanism of process socialization also draws upon tacit knowing and interpersonal and team communication, in the recursive formation of new practices within the community of process practitioners. Socialization encourages the agency of all participants to identify congruence between their values and the proposed routines and structures of the strategic initiative or target process. It also affords an "unfreezing" period to suspend judgment on current practices, allowing for trial and error within a learning phase. Socialization provides latitude to explore the contradictions

and resistances that emerge when prior process routines are challenged. Explicit process change triggers conflicts with long-standing values embedded within current practices; a socialization approach to process change must allow for dialogue among participants to ensure that critical values remain respected, or chosen, in the new functions.

Process socialization was developed empirically, as an alternative to planned, authoritative (top-down) institutionalization for the introduction of new knowledge-based practices in the organizations studied in this research. Theoretical support for socialization draws from organizational structuration (Orlikowski, 2002; Orlikowski & Robey, 1991) and social networks in knowledge practices (Liebeskind, Oliver, Zucker & Brewer, 1996). The essential claim argues for practice-level constitution of processes and the inscription of defined values, as two necessary components of process structure. Strategically-motivated processes are constructed by organizational teams and experts most closely involved with the performance of the process. Process values originate with and are owned by the communities of practice engaged in the process as an organizational structure. Unlike the expectations set by "alignment," values are not defined by management and carried into the process. Process values are not necessarily shared in kind with management values; deliberate difference between these communities should be encouraged to ensure sufficient variety of perspectives is promoted in the organizational ecology. The shared values system is mutually constructed with management in the specification of deliverables produced by the process for internal customers. The process customers, receiving these deliverables, will normally identify and negotiate requirements that reflect their values for use, which may be represented as specifications for quality, measures of performance, or economic priorities. This processual view of strategically motivated change corresponds to the recursive interplay between the agency of participants and organizational structures (recurrent practices and rules), in the perspective of structuration (Orlikowski, 2000, 2002).

The theoretical orientation of structuration, originated by Giddens (1979, 1984) and adapted as a lens for technology-adapted social systems by Orlikowski (1992) and DeSanctis and Poole (1994), explains the evolution of structures in organizations as mutually co-constructed by participants and the structures they develop and institutionalize over time. Structures, such as business processes and established practices, are conceived of as enduring yet flexible sets of rules and systems around and toward which individual *agency* intervenes and responds. Individuals and group processes recursively develop structures that produce intentional group outcomes. Both strategic management (typically executives) and practice-level leaders create structures and inscribe associated values in the communication and diffusion of those structures. Participating actors negotiate from agency (and their own values systems) to adapt their personal values and practices to new structures, or to negotiate changes to structures (e.g., business strategy or process).

Structuration further informs the notion that individual values (norms) and organizational values co-evolve with structures. Certain individual values, promoted in practice, survive organizational challenges to become "legitimated" and recognized as reinforcing the values and practices important to strategy. For example, socializing the process of user-centered design in a product organization necessitates a corresponding commitment to new values identified with a product's "user" as a significant and competing representation of the "customer." Not only are new practices introduced to study, observe, and design for the "user," but new values are socialized through distinctions made about the value of users, the business value of user data, and the competitive value of user preference. These distinctions encounter resistance from pre-existing, enduring commitments (e.g., customer) which are negotiated, not replaced. Over time, deeply held values associated with both users and customers are evidenced throughout the organization, creating an organic internal demand for the new process and technical practices associated with the values system. This socialization process may be a critical, yet overlooked, function in the distribution of new knowledge and developing values systems within organizations. As a theory of process, socialization accounts for all three key structural factors of structuration in KM as represented by Timbrell, Delaney, Chan, Yue, and Gable (2005): the signification or interpretive scheme of *strategy*, the *legitimation* of norms and values, and the distribution of *power* in values-oriented decisions.

The Socialization of Values to Strategy

The socialization of processes requires knowledge integration at the level of *practice*. Individuals in defined practices or belonging to practice communities (Brown & Duguid, 1991; Lave & Wenger, 1991) generally hold education and expertise in a skill area (e.g., engineering, design, or planning) as well as in the business domain. While values disclosure within practice communities evolves over the course of collaboration and knowledge sharing, socialization accelerates deployment across functions and communities. The opportunities to identify and disclose values in-use occur with *values conflicts* during the coordination of activities in organizational processes, working in teams with members of other organizational functions (Jones, 2002a). Both managers and practice leaders must learn to identify and communicate the values conflicts that occur in process redesign and transition.

Given the importance and leverage of embedded values (persistent values in-use), a knowledge strategy should propose alternative values systems within the context of process socialization. Alternatives are represented as new priorities and metaphors for action associated with the adapted process and clarified in the course of everyday decision making. Values alternatives sets may be identified as priorities and key process objectives. Practice leaders (as process owners) serve as stewards of both process and practice-level values, and can take responsibility for identifying competing values systems and negotiating conflicts. The resolution of values conflicts results in integrating the contribution as new learning (knowledge) in responsible processes.

Given the social leverage of values *in-use*, a function of knowledge strategy should be to develop values "alternatives" within the context of knowledge management activities, identified and clarified in the course of everyday decision making. Stewards of these practice-level values can take responsibility for identifying competing values systems and even negotiating conflicts. In management practice, this shows up as "ownership" of job functions or new processes.

While originating with individuals, knowledge and values develop *from* individual knowing and learning, becoming not so much encoded but enculturated in the organization. Through numerous conversations, communication, and enacted practices in the organization (e.g., in the everyday practices within the process, design reviews, requirements negotiation, walkthroughs, prototyping), individual knowing, methods and procedures, and values continually exchange through the course of production work. While new organizational routines and resources are introduced into teams and projects through formal training and new methods and practices, they will remain constrained or become diffused by the context within which knowledge is recognized and deployed in the organization.

CONCLUSION

The knowledge strategy perspective does not replace competitive business strategy as practiced; rather it offers complementary guidance within a resource-based strategic perspective. However, traditional strategic planning has become regarded by research as a poor instrument for long-range business strategy, due to rapid unforeseen market changes and the environmental complexity of modern business. The socialization of processes and leadership toward enhanced values systems asserts a more enduring and sustainable path to a desired competitive standing. It is argued that to deploy a knowledge strategy the firm must undergo a significant reconfiguration of the processes and values responsive to strategic intent, to achieve the dynamic capabilities realized by knowledge integration.

Organizational processes are the coordination capacities and defined routines within which individual tacit knowing is located. Processes and routines must be refreshed by knowledge creation and transfer, but not merely within projects or skillcraft practices. To develop nonreplicable, competitive knowledge processes, unique practices learned in the "art of doing" must be re-integrated within the overall schema of production and coordination.

Organizational values are institutionalized guiding principles and priorities that influence behavior and decision making. Changing embedded values systems requires identifying the values in-use throughout the organization or the processes of strategic interest. As opposed to changing explicit company "slogans," the espoused values on a wall plaque, cannot be easily accomplished directly. Consistent with the definition of institutionalization, over time people accept the underlying culture and its values as given. Values in-use might be accessible to intervention if they were not deeply embedded, but they would also be much less powerful in the social functions they also serve, the purpose of orienting action and simplifying decisions based on understood (yet often unexplicated) priorities.

This model proposes a strategic function for values, following a methodology known as socialization, complementary to organizational authority. Overt programs and actions taken by new managers often fail due to the resistance inherent in deeply socialized, highly stable values systems. Any successful attempt to leverage deep knowledge as a competitive strategic resource must acknowledge the existing values systems that reward, enable, and deploy organizational knowing within an intact social system.

Socialization as a management function involves values leadership, including the introduction of new opportunities (career, project, organizational) aligned with values oriented toward the outcome of knowledge practices. The embedded organizational values anticipated to follow socialization should also be considered, since these underlying values systems will persist after socialization, and theoretically until business strategy significantly shifts. While this requires an authentic, long-term commitment, the returns to the organizational culture from the commitment to change accrue immediately.

Given the ever-increasing complexity and interconnectedness of business and technology, strategic management must become more collaborative and draw on the collective knowledge of many contributors. A socialization approach mitigates the problem of analyzing complex relationships by distributing the sensing and opportunity/threat analysis across the organization. Socialization delegates strategic intent and attention, while locating individual responsibility firmly in the processes within which one has expertise and experience.

Values leadership and socialization have the potential to significantly enhance organizational effectiveness and competitiveness. Organizationally, a strong values consensus establishes a set of decision criteria for management and resource deployment. Without the pragmatic direction of management (i.e., leadership and socialization), the historically embedded (sedimented) values of the organizational culture will bend vulnerable practices back toward the status quo. Redesigned processes tend to revert to prior states of practice, due to prior ad hoc socialization created as recurrent social practices (Giddens, 1984). Therefore, values offer a pivotal standpoint for leadership, allowing managers to identify and orchestrate examples of behavioral and practice in reference to competitive strategy.

By managing *to values* and not processes, managers empower practice leaders (across processes and project teams) to intellectually invest in their processes and continually integrate new learning to ensure competitive renewal. Disclosing and exchanging values that emerge within the context of process coordination allows participants to understand the organizational commitment to strategic goals. People do not respond emotionally to strategies, but they are motivated by and respond immediately to values, and can identify values conflicts. Values conflicts reveal meaningful opportunities for engagement, dialogue, and reconfiguration of organizational practices. From a strategic perspective, values conflicts return organizational feedback to managers from the distributed, delegated attention inherent in socialization. Strategic intent becomes socially meaningful when values differences are honored, becoming instruments of organizational learning and listening rather than merely positions in decision making.

FUTURE RESEARCH DIRECTIONS

An approach is described for developing a knowledge strategy that attempts to resolve the contradictions between the management concerns of organizational strategy and values, and the everyday concerns for action based on knowledge. This approach synthesizes both theoretical research and practical management concerns, with a dual intent of dispelling unworkable orientations to knowledge management strategies and improving strategic management practice. Both of these intents are supported by seminal foundation studies and current research, as well as experience and empirical observations over the course of organizational consulting projects.

Profitable future research directions should support both of these intents. The most valuable research contributions will be those that strengthen the theoretical and empirical bases for the organizational practices of strategy building and process design and deployment. Yet the most valuable pragmatic contributions are those that enable practical, effective management action.

The most profitable directions for knowledge strategy, and knowledge management, are those that extend our collective learning from organizational and management sciences. The KM literature has developed from a strong focus on enabling information technology. We now have a sufficient number of studies of knowledge management in actual organizational practice to offset the far-reaching claims of information technology enabling knowledge practices. New research should balance the predominance of technology with studies of organizational cognition and the successful development of new knowledge practices. And given the interdisciplinary nature of all research in knowledge, management, and organization, we must do a better job of integrating our knowledge across the social sciences and management disciplines.

The reported research did not deliberately exclude information technology from its treatment of organizational knowledge management; it was merely unnecessary given the focus and structure of the claims. While some studies of IT integration make well-founded claims for practice and

process transformation, knowledge management research should advance management practice. As an interdisciplinary research area, KM researchers should evaluate and integrate current thinking in cognitive science (e.g., distributed cognition and cognitive engineering), cognitive anthropology (e.g., activity theory research), organizational sociology (e.g., structuration and institutionalization), as well as information science (e.g., contextual information practices).

A significant direction of pursuit may be to examine and validate in theory and organizational settings the empirically-developed approaches to strategy making and deployment. To better inform and enable management practice, we should be eliciting the most empirically effective models and identifying their core relationships to identify generalizable functions expressed by the model. Strategic design models such as Christensen's RPV have been developed through iterations and observations in practice. These should be rigorously "reverse-engineered," returning their empirical claims and mechanisms to theoretical form, to learn from the process to understand its connection to management practice and organizational dynamics.

Moreover, the directionality of research and practice can be profitably reversed in strategic research, similar to the research trajectories of many human sciences (clinical psychology), practices (medicine, law), and interdisciplinary research (human-computer interaction). In all these domains, theory-led proposals have often failed, and yet many scholars resist drawing from practice due to concerns for originality or academic "rigor." Mahoney and Sanchez (2004) have argued for a stronger integration of pragmatic and deductive theory. Researchers should go further than this, and conduct ethnographies of firms that successfully demonstrate the principles of strategic thinking and deployment as an organizational practice.

Strategic management itself is a creative and collaborative organizational *practice*. Strategy building requires experientially-grounded theory-creation and theory-testing within a complex fusion of business and organizational domains. The purpose of competitive business strategy is essentially to construct descriptive and predictive models of business dynamics to inform executive decision making. Organizational strategy that follows a theory-of-competition model must be deployed based on human, not economic, theories. Therefore motivation (values), productivity and innovation (cognitive effectiveness), and reorganization (process and practice) emerge as the foremost lever-variables. These are the internal resources available within the organization, all forms of knowledge and knowing. Knowledge resources will be created and sustained by people performing within the context of these process structures. Research should be conducted on the relationship between these strategy-related variables and the development of competitive knowledge resources as an outcome of organizational process and structure.

Research in knowledge strategy, in particular, should progress beyond the theoretical dimensions of strategic resource economics and identify effective relationships between strategy building and the collective intelligence available from within organizations, their people, and processes.

REFERENCES

Argyris, C. (1992). Why individuals and organizations have difficulty in double loop learning. In *On organizational learning* (pp. 7-38). Cambridge: Blackwell Publishers.

Argyris, C., & Schön, D. (1978). *Organizational learning: A theory of action perspective*. New York: McGraw-Hill.

Banathy, B.H. (1996). *Designing social systems in a changing world*. New York: Plenum Publishing Co.

Barney, J.B. (1986). Organizational culture: Can it be a source of sustained competitive advantage? *The Academy of Management Review, 11*(3), 656-665.

Baron, J., & Spranca, M. (1997). Protected values. *Organizational Behavior and Human Decision Processes, 70*(1), 1–16.

Beinhocker, E.D. (1999, March). Robust adaptive strategies. *Sloan Management Review,* p. 22.

Braithwaite, V.A., & Law, H.G. (1985). Structure of human values: Testing the adequacy of the Rokeach Value Survey. *Journal of Personality and Social Psychology, 49*, 250-262.

Brown, J.S., & Duguid, P. (1991). Organizational learning and communities of practice: Toward a unified view of working, learning and innovation. *Organization Science, 2*, 40-57.

Chae, B., & Bloodgood, J.M. (2006). The paradoxes of knowledge management: An eastern philosophical perspective. *Information and Organization, 16*(1), 1-26.

Choo, C.W. (1998). *The knowing organization: How organizations use information to construct meaning, create knowledge, and make decisions*. New York: Oxford University Press.

Christensen, C.M. (1997). *The innovator's dilemma*. Boston: Harvard Business School Press.

Ciborra, C.U. (1998). Crisis and foundations: An inquiry into the nature and limits of models and methods in the information systems discipline. *Journal of Strategic Information Systems, 7*, 5-16.

Collins, J.C., & Porras, J.I. (1996, September-October). Building your company's vision. *Harvard Business Review,* pp. 65-88.

Crosby, L.A., Bitner, M.J., & Gill, J.D. (1990). Organizational structure of values. *Journal of Business Research, 20*(2), 123-134.

Davenport, T., Thomas, H., & Short, J.E. (1990, Summer). The new industrial engineering: Information technology and business process redesign. *Sloan Management Review,* pp. 11–26.

DeSanctis, G., & Poole, M.S. (1994). Capturing the complexity in advanced technology use: Adaptive structuration theory. *Organization Science, 5*(2), 121-145.

Dose, J.J. (1997). Work values: An integrative framework and illustrative application to organizational socialization. *Journal of Occupational and Organizational Psychology, 70,* 219 -240.

Dose, J.J., &. Klimoski, R.J. (1999). The diversity of diversity: Work values effects on formative team processes. *Human Resource Management Review, 9*(1), 83-108.

Drew, S. (1999). Building knowledge management into strategy: Making sense of a new perspective. *Long Range Planning, 32*(1), 130-136.

Ellis, R.K., & Hall, M.L.W. (1994). Systems and values: An approach for practical organizational intervention. *Proceedings of the ISSS, 94.*

Friedman, B. (1997). *Human values and the design of computer technology.* Cambridge, UK: Cambridge University Press.

George, J.M., & Jones, G.R. (1997). Experiencing work: Values, attitudes, and moods. *Human Relations, 50*(4), 393-417.

Giddens, A. (1979). *Central problems in social theory: Action, structure, and contradiction in social analysis.* London: MacMillan Press, Ltd.

Giddens, A. (1984). *The constitution of society: Outline of the theory of structuration.* Berkeley, CA: University of California Press.

Grant, R.M. (1991). The resource-based theory of competitive advantage: Implications for strategy formulation. *California Management Review, 33*(3), 114-135.

Grant, R.M. (1996). Prospering in dynamically competitive environments: Organizational capability as knowledge integration. *Organization Science, 7*(4), 375-387.

Hall, R. (1993). A framework linking intangible resources and capabilities to sustainable competitive advantage. *Strategic Management Journal, 14,* 607–618.

Hammer, M., & Champy, J. (1993). *Reengineering the corporation.* New York: Harper Collins.

Heusinkveld, S., & Benders, J. (2001). Surges and sediments: Shaping the reception of reengineering. *Information & Management, 38*(4), 239-251.

Johnson, D.G. (1997). Is the global information infrastructure a democratic technology? *ACM SIGCAS Computers and Society, 27*(3), 20-26.

Jones, P.H. (2000). *Embedded values in innovation practice: Toward a theory of power and participation in organizations.* Ann Arbor, MI: Dissertation Abstracts International.

Jones, P.H. (2002a, June). Embedded values in process and practice: Interactions between disciplinary practice and formal innovation processes. In *Proceedings of the 11ᵗʰ International Forum on Design Management Research*, Boston, Massachusetts.

Jones, P.H. (2002b). When successful products prevent strategic innovation. *Design Management Journal, 13*(2), 30-37.

Kalthoff, O., Nonaka, I., & Nueno, P. (2001). *The light and the shadow: How breakthrough innovation is shaping European business.* Oxford: Capstone Publishing Ltd.

King, A.W., & Zeithaml, C.P. (2003). Measuring organizational knowledge: A conceptual and methodological framework. *Strategic Management Journal, 24,* 763-772.

Kling, R. (1996). The centrality of organizations in the computerization of society. In R. Kling (Ed.), *Computerization and controversy: Value conflicts and social choices* (2nd ed., pp. 108-112). New York: Academic Press.

Kogut, B., & Zander, U. (1996). What firms do: Coordination, identity and learning. *Organization Science, 7*, 502-518.

Kraimer, M.L. (1997). Organizational goals and values: A socialization model. *Human Resource Management Review, 7*(4), 425-447.

Kumar, K., & Bjorn-Anderson, N. (1990). A cross-cultural comparison of IS designer values. *Communications of the ACM, 33*(5), 528-538.

Liebeskind, J.P., Oliver, A.L., Zucker, L.G., & Brewer, M.B. (1996). Social networks, learning and flexibility: Sourcing scientific knowledge in new biotechnology firms. *Organization Science, 7*(4), 428–443.

Lave, J., & Wenger, E. (1991). *Situated learning: Legitimate peripheral participation*. Cambridge, UK: Cambridge University Press.

Louis, M.R. (1980). Surprise and sense making: What newcomers experience in entering unfamiliar organizational settings. *Administrative Science Quarterly, 25*, 226–248.

Mahoney, J.T., & Sanchez, R. (2004). Building new management theory by integrating processes and products of thought. *Journal Of Management Inquiry, 13*(1), 34-47.

Malhotra, Y. (2004). Why do knowledge management systems fail? Enablers and constraints of knowledge management in human enterprises. In M.E. Koenig & T.K. Srikantaiah (Eds.), *Knowledge management lessons learned: What works and what doesn't* (pp. 87-112). Silver Spring MD: Information Today (ASIST Monograph Series).

Maslow, A.H. (1965). *Eupsychian management: A journal*. Homewood, IL: The Dorsey Press.

Maslow, A.H. (1971). *The farther reaches of human nature*. New York: Viking Press.

Mertins, K., Heisig, P., & Vorbeck, J. (2001). *Knowledge management: Best practices in Europe*. Springer-Verlag.

Mintzberg, H. (1990). The design school: Reconsidering the basic premises of strategic management. *Strategic Management Journal, 11*, 171-1965.

Mintzberg, H. (1994). *The rise and fall of strategic planning*. New York: Free Press.

Nelson, R., & Winter, S. (1982). *An evolutionary theory of economic change*. Cambridge, MA: Harvard University Press.

Nonaka, I. (1991, November-December). The knowledge-creating company. *Harvard Business Review*, pp. 14-36.

Nonaka, I. (1996, February 23). *Knowledge has to do with truth, goodness, and beauty: A conversation with Professor Ikujiro Nonaka*. Claus Otto Scharmer. Tokyo.

Nonaka, I., & Nishiguchi, T. (2001). *Knowledge emergence: Social, technical, and evolutionary dimensions of knowledge creation*. Oxford, UK: Oxford University Press.

Normann, R., & Ramirez, R. (1993, July-August). From value chain to value constellation: Designing interactive strategy. *Harvard Business Review*, pp. 65-77.

Oliver, B.L. (1999). Comparing corporate managers' personal values over three decades, 1967-1995. *Journal of Business Ethics, 20*(2), 147-161.

Orlikowski, W.J. (1992). The duality of technology: Rethinking the concept of structure in organizations. *Organization Science, 3*(3), 398-427.

Orlikowski, W.J. (2000). Using technology and constituting structures: A practice lens for studying technology in organizations. *Organization Science, 11*(4), 404-428.

Orlikowski, W.J. (2002). Knowing in practice: Enacting a collective capability in distributed organizing. *Organization Science, 13*(4), 249-273.

Orlikowski, W.J., & Robey, D. (1991). Information technology and the structuring of organizations. *Information Systems Research, 2*(2), 143-169.

Penrose, E.T. (1959). *The theory of the growth of the firm.* New York: Wiley & Sons.

Polanyi, M. (1967). *The tacit dimension.* New York: Doubleday and Co.

Porter, M.E. (1980). *Competitive strategy: Techniques for analyzing industries and competitors.* New York: Free Press.

Porter, M.E. (1998). *Competitive advantage: Creating and sustaining superior performance.* New York: Free Press.

Rokeach, M. (1973). *The nature of human values.* New York: Free Press.

Schwartz, S.H. (1994). Are there universal aspects in the structure and contents of human values? *Journal of Social Issues, 50*(4), 19-46.

Spender, J.-C. (1994). Organizational knowledge, collective practice, and Penrose rents. *International Business Review, 3*(4), 353-367.

Teece, D.J. (1984). Economic analysis and strategic management. *California Management Review, 26*(3), 87-110.

Teece, D.J. (1998). Capturing value from knowledge assets: The new economy, markets for know-how, and intangible assets. *California Management Review, 40*(3), 55-79.

Teece, D.J., Pisano, G., & Schuen, A. (1997). Dynamic capabilities and strategic management. *Strategic Management Journal, 26*(3), 87-110.

Tierney, T. (1999). What's your strategy for managing knowledge? *Harvard Business Review, 77*(2), 106-116.

Timbrell, G., Delaney, P., Chan, T., Yue, A., & Gable, G. (2005). A structurationist review of knowledge management theories. In *Proceedings of the 26th Annual Conference on Information Systems* (pp. 247-259), Las Vegas, Nevada.

Venkatraman, N., & Tanriverdi, H. (2005). Reflecting "knowledge" in strategy research: Conceptual issues and methodological challenges. *Research Methodology in Strategy and Management, 1*, 33-65.

Walsham, G., & Waema, T. (1994). Information systems strategy and implementation: A case study of a building society. *ACM Transactions on Information Systems, 12*(2), 150-173.

Weick, K. E. (1995). *Sensemaking in organizations.* London: Sage Publications.

Wilson, T.D. (2002). The nonsense of "knowledge management." *Information Research, 8*(1), paper 144. Retrieved May 21, 2007, from http://InformationR.net/ir/8-1/paper144.html

Winter, S.G. (1987). Knowledge and competence as strategic assets. In D. Teece (ed.), *The competitive challenge: Strategies for industrial innovation and renewal.* Cambridge, MA: Ballinger Publishing Co., 159-184.

Wu, I.-L. (2002). A model for implementing BPR based on strategic perspectives: An empirical study. *Information and Management, 39*(4), 313-324.

Zack, M.H. (1999). Developing a knowledge strategy. *California Management Review, 41*(3), 125-145.

Zander, U., & Kogut, B. (1995). Knowledge and the speed of the transfer and imitation of organizational capabilities: An empirical test. *Organization Science, 6*, 76–91.

Additional Reading

Ackoff, R.L. (1994). *The democratic corporation.* New York: Oxford University Press.

Amburgey, T.L., Kelly, D., & Barnett, W.P. (1993). Resetting the clock: The dynamics of organizational change and failure. *Administrative Science Quarterly, 38*, 51-73.

Barrett, M., Cappleman, S., Shoib, G., & Walsham, G. (2004). Learning in knowledge communities: Managing technology and context. *European Management Journal, 22*(1), 1-11.

Blackler, F. (1993). Knowledge and the theory of organisations: Organisations as activity systems and the reframing of management. *Journal of Management Studies, 30*, 863-884.

Bloomfield, B.P., & Vurdubakis, T. (1997). Visions of organization and organizations of vision: The representational practices of information systems development. *Accounting, Organizations and Society, 22*(7), 639-668.

Boland, R.J., & Collopy, F. (2004). *Managing as designing.* Stanford, CA: Stanford University Press.

Christensen, C.M., & Raynor, M.E. (2003). *The innovator's solution: Creating and sustaining successful growth.* Boston: Harvard Business School Press.

Ciborra, C.U. (2004). *The labyrinths of information: Challenging the wisdom of systems.* Oxford, UK: Oxford University Press.

Cole, M., & Engeström, Y. (1991). A cultural historical approach to distributed cognition. In G. Salamon (Ed.), *Distributed cognition* (pp. 1-47). Cambridge: Cambridge University Press.

Collins, J.C., & Porras, J.I. (1996, September-October). Building your company's vision. *Harvard Business Review,* pp. 65-88.

Eisenhardt, K. (1988). Agency and institutional theory explanations: The case of retail sales competition. *Academy of Management Journal, 30*, 488-511.

Ellingsen, G., & Monteiro, E. (2003). Mechanisms for producing a working knowledge: Enacting, orchestrating, and organizing. *Information and Organization, 13*, 203-229.

Ellis, R.K., & Hall, M.L.W. (1994). Systems and values: An approach for practical organizational intervention. *Proceedings of the ISSS, 94.*

Hannan, M.T., & Freeman, J.H. (1989). *Organizational ecology.* Cambridge. MA: Harvard University Press.

Hanseth, O., & Monteiro, E. (1997). Navigating future research: Judging the relevance of information systems development research. *Accounting, Management, and Information Technology, 6*(1/2), 77-85.

Hinings, C.R., Thibault, L., Slack, T., & Kikulis, L.M. (1996). Values and organizational structure. *Human Relations, 49*(7), 885-917.

Keeney, R.L. (1994). Creativity in decision making with value-focused thinking. *Sloan Management Review, 35*, 33-41.

Kohlberg, L. (1969). Stage and sequence: The cognitive development approach to socialization. In D.A. Goslin (Ed.), *Handbook of socialization theory and research* (pp. 347-480). Chicago: Rand McNally.

Lave, J. (1988). *Cognition in practice.* Cambridge, UK: Cambridge University Press.

Nevis, E.C., DiBella, A.J., & Gould, J.M. (1995). Understanding organizations as learning systems. *Sloan Management Review, 36*, 73-85.

Norrgren, F., & Schaller, J. (1999). Leadership style: Its impact on cross-functional product development. *Journal of Product Innovation Management, 16*(4), 377-384.

Parolini, C. (1999). *The value net: A tool for competitive strategy.* Great Britain: John Wiley & Sons Ltd.

Raynor, M. E. (2007). *The strategy paradox: Why committing to success leads to failure (and what to do about it).* New York: Doubleday.

Rouse, W. (2005). A theory of enterprise transformation. *Systems Engineering, 8*(4), 279-295.

Sauer, C., & Willcocks, L. (2003). Establishing the business of the future: The role of organizational architecture and information technologies. *European Management Journal, 21*(4), 497-508.

Star, S.L., & Ruhleder, K. (1994, October 22-26). Steps toward an ecology of infrastructure. In *Proceedings of CSCW, 94, 253–264,* Chapel Hill, North Carolina.

Storck, J., & Hill, P.A. (2000). Knowledge diffusion through "strategic communities." *Sloan Management Review, 41*, 63-74.

Thompson, M.P.A., & Walsham, G. (2004). Placing knowledge management in context. *Journal of Management Studies, 41*(5), 725-747.

Tolbert, P.S., & Zucker, L.G. (1999). The institutionalization of institutional theory. In S.R. Clegg & C. Hardy (Eds.), *Studying organization.* London: SAGE Publications.

Vaast, E., & Walsham, G. (2005). Representations and actions: The transformation of work practices with IT use. *Information and Organization, 15*(1), 65-89.

van Maanen, J., & Barley, S.R. (1984). Occupational communities: Culture and control in organizations. In B.M. Staw (Ed.), *Research in organizational behavior* (vol. 6). Greenwich, CT: JAI Press.

von Krogh, G., & Roos, J. (1995). *Organizational epistemology.* New York: St. Martin's.

Walsham, G. (2001). Knowledge management: The benefits and limitations of computer systems. *European Management Journal, 19*(6), 599-608.

Weick, K.E. (1989). Theory construction as disciplined imagination. *Academy of Management Review, 14*, 532-550.

Weick, K.E. (1990). Technology as equivoque: Sensemaking in new technologies. In P. Goodman et al. (Eds.), *Technology and organizations* (pp. 1-44). San Francisco: Jossey-Bass.

Weick, K.E., & Bougon, M.G. (1986). Organizations as cognitive maps: Charting ways to success and failure. In *The thinking organization* (pp. 102-135). San Francisco: Jossey-Bass.

Wynn, E. (1991). Taking practice seriously. In J. Greenbaum & M. Kyng (Eds.), *Design at work.* Hillsdale, NJ: Lawrence Erlbaum Associates.

Yasai-Ardekani, M., & Haug, R.S. (1997). Contextual determinants of strategic planning processes. *Journal of Management Studies, 5*(34), 729-741.

Yates, J., & Orlikowski, W.J. (1992). Genres of organizational communication: A structurational approach to studying communication and media. *The Academy of Management Review, 17*(2), 299-326.

Zuboff, S. (1988). *In the age of the smart machine.* New York: Basic Books.

Chapter VIII
A Technology–Focused Framework for Integrating Knowledge Management into Strategic Innovation Management

Marc Henselewski
Deloitte Consulting GmbH, Germany

Stefan Smolnik
European Business School, Germany

Gerold Riempp
European Business School, Germany

ABSTRACT

Today's business environment is characterized by highly transparent markets and global competition. Technology life cycles are decreasing due to the fast pace at which development of new technologies is progressing. To compete in this environment, it is necessary to identify upcoming innovations and trends as early as possible to decrease uncertainty, implement technology leadership, and create competitive advantage. In a parallel development, the amount of information available is already vast and increasing daily. As a result of these developments, strategic innovation management has become increasingly challenging. The goal of our chapter is to investigate to what extent knowledge management technologies support and improve strategic innovation management to face the aforementioned problems successfully. Consequently, we will develop a characterization scheme which works as a framework for the subsequent evaluation of knowledge management technologies and apply this to a real-world case.

INTRODUCTION

Competition in today's business environment is intense. The influences of the rapid pace of globalization, and of national and international markets' on-going liberalization lead to the emergence of new problem settings and, consequently, increased pressure on companies. Companies therefore face greater risks due to the higher number of players in the market. However, environmental influences created outside the market are not the only factors that have an impact on companies' complexity. The increasing speed at which innovations and new developments occur, the resultant shorter product life cycles, and decreasing production costs also add to the pressure felt by firms and their decision-makers. High technology companies that have high research and development (R&D) expenditures, have to specifically plan their research programs more carefully, because they run a higher risk of losing the competitive advantage when "going the wrong way". Consequently, decision-makers have a greater need to anticipate or forecast future developments and apply these insights in business strategies and strategic innovation management in order to keep risk levels low and the company competitive. According to Bright (1979), all "firms and governments dealing with technology have been and are doing technology forecasting. This is because each decision to explore, support, oppose or ignore a technological prospect incorporates the decision-maker's assumptions about that technology and its viability in the future" (p. 228).

Over the last few years, firms have increasingly realized that knowledge plays a key role in the development of strategies for future success and stronger market positions. The most striking examples of such firms are technology and service-oriented companies, but retailers also engage in activities to use knowledge as factors of competitive advantage. A paradigm shift can be observed in business strategies: from a focus on tangible assets to one that prioritizes intangible assets (Drucker, 1996, p. 203; Stewart, 1997, p. 23). However, information and information sources' quantity is continuously increasing, and what at first seemed to be the solution to several business problems has itself become a unique problem for today's companies—too much information. In order to gain from information and to facilitate knowledge creation within a company, new ways of filtering and selecting information have to be applied. Furthermore, the nature of knowledge is highly dynamic. The value of knowledge is difficult to measure and can change from one moment to another. Companies try to control this uncertainty to some extent and to obtain as much advantage as possible from their knowledge by integrating knowledge management paradigms into competitive strategies.

The question arises if it is possible to successfully support knowledge and strategic innovation management alignment on an operational level. With technology forecasting being an essential discipline of today's innovation and innovation management processes, it is of specific interest to know whether technology forecasting can be improved by integrating knowledge management—particularly by means of current knowledge management technologies. In the following, we understand the latter as instruments of information and communication technologies that support knowledge management processes.

In order to answer the stated question, this chapter's objective is to develop a characterization scheme that integrates aspects of both fields: knowledge management as well as innovation management process's technology forecasting. Furthermore, selected knowledge management technologies will be evaluated by applying this scheme to derive conclusions regarding the most promising solutions with which to support technology forecasting.

The section following this one introduces and defines technology forecasting and illustrates the associated standard technology forecasting process, which is tailored to comply with strategic innovation management. Thereafter, an overview of several forecasting methods is given. The section *Knowledge Management Needs Within Technology Forecasting* explains the motivation for knowledge management's integration into technology forecasting and describes the strategic and organizational reasons. The subsequent section leads to the development of a characterization scheme in order to evaluate the knowledge management technologies data mining, case-based reasoning, information retrieval, topic maps, and ontologies. The next section comprises the actual evaluation of the mentioned technologies and is followed by an integrative discussion of the findings to close the evaluation. The transfer of the developed insights to the real world through discussion of an example case is covered in the section *Towards an Exploratory Case Study*. This is taken from an innovation project at DETECON Inc., conducted for Deutsche Telekom AG. The subsequent section summarizes the main results and the concluding section suggests fields for further research.

DELIMITATION AND CONCEPTUAL DEFINITIONS

Technology Forecasting

As Granger points out, technology forecasting evolved from the argument that, in the long run, technological change is one of the most important influencing factors of economies (Granger, 1989, p. 209). Thus, technology forecasting seems to be most valuable when applied to long time horizons, which becomes even more important in strategic innovation management. For example, decisions pertaining to general strategic business planning are often based on a forecast time horizon of three to twenty years (DeLurgio, 1998, p. 8).

Besides longer time horizons, the scope of the results is another specific property of technology forecasting. Such forecasts "are generally con-

cerned with the characteristics of a technology rather than how these are achieved" (Granger, 1989, p. 210). It was Bright (1979) who incorporated this fact into a definition of technology forecasting:

Technology forecasting is a quantified statement of the timing, the character or the degree of change in technical parameters and attributes in the design, production and application of devices, materials and processes, arrived at through a specified system of reasoning. (p. 235)

Other authors (for example, DeLurgio, 1998, p. 10) stress that uncertainties about future developments can be modeled with the help of probabilities that help decision-makers plan for a variety of contingencies and scenarios. For this reason and the fact that technology forecasting mostly deals with long time horizons, we revised Bright's definition to attain a more rigorous and precise definition of technology forecasting:

Technology forecasting is a probabilistic, long-term estimate of the timing, the character or the degree of change in technical parameters and attributes in the design, production, and application of devices, materials, and processes, arrived at through a system of reasoning consciously applied by the forecaster and exposed to the recipient.

In different situations, the exact technology-forecasting process can vary from a relatively simple process with just a few stages, to a process comprising a complex structure of stages and subprocesses (DeLurgio, 1998, p. 26). Armstrong (2001) divides the process into six basic steps: formulate problem, obtain information, select methods, implement methods, evaluate methods, and use forecasts (p. 8). These steps also appear in other literature, in the same or a very similar order (DeLurgio, 1998, p. 27; Reger, 2001, p.538), sometimes in combination with additional stages.

Figure 1. The technology-forecasting process (following Armstrong, 2001)

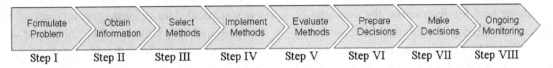

In addition to this process structure, DeLurgio (1998) mentions that on-going maintenance and verification are necessary to ensure that the results are valid and effective (p. 27). Hence, it is recommended that reality be monitored and compared to the forecasting results in order to respond to possible inaccuracies. In the context of innovation management, the suggested on-going monitoring becomes even more important, since companies have to respond to changes as quickly as possible to stay competitive. Moreover, it can be assumed that in a large company, the individuals who conduct the forecast and the decision-makers are not the same persons. Additional steps to prepare and make decisions are therefore necessary for a complete view of the process. To include these thoughts into the process, the last step of the process has to be split and a more detailed structure created. The resulting technology-forecasting process for strategic innovation management is shown in Figure 1.

Overview of Forecasting Methods

For the later discussion of technology forecasting, it is important to get a basic understanding of available classes of forecasting methods. This section is based on the "Methodology Tree" by Armstrong which illustrates the characteristics of forecasting methods and their relationships. Figure 2 depicts the Methodology Tree.

Armstrong begins with a separation of judgmental and statistical methods. He mentions, however, that judgment pervades all aspects of forecasting (Armstrong, 2001, p. 9). The further down a method is positioned in the tree, the higher the amount of judgmental and statistical integration. On the judgmental side of the tree, the methods are split into those predicting one's own behavior and those predicting the behavior of others, mostly by including experts into the forecasting process. On the side of method types predicting one's own behavior, the methods are

Figure 2. Methodology tree by Armstrong (2001, p. 9); dotted lines present possible relationships

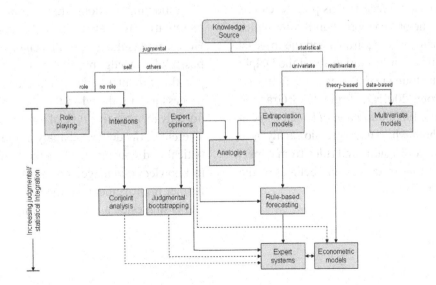

characterized by the influence of a role. If a role influences the decision to make, *role playing* is a valuable tool for forecasting the outcome of the decision through the simulated interaction of roles affected by the decision. In case there is no influence of a role, the *intentions method* can be used in which people predict their own behavior in different situations. *Conjoint analysis* goes a step further than the *intentions method* by trying to create a connection between personal intentions and certain features of a situation through statistical analysis. For example, "a forecaster could show various designs for a computer and ask people about their intentions to purchase each version" (Armstrong, 2001, p. 9).

Forecasting methods within the *others* branch are based on *expert opinions* about how organizations or others will behave. There is a broad number of forecasting methods which belong to this type, with the Delphi method being the most famous one. In this method, questionnaires are sent out to experts in the targeted fields who answer the questions by the use of their subjective judgment. Once the questionnaires are sent back and analyzed, they are sent out again to the same experts together with the results of the first round in order to get a second estimation. The reason for this is to share the results and create a common knowledge base among all participants of the forecast. This process can be repeated for one or two more rounds after which the final conclusions are drawn and the forecast is created. Further information about the Delphi method can be found in the forecasting literature (e.g., Armstrong, 2001; DeLurgio, 1998; Granger, 1989; Martino, 1983). *Judgmental bootstrapping* refers to methods which use regression analysis in order to draw conclusions and rules from expert opinions and, to a certain extent, belongs to the class of expert systems.

Judgment and statistics are merged into one method type when *analogies* are used. Based on statistical data, experts try to forecast the development of a situation. The success of such an approach depends on the degree of similarity between the situation which has to be predicted and the one the statistical data are taken from.

The statistical side of the tree is split into univariate and multivariate methods. The *univariate* part of the tree contains extrapolation methods (Armstrong, 2001, p. 10); that is, values are predicted by the use of older values within a (time-) series. The simplest method of this type is using today's number of sales to predict tomorrow's number. When domain knowledge and knowledge about forecasting procedures is combined in a type of expert system to achieve this task, one speaks of *rule-based forecasting*. Full *expert systems* utilize an even greater integration of expert rules (rules which are similar to the way experts create their judgments) in order to support forecasting.

Multivariate forecasting methods are distinguished whether they are based on statistical data or theory. The latter leads to *econometric models* which base on domain knowledge or findings from prior research. "Econometric models provide an ideal way to integrate judgmental and statistical sources" (Armstrong, 2001, p. 10).

In general, one can argue that the focus of the following sections lies within the area of quantitative or statistical forecasting methods. However, it is the goal of this chapter to identify possible knowledge management technology support throughout the entire technology forecasting process as introduced in the section before and not only for a specific type of forecasting method. Therefore, the dedicated analysis of specific statistical and nonstatistical methods with regards to knowledge management needs could lead to further improvements of the forecasting quality and is suggested as an area of future research.

KNOWLEDGE MANAGEMENT NEEDS WITHIN TECHNOLOGY FORECASTING

There are three major perspectives that have to be considered in order to determine the need for knowledge management within technology forecasting. First, knowledge management needs within technology forecasting can be considered natural implications emerging from business and knowledge strategies which companies formulate to sustain or increase their competitive advantage. Second, the topic can be approached from an inside-the-company view: which other strategic, technological, or organizational factors within a company necessitate integrating knowledge management into the technology-forecasting process? Third, a company's forecasting process is obviously influenced by the company's environment. Therefore, an analysis from an outside-the-company perspective is also crucial to achieve a complete view of the need for knowledge management within technology forecasting.

Business and Knowledge Strategy Implications

As business strategies are formulated to set the overall company goals and define a company's unique strategy to gain profits, one needs to understand that these strategies are built from different components, each delivering a fundamental part to realize a company's objectives. Various authors, for example, Geschka (1992), broadly accept that "the innovation strategy is one means to achieve overall strategic company goals" (p. 70). Therefore, innovation is becoming increasingly important within companies and is moving from an activity often conducted solely within marketing or research and development departments to a process spanning several departments steered by dedicated innovation management. Furthermore, the nature of innovation is such that it can

be the sole source of a company's competitive advantage and business success. O'Hare (1988) states that "truly successful innovation does not just lead to some extra sales volume, or a temporary improvement in performance. ... Rather, it is about achieving fundamental improvement in competitive position, about re-establishing the competitive equilibrium at a new, more favorable point" (pp. 39-40). However, the value of innovation and, therefore, its ability to function as a basis for competitive advantage, declines over time. This can be observed on a daily basis and examples can be found everywhere, from food to consumer technology and from health care to aviation; what seems to be a unique and exclusive product justifying a premium price today becomes a commodity product tomorrow.

It is essential to continue the development of further innovations to successfully build and sustain competitive advantage based on innovation. This undertaking is, however, influenced by many factors that determine the future of a company as well as the economy and society to which the company belongs. These factors could, for example, belong to political regulations, trends, and hypes within a society, or technological and scientific breakthroughs. Therefore, the development of innovation faces risks and uncertainty that are all future related and with which the company needs to cope through stringent innovation management. It is essential to recognize that this uncertainty with regard to future developments is the main reason for technology forecasting being a core part of current companies' efforts to plan innovation roadmaps and business strategies in keeping with future challenges. Armstrong (2001) says that:

We have no need to forecast whether the sun will rise tomorrow. There is also no uncertainty when events can be controlled; for example, you do not need to predict the temperature in your home. Many decisions, however, involve uncertainty, and in these cases, formal forecasting procedures ... can be useful. (p. 2)

A knowledge management strategy defines the basic direction of an organization's knowledge management structures and activities (Riempp, 2004, p. 77). The overall aim of these structures and activities is the improved utilization of knowledge that contributes to the better achievement of an organization's goals; that is, the knowledge management strategy is part of the overall business strategy. When thinking about technology forecasting and transferring it to the domain of knowledge strategies, technology forecasting can be regarded as a means to define and evaluate what Abou-Zeid (2005) calls the Knowledge-Scope (K-Scope); "K-Scope deals with the specific domains of knowledge that are critical to the firm's survival and advancement strategies" (p. 100). In other words, technology forecasting helps a company to understand which path technological innovations will follow to identify the implications for the company's own innovation roadmap and its overall competitive strategy. According to Abou-Zeid (2005), this is part of the Knowledge Strategy External Domain (p. 100). Thereby, technology forecasting is a means to support knowledge strategy creation by supporting the Knowledge-Scope definition as well as an essential part of a company's innovation management by being a driver for innovation strategy formulation.

Needs Emerging from Inside the Company

Inside a company, technology forecasting is closely linked with decision-making processes. It is part of the activities incorporated in strategic innovation management in order to support planning of innovation and R&D programs. DeLurgio (1998) argues that "it is important to recognize the role of forecasting in expanding the knowledge base of organizations and whole societies" (p. 6). Thus, technology forecasting itself can be regarded as a knowledge-creating activity; that is, knowledge in the sense of enabling managers to make strategic decisions, plan a technological in-

novation path for the company, and adjust business strategies. Therefore, decision-makers need an as comprehensive view of future developments as possible, which cannot be achieved with the help of technology forecasting alone. The end product of forecasting activities is, in most cases, some sort of study or report that represents all analyzed future developments. However, it can be assumed that this report does not contain enough information for a decision-maker to recreate all the knowledge that has been created by participants through the entire forecasting process. Knowledge, like perspectives and prior experiences shared by forecasters, might be valuable for a decision-maker. This facilitates interpretation of the information contained within the reports in a more efficient and comprehensive fashion, thus leading to decreased uncertainty and better-informed decisions. Moreover, reports cannot contain all the information available to the forecasters. In order to provide precise information and to reduce the document's complexity, some information has to be omitted. However, this information might become useful later in the decision process. Without efficient ways of recovering the missing information, the decision process is either slowed down, due to the additional time spent analyzing or acquiring the missing information for a second time, or it becomes less accurate.

In summary, from an inside-the-company perspective, two major reasons can be identified for the emerging need of knowledge management support for technology forecasting within strategic innovation management. Moreover, the last two major reasons have the potential to improve the quality and efficiency of the process:

- Technology forecasting is itself a knowledge-creating process.
- Knowledge that has been created during the process is not transferred to decision-makers due to, for example, the limited amount of information that can be conveyed via documentation.

Needs Emerging from Outside the Company

Making the right decisions with respect to future developments and technologies is vital for a company's competitiveness. One reason for this is the decreasing length of technological life cycles as "technological change is one of the most important forces affecting a firm's competitive position" (Burgelman, Maidique & Wheelwright, 1996, p. 6). Additional dynamics and uncertainty are created by the phenomenon of unexpected, disruptive innovations with which a company has to cope and which can never be fully excluded. Another factor that increases the pressure felt by decision-makers is cost. Vanston (1996) states that "under pressure to contain these [higher] costs, it has become increasingly important for R&D programs to focus on projects that will result in enhanced profits and sustainable competitive advantage" (p. 57). All these factors are evidence of how crucial it is for a company to make the right decisions in a constantly decreasing time frame.

On the other hand, the same reasons lead companies to face increasing uncertainty with respect to future developments. In order to deal with this uncertainty, companies have to collect and assess more information swifter and more efficiently than they used to. This is also true in the context of technology forecasting within strategic innovation management. It can be assumed that more information leads to a reduced uncertainty and thus to a better-informed decision. At the same time, however, more information also leads to greater complexity and, consequently, to a decrease in efficiency and a slower process. The amount of information required to decrease uncertainty and the time needed to collect, assess, and process information are in inverse proportion to each other. As far as possible, companies should therefore find equilibrium on the information side to keep uncertainty low, while keeping complexity on a level that the forecaster can still handle.

Hence, two main factors—related to a technology-forecasting process's efficiency and emerging from outside the company—that influence a company's competitive advantage and business strategy, and create a need for knowledge management within technology forecasting, are:

- Decisions have to be made faster to stay ahead of competition.
- More information with an increasingly complex relational structure has to be collected, assessed, and processed to decrease uncertainty.

DEVELOPMENT OF A CHARACTERIZATION SCHEME FOR KNOWLEDGE MANAGEMENT TECHNOLOGIES

In this chapter, we will develop a characterization scheme to evaluate and delineate knowledge management technologies. Since these technologies differ with respect to knowledge management as well as technology forecasting, the scheme will combine these two fields by integrating a dimension for each of them.

We have shown that one can argue that technology forecasting itself is a knowledge-creating process. A second look at the forecasting process reveals that each step can be regarded as a transformation process with specific inputs and outputs. Step II, for example, needs the definition of the forecasting objectives, the scope, and the time horizon as inputs. This information is utilized within the process step's activities and transformed into information of a greater complexity by combining the input with new information. New relations are identified between certain information objects, leading to the observed information structure's greater complexity. The subsequent step III also requires input from the preceding steps. It is, however, different from step II with respect to the transformation of information.

Figure 3. Information-structure complexity

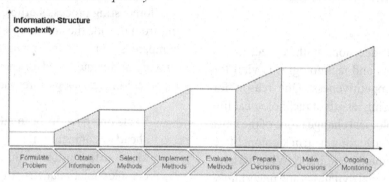

While the activities of process step II increase the information structure's overall complexity, the complexity remains constant during step III, because the information is only analyzed to select suitable forecasting methods. An analysis of the other process steps reveals that the technology-forecasting process's steps can be characterized by their varying degree of complexity; in other words, either the level of complexity is increased or it remains unaltered. Figure 3 illustrates this relation on an abstract level without claiming to represent the actual degree of complexity increase.

On examining Figure 3, it is possible to identify four steps that cause the information structure's increasing complexity within the forecasting process. These steps are: obtain information, implement methods, prepare decisions, and on-going monitoring. Reasons can be found for these four steps' contribution to the complexity when comparing each step's activities. They all have the combination of previous steps' results and newly acquired information in common, which leads to the creation of new knowledge. Such knowledge is needed to complete each process step's tasks.

Accordingly, the level of the information structure's complexity is chosen as a dimension of technology forecasting and is expressed by the four process steps identified. This dimension enables knowledge management technologies to be classified according to their capability to support

these four process steps, and allows an implicit description of the level of information complexity within the technology-forecasting process that a knowledge management technology supports.

While the development of the technology forecasting dimension is based on the analysis of the forecasting process, a different approach has to be found to define the knowledge management dimension. As a starting point, the definitions of data, information, and knowledge should be considered. Since there is a defined difference between these terms, one can argue that data, information, and knowledge's definitions could be used as a structure with which to categorize knowledge management technologies; for example, the category "information" contains all those technologies that target information. Furthermore, transformation processes are required to turn data into information and information into knowledge. A categorization structure based only on the definitions of the three terms is not capable of integrating such transformation processes, and it is obvious that there are knowledge management technologies that, for example, specifically support the transformation of data into information. Aamodt and Nygård (1995) propose a model for data, information, and knowledge that takes the three terms' specific relationships into account (p. 8). The model explains the processes that are needed to transform, for example, data into information, in addition to providing data, information, and knowledge's basic structure. However, with regard to the development of a dimension for knowledge management technologies' characterization from a knowledge management point of view, it can be argued that this model is not applicable. Knowledge, as understood in this chapter, is closely linked with human action and the human mind, with learning being one way of creating knowledge. While there might be a number of knowledge management technologies that support learning, it is impossible for technologies to target knowledge itself.

Another disadvantage of such a model is its granularity. It can be assumed that there are several types of knowledge management technologies that target information, but each with a different focus or different application areas. Consequently, a finer granularity is needed which, in an optimal case, can be based on a single and continuous criterion to facilitate adoption and the development of a knowledge management dimension for the characterization scheme as stated previously.

Smolnik et al. (2005) suggest an approach called "the continuum of context explication", which fulfills the mentioned requirements and is based on the importance of context. Here, context explication means "discovering implicit meanings and expressing those meanings explicitly" (p. 28). The authors stress that context is an important aspect that many definitions of knowledge have in common (Smolnik et al., 2005, p. 30) and they compare several definitions of context. Dey and Abowd (2000), for example, define context as follows:

Context is any information that can be used to characterize the situation of an entity. An entity is a person, place, or object that is considered relevant to the interaction between a user and an application, including the user and applications themselves. (pp. 3-4)

Besides its role in the definition of knowledge, context also plays an important role in the defini-

tion of information. Nonaka and Takeuchi (1995) argue that "knowledge, like information, is … context-specific and relational" (p. 58). Smolnik et al. (2005) found that knowledge management technologies "focus on contextual information in different ways and with varying intensity" (p. 36). Consequently, the authors present five approaches to "find and use information objects and contextual information …, each with a differing degree of context and explication ease" (Smolnik et al., 2005, p. 36). The continuum distinguishes the following five approaches:

- **The data approach:** Data are symbols or signs without a meaning or context. Thus, context cannot be explicated. Nevertheless, technologies can be applied to transform data into information or domain-specific knowledge. The data approach encompasses these methods.

- **The information approach:** Most important for the definition of information is that information includes meaning and a specific context. However, the "context is … interwoven with the content and difficult to conceptualize, which means that the methods implemented to find requested information objects have to rely on the content and cannot access contextual information" (Smolnik et al., 2005, p. 37).

- **The descriptor approach:** The addition of explicit contextual information to information objects, thereby providing context-aware methods for information search and discovery, is called a descriptor approach.

- **The metacontext approach:** This approach extends the descriptor approach, as explicit contextual information no longer resides only within information objects, but is integrated into a metalayer that lies above and spans a variety of information.

- **The knowledge approach:** The knowledge approach focuses on the human being and considers characteristics of knowledge. It is about knowledge creation through actions like communication, construction, or cognition.

The continuum's consideration of context and its explication offers a continuous criterion through which it is possible to distinguish different knowledge management technologies. This makes the continuum of context explication an ideal basis for the development of a knowledge management dimension. Each approach forms one category that can be used to classify knowledge management technologies. The only exception is the knowledge approach. Since it is closely linked to the human mind and human action, knowledge management technologies cannot explicate the person-specific context. This approach is therefore not used within the knowledge management dimension.

The combination of the developed technology-forecasting dimension with the knowledge management perspective dimension results in the context-complexity matrix. This matrix allows the characterization of knowledge management technologies with regard to the degree of context as well as to the technology-forecasting process's degree of information structure complexity. The background of each dimension implicitly provides further characteristics of the classified knowledge management technologies. A categorization of, for example, the metacontext approach within the knowledge management domain and step VIII of the technology-forecasting domain means that the knowledge management technology is capable of supporting step VIII's great information structure complexity and also comprises a high level of explicit contextual information.

EVALUATION OF KNOWLEDGE MANAGEMENT TECHNOLOGIES

The breadth of available knowledge management technologies ranges from very simple to very complex. The set of knowledge management tech-

nologies for the following evaluation has therefore been selected to represent this breadth, namely, data mining, case-based reasoning, information retrieval, topic maps, and ontologies. We evaluate these technologies in the following with respect to the presented characterization scheme.

Data Mining

Authors in the field of data mining often state that the identification of specific patterns enables the extraction of knowledge embedded within databases (e.g., Han & Kamber, 2001, p. 4; Lusti, 2002, p. 260). This view is not absolutely precise. The consideration of data-mining applications like market basket analysis, fraud detection, or risk analysis leads to the thought that data-mining functionalities enrich data through the identification of patterns or classes in a way that a person familiar with the domain is capable of deriving a meaning from the presented results. Hence, domain-specific information is generated, which can then be combined with other information and knowledge to create new knowledge. But data mining contains no functionality that specifically supports this combination of information. By considering the continuum of context explication as a dimension for a knowledge management categorization, the discussion above can be summarized by assigning data mining to the category "data approach".

With respect to technology forecasting, Armstrong (2001) argues that "an immense amount of research effort has so far produced little evidence that data-mining models can improve forecasting accuracy" (p. 10). Thus, the quality of forecasts that are solely based on data mining is debatable and, consequently, so is the support of step IV. However, it is our opinion that with the exception of the implementation of forecasting methods, data mining can be successfully utilized to facilitate specific tasks within the technology forecasting process's steps. As we explained in the previous section, step II and step VIII require the analysis of great amounts of information with respect to specified criteria. In step II, information is needed that can be associated with the forecast's objectives as defined during step I, while an on-going analysis of information based on the results of a forecast is required within step VIII. In combination with other technologies, data mining might be a suitable way to improve the efficiency of identifying interesting information objects through classification and association analysis. Data mining can therefore be assigned to the categories "step II" and "step VIII" of the technology-forecasting dimension.

Case-Based Reasoning

Compared to data mining, case-based reasoning is a concept which targets information rather than data. A case provides the solution to some problems, which can basically be viewed as providing domain-specific information (Riesbeck & Schank, 1989, p. 24). Case-based reasoning comprises certain functionalities that allow the emulation of cognitive processes in order to generate solutions (Riesbeck & Schank, 1989, p. 24). These functionalities are the capability to adapt old cases to suit the needs of new cases and the fact that a system enlarges its case base by evaluating and retaining cases that have either been solved, or provide information about faults. Systems following the structural case-based reasoning approach (Bergmann, Althoff, Breen, Göker, Manago, Traphöner & Wess, 2003, p. 21) integrate these functionalities and apply general domain knowledge to a model to improve case storage and retrieval, thereby putting the different cases into a certain context. The context is defined by a set of features that are used to index a case and to determine similarity between different cases (Aamodt & Plaza, 1994, p. 50). Thus, features are descriptors of information objects and the corresponding context.

On the other hand, there are also case-based reasoning systems that do not have an underlying domain model, like those that use the textual case-based reasoning approach (Bergmann et al., 2003, p. 21). Such systems work directly on the information and utilize certain algorithms to compare and match new cases with those contained in the case base. Consequently, with respect to the knowledge management dimension, case-based reasoning belongs equally to the category "information approach" and to the category "descriptor approach".

With regard to the dimension for technology forecasting, an appropriate characterization and the corresponding identification of the potential for supporting the technology-forecasting process is a more difficult task. Gaines and Shaw (1986) argue that as far as technology and innovations are concerned, it seems that the past is not appropriate for predicting the future (p. 3). Case-based reasoning is, however, designed around previous experiences. This leads to the conclusion that case-based reasoning cannot be applied to technology-forecasting activities. It cannot therefore be assigned to the category "step IV" of the technology-forecasting dimension. Moreover, taking the requirements of step II and step VIII into account, it is doubtful that case-based reasoning is a useful method with which to support these activities. Both steps need to handle a great amount of new information and need to put this information into context to achieve a clearer perspective of the forecast's scope as well as to collect information with which to monitor the forecast's results. Case-based reasoning is not a method that is intended for the identification of new information. It cannot therefore be assigned to the categories "step II" or "step VIII" of the technology-forecasting dimension.

Nevertheless, it is case-based reasoning's purpose to support decisions and to solve problems. Therefore, it is an appropriate technology for application during step VI. More precisely, case-based reasoning can be used to support planning activities (Lenz, Bartsch-Spörl, Burkhardt & Wess, 1998, p. 14). A company that has a long experience of pursuing and developing innovative technologies might profit from its knowledge when a new technology is about to be developed or integrated.

Information Retrieval

On considering the definitions of each single category of the knowledge management dimension, it seems obvious that information retrieval belongs to the category "information approach". In general, such a categorization appears to be reasonable since information retrieval targets raw information. Smolnik et al. (2005) argue that although information itself comprises content and context, the context is interwoven with the content and thus difficult to explicate (p. 37). As a result, technologies that do not include additional explicit contextual information only rely on content or its representation within search functionalities. Clearly, this is true of most conceptual information retrieval models.

On the other hand, one can argue that some forms of information retrieval also integrate explicit contextual information into search and retrieval methods. While Smolnik et al. (2005) state that "authors have to provide [explicit contextual] information at the time of creation" (p. 37), the consideration of the concept of aboutness, as introduced by Ingwersen (1992, p. 50), allows an additional perspective. On considering the fact that some information retrieval systems are based on the creation of index terms through document analysis and alignment with a specific domain by individuals, we argue that such indexes represent the indexer's aboutness and therefore also the context of the individual who analyzes the documents and creates the index. Nevertheless, in the same way that indexer aboutness differs from author aboutness, the author and indexer's contexts vary. In general, the characterization of information retrieval by assigning it to the category "information approach" within the knowledge management dimension is a reasonable outcome; however, the

exceptions as discussed previously should be taken into account. Information retrieval will therefore be categorized by mainly assigning it to the category "information approach" as well as partially to the category "descriptor approach".

Within technology forecasting, certain process steps include the need to identify information when a large amount of it is available, namely in step II, step IV, and step VIII. The difference between these steps' information need is that the first two steps require a broad range of new information with respect to the selected forecasting scope, while the latter step utilizes specific information that is closely linked with the developed technology forecasts in order to compare them to reality. Therefore, an efficient way to identify and assess relations and derive consequences from specific information objects is more important than the mere retrieval of interesting information from a large amount and variety of information. It is a common assumption among information retrieval researchers that searching within such systems is an iterative process (Salton & McGill, 1983, p. 3). A user starts with some sort of query and evaluates his or her own understanding of the information needed with the help of the first result set. Either the information is sufficient—it results in the retrieval of additional information through references or the like—or a user realizes that the request has to be completely revised. Reasons for this can be found when taking into account that users are only able to describe what they need, which is in turn based on what they already know. These arguments lead to the conclusion that information retrieval is not applicable to step VIII of the technology-forecasting process and, instead, can be characterized as able to support steps with a need for a wide range of new information, thus step II and step IV.

Topic Maps

Topic maps provide methods with which to navigate associatively across large amounts of information in a conscious manner, enabling a systematic identification of information and creation of new knowledge by the user. This is possible by detaching the information source from the context used to find the information, which results in topic maps being "information assets in their own right, irrespective of whether they are actually connected to any information resources or not" (Rath & Pepper, 1999, p. 9). Moreover, topic maps support "managing the meaning of the information, rather than just the information" (Garshol, 2002, p. 2). An explicit context, called metacontext, is used to organize available information in such a way that more efficient search methods can be applied. Hence, the metacontext is the most characterizing aspect when discussing topic maps; they thus clearly belong to the category "metacontext approach" when considering the knowledge management dimension of the context-complexity matrix.

Because a topic map describes certain domain knowledge, it can be very useful when created to represent the forecast's scope. Such a topic map comprises the different technologies and research areas within the focus of the company that conducts the forecast. Associations can be used to link technologies to express their influences and relations. Any information, to which the topic map is applied, can then be categorized with respect to the forecast's scope, facilitating identification of valuable information. Furthermore, once there is a comprehensive information repository, the topic map can be used to relocate information and to relate it to the forecasting activities' results. Hence, topic maps also provide additional value when used within step IV and step VI. Identifying specific information that correlates with the forecasting activities' results is especially important within step VIII. Topic maps' filtering and localization capabilities help to achieve a more precise analysis of available information and, hence, a more efficient monitoring process overall. In general, topic maps have the potential to increase the efficiency of each technology-forecasting step

in the context-complexity matrix, because they can be tailored to a forecast's scope and thereby reduce the available information's complexity to a manageable level.

Ontologies

Ontologies are a means to provide a resource that unambiguously determines the meaning of terms and their relations to other terms within a certain domain (Benjamins, Fensel, & Gómez Pérez, 1998, p. 2). This structure is an autonomous construct without links to specific information resources. With respect to the knowledge management dimension of the context-complexity matrix, it is quite obvious that ontologies belong to the category "metacontext approach", as explicit context structures are created that are independent of specific information resources and can themselves be viewed as an information resource. Therefore, relations have to be created between an information resource and ontologies by means of explicit contextual information and specific references that are added to the information resource. This methodology clearly does not fit into any other category on the knowledge management dimension than the metacontext approach.

The same reasons that lead to the obvious characterization of ontologies as a metacontext approach hamper categorization with regard to technology forecasting. The question arises: which of the technology-forecasting process's steps and activities benefit from the development and application of an ontology? Following the premises regarding the benefits of ontology application as presented by Zelewski (2001, p. 4), possible applications can be derived for ontologies within technology forecasting. Zelewski (2001) argues that the knowledge intensity of the tasks to be accomplished and the degree to which the knowledge backgrounds of the parties involved in an interaction differ both influence ontologies' importance as a means to improve the considered process tasks' efficiency (p. 4). When conducted for strategic innovation management, many technology-forecasting methods such as, for example, the Delphi method (e.g., Armstrong, 2001; DeLurgio, 1998), are aimed at transforming individuals with different backgrounds' specific knowledge into statements about future technological innovations and developments. Thus, Zelewski's premises are true with regards to technology forecasting. As a result, only the category "step IV" seems to be suitable for ontology application's characterization within technology forecasting for strategic innovation management, but it is limited by the chosen technology-forecasting methods.

DISCUSSIONS

Obviously, some of the technology-forecasting process's steps can be supported by more than one knowledge management technology. Therefore, the question arises: which single technology or which combination appears to be the most promising with which to support and

improve this process? To answer this question, it is helpful to consider technology forecasting for strategic innovation management with respect to the type of input each process step requires. We have shown that the complexity of the information structure within the technology-forecasting process increases in the course of the process. We argue that context too becomes more and more important. At the beginning of the process, the importance of context as well as the information structure's complexity is rather modest, but in the end, the degree of complexity and context importance reaches a maximum. As a result, the context-complexity matrix has to be refined to integrate strategic innovation management's focus in such a way that only the upper left triangle represents possible solutions, which are promising ways of supporting technology-forecasting steps through knowledge management technologies as presented in Figure 4.

A striking point of the context-complexity matrix is the fact that topic maps are capable of supporting each process step in a certain way.

Figure 4. The context-complexity matrix

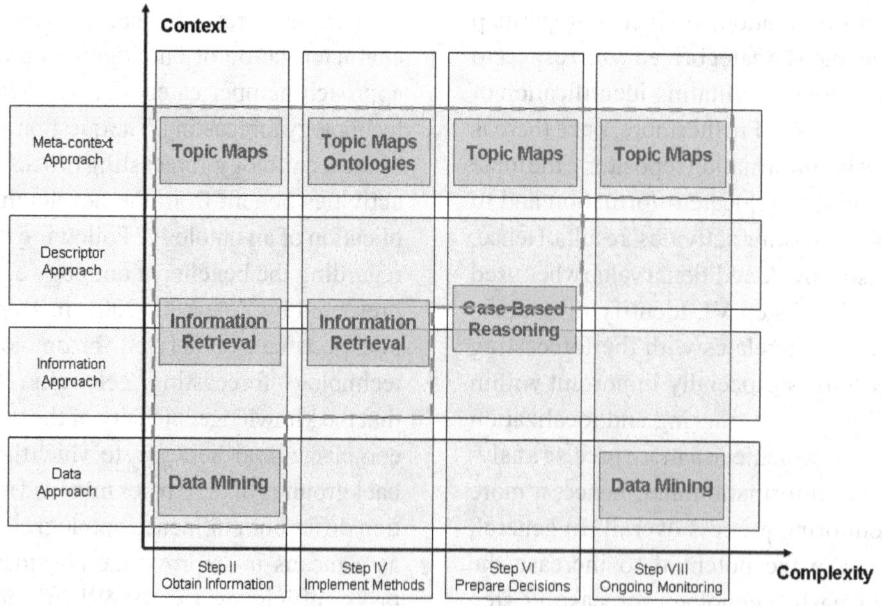

However, topic maps require some knowledge about the domain and its topics for their generation, while information retrieval provides functionalities that require less prior knowledge and can be used to gather a first broad variety of information. This can be especially helpful during the first phases of technology-forecasting research efforts. Such information can then be analyzed to generate the needed topic map, which corresponds with a technology forecast's scope. Later on, the topic map can be used to classify and organize further information and, hence, allows a more systematic way of discovering additional information.

In summary, we can state that a knowledge management system that is based on topic map technologies and integrates information retrieval functionalities as extensions to those provided by the topic map, is the most promising solution with which to support technology forecasting for strategic innovation management. In order to verify the theoretical results, we test them within a real-world scenario.

TOWARDS AN EXPLORATORY CASE STUDY

We applied our findings to a project conducted for Deutsche Telekom AG at DETECON Inc., a technology and management consulting company with a focus on innovation engineering. The main objectives of the project were the identification of technology trends and developments that are able to open new opportunities and the assessment of their innovation potential in order to define innovation strategies and achieve company goals. The technology forecasting process at DETECON Inc. differs in two main aspects from the generic process as presented in this chapter. First of all, people at DETECON Inc. distinguish between *inductive* and *deductive* approaches toward innovation and trend identification. This is comparable to what Reger (2001) calls "core technologies" and "white spaces" (p. 539). Inductive methods

begin with the identification and formulation of a certain problem setting. In this case, the term *problem* refers to certain needs which emerge from inside Deutsche Telekom and are derived from, for example, internal developments or processes.

After problem formulation, specific information is obtained which is related to the problem and helps finding innovative solutions. In other cases the appearance of information about certain technology developments and innovations precedes the identification of a problem. Emerging trends and innovations are monitored by DETECON Inc. and assessed with respect to their potential influence on Deutsche Telekom AG's business or innovation strategy. An example for technological trends which lead to an innovation need from outside Deutsche Telekom is Voice-over-Internet protocol (VOIP) which, in the long run, can be considered a threat to Telekom's integrated services digital network (ISDN) landline product.

In summary, a forecasting process at DETECON Inc. can be initiated in basically two ways (Figure 5): either problem precedes information or information precedes problem. Furthermore, the technology forecasting process for Deutsche Telekom AG can be considered an iterative process. A first iteration gives a broad overview of potential interesting technologies which are then communicated on a very high level towards Deutsche Telekom AG. On the base of interest, Deutsche Telekom AG requests an additional iteration with an increased analysis depth and a more precise technology scope which results in the development of *technology profile documents*. The process leaves DETECON Inc. in a phase comparable to step VI of the general process of technology forecasting for innovation management. From this point on, Deutsche Telekom AG is responsible for the remaining steps and activities and the integration of the acquired knowledge into its innovation strategy.

In the light of the previous section's results, a system based on the central utilization of topic maps seems most promising to improve technology forecasting's efficiency.

Figure 5. Technology-forecasting process at DETECON, Inc. for Deutsche Telekom AG

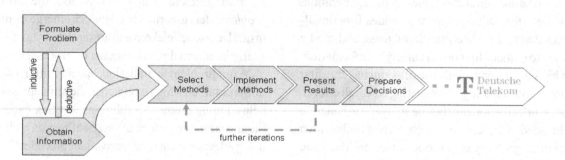

One characterizing aspect of technology forecasting at DETECON Inc. is the flexible scope required by the different steps and activities inside the process. Topic maps can be tailored to suit this flexible use. Regarding the process at DETECON Inc., the development of a single comprehensive topic map that represents the applied domain knowledge's basic structure as, for example, technologies and their relations and influences, could offer a solution. Sophisticated methods, like a topic map concept called scope, can then be used to restrict this topic map to the necessary range for single activities. This is sufficient because all DETECON Inc.'s forecasting activities deal with technology and innovation developments and their influences on Deutsche Telekom's technology and business situation. A topic map that has been built and maintained for the corresponding domain, and which can be tailored to represent only the available information's subparts through the exploitation of topic maps' scope attribute, provides an efficient solution to the flexibility requirement.

Obviously, the nature of a topic map also facilitates the organization and reuse of information, and therefore fulfills another requirement with respect to technology forecasting at DETECON Inc.: information that has been used once can be stored in a repository and can be accessed through the topic map. It is also associated with analyses, contacts, or other related information. Therefore, knowledge structures, once generated,

can be represented by the topic map, facilitating the recovery of these structures. In addition, a topic map can be used to categorize new information by determining the topics that occur in the new information. This functionality can be combined with automated information retrieval methods. The information is retrieved from a source (most likely within the WWW); it is analyzed with respect to the occurring topics, and then added to the information repository. This process facilitates the identification of valuable new information without the need to analyze all new information manually. Because the information is available through the topic map, it can be accessed when needed.

Switching control of and responsibility for the process from DETECON Inc. to Deutsche Telekom AG, leads to knowledge transfer being facilitated—another requirement of a system to support technology forecasting at DETECON Inc. Once Deutsche Telekom AG considers a technology interesting and relevant, a more detailed technology profile is created, which is then sent to Deutsche Telekom AG. The integration of the mentioned profile documents into the structure of a topic map, as well as their association with the main topics and further relevant information about the corresponding technologies, facilitates this task. The technology-related knowledge can be transferred with the help of the topic map by allowing access to the profile documents and their related information. Personal meetings can then be used to discuss the technology and business consequences, creating additional knowledge that goes beyond the technology itself.

The challenge of such a system is, however, maintaining the topic map. A fully manual maintenance implies the awareness of new developments. Therefore, methods have to be found that can facilitate this task by suggesting new topics and associations. Statistical methods as applied within automatic indexing can provide a useful starting point to solve this problem.

It is obvious that the intense communication and collaboration between the two organizations cannot only rely on an underlying knowledge management system. Therefore, it can be considered valuable future research to include non-codified knowledge management processes into the analysis of knowledge management support within technology forecasting. One starting point can be to map the socialization, externalization, internalization and combination (SECI) model as presented by Nonaka and Takeuchi of organizational knowledge creation with the technology forecasting process to determine those stages which rely on non-codified knowledge creation to improve the overall forecasting process (Nonaka & Takeuchi, 1995, p. 70).

In summary, topic maps provide the needed degree of flexibility, facilitate information organization and reuse as well as knowledge transfer. Therefore, a system that is based on topic maps will be considered the solution to the increasing difficulties with technology forecasting at DETECON Inc.

CONCLUSION

As shown, knowledge management technologies play an important role in supporting the technology forecasting process as a part of strategic innovation management and overall competitive strategies. As there are several possible knowledge management technologies, the real task for technology forecasting begins with the selection of the appropriate technologies for each process step. We have therefore evaluated several knowledge management technologies, each explained according to its main characteristics, benefits, and constraints, focusing on its support of the technology forecasting process's different steps. We have furthermore aligned them all in the proposed context-complexity matrix. The successful application of our theoretical findings was revealed by the case study, realized at DETECON Inc. and Deutsche Telekom AG.

FUTURE RESEARCH DIRECTIONS

To enrich our proposed context-complexity model, we envisage the following areas of future research:

- First, within innovation management, most forecasting is done via the analysis of information as exemplified by DETECON Inc. and Deutsche Telekom AG. We have to determine whether the integration of other forecasting methods, for example, extrapolation methods, into the supporting system could lead to a higher forecasting quality and decreased uncertainty, with the aim of automating a major part of the forecasting process and achieving improved decision support.
- Second, we have to determine whether knowledge management technologies are also capable of supporting single technology forecasting methods.
- Third, we have to validate and expand our findings in further real-world cases in order to verify the theoretical results and ideas of this chapter and to identify further aspects that could potentially increase technology forecasting efficiency, improve innovation strategy formulation, and thus create and sustain competitive advantage.

- Fourth, efficient knowledge management also depends on organizational issues to a certain extent. While this chapter considers knowledge management technologies to be the focal point for knowledge management support within technology forecasting, we have to determine to what extent organizational knowledge management concepts influence technology forecasting. We assume that organizational concepts depend on the structure of a forecasting process. Processes which are conducted completely inside a single company might benefit more from organizational knowledge management concepts than processes which a scattered over one, two, or more companies. Further research in this area should discuss which combination of technological and organizational process support results into the highest value for competitive advantage and company success.

- Fifth, the main objective of this chapter is to introduce a technology focused framework for integrating knowledge management into quantitative technology forecasting. However, further research should also focus on the support of qualitative technological forecasting, for example, using methods such as scenarios, as well as on the support by noncodified knowledge management processes like those defined by Nonaka and Takeuchi's SECI model and respective technologies such as collaboration supporting tools.

The development of the context-complexity matrix and its application to selected knowledge management technologies has shown that, within technology forecasting, increasing information structure complexity leads to an increasing need for context explication. Information repositories are less useful without the application of explicit metacontexts that facilitate the discovery of needed information. While technologies like data mining or case-based reasoning provide only a marginal efficiency increase, topic maps possess a broad applicability and have the potential to increase efficiency greatly.

By returning the conclusion to the level of innovation and knowledge strategies, we can state that technology forecasting, which was originally a means of supporting an innovation strategy definition, simultaneously supports a knowledge strategy definition by presenting a basis for knowledge-scope determination. The integration of knowledge management technologies and technology forecasting by applying the proposed framework, can therefore be considered a method with which to support business and knowledge strategy alignment on an operational level.

REFERENCES

Aamodt, A., & Nygård, M. (1995). Different roles and mutual dependencies of data, information, and knowledge: An AI perspective on their integration. *Data and Knowledge Engineering, 16*, 191-222.

Aamodt, A., & Plaza, E. (1994). Case-based reasoning: Foundational issues, methodological variations, and system approaches. *AI Communications, 7*(1), 39-59.

Abou-Zeid, E. (2005). Alignment of business and knowledge management strategies. In M. Khosrow-Pour (Ed.), *Encyclopedia of information science and technology* (Vol. 1, pp. 98-103). Hershey, PA: Idea Group Publishing.

Armstrong, J.S. (2001). *Principles of forecasting: A handbook for researchers and practitioners.* Boston: Kluwer.

Benjamins, V.R., Fensel, D., & Gómez Pérez, A.G. (1998). Knowledge management through ontologies. In *Proceedings of the 2nd International Conference on Practical Aspects of Knowledge*

Management (PAKM98) (pp. 5.1-5.12). Basel, Switzerland.

Bergmann, R., Althoff, K., Breen, S., Göker, M., Manago, M., Traphöner, R., & Wess, S. (2003). *Developing industrial case-based reasoning applications* (2nd ed.). Berlin: Springer-Verlag.

Bright, J.R. (1979). Technology forecasting as an influence on technological innovation: Past examples and future expectations. In M.J. Baker (Ed.), *Industrial innovation* (pp. 228-255). Basingstoke, UK: The Macmillan Press Ltd.

Burgelman, R.A., Maidique, M.A., & Wheelwright, S.C. (1996). *Strategic management of technology and innovation* (2nd ed.). Boston: Irwin/McGraw-Hill.

DeLurgio, S.A. (1998). *Forecasting principles and applications.* Boston: Irwin/McGraw-Hill.

Dey, A.K., & Abowd, G.D. (2000). *Towards a better understanding of context and context-awareness.* Atlanta: Graphics, Visualization and Usability Center and College of Computing, Georgia Institute of Technology.

Drucker, P.F. (1996). *Managing in a time of great change.* Boston: Butterwort-Heinemann.

Gaines, B.R., & Shaw, M.L.G. (1986). A learning model for forecasting the future of information technology. *Future Computing Systems, 1*(1), 31-69.

Garshol, L.M. (2002). What are topic maps? Retrieved May 22, 2007, from http://www.XML.com

Geschka, H. (1992). The strategic aspect in the process of innovation. In H. Geschka & H. Hubner (Eds.), *Innovation strategies: Theoretical approaches - experiences - improvements* (pp. 69-78). Amsterdam: Elsevier Science Publishers.

Granger, C.W.J. (1989). *Forecasting in business and economics.* San Diego: Academic Press.

Han, J., & Kamber, M. (2001). *Data mining: Concepts and techniques.* San Diego: Academic Press.

Ingwersen, P. (1992). *Information retrieval interaction.* London: Taylor Graham Publishing.

Lenz, M., Bartsch-Spörl, B., Burkhardt, H., & Wess, S. (1998). *Case-based reasoning technology: From foundations to applications.* Berlin: Springer-Verlag.

Lusti, M. (2002). *Data warehousing und data mining: Eine Einführung in entscheidungs-unterstützende Systeme.* Berlin: Springer-Verlag.

Martino, J.P. (1983). *Technological forecasting for decision making.* New York: Elsevier Science Publishers.

Nonaka, I., & Takeuchi, H. (1995). *The knowledge-creating company: How Japanese companies create the dynamics of innovation.* New York: Oxford University Press.

O'Hare, M. (1988). *Innovate! How to gain and sustain competitive advantage.* Oxford: Basil Blackwell Ltd.

Rath, H.H., & Pepper, S. (1999). Topic maps: Introduction and Allegro. In *Proceedings of the Markup Technologies, 99.* Philadelphia, USA.

Reger, G. (2001). Technology foresight in companies: From an indicator to a network and process perspective. *Technology Analysis & Strategic Management, 13*(4), 533-553.

Riempp, G. (2004). *Integrierte wissensmanagement-systeme—Architektur und praktische anwendung.* Berlin: Springer.

Riesbeck, C.K., & Schank, R.C. (1989). *Inside case-based reasoning.* Hillsdale: Lawrence Erlbaum Associates.

Salton, G., & McGill, M.J. (1983). *Introduction to modern information retrieval.* New York: McGraw-Hill.

Smolnik, S., Kremer, S., & Kolbe, L. (2005). Continuum of context explication: Knowledge discovery through process-oriented portals. *International Journal of Knowledge Management, 1*(1), 27-46.

Stewart, T.A. (1997). *Intellectual capital: The new wealth of organization.* Currency New York: Doubleday.

Vanston, J.H. (1996). Technology forecasting: A practical tool for rationalizing the R&D process. *The New Telecom Quarterly, 4*(1), 57-62. Technology Futures Inc.

Zelewski, S. (2001). Ontologien—ein Überblick über betriebswirtschaftliche Anwendungsbereiche. In Workshop Forschung in schnellebiger Zeit", Beitrag 5, Appenzell.

Additional Reading

Alavi, M., & Leidner, D.E. (1999). Knowledge management systems: Issues, challenges, and benefits. *Communication of the AIS, 1*(2), Article 7.

Alavi, M., & Leidner, D.E. (2001, March). Review: Knowledge management and knowledge management systems: Conceptual foundations and research issues. *MIS Quarterly, 25*(1), 107-136. MIS Quarterly and The Society for Information Management, Minneapolis, Minnesota.

Allesch, J. (1986). Situative model of the innovation process in the area of tension between market and technology. In H. Hubner (Ed.), *The Art and Science of Innovation Management* (pp. 3-13). Amsterdam: Elsevier Science Publishers.

Baeza-Yates, R.A., & Ribeiro-Neto, B. (1999). *Modern information retrieval.* Boston: Addison-Wesley Publishing.

Berners-Lee, T., Hendler, J., & Lassila, O. (2001). The Semantic Web. *Scientific American, 284*(5), 34-43. Stuttgart: Verlagsgruppe Georg von Holtzbrinck.

Bruckner, R.M., Ling, T.W., Mangisengi, O., & Tjoa, A.M. (2001). A framework for a multidimensional OLAP model using topic maps. In *Proceedings of the Second International Conference on Web Information Systems Engineering (WISE 2001), Web Semantics Workshop* (Vol. 2, pp. 109-118), Kyoto, Japan. Los Alamitos CA: IEEE Computer Society Press.

Davenport, T.H., & Prusak, L. (1998). *Working knowledge: How organizations manage what they know.* Boston: Harvard Business School Press, Boston (Excerpt from the ACM Digital Library). Retrieved May 22, 2007, from http://www.acm.org/ubiquity/book/t_davenport_1.html

David, F.R. (1986). Fundamentals of strategic management. London: Merrill Publishing Company.

Dussauge, P., Ramanantsoa, B., & Hart, S. (1992). *Strategic technology management: integrating product technology into global business strategies for the 1990s.* Hoboken, NJ: John Wiley & Sons Ltd.

Fayyad, U.M., Piatetsky-Shapiro, G., Smyth, P., & Uthurusamy, R. (1996). Advances in knowledge discovery and data mining. Menlo Park, CA: American Association for Artificial Intelligence.

Fensel, D. (2001). *Ontologies: A silver bullet for knowledge management and electronic commerce.* Berlin: Springer.

Fensel, D., Wahlster, W., Lieberman, H., & Hendler, J. (2003). *Spinning the Semantic Web: Bringing the World Wide Web to its full potential.* Cambridge, MA: MIT Press.

Frakes, W.B., & Baeza-Yates, R.A. (1992). *Information retrieval: Data structures & algorithms.* Upple Saddle River, NJ: Prentice Hall.

Gallupe, B. (2001, March). Knowledge management systems: Surveying the landscape. *International Journal of Management Reviews, 3*(1) 61-77. Oxford: Blackwell Publishing Limited.

Gruber, T.R. (1993). A translation approach to portable ontology specifications. *Knowledge Acquisition, 5*(2), 199-220.

Gruninger, M., & Lee, J. (2002). Ontology applications and design. *Communications of the ACM, 45*(2), 39-41.

Hovy, E. (2003). Using an ontology to simplify data access. *Communications of the ACM, 46*(1), 47-49.

Kolodner, J. (1993). *Case-based reasoning.* San Mateo, CA: Morgan Kaufmann Publishers.

Loveridge, D. (1997). *Technology forecasting and foresight: Pedantry or disciplined vision?* The University of Manchester, Policy Research in Engineering, Science and Technology.

Lyles, M.A., & Schwenk, C.R. (1992, March). Top management, strategy and organizational knowledge structures. *Journal of Management Studies, 29*(2), 155-174. Oxford: Blackwell Publishing Limited.

Maedche, A., Motik, B., Stojanovic, L., Studer, R., & Volz, R. (2003). Ontologies for enterprise knowledge management. *IEEE Intelligent Systems, 18*(2), 26-33.

Maier, R. (2002). *Knowledge management systems: Information and communication technologies for knowledge management.* Berlin: Springer.

Martin, B.R. (1995). Foresight in science and technology. *Technology Analysis & Strategic Management, 7*(2), 139-168.

McInerney, C. (2002). Knowledge management and the dynamic nature of knowledge. *Journal of the American Society for Information Science and Technology, 53*(12), 1009-1018.

Nonaka, I. (1994, February). A dynamic theory of organizational knowledge creation. *Organization Science: A Journal of the Institute of Management Sciences, 5*(1), 14-37. Linthicum, MD: Institute for Operations Research (INFORMS).

Nonaka, I., Toyama, R., & Konno, N. (2001). SECI, ba and leadership: A unified model of dynamic knowledge creation. In I. Nonaka & D.J. Teece (Eds.), *Managing industrial knowledge* (pp. 13-43). London: SAGE Publications.

Pao, M.L. (1989). *Concepts of information retrieval.* Englewood, CO: Libraries Unlimited.

Park, J., & Hunting, S. (2003). *XML topic maps: Creating and using topic maps for the Web.* Boston: Addison-Wesley.

Pearce II, J.A., & Robinson, R.B., Jr. (2000). *Strategic management: Formulation, implementation, and control.* Boston: Irwin/McGraw-Hill.

Polanyi, M. (1966). *The tacit dimension.* Gloucester: Routledge & Kegan Paul.

Rumelt, R.P., Schendel, D., & Teece, D.J. (1991). Strategic management and economics. *Strategic Management Journal, 12*, 5-29.

Russell, S.J., & Norvig, P. (2003). *Artificial intelligence: A modern approach* (2nd ed.). Upper Saddle River, NJ: Pearson Education.

Sanchez, R., & Heene, A. (2004). *The new strategic management: Organization, competition, and competence.* New York: John Wiley & Sons.

Smolnik, S., & Erdmann, I. (2003). Visual navigation of distributed knowledge structures in groupware-based organizational memories [Special Issue: Knowledge Management and Organizations: Process, System, and Strategy]. *Business Process Management Journal, 9*(3), 261-280. West Yorkshire, UK: Emerald, Bradford.

Sowa, J.F. (1991). *Principles of semantic networks.* San Mateo, CA: Morgan Kaufmann Publishers.

Sowa, J.F. (2000). *Knowledge representation: Logical, philosophical, and computational foundations.* Pacific Grove, CA: Brooks/Cole.

Tsoukas, H. (2003). Do we really understand "tacit knowledge"? In M. Easterby-Smith & M.A. Lyles (Eds.), *The Blackwell handbook of organizational learning and knowledge management* (pp. 410-427). Malden, MA: Blackwell Publishers.

Tsoukas, H., & Vladimirou, E. (2001). What is organizational knowledge? *Journal of Management Studies, 38*(7), 973-993.

Von Krogh, G., Ichijo, K., & Nonaka, I. (2000). *Enabling knowledge creation: How to unlock the mystery of tacit knowledge and release the power of innovation.* New York: Oxford University Press.

Von Krogh, G., & Roos, J. (1996). The epistemological challenge: Managing knowledge and intellectual capital. *European Management Journal, 14*(4), 333-337. Amsterdam: Elsevier B. V.

Weiss, S.M., Indurkhya, N., Zhang, T., & Damerau, F. (2004). *Text mining: Predictive methods for analyzing unstructured information.* New York: Springer.

Wiig, K.M. (1993). *Knowledge management foundations: Thinking about thinking—How people and organizations create, represent, and use knowledge.* Arlington, TX: Schema Press.

Wiig, K.M. (1999). *Knowledge management: An emerging discipline rooted in a long history.* Knowledge Research Institute, Inc.

Zack, M.H. (1999). Managing codified knowledge. *Sloan Management Review, 40*(4), 45-58.

Section III
Business and KM Strategies Alignment

Chapter IX
Knowledge Strategic Alignment:
Research Framework, Models, and Concepts

Derek A. Asoh
Southern Illinois University, USA
University of Yaounde I, Cameroon

Salvatore Belardo
University at Albany State University of New York, USA

Peter Duchessi
University at Albany State University of New York, USA

ABSTRACT

Knowledge has been recognized as a key organizational resource. Yet, despite commitment in knowledge management (KM), many researchers and organizations overlook the need to engage in the alignment of knowledge-related resources with business-related strategies (knowledge strategic alignment). Although many reasons may be advanced for the lack of research and practice on knowledge strategic alignment, two reasons stand out. First, the alignment concept is difficult to understand and measure (Chan, Huff, Barclay & Copeland, 1997), and second, the KM field is relatively new and lacks appropriate frameworks, models, and methodologies for expected research and practice (Earl, 2001). The objectives of this chapter are twofold: The first is an attempt to respond to the call for frameworks, models, and methodologies for research in KM; and the second is an attempt to "simplify" the understanding of the alignment concept within the KM field. To attain both objectives, we first review the KM literature, and then opine on research from the alignment "reference fields" (Information Systems/Information Technology (IS/IT) and strategic management), where the alignment concept is well researched and practiced to propose a framework for research on alignment in the KM field. We identify relevant research models, discuss conceptualizations of alignment in KM, and illustrate the application of the framework, models, and alignment concepts.

INTRODUCTION

The recognition of knowledge as the new important production resource of the firm has motivated researchers and practitioners to give considerable thought to how to manage knowledge. As a result, knowledge management (KM) has emerged as a formal field of research and practice. However, as a formal field of activity, KM is still in its infancy and is not well understood by many organizations (Earl, 2001; Zack, 1999a)

Although some adopters of KM, such as Skandia, BP Amoco, Dow Chemical, IBM, Hewlett-Packard (HP), Bain & Co., and Xerox (Belardo & Belardo, 2002; Earl, 2001), have realized and reported significant benefits from their efforts, a good number of others appear to still be struggling with KM. For these struggling organizations, significant benefits are yet to be accrued because of multiple difficulties associated with the initiation and implementation of KM. Earl (2001) eloquently describes the state of affairs and the difficulties confronting organizations that have embarked on the formal but relatively new practice of managing knowledge. Following a study aimed at developing a taxonomy of the strategies used by organizations engaged in KM, Earl (2001) notes: "once organizations embraced the concept that knowledge could make a difference to performance and that somehow it should be managed better, they often have not known where to start … initiating a knowledge management program was a nontrivial issue. One approach was to appoint a chief knowledge officer … but then he faced the same dilemma—where or how to begin" (p. 216).

Questions regarding where or how to begin, and even how, when, and why to proceed, in KM are implicit in the concept of alignment. Though highly developed and practiced in other fields, such as information systems/information technology (IS/IT) and management, little or no research has been carried out on alignment in the KM field (Asoh, Belardo, & Duchessi, 2003).

One is left to wonder why, given the value of knowledge and the interest in managing knowledge, research on alignment of knowledge-related resources with business strategies has lagged compared to research on alignment of other resources with business strategies. One explanation for the paucity of research on alignment in the KM field is the absence of research frameworks and models. In fact, to further the discipline and practice of KM, Earl (2001) suggests "there is a need for models, frameworks, or methodologies that can help [researchers and] corporate executives both to understand the sorts of knowledge management initiatives or investments that are possible and to identify those that make sense in their context" (p. 216).

This chapter is a contribution in response to the call for models, frameworks, or methodologies in KM by Earl (2001). Specifically, we draw from the body of knowledge from the KM field and the IS/IT and management fields (referred here as the "alignment reference fields") to propose an alignment research reference framework to guide research and practice of knowledge strategic alignment. We also highlight alignment research models and elaborate on various conceptualizations of alignment for knowledge strategic alignment. We are interested in strategic knowledge alignment because knowledge has been recognized as a key organizational resource; yet, despite commitment in KM, many organizations overlook the need to align knowledge-related resources with business and other organizational strategies, just as is done with other resources. We believe researchers and executives would stand to benefit from an understanding of the application and implications of the alignment concept when it comes to committing and engaging in the management of today's most valuable resource—knowledge.

The rest of this chapter is organized in seven sections. In section two, we present the background to our discussions. We first synthesize the literature on alignment and its importance as a general organizational and specific KM concept. Next we review the current literature on alignment in the KM field and conclude the section by reflecting on the reasons for the lack of research on alignment in the KM field. In section three, we discuss theories that cast knowledge as a resource and KM as a strategic imperative. We end the section by delineating key alignment-related KM issues. In section four, we present some lessons on alignment from the "alignment reference fields" which we think are important for research and practice on alignment in the KM field. Specifically, we examine IT alignment models, IT strategic levels, and various conceptualizations of alignment. In section five, we opine on the background discussions and lessons from the "alignment reference fields" to propose a two-level strategy concept in KM. Subsequently, we propose and discuss a generic alignment reference framework for KM research, anchoring knowledge-, business-, and information-related strategies as its dimensions. In section six, we highlight various alignment models, and elaborate on various conceptualizations of alignment in the KM field based on conceptualizations from the "reference fields". We illustrate the application of the generic alignment framework with a discussion of research questions, constructs, model testing, and data analytical techniques. We conclude the chapter in section seven with a discussion of the limitation and contribution of our work and direction for future research.

BACKGROUND

Alignment and the Importance of Alignment to Organizations

Alignment has been noted as a consistent perennial top management issue in the IS/IT field worldwide (Gottschalk, 2000; Luftman, 2003; Moody, 2003). But what is alignment? Alignment is a general concept that pertains to the organization and its environment (internal and external). Miles and Snow (1978) point out that the organization is "a total system—a collection of people, structures, and processes that must be effectively aligned with the organization's chosen environment" (p. 6). What this means is that alignment implies or requires strategic fit and functional integration respectively for the external and internal environments (Henderson & Venkatraman, 1999). Alternatively, alignment is considered consistency between organizational functions and overall business strategy (BS) of the firm (Porter, 1996). But why is alignment so important?

Several arguments are advanced in support of the importance of alignment. For example, aligning organizational processes, including strategic decisions in general, leads to competitive advantage (Powell, 1992) because alignment improves performance results (Hall, 2002). Empirical research indicates a positive performance impact of environment-strategy alignment (Miller, 1992; Venkatraman & Prescott, 1990). Strategic fit among various organizational functions creates competitive advantage and superior profits to organizations (Porter, 1996). This is possible because among many things, fit means consistency between each function performed and the overall BS of the firm. Such consistency ensures that the competitive advantages of various activities or functions accumulate and do not cancel themselves out. Furthermore, when there is fit, activities are reinforcing, and it is possible to optimize coordination and other efforts in the organization (Porter, 1996). Superior fit among primary and support value chain activities creates an activity system, which helps firms establish and exploit their strategic positions (Hoskisson, Hitt, & Ireland, 2004).

For the specific case of KM, alignment is important because being able to use knowledge requires that knowledge be aligned with itself (Abou-Zeid, 2002). Equally, being able to accurately identify, capture, transfer, and apply knowledge within the organization is predicated on the alignment of these activities with the organizational strategic objectives (Malone, 2002). For effective KM to take place, it is necessary to align knowledge processes with the organization's mission, vision, strategy, and goal (van den Hooff, Vijvers & de Ridder, 2003). Furthermore, in order to be able to effectively manage knowledge, organizations must undertake some significant cultural changes (Belardo & Belardo, 2002). But it turns out that lack of fit is a major impediment to successful change implementation (Saint-Onge, 1999). In addition, the lack of alignment leads to poor strategic planning, which in turn, leads to misallocation of resources (Cascella, 2002; Luftman, Papp, & Brier, 2002) which is counterproductive for organizational performance (OP).

Finally, since many organizations engage in KM so that they can develop the core competences (Prahalad & Hamel, 1999) they need for innovation and dynamic capabilities (Teece, Pisano & Shuen, 1999) in order to stay competitive, KM can be characterized as an effort to develop and secure capabilities by the firm to perform in its environment. In discussing the tension that exists between the strategic requirements of the environment and the capabilities of organizations, Saint-Onge (1999) comments:

In order to keep pace with a fast changing business environment, organizations have to continuously regenerate their core strategies. If their strategies are out of phase with the business environment, the enhancement of internal effectiveness will not significantly improve performance, while on the other hand, the adoption of strategies must take into account the capabilities of the organization to implement them. (p. 228)

The above quote stresses the importance of aligning capabilities and other resources with strategy in order to better attain performance goals.

Alignment in KM would mean that KM activities are being directed to provide knowledge-related resources and capabilities that are in line with the needs and priorities of the business processes they support. Given the foregoing discussion, a closer look at knowledge as a resource as well as the strategic perspective of KM will enhance understanding and the ability to develop appropriate frameworks and models for alignment research in KM. But before we proceed, we first take a look at the current state of alignment research in the reference (IS/IT and management) and KM fields.

Alignment Research in the KM Field

Unlike the IS/IT and management fields, where significant work has been done on alignment, our literature search revealed a paucity of alignment studies in the KM field. We found only three studies on alignment which we consider worthy to review here (the first two, theoretical, and the last one, empirical).

The first theoretical work (Abou-Zeid, 2002) builds on the IT strategic alignment model (ITSAM) (Henderson & Venkatraman, 1999) and suggests that the alignment of business and knowledge strategies is the basis upon which business value can be realized from KM investments. The author proposes a knowledge management strategic alignment model (KMSAM) as a direct translation of the ITSAM. The premise of KMSAM is that "the effective and efficient use of organizational knowledge requires the alignment of knowledge strategies with business strategies" (p. 159). Based on this premise, Abou-Zeid (2002) discusses the external and internal knowledge strategy domains as a direct mapping of the elements within ITSAM.

Although Abou-Zeid (2002) succinctly discusses the KM initiative at Buckman Laboratories to illustrate the "interpretive power" of KMSAM, it is not clear however, how researchers could pursue empirical research on alignment in KM. Nevertheless, the author recognizes the necessity for empirical research and calls for cross-sectional and longitudinal studies of KM initiatives that would help identify the patterns of knowledge and business strategies alignment.

The second theoretical work on alignment in KM research (Asoh et al., 2003) builds on ITSAM (Henderson & Venkatraman, 1999) and the IT strategic levels model (Earl, 1989) to propose a knowledge strategic alignment model (KSAM). The basis for KSAM is that knowledge is a resource, just as any other resource that needs to be aligned with business strategy if the firm expects to derive maximum benefit from it. Like Abou-Zeid (2002). Asoh et al. (2003) recognize the need for empirical studies but do not provide any framework for researchers interested in pursuing alignment in KM research.

The third and only empirical work (Asoh, 2004) builds on the works of Abou-Zeid (2002) and Asoh et al. (2003). Asoh (2004) elaborated the idea of strategic knowledge orientation with two components (knowledge- and learning-oriented). The premise is that knowledge and learning are intrinsically related and strategic knowledge orientation requires both components. The author subsequently investigated the alignment of the knowledge-related component with business strategy. Asoh (2004) considered alignment in terms of mediation, and found that while both KS and BS individually and positively impact OP, BS was a better mediator of the KS–OP link than KS was of the BS–OP link.

From the above review, it is evident that alignment continues to remain a missing link in KM research (Asoh et al., 2003). We reflect on some of the reasons for the paucity of alignment research in the KM field.

Reasons for Lack of Alignment Research in the KM field

We believe alignment is a missing link in KM research for a number of reasons. First, the field lacks appropriate frameworks and models required for alignment research. Second, the different perspectives of knowledge and KM may mean that researchers cannot come to terms concerning what exactly has to be aligned. Third, there is persistent confusion between the terms information and knowledge. Some researchers incorrectly use the terms interchangeable (see Alavi & Leidner, 1999, 2001 for various definitions). Fourth, because of the confusion between information and knowledge, researchers may think they are working on KM when in fact they are researching IS/IT, there is a similar degree of confusion between knowledge strategy (KS) and knowledge management strategy (KMS). Again, some authors use these terms interchangeably or fail to make any distinctions (e. g., Hansen, Nohria & Tierney, 2001). Others even create new appellations such as KM styles (e. g., Choi & Lee, 2003) that add to the confusion. Consequently, readers are left to believe that KS and KMS mean the same thing, which is incorrect. Finally, researchers may be avoiding research on alignment in KM because the alignment concept is "difficult to understand and measure" (Chan et al., 1997, p. 126).

ALIGNMENT-RELATED PERSPECTIVES OF KNOWLEDGE AND KM

Resource Perspective of Knowledge

Many perspectives of knowledge have been discussed in the literature. Within the IS/IT fields, the most elaborate discussions are those by Alavi and Leidner (2001) and Holsapple and Joshi (2002). According to Alavi and Leidner (2001), knowledge can be examined and understood from six perspectives: (1) knowledge in relation to data and information, (2) knowledge as a state of mind, (3) knowledge as an object to be stored and manipulated, (4) knowledge as a process, (5) knowledge as access to information, and (6) knowledge as capability. Although knowledge in any of the above perspectives may be amenable to alignment, the perspective of knowledge as a resource has not been directly and widely discussed in the IS/IT literature. It is possible to consider each of the six perspectives (and especially the capability perspective of knowledge) as a resource. This consideration is reinforced by the work of Holsapple and Joshi (2002).

Taking a knowledge-centric view of organizations, Holsapple and Joshi (2002) maintain that the knowledge of an organization can be stored, embedded, or represented as any or a combination of six distinct kinds of resources: (1) participants' knowledge, (2) culture, (3) infrastructure, (4) knowledge artifacts, (5) purpose, and (6) strategy. Just as in the case of the six knowledge perspectives proposed by Alavi and Leidner (2001), each of the six kinds of knowledge resources proposed by Holsapple and Joshi (2002) is amendable to alignment. For the purpose of this chapter, we will discuss alignment of strategy-related resources. Aligning other resources (especially culture, participants' knowledge, human resources, and purpose) within the organization is equally important. However, discussing only the alignment of strategy-related resources here is meant to ensure a better focus for the chapter, and in no way undermines the necessity to align other organizational resources.

With limited research on knowledge resources in the IS/IT field, for a better understanding of knowledge as a resource, we turn to the strategic management field (the other "alignment reference field"), where key theories of the resource perspective of knowledge have been elaborated. Attention to the strategic management field is of merit because knowledge strategic alignment compels direct and indirect discussions of strategy and management. Examining knowledge as a resource will pave the way for a discussion on the strategic perspective of KM, since as a resource, knowledge must be aligned with all areas of strategy for the efficient and effective conduit of the organization's operational and strategic activities (Zack, 2002).

Researchers and practitioners have long been struggling to understand organizational performance (OP) differentials primarily in terms of traditional production resources such as land, labor, and capital owned or available to organizations. As these resources are subject to inevitable economic laws of diminishing returns, a wider view on OP determinants has been in order.

Penrose (1959) theory of firm growth set the pace for broadening the set of firm resources. According to Penrose, a firm is a bundle of resources that can be employed for the provision of different services for production opportunities. Such resources include not only the tangible things a firm can buy (e. g., land, labor, capital, information, etc.) but also the intangible things it possesses or develops (e. g., capabilities, culture, knowledge, etc.) (Hall, 1999).

The subsequent development of the resource-based view of the firm (Wernerfelt, 1984) contributed to the recognition that intangible resources are determinants of competitive advantage and performance (Barney, 1991; Grant, 1999). Researchers characterize intangible resources from various perspectives in attempts to better understand performance. For example, Barney (1991) indicates that a resource has to be valuable, rare, and inimitable before it can be considered as a source of competitive advantage. In essence, resources are the basis of effective business strategy (BS), and to sustain a profitable strategy, a resource must pass external market value tests including inimitability, durability, appropriability, substitutability, and competitive superiority (Collis & Montgomery, 1999).

Among intangible resources, knowledge is *the only resource that readily meets all the criteria of sustained competitive advantage and passes all the external market tests*. This versatility of knowledge as a key resource ushered attention toward the knowledge-based view of the firm (Grant, 1996). This view considers firms to be composed of knowledge-holding individuals where the firm's role is to coordinate these individuals so that they can create value for the firm. The rationale is that knowledge endows firms with knowledge-derived intangibles that account for firm performance differentials. Such intangibles include core competencies (Prahalad & Hamel, 1999) and dynamic capabilities (Teece et al., 1999).

Knowledge has also been recognized as a (re)source of innovation (Drucker, 2002), and plays a role in the development of firms' innovative capacity, another intangible that impacts performance.

Strategic Perspective of KM

As organizations differentiate themselves in the business environment in terms of their knowledge (Zack, 1999a), it matters where they focus regarding exploring and exploiting knowledge (Bierly & Chakrabarti, 1999) and/or codifying and personalizing knowledge (Hansen et al., 2001). Whatever the focus, the ultimate goal is to make knowledge available to the right person at the right time to ensure performance (Baird & Henderson, 2001). However, it cannot be taken for granted, because something is being done regarding knowledge in organizations; the strategic management of knowledge is always implied. Although some authors have already articulated the strategic management of knowledge as discussed later, no models or frameworks have been adequately developed and advanced to meet the needs of researchers and practitioners.

The necessity for a strategic perspective of managing knowledge is based on the grounds of the resource-based view of knowledge (RBV) and the knowledge-based view (KBV) of the firm. Both views culminate in the recognition and acceptance that society has moved from the industrial age business era to the knowledge age business era (Lieibold, Probst & Gilbert, 2002; Zack, 2002).

According to Zack (2002), if the RBV and KBV are to be useful, firms must explicitly address questions regarding the creation, development, and maintenance of knowledge as a strategic resource. A strategic perspective of knowledge requires firms to close their knowing-doing gaps. That is to say, firms must balance their knowledge resources and knowledge processing capabilities with the knowledge required to create products and services to meet customers' needs in ways superior to competitors.

Lieibold et al. (2002) argue that the management task today is not only radically different from what it used to be, but it also requires a strategic view of KM. Specifically, these authors maintain that the new task of management today is to figure out:

How organizations can continuously adapt, shape, change, innovate, create and network to survive and prosper in global markets environments that are quickly becoming more unpredictable, with organizations that have become more virtual, mobile, and porous, with technologies that are becoming revolutionary and integrative, and with people that are more independent, knowledgeable, assertive and mobile. A new overall organizational purpose, or strategic thrust, seems to emerge [as a way of competing in the knowledge age business era]: unlocking the mystery of organizational self-renewal, resulting from knowledge-based creativity and innovation. (p. 18)

Since creativity and innovation are the cornerstones of performance, if knowledge is recognized as the (re)source of innovation and key performance differentiator in today's economy, then, in order to address the emergent management task, summarized earlier by Lieibold et al. (2002) and Zack (2002), a strategic perspective of KM is an imperative and not an option.

A strategic perspective of KM requires a minimum understanding of the concept of business strategy (BS). Without going into elaborate discussions and definitions of BS from the strategic management field, it is sufficient to understand that BS is about direction and cohesion, and its main elements are arenas, vehicles, differentiators, staging, and economic logic (Hambrick & Fredrickson, 2001). When KM is considered from a strategic perspective, the management of organizational knowledge is grounded in business strategy through the process of alignment. What this means is that the strategic perspective of KM considers the role knowledge plays in all elements of BS stipulated by Hambrick and Fredrickson (2001).

For strategic KM, the arena is where the firm should leverage its knowledge; the vehicles are the means for ensuring that knowledge is made available in the arena; the differentiators refer to how the firm distinguishes itself in the marketplace by virtue of its knowledge assets; staging refers to the nature of learning and the type of knowledge base developed in the arena; and economic logic for strategic management of knowledge is reflected by the essence and subsequent impact of the knowledge differentiating activities (Asoh, 2004).

As an example, in order to define a new product/service as a company's differentiator based on knowledge, the company needs knowledge about three elements: *who* (customers to be served), *what* (applications or customer needs), and *how* (technology to develop the product/service) (Cooper, 1987).

To summarize, a strategic perspective of KM requires that the managing of knowledge in organizations as a resource be grounded in, and aligned with, the organizational business strategy (BS). To meet the foregoing requirement in a holistic manner, pertinent alignment-related key issues in KM must be considered at all times.

Alignment-Related Key Issues in KM

KM is a broad field, and considering the importance of knowledge and KM to organizations, researchers and practitioners have raised a number of issues and questions regarding knowledge and KM within organizations.

Since it would be impractical to attempt to catalogue all the issues and questions that have been raised in the literature, for the purpose of this chapter, we first identify business strategy as the number one key business related issue confronting organizations. Second, we identify and limit ourselves to eight KM key issues that can be related to business strategy: (1) knowledge, (2) knowledge strategy (KS), (3) operational KM, (4) strategic KM, (5) KM systems, (6) KM strategy, (7) KM, and (8) sociotechnical KM. Finally, we identify associated questions that warrant the invocation of alignment by organizations engaged in KM. We believe the KM field can be unambiguously characterized by examining these issues and related questions when contemplating the alignment of knowledge-related resources (see Table 1).

The key issues and related questions have been discussed in the literature to various degrees in the sources cited. The relevance of alignment in KM can be understood by looking at each key question to see whether it makes sense, when considered alongside the key BS question. An understanding of the issues in Table 1 is implicit in the questions. For example, if we were to ask what KS is (issue #3), Zack (1999a, b, c, 2002) would respond that KS is about identifying the knowledge gaps of the organization. Similarly, Bierly and Chakrabarti (1999) would respond that KS is about the strategic choices firms make to shape their learning and knowledge base. Although we consider some of the issues later, we refer the reader to the cited sources for further details on the key issues and questions.

Given the background discussions and the key issues in Table 1, we take a look at some important alignment lessons from the "alignment reference fields" to guide the development of an alignment research framework and concepts in the next section.

Table 1. Key issues and questions of KM

#	Issue(s)	Q#	Question(s)	Author(s)
1	Business Strategy (BS)	1	How do we compete in our business?	(Hoskisson et al., 2004)
2	Knowledge	2	What perspectives of knowledge do we have in our organization?	Alavi & Leidner (2001)
		3	What are the distinct knowledge resources of our organization?	Holsapple & Joshi (2002)
3	Knowledge Strategy (KS)	4	What knowledge is needed for our business?	Zack (1999a, b, c, 2002)
		5	What strategic choices should shape our learning and knowledge base?	Bierly & Chakrabarti (1999)
		6	What strategies can we adopt to create future wealth?	Skyrme (2000)
		7	How do we develop intellectual capital?	Bierly & Daly (2002)
4	Operational KM	8	How do we use our knowledge for daily business purposes?	Zack (2002)
5	Strategic KM	9	How do we get the knowledge for strategy formulation?	Earl (2001); Zack (2002)
6	KM Strategy (KMS)	10	What processes and techniques do we need to ensure we get the knowledge we need?	Zack (1999a, b, 2002)
7	KM Systems	11	How do we provide decision makers with insights into patterns and trends that affect their domains, especially by tracking and evaluating critical success factors?	Thierauf (1999)
		12	How do we support creation, transfer, and application of knowledge?	Alavi & Leidner (2001)
8	Knowledge Management (KM)	13	How can we deliberately design processes, tools, and structures so as to increase, renew, share, and improve the use of knowledge?	Seemann, De Long, Stucky & Guthrie (2000)
		14	How do we build core competencies and understand strategic know-how?	Alavi & Leidner (2001)
		15	How can our organization manage its knowledge to become/ remain viable?	Achterbergh & Vriens (2002)
9	Socio-Technical KM	16	How do we amalgamate the dualism of people and technology to ensure organizational adaptation in the environment?	Coakes, Willis & Clarke (2002)

ALIGNMENT RESEARCH LESSONS FROM THE "REFERENCE FIELDS"

In order to develop a framework for research on alignment in KM, we take the sage approaches and recommendations of Abou-Zeid (2002), Asoh et al. (2003), and Asoh (2004). According to these authors, researchers should look and learn from other fields rather than trying to re-invent the wheel. Consequently, we examine and build on the literature in the reference fields, where pertinent lessons pertaining to IT alignment models, IT strategic levels, and conceptualization of alignment are useful in developing the concept of strategy levels in KM, the generic alignment research framework, and alignment models and research questions in KM.

IT Alignment Model

Many models have been proposed to address alignment-related issues in organizations, for example, balanced scorecard (Kaplan & Norton, 2001) and strategic alignment (Henderson & Venkatraman, 1999). The strategic alignment model (Henderson & Venkatraman, 1999) (H&V model) has found wide application in the IS/IT fields. The H&V model is relevant because of its broad examination of alignment issues. The H&V model attempts to explain organizational performance in terms of organizational alignment. Alignment is thought to exist in four domains under management control: BS (scope, distinctive components, and business governance), IT strategy (technology scope, systemic competencies, and IT governance), organizational infrastructure and processes (administration, processes, and skills), and IT infrastructure and processes (architecture, processes, and skills).

BS and IT strategy are outward-looking domains, while organizational infrastructure and processes and IT infrastructure and processes are inward-looking domains. Alignment is then viewed from two perspectives, strategic fit and functional fit (integration). Strategic fit relates the inward-looking domains with the outward-looking domains while functional fit relates each of the two domains within the inward- and outward-looking configuration. In other words, strategic fit considers how strategy is shaped by factors external to organizations and how organizations' internally controlled infrastructure and processes are related to the strategy. Similarly, functional fit considers how business oriented processes fit or integrate with the infrastructure and other processes of the organization.

Based on the examination of the H&V model, it is plausible to substitute relevant key issues of KM for IT and maintain the same model. The discussion of infrastructure and processes in KM (e. g., Zack, 1999c) is concise and its substitution poses no problem. However, trying to substitute for strategy is problematic, particularly because of the confusion on what constitutes strategy in KM. A look at the IT strategic levels in the reference fields is helpful.

IT Strategic Levels

We believe that alignment research in the IS/IT fields has been facilitated by the existence of standard frameworks linking the concepts in these fields. The framework of information-related strategies proposed by Earl (1989) offers good lessons for KM; and of interest are three predominant strategies: information management (IM) strategy, information systems (IS) strategy, and information technology (IT) strategy.

The IS strategy deals with the *what* questions (e. g., what should we do with technology?), the IT strategy deals with *how* questions (e. g., how do we do it?), and the IM strategy deals with questions of *whereof/which* way and so focuses on structures and roles for managing IS and IT (e. g., management responsibilities and control, relationship between specialists and users, and performance measurement) (Earl, 1989).

The framework proposed by Earl (1989) puts the three information-related strategies at different levels. The IS strategy is at the topmost level and IT strategy at the lower level. A firm must first answer the business-focused *what* questions (the top level) before looking at the activity-focused *how* questions (lower level). IM strategy mediates the top and lower levels.

Alignment Concepts

Although alignment has been noted as a difficult concept to understand and investigate, KM researchers can benefit from an understanding of alignment concepts that have been developed and used in the "alignment reference fields. " The alignment concepts we identified that have been widely used in the reference fields include moderation, mediation, matching, covariation, deviation, and gestalts (Venkatraman, 1989a; Venkatraman & Camillus, 1984). In continuing our discussions, we will use the term "fit" as the need arises to refer to alignment in order to maintain consistency of discussions on the alignment concepts as proposed by the above authors.

The degree to which KM researchers can use the alignment concepts depends on how the concepts can be successful interpreted from the KM perspective. Four criteria have been delineated for use as a guide in the interpretation and application of the concepts (Venkatraman, 1989a): first, is the criterion whether the conceptualization of fit is criterion specific or is criterion free? Second, is the relationship how the key variables in the conceptualization of fit relate among themselves? Third, is the verbalization what the fit is meant to be? Finally, are the analytics what data analytical technique(s) can be used to investigate the research model? These conceptualizations of fit and corresponding criteria are useful in developing analogous concepts in KM as presented in the next section.

STRATEGIC KNOWLEDGE ALIGNMENT RESEARCH FRAMEWORK

Strategic Levels in KM

Earlier, we pointed to confusion concerning the definition and use of concepts in the KM field. Without clarifying some of the confusion, a meaningful framework cannot be developed. To help clarify some of the confusion, we contend that:

1. Information is different from knowledge, and
2. Knowledge strategy (KS) is different from knowledge management strategy (KMS).

To support our contention, some definitions are in order. We define information as organized data and facts of all kinds that exist independently of an individual or group of individuals (i. e., information resides outside the mind of individuals or group of individuals). Knowledge is the personal capability and capacity (skills, experience, expertise, and competencies) of individuals or groups of individuals to assess signals and perform specific actions.

Given the above definitions, we further contend that information is to the IS/IT field as knowledge is to the KM field; and we define KM as the management discipline that attempts to address the knowledge-related imperatives of an individual or group of individuals to meet specific goals (Asoh, 2004). In effect, these imperatives which include the: (1) perception, (2) interpretation, and (3) evaluation of signals as well as the (4) articulation, (5) selection, and (6) implementation of specific actions to meet specific goals provide the raison d'être of KM (Acheterbergh & Vriens, 2002).

We examine the contention that KS is different from KMS and subsequently present a definition for each of these two concepts. In the KM field, the core concepts are analogous to those in the IS/IT field. Based on the IT strategic levels logic, we further contend that:

3. KS level is analogous to IS strategy level, and
4. KMS level is analogous to IT strategy level.

Contentions 3 and 4 depict a two-level arrangement of strategy in the KM field; that is, KS is at the top level while KMS is at the lower level. At the top level, KS parallels IS strategy. From the business perspective, we believe that prior to their BS, organizations must first identify the knowledge required for business activities. For successful business activities, organizations must consider all five elements (components) of business strategy, in what is referred to as the strategy diamond: (1) arenas, (2) vehicles, (3) differentiators, (4) staging, and (5) economic logic (Hambrick & Fredrickson, 2001). Knowledge is required for all business activities and consequently in each component of the strategy diamond. Therefore, examining KM within the strategy diamond framework is an opportunity for organizations to develop the best strategies for managing organizational knowledge. For example, through a knowledge strength, weaknesses, opportunities, and threats (K-SWOT) analyses, an organizations can develop its KS (Zack, 1999a).

A KS enables an organization to answer "what," "where," "when," "why," and "who" questions pertaining to its knowledge resources and activities and is defined as an integrated set of strategic knowledge-related choices an organization makes and executes to orientate its knowledge-related resources so as to ensure OP (Asoh, 2004). In other words, KS is the collective response of managers to the strategic knowledge needs of the organization to meet performance goals (Bierly & Chakrabarti, 1999). Making strategic knowledge choices is important because no single KM activity can lead to the best performance benefits of KM and it is not feasible for an organization to undertake all KM activities. Consequently, the strategic choices involve trade-offs such as codification vs. personification of knowledge; exploration vs. exploitation of knowledge; internal vs. external sourcing of knowledge; and maintaining deep vs. a broad knowledge base (Asoh, 2004).

After an organization has answered "what," "where," "when," "why," and "who" questions pertaining to its knowledge resources and activities, it is then possible to look at low-level "how" questions which is the object of a KMS. A KMS focuses on *how* to do what the KS has identified at the right place, at the right time, for the right reason, and by the right person and is defined as the tactical activities executed by an organization in response to its KS (Asoh, 2004). To summarize, both the KS and the KMS are complementary. A KS acts as a compass, and points to *what* must be done in KM; a KMS focuses on *how* to do what the KS identifies. For example, if as a result of its KS, an organization makes the strategic decision of knowledge personification, the organization's KMS will seek to address the question of how the organization can personify its knowledge so as to meet OP goals and objectives.

Within the IT strategic level model, strategic choice is implicit in the IS strategy (top level) focus on IS applications: no organization can pursue all IS applications, and no single IS application can provide the best OP. The IT strategy (lower level) focus on delivery of IS applications is tactical, and deals with *how* questions (e. g., how does the organization delivers the selected IS applications?) (Earl, 1989). Finally, unlike IM strategy that mediates the top (IS strategy) and the lower (IT strategy) levels within the IT strategic level model, within the two-level knowledge strategic level model discussed here, IT strategy may mediate and/or moderate the relationship between the KS and KMS.

A Generic Alignment Reference Framework

As previously discussed in the section *Alignment-Related KM Issues*, many resources can be, and need to be, aligned with business strategies. For the purpose of this chapter, we delineate and limit the discussions on alignment to consist of three broad dimensions (business-related, information-related, and knowledge-related) (Figure 1).

The first dimension pertains to business-related strategies. Companies use different business strategies and models depending on their environments. For example, we know of strategic business typologies (e. g., Miles & Snow, 1978; Porter, 1980) and fine-grained business strategies such as the strategic orientation of business organizations (e. g., Venkatraman, 1989b). The second dimension pertains to information-related strategies. Here researchers would consider strategies related to IT, IS, information management, and information resources (e. g., Earl, 1989). The third dimension pertains to knowledge-related strategies. Here, holistic strategies pertaining to knowledge such as discussed by Abou-Zeid (2002), Asoh et al. (2003), and Asoh (2004) can be considered, including typologies of knowledge strategies (e. g., Bierly, 1999; Zack, 1999a) and tactical aspects of operational and strategic KM (e. g., Earl, 2001; Zack, 2002).

Figure 1. Generic alignment research reference framework

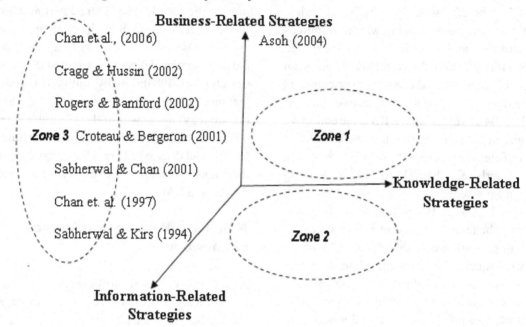

Alignment Zones and Research Questions

To frame research questions based on the generic alignment reference framework presented in Figure 1, three zones of alignment (Zone 1, Zone 2, and Zone 3) are considered, corresponding respectively to the pairwise consideration of any two dimensions (business- and knowledge-related strategies, knowledge- and information related strategies, and information- and business-related strategies).

No matter which zone is considered, two primary research questions can be investigated. The first relates to the degree to which a particular strategy from one dimension is aligned with the strategy from the other dimension. The second relates to the performance impact of the alignment between the strategies from two dimensions. A secondary question pertains to the individual performance impact of each strategy within each zone.

Empirical research that has attempted to answer the primary and secondary alignment

questions in one form or another are depicted in Figure 1. Much of the published work on alignment in the reference field has focused only in Zone 3 (e. g., Chan, 1992; Chan et al., 1997; Chan, Sabherwal & Thatcher, 2006; Sabherwal & Kirs, 1994; Cragg, King & Hussin, 2002; Croteau & Bergeron, 2001; Luftman et al., 1993; Luftman et al., 2002; Ragu-Nathan, Ragu-Nathan, Tu & Shi, 2001; Rogers & Bamford, 2002; Sabherwal & Chan, 2001). The only empirical research we found in zone 1 is the work by Asoh (2004). We did not find any empirical research in zone 2 (*indicated with a question mark* "**?**").

ALIGNMENT MODELS AND CONCEPTS IN KM RESEARCH

Alignment Models in KM

As a first step in the investigation of strategic knowledge alignment, the generic alignment research framework makes it easy to identify alignment research zones and research questions.

As presented and discussed in the last subsection, this first step is easy and intuitive. It is sufficient for the researcher to identify an appropriate research zone, and everything else should follow. For example, if the area of interest is identified as zone 1, researchers could immediately decide to use either the KMSAM model (Abou-Zeid, 2002) or the KSAM model (Asoh, 2004; Asoh et al., 2003).

The only possible problems with using the above holistic models are the need to instantiate each model with a specific knowledge-related strategy (e. g., KS vs. KMS) and a specific business strategy, operationalize the strategies, and then develop data collection instruments. In comparing the KMSAM and KSAM, for a given BS, we note that the KSAM has been instantiated with KS, and operationalized (Asoh, 2004). Availability of operationalized constructs makes for easy replication of research.

Alignment Concepts in KM

After selecting the appropriate alignment model, deciding which conceptualization of alignment (or fit) to use may pose some problems since greater understanding is required of the various alignment conceptualizations available within the reference fields. As discussed in the previous section, the six major alignment conceptualizations identified in the reference field include moderation, mediation, matching, covariation, deviation, and gestalts (Venkatraman, 1989a; Venkatraman & Camillus, 1984). Using the four criteria listed as a guide, we will conceptualize alignment in KM in the rest of this section. Again, for consistency of discussions we will use the term "fit" as needed to refer to alignment in line with discussions by the above authors.

Fit as Moderation is criterion specific (i. e., a specification of a criterion is required for analysis), is conceptualized as interaction between BS and KS, and is verbalized as the performance implications of the interactive effect of BS and

KS. The testing technique used is correlations of various subsamples.

Fit as Mediation is also criterion specific, is conceptualized as intervening variables (KS) between the antecedent (BS) and the consequent (OP), and is verbalized to mean KS is an intervening variable between BS and OP. Alternately, mediation may be verbalized to mean BS is an intervening variable between KS and OP. The data analytic techniques used for mediation are path analysis and structural equation modeling (SEM) approach.

Fit as Matching is criterion free (i. e., no specification of a criterion is required or referenced), is conceptualized as the match between BS and KS, and is verbalized to mean fit in BS orientation exists when KS orientation matches the BS orientation. The data analytic testing techniques are score analysis, residual analysis, and and analysis of variance (ANOVA).

Fit as Covariation is criteria free, is conceptualized as "a pattern of covariation or internal consistency among a set of underlying theoretically related variables" (Venkatraman, 1989a) (p. 435), and is verbalized to mean the appropriate co-alignment between BS and KS has performance implications.

Fit as Profile Deviation is criterion specific, is conceptualized as the internal consistencies of multiple contingencies, and is verbalized to mean the degree of adherence to a specified profile of BS and KS has performance implications. What this means is that an ideal profile is assumed to exist, and the deviation or nondeviation from this profile has performance implications. A popular approach to create the ideal profile is to consider the topmost 10% of performers as the "ideal sample." The BS orientation (independent variable) of the 10% sample is estimated. This "ideal sample" is not included in the other computations, except for the purpose of comparing. The testing technique attempts to verify the degree of adherence of the remaining 90% of the sample to the ideal profile as obtained by calculating Euclidean distances in an n-dimensional space; the further the distance, the poorer the performance.

Fit as Gestalts is criterion free and is conceptualized internal congruence, whereby fit is seen as patterns (i. e., set of relationships which are in a temporary state of balance). This perspective means, "instead of looking at few variables or at linear associations among such variables, we should be trying to find frequently occurring clusters of attributes or gestalts" (Venkatraman, 1989a, p. 432). The testing techniques are numerical classification methods that simultaneously look at many variables, for example, cluster analysis and q-factor analysis.

Having presented and characterized various conceptualizations of alignment in KM, the next logical step is to discuss and illustrate model testing and data analytical approaches available to KM researchers. This is the subject of the next subsection.

Model Testing and Data Analytic Techniques and Tools: An Illustration

We illustrate the use of the alignment framework, alignment model, and alignment conceptualization by considering alignment as covariation. We also include and discuss relevant hypotheses.

We position ourselves in zone 1 of the generic alignment reference framework. Our example is the case of aligning BS and KS based on the KSAM model (Asoh et al., 2003). The research model includes four constructs (BS, KS, AL (alignment), and OP (organizational performance)). As a hint, the *primary research questions are reformulated based on how fit is conceptualized and verbalized.* The testing techniques described pertain to the data analytical methodology that may be used, and the number of possible tests depends on the modeling tool used. Figure 2 presents a research model with the four constructs (BS, KS, AL, and OP) and four testable hypotheses (discussed in the next subsection).

For the covariation alignment model (Figure 2), the option of second-order factor analysis opens many opportunities to researchers for testing the four hypotheses. The example depicts alignment as covariation with four hypotheses (H1–H4) from a contingency perspective. We have ordered these hypotheses to emphasize the sequence in which we think research questions can best be asked and answered using this approach.

Hypothesis H1 tests the relationship between BS and OP (i. e., how OP is contingent upon the BS adopted). Most of the work on alignment within zone 3 of the generic alignment reference framework has tested the BS–OP link. This link

Figure 2. Alignment research questions, model, and hypothesis (Adapted from Asoh et al., 2003)

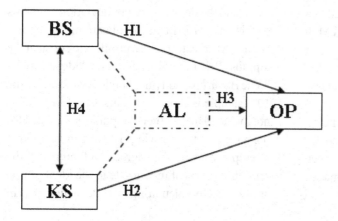

Legend:
BS: Business-related strategies
KS: Knowledge-related strategies
OP: Organizational Performance
AL: Alignment

H1, H2, H3, H4: Hypotheses (discussed in the text)

may serve the purpose of validation in subsequent research models.

Hypothesis H2 tests the relationship between KS and OP (i. e., how OP is contingent on KS) and is mandatory. When covariation is not being considered, AL may be computed and once H1 and H2 have been tested, then testing hypothesis H3 makes sense. One would investigate whether or not the computed alignment has an impact on performance, and how the impact (if any) compares with the direct impacts of KS and BS.

Finally, hypothesis H4 relates BS and KS. The bidirectional arrow indicates that BS can drive or enable KS and vice versa, in line with Zack (1999a). The H4 hypothesis is typical of covariation analysis. Here researchers would attempt to answer the question pertaining to how covariation between BS and KS impacts OP.

Although four top level hypothesis could be investigated as indicated previously, many more hypotheses could be generated and tested when BS, KS, and OP are modeled as higher-order factors. In this case, specific hypotheses relating the individual dimensions of BS, KS, and OP could be investigated in what is often referred to as bivariate analysis.

In terms of data analysis and data analytic tools, the structural equation modeling (SEM) approach has been widely used with either the covariance based analytic tools such as linear structural relationships (LISREL) (Joreskog & Sorbom, 2002) or the variance-based tools such as partial least squares (PLS) (Chin, 2006). The SEM approach is preferred over traditional regression analysis because it gives the researcher the opportunity to model measurement errors, confront *a priori* theory and hypotheses with data (Fornell, 1982), map paths to multiple latent variables in the same model, analyze multiple paths simultaneously, and combine reflective and formative variables (Barclay, Higgins & Thompson, 1995; Gefen, Straub & Boudreau, 2000).

Although SEM techniques appear very appealing, it is important for researchers to weigh the pros and cons of using these techniques and compare them with conventional techniques for data analysis. Researchers would do well to understand the scope, advantages, and limitations of each tool before retaining it for serious work. A note of caution on the use of SEM analytic tools has been given by Chin and Todd (1995). A comparison between the SEM and traditional tools such as regression has been detailed in the literature. We refer the reader to such comparisons in Gefen et al. (2000).

CONCLUSION

In this chapter, we argued that alignment is an important, yet neglected research area in the KM field. We recognize that the lack of research on alignment is not only due to the fact that the concept is difficult to understand but also because of the absence of appropriate frameworks, models, or methodologies. The contribution of this work is the development of a generic alignment research reference framework in response to the call by Earl (2001) for frameworks and models to help researchers and practitioners in KM.

The framework encompasses key issues relating to alignment in KM and presents a unified approach to knowledge strategic alignment. We believe knowledge-related strategies have to be aligned, not just with business-related strategies, but also with information-related strategies. Therefore, the framework presents researchers with an opportunity to investigate information-related strategic alignment, knowledge-related strategic alignment, and alignment between information- and knowledge-related strategies.

In addition, we also identified holistic alignment models such as KMSAM and KSAM and discussed research questions, alignment models and concepts, data analysis techniques, and modeling tools. We believe the proposed framework, the alignment models identified, and the discussions on the conceptualization of alignment in the KM field will foster research to inform and benefit both academicians and practitioners.

FUTURE RESEARCH DIRECTIONS

Based on the proposed research framework and associated models and concepts discussed in relationship to strategic knowledge alignment, this work provides a solid foundation for future research in a number of areas: first, researchers would recognize that we did not consider the alignment of all knowledge-related resources proposed in the literature. For example, we did not consider the alignment of other important knowledge resources such as culture and human resources because we wanted to keep our discussion more focused. Therefore, researchers would want to examine how these and other knowledge resources can be aligned. Second, while our focus was on the strategy resource, we did not consider alignment of all resource-related strategies. For example, human resources (HR) management is an important organization process. The strategies used in the management of HR need to be aligned with business strategy and knowledge strategy as well. Omitting the discussion on HR strategies was also deliberate, to maintain a better focus of the chapter. For future research, an extension of our framework would be to include additional dimensions (e. g., HR-related strategies), and review the literature to find out if any research has been done on alignment in the area.

Third, we did not address issues of measurement scales for the various constructs in the alignment models. In carrying out research on alignment in general using the framework of Figure 1, researchers need a minimum of four scales to measure: (1) business-related, (2) information-related, (3) knowledge-related strategies, and (4) organizational performance. Specific research within an area of interest (such as the zones depicted in Figure 1) requires just three measurement scales. While the literature is replete with various scales to measure business-related strategies, information-related strategies, and organizational performance, there are virtually no such scales for knowledge-related strategies conceived for the purpose of studying alignment. Developing scales for knowledge-related strategies is a fertile area of future research. Forth, future research is suggested on alignment in zones 1 and 2. Compared to zone 3, these two zones are in dire need of research. Fifth, another direction of future research is to investigate the success factors of alignment in KM while a sixth area will be to investigate the antecedents of knowledge strategic alignment. A seventh area of research will be to investigate the mediating/moderating role of IT between KS and KMS as proposed in this work.

REFERENCES

Abou-Zeid, E. -S. (2002). Developing business aligned knowledge management strategy. In E. Coakes (Ed.), *Knowledge management: Current issues and challenges* (pp. 157-173). Hershey, PA: Idea Group.

Achterbergh, J., & Vriens, D. (2002). Managing viable knowledge. *Systems Research and Behavioral Science, 19*, 223-241.

Alavi, M., & Leidner, D. E. (1999). Knowledge management systems: Issues, challenges and benefits. *Communications of the Association for Information Systems, 1*(Article 7), 1-37.

Alavi, M., & Leidner, D. E. (2001). Review: Knowledge management and knowledge management systems: Conceptual foundations and research issues. *MIS Quarterly, 25*(1), 107-136.

Asoh, D. A. (2004). *Business and knowledge strategies: Alignment and performance impact analysis.* (Doctoral Dissertation, UMI ProQuest Dissertation Publication Reference # 3134655). University at Albany, Albany, NY.

Asoh, D. A., Belardo, S., & Duchessi, P. (2003). *Alignment: The missing link in knowledge management research.* Paper presented at the 4th European Conference on Knowledge Management, Oriel, Oxford.

Baird, L., & Henderson, J. C. (2001). *The knowledge engine.* San Francisco: Berret-Koehler Publishers, Inc.

Barclay, D., Higgins, C., & Thompson, R. (1995). The partial least square (PLS) approach to causal modeling: Personal computer adoption and use as an illustration. *Technology Studies, 2*(2), 285-309.

Barney, J. B. (1991). Firm resources and sustained competitive advantage. *Journal of Management, 17*(1), 99-120.

Belardo, S., & Belardo, A. W. (2002). *Innovation through learning: What leaders need to know in the 21st century.* Albany, NY: Whitston Publishing Company, Inc.

Bierly, P. E. (1999). Development of a generic knowledge strategy typology. *Journal of Business Strategies., 16*(1), 1-26.

Bierly, P., & Chakrabarti, A. (1999). Generic knowledge strategies in the U. S. pharmaceutical industry. In M. H. Zack (Ed.), *Knowledge and strategy* (pp. 231-250). Boston: Butterworth Heinemann.

Bierly, P. E., & Daly, P. (2002). Aligning human resource management practices and knowledge strategies. In C. W. Choo & N. Bontis (Eds.), *The strategic management of intellectual capital and organizational knowledge* (pp. 277-295). Oxford: Oxford University Press.

Cascella, V. (2002, November). Effective strategic planning: Processes, measurements and accountability are keys to success. *Quality Progress*, pp. 62-67.

Chan, Y. E. (1992). *Business strategy, information systems strategy, and strategic fit: Measurement and performance impact* (Dissertation Summary). London, Ontario: University of Western Ontario.

Chan, Y. E., Huff, S. L., Barclay, D. W., & Copeland, D. G. (1997). Business strategic orientation, information systems strategic orientation, and strategic alignment. *Information Systems Research, 8*(2), 125-150.

Chan, Y. E., Sabherwal, R., & Thatcher, J. B. (2006). Antecedents and outcomes of strategic IS alignment: An empirical investigation. *IEEE Transactions on Engineering Management, 53*(1), 27-47.

Chin, W. W. (2006). *PLS-Graph (Version 3. 0).* Soft Modeling Inc.

Chin, W. W., & Todd, P. A. (1995, June). On the use, usefulness, and ease of use of structural equation modeling in MIS research: A note of caution. *MISQ*, pp. 237-246.

Choi, B., & Lee, H. (2003). An empirical investigation of KM styles and their effects on corporate performance. *Information and Management, 40*, 403-417.

Coakes, E., Willis, D., & Clarke, S. (2002). Introduction. In E. Coakes, D. Willis & S. Clarke (Eds.), *Knowledge management in the socio-technical world: The graffitti continues* (pp. 1-3). London: Springer-Verlag.

Collis, D. J., & Montgomery, C. A. (1999). Competing on resources: Strategies in the 1990s. In M. H. Zack (Ed.), *Knowledge and strategy* (pp. 25-40). Boston: Butterworth Heinemann.

Cooper, R. G. (1987). Defining the new product strategy. *IEEE Transactions on Engineering Management, EM-34*(3), 184-193.

Cragg, P., King, M., & Hussin, H. (2002). IT alignment and firm performance in small manufacturing firms. *Journal of Strategic Information Systems, 11*, 109-132.

Croteau, A. -M., & Bergeron, F. (2001). An information technology trilogy: Business strategy, technological deployment and organizational performance. *Strategic Information Systems, 10*, 77-99.

Drucker, P. F. (2002, August). The discipline of innovation [Special issue: The Innovative Enterprise]. *Harvard Business Review,* pp. 95-102.

Earl, M. J. (1989). *Management strategies for information technology.* New York: Prentice Hall.

Earl, M. (2001). Knowledge management strategies: Toward a taxonomy. *Journal of Management Information Systems, 18*(1), 215-233.

Fornell, C. (1982). *A second generation of multivariate analysis. Volume 2: Measurement and evaluation.* New York: Praeger Publishers.

Gefen, D., Straub, D. W., & Boudreau, M. -C. (2000). Structural equation modeling and regression: Guidelines for research practice. *Communications of the Association for Information Systems, 4,* Article 7, 1-77.

Gottschalk, P. (2000). Studies of key issues in IS management around the world. *International Journal of Information Management, 20*, 169-180.

Grant, R. M. (1996, Winter). Toward a knowledge-based theory of the firm. *Strategic Management Journal, 17*, 109-122.

Grant, R. M. (1999). The resource-based theory of competitive advantage: Implications for strategy formulation. In M. H. Zack (Ed.), *Knowledge and strategy* (pp. 3-23). Boston: Butterworth Heinemann.

Hall, R. (1999). The strategic analysis of intangible resources. In M. H. Zack (Ed.), *Knowledge and strategy* (pp. 181-195). Boston: Butterworth Heinemann.

Hall, M. -J. (2002, Summer). Aligning the organization to increase performance results. *The Public Manager,* pp. 7-10.

Hambrick, D. C., & Fredrickson, J. W. (2001). Are you sure you have a strategy? *Academy of Management Executive, 15*(4), 48-59.

Hansen, M. T., Nohria, N., & Tierney, T. (2001). What's your strategy for managing knowledge? *Harvard Business Review on Organizational Learning,* 61-86.

Henderson, J. C., & Venkatraman, N. (1999). Strategic alignment: Leveraging information technology for transforming organizations. *IBM Systems Journal, 38*(2/3), 472-484.

Holsapple, C. W., & Joshi, K. D. (2002). Knowledge management: A threefold framework. *The Information Society, 18,* 47-64.

Hoskisson, R. E., Hitt, M. A., & Ireland, R. D. (2004). *Competing for advantage.* Australia: Thompson South-Western.

Joreskog, K., & Sorbom, D. (2002). *LISREL (Version 8. 52).* Lincolnwood, IL: Scientific Software International, Inc.

Kaplan, R. S., & Norton, D. P. (2001). *The strategy-focused organization.* Boston: Harvard Business School Press.

Lieibold, M., Probst, G., & Gilbert, M. (2002). *Strategic management in the knowledge economy: New approaches and business applications.* Erlangen, Germany: Publicis Corporate Publishing and Wiley-VCH-Verlag.

Luftman, J. (2003, Fall). Assessing IT/business alignment. *Information Systems Management,* pp. 9-15.

Luftman, J. N., Lewis, P. R., & Oldach, S. H. (1993). Transforming the enterprise: The alignment of business and information technologies strategies. *IBM Systems Journal, 32*(1), 198-221.

Luftman, J. N., Papp, R., & Brier, T. (2002, September). Enablers and inhibitors of business-IT alignment. *IBM Advanced Business Institute (ABInsight)*, pp. 1-26.

Malone, D. (2002). Knowledge management: A model for organizational learning. *International Journal of Accounting Information Systems, 3*, 111-123.

Miles, R. E., & Snow, C. C. (1978). *Organizational strategy, structure, and processes.* New York: McGraw-Hill.

Miller, D. (1992). Environmental fit versus internal fit. *Organization Science, 3*(2), 159-178.

Moody, K. W. (2003, Fall). New meaning to IT alignment. *Information Systems Management*, pp. 30-35.

Penrose, E. T. (1959). *The theory of the growth of the firm* (3rd ed.). New York: Wiley.

Porter, M. E. (1980). *Competitive strategy.* New York: Free Press.

Porter, M. E. (1996). What is strategy? *Harvard Business Review, 74*(6), 61-78.

Powell, T. C. (1992). Organizational alignment as competitive advantage. *Strategic Management Journal, 13*(2), 119-134.

Prahalad, C. K., & Hamel, G. (1999). The core competence of the corporation. In M. H. Zack (Ed.), *Knowledge and strategy* (pp. 41-59). Boston: Butterworth Heinemann.

Ragu-Nathan, B., Ragu-Nathan, T. S., Tu, Q., & Shi, Z. (2001). Information management (IM) strategy: The construct and its measurement. *Journal of Strategic Information Systems, 10*, 265-289.

Rogers, P. R., & Bamford, C. E. (2002). Information planning process and strategic orientation: The importance of fit in high-performance organizations. *Journal of Business Research, 55*, 205-215.

Sabherwal, R., & Chan, Y. E. (2001). Alignment between business and IS strategies: A study of prospectors, analyzers, and defenders. *Information Systems Research, 12*(1), 11-33.

Sabherwal, R., & Kirs, P. (1994). The alignment between organizational critical success factors and information technology capability in academic institutions. *Decision Sciences, 25*(2), 301-330.

Saint-Onge, H. (1999). Tacit knowledge: The key to strategic alignment of intellectual capital. In M. H. Zack (Ed.), *Knowledge and strategy* (pp. 223-230). Boston: Butterworth Heinemann.

Seemann, P., De Long, D., Stucky, S., & Guthrie, E. (2000). Building intangible assets: A strategic framework for investing in intellectual capital. In D. Morey, M. Maybury & B. Thuraisingham (Eds.), *Knowledge management: Classic and contemporary works* (pp. 85-98). Cambridge: The MIT Press.

Skyrme, D. J. (2000). *Knowledge networking: Creating the collaborative enterprise.* Oxford: Butterworth Heinemann.

Teece, D. J., Pisano, G., & Shuen, A. (1999). Dynamic capabilities and strategic management. In M. H. Zack (Ed.), *Knowledge and strategy* (pp. 77-115). Boston: Butterworth Heinemann.

Thierauf, R. J. (1999). *Knowledge management systems for business* (1st ed.). Westport: Quorum Books.

van den Hooff, B., Vijvers, J., & de Ridder, J. (2003). Foundations and applications of a knowledge management scan. *European Management Journal, 21*(2), 237-246.

Venkatraman, N. (1989a). The concept of fit in strategy research: Toward verbal and statistical correspondence. *Academy of Management Review, 14*(3), 423-444.

Venkatraman, N. (1989b). Strategic orientation of business enterprises: The construct, dimensionality and measurement. *Management Science, 35*(8), 942-962.

Venkatraman, N., & Camillus, J. C. (1984). Exploring the concept of "fit" in strategic management. *Academy of Management Review, 9*(3), 513-525.

Venkatraman, N., & Prescott, J. E. (1990). Environment-strategy coalignment: An empirical test of its performance implication. *Strategic Management Journal, 11*, 1-23.

Wernerfelt, B. (1984). A resource-based view of the firm. *Management Journal, 5*(2), 171-180.

Zack, M. H. (1999a). Developing a knowledge strategy. *California Management Review., 41*(3), 125-145.

Zack, M. H. (1999b). Introduction. In M. H. Zack (Ed.), *Knowledge and strategy* (pp. vii-xii). Boston: Butterworth Heinemann.

Zack, M. H. (1999c, Summer). Managing codified knowledge. *Sloan Management Review*, pp. 45-58.

Zack, M. H. (2002). Epilogue: Developing a knowledge strategy. In C. W. Choo & N. Bontis (Eds.), *The strategic management of intellectual capital and organizational knowledge* (pp. 268-276). Oxford: Oxford University Press.

Additional Reading

Benson, R. J., Bugnitz, T. L., & Walton, W. B. (2004). *From business strategy to IT action: Right decisions for better bottom line*. Hoboken, NJ: John Wiley & Sons.

Boar, B. H. (1994). *Practical steps for aligning information technology with business strategies: How to achieve a competitive advantage*. Hoboken, NJ: John Wiley & Sons.

Hayles, R. A., Jr. *Practical strategy: Aligning business and information technology*. Dubuque, IA: Kendall/Hunt Publishing Company.

Kaplan, R. S., & Norton, D. P. (2006). *Alignment: Using the balanced scorecard to create corporate synergies*. Boston: Harvard Business School Press.

Lufman, J. N. (2003). *Competing in the information age: Align in the sand*. New York: Oxford University Press.

Luftman, J. N. (1996). *Competing in the information age: Strategic alignment in practice*. New York: Oxford University Press.

Chapter X
Integrating Knowledge Management Services:
Strategy and Infrastructure

Ronald Maier
University of Innsbruck, Austria

Ulrich Remus
University of Canterbury, New Zealand

ABSTRACT

Many organizations have established knowledge management initiatives, but most of them have developed instruments bottom-up, often in parallel and without strategic considerations. Many of those instruments involve information and communication technologies (ICT) which therefore are fragmented and cannot be easily reused outside their original intended organizational unit. This chapter proposes a three-layered service infrastructure that composes services from heterogeneous applications into specific knowledge management (KM) services. The infrastructure supports discovery, call, and provision of KM services from activities within business processes. It argues that integration of KM services in organizations requires alignment of the IT infrastructure, particularly its knowledge-oriented part, with the KM portion of business strategy, that is, KM strategy. This alignment can be achieved by introducing a service infrastructure that uses the concept of KM service in order to connect the customer-oriented materialization of strategic decisions on a conceptual level, that is, business processes, with their technical counterpart on the ICT level, that is, software services.

INTRODUCTION

Work in organizations is increasingly information- and knowledge-intensive and the share of knowledge work has risen continuously during the last decades (Wolff, 2005). Since the late 1990s, after a period of high attention to the increase in efficiency of business processes, organizations have been faced with the transformation to knowledge-intensive organizations in order to significantly increase speed of innovation and improve productivity of knowledge work (Drucker, 1994). However, compared to more traditional, predominantly manual, data- or service-oriented work, the unstructured, creative, and expertise-driven knowledge work cannot be designed with standardized business process management approaches and cannot be easily supported by information and communication technologies (ICT), for example, workflows or single application systems. As a result, an enormous number of fragmented knowledge management (KM) measures, procedures, instruments, or tools have been proposed which claim to solve particular knowledge-related problems, but are not connected or integrated. Even though many authors have studied the strategic perspective of KM (April, 2002; Hansen, Nohria, & Tierney, 1999; Ordóñez de Pablos, 2002; Zack, 1999a) and process-oriented KM strategies in particular (Davenport, Jarvenpaa & Beers, 1996; Maier & Remus, 2003), in order to integrate KM initiatives and guide their organization-wide implementation, these considerations still remain on an abstract, strategic level and are not connected with the manifold fragmented KM measures, procedures, instruments, and tools as proposed in the literature and experimented in businesses and organizations.

During recent years, a number of empirical studies found that many businesses and organizations have established numerous initiatives in order to implement KM (Maier, 2004, pp. 359-512). In many initiatives, KM measures and

tools have been bundled as KM instruments to provide specific KM services. KM services cater to the special needs of one or a small number of organizational units, for example, a process, work group, department or subsidiary, factory, or outlet in order to provide a solution to a defined business problem. As opposed to strategic, enterprise-wide KM approaches guided by a knowledge or business strategy, these KM services are designed bottom-up, often in parallel and without considering or even noticing each other.

KM services typically concentrate on one out of four specific KM focus areas identified by Wiig (1999, p. 158). Examples for KM services are (1) management of patents and licenses or KM scorecards in the intellectual asset focus; (2) competence management, communities, and networks of experts in the people focus; (3) lessons learned, good/best practices, and knowledge process re-engineering in the enterprise effectiveness focus; and (4) knowledge portals, semantic content management systems, or skill management systems in the information technology focus. Activities implementing these KM services are often applied in isolation suffering from a lack of integration with other activities. Consequently, the deployment of KM services in organizations might profit substantially from both the integration and the corresponding alignment with strategic goals.

This chapter argues that integration of KM services in organizations requires alignment of the KM portion of business strategy, that is, KM strategy and IT infrastructures, particularly their knowledge-oriented part and customer orientation. This alignment can be achieved by connecting KM services to the customer-oriented materialization of strategic decisions on a conceptual level, that is, business processes, with their technical counterpart on an ICT level, that is, software services.

Integration on the level of business processes means defining which services are required in which core business processes, which services are offered by what service processes, who is responsible for them, and what resources are allocated to fulfill them. Concepts of process-oriented KM (Remus & Schub, 2003) can especially help to analyze, understand, and improve business processes with regard to a knowledge-oriented and, at the same time, strategic perspective on KM services in business processes.

In contrast, integration on the ICT level involves building these services with the help of technologies such as application components, Web services, and their composition. In the context of KM services, ICT integration comprises data, function, and process integration and particularly supports access to a variety of structured and unstructured data sources such as enterprise systems, Web sites, databases, data warehouses, document bases, or messaging systems.

The main challenge is how to integrate both levels. We suggest a KM service infrastructure that composes services from heterogeneous applications into specific KM services and supports their discovery, call, and provision from activities within business processes. The KM service infrastructure is defined by a blueprint that represents KM services as the output of knowledge processes.

The second section of this chapter describes the background, both practical, as state-of-practice of KM, and theoretical, as approaches to process-oriented KM, that explains the need for the definition of a service layer architecture for KM services. The third section details the concept of KM service and thus helps to define KM initiatives from a management and IT perspective. The fourth through sixth sections conceptualize a three-layered KM service infrastructure. On a conceptual layer, KM services are offered by knowledge processes. An intermediate layer shows the composition of basic into complex KM services and maps them to IT services, that is, defined interfaces offering methods of heterogeneous KM-related applications. The ICT layer describes all KM-related services offered by the

IT infrastructure of a business or organization. Finally, the last section concludes the chapter by addressing the challenges of implementing KM service infrastructures and gives an outlook on future research questions.

BACKGROUND: KM STRATEGIES AND INITIATIVES

State-of-Practice

Along with a deeper understanding of the application of KM concepts during recent years, it became evident that both the human-oriented and the technology-oriented approaches have to be integrated into a more "holistic" KM approach. Information and communication technology plays an important role in the implementation of KM concepts and a badly designed ICT context can create substantial barriers, for example, for knowledge documentation, integration, transfer, refinement, and reuse. However, the sole focus on ICT in KM initiatives, instead of balancing technology, processes, people, and content seems to be one factor of an increasing number of failed KM projects (Malhotra, 2005; Rollet, 2003; Tsui, 2005). ICT can play an important role as accelerator for or even enabler of the introduction and buy-in of a KM initiative, but has to be aligned with a KM strategy (Tsui, 2005).

Although KM concepts have found their way into many organizations, there are comparably few organizations that have gone to the trouble of developing a KM strategy or implement other instruments coordinating their KM efforts throughout the enterprise. Empirically, four scenarios have been found that describe what organizations are pursuing when implementing KM. These KM scenarios aim at bridging the gap between human-oriented and technology-oriented KM, between a personalization and a codification strategy (Hansen et al., 1999), and between an interactive and integrative knowledge management system (KMS) (Zack, 1999b). Organizational and ICT instruments are combined in a sociotechnical perspective in knowledge processes that support the sharing of both tacit and explicit knowledge. In Maier (2004), the following four scenarios are described together with recommendations for an implementation of the strategies:

- **Scenario 1:** *Knowledge management starter* is characterized in detail in the following;
- **Scenario 2:** *Centralized "market and hierarchy"* reflects a central coordinating organizational unit responsible for establishing concepts, rules, and procedures and developing tools, instruments, and knowledge products and services that are then applied decentrally in a market-type and/or hierarchical situation in the business units;
- **Scenario 3:** *Decentralized "network and community"* strengthens informal networks for knowledge exchange where collective initiatives have to be supported by knowledge sponsors or champions. Existing networks gain visibility and thus are strengthened and new networks and communities are founded as a supported bottom-up initiative by interested groups of people;
- **Scenario 4:** *Personal "idea and individual"* describes a more recent approach that can be found in highly expert-dependent organizations. The main focus is to individualize the organization's KM efforts and to have every employee ideally responsible for his or her own handling of knowledge. The organization creates an environment (organizational and ICT infrastructure, career, and reward system) conducive for individuals to commit to an improved handling of knowledge.

From a strategic perspective, the situation in most organizations still can be best described by the scenario of a KM starter. The scenario is characterized by a number of uncoordinated

initiatives that comprise a relatively small number of employees being aware of the potential benefits of KM who have started to market the approach in their respective domain, but not enterprise-wide. Projects under way, for example, a new release of the corporate Intranet or the introduction of a document management system, are used as vehicles to establish those KM instruments that promise the most benefits from the perspectives of the people involved (e. g., an IT perspective, human resource management perspective, research and development perspective, or marketing perspective). In each initiative, a small core group of employees enthusiastic about KM analyzes its potentials for their respective domain. The core group or network can either be fueled by the enthusiasm of the group itself, assigned by senior management, or developed as part of a project with a goal complementary to KM. The goal is to create awareness of the potentials of KM, to show some quick fixes of immanent problems and to gain support for a consecutive implementation of a coordinated KM program. The approach taken, gaps identified, and instruments considered by the initiatives in this scenario vary widely depending on the background of the employees who are members of the core group.

As for KM roles, if any, there is only one specific KM role established in this scenario, namely, one coordinator for each KM initiative. This can either be an individual determined by the core group or the core group altogether coordinates the approach. Regularly, there is a speaker for the core group who takes on responsibility to coordinate the KM activities in the organization. KM initiatives either have a sponsor, senior manager supportive of KM, or are searching for a supporter. The funding of the initiative is frequently provided by the projects that have a complementary focus and create synergies when combined with the KM initiatives. Additionally, it is the core group's own commitment that provides the funding so that budgets (if any) stem from the business units participating in the efforts.

The core group regularly tries to design and implement ICT tools supportive of KM. The focus is on a secure ICT infrastructure accessible to as many employees as possible, an enterprise knowledge infrastructure. An enterprise knowledge infrastructure is a comprehensive ICT platform for collaboration and knowledge sharing with advanced KM services built on top that are contextualized, integrated on the basis of a shared ontology, and personalized for participants networked in communities that fosters the implementation of KM instruments in support of knowledge processes targeted at increasing productivity of knowledge work (EKI) (Maier, Hädrich & Peinl, 2005). This requires integrated access to the most important electronic data and knowledge sources that already exist within the domain of the initiative and provides basic support for communication between the participants. The services offered by differing tools and systems designed in the KM initiatives cover infrastructure, integration, discovery, publication, collaboration, learning, personalization, and access services (see section 5).

The state of practice according to ICT services for KM can be described as follows (Maier et al., 2005, p. 370ff). Major vendors seem to understand the need for comprehensive, yet modular systems and have supplemented their offerings to provide at least partial solutions for the whole range of services. The market for enterprise knowledge infrastructure solutions has been consolidated and technologies of different vendors have been integrated into product offerings of major software companies such as IBM or Microsoft, or of leading vendors of enterprise knowledge infrastructure technology, such as Hyperwave or Open Text. However, there are still many small companies offering innovative tools that require integration with other application systems and platforms.

Many organizations have undergone substantial reorganization during the last 10 years when they exchanged proprietary, unintegrated solutions for standard enterprise resource planning systems. Both horizontal and vertical integration of structured data stored in relational databases has substantially improved transparency of business transactions in organizations and increased data quality and flexibility of the organization's business processes and reporting system. Recently, application functions of major standard enterprise resource planning systems have been described as Web services. When realizing KM services, enterprise resource planning services thus can be accessed in a standardized way. Moreover, KM services often aim at the integration of semistructured data dispersed in numerous servers and individual PCs, largely unintegrated and consequently hindering knowledge work. Both enterprise resource planning services as well as KM services are needed in—and called from—weakly structured knowledge processes as much as from mostly well-structured business processes.

Summing up, the situation in many organizations is that there are a number of KM initiatives similar to the ones described previously under way with no systematic strategic considerations on how these can be coordinated, on how double efforts and redundancies can be avoided, on how ICT services relevant for KM can be integrated, and on how KM initiatives and activities can be aligned with the organization's business strategy. We will pick up this idea and explore some of the main drivers of these "scattered" KM initiatives, where this balancing has not yet taken place. Current KM initiatives may suffer from the following problems:

- **Lack of strategic alignment:** Often, technology-oriented KM initiatives are not sufficiently or not at all aligned with a KM strategy and the corresponding business strategy. Alignment is important, though, for putting emphasis on business performance outcome as the key driver ensuring that relevant processes, activities, and related ICT are adopted, modified, rejected, replaced, or enhanced in service of business performance (Malhotra, 2005, p. 16).

- **Lack of business process orientation:** A reasonable process-orientation is regarded to be beneficial for successful KM initiatives, as knowledge that contributes to value added activities is successfully linked to activities in business processes (Maier & Remus, 2002). This seems to be one of the most pressing and challenging theoretical research issues in KM (Scholl, König, Meyer & Heisig, 2004).

- **KM fragmentation:** Isolated applied KM measures, procedures, instruments, tools, or services have been implemented to solve particular knowledge-related problems, but are not connected or integrated with each other. The authors have consulted numerous organizations in the development of their KM initiative and almost always have seen numerous KM programs in parallel that often have not even taken notice of each other. Although KM set out to help organizations avoid re-inventing the wheel, KM initiatives often follow the same pattern and implement activities redundantly.

Often, proposed top-down KM approaches are not successful, first, because they ignore that a large number of KM measures, instruments, and tools are already in place or under way, and second, because top-down approaches are often not supported by people actually working with KM in their daily tasks. We agree that a strategy-pull model as proposed by Malhotra (2005), in contrast to a technology-push model of KM, could solve some of the problems mentioned. However, practical approaches to implement this type of strategy are still missing. We believe that a process-oriented KM strategy needs to design an organizational infrastructure suitable to implement strategy-pull models of KM without losing the momentum created in many fragmented KM projects in an organization.

Process-Oriented Knowledge Management

Process-oriented knowledge management (pKM) aims at the integration of business processes and knowledge management (Allweyer, 1999; Davenport et al., 1996; Eppler, Seifried, & Röpnack, 1999; Heisig, 2001; Maier, 2004; Remus, 2002) offering a number of advantages for KM such as orienting KM towards the value chain, providing relevant context, and aiding navigation in enterprise knowledge infrastructures, applying widely accepted management methods, thus supporting pKM, particularly design, implementation, and integration of enterprise knowledge infrastructures (Maier & Remus, 2002). In order to implement pKM and thus provide knowledge for value-adding activities within the business processes, KM instruments and ICT services for KM have to be adapted to business and knowledge processes. In detail, KM instruments, such as content management, skill management, lessons learned, communities, and the corresponding bundles of ICT services that support their implementation, have to be assigned to KM activities and processes. Models and patterns that describe generic pKM processes (Remus & Schub, 2003) can build a blueprint for the implementation and support the stepwise integration of business processes into the knowledge life cycle. Fundamental to pKM is that all instruments, measures, and methods described in the following levels are responsible for setting up and fostering the "flow of knowledge" within and between (knowledge-intensive) business processes which correspond to the concept of a closed knowledge life cycle. A complete knowledge life cycle consists of the KM activities creation, acquisition, organization, distribution, application, and improvement of knowledge (e. g., Nissen, Kamel, & Sengupta, 2000). Central levels of intervention in the light of a pKM approach are (Maier & Remus, 2003):

- **Strategy:** The starting point of a pKM initiative is the definition of a pKM strategy guiding the implementation of the other levels of intervention. The role of a pKM strategy is to guide the design of business and knowledge processes that avoid the problems of "core rigidity" (Leonard-Barton, 1992) in the case of resource orientation (Wernerfelt, 1984) and strategic overstretching of competencies in the case of market orientation (Porter, 1996). A pKM strategy should be able to balance both orientations by considering the organization's core competencies and, at the same time, its market and customer orientation, respectively.

- **Topics/content:** A pKM initiative extends the knowledge base by knowledge about processes which is typically embodied in process models and process warehouses, and by knowledge which is created and used within processes. Knowledge about processes can provide part of the context that is important for the interpretation and construction of process-relevant knowledge. A process-oriented knowledge structure can help to avoid information overload by filtering and presenting knowledge from a variety of sources internal and external to the organization according to the specific needs of a certain activity in a business process.

- **Instruments and systems:** Typical KM instruments are content management, yellow pages, process communities and knowledge networks, knowledge maps, lessons learned, and best practices. Additionally, a pKM approach considers instruments originally developed for process management like continuous process improvement and process modeling. Activities, roles, and responsibilities as well as resources (e. g., ICT systems) have to be defined for each of these instruments and combined into knowledge processes. Enterprise knowledge in-frastructures are expanded, for example, by functions for managing process knowledge, by functions supporting ad-hoc workflows, task, and project management, by functions to build and navigate process-oriented knowledge structures as well as functions that realize process-oriented push and pull of knowledge elements. Process-oriented enterprise knowledge infrastructures should also have strong links to tools for modeling, simulation, monitoring, and controlling knowledge processes.

- **KM organization and processes:** So-called knowledge-intensive business processes, knowledge processes, and KM processes implement specific KM instruments and activities. *Knowledge-intensive operative business processes* are often core processes along the value chain and primarily use knowledge in order to create process outputs. *Knowledge processes* are service processes that support the exchange of knowledge between business units and business processes. Examples are processes that support the collection, organization, storing, and distribution of knowledge as an outcome of business processes or processes that manage the allocation of skills and expertise to business processes or projects. *Knowledge management processes* control and manage the organizational knowledge base and realize an external management cycle, for example, the continuous improvement of the knowledge base. In pKM, activities of the knowledge life cycle are combined into knowledge processes. These processes have to be linked to other knowledge processes and also business processes, for example, enhancing existing activities in business processes with specific KM activities, such as documenting lessons learned or modeling process knowledge.

KM SERVICE INFRASTRUCTURE

In this section, we outline the idea of a KM service infrastructure where, similar to the concept of service-oriented architecture (SOA) (e. g., Papazoglou & Georgakopoulos, 2003), so-called KM services are utilized to develop an integrated, process-oriented KM. KM services are first structured from a strategic perspective with the help of Wiig's focus areas and then their implementation is sketched with the help of a service layer architecture.

KM Services According to Wiig's Focus Areas

Often, KM measures and tools have been bundled as KM instruments to provide specific KM services, concentrating on one out of four specific KM focus areas identified by Wiig (1999, p. 158). Table 1 briefly describes Wiig's four KM focus areas and gives examples for KM instruments and KM tools and systems for each of these areas.

The focus areas are well suited to structure KM instruments and tools as can be found in the literature. They help organizations concentrate their KM efforts towards specific goals. This focusing would represent a strategic decision. Consequently, a process-oriented KM strategy could set an enterprise effectiveness focus whereas

a different KM intervention could concentrate on the human resource management side of KM in a people focus. However, practical KM initiatives in organizations regularly are not restricted to one of these focus areas, but implement organizational (instruments) and technical (tools and systems) solutions for more than one focus area. Strategically, the focus areas could provide a tactical plan for subsequently engaging in KM efforts with each step targeted at one of the focus areas. In the end, solutions in all four focus areas could positively affect the organization's competitive position. The KM tools and systems in the last column can be described as collections of services. Their integration requires the composition of services which is typically implemented with the help of a service-oriented architecture.

KM Services and Service Layer Architecture

Generally, a service is an abstract resource that represents a capability of performing tasks that form a coherent functionality from the point of view of providers entities and requesters entities (W3C, 2004a). It consists of a contract, interfaces, and implementation and has a distinctive functional meaning typically reflecting some high-level business concept covering data and business logic (Krafzig, Banke & Slama, 2005,

Table 1. KM focus areas, instruments, and tools

focus area	description	examples for KM instruments	examples for KM tools and systems
intellectual asset	maximize building and value re-allocation of intellectual capital	management of patents and licenses, KM scorecards	management information system, reporting system
people	maximize effectiveness of people-centric learning organization	competence management, communities, knowledge networks, coaching, mentoring	skill management system, yellow pages, social software, Weblog, Wiki, Web-based training
enterprise effectiveness	maximize use of knowledge assets; operational effectiveness	lessons learned, good/best practices, knowledge process re-engineering	lessons learned database, case-based reasoning, process warehouse
information technology	use IT and IM to maximize the capture, transformation, storage, retrieval, and development of knowledge	semantic content management, instruments for discovery, publication, collaboration and learning, personalization, and adaptation	knowledge portal, knowledge management system, learning infrastructure

pp. 57-59). The service concept has gained much popularity with the advent of a set of standards that allow for open interaction between software applications using Web services. A Web service is a software system, identified by a URI, whose public interfaces and bindings are defined and described using XML. Its definition can be discovered by other software systems. These systems may then interact with the Web service in a manner prescribed by its definition, using XML-based messages conveyed by Internet protocols (W3C, 2004b; see also Alonso, 2004). Web services are one way of implementing business and technical services in a service-oriented architecture. A service-oriented architecture is based on the concepts of an application front-end, services, service repository, and service bus (Krafzig et al., 2005, p. 57) which together make business and technical functions available as independent services that can be accessed without any information of their implementation.

Consequently, KM services are a subset of services offered in an organization, both basic and composed, whose functionality supports high-level KM instruments as part of on-demand KM initiatives. [1] Examples for these services are "find expert", "submit experience", "publish skill profile", "revisit learning resource", or "join community-of-interest". Services are offered by service providers who procure the service implementations, supply their service descriptions, and provide the necessary support. Often, KM services cater to the special needs of one or a small number of organizational units, for example, a process, work group, department or subsidiary, factory, or outlet, in order to provide a solution to a defined business problem. KM services describe individual aspects of KM instruments implemented in heterogenous application systems that can be combined into an enterprise knowledge infrastructure.

Figure 1. KM service infrastructure

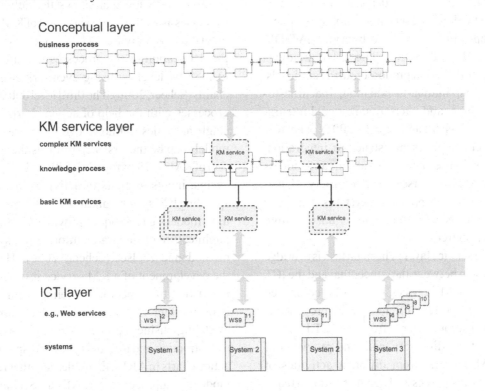

Basic services can be composed into new composite services enabling larger integrated KM services. In addition, service descriptions have to be published in order to provide information about service capability, interface, behavior, and quality (Papazoglou & Georgakopoulos, 2003). Figure 1 shows the main layers of a KM service infrastructure.

- **Conceptual layer:** Based on process descriptions, the conceptual layer defines which services are required in which core business processes, which services are offered by what service processes, who is responsible for them, and what resources are allocated to fulfill them. Concepts of process-oriented KM can especially help to analyze, understand, and design business and knowledge processes with regard to a knowledge-oriented and, at the same time, strategic perspective on KM services in business processes.

- **ICT layer:** Services are described, discovered, and invoked with the help of negotiated or standardized sets of technologies, for example, in the case of Web services, WSDL, UDDI, and SOAP. These technologies support the integration on different levels, that is, human-to-machine, machine-to-machine, and inter-organizational integration (Puschmann & Alt, 2005). The ICT layer comprises infrastructure, integration, knowledge, personalization, and access services dispersed over a variety of heterogeneous application systems that cover structured as well as semi or unstructured data sources.

- **KM service layer:** The main task is to bridge the gap between the conceptual and the ICT layer. KM services have to be composed using services offered by heterogeneous application systems from the ICT layer. In addition, discovery, call, and provision of KM services from different activities of business processes have to be supported.

In the next three sections, these three layers will be described in detail.

CONCEPTUAL LAYER

In this section, we will demonstrate our idea of a KM service infrastructure using a real-life example of a knowledge process and its composition by KM services. One important prerequisite is the identification, separation, and description of relevant processes.

We draw from a pKM modeling project aimed at extending quality management in order to improve knowledge sharing within and between the core business processes for the transaction business of one of the five largest German universal banks. A complex process landscape consisting of several knowledge processes was defined and modeled (Maier & Remus, 2003; Remus & Schub, 2003). Our conceptual layer provides different levels of abstraction.

The highest level displays the activity and process landscape that shows the definition of processes as well as the assignment of KM instruments to KM activities. The second level refines the delineation of the processes that are shown in the first level by using event-driven process chains (Scheer, 2000). The third level details these processes with the help of action charts linking single activities to knowledge structures. These models can be the first step towards the description of KM services together with their triggering events, inputs, outputs of activities, and corresponding ICT systems and tools. In this project, we used modeling techniques provided by the ARIS (architecture of integrated information systems) method and toolset (Scheer, 2000). However, the development of a KM service infrastructure is not tied to a specific modeling technique as long as other methods provide techniques for modeling business processes on different levels of abstraction and a model type corresponding to action charts in ARIS. Examples for other relevant modeling approaches are ADONIS (Junginger et al., 2000), ARIS (Scheer, 2000), PROMET for process development (PROMET BPR), and for process-oriented introduction of standard software (PROMET SSW) (Österle, 1995), semantic object modeling (SOM) (Ferstl & Sinz, 1995), or business process modeling methods on the basis of the unified modeling language (UML) (Oestereich, 2003). *Action charts* illustrate which service objects are consumed, produced, and transformed. In case of the implementation of a pKM initiative, these service objects are typically knowledge objects.

In general, service descriptions have to provide information about (Papazoglou & Georgakopoulos, 2003):

- **service capability,** stating the conceptual purpose and expected result of the service by the description of output objects;

- **Service interface,** publishing the services signature (input/output/error parameters and message types);
- **Service behaviour,** which can be described as a detailed workflow process invoking other services; and
- **Quality of service,** publishing important functional and nonfunctional service quality attributes (e. g., service metering, costs, performance metrics, security attributes).

Figure 2 shows the example knowledge process "*knowledge documentation*", consisting of the two parallel subprocesses, content and skill management, with its main activities and triggering events. We used event-driven process chains for modeling processes (Scheer, 2000).

Every event-driven process chain is represented as a diagram. The recommended direction

Figure 2. KM services of the knowledge documentation process

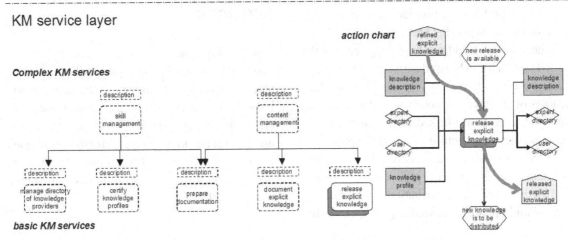

219

of reading is from left to right. Functions represent tasks or activities performed as part of the interactions from one or more objects. They are displayed as a rectangle with rounded corners. Functions produce events or states which in turn can cause a change of states of these objects or the execution of other functions. Events specify relevant states for objects that must be satisfied before functions can be executed and are displayed as hexagons. To display possible alternatives of similar business processes in one diagram, the event-driven process chain contains logical operators (OR, XOR, AND) that are used to describe different sequences of actions.

Experiences (i. e., lessons learned) that have been documented during the execution of business processes have to be managed regularly by initiating the process "knowledge documentation". In order to avoid information overload and to guarantee a high quality standard of the knowledge base, changes within the knowledge base have to be evaluated. Therefore, appropriate measures to value, refine, certify, and release knowledge have to be carried out (link to the process "enhancement of the knowledge base"). It is important to distinguish between explicit and implicit knowledge, since both types need different measures in handling knowledge. Explicit knowledge can be documented directly whereas implicit knowledge can only be addressed by developing and maintaining an expert and user directory in which knowledge profiles are provided and linked to content in the knowledge base.

The result is an updated knowledge base with knowledge that can be used actively within business processes. It contains updated knowledge profiles of employees together with documented knowledge. Both are linked to functions in the business processes with the help of the process-oriented knowledge structure. A subject matter specialist can then release parts of the updated knowledge base for distribution. In addition, refined and updated knowledge profiles have to

be certified by discussions between employers and employees.

The next step is to determine which services are required to fulfill the process. At one extreme, the process can be viewed as one single, but complex, service; at the other extreme, service granularity could be so fine that the process can be constructed from multiple services. Similar to concepts in SOA, the choice is made by balancing quality of service characteristics (QoS), ubiquitous service reuse, and reduction of complexity for service composition (Crawford, Bate, Cgerbakov, Holley & Tsocanos, 2005).

In our case, KM services can be viewed as encapsulated KM activities, accessible by an interface and described by action charts (providing an initial service description). The composition of KM services is presented in Figure 2, together with one detailed service description (as action chart) for the KM service "release explicit knowledge" in our knowledge documentation process. This KM service approves content and makes it accessible to the employees of the company. It releases knowledge descriptions, user and expert dictionaries, and assigns appropriate user privileges for the envisioned target group. It is based on the input "refined explicit knowledge" and produces the output "released explicit knowledge".

ICT LAYER: INFRASTRUCTURE SERVICES

The ICT layer describes the services offered by heterogeneous application systems that have to be selected, called, and combined in order to provide basic KM services. A comprehensive platform-type solution for these services has been termed an enterprise knowledge infrastructure (see section 2. 1). From an ICT perspective, services can be structured into the following categories (Maier, 2004):

Infrastructure services: The Intranet infrastructure provides basic functionality for (1) communication, that is, synchronous and asynchronous communication and the sharing of data and documents; (2) storage, that is, the management of electronic assets in general and of Web content in particular; and (3) processing, that is, in analogy to data warehousing, extract, transformation, and loading tools that provide access to data sources which can be organization-internal or -external, structured or semistructured data sources. Inspection services (viewer) are required for heterogeneous data and document formats.

Integration services: Learning objects or knowledge elements have to be described by metadata. Metadata are represented, stored, extracted, queried, typed, and connected with the help of an ontology that meaningfully organizes and links knowledge elements that come from a variety of sources and are used to analyze the semantics of the organizational knowledge base (Maier & Peinl, 2005). Generally, an ontology is an explicit specification of a shared conceptualization (Gruber, 1993, p. 199). Ontologies in KM are formal models of an application domain that help to exchange and share knowledge with the help of ICT systems and, as an integration tool, within and between application systems. Synchronization services export a portion of the knowledge workspace for work off-line and (re)integrate the results of work on knowledge elements that has been done off-line.

Knowledge services: The core knowledge processes search and retrieval, publication, collaboration, and learning are supported by knowledge services. These are key components of the enterprise knowledge infrastructure and provide intelligent functions for:

- **Discovery:** search, retrieval, and presentation of knowledge elements and experts with the help of, for example, mining, visualization, mapping, and navigation tools;

- **Publication:** the joint authoring, structuring, contextualization, and release of knowledge elements supported by workflows;

- **Collaboration:** supports the joint creation, sharing, and application of knowledge by knowledge providers and seekers with the help of, for example, contextualized communication and coordination tools, location and awareness management tools, community home spaces, and experience management tools; and

- **Learning:** supported, for example, by authoring tools and tools for managing courses, tutoring, learning paths, and examinations.

Personalization services: The main aim of personalization services is to provide a more effective access to the large amounts of knowledge elements. Subject matter specialists or managers of knowledge processes can organize a portion of the contents and services for specific roles or develop role-oriented push services. Also, both the portal and the services can be personalized with the help of, for example, interest profiles, personal category nets, and personalizable portals. Automated profiling can aid personalization of functions, contents, and services.

Access services: The participant accesses the organization's enterprise knowledge infrastructure with the help of a variety of services that translate and transform the contents and communication between infrastructure and heterogeneous applications and appliances. This layer integrates the services of the other layers into the application systems designed for and used in the various business processes that have to be supported. Also, the infrastructure has to be protected against eavesdropping and unauthorized use by tools for authentication and authorization.

These categories help to structure existing services offered by different application systems. Next to semantic integration between these services, process integration is required in the form of KM service composition which is explained in the following section.

KM Service Layer

Regardless of the implementation, it is important to understand the steps required to decompose a process into a series of complex and basic services and operational characteristics (Crawford et al., 2005). Composing KM services means specifying how these services have to be discovered and selected (discovery), how they have to be accessed from different activities of business processes (call), and finally how these services are provided by the service infrastructure accessing heterogeneous application systems from the ICT layer (binding, provision). Modeling techniques help define the composition of services (Crawford et al., 2005). Figure 3 shows the interplay between conceptual and ICT layers by the example of

invoking the complex KM service "search for experts" from the *business process layer*. On the *conceptual layer*, this KM service has to be described using *knowledge process descriptions* and *action charts* specifying basic input and output parameters. The area of expertise is required as the minimum input parameter. Further input parameters can be specified that describe the context of the situation in which the service is invoked. Examples for context parameters are (1) process, that is, the business process or task that the person is currently engaged in; (2) person, that is, the profile of the person invoking the service, for example, areas of expertise or skill levels; (3) preferences, for example, for synchronous vs. asynchronous communication channels; (4) products, that is, electronic resources concerning the area of expertise that have already been collected and/or analyzed by the person, for example, learning resources, handbooks, reports, or lessons learned; (5) applications and appliances,

Figure 3. KM service invocation

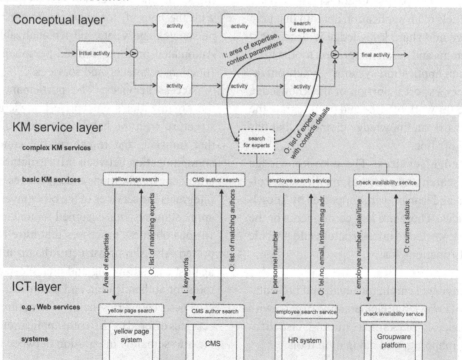

for example, a Web browser on a desktop PC or a mobile application on a smartphone; (6) location and time, for example, the GPS coordinates or the connection, such as wired LAN, wireless LAN, or UMTS connection as well as the date and time, normalized according to the time zone, which might help to determine the appropriate way of contacting experts; and (7) urgency of the need for an expert. The execution of the service results in a list of experts, brief descriptions, contact history, and information about the (social) relationship to the searcher, for example, common business acquaintances and the contact and availability details, ordered according to the preferences of the experts together with links to further KM services that can be invoked in order to establish a connection to the selected expert.

The middle layer in Figure 3 shows the composition of a number of basic KM services into one complex KM service and maps the required basic KM services to actual, "real" services offered as part of the ICT layer. The complex KM service "search for experts" is composed of the basic KM services 1-"yellow page search", 2-"CMS author search", 3-"employee search service", and 4-"check availability service". The yellow page search service delivers a list of IDs (e. g., personnel numbers) for experts matching the input parameter of an area of expertise. The "CMS author search" requires a list of keywords describing the area of expertise. The complex KM service "search for experts" invokes an integration service (see section 5) for the task of finding keywords that describe the area of expertise. The keywords are assigned to areas of expertise either in a simple database solution or in a more advanced solution using an ontology. With the help of an inference engine, these relationships together with rules in the ontology can be used to determine a list of keywords. The "CMS author search" then returns a list of IDs of matching authors or active contributors to the CMS respectively. An "employee search service" takes the personnel numbers found in the "yellow

page search" and the "CMS author search" and returns contact details, for example, telephone number, e-mail address, or instant messaging address. Finally, the "check availability service" delivers the current status of the experts and a decision on their availability.

The *ICT layer* binds the basic KM services of the conceptual layer to actual application systems in the current work environment of the searcher that are able to deliver these services. In the case example, there are a yellow page system, two CMSs, a HR system, a groupware platform, and an instant messaging system that offer Web services fitting to the descriptions of the basic KM services on the conceptual layer. Depending on which systems are accessible to the calling complex KM service, the actual implementation could consist, for example, of basic services 1 and 3; 2 and 3; 1, 3, and 4; or 1, 2, 3, and 4, respectively. Consequently, the description of the complex KM service needs to include some specification of what basic KM services are mandatory and what combinations of basic KM services are allowed. Figure 3 shows the three layers and an example of calls of KM services from activities in business processes and their binding to the corresponding Web services on the ICT layer.

CONCLUSION

When designing and implementing KM infrastructures, KM initiatives can employ service orientation as an additional strategic guideline. We proposed a three-layered KM service infrastructure that composes services from heterogeneous applications into specific KM services and supports discovery, call, and provision of KM services from activities within business processes. This infrastructure will help solve the problems mentioned earlier:

Strategic alignment is realized by connecting KM services to the materialization of strategic decisions (e. g., customer orientation) in the form of business processes and corresponding application systems on the ICT level. The deployment of KM services in organizations might profit substantially from both the integration and the corresponding alignment with strategic goals.

Process orientation is realized by not only focusing on business processes as main drivers for calling KM services, but also on knowledge processes, which comprise a procedural view of a bundle of KM instruments implemented by KM services that are in turn described with the help of action charts. The numerous KM measures, procedures, instruments, or tools applied in isolation from each other are integrated by bundling KM instruments to provide complex KM services. Business processes determine which KM services are required in which core business processes, are offered by what service processes, who is responsible for them, and what resources are allocated to fulfill them.

A concise KM architecture consisting of a KM service infrastructure on different levels will help reduce the complexity and improve the flexibility of current KM initiatives. A set of accompanying procedures, models, and tools, for example, a blueprint defining reference processes (Remus & Schub, 2003), corresponding modeling techniques for business and knowledge processes, and KM services and tools will support the deployment and improvement of the KM service infrastructure.

FUTURE RESEARCH DIRECTIONS

In today's global hypercompetition, projects and business processes are becoming increasingly knowledge-intensive. Borders between projects and more rigid processes begin to blur. This is due to the organizations' intentions to increase their flexibility by designing business processes and supporting ICT infrastructures to become more agile and adaptive, including highly flexible project-oriented tasks. In order to take into account these new developments, future KM approaches

will have to become more and more "on-demand" and "just-in-time" (Davenport & Glaser, 2002; Tsui, 2005). Consequently, KM technologies have to operate increasingly on infrastructures that support rapid deployment of relevant tools and systems for ad-hoc, intensive, and inter-organizational collaborations (Tsui, 2005).

Organizations are also increasingly dependent on knowledge assets as primary sources of competitive advantage. More flexibility and opening up of knowledge-intensive business processes with the help of KM initiatives typically aims at increasing transparency of knowledge and enhancing knowledge sharing in order to accelerate the pace of reusing knowledge assets. This also bears risks that knowledge-based competitive advantages are diluted. Another future research direction thus will focus on management of knowledge risks and aim at finding ways for protecting sensitive knowledge assets while at the same time increasing sharing of nonsensitive knowledge assets.

Designing more flexible business processes and infrastructures could also increase activity costs, both of primary activities and of support activities that have to quickly adapt to changed requirements by primary activities. Thus, it will be important to work towards an optimum level of agility that balances the needs to adapt to an ever-changing environment with the efforts to design, implement, and deploy such an infrastructure. One of the major advantages of a KM service infrastructure is the ability to build it once and reuse it frequently. However, the efforts to implement a KM service infrastructure should not be underestimated. Already established KM services have to be identified and made available. New KM services have to be implemented. KM services have to be composed and decomposed finding the appropriate level of detail. Quality of KM services has to be assessed and documented in order to provide a constant level of quality throughout the knowledge life cycle. Still, a procedure model or a roadmap is required which guides building and improving KM service infrastructures.

Another key issue is the further development of standards in order to describe and model KM services in terms of service capability, service interface, service behavior, and quality of service. These standards create the potential to support KM initiatives, in which KM services, located across multiple organizations can be integrated. With regard to increasing process standards, it will be interesting to see whether there will be a similar movement towards standardization of knowledge-intensive business processes and knowledge processes. This could lead to process standards similar to the ones already established for specific domains, for example, the capability maturity model for global standards in software development processes (Davenport, 2005). Our approach can be seen as a first step towards this direction.

REFERENCES

Allweyer, T. (1999). A framework for redesigning and managing knowledge processes. Retrieved May 22, 2007, from http://www. processworld. com/ content/docs/8. doc/

Alonso, G., Casati, F., Kuno, H., & Machiraju, V. (2004). *Web services: Concepts, architectures and applications*. Berlin: Springer.

April, K. A. (2002). Guidelines for developing a k-strategy. *Journal of Knowledge Management, 6*(5), 445-456.

Crawford, C. H., Bate, B. P., Cgerbakov, L., Holley, K., & Tsocanos, C. (2005). Toward an on demand service-oriented architecture. *IBM Systems Journal, 44*(1), 81-107.

Davenport, T. H. (2005, June). The coming commoditization of processes. *Harvard Business Review, 83*(6), 101-108.

Davenport, T. H., & Glaser, J. (2002). Just-in-time delivery comes to knowledge management. *Harvard Business Review*(July 2002), 5-9.

Davenport, T. H., Jarvenpaa, S. L., & Beers, M. C. (1996). Improving knowledge work processes. *Sloan Management Review, 37*(4), 53-65.

Drucker, P. F. (1994). The age of social transformation. *The Atlantic Monthly, 274*(5), 53-80.

Eppler, M., Seifried, P., & Röpnack, A. (1999). *Improving knowledge intensive processes through an enterprise knowledge medium*. Paper presented at the 1999 ACM SIGPR CONFERENCE, New Orleans, Louisiana.

Ferstl, O. K., & Sinz, E. J. (1995). Der Ansatz des Semantischen Objektmodells (SOM) zur Modellierung von Geschäftsprozessen. *Wirtschaftsinformatik, 37*(3), 209-220.

Gruber, T. R. (1993). A translation approach to portable ontology specifications. *Knowledge Acquisition, 5*(2), 199-220.

Hansen, M. T., Nohria, N., & Tierney, T. (1999, March-April). What's your strategy for managing knowledge. *Harvard Business Review*, pp. 680-689.

Heisig, P. (2001). Business process oriented knowledge management. In K. Mertins, P. Heisig & J. Vorbeck (Eds.), *Knowledge management: Best practices in Europe* (pp. 13-26). Berlin: Springer.

Junginger, S., et al. (2000). Ein Geschäftsprozessmanagementwerkzeug der nächsten Generation - adonis: Konzeption und Anwendungen. *Wirtschaftsinformatik, 42*(5), 392-401.

Krafzig, D., Banke, K., & Slama, D. (2005). *Enterprise SOA: Service-oriented architecture best practices*. Upper Saddle River, NJ.

Leonard-Barton, D. (1992). Core capabilities and core rigidities: A paradox in managing new product development. *Strategic Management Journal, 13*, 111-125.

Maier, R. (2004). *Knowledge management systems: Information and communication technologies for knowledge management* (2nd ed.). Berlin: Springer-Verlag.

Maier, R., Hädrich, T., & Peinl, R. (2005). *Enterprise knowledge infrastructures.* Berlin: Springer-Verlag.

Maier, R., & Peinl, R. (2005). Semantische Dokumentbeschreibung in Enterprise Knowledge Infrastructures. *HMD - Praxis der Wirtschaftsinformatik*(246), 84-92.

Maier, R., & Remus, U. (2002). Defining process-oriented knowledge management strategies. *Journal of Process- and Knowledge Management, 9*(2), 103-118.

Maier, R., & Remus, U. (2003). Implementing process-oriented knowledge management strategies. *Journal of Knowledge Management, 7*(4), 62-74.

Malhotra, Y. (2005). Integrating knowledge management technologies in organizational business processes: Getting real time enterprises to deliver real business performance. *Journal of Knowledge Management, 9*(1), 7-26.

Nissen, M., Kamel, M., & Sengupta, K. (2000, January-March). Integrated analysis and design of knowledge systems and processes. *Information Resources Management Journal, 13*(1), 24-43.

Oestereich, B., et al. (2003). *Objektorientierte Geschäftsprozessmodellierung mit der UML.* Heidelberg: dpunkt.

Ordóñez de Pablos, P. (2002). Knowledge management and organizational learning: Typologies of knowledge strategies in the Spanish manufacturing industry from 1995 to 1999. *Journal of Knowledge Management, 6*(1), 52-62.

Österle, H. (1995). *Business engineering: Prozeß- und Systementwicklung. Band 1: Entwurfstechniken.* Berlin et al.

Papazoglou, M. P., & Georgakopoulos, D. (2003). Service-oriented computing. *Communication of the ACM, 46*(10), 25-28.

Porter, M. E. (1996). What is strategy? *Harvard Business Review, 74*(5-6), 61-78.

Puschmann, T., & Alt, R. (2005). Developing an integration architecture for process portals. *European Journal of Information Systems, 14*(2), 121-134.

Remus, U. (2002). *Prozessorientiertes Wissensmanagement, Konzepte und Modellierung.* PhD thesis, University of Regensburg, Regensburg.

Remus, U., & Schub, S. (2003). A blueprint for the implementation of process-oriented knowledge management. *Journal of Process- and Knowledge Management, 10*(4), 237-253.

Rollet, H. (2003). *Knowledge management: Processes and technologies.* Dordrecht: Kluwer.

Scheer, A. (2000). *Aris: Business process modelling* (3rd ed.). Berlin.

Scholl, W., König, C., Meyer, B., & Heisig, P. (2004). The future of knowledge management: An international Deplhi study. *Journal of Knowledge Management, 8*(2), 19-35.

Tsui, E. (2005). The role of it in KM: Where are we now and where are we heading? *Journal of Knowledge Management, 9*(1), 3-6.

W3C. (2004a). Web services architecture requirements. Retrieved May 22, 2007, from *http://www.w3.org/TR/wsa-reqs/*

W3C. (2004b). Web services glossary. Retrieved May 22, 2007, from http://www.w3.org/TR/2004/NOTE-ws-gloss-20040211/

Wernerfelt, B. (1984). A resource-based view of the firm. *Strategic Management Journal, 5*(2), 171-180.

Wiig, K. M. (1999). What future knowledge management users may expect. *Journal of Knowledge Management, 3*(2), 155-165.

Wolff, E. N. (2005). The growth of information workers. *Communications of the ACM, 48*(10), 37-42.

Zack, M. H. (1999a). Developing a knowledge strategy. *California Management Review, 41*(3), 125-145.

Zack, M. H. (1999b). Managing codified knowledge. *Sloan Management Review, 40*(4), 45-58.

ADDITIONAL READING

Alonso, G., Casati, F., Kuno, H., & Machiraju, V. (2004). *Web services: Concepts, architectures and applications.* Berlin.

Bayer, F., & Maier, R. (2006, September) Knowledge risks in inter-organizational knowledge transfer. In K. Tochtermann & H. Maurer (Eds.), *Proceedings of the 6th International Conference on Knowledge Management (I-Know '06)* (pp. 76-84).

Chen, Y., Zhou, L., & Zhang, D. (2006). Ontology-supported Web service composition: An approach to service-oriented knowledge management in corporate financial services. *Journal of Database Management, 17*(1), 67-84.

Collins, H. (2003). *Enterprise knowledge portals.* New York.

Davenport, T. H., & Glaser, J. (2002, July). Just-in-time delivery comes to knowledge management. *Harvard Business Review*, pp. 5-9.

Desouza, K. C. (Ed.). (2005). *New frontiers of knowledge management.* Basingstoke.

Dumas, M., van der Aalst, W., & Hofstede, A. t. (2005). *Process aware information systems: Bridging people and software through process technology.* New York.

Firestone, J. M. (2003). *Enterprise information portals and knowledge management.* Amsterdam.

Holsapple, C. W. (Ed.). (2003). *Handbook on knowledge management* (Vol. 1-2). Berlin.

Illeris, K. (2003). Workplace learning and learning theory. *Journal of Workplace Learning, 15*(4), 167-178.

Jennex, M. E. (Ed.). (2005). *Case studies in knowledge management.* Hershey, PA.

Jordan, J., & Lowe, J. (2004). Protecting strategic knowledge: Insights from collaborative agreements in the aerospace sector. *Technology Analysis and Strategic Management, 16*(2), 241-259.

Krafzig, D., Banke, K., & Slama, D. (2005). *Enterprise SOA: Service-oriented architecture best practices.* Upper Saddle River, NJ.

Kwan, M., & Balasubramanian, P. (2003). Process-oriented knowledge management: A case study. *The Journal of the Operational Research Society, 54*(2), 204-211.

Maier, R. (2007). *Knowledge management systems. Information and communication technologies for knowledge management* (3rd ed.). Berlin: Springer-Verlag.

Marjanovic, O. (2005). Towards IS supported coordination in emergent business processes. *Business Process Management Journal, 11*(5), 476-487.

Marks, E. A., & Bell, M. (2006). *Service-oriented architecture (SOA): A planning and implementation guide for business and technology.* New York.

Miltiadis, D. L., & Naeve, A. (Eds.). (2006). *Intelligent learning infrastructures for knowledge-intensive organisations.* London.

Papazoglou, M. P., & Georgakopoulos, D. (2003). Service-oriented computing. *Communications of the ACM, Vol. 46*(10), 25-28.

Sambamurthy, V., & Subramani, M. (2005). Special issue on information technologies and knowledge management. *MIS Quarterly, 29*(1), 1-7.

Sampson, D., Karagiannidis, C., Schenone, A., & Cardinali, F. (2002). Knowledge-on-demand in e-learning and e-working settings [Special Issue on Integrating Technology into Learning and Working]. *Educational Technology & Society Journal, 5*(2), 107-112.

Strohmaier, M., & Tochtermann, K. (2005). B-KIDE: A framework and a tool for business process-oriented knowledge infrastructure development. *Knowledge and Process Management, 12*(3), 171.

Woitsch, R., & Karagiannis, D. (2002). Process-oriented knowledge management systems based on KM-services: The PROMOTE(R) approach. *International Journal of Intelligent Systems in Accounting, Finance and Management, 11*(4), 253-267.

Wolff, E. N. (2005). The growth of information workers. *Communications of the ACM, 48*(10), 37-42.

Zack, M. H. (1999) (Ed.). *Knowledge and strategy.* Boston.

Zyngier, S., Burstein, F., & McKay, J. (2006, January 4-7). The role of knowledge management governance in the implementation of strategy. In *Proceedings of the 39th Hawaii International Conference on System Science*, Kauai, Hawaii. Knowledge Management Systems Track.

ENDNOTE

[1] The terms knowledge service and knowledge management service both reflect components in support of KM initiatives and thus are treated as synonyms in this paper.

Chapter XI
Aligning Knowledge and Business Strategies within an Artificial *Ba* Context[1]

Hannu Kivijärvi
Helsinki School of Economics, Finland

ABSTRACT

Knowledge is the capability to make decisions and the primary resource for all organizational transformations. It allows strategic decision making, the planning and control of organizational activities, the management of everyday business operations as well as our personal behaviour. Knowledge exists at various levels, not only at the personal level but also at group and organizational levels. Organizational knowledge is a special type of knowledge, 'collective understanding', that is valid in a specific organizational context. The focus and contribution of this chapter is first to provide a theoretical basis for a knowledge strategy called artificial Ba and, secondly, to develop a concrete, artificial Ba that supports the alignment of knowledge and business strategies. The proposed system is a complete 'artifact', a supportive environment in which knowledge accumulates and is shared, a system that is built to activate existing knowledge and to support the creation of valuable new knowledge in an organization.

INTRODUCTION

As far as we know, the world we are living in consists only of two things: matter and energy. From a strictly physical point of view there does not exist anything else. Knowledge and information, for example, are thus only an illusion. However, in the social sciences, information, knowledge and their processing are valued as the key characteristics of human beings and the growth engine of teams, organisations and the whole society. Over modern history, but particularly during the last few decades, the underlying properties of knowledge and knowledge management have continually been investigated in the relevant literature, especially in the philosophical, managerial, sociological, and information sciences.

Because knowledge is a complex, ambiguous, and multidimensional concept it has been interpreted, understood and classified in a number of ways. Most of us are Polanyi's prisoners within his concept of personal knowledge and the dichotomy between tacit and explicit knowledge (Polanyi, 1962). Polanyi's stress on the personal dimension of all knowledge has directed relevant research in the field during last forty years more than any other conceptual innovation. Although it may be true that 'all knowing is personal knowing', all knowledge is not necessarily personal knowledge. Organizations have a common capability to act, i.e. knowledge capacity or intellectual capital (Stewart, 1999), the lack of which would inevitably prevent organizational action and would lead to an unpredictable disorder and confusion.

Knowledge is today more than ever the most critical resource of organizations. As for any other critical resource, organizations should have an explicit strategy for the management of knowledge resources, too. The focus and contribution of this chapter is first to provide a theoretical basis for the definition of the key elements of knowledge strategy and then to define the knowledge strategy in a form of an artificial context that can be used to create and evaluate business strategies. The developed system allows investigating alternative business strategies and their organizational implications. The proposed approach guarantees that the knowledge strategy and business strategy are integrated and aligned at definitional, structural and procedural levels.

The next section is rather theoretical discussing e.g. the following epistemological concepts: personal and organizational knowledge, knowledge vs. knowing, knowledge definition, problems of knowledge conversion, dimensions of knowledge, organizational context, knowledge strategy, and aligning knowledge and business strategies. In section 3, the structural and procedural aspects of

alignment are of interest. Based on the conceptual discussion, we demonstrate an actual artificial environment where personal knowledge can be converted into organizational usage, new knowledge can be created, shared and expressed in the form of business strategies. We constructively show how even hidden, tacit aspects of individual knowledge can be externalized into an explicit form and generalized to organizational usage.

KNOWLEDGE CONCEPTUALIZATION

What is Knowledge?

Knowledge is an inner-centric concept. It requires human judgement, is closely related to action, and presupposes values and beliefs. Polanyi (1962) tied personal dimension to all knowledge and his master-dichotomy between tacit and explicit knowledge has shaped practically all epistemological discussion, especially since the rediscovery and popularization made by Nonaka and Takeuchi (1995). The deepest nature of explicit and specially tacit knowledge is discussed and interpreted widely. Perhaps the largest disagreement is that whether it is possible or not to 'convert' or 'transform' personal tacit knowledge to any explicit form.

Nonaka and Takeuchi (1995) proposed and Nonaka and Toyama (2003) revised four modes of knowledge conversion and their knowledge spiral assumes that both types of knowledge are fully convertible with each other. They assume that tacit knowledge can be converted into explicit knowledge by sequential use of metaphor, analogy, and model. In managerial studies this conception is widely accepted and elaborated further (Davenport & Prusak, 1998, Leonard & Sensiper, 1998). The conversion process has been conceptualized and named differently like 'articulation' (Håkanson, 2001), 'codification' (Cowan et al., 2000, Hansen et al., 1999) or 'sharing' (von Krogh, 2003, Hayes & Walsham, 2003).

However, the conversion-principle is also denied, specially in epistemological writings (Cook & Brown, 1999, Tsoukas, 2003). "Tacit knowledge cannot be turned into explicit, nor can explicit knowledge be turned into tacit" (Cook & Brown, 1999, p. 385). According to Polanyi the two ingredients of tacit knowledge, subsidiary particulars and focal target (proximal and distal, Polanyi, 1966, p. 10), are joined by the third, knower. "No knowledge is possible without the integration of the subsidiaries to the focal target by a person". (Tsoukas, 2003, p. 415). Subsidiary particulars are instrumental in the sense that they are not explicitly known by the knower during the knowing process and therefore they remain tacit. Thus, "we can know more than we can tell" (Polanyi, 1966, p. 4) or even "we can often know more than we can realise" (Leonard & Sensiper, 1998, p. 114) and we cannot directly convert tacit knowledge to explicit knowledge.

As noted above, Polanyi (1962) added the personal dimension to all knowledge. The question is: what are the other dimensions?

Three Dimensions of the World

Karl Popper (1979) divides all that exists into three domains: World 1, World 2, and World 3. World 1 consists of physical objects and events. It is the world of physics, chemistry, and biology. World 2 is the world of subjective experiences, the world of our psychological or mental states, episodes, dispositions and processes. World 3 is the entity that we create with our own intellect and it includes all abstract products of the human mind as well as their physical manifestations like the contents of libraries. It is 'the world of objective contents of thought' (Popper, 1979, p. 106). Generally, creating knowledge means adding some useful models to World 3. According to Popper's logic, World 1 and World 2 are in immediate interchange. World 2 and World 3 are equally related. On the other hand, World 1 and World 3 interact only through World 2. Because

knowledge creation, ie contributing to World 3, depends not only on World 1 and World 2 but also on existing knowledge, knowledge creation is an iterative process. The contents of World 3 that are already embodied are used to discover the 'unembodied World 3 objects'.

Popper's works have been attacked and criticized widely (e.g. Suppe, 1974). Habermas (1984) revises Popper's three-world theory when creating his theory of communicative action. He also defines three different worlds but with different terms and contents—the objective, social, and subjective worlds. The objective world contains the actual and possible states of affairs and is independent of human beings, the social world consists of normatively regulated interpersonal relations (normative context), and the subjective world of personal experiences, beliefs, feelings, cognitions, needs, desires, values, and intentions.

As discussed earlier, Polanyi (1962) related personal dimension to all knowledge. Here we assume that knowledge is a three-dimensional model (representation) of the subjective (personal), social and material worlds. Only the model can be stored in our heads, books, computers, etc., not the worlds themselves. To attain a better insight into the dimensions of knowledge let us take the famous example of riding a bicycle. The tacit nature of this case has been discussed thoroughly in a number of connections (Polanyi, 1962, Tsoukas, 2003, Cook & Brown, 1999). It is obvious that the knowledge has a strong personal dimension.

Let us assume that a young boy cannot ride a bicycle yet. We can only imagine the pressures he meets from his fellows that already have the magic ability. This pressure pushes the boy to practice more and more. And one day he learns. How proud he is of his new skill. He compares his skills to those of the other boys, develops special tricks, jumps, etc. It is possible that without this social dimension of knowledge he would not have learnt to ride a bicycle at all or perhaps much later or he would not be such a master.

What about the material dimension? It reflects the bicycle itself, quality of the roads, downhills and uphills, position of the saddle, air pressures in rears, etc. The rider learns the basic construction of his bicycle soon, is careful with the holes in the road, uses the brakes to limit his speed in downhills, etc. All of this forms the material dimension of the knowledge to ride a bicycle.

Thus, in the forthcoming discussion we relay on the three-dimensional knowledge.

Knowledge in Action: Knowing

In the discussion above we concluded that the different types of knowledge cannot be directly converted from one type to another. However, in practice, we de facto quite easily learn to ride a bicycle, use a hammer, play the piano, make bread, etc. Somehow even tacit knowledge 'moves' from a father to a son, from a teacher to a student, from an expert to a novice, etc. How does it happen?

In his later works, when Polanyi talks of knowledge, especially of tacit knowledge, he actually refers to a process rather than things (Polanyi 1966). He summarizes as follows: "Knowledge is an activity which would be better described as a process of knowing." (Polanyi, 1961, p. 466). Consequently, we should pay more attention to the tacit knowing rather than to tacit knowledge. From the epistemological point of view, it is of interest how we connect the subsidiary particulars to the focal targets not the ingredients themselves. Thus, "all knowing is personal knowing" (Polanyi & Prosch, 1975, p. 44).

Cook and Brown (1999) emphasize that knowing is an important aspect of all actions and knowing has its own epistemic content. It is that part of action that 'does epistemic work'. Basically, knowing is a relation where two entities are connected tacitly—particulars (subsidiaries) to focal target. One of the propositions of Cook and Brown (1999) is that 'each form of knowledge can be used as an aid in acquiring the other (p. 385)' and they see 'knowledge as

Figure 1. Generative dance within the three worlds

a tool at the service of knowing (p. 388)'. Thus, tacit knowledge most easily comes out when it is used, that is, it will manifest itself during the knowing process. Instead of using the concept of 'knowledge creation' Cook and Brown offer another concept, '*generative dance*', to describe the interactive process between knowledge and knowing. Knowing forms an interaction between the knower(s) and the world. If we continue with the three dimensions of the world, knowing is 'generative dance' between a knower and the three worlds as described in Figure 1.

In Figure 1, the worlds are named according to Habermas (1984). Because all knowledge has three dimensions, all worlds are involved and interrelated in the 'generative dance' of knowledge creation. The knower is surrounded by all those three worlds. Also, the iterative or cyclical nature of knowledge creation, generative dance, is described in Figure 1.

Knowledge as an Ability to Make Decisions

If decision-making is not a synonym of management, as Simon (1960) has argued, decision-making is in any case at the core of all managerial functions. When a decision is made the epistemic work has been done and the physical work to implement the decisions can start.

In defining knowledge, Tsoukas and Vladimirou (2001, p. 979) relate knowledge to the person's ability to draw distinctions: "Knowledge is the individual ability to draw distinctions, within a collective domain of action, based on an appreciation of context or theory, or both." According to this definition, a person is more knowledgeable if she/he can draw finer distinctions.

Here, we elaborate the above characterization of knowledge further and identify knowledge as the individual or organizational *ability to make decisions*. All actions are consequences of decisions. The *value of knowledge and information* are finally evaluated by the quality of decisions made. Making decisions involves also making distinctions, categorizations and judgements—we need to search and structure alternatives.

When defining knowledge we should note that decisions are more than distinctions; they are value-driven in the sense that they aim to achieve a specific *goal* or a set of goals. Individual behavior as well as organizational processes are at bottom based on values. Values are those grounding preferences that guide our selections in different decision situations. In Rokeach's definition values are seen as forms of beliefs: A value is "an enduring belief that a specific mode of conduct or end-state of existence is personally or socially preferable to an opposite or converse mode of conduct or end-state of existence" (Rokeach, 1973, p. 5). Instead of a single value, a person's behavior is guided by a cluster of values or by a value system where hierarchical relations (*hierarchical goal structure*) typically exist as Fritzsche states: "A series of clusters of values together form a person's value system consisting of a value hierarchy or priority structure based upon the relative importance of the individual values" (Fritzsche, 1995, p. 910).

If we return to the conceptualization of knowing the respective epistemic activity for knowing is *decision making*. Here, the concept of decision making is understood widely including all phases of information and knowledge gatherings (intel-ligence and design, (Simon, 1976)—not just the choice phase. It is the 'generative dance' (Cook & Brown, 1999) between decision maker(s) as knower and the three worlds.

Because knowledge is closely linked to the people who hold it, knowledge is context specific. Without a context, it is just information. One potential context of knowledge creation and use is the organizational context.

Organizational Knowledge in Context

Organizational Knowledge

Borrowing from biology, organizational context is the kind of 'ecology' where the organization and its members live and where they seek for the 'ecological fitness.' In organizational context, *equivocality* means that the members of the organization do not have a single knowledge scheme, framework, representing the 'ecology' and the actions needed for 'fitness'. *Uncertainty*, on the other hand, is the kind of empirical confusion; all the characteristics of the ecology are not known and their likelihood of occurrence is not known by the members. Some of an organization's decision processes reflect both, uncertainty and equivocality, for example, the strategic decision making process, but some of them are more definite.

Knowledge and knowing always reflect their context. The individual capacity to exercise judgement and take actions is based on appreciation of 'context or theory, or both' (Tsoukas & Vladimirou, 2001, p. 979). 'Theory' is understood very broadly as a mean to generalize from a context to another. Because organizational context includes the general rules, generally accepted working routines, etc, there is no need to make difference between 'theory' and 'organizational context' in the definition of organizational knowledge.

"Organizational knowledge is the set of collective understanding embedded in a firm" (Tsoukas & Vladimirou, 2001, p. 981). It is "the capability members of an organization have developed to *draw distinctions* in the process of carrying out their work, in particular *concrete contexts*, by enacting sets of generalizations *(propositional statements)* whose application depends on historically evolved *collective understandings* and experiences" (Tsoukas & Vladimirou, 2001, p. 983). Similarly, as we extended the definition of personal knowledge, we extend the above definition of organizational knowledge as the capability members of an organization have developed to *make decisions* in the process of carrying out their work in *organizational contexts*. Part of personal knowledge (subsidiary particulars) is *instrumental* in the sense that it is tacit. Similarly, part of organizational knowledge is used instrumentally (without explication) in the organizational decision making routines.

Organizational decision making (knowing) is an action between organizational knowledge and the members in an organization. Creating new organizational knowledge (capability to make organizational decisions) is also a generative dance—actually a generative square dance—where each individual not only makes his/her own steps but also follows the general rules of the dance and the movement of the others. A part of organizational knowledge remains tacit, unknown for the members of the organization. Everyone in the organization does not have or need all the knowledge available in organization. We only know the domain what one knows, we do not know exactly what one knows or how one does something. Part of the knowledge serves as a 'subsidiary particular' for the organizational knowing. Specialization aims to organizational efficiency.

If organizational knowledge is understood as a system, the structure of organizational knowledge follows the organizational structure and is typically arranged hierarchically. For example, the knowledge needed to make a strategic investment decision in a manufacturing corporation is diversified all over the organization and collected during the strategy process.

In organizational context, "organizational value systems provide guides for organizational goals, policies, and strategies" (Wiener, 1988, p. 536). Organizational values (value system) guide firms to make strategic choices, set goals and objectives or run the everyday business. Values influence on the search of alternatives, they manifest in the *goals and goals structure*, and they are present when the alternatives are evaluated. Although the values are relatively fixed they may change even in short run, or at least they can be explicated differently.

Knowledge as a Strategic Resource

A perspective to the strategic decision making and management and the economic theory of an organization, specially that of the firm, is the resource-based view of the firm (Barney 1986, Penrose 1959, Wernerfelt, 1984). This approach suggests that firms should position themselves strategically based on their rare, valuable, nonsubstitutable, and imperfectly imitable resources and capabilities instead of the products and services. It is assumed that the collection of resources including tangible and intangibles assets, knowledge and skills are the primary predictors also of the market-based and financial-based performance. According to this approach the competitive advantage of a firm is finally based on resource heterogeneity and resource immobility. In the markets, there are not similar organizations with similar resource-bases and competitors find it impossible or difficult to imitate or substitute these resources.

Because knowledge resource is at least partly tacit and contextual, organization specific, it cannot be directly explicated, purchased from markets, and moved from an organization to another. The organizational strategies are based on experience, continuous learning and routines. In order to create similar knowledge, competitors have to engage similar experience, create similar routines, etc. It is a process that takes time and thus, the business strategies of an organization based on its unique intellectual resources are more competitive and sustainable.

Strategic knowledge, according to the discussion above, is the ability to make strategic decisions. It may be held by individuals but usually it is a type of organizational knowledge. Uncertainty and equivocality are typical in the strategic decision making (knowing), the final value of the strategic knowledge can be evaluated thru the outcomes of the strategies, and organizational values are explicated by the strategic goals and goal hierarchies.

A KNOWLEDGE STRATEGY: *BA*

Knowledge strategy is the way or a scheme to do epistemic work in organizational context, that is, to create, convert, share, storage, secure, use, and evaluate knowledge resources in organizational context. In literature, knowledge strategy is defined e.g. through the following choices:

- Codification vs. personalization (Hansen et al., 1999)
- External vs. internal learning, radical vs. incremental learning, learning speed, and the breadth of knowledge base (Bierly and Chakrabarti, 1996)
- Exploitation of existing knowledge vs. exploration of new knowledge, internal vs. external knowledge (Zack, 1999)

Next, one potential knowledge strategy, *Ba*, is discussed.

Nonaka and Konno (1998) have introduced the concept of *Ba* to the western community as a multi-context place for knowledge creation. Nonaka, Toyama & Konno (2001, p. 22) define *Ba* as 'a shared context in which knowledge is shared, created and utilized'. It is a time-place location where physical, virtual, and mental spaces are incorporated to increase the interactions between individuals. It is the context where knowledge

sharing takes place. Also '*ba* is a place where information is interpreted to become knowledge' (Nonaka et al 2001, p. 22). "*Ba* opens a dynamic process that surpasses individual limits and it comes to reality through a platform where common language is used to achieve community aims and goals. *Ba* is focused on knowledge front and the human energy it uses can be extended and optimized with information and communication technologies capabilities (ICT)" (Fayard, 2003, p. 28).

Nonaka et al (2001) propose four types of *Bas*—originating, dialoguing, systemizing, and exercising *Ba*—and integrates them into the concept of knowledge creation: the SECI-model. Originating *Ba* offers a context for physical face-to-face discussions, socialization. Dialoguing *Ba* supports the conversion and articulation of tacit knowledge into a more external form. Systemizing *Ba* offers a context for combining explicit knowledge, whereas exercising *Ba* offers a context for the internalization of the knowledge again.

The organizational context forms the circumstances needed for *Bas*. In the organizational context, different kinds of working groups and teams, their roles and rules, offer natural settings for *Bas*. In those groups, the interacting participants activate knowledge creation. Like organizations in general, *Bas* can also be arranged hierarchically, forming greater *Bas* or *Bashos* (Nonaka & Konno, 1998).

Aligning Knowledge and Business Strategies

"Organizational alignment is the degree to which an organization's design, strategy, and culture are cooperating to achieve the same desired goals." (Semler 1997, p. 23). The predecessor concept to alignment was the concept of concurrence as proposed by Nadler and Tushman (1989). In their system model of organization the whole organization performed better or worse depending on the degree of congruence or fit between each pair of system elements. Thus, when discussing about alignment we need to examine things in pairs, like knowledge and business strategies, and make sure that they are aiming at the same desired goals. However, the broad concept of alignment can be considered from different perspectives and different aspects of alignment can be of interest. Semper (1997), for example, builds his theory of organizational alignment on structural, cultural, performance, and environmental aspects. Here we distinguish between three aspects when aligning business and knowledge strategies at organizational context: definitional, structural and procedural alignment.

A business strategy is one of the most important pieces of organizational knowledge. Thus, if *Ba* is a context to create, convert, share, storage, secure, use, and evaluate knowledge resources then strategic *Ba* would be a strategic context to create, convert, share, storage, secure, use, and evaluate strategic knowledge, i.e. ability to make strategic (business) decisions. By this chained definition business strategies and knowledge strategies are aligned at definitional level indicating that they are aiming at the same goals, are intertwined and cannot be separated.

Structural alignment guarantees that knowledge management and strategic business management have common arrangements and facilities that guarantee the goal attainment of both strategies. The substance of the knowledge strategy has to be the business strategies. Knowledge strategy must be based on epistemological requirements but the requirements of strategic management have to be met or at least supported by the arrangements. The structural alignment of knowledge and business strategies is discussed in *Structural Alignment: Design of an Artificial* Ba.

The structure of any system determines the necessary conditions for the process of that system. If the structural aspects of the alignment are in order then there are good possibilities that the strategy and knowledge processes are aligned towards the same goals. The procedural alignment,

however, is more situational and the contextual factors determine the actual process and the quality of procedural alignment. Therefore, the procedural alignment is discussed by an actual case in *Procedural Alignment: Indwelling in the Artificial* Ba *Context.*

AN ARTIFICIAL *BA* CONTEXT FOR STRATEGIC BUSINESS MANAGEMENT

Next, we propose an artificial (virtual) *Ba* environment as a knowledge strategy for supporting strategic management in organizational context. The proposed system is a complete 'artifact' (Simon, 1996), a supportive environment in which knowledge accumulates and is shared, a system that is intentionally built to activate existing knowledge resources and to support the creation of valuable new knowledge in an organization.

Epistemological Choices for a Knowledge Strategy within an Artificial *Ba* Setting

In Table 1, 10 most fundamental epistemological concepts discussed earlier are summed up and the respective choices for the knowledge strategy as implemented by artificial *Ba* context are described. The final content of the artificial *Ba* depends on the actual strategic choices made and implemented.

Because all knowledge has three dimensions and because it is context-specific, the artificial *Ba* has to be built on the representatives of those *three worlds*. Missing any of them will nullify the whole construct.

Although the system relies on information technology, it cannot be any form of automata but *human agency* has to be involved directly. Without a possibility of free, living discussion among participants, no knowledge originates. A necessary requirement for the system is that it

Table 1. Constitution of the Ba based knowledge strategy

Epistemological concept	Strategic choice
1. Three worlds	How are the subjective, social and material worlds represented?
2. Knower(s)	How is the human agency involved?
3. Generative dance	How are the different forms of knowledge available and used in the knowing process?
4. Instrumentalization	How is the knowledge instrumentalized through experimentation?
5. Organizational context	How are the external and internal organizational contexts imitated?
6. Knowledge hierarchy	How are data, information, and knowledge tied together at operational, tactical, and strategic planning levels.
7. Uncertainty and equivocality	How are uncertainty and equivocality reduced?
8. Knowledge value	How are the outcomes of decisions evaluated?
9. Goals and goal structure	How are the personal and organizational values represented as goals and a goal system?
10. Knowledge	How is strategic decision making supported?

should offer circumstances to stimulate creativity. Creativity adds knowledge, extends and reshapes prior knowledge. New and surprising information, connections between the knowledge items, innovative experiments, etc, can substantially stimulate participants' creativity. The possibility to present ideas, critique, make assessments, question sensitive topics, etc, anonymously, must be granted.

Existing and new knowledge are tools used in action, part of which is the 'epistemic work', *knowing*. Artificial *Ba* needs to support such interaction between knowledge, knowing and action.

Creating a new tacit knowledge requires that the subsidiary particulars of knowledge go 'under our skin', i.e., they are *instrumentalized*. This can happen only through action, or quasi-action, by experimentation. Artificial *Ba* must offer an artificial context for artificial action through experimentation. A proper place for

innovative knowledge creation offers not only a shared context in cognition but also a shared context in action. Models in the artificial *Ba* can be used for experimentation without committing the organization to risky actions. By these experiments, the value of knowledge is tested and if the experimental results can also be negotiated and arbitrated then the outcomes are internalized more intensely.

Artificial *Ba* is an artificial context and it has to imitate the original *organizational context*. Otherwise the converted or created knowledge would not have any usage. Management of *data, information and knowledge flows between the participants from different organizational levels* is an essential requirement for the artificial *Ba*. Dialogue among participants is essential for knowledge creation. The mental models of the participants are shared and externalized by dialogues. Networking diversified participants and establishing collaborative sessions are examples of means to urge dialogue between members. Easy transmission of data and information in different forms (texts, figures, numbers, tables, etc) between group members activates the dialogue.

Because the members of the organization do not have a single, uniform knowledge framework they see differently the organizational context ('ecology') as well as the necessary actions to be taken. Similarly all characteristics of the organizational context are not known or their likelihood of occurrence is not known. A significant purpose of an artificial *Ba* is to reduce *equivocality and uncertainty* by uniforming the knowledge framework and collecting information about organizational context. Public justification or making 'validity claims' (Habermas, 1984) in a *Ba* context makes the whole process of creating knowledge different.

As discussed earlier the *value* of organizational knowledge is finally evaluated through the quality of organizational decisions. If the quality of decisions is not improved, the *Ba* context is useless. Finally, the artificial *Ba* needs to represent organizational values and explicate them by *goals and goal structure* guiding actual decision making. In sum, due to the definition of knowledge, the artificial *Ba* has to support *strategic decision making*.

The ten epistemological concepts above form a basis and necessary conditions for the development of an environment aimed to encourage knowledge innovation in strategic management.

Because *Ba* 'constantly changes' (Nonaka et al., 2001, p. 24), artificial *Ba*s must also be easily adapted to changing circumstances, modified flexibly by the knowledge type sought after, and developed further according to the accomplished experiences. In order to increase users' involvement, participative development methods need to be used during the system development. The existing organizational knowledge must be embedded into it. Because there are no general *Ba*s—the *Ba*s are context specific—artificial *Ba*s must be developed, tested and validated organizationally. Although *Ba*s are primarily open places for knowledge creation, *Ba*s also set some boundaries for interaction. They are platforms where everything is not allowed. Similarly in the artificial environment, themes for group discussions are agreed, model boundaries are relatively fixed, valuation procedures follow their logical steps, etc.

Structural Alignment: Design of an Artificial *Ba*

Information and communication technology (ICT) offers many means for building an artificial (virtual) *Ba* context. They represent a wide variety of tools, starting from simple electronic mails and ending with collaboration technologies and knowledge archives. Communication networks (internet, intranets, extranets), videoconferencing, multimedia mail, data warehousing and data mining, intelligent agents, group support systems and collaborative tools, document management

systems, web content management tools, etc, are just some examples of the tools that can be used in knowledge management. In summary, there are endless possibilities to employ modern ICT in knowledge creation.

In order to meet the epistemological requirements of an artificial *Ba* context (Table 1) with the ontological premises (Figure 1), we propose a context that consists of three subsystems:

1. Organization-wide simulation model (OWSM), representing the material world
2. Valuation procedure, representing the subjective world
3. Group Support System, representing the social world

These three subsystems directly represent the three worlds discussed earlier. Together, they form a context that can be used in transforming personal knowledge into organizational decisions, to interpret information to knowledge, and to create new knowledge. Because business strategies are a significant piece of organizational knowledge, strategic management inevitable involves the three words discussed earlier. Therefore the knowledge strategy based on an artificial *Ba* and business strategies are aligned, aiming at same goals, finally at business success thru superior knowledge resources. A description of the system structure is presented in Figure 2.

The core of the proposed context is an organization-wide simulation model. The structure of an OWSM is always represented as an analogue to the object organization. Although OWSM is mainly intended to approximate the material world (in Habermas's terms, 1984) it can include some properties of the subjective world as well. Because the construction process of the model fully depends on personal and organizational knowledge, the model is also a representation of that knowledge. Especially if we use participative methodologies in the modeling process where the flows of explicit knowledge and information are

Figure 2. The structure of an artificial Ba

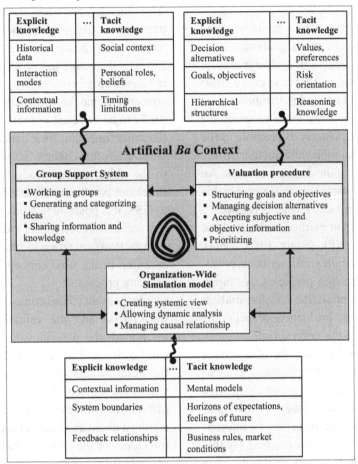

replicated, then OWSM is also a representation of personal and organizational knowledge.

The structure of the OWSM cannot be fixed but its structure must evolve as part of the 'generative dance' to convert personal knowledge to organizational decisions. In knowledge transformation, metaphors are used to externalize tacit knowledge to explicit knowledge. The simulation model and its usage form a dynamic metaphor of the organization.

Organizational knowledge is always at least partly a by-product of organizational action. OWSM is an environment where connections between knowledge and action can be created and evaluated. Participants can easily test the value of their embodying knowledge without risk of

organizational or personal hazards. In addition to observation experience, OWSM can also offer action experience that might be of special value in knowledge creation.

The second element in the structural design of an artificial context is a subsystem to manage the whole organizational value structure, i.e. all intentional knowledge of individuals (subjective world) and those of the organization. As discussed earlier, individual behaviour as well as organizational processes are based on values or value systems. Organizations operate and survive through organizationally accepted rules that are justified by goals or a hierarchical goal system. Within organizations there are individual goals, objectives, desires, wishes, intentions, etc., as well as organizational goals, objectives, missions, etc.

In the organizational context, an intertwined set of personal and organizational goals and objectives and other intentional logic is always present in every decision situation, that is, in every effort to create valuable new knowledge. In multicriteria decision making, efforts are made to relate the whole value system as closely as possible to the knowledge of the situation, and further to the priorities and choices of the decision courses. An effective method to stimulate and manage this whole set of intentional knowledge is needed.

A potential valuation method is the analytic hierarchy process (AHP), (Saaty 1980, 1994), developed to tackle complex, multicriteria, political and economic decision problems. As input, AHP uses the judgements of the decision-makers about the alternatives, evaluation criteria, the relationships between the criteria (importance), and the relationships between the alternatives (preference). In the valuation process, subjective values, personal knowledge, and objective information can be linked together. As an output, a goal hierarchy, and the priorities of alternatives, and their sensitivities, are reached. By this routine, it is possible to structure the decision problem into a hierarchy that reflects the values, goals, objectives, and desires of the participants in their knowledge creation process. AHP is just an example of valuation methods available.

The third structural element of the proposed artificial context for knowledge creation is a group support system (GSS). By GSS it is possible to approximate the interpersonal relationships of the social world within the organization. A group (decision) support system is an interactive computer-based system, which facilitates the solution of unstructured problems by a set of decision makers working together as a group. Because internal communication over organizational levels or over functional barriers in a large organization is typically rather poor, a GSS can be used to diminish these problems. Collaboration and communication technologies are key foundations of GSSs.

The artificial *Ba* may change the concept of time considerably. First, the time concept of the participants (subjective time) may change from linear, monochronicity to polychronicity (Hall 1959). If the actors in knowledge creation prefer to engage only in one activity at a time their time concept is monochronic. On the other hand, if they prefer to be engaged in two or more activities at the same time their time concept is polychronic. GSSs allow this change. Second, the time related to the object of knowledge creation (objective time) can be altered. By connecting the OWSM to GSS, it is possible to study and discuss the direct and indirect effects of today's decisions over the whole organization in future. This gives new meaning to the time concept in the knowledge creation process.

Our present values come from the past. When the OWSM and the valuation subsystem are integrated, the present values of the members can be changed by the simulated future and in the iterative knowledge creation process those values are applied to. At the concrete level, it is difficult to evaluate the large set of simulation results without a valuation procedure that reflects the values of the decision makers and the needs of strategic planning.

Using GSS together with OWSM, it is possible to integrate the results of the simulations with the discussions in GSS and examine the direct and indirect consequences of today's strategic decisions over the whole organization in future. Joint use of GSS and the valuation method helps to structure sometimes diversifying discussions. When goals and objectives are structured, the ensuing discussion will become more purposeful and goal seeking.

If the final value of the knowledge is measured through the improved decisions, the knowledge creation process and the decision process are aligned except that one phase of the decision making process may include all phases of the iterative knowledge creation process. For example, the intelligence phase in Simon's process model (Simon, 1976) may activate all phases of the

Nonaka-Takeuchi model (Nonaka & Takeuchi, 1995).

The interaction between the experimentation by the artificial *Ba* and knowledge growth is interesting. It is clear that the present knowledge shapes the whole structure of the artificial *Ba*, every detail of it, as well as its usage. On the other hand, the experimentation might change the existing knowledge structure substantially. The spiral of knowledge creation is complete. The interplay between experimentation and knowledge can be recurring and continuing.

Procedural Alignment: Indwelling in the Artificial *Ba* Context

The artificial context outlined above was implemented and used in one of the world-leading wood processing corporation. The purpose of the preliminary experiment was to study the structural, but especially the procedural alignment of knowledge and business strategies in a real organizational context. The purpose of the experiments was not to provide final prove of anything or test empirically in traditional sense anything. The purpose was rather to make a very initial assessment of the proposed concepts in a real context.

Strategic management in the forest industry covers the whole corporation, indicating that every subsidiary and department in the company is understood as a part of the whole, not as an isolated entity. Thus, the respective artificial *Ba* context also has to adopt a systemic, corporate-wide perspective. The system has to cover the whole company and all its functions, like finance, production, and marketing.

The strategy process is a multivalued and inter-related process but the process typically contains the following activities: Review the behavior of the present system, identify goals and objectives, formulate business strategies, evaluate the outcomes of strategies, prioritize strategies and select the best strategy. Such kinds of descriptions of the

Figure 3. Knowledge spiral in artificial Ba context

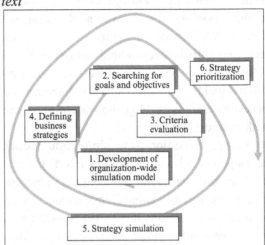

strategy process are, of course, highly simplistic and serve only for conceptual purposes. For example, iterations may exist during the strategy process.

The development of the artificial *Ba* context in the case company took a couple of years but the development process itself was a fruitful knowledge creation process. The main phases of the development and use process are described in Figure 3. Although the support process is divided into distinct phases in Figure 3, the process was completely iterative; specially the structure of the organization-wide simulation model was evolved during other phases as part of the dialogue among participants

In the following discussion of knowledge creation, emphasis is, of course, on explicit organizational knowledge. Much tacit knowledge was certainly also created and used but because of its hidden nature it remains unarticulated.

Development of Organization-Wide Simulation Model

The OWSM was developed according to the principles of System Dynamics and it covers the mechanical wood-processing (saw, plywood), pulp, and paper industries. A number of people from different organizational units were involved in the modeling process but the responsibility of the modeling process was at the strategic department. Outside consultation help was also received from a business school and a technological university. During the process, a couple of restarts had to be made to sharpen the purposes of development and to align the modeling process with business goals.

The organization-wide simulation model developed in this case is divided into two main modules: production and finance. The production component includes some elements concerning marketing as well, and it is further divided into four analogically similar sub-modules: sawing, pulp, paper, and plywood. As an output of the model, the behavior of over 400 interrelated variables was achieved. In the wood-processing industry, the planning horizon is usually long. For example, the life-cycle of production capacity is several decades and the technical solutions are long lasting. Therefore the planning horizon in the model, and hence the solution, is 30 years, enabling superior knowledge for the strategy process of the company. As a summary, the whole structure of the developed OWSM is graphically described in Appendix 1.

The biggest problems in the modeling process were the data collection, information gathering and knowledge search. Fortunately, the modeling method (System Dynamics) is flexible enough to accept data sources in different forms. Objective, historical data, as well as subjective, future oriented opinions can be easily used and integrated. As a result, the general understanding of the organizational processes and structures behind them was increased—the equivocality in strategic management was reduced.

The structure of the OWSM was not permanent but it was evolved as a part of the 'generative dance' in knowledge conversion. However, the final version of the whole model was used in an instrumental fashion. The participants did not pay any attention to the model (subsidiary) itself but they concentrated on the actual strategic issues (specifics) like finance, pricing, production capacity, etc. Participants were 'indwelling' within the model and all knowledge behind the model was converted at least partly to tacit organizational knowledge.

Searching for Goals and Objectives

After a descriptive understanding of the corporate behavior was achieved, i.e. the OWSM was developed, it was necessary to gather knowledge concerning the goals and objectives of the corporation (value system). For this purpose, electronic brainstorming was used to gather ideas, beliefs and comments about the goals and objectives of the organization. In a GSS session, this partly tacit knowledge was elicited from the management team of the company. In addition to the strategic management, the members of the management team represented the expertise and experience of production, finance, and information technology.

During the session, the participants generated over twenty goals and objectives they believed the corporation was striving towards or goals and objectives the company should strive towards. The participants responded to questions and comments of the others in a divergent process helped the group to rapidly generate a free flow of knowledge. The participants contributed simultaneously and anonymously to a discussion that could be used as such or sorted in appropriate ways.

After this free idealization session, the generated goals and objectives, with the comment, were categorized and similarities excluded. As an explicit output, a list of organizational goals and objectives was achieved (Table 2). In the fourth column of the table, the respective variable names of the OWSM are defined. Because the OWSM is not fully isomorphic with reality, all the goals of the organization cannot be studied through the model, but must be evaluated, for example, subjectively.

Table 2. Organizational goals and goal hierarchy

Main goal	2. level goal	3. level goal	Respective variable in OWSM
Well-being of a wood-processing company	Profit-ability (0.334)	Maximum return on investment	ROI
		Belonging to the Top Three in the entire industry	Reference ROI
		High value added degree of processing	Added value
	Growth (0.031)	High turnover	Sales
		Large scale balance sheet	Total assets
		Growth rate of the corporation equal to its key competitors	Industry growth
		Production activities in several countries	NA
		Growth by using acquisitions during favourable business cycles	NA
	Finance (0.087)	Healthy balance sheet structure	Debt-Equity ratio
		Working capital on proper level	Working capital
		Good liquidity	Current ratio
		Creditworthiness AAA	Credit ratio
	Customers and markets (0.263)	Satisfied customers	Levels of order backlogs
		Market leader in its chosen paper business	Market shares
		Steady production levels	Production completions
	Societal relations (0.031)	Basing activities on sustainable development	Environmental effects
	Production technology (0.062)	Modern technology	NA
	Personnel (0.091)	Motivated, internationally oriented and multiskilled personnel	Satisfaction level
	Investors (0.101)	The best ROI within the forest industry	Earnings per share
		Shareholders are satisfied with the corporation's ability to pay stable and high dividends	Dividends

The whole set of intentions justifies all the actions taken in an organization as well as all the efforts to create new knowledge. Goals and objectives direct all the activities of individuals as well as those of the whole organization. In subsequent phases, the goals and objectives serve as decision criteria. The whole set of goals and objectives include more, and less, important ones. Therefore they had to be weighted by some means or other.

Criteria Evaluation

In this phase, the relative importance of the strategic goals and objectives were evaluated. In evaluating goals and objectives a multi-criteria evaluation procedure, the analytic hierarchy process (Saaty 1980, 1994), was used. The AHP is designed to cope with both explicit and tacit knowledge and to select the best one from a number of discrete alternatives evaluated with respect to multiple criteria. In this process of knowledge creation, the decision makers (management team) carry out simple pairwise comparisons, which are then used to rank the goals and objectives.

Searching for goals and objectives and especially evaluating their relative importance requires personal judgement. These processes are not, however, pure individualistic activities, but communication and cooperation within a group changes the initial attitudes, values, and beliefs of the members. Working in groups in an artificial *Ba* context converts personal knowledge into organizational knowledge.

Defining Business Strategies

In the organizational context, it is most important to generate and choose proper business strategies. After the goals and objectives of the company were evaluated, in the next step the properties of electronic brainstorming and the categorizer in GSS were used again to search for potential business strategies of the case company. In this session, the management team of the company generated and organized ideas for potential corporate strategies.

After a brainstorming session, the generated raw list of potential strategies was categorized into the following 8 strategy groups: financial, growth, sustainable development and environment, core businesses, production, investor, marketing, and resource strategies. Financial strategies, for example, included 15 potential strategies.

The session for strategy generation shows how wide and multidimensional are the strategic insights the members of the company have. The hidden knowledge of the strategic potential only needs to be manifested. Of course, this is partly due to the fact that in this phase there is no need to evaluate the consequences of each strategy. The direct and indirect consequences of the strategies are assessed by OWSM in the next phase of the knowledge spiral.

Strategy Simulation

Due to the limits of the OWSM, only a subset of the generated strategies can be replicated by the simulation model, some strategies can be discussed and evaluated only subjectively. However, in this case the most interesting strategic alternatives were evaluated by the model. The (explicit) knowledge created by the model can be presented in different forms (numeric, graphic). In Figure 4, the behavior of some goal variables under one single strategy is described in graphic form.

By doing strategy simulations (experiments) the participants can evaluate their present knowledge concerning the strategic issues and develop

Figure 4. Examples of the output of strategy simulation

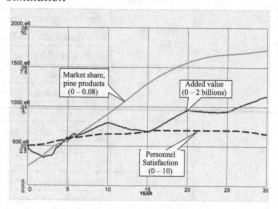

it further. They can use their personal tacit knowledge as an instrument to create organizational knowledge.

Strategy Prioritization

In the next phase of the knowledge creation process, the simulated strategies are evaluated by the goal hierarchy described in Table 2. In strategy evaluation all strategy alternatives are compared with respect to each criterion. This means that the outputs of the OWSM generated by each strategy are compared pairwise by each criterion at the lowest level.

Analyzing corporate strategies is a challenging task because all relevant inputs are subject to uncertainty and equivocality and they are based on qualitative and quantitative data, subjective judgements, and conflicting goals. Values, preferences and goals, and strategic alternatives are not unambiguous but they can be re-evaluated, ordered differently, described in more detail, etc.

After the comparisons, the total priorities of the strategies were synthesized (Table 3). The table indicates that the best strategy with respect to the well-being of the forest industry corporation is 'The prices of paper and pine products are tied to the respective order backlogs and inventories' strategy. The next best strategy is the 'Smooth dividends per share relationship' strategy.

Table 3. Strategy prioritization

Strategy	Relative Value
The prices of paper and pine products are tied to the respective order backlogs and inventories	0.160
Smooth dividends per share relationship	0.151
Present system	0.113
Smaller inventories	0.107
Investments are closely tied to return on sales	0.102
Investments are not closely tied to return on sales	0.102
Salary and wage levels are tied to the profitability of the company	0.094
Smooth growth in salary and wage levels	0.087
Investing in environment-oriented technology	0.085

The results of the strategy prioritization represent the highest form of knowledge (ability to make strategic decisions) that can be created in the present artificial *Ba* context. Despite the simplified outlook, this output represents the top of the cumulative chain of knowledge conversion beginning from the first thoughts for the construction of an organization-wide simulation model. It is based on all knowledge about the structural relationships within the company, material, money, and information flows between units, personal values, desires, motives, and insights of the managerial team and their organizational representations in the goals and objectives the company is striving towards.

Table 4. Examples of strategic knowledge created

Phases of strategy process	Support Content	Examples of knowledge created	
		Explicit knowledge	Tacit knowledge
Review the behavior of the present system	Development of corporate-wide simulation model	• Structure of the organization • Flows between organizational units • OWSM in graphic and computerized form	• Feeling that everything depends on everything else • Familiarity with other functions and levels in the company • Understanding the limits of computerized models • Modeling is a never-ending process • Increased modeling capability
Identify goals and objectives	Searching for goals and objectives	• Goals and objectives of the organization	• Changed values • Changed ways of reasoning • Contradictions between personal and organizational goals
	Criteria evaluation	• Goal hierarchy • Relative weights within the hierarchy	• Insights into power and politics • Doubts about the hierarchy concept • Hesitation concerning the weights
Formulate business strategies	Defining business strategies	• Most important strategies	• Imaging the thousands of potential directions for the company • Changed personal problem-solving models
Evaluate the outcomes of strategies	Strategy simulation by the corporate-wide model	• Scenarios for balance sheets, income statements, production and inventory levels, demands, etc. • Goal attainment under each strategy	• Recognition of the interlinkages between strategies and goals • Extended horizon of expectations • Risks involved
Prioritize strategies and select the best strategy	Choice of the best strategy	• Priority of strategic alternatives	• Long term consequences of decisions • Understanding the sensitivity of the priorities

Examples of the Strategic Knowledge Created

In summary, many different types of knowledge were created within the artificial *Ba* context. Because of the structural and procedural alignment of knowledge and business strategies it is, however, difficult to differentiate the development of the context and its use; they are strictly interlinked. And because the artificial *Ba* context is a part of the organizational context, it is also difficult to indicate the primary origin of the strategic knowledge. A piece of knowledge may be originated in the artificial *Ba* context but it is finally materialized in the original organizational context.

Because created explicit knowledge is somehow articulated it is relatively easy to identify it. Tacit knowledge, on the other hand, remains hidden. Notwithstanding these difficulties, an attempt is made in Table 4 to integrate and classify the created knowledge is integrated and classified. As a primary classification criterion, we use the main phases of the strategy process, which are tied to the organizational context of the forest industry corporation.

DISCUSSION AND CONCLUSION

In this chapter, we have proposed and evaluated a new model for aligning business and knowledge strategies. Three aspects of the alignment have been of interest: definitional, structural and procedural alignment. We first provide a theoretical basis for the definition of the key elements of knowledge strategy and then define the knowledge strategy in the form of an artificial context that can be used to create and evaluate business strategies. The developed context forms a set of artificial conditions to test alternative business strategies and their organizational implications. The proposed system is a complete 'artifact', a supportive environment in which knowledge accumulates and is shared, a system that is built to activate existing knowledge and to support the creation of valuable new knowledge in an organization. It supports the natural characteristics of human being to act as a group and to learn new, qualified knowledge. The proposed approach guarantees that the knowledge strategy and business strategy are integrated and aligned at definitional, structural and procedural levels.

The proposed artificial context forms the connection from personal knowledge to organizational decisions. Thus, it is a place where knowing happens by definition (creation a relation from particulars (subsidiaries) to focal target). Due to the nature of knowledge, the receiver in knowledge conversion, in order to become knowledgeable, has to become involved in the knowledge creation process. In the artificial context, a number of parties are directly involved in knowledge creation. Organizational knowledge is not a static commodity that can be easily transmitted, but a continuous, dynamic process within the involved parties and the organizational context. The proposed context facilitates the process and is accelerated by the permanent interplay between knowledge and experimentation.

Habermas (1984) proposes three types of validity claims (propositional truth, normative rightness, and subjective truthfulness) to ensure the success of a communicative action. Similarly, we can challenge the validity of an artificial *Ba* by evaluating the quality of the created knowledge in relation to objective, social and subjective worlds. We need to evaluate whether the OWSM represents the objective world well enough, if the social relations are properly maintained in GSS sessions, and if our personal values, goals, intentions, and desires are correctly approximated by the valuation procedure with the goal hierarchy.

Personal knowledge is tied to personal action. If this logic is followed through, then organizational knowledge is tied to organizational action. In order to accumulate and share organizational knowledge, the developed *Ba* context imitates organizational activities as far as possible. First, the structure of the object organization (system) is represented by an organization-wide simulation model. According to the key principles of system thinking, the structure also determines the behavior of the system that is animated by the dynamic simulation. Second, although in the organizational context there cannot be any given automata to generate alternative strategies, the generation and evaluation of the consequences of those strategies can be supported. Thirdly, numerous experiences are generally crystallized into the goals and objectives of an organization. When stating and weighting goals and objectives, we at the same time evaluate our earlier experiences—what is worth striving for, what is not. The proposed *Ba* environment allows the transformation of our personal, subjective experiences and judgements into a consistent goal hierarchy. Even though the developed context has much potential and has proved to be effective in actual use, it can be improved in a number of dimensions. Present information and communication technology offers a number of means to enrich the contents of the artificial *Ba* context and to enhance the alignment of knowledge and business strategies.

FUTURE RESEARCH DIRECTIONS

The proposed approach for aligning business and knowledge strategies suggests and would certainly benefit from further theoretical and empirical work. The proposed artificial context is based on ten epistemological concepts and the conceptual base can be extended to a number of dimensions or some of the conceptual considerations can be even challenged. For example, the perspective of the three worlds can be possibly substituted by systems philosophy, systems theory and systems approach. Our understanding how the highly situational organizational knowledge can be exploited to wider organizational usage is still imperfect. Deeper conceptual integration to the theories of the strategic management and

organizational behavior would also be of benefits. Artificial *Ba* is only a knowledge strategy among other strategies. Under what conditions should it be applied?

Secondly, there is a need for more empirical case studies. Researchers on knowledge management should be encouraged to replicate the artificial context and develop it further. Even though the developed context has much potential and has proved to be effective in actual use, it can be improved in a number of dimensions. Present information and communication technology offers a number of means to enrich the contents of the artificial *Ba* context and to enhance the alignment of knowledge and business strategies. Communication networks, videoconferencing, multimedia mail, data warehousing and data mining, software agents, group support systems and collaborative tools, expert systems, case based reasoning, document management systems, web content management tools, etc, are just some examples of the tools that can be integrated to an artificial context of knowledge creation and sharing and further aligned to business strategy process.

Because the final value of the strategic knowledge can be evaluated thru the success of the strategies, longitudinal studies are needed to evaluate the final value of the types of artificial *Bas* illustrated here. In addition, more sophisticated approaches to evaluate the developed context are needed. Among the numerous questions the further work could concentrate on the following questions: What types of strategies are generated by the artificial context? How successful have those strategies been? What advantages or disadvantages have been observed within each subsystem of the context?

Equally important to the technological progress is the emergence of new organizational forms that presents both opportunities and challenges to organizational knowledge creation and sharing. These new forms require cooperation and alignment rather than command and control to harness the capabilities and insights of all their organizational members.

The proposed approach can be of value in the future case studies without attempting to develop any artificial context but the conceptual base can be used to evaluate the existing knowledge systems and their alignment to strategic management. For example it would be worth studying how well the material, social or subjective dimensions of the knowledge are represented or supported in organizations.

Although the proposed context is intended to stimulate knowledge creation and sharing of in strategic management the context can at the same time serve as a laboratory for researching knowledge creation and alignment with the organizational strategy process.

REFERENCES

Barney, J.B. (1986). Organizational culture: Can it be a source of sustained competitive advantage? *The Academy of Management Review*, 11(3), 656-665.

Bierly, P., & Chakrabarti, A. (1996). Generic knowledge strategies in the U.S. pharmaceutical industry, *Strategic Management Journal*, 17, Winter 1996, 123-135.

Cook, S.D.N., & Brown, J.S. (1999). Bridging Epistemologies: The Generative Dance Between Organizational Knowledge and Organizational Knowing, *Organization Science*, 10(4), 381-400.

Cowan, R., David, P.A., & Fory, D. (2000). The Explicit Economics of Knowledge Codification and Tacitness, *Industrial and Corporate Change*, 9(2), 211-253.

Davenport, T.H., & Prusak, L. (1998). *Working knowledge: how organizations manage what they know*, Boston, MA: Harvard Business School Press.

Fayard, P. (2003). Strategic communities for knowledge creation: A Western proposal for the Japanese concept of Ba, *Journal of Knowledge Management*, 7(5), 25-31.

Fritzsche, D.J. (1995). Personal Values: Potential Keys to Ethical Decision Making, *Journal of Business Ethics*, 14, 909-922.

Habermas, J. (1984). *The Theory of Communicative Action*, Polity Press.

Hall, E.T. (1959). *The Silent Language*, Anchor Books, New York.

Hansen, M.T., Nohria, N., & Tierney, T. (1999). What is your Strategy for Managing Knowledge, *Harvard Business Review*, 77(2), 106-116.

Hayes, N., & Walsham, G. (2003). Knowledge Sharing and ICTs: A Relational Perspective. In M. Easterby-Smith, & M. Lyles (Eds.), *The Blackwell Handbook of Organizational Learning and Knowledge Management* (pp. 54-77). Blackwell Publishing.

Håkanson, L. (2001). The rediscovery of articulation, *European Business Forum*, 5, 29-36.

Kivijärvi, H. (2004). Knowledge Conversion in Organizational Contexts: A Framework and Experiments, *Proceedings of the 37th Hawaii International Conference on System Sciences*. Retrieved August 23, 2007 from http://csdl2.computer.org/comp/proceedings/hicss/2004/2056/08/205680242a.pdf

von Krogh, G. (2003). Knowledge Sharing and the Communal Resource, In M. Easterby-Smith & M. Lyles (Eds.), *The Blackwell Handbook of Organizational Learning and Knowledge Management* (pp. 372-392). Blackwell Publishing.

Leonard, D., & Sensiper, S. (1998). The Role of Tacit Knowledge in Group Innovation, *California Management Review*, 40(3), 112-132.

Nadler, D.A., & Tushman, M.I. (1989). A model for diagnosing organizational behavior, Applying congruence perspective, In D.A. Nadler, M.L. Tushman & C. O'Reilly, (Eds), *The management of organizations: Strategic, tactics, analyses*, (pp. 91-106). Harper & Row, New York

Nonaka, I., & Konno, N. (1998). The concept of Ba, Building a Foundation for Knowledge Creation, *California Management Review*, 40(8), 40-54.

Nonaka, I., & Takeuchi, H. (1995). *The Knowledge Creating Company*, Oxford University Press, New York.

Nonaka, I., & Toyama, R. (2003). The knowledge-creating theory revisited: knowledge creation as a synthesizing process, *Knowledge Management Research and Practice*, 1(1), 2-10.

Nonaka, I., Toyama, R., & Konno, N. (2001). SECI, Ba and Leadership: A Unified Model of Dynamic Knowledge Creation, In I. Nonaka, & D.J. Teece, (Eds.), *Managing Industrial Knowledge* (pp. 13-43). Sage Publications, London.

Penrose, E.T. (1959). *The theory of the growth of the firm*, New York: Wiley and Sons.

Polanyi, M. (1962). *Personal Knowledge*, University of the Chicago Press, Chicago.

Polanyi, M. (1966). *The Tacit Dimension*, Doubleday & Co., Reprinted Peter Smith, Gloucester, Massachusetts.

Polanyi, M. (1961). Knowing and Being, *Mind*, New Series, 70(280), 458-70.

Polanyi, M., & Prosch, H. (1975). *Meaning*, The University of Chicago Press.

Popper, K.R. (1979). *Objective Knowledge*, Oxford University Press, Oxford.

Rokeach, M. (1973). *The nature of human values*, Free Press, New York.

Saaty, T.L. (1980). *The Analytic Hierarchy Process*, McGraw-Hill, New York.

Saaty, T.L. (1994). *Fundamentals of Decision Making and Priority Theory with the Analytic Hierarchy Process*. Pittsburgh: RWS Publications.

Semler, S. W. (1997), Systematic Agreement: A Theory of Organizational Alignment, *Human Resource Development Quarterly*, 8(1), 23-40.

Simon, H A. (1960). *The New Science of Management Decisions*, New York: Harper Brothers.

Simon, H. (1976). *Administrative Behavior*, Free Press, New York.

Simon, H.A. (1996). *The Sciences of the Artificial*, Cambridge, Mass. MIT Press.

Stewart, T. (1999). *Intellectual Capital, The New Wealth of Organizations*, Currency Doubleday, New York.

Suppe, F. (1974). *The Structure of Scientific Theories*, Urbana, IL: University of Illinois Press.

Tsoukas, H. (2003). Do we relay understand tacit knowledge, In M. Easterby-Smith & M. Lyles (Eds.), *The Blackwell Handbook of Organizational Learning and Knowledge Management* (pp. 410-427). Blackwell Publishing.

Tsoukas, H., & Vladimirou, E. (2001). What is Organizational Knowledge?, *Journal of Management Studies*, 38(7), 973-993.

Wernerfelt, B. (1984). A Resource-Based View of the Firm, *Strategic Management Journal*, 5(2), 171-180.

Wiener, Y. (1988). Forms of Value Systems: A Focus on Organizational Effectiveness and Cultural Change and Maintenance, *The Academy of Management Review*, 13(4), 534-545.

Zack, M.H. (1999). Developing a Knowledge Strategy, *California Management Review*, 41(3), 125-145.

Additional Reading

Brown, C.V., & Magill, S.L. (1994). Aligning the IS Functions with the Enterprise: Toward a Model of Antecedents, *MIS Quarterly*, 18(4), 371-403.

Chan, Y. E. (2001). Information Systems Strategy, Structure and Alignment, In R. Papp, (Ed.), *Strategic Information Technology: Opportunities for Competetive Advantage* (pp. 56-81). Idea Group Publishing,

Chan, Y.E., Huff, S. L., Barclay, D.W., & Copeland, D.G. (1997). Business Strategic Orientation, Information Systems Strategic Orientation and Strategic Alignments, *Information Systems Research*, 8 (2), 125-150.

Daft, R.L., & Lengel, R.H. (1986). Organizational Information Requirements, Media Richness and Structural Design, *Management Science*, 32(5), 554-571.

Davenport, T.H., De Long, D.W., & Beers, M.C. (1998). Successful knowledge management projects, *Sloan Management Review*; Cambridge, 39(2), 43-57.

DeSantictis, G., & Gallupe, R.B. (1987). A Foundation for the Study of Group Decision Support Systems, *Management Science*, 33(5), 589-609.

Disterer, G. (2001). Individual and Social Barriers to Knowledge Transfer, *Proceedings of the 34th Hawaii International Conference on System Sciences.*

Drazin, R. & Van de Ven, A. H. (1985). Alternative Forms of Fit in Contingency Theory, *Administrative Science Quarterly,* 30(4), 514-539.

Estes Z., & Hasson, U. (2004). The Importance of Being Nonalignable: A Critical Test of the Structural Alignment Theory of Similarity, *Journal of Experimental Psychology: Learning, Memory, and Cognition,* 30(5), 1082–1092.

Galbraith, J. R. (1977). *Organization Design,* Reading, MS, Addison-Wesley.

Gentner, D. (1983). Structure-mapping: A theoretical framework for analogy, *Cognitive Science, 7,* 155–170.

Henderson, J.C., & Venkatraman, N. (1993). Strategic Alignment: Leveraging Information Technology for Transforming Organizations, *IBM Systems Journal*, 32(1), 4-16.

Keane, M. T., & Costello, F. J. (2001). Setting Limits on Analogy: Why Conceptual Combination is Not Structural Alignment, in 'The Analogical Mind: Perspectives from Cognitive Science,' D Gentner, K. J. Holyoak, B. N. Kokinov (Eds.) (pp. 172-198). Cambridge, MA: MIT Press.

Khazanchi, D. (2005). Information Technology (IT) Appropriateness: The Contingency Theory Of "Fit" And It Implementation In Small And Medium Enterprises, *The Journal of Computer Information Systems*, 45(3), 88-95.

Locke, E. A., & Latham, G. (1990). *A theory of goal-setting and task performance.* Englewood-Cliffs, NJ: Prentice-Hall.

Luftman, J. (2004). Assessing Business-IT Alignment Maturity, In W. Van Grembergen (Ed.), *Strategies for Information Technology Governance* (pp.99-128). Idea Group Publishing, London.

Markman, A. B., & Medin, D. L. (1995). Similarity and alignment in choice, *Organizational Behavior and Human Decision Processes, 63,* 117–130.

Middleton, P., & Harper, K. (2004). Organizational alignment: a precondition for information systems success?, *Journal of Change Management,* 4(4), 327-338.

Nonaka, I., & Teece, D. (2001). *Managing Industrial Knowledge*, Sage Publications, London.

Poitrenaud, S., Richard J., & Tijus, C. (2005). Properties, categories, and categorisation, *Thinking & Reasoning*, 11(2), 151–208.

Reich B.H., & Benbasat I. (1996). Measuring the Linkage between Business and Information Technology Objectives, *MIS Quarterly*, 20(1), 55-81.

Reich B.H., & Benbasat I. (2000). Factors that Influence the Social Dimension of Alignment between Business and Information Technology Objectives, *MIS Quarterly*, 24(1), 81-113.

Robinson. A.G., & Stem. S. (1997). *Corporate Creativity—How Innovation and Improvement Actually Happen,* Berrett-Koehler Publishers, San Francisco, CA.

Sabherval, R., & Chan, Y.E. (2001). Alignment between Business and IS Strategies: A Study of Prospectors, Analyzers and Defenders, *Information Systems Research*, 12(1), 11-33.

Sledgianowski, D., & Luftman, J. (2005). IT-Business Strategic Alignment Maturity: A Case Study, *Journal of Cases on Information Technology*, 7(2), 102-120.

Sterman, J.D. (2000). *Business Dynamics; Systems Thinking and Modeling for a Complex World*, Irwin McGraw-Hill.

Stewart, T. A. (2001). *The Wealth of Knowledge: Intellectual Capital and the Twenty-first Century Organization*, Nicholas Brealey Publishing, London.

Sveiby, K.E. (1997). *The New Organizational Wealth—Managing and Measuring Knowledge-based Assets*, Berrett-Kehler Publishers, Inc., San Francisco.

Venkatraman, N. (1989). The Concept of Fit in Strategy Research: Toward Verbal and Statistical Correspondence, *The Academy of Management Review,* 14(3), 423-444.

Venkatraman, N., & Camillus, J.C. (1984). Exploring the Concept of 'Fit' in Strategic Management, *The Academy of Management Journal*, 9 (3), 513-525.

Wisniewski, E. J. (1997). When concepts combine. *Psychonomic Bulletin & Review, 4*(2), 167-183.

Zigurs, I., & Buckland, B. (1998). A Theory of Task/Technology Fit and Group Support Systems Effectiveness, *MIS Quarterly*, 22:3, 313-334.

ENDNOTE

[1] Portions of this chapter are reprinted, with permission, from Kivijärvi, H. (2004). Knowledge Conversion in Organizational Contexts: A Framework and Experiments, *Proceedings of the 37th Hawaii International Conference on System Sciences.* © 2004 IEEE.

APPENDIX 1 CAUSAL DIAGRAM OF THE ORGANIZATION-WIDE SIMULATION MODEL

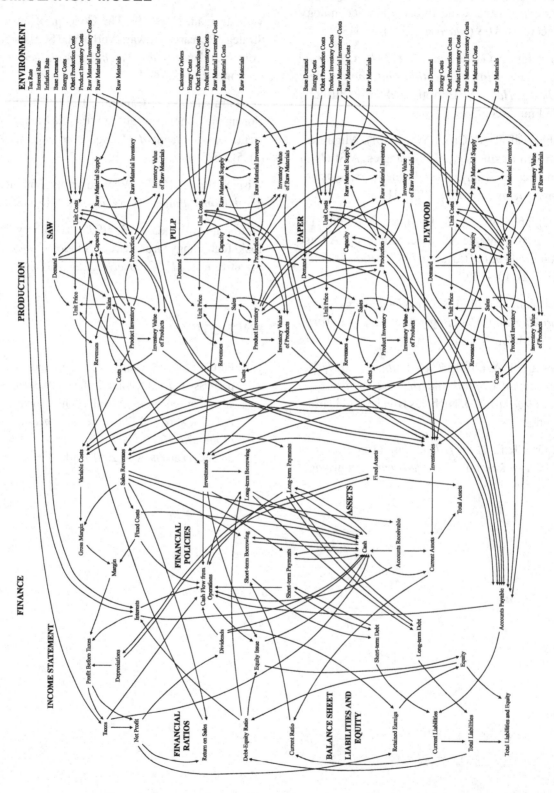

Chapter XII
The Activity Domain Theory:
Informing the Alignment of Business and Knowledge Management Strategies

Lars Taxén
Linköping University, Sweden

ABSTRACT

In this chapter, the activity domain theory is introduced as a theoretical lens for guiding the alignment of business and knowledge strategies. Alignment is focused around the activity domain, which can be comprehended as a human workpractice where socially organized actors process a work object into a required outcome. An organization is seen as a constellation of activity domains, each providing a specific outcome. The products or services provided by the organization are realized by coordinating the domains. The main target for the business strategy is the constellation of activity domains. The target of the knowledge strategy is the knowledge needed to produce the outcome of each domain and the knowledge needed to coordinate the domains. In this way, the activity domain provides a common target for business and knowledge strategies. We argue that this approach makes it possible to operationalize an integrated alignment of business and knowledge strategies.

INTRODUCTION

The importance of aligning business (B) and knowledge (K) strategies[1] is well-recognized (Abou-Zeid, this volume). In order to operationalize alignment, these strategies should be grounded in a common foundation from which general definitions or theories can be transformed into elements that can be manipulated, measured or observed in practical situations. In particular, such a foundation must consider the socio-technical nature of alignment (Tuomi, 2002). By this we mean that the social and technological context in which alignment takes place, must be taken into account.

The purpose of this contribution is to investigate alignment based on the *activity domain theory* (ADT) (Taxén, 2003, 2004, 2005a, 2005b,

2006). The ADT matured from a long term effort to comprehend and inform the coordination of large, extraordinary complex system development projects at Ericsson, a major supplier of telecommunication equipments world-wide. In particular, the theory addresses the construction of shared, or communal, meaning about how coordination should be conceived.

The roots of ADT are found in the notion of praxis (Kosík, 1976; Israel, 1979) and activity theory (e.g., Engeström, 1999), which implies that ADT is a contribution to the discourse that considers the *practice* as the nexus of human activity (Schatzki, 2001). A practice is conceived of as "embodied, materially mediated arrays of human activity centrally organized around shared practical understanding" (p. 2). According to practice theory, the human mind is "at least to a significant extent 'constituted' within practices. However much the contents and properties that compose and define mind have biophysical sources and continuous neurophysiological underpinnings, they depend, both causally and ontologically, on participation in social practices." (p. 11). This point is also iterated by Orlikowski (2002), who suggests that knowing is constituted and reconstituted as individuals engage the world in purposeful, everyday practice. Hence, we claim that the practice is a suitable point of departure for integrative socio-technical approaches that regard individual, technological and social aspects of human activity as highly interrelated.

Taking the practice as the unit of analysis makes it possible to conceive of a common target for aligning B and K strategies. In ADT, this target is provided by the *activity domain*, which can be comprehended as a practice where socially organized actors process a work object into an outcome fulfilling certain social needs. Such practices have been called workpractices (Goldkuhl & Röstlinger, 2003). An organization is seen as a constellation of activity domains, each providing a specific outcome needed to produce the products or services that the organization offers. Thus, the activity domain provides an intermediate, shielding construct between the daily practice of each individual actor and the organization as a whole.

The outcome of the organization is achieved by coordinating the outcomes of the activity domains. Consequently, a main target for the B strategy is the constellation and coordination of the activity domains. The target of the K strategy is two-fold. First, in each activity domain, the nature of the work object determines the kind of knowledge needed in order to produce the outcome. Thus, the K strategy should address how to achieve this knowledge. Second, this strategy should attend to the knowledge needed to coordinate the outcomes of the domains.

In this chapter we shall inquire into this line of thought. The outline is as follows. In the first section (*Reconstruction of Strategy Alignment*) we reconstruct our understanding of the B/K alignment discourse in order to position our contribution relative to this discourse. In the next section (*Positions Taken*) our stances on knowledge in relation to the individual and the organization are outlined. The point of departure is the concept of *meaning*, which is seen as the foundation for all aspects of knowledge. By analyzing various facets of meaning, we suggest that knowledge is situated, located in the individual, and constructed in social interaction in practices. Moreover, we assume that manifestations of activity in the human mind and in the practice are in some sense *congruent*. The phylogenetic constitution of humans is reflected in our constructed social reality, which in turn is reflected in the ontogenetic constitution of the individual in a particular practice. For example, the ability to learn a language is a result of the phylogenetic evolution of man, while the ontogenetic acquisition of a particular language by an individual is determined by the historical and cultural context in which the individual is immersed.

The section is concluded with a discussion of knowledge in organizations. We introduce the concept of 'activity' as it is understood in the Russian theory of activity (Bedny & Meister, 1997; Engeström, 1999) in order to understand the specific nature of knowledge in organizations.

In the following section (*The Activity Domain Theory*), a general view on human activity is elaborated. We propose that the construction of the human mind and the socio-technical reality in activity domains proceed along certain dimensions called *activity modalities*. These modalities denote fundamental human capabilities to coordinate actions. For example, the innate capacity of humans to separate spatial dimensions from temporal ones is apprehended in ADT as two distinct, albeit dialectically related activity modalities: spatialization and temporalization. The congruence principle enables us to operationalize the construction of meaning concerning coordination by manipulating tangible manifestations of the activity modalities.

At this point, we are in a position to discuss the alignment of B/K strategies as seen from the ADT perspective (*Aligning Business and Knowledge Strategies*). In this section, we also compare our approach to some other alignment approaches found in the literature. In the next section (*Discussion*) we examine some implications of our approach. In particular we address the issues stated by Abou-Zeid (editor's preface, this volume):

- How to model the relationship between an organization's competitive B strategy and its K strategies?
- How to align K strategies with the organization's competitive B strategy, i.e., the dynamics of alignment?
- What are enablers and inhibitors of B and K strategies alignment?
- What are the roles of top/middle managers in alignment process?

- What are the impacts of culture (organizational and national) on alignment process?

The implications should be regarded as opportunities for further research rather than elaborated and decisive results. Our main conclusion is that the ADT provides a promising approach towards informing the alignment of B and K strategies that may open up hitherto untrodden paths of research.

RECONSTRUCTION OF STRATEGY ALIGNMENT

In order to position our approach we will reconstruct our understanding of the B/K strategy alignment discourse. A suitable point of departure is provided by Tuomi (2002), who states that the sources of knowledge management (KM) can be separated into four intertwined clusters. The first one, *organizational information processing*, has its roots in the artificial intelligence community and is concerned with building corporate-wide information systems and expert systems. The core idea is that knowledge can be stored and shared with the help of computer systems. In this cluster, technology is in focus.

In the next cluster, *business intelligence*, the focus is on categorizing, searching and distributing information that is considered vital for the business. Knowledge sharing is a prime task for corporate librarians and intelligence professionals. This task is facilitated by the access to large databases and the Internet. However, information overload is an issue. This in turn brings the relevance of the information to the foreground. Ultimately, the problem of knowledge representation is reduced to the idea that "all knowledge can be represented as documents and associations between them" (Tuomi, 2002, p. 5). Making sense of the information is left to the reader.

In the third cluster, *organizational cognition*, organizational sense-making and the active process of knowledge construction are emphasized. The focus is on the effective use of human experts and the establishment of social and communicative networks. A more interpretationistic approach towards knowledge is taken where tacit and situated knowledge are highlighted.

The fourth cluster, *organizational development*, brings knowledge and social action to the foreground. The concept of the 'learning organization' is coined and the knowledge creation process becomes subject to management. In this cluster, KM is linked to the B strategy, that is, the KM strategy is turned into a K strategy. Resource-based strategies, including analysis of competitive strengths and weaknesses, evolve to competence-based strategies. Knowledge is considered an asset in the balance sheet, and intellectual property is protected. The strategic needs of the organization are linked to the aggregation of individual skills by human resource

(HR) management initiatives. The basic idea is to identify and fill in gaps in knowledge in order to execute the B strategy, which in turn is grounded in organizational sciences. Thus, the HR department becomes the link between K and B strategies as illustrated in Figure 1.

The clusters described emerged more or less sequentially between 1993-1996. Tuomi (2002) calls this period the 'first generation of KM'. It is characterized by its focus on information sharing, repositories and intellectual capital management. In the second period, which started around 1997, companies include KM as part of their everyday organizational discourse. Specific KM positions and departments are established. Issues of tacit knowledge, social learning, situated and embedded knowledge, and communities of practice are in focus (p. 10).

Tuomi maintains that the first and second generations of KM will remain vital. A third generation of KM will in addition emphasize the role of information systems as support for

Figure 1. The linking of K and B strategies

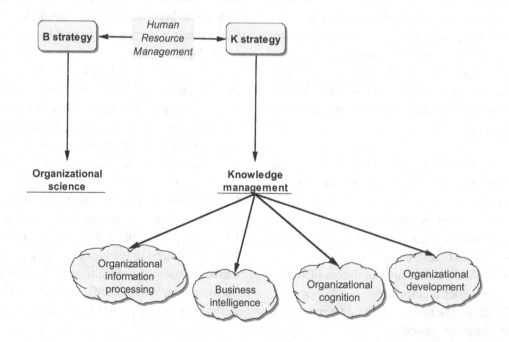

knowledge construction and human sense-making. Knowledge will be viewed from a constructivistic and pragmatic perspective. The action character of knowledge will be in focus as well as social aspects of knowledge. This will require a better understanding of the cultural basis of knowledge.

The ADT is an attempt to contribute to such an understanding. The HR initiative tried to link individual knowledge directly to the organization's strategical needs. In our opinion, this is a dead end since the workpractice basis of knowledge is overlooked. As an alternative, we suggest that the link between the B and K strategies should be the activity domain. In the following, we shall elaborate on this idea.

POSITIONS TAKEN

The alignment of B and KM strategies is indeed a challenging task that is aggravated by the problems of defining knowledge in general and organizational knowledge in particular. This makes it necessary to be specific about our positions in these areas.

Before we develop these positions we need some basic definitions of business strategy, knowledge strategy and alignment. According to Porter, activities are the basic units of competitive advantage (Porter, 1996). Strategic positioning means "performing *different* activities from rivals' or performing similar activities in *different ways*." (p. 62, italics in original). From this follows that "strategy is the creation of a unique and valuable position, involving a different set of activities." (p. 68).

Business strategy has been defined as "the determination of the basic long-term goals and objectives of an enterprise, and the adoption of courses of action and the allocation of resources necessary for carrying out these goals" (Chandler, 1966, p. 16). A business strategy is unique

to an organization, sometimes unique in time, and always shaped by the cultural values of the stakeholders, constituencies, the communities the organization serves, and by marketplace considerations (Bishoff & Allen, 2004).

A *knowledge strategy* is a plan that describes how an organization will manage its knowledge better for the benefit of the organization and its stakeholders. A good knowledge strategy is closely aligned with the organization's overall strategy and objectives. According to Zack (1999), a "knowledge strategy [...] describes the overall approach an organization intends to take to align its knowledge resources and capabilities to the intellectual requirements of its [business] strategy." (p. 135). This strategy "can be thought of as balancing knowledge-based resources and capabilities to the knowledge required for providing products or services in ways superior to those of competitors." (p. 131). In order to become operational, the strategy must be translated into an organizational and technological architecture to support knowledge creation, management, and utilization processes for closing those gaps (p. 142). In doing so, firms need some model, which "strategically guide their knowledge management efforts, bolstering their knowledge advantages and reducing their knowledge weaknesses" (p. 131).

Alignment can be seen as the efforts of an organization to balance different stakeholder needs in order to survive in a changing environment (Regev & Wegmann, 2004). However, alignment, or fit, is an imprecise concept. According to Knoll & Jarvenpaa (1994), alignment has several dimensions such as the number of components involved, external vs. internal alignment and static vs. dynamic alignment. In addition, Regev & Wegmann (1994) state that alignment is a point of view. Hence, people are likely to disagree on the meaning of alignment. This situation is further aggravated due to vagueness in central concepts like business goal, business structure, and informal organization structure (Chan, 2002). Chan (ibid.)

sees alignment as consisting of "simultaneous component alignments that bring together an organization's structure, strategy, and culture at multiple (IT, business unit, and corporate) levels, with all their inherent demands." (p. 99). We shall adopt this view of alignment since it goes well with the activity domain construct.

The Point of Departure: Meaning

Download knowledge directly to the brain! Today the actual learning process takes too long. In the future we will download knowledge directly to the brain. Connect in to something which contains specific know how and transfer it over. (Framed statement hanging on the wall at Corporate IT, Ericsson, July 2000)

Many different characterizations of knowledge have been suggested in the KM discourse (e.g., Blumentritt & Johnston, 1999). Most of these state that knowledge can be encoded or embedded in artefacts such as, for example, books and symbols. Often, a distinction is drawn between codified knowledge and personal knowledge (e.g., Hansen et al., 1999; Dennis & Vessey, 2005). Codified knowledge is formally identified, coded and stored in a KM system.

We challenge this view of knowledge as being too shallow for grounding an integrated approach towards alignment. There is a need to distinguish between data, information and competence (Mathiassen, 1996). The concepts of data and information emphasize the difference between formal representation of information (to be processed by, for example a KM system) and interpretation of representations (being performed by human beings). The concepts of information and competence clarify the difference between, on the one hand, knowing and being able to explicitly describe, and, on the other hand, doing and being able to perform (p. 128). "Competence [is] a situated knowing constituted by a person acting in a particular setting and engaging aspects of the self, the body, and the physical and social worlds." (Orlikowski, 2002, p. 252). Thus, an intrinsic aspect of knowledge is its anchoring in the individual. There is no knowledge without someone knowing it (Fahey & Prusak, 1998). However, this is not the whole story.

We suggest that the underlying concept for integrating data, information and competence is *meaning*. Only meaningful sensory impression can be informative and acted upon. Meaning has been proposed as fundamental for understanding the human mind. For example, Bruner (1990) suggests that "[T]he central concept of a human psychology is meaning and the processes and transactions involved in the construction of meanings" (p. 33). Meaning is intrinsically related to culture and human action:

[C]ulture and the quest for meaning within culture are the proper causes of human action. The biological substrate, the so-called universals of human nature, is not a cause of action but, at most, a constraint upon it or a condition for it. (Bruner, 1990, p. 20)

Through interaction with its environment, the individual gradually constructs a meaningful world ranging from the meaning of near-sensory impressions to, in due time, abstract symbols in a specific culture. Each individual acquires her own, particular understanding of the world. This understanding is located in the mind and body of the individual. Thus, on the one hand, meaning is idiosyncratic. On the other hand, meaning is inherently social. In order to construct meaning, an individual needs to interact with her social and physical environment, including other individuals:

Every function in the child's cultural development appears twice: first, on the social level, and later, on the individual level; first, between people (interpsychological), and then inside the child (intrapsychological). (Vygotsky, 1978, p. 57, italics in original)

Thus, meaning has a dual nature. The mediator between the social and individual aspects is the *sign*. The sign bridges internal, mental processes and external physical and social reality:

By its very existential nature, the subjective psyche is to be localized somewhere between the organism and the outside world, on the borderline separating these two spheres of reality. [...] the organism and the outside world meet here in the sign. (Vološinov, 1986, p. 26)

In the Russian theory of activity, the difference between subjective, personal 'sense' and objective 'meaning' is central (Leont'ev, 1978). Objective meaning refers to the meaning of a word given in a dictionary. This meaning is "independent of any particular individual and is thus trans-individual, but [it] exist only through the activity and reason of individuals" (Kosík, 1976, p. 146).

In the literature, it is common to describe objective meaning as 'shared'. However, from the discussion above it is clear that meaning cannot be shared in the same sense as two individuals share, for example, an apartment. This has also been pointed out by Boland (1996) and Walsham (2005). Hence, the term 'communal', with its connotations of contextuality and social action, appears to be more appropriate: "By virtue of [its] actualization in culture, meaning achieves a form that is public and communal rather than private and autistic" (Bruner, 1990, p. 33).

The social foundation of meaning implies that meaning is historically and culturally dependent. Different meanings evolve in different cultures separated in time and space. The interactions

between individuals in a particular society bring about a communal meaning that stabilizes the social system:

All social interaction is situated interaction - situated in time and space. It can be understood as the fitful yet routinised occurrence of encounters, fading away in time and space, yet constantly reconstituted within different areas of time-space. The regular or routine features of encounters, in time as well as space, represent institutionalized features of social systems. (Giddens, 1984, p. 86, in Rose & Scheepers, 2001, p. 221)

Signification occurs through physical stimuli picked up by sensory organs in various modalities such as sight, sound, taste, smell, and touch. Everything that possesses meaning is ultimately physical in origin. The sign is a material phenomenon:

Signs [...] are particular, material things; and [...] any item of nature, technology or consumption can become a sign, acquiring in the process a meaning that goes beyond its given particularity. A sign does not simply exist as part of a reality - it reflects and refracts another reality. (Vološinov, 1986, p. 10)

In summary, meaning integrates individual, social and technological / material aspects of social reality. Knowledge is acquired through social interaction in which physical sensory impressions become meaningful in a certain situated and historical context. Thus, meaning and knowledge have a dualistic and multi-faceted nature (Hildreth & Kimble, 2002; Blackler, 1995). It is embodied in the individual mind and body and reflected in the artefacts and symbols that emerge as meaningful in a culture. Moreover, meaning is simultaneously idiosyncratic and communal, mediated by signs that relate the external physical and social reality with the psychological reality in the minds of human beings. Human social reality is a reality where processes of semiosis are inseparably intertwined with material processes:

Semiotic formations [...] are essential elements in the material dynamics of human communities, and this material-semiotic coupling is reciprocal. There cannot be two systems here, changing according to separate laws, relatively independent of one another. There can be only one unitary ecosocial system, material and semiotic, with a single unified dynamics, described under two aspects, by two different sorts of culture-specific discourses. (Lemke, 1993)

The Congruence of Mind and Activity

The dualistic nature of meaning is still being discussed among scholars (e.g. Zinchenko, 2001). Usually, this discussion is framed in terms of internalization and externalization. In object-related activity, the human mind is externalized into the objectified social world, which in turn is internalized into the consciousness in the course of socialization (Berger & Luckmann, 1991). However, in this discourse the idea that the human mind does not have its own structure and logic of development, distinct from the structure of object-related activity, has been lost (Stetsenko, 1999, p. 246). According to Zinchenko (2001), we should assume that "what is considered mental, or subjective, is objective at the same time" (p. 138). The mind, just like culture, does not have its own enclosed territory, but is "situated instead at the borders between own and not-own" (p. 139).

The consequence of this position is that the structure of communal meaning in the human mind will develop in congruence with the structure of object-related activity. In a superficial way, this is quite obvious. Cars, trains, buildings, books or whatever artifacts constructed, are all adapted to the measures of human. This is valid also for symbols like the alphabet, traffic signals and the like. Conversely, only physical stimuli accessible by our sensory organs can become meaningful. Stimuli not directly accessible by human senses, for example, ultraviolet light and high-pitch sounds, are made meaningful only through some translation and processing.

The congruence principle implies that two forms of objectivizing are constructed in human activity. The transformation of the world into artifacts such as tools, institutions and organizations is *objectification* ('Vergegenständlichung') (Kosík, 1976). This process is dialectically intertwined with a process where the individual is integrated in a trans-individual whole as one of its elements: "The subject abstracts from his subjectivity and becomes an object and an element of the system" (p. 50). This second form of objectivizing is *objectivation* ('Objektivierung') (p. 131). The essence of objectivation is the appropriation of communal meaning necessary to perform coordinated actions.

We can exemplify the objectification—objectivation process with the activity of playing in an ensemble. First, there are obvious objectified elements involved, like the instruments and the musical score. Each individual actor/player has to appropriate her instrument by a long and intense interaction with it. Technical and musical abilities must be learned. However, in order to bring forth music the musicians cannot act one by one. They have to appropriate a communal meaning of context-relevant elements such as, for example, scores, notes, tuning procedures and performance manners. In short, they have to be integrated in a trans-individual whole—the activity of playing—where they start playing at the same time, use the same phrasing and dynamics, and so on. Without going through this objectivation process, the musicians cannot coordinate their actions.

The Organizational Context

In the literature organizational knowledge is often discussed in anthropocentric terms. Organizational knowledge is apprehended as similar to, yet different from human knowledge. This view can be traced in expressions like organizational knowledge, organizational memory, organizational cognitive structures (Nicolini & Meznar, 1995), and the like. At the extreme, organizations are conceived as living entities (Hall, 2005; Örtenblad, 2005). We reject this understanding of organizations.

From our point of view, organizations are specific forms of human, situated activity where the positions stated in the previous sections remain valid. The main distinguishing element is that organizations are intentionally created to fulfill social needs. As a consequence, knowledge in organizations is used for productive purposes in a certain context. The primary role of the firm is in the "application of existing knowledge to the production of goods and services" (Grant, 1996, p.112). This position is also emphasized by Burstein and Linger (2003), who maintains that knowledge must be seen in relation to the task at hand.

Ultimately, all differences between companies in cost or price derive from the hundreds of activities required to create, produce, sell, and deliver their products or services, such as calling on customers, assembling final products, and training employees (Porter, 1996, p. 62). These activities need to be coordinated, regardless of whether they reside inside or outside the organization. Thus, core knowledge in an organization concerns the coordination of a certain constellation of units, some of which are part of the organization and others are not. This point is strongly emphasized by Grant (1996), who maintains that the firm should be conceptualized as an institution for integrating knowledge by coordinating the efforts of individual specialists possessing different types of knowledge. This coordination can only be carried out if a certain degree of communal meaning concerning the coordination is achieved.

In order to ground these general observations theoretically, we will make use of the concept of 'activity' in the Russian theory of activity (Bedny & Meistner, 1997). An activity ('*deyatelnost*' in Russian) has a very specific meaning in this theory. It is defined as "a coherent system of internal mental processes, external behavior, and motivational processes that are combined and directed to achieve conscious goals" (p. 3). The activity frames the social context within which individual actions are meaningful. For example, the action of a beater to drive wild game away is meaningful only in the activity of socially organized hunting.

The existence of an activity is motivated by the transformation of a *work object* into an outcome fulfilling a social need. The work object is the key element that defines the activity and separates activities from each other. Work objects can be material or intangible things as long as they can be shared for manipulation and transformation by the participants of the activity (Virkkunen & Kuutti, 2000, p. 301). In what follows, we will use the activity as the basis for the further theoretical elaboration in the next section. In this respect, our approach differs from that of Grant (1996), who emphasizes the integration of *individual*, specialized knowledge: "Given the efficiency gains of specialization, the fundamental task of organization is to coordinate the efforts of many specialists" (p. 113).

To summarize, our position on organizational knowledge is that such knowledge is, in principle, not different from knowledge in general. By working in an organized manner, a communal meaning is constructed concerning the actions needed to produce the outcome. This meaning is acquired in the interaction between actors and meaningful artifacts in the context of the organization. A similar position has been advocated by Orlikowski

(2002) who uses 'organizational knowing' instead of 'organizational knowledge' to emphasize that knowing is enacted in practice:

Knowledgeability or knowing-in-practice is continually enacted through people's everyday activity; it does not exist "out there" (incorporated in external objects, routines, or systems) or "in here" (inscribed in human brains, bodies, or communities). Rather, knowing is an ongoing social accomplishment, constituted and reconstituted in everyday practice. (Orlikowski, 2002, p. 252)

The coordination of actions is taking place both within the activity and between activities. Accordingly, we can identify two aspects of knowledge that may be subject to management. The first aspect concerns the knowledge needed to produce the outcome of a certain activity. The second aspect concerns the knowledge needed to coordinate the outcomes of these activities. Thus, in line with Fahey & Prusak (1998), we suggest that the target of knowledge strategies should be the construction of a certain degree of communal meaning of an organization's external and internal worlds and how these worlds are connected.

THE ACTIVITY DOMAIN THEORY

The activity domain theory (ADT) originated in the development practice of Ericsson, where it influenced and was influenced by the activity to coordinate large, extraordinary complex system development projects (Taxén, 2003, 2004, 2005a, 2005b, 2006). Thus, ADT is empirically rooted in a concrete practical setting. Its philosophical and theoretical roots are found in the notion of praxis (Kosík, 1976; Israel, 1979) and the Russian theory of activity (Bedny & Meister, 1997; Engeström, 1999). The focus of ADT is the construction of communal meaning concerning coordination, which turned out to be a major issue in the Ericsson practice. From the outset, an ambition with ADT has been to provide an operationalizable theoretical foundation that can be efficiently applied to demanding coordination tasks.

The central construct in ADT is the *activity domain*, which can be conceived of as an activity structured from a coordination point of view. From activity theory, ADT has appropriated the notions of the *work object* and the *motive* as the main drivers of the constitution of the domain. The praxis perspective emphasizes certain quali-

Figure 2. A model of the activity domain

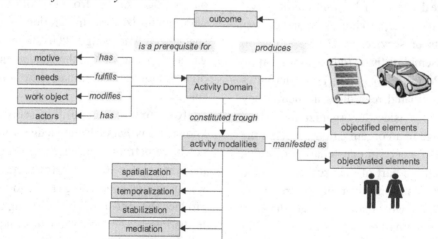

ties of human activity such as historicity, cultural specificity, and dialectical interaction. The activity domain is considered to be in constant motion and development. Through the emergence and resolution of inner contradictions, the structure of the activity domain evolves to meet new needs. In ADT, we strive to maintain these qualities while simultaneously giving praxis a structure that is suitable for analytical and constructive purposes related to coordination.

Since we assume that one premise for the meaning construction process is the biological 'substrate' brought about during the phylogenetic evolution of mankind, we may hypothesize that manifestations of this process are in some sense trans-situational. In other words, regardless of the particular motive and work object of an activity domain, certain regular features should prevail between different domains. An indication of such features is provided by the empirical observations from the Ericsson development practice (Taxén, 2003). The analysis of these observations indicates that the evolution of activity domains proceeds along certain, dialectically interdependent dimensions, which have been coined *activity modalities* in ADT. As the name indicates, these modalities should be seen as fundamental dimensions of human socially organized activity. These dimensions are, at least to some extent, determined by the biological constitution of human beings.

What does this mean? For example, one activity modality is *temporalization*. The construction of communal meaning in this modality is manifested as objectified artifacts such as, for example, business process models. These signify a temporal dimension of activity. To become effective in the organization, the actors must acquire communal meaning about how to interpret and make use of these models. This meaning is manifested as objectivated elements in the minds of the actors. Thus, the construction of a coordinating instrument in any modality implies two types of results—a tangible, objectified result in the domain and an intangible, objectivated result in the minds of the actors.

In Figure 2, a model of the activity domain is depicted. In the text that follows, we describe this model in detail.

The existence of the *activity domain* is *motivated* by some social *need*. This need is fulfilled by the modification of a *work object* by socially organized *actors* into an *outcome*. The work object and the motive are the key elements that define the domain and separate different domains from each other. The outcome may be the *prerequisite* for the other domains. This means that the activity domain construct is recursive. The same structure applies to all activity domains.

The activity domain is constituted through the actions of the actors along the activity modalities. These modalities are manifested as *objectified*, tangible elements in the activity domain, and intangible, *objectivated* elements in the human minds of the actors. In the analysis of the empirical results from Ericsson, the following activity modalities were found to be particularly important for coordination (Taxén, 2003):

- **Spatialization** manifests a spatial framing that enables the actors to acquire a communal meaning of what entities are relevant, how these entities should be characterized and related to each other, and in what state or condition they are. Examples of organizational manifestations of spatialization are information models, product structures, and conceptual models. Spatialization can refer both to direct, physical objects or signs signifying such objects. For example, both a map of a city and the city itself are examples of spatialization.

- **Temporalization** manifests a temporal framing that enables the actors to acquire a communal meaning about actions and the dependencies between them. In this sense, manifestations of temporality are coordinating elements according to the definition given by Malone & Crowston (1994): "Coordination is managing dependencies between [actions][2]" (p. 90). Examples of organizational manifestations of temporalization are business process models, interaction diagrams, and use cases.

- **Stabilization** manifests stability in the domain as provided by, for example, norms, values, habits, routines, rules, standards, and domain specific languages. Without stabilizing elements, coordination is impossible. Such elements have the function of "... reducing the infinite number of things in the world, potential or actual—to a moderate number of well-defined varieties" (March & Simon, 1958, p. 181). Together, the stabilizing elements constitute an *ideology*, that is, a wide-ranging system of belief or thought. Some elements of the ideology may be common to several domains, but in general, these elements vary between domains.

Organizational manifestations of stabilization are, for example, naming conventions, business rules, and standards.

- **Mediation** manifests resources by which actions are accomplished. 'Mediation', which can be material and semiotic in nature, is a key concept in activity theory (e.g., Susi, 2006), and refer to the idea that humans always put something between themselves and their work object. Organizational manifestations of mediation are, for example, information systems, mail systems and financial resources.

- **Contextualization** manifests a contextual framing of human activity. In ADT, framing is mainly determined by the motive of the domain. A capability to contextualize appears to be innate in humans. For example, our visual system simplifies a visual scene into a figure attended in the foreground and other things unattended in the background (Jackendoff, 1983, p. 42). Contextualization

Figure 3. Spatial domain model from Ericsson (1998)

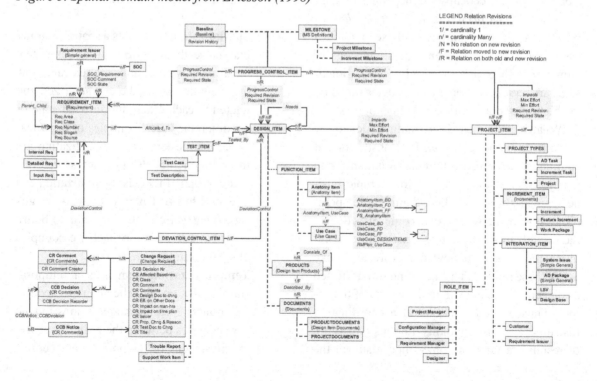

implies that meaning is context dependent. This means that same object will be characterized differently depending on the motive of the domain. For example, a product will be described differently in the contexts of marketing, development and production. Organizational manifestations of contextualization are, for example, organizational units, teams, and projects.

• **Transition** In general, activity domains have to interact in order to fulfill a certain need. Since communal meaning differs between domains, a particular outcome from one domain may be characterized differently in other domains. Transitional elements provide a mapping and translation between meanings that enables the actors to cooperate. Organizational manifestations of transitional elements are, for example, interface specifications and dictionaries for translating between organization specific languages such as product identification conventions. The coordination of a constellation of activity domains is enabled by the transition modality.

Operationalization of Meaning Construction

According to ADT, the activity modalities are manifested both in the domain and the minds of the actors. Both these aspects must be considered in the operationalisation of the theory. This is done by identifying objectified elements of the modalities, and using these in a process for constructing objectivated, communal meaning concerning these elements.

In general, modality manifestations are signified by models and artifacts corresponding to each modality (Taxén, 2003). For example, spatialization can be manifested as *spatial domain models* realized by OMT diagrams (Object Modeling Technique, Rumbaugh et al., 1991). In order to alleviate the construction of communal meaning, the nomenclature in the model should be easily comprehended by the actors. An example of a spatial domain model is given in Figure 3.

The figure shows entities (square boxes) and relations between these (arrowed lines). Attributes may be used to characterize entities (bottom part of the boxes) and relations. State set names,

Figure 4. The construction of communal meaning

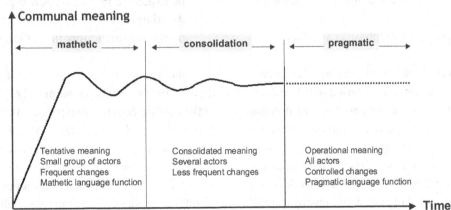

indicating the states a certain entity can take, are given within {} brackets. Class relationships (*is_a*) are signified by dotted lines. Finally, rules for managing relations when an entity is revised, are given in the legend in the upper right corner. All in one, approximately 600 items are specified in the model. This model, as well as other models corresponding to other modalities is implemented in an information system.

In order to construct a communal meaning about models like the one in Figure 3, which is indeed a formidable task, a *domain construction process* has been suggested in ADT. As the name indicates, the gist of this process is in fact the construction of the entire activity domain, including communal meaning and meaningful artifacts. The process, which is based on an experiential learning approach (Kolb, 1984), is carried out in three phases: the *mathetic, consolidation* and *pragmatic* ones (see Figure 4).

The terms mathetic and pragmatic are adopted from Halliday (1975), who distinguishes between pragmatic and mathetic functions of language. Pragmatic functions involve coordination of actions when a communal meaning is established, while mathetic functions have to do with the construction of communal meanings. The gist of the process is an ongoing iteration between reflection and action, resulting in a communal meaning being gradually established among the actors. In this process, a gradual shift is made from the mathetic to the pragmatic functions of language.

The purpose of each phase is as follows:

- **Mathetic:** In this phase, the initial construction of the domain is carried out. The main purpose is to achieve a tentative domain structure in terms of a communal meaning and corresponding objectified artifacts such as domain models and their implementation in the information system. The work is carried out in a 'daily build' manner by a small 'task force'. Provisionary domain models, rules, etc., are suggested and implemented in the information system. The results are discussed and evaluated with respect to usefulness. Changes are suggested to the domain models and implemented anew in the information system. In this way a communal meaning is gradually constructed. The iteration is continued until a working consensus is achieved. The focus in this phase is on the mathetic function of language.

- **Consolidation:** The purpose of this phase is to boost the trust about the feasibility of the domain as constructed in the mathetic phase. Key issues are getting all actors to trust the data in the information system. This may be done in an on-going development project, that is, a project that develops a product for a customer. The task force is still driving the construction. Additional user roles around the project are involved and immediate, personalized support is provided. The construction of the domain in the consolidation phase progresses by controlled changes. No major reconstruction of the domain is allowed at this stage.

- **Pragmatic:** In this phase, actors in several projects may be included in the domain. As in the consolidation phase, the construction is done by controlled changes, however now in a formalized way. The domain may also be expanded to include new types of coordination entities. The focus in this phase is on the pragmatic function of language.

This process was applied successfully at Ericsson (Taxén, 2003). To summarize, the result of the domain construction process is an activity domain that produces a certain outcome needed by an organization. The construction of the domain includes both objectified elements such as models and tools, and objectivated communal meaning among the actors concerning theses elements.

ALIGNING BUSINESS AND KNOWLEDGE STRATEGIES

In this section, we examine some aspects of B/K strategy alignment that are brought to the fore by the ADT perspective.

B Strategy Focus

The activity domain view of the organization suggests that a main target of the B strategy should be the constellation and coordination of activity domains. It is beyond the scope of this contribution to discuss coordination in detail (see, e.g., Mintzberg, 1983; Larsson, 1990; Malone & Crowston, 1994). However, a key point in ADT is that all modalities as well as their interdependencies are involved in the coordination. Some of the issues that need to be considered are:

- **The constellation of activity domains:** Which domains are needed to fulfill the strategic intents of the organization?
- **Business level coordination:** How are the activity domains coordinated from the top-level domain, that is, the organization itself? In general, this coordination is signified by a business process model. How should this model be expressed in order to enhance the construction of communal meaning about it? A discussion of this issue is found in Taxén and Svensson (2005).
- **Internal or external:** Which domains should remain within the control of the business, that is, internal to the organization? Which ones should be external? Should we out-source or in-source some domains?
- **Transitions between activity domains:** Are there business critical transitions between activity domains? How should these be managed? For example, an organization may choose to out-source the operation of its IT-platform to another organization. An

issue that may appear in such a case is the translation between different organizational languages. Other issues concern the pragmatic functions of language. Which assignments, contracts, agreements, responsibilities, etc., are needed to regulate the cooperations between organizations?

- **Central versus local control:** Since each activity domain has a particular motive and produces a specific outcome, each domain is unique to some extent. However, the coordination of activity domains calls for some communal meaning across activity domains. This raises the question of maintaining an optimal balance between what is centrally controlled and what can be left to each domain to control locally. This balance affects all the activity modalities.
- **IT architecture:** How should the IT architecture of the organization be designed in order to support the coordination of activity domains?

K Strategy Focus

So far, most KM initiatives have taken as a point of departure the knowledge needed for an actor to carry out a certain task, for example, writing software code in C++. This is certainly valid also in our approach. However, with the introduction of the activity domain, individual actions are immersed in a social context where these actions make sense only in relation to the motive of the domain. Thus, the communal and situated aspects of individual knowledge are brought to the fore. This means that knowledge about how to coordinate individual actions becomes crucial. Based on these considerations, two focal areas for K strategies can be discerned: the knowledge needed to perform a certain action in order to transform the work object of the domain, and knowledge needed to coordinate such actions in the domain.

We suggest that K strategies for constructing and maintaining knowledge should be targeted to these focal areas. The management of transformational knowledge needs to be related to the motive and object of the activity domain. Actors in a domain producing printed circuit boards need very different kinds of knowledge as compared to actors in a domain producing software in C++. Strategies for constructing coordination knowledge should be based on the principles described in the section (Operationalization of Meaning Construction). In general, all activity modalities should be attended. In particular, the interdependencies between these modalities need to be managed as well as the transitions between activity domains.

Since the activity domain is a recursive construct, the entire organization is also regarded as an activity domain. In this sense, it is no different from other domains. The actors in this domain, for example, the CEO and his or hers steering group need to acquire the particular competences needed. Moreover, their actions need to be coordinated. Thus, the same two focal areas for K strategies apply also to this domain.

KM Systems

The storing, distribution and retrieving of information in a KM system should be structured from an activity domain perspective. Some conceivable functions of such systems are:

- Listing activity domains and their characteristics, for example, their motives, what needs they fulfill, and what kinds of work objects are manipulated.
- Keeping track of the dependencies between activity domains.
- Matching activity domains with similar characteristics where actors with similar knowledge may be found.
- Listing individuals with expert knowledge related to a particular domain.

It has been noted that the predominant use of KM systems is to capture, store and transmit 'commodified knowledge' in the form of patents, documents, experiences, etc. (e.g. Hildreth & Kimble, 2002). From the ADT point of view, this kind of management concerns only the objectified manifestations of the activity in various activity domains. Thus, only one side of the dualistic nature of knowledge is managed. In order to manage the objectivation aspect, KM systems need to support the entire spectrum of meaning and knowledge implicit in the activity domain construct. This is in line with Tuomi when he suggests that:

"[I]nformation systems for knowledge management and organizational memory should be seen as media that is used as an interpersonal cognitive artifact. A critical factor in designing such artifacts is to consider those knowledge stocks that are needed to make sense of the information stored in the system" (Tuomi, 1999, p. 9).

If two domains have similar motives and objects, the objectivated manifestations of activity modalities, that is, what is embodied in the minds of the actors will be similar. Communities of Practices (CoPs) (Wenger et al., 2002), consisting of actors from different domains, can be cultivated based on these considerations. In CoPs, actors can exchange experiences and look for solutions to similar problems.

It can also be noted that systems, which are used in manipulating the work object, for example, configuration management systems, contribute to the knowledge construction in the domain. They are an intrinsic part of the construction of the domain, and should be designed to facilitate the construction of communal meaning. This implies, for example, that the semiotic aspects of such systems should be given a high priority when designed. The action character of cues, symbols, and help texts should be made as evident as possible.

Comparison with other Alignment Approaches

In this section we shall compare the ADT approach with some other alignment approaches reported in the literature. This comparison can only be superficial, given the width and depth of the subject area. We will use the following categories as reference:

- **Integrative perspective:** Is the approach based on an integrative socio-technical perspective?
- **Practice based:** Is there a practice construct akin to the activity domain in the approach?
- **Communal meaning:** Is the issue of shared or communal meaning salient?
- **Dualistic view of knowledge:** Is there a dialectical view on the construction of objectivated elements in the mind and objectified elements in the work context?
- **Emphasis on the work object:** Does the approach emphasize the work object as a focus for B/K strategy alignment?
- **Coordination:** Is coordination an essential theme in the approach?

Earl (2001) has made a thorough investigation of various approaches to KM. He reports on seven 'schools' of KM and suggests how these can be used as points of departures for alignment initiatives. These schools are related to the ADT approach as follows[3].

Systems School

Here, the purpose is to capture specialist knowledge. Domain specific knowledge is codified and stored in knowledge databases. Technical know-how is provided to those qualified to use it. The KM systems have virtually the same role as information systems. Knowledge is generated from objective data and experience through practice.

In this school, there is a practice touch since the domain specificity of the knowledge is emphasized. The objectification aspect of the dualistic view of knowledge is in focus. However, there is less focus on the actual construction of knowledge.

Cartographic School

This school tries to map the knowledge of the organization: who in the organization knows what? This information is stored in knowledge directories, similar to the 'yellow pages' in a phone directory. The individual and tacit aspects of knowledge are communicated to other individuals. IT supports the connection of people.

The domain aspect is present in this school since individual knowledge acquired in one practice is supposed to be transferred to other, similar practices. The objectivation aspect of knowledge is emphasized.

Process School

In the process school contextual and best practice knowledge related to tasks are emphasized. Learning from experience is shared, based on similarity of tasks in key knowledge areas. Improvements made in particular practices are collected and distributed within the organization. The role of IT is the unrestricted provision of knowledge by shared data bases.

This school is related to the ADT approach in several ways. The constructive aspect of learning is emphasized. Contextual and best practice aspects as well as 'knowledge areas' are related to the activity domain construct. Moreover, different KM strategies are advocated, which is an indication of differentiation based on type of process or practice. It appears that the process school tries to 'balance' several of the activity modalities in

ADT. However, the emphasis on process indicates that the temporalization modality is in focus.

Organizational School

The organizational school nurses knowledge communities in which participants can exchange and share knowledge interactively. This takes place outside their daily practice. The communities are organized as networks of domain specific knowledge across business units, sites, and countries. Groupware IT support is heavily employed.

This school is similar to the ADT approach in the sense that the community is in focus. However, in the knowledge community the work object in the activity domain is only indirectly present. The knowledge that is shared in a knowledge community has been constructed elsewhere, in the activity domain.

Strategic School

In the strategic school, knowledge is the key resource. KM is the essence of the B strategy. Intellectual capital and a learning organization are heavily stressed. Knowledge achieved through systems, processes, and people is converted into knowledge-based products or services. The domain specificity of knowledge is recognized as captured in the slogan 'multi-local, multi-national'.

As in ADT, the strategic school takes an integrative view of knowledge. Knowledge is needed in every practice and is situated in nature. However, in these practices, the work object is subdued in the focus on knowledge itself as the essence of the organization.

In Table 1 below we have made a qualitative mapping of the ADT approach to the schools above. More stars indicate a stronger relation.

Although the mapping is indeed crude, some observations can be made. First, none of the schools can be directly mapped onto the categories of ADT. The process school is the one that has most in common with our approach. It seems that the various schools highlight one or several of the ADT categories. This may be a consequence of the fact that the schools are grounded in different views or 'philosophies' of knowledge (Earl, 2001, p. 217). Second, only the strategic school appears to take an integrative view of knowledge. However, the relation of knowledge to the organization's competitive products or services is not salient. Third, the categories of meaning, work object, and coordination are by and large absent in the different schools.

Zack (1999) suggests that the link between K and B strategies has been widely ignored. There is a need for pragmatic and theoretically sound models that enable executives to relate the firm's competitive strategy to capabilities and intellectual resources. According to Zack, a knowledge

Table 1. Mapping the ADT approach to KM schools according to Earl (2001)

	Systems	Cartographic	Process	Organizational	Strategic
Integrative			*		***
Practice	*	**	***	***	**
Meaning			*		
Objectification	***		**		
Objectivation		***	*		
Work object			**	*	
Coordination			*		

strategy should identify "which knowledge-based resources and capabilities are valuable, unique, and inimitable as well as how those resources and capabilities support the firm's product and market" (p. 131).

This position goes well with the ADT approach. The coordination of activity domains provides the products or services of the firm. By analyzing the knowledge needed to coordinate the outcomes and to produce the outcome of each individual activity domain, a strategy for knowledge management can be devised that matches the B strategy. In doing so the classification of knowledge into core, advanced and innovative knowledge suggested by Zack (1999) can be applied to each activity domain as well as to coordination knowledge. Moreover, Zack advocates that B and K strategies should be simultaneously aligned (p. 135). In ADT this is provided by targeting both strategies to the activity domain construct.

Abou-Zeid (2005) suggests a model for aligning B and K strategies based on the Henderson & Venkatraman (1993) Strategic Alignment Model for aligning IT to the B strategy. The K strategy is considered as a balance between external opportunities / threats and internal capabilities / arrangements. Three external dimensions are identified: *K-scope* (what the firm must know), *K-Systemic* (what are the critical characteristics of the required knowledge) and *K-Governance* (how to obtain the required K-competencies). The K-Scope is modeled as a business domain versus knowledge 'things' matrix in which each matrix element state the current / required state of knowledge of either a survival or advancement character.

Abou-Zeid is not specific about the nature of the business domains. However, if these are regarded as activity domains, there exists a straight-forward mapping between the K-scope matrix and the ADT approach. Each activity domain corresponds to a row in the matrix. Thus, a knowledge characterization for the K-scope dimension can be related to

Figure 5. The mediating role of the activity domain

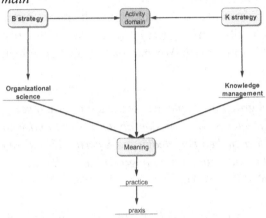

each activity domain. Whether the other external dimension, as well as internal dimensions of knowledge, can be related to the ADT approach require an extensive analysis that is outside the scope of this contribution.

DISCUSSION

The gist of the ADT approach towards alignment is the introduction of the activity domain as a common target for B and K strategies. In essence, we have replaced the HR department with the activity domain as the mediator between these strategies. Moreover, we suggest that meaning is a proper point of departure for knowledge and organizational discourses (see Figure 5). In this section we shall discuss some consequences of this way of addressing the alignment problem.

The Practice Turn in KM

A practice based approach has been suggested in several recent contributions to the KM discourse (e.g., Brown & Duguid, 1991; Gherardi, 2000; Tuomi, 2002; Hildreth & Kimble, 2002; Peltonen & Lämsä, 2004; Gorelick & Tantawy-Monsou, 2005). The reason for the interest in the practice is a growing discontent with the disentangled views of knowledge as either a commodity or residing in the head of individuals.

In order to overcome this dilemma, many contributions suggest a Community of Practice (CoP) approach (Wenger, 1998). A CoP is defined as ():

A group of people who share a concern, a set of problems, or a passion about a topic, and who deepen their knowledge and expertise in this area by interacting on an ongoing basis. (Wenger et al., 2002, p. 4)

An example of a CoP is given by engineers who design a certain kind of electronic circuits called phase-lock loops. They "find it useful to compare designs regularly and to discuss the intricacies of their esoteric specialty." (Wenger et al., 2002, p. 4). Thus, a CoP is primarily a context outside the workpractice, where actors from domains with similar or identical work objects can share experiences and knowledge. As such, a CoP may become important in the K strategy as a mean to transfer knowledge.

However, in order to anchor the knowledge creation process in organizations, the work object is central (Grant, 1996; Burstein & Linger, 2003). The primacy of the work object is recognized in activity theory, and some contributions in the KM literature have exploited this line of inquiry (Blackler, 1995; Virkkunen & Kuutti, 2000). For example, Blackler states that "Central to activity theory is the idea that collective action is driven by the conceptions people have of the object of their activities" (Blackler, 1995, p. 1041). In line with this we argue that the work object, as determinant for the formation of the activity domain, is crucial for the alignment of B and K strategies.

An Integrated View on Knowledge

The grounding of knowledge in meaning makes it possible to integrate individual, social and technological aspects of human object-related activity. Based on this perspective we may re-interpret espoused concepts in the KM discourse as follows:

- **Commodification of knowledge, embedded knowledge:** the tendency to focus on objectified manifestations of activity.
- **Mentalistic view of knowledge:** The tendency to focus on objectivated elements in the mind.
- **Organizational memory:** The objectified manifestations (artifacts) of object-related activity. Since an organization can employ different types of activity domains, depending on the type of object, various types of organizational memory will exist in an organization.
- **Organizational learning:** The learning among actors that takes place in various activity domains in accordance with the overall motive of the organization.

Moreover, grounding knowledge in the concept of meaning makes it possible to address many of the problems found in existing KM practices. Fahey & Prusak (1998) listed "The Eleven Deadliest Sins of Knowledge Management":

1. Not developing a working definition of knowledge.
2. Emphasizing knowledge stock to the detriment of knowledge flow.
3. Viewing knowledge as existing predominantly outside the heads of individuals.
4. Not understanding that a fundamental intermediate purpose of managing knowledge is to create shared context.
5. Paying little heed to the role and importance of tacit knowledge.
6. Disentangling knowledge from its uses.
7. Downplaying thinking and reasoning.
8. Focusing on the past and the present and not the future.

9. Failing to recognize the importance of experimentation.
10. Substituting technological contact for human interface.
11. Seeking to develop direct measures of knowledge.

Many of these points are attended to in the ADT approach. Point 1—a working definition of knowledge is given in the section (The Point of Departure—Meaning). Points 2, 3, 7, and 9—objectified ('knowledge stock') and objectivated ('in the head') manifestations are constructed in social interaction in the activity domain. This also implies that it is futile to develop measures of knowledge (point 11). Point 4—meaning is intrinsically communal ('shared') as well as individual since it is achieved in social settings. Point 5—tacit knowledge is apprehended as objectivated elements in the mind constructed in interaction. Point 6—actions are directed to the work object, which means that knowledge is intrinsically bound to its uses.

In summary, we claim that grounding knowledge in meaning makes it possible to find an integrating view on individual, organizational and technological aspects of knowledge.

DIRECTIONS OF FUTURE RESEARCH

The list of issues provided by Abou-Zeid (editor's preface, this volume) can be seen as research questions concerning the alignment of B and K strategies. From the ADT perspective, we may indicate some directions of future research as follows:

- **How to model the relationship between an organization's competitive B strategy and its K strategies?** We suggest that there is a need for constructs that mediate the actions of individuals with the multitude of different kinds of knowledge needed in large and possibly globally distributed organizations. In ADT, this mediating construct is the activity domain. Without such a construct the task of coordinating the specialist knowledge of individuals becomes overwhelming. Thus, the unit of analysis should be neither the individual, nor the organization, but some intermediate, practice oriented construct like the activity domain.

- **How to align K strategies with organization's competitive B strategy, i.e., the dynamics of alignment?** Again, we argue that the dynamics of alignment needs a practice oriented construct that mediates between the K and B strategies. Alignment implies that the constellation and coordination of activity domains must be rearranged to reflect changes in the organization's strategic positioning on the market. Some domains may become obsolete and others may have to be constructed. In this effort, the domain construction process provides guidelines of how to construct the new domains in such a way that both objectified elements (such as artifacts, tools, and institutions), and objectivated elements (communal meaning among actors about coordination of actions) are manifested according to the motive of the domain.

- **What are the enablers of B and K strategies alignment?** The indications from ADT in researching this question are as follows. A first enabler is to take the activity domain, or any similar practice based construct, as the main unit of analysis. Without such a unit the complexity of the analysis cannot be mastered. Next, an integrative perspective of knowledge is needed where objectivated ('in the head') and objectified ('commodified') forms of knowledge are seen as a dualistic unity. These forms of knowledge are constructed by actors working on a common work object. Thus, a second enabler is to emphasize the work object, that is, the target for the actions in the domain. A third enabler may be to bring coordination into the KM discourse as one way to relate B and K strategies.

- **What are the inhibitors of B and K strategies alignment?** Here, the ADT approach indicates that the main inhibitor of alignment is the disjoint views on knowledge represented by the commodification view and the mentalistic view. If this disentangled view persists, the fundamental dualism between objectified and objectivated forms of knowledge will remain unattended. This means that the dynamics of knowledge construction is not considered, which in turn implies that the full scope of alignment cannot be mastered.

- **What are the roles of top managers in alignment process?** Basing the alignment on some practice construct indicates that the organization must be envisaged as consisting of a number of more or less independent units, the outcomes of which need to be coordinated. This implies that espoused views on organizations as a homogenous entity need to be revised. In this process, top management has a key role in 'spreading the word'. Furthermore, top management is responsible for the implementation of the K and B strategies along the principles outlined in this contribution.

- **What are the roles of middle managers in alignment process?** A natural consequence from the ADT approach is that middle managers take on the responsibility for the activity domains. One side of this responsibility is directed towards the interior of the domain. The manager must secure that actors are knowledgeable in producing the outcome. This amounts to implementing the K strategy in the domain. The other side is externally oriented towards the coordination with other domains. As such the manager

is involved in implementing the B strategy of the organization as a whole.

- **What are the impacts of culture (organizational and national) on alignment process?** Here, the indications from the ADT approach is that culture cannot be seen as a detached element that can be managed separately. On the contrary, culture is constituted by meaningful activity:

Socially meaningful doings constitute cultures (social semiotic systems): [...] cultures are systems of interlinking, socially meaningful practices by which we make sense to and of others, not merely in explicit communication, but through all forms of socially meaningful action. (Lemke, 1993).

Consequently, culture expressed as various communal meanings needs to somehow be reconciled if different domains shall be able to coordinate their work. An indication of how to research this issue is given by the transition modality in ADT. Manifestations of this modality signify ways that actors enact in order to coordinate domains harboring different communal meanings.

LIMITATIONS AND FUTURE OPPORTUNITIES

The approach presented in this contribution is an attempt to address a major problem in alignment—how to operationalize an integrated B/K alignment strategy where individual, social and technological aspects are considered. The approach is based on openly declared positions with respect to knowledge and the nature of the organization. These positions may certainly be contested. However, given that they are accepted, our line of argumentation from the very basic concept of meaning to the operationalization of the B/K alignment strategy needs to be further articulated and grounded in both literature and empirical research.

This said and done, we claim that our approach indicates new directions for researching the B/K alignment problem. An integrative, socio-technical perspective of grounding knowledge is necessary. We suggest that meaning provides such a grounding. In addition, the organizational discourse needs to be grounded in some practice perspective where the coordination of different workpractices is emphasized. Such a perspective is provided by the activity domain.

CONCLUSION

We have proposed the activity domain theory as a theoretical framework for informing the alignment of business and knowledge strategies. In this theory, the activity domain is seen as a mediator between these strategies. Thus, the elaboration of business and knowledge strategies as well as their alignment cannot be considered as separate tasks. On the contrary, these tasks are highly interdependent. The suggested approach provides an integrating perspective on individual, organizational and technological aspects of knowledge, based on the concept of meaning. In this respect, the approach is well suited to address the so called third generation of knowledge management in which knowledge construction, tacit and situated knowledge, and a social understanding of technology are emphasized. However, the viability of our approach needs to be validated by future research. At best, the ADT provides a promising approach towards informing the alignment of B and K strategies that may open up hitherto untrodden paths of research.

REFERENCES

Abou-Zeid, E. (2006). Introduction (this volume).

Abou-Zeid, E. (2005). Alignment of Business and Knowledge Management Strategies. In M. Khosrow-Pour (Ed.), *Encyclopedia of Information Science and Technology* (pp. 98-103). Hershey, PA: Idea Publishing Group.

Bedny, G., & Meister, D. (1997). *The Russian Theory of Activity: Current Applications to Design and Learning*. Mahwah, NJ: Lawrence Erlbaum Associates.

Berger, P., & Luckmann, T. (1991). *The Social Construction of Reality*. London: Penguin Books. Original work published in 1966.

Bishoff, L., & Allen, N. (2004). *Business Planning for Cultural Heritage Institutions*. Washington, D.C.: Council on Library and Information Resources.

Blackler, F. (1995). Knowledge, Knowledge Work and Organization: An Overview and Interpretation. *Organization Studies*, 16(6), 1021-1046.

Blumentritt R., & Johnson, R. (1999). Towards a Strategy for Knowledge Management. *Technology Analysis & Strategic Management*, 11(3), 287-300.

Boland, R.J. (1996). Why shared meanings have no place in structuration theory: A reply to Scapens and Macintosh. *Accounting, Organizations and Society*, 21(7/8), 691-697.

Brown, J. S., & Duguid, P. (1991). Organizational Learning and Communities of Practice: Towards a Unified View of Working, Learning, and Innovation. *Organization Science*, 2(1), 40-57.

Bruner, J. (1990). *Acts of Meaning*. Cambridge MA: Harvard University Press.

Burstein, F., & Linger, H. (2003). Supporting post-Fordist work practices. A knowledge management framework for supporting knowledge work. *Information Technology & People*, 16(3), 289-305.

Chan, Y. (2002). Why haven't we mastered alignment? The importance of the Informal Organization Structure. *MIS Quarterly Executive,* 1(21), 76-112.

Chandler, A. (1966). *Strategy and Structure.* Garden City, N.Y.: Doubleday & Company.

Dennis, A., Vessey, I. (2005). Three Knowledge Management Strategies: Knowledge Hierarchies, Knowledge Markets, and Knowledge Communities. *MIS Quarterly Executive*, 4(4), 399-412.

Earl, M. J. (2001). Knowledge Management Strategies: Toward a Taxonomy. *Journal of Management Information Systems*, 18(1), 215-233.

Engeström, Y. (1999). Activity theory and individual and social transformation. In Y. Engeström, R. Miettinen, & R. L. Punamäki (Eds.), *Perspectives on Activity Theory* (pp. 19-38). Cambridge UK: Cambridge University Press.

Fahey, L., & Prusak, L. (1998). The eleven deadliest sins of knowledge management. *California Management Review*, 40 (3), 265-276.

Gherardi, S. (2000). Practice-based Theorizing on Learning and Knowing in Organizations. *Organization*, 7(2), 211–223.

Giddens, A. (1984). *The Constitution of Society.* Cambridge: Polity Press.

Goldkuhl, G., & Röstlinger, A. (2003). The significance of workpractice diagnosis: Socio-pragmatic ontology and epistemology of change analysis. In *The International workshop on Action in Language, Organisations and Information Systems (ALOIS-2003)*. Linköping University. Retrieved October 19, 2006, from http://www.vits.org/?pageId=161

Gorelick, C., & Tantawy-Monsou, B. (2006). For performance through learning, knowledge management is the critical practice. *The Learning Organization*, 12(2), 125-139.

Grant, R. (1996). Toward a Knowledge-Based Theory of the Firm. *Strategic Management Journal,* 17 (Winter Special Issue), 109-122.

Hall, W. (2005). Biological nature of knowledge in the learning organization. *The Learning Organisation*, 12(2), 169-188.

Halliday, M. (1975). *Learning How to Mean.* London: Edward Arnold.

Hansen, M., Nohria, N., & Tierney, T. (1999). What's Your Strategy for Managing Knowledge? *Harvard Business Review*, March-April 1999, 106-116.

Henderson, J., & Venkatraman, N. (1993). Strategic Alignment: Leveraging Information Technology for Transforming Organization. *IBM Systems Journal*, 32(1), 4-16.

Hildreth, P. M., & Kimble, C. (2002). The duality of knowledge. *Information Research*, 8(1). Retrieved October 18, 2006, from http://informationr.net/ir/8-1/paper142.html

Israel, J. (1979). *The language of dialectics and the dialectics of language.* New York: Humanities Press.

Jackendoff, R. (1983). *Semantics and Cognition.* Cambridge, MA: MIT Press.

Knoll, K., & Jarvenpaa, S. L. (1994). Information technology alignment or "fit" in highly turbulent environments: the concept of flexibility. In *Proceedings of the 1994 computer personnel research conference on Reinventing IS* (pp. 1-14). Alexandria, Virginia, United States.

Kolb, D. A. (1984). *Experiential Learning: Experience as the Source of Learning and Development.* Englewood Cliffs, New Jersey: Prentice Hall.

Kosík, K. (1976). *Dialectics of the concrete.* Dordrecht: Reidel.

Larsson, R. (1990). *Coordination of Action in Mergers and Acquisitions - Interpretative and Systems Approaches towards Synergy*. Dissertation No. 10, Lund Studies in Economics and Management, The Institute of Economic Research. Lund: Lund University Press.

Lemke, J. L. (1993). Discourse, Dynamics, and Social Change. *Cultural Dynamics* 6(1), 243-275. In *Language as Cultural Dynamic*, M.A.K. Halliday (Ed.) Leiden: Brill. Retrieved October 18, 2006, from http://academic.brooklyn.cuny.edu/education/jlemke/cult-dyn.htm

Leont'ev, A. N. (1978). *Activity, consciousness, and personality*. Englewood Cliffs, N. J.: Prentice-Hall. Original work published 1975. Retrieved October 18, 2006, from http://lchc.ucsd.edu/MCA/Paper/leontev/

Malone, T., & Crowston, K. (1994). The Interdisciplinary Study of Coordination. *ACM Computing Services,* 26(1), 87-119.

March, J. G., & Simon, H. A. (1958). *Organizations*, 2nd edition. Cambridge, Massachusetts, USA: Blackwell Publishers.

Mathiassen, L. (1996). Information Systems Development: Reflections on a Discipline. *Accounting, Management and Information Technologies,* 6(1/2), 127-132.

Mintzberg, H. (1983). *Structures in Fives: Designing Effective Organizations*. New Jersey: Prentice-Hall.

Nicolini, D., & Meznar, M. (1995). The Social Construction of Organizational Learning: Conceptual and Practical Issues in the Field. *Human Relations*, 48(7), 727-746.

Orlikowski, W. (2002). Knowing in Practice: Enacting a Collective Capability in Distributed Organizing. *Organization Science*, 13(3), 249-273.

Peltonen, T., & Lämsä, T. (2004). 'Communities of Practice' and the Social Process of Knowledge Creation: Towards a New Vocabulary for Making Sense of Organizational Learning. *Problems and Perspectives in Management*, 4/2004, 249-262.

Porter, M. (1996). What Is Strategy? *Harvard Business Review*, November-December 1996, 61-78.

Regev, G., & Wegmann, A. (2004). Remaining Fit: On the Creation and Maintenance of Fit. In *The 5th BPMDS Workshop on Creating and Maintaining the Fit between Business Processes and Support System* (pp. 131-137). Riga, Latvia.

Rose, J., & Scheepers, R. (2001). Structuration theory and information systems development; frameworks for practice. In S. Smithson and S. Avgerinou (Eds.), *The 9th European Conference on Information Systems* (pp. 217-231). Bled, Slovenia, June 27-29, 2001.

Rumbaugh, J., Blaha, M., Premerlani, W., Eddy, F., & Lorensen, W. (1991). *Object-Oriented Modeling and Design*. New Jersey: Prentice-Hall International, Inc.

Schatzki, T. R. (2001). Introduction: Practice theory. In T. R. Schatzki, C. Knorr Cetina, & E. von Savigny (Eds.), *The practice turn in contemporary theory* (pp. 1-14). London: Routledge.

Stetsenko, A. (1999). Social Interaction, Cultural Tools and the Zone of Proximal Development: In Search of a Synthesis. In S. Chaiklin, M. Hedegaard, U. J. Jensen (Eds.), *Activity Theory and Social Practice: Cultural-Historical Approaches* (pp. 235-252). Aarhus: Aarhus University Press.

Susi, T. (2006). *The Puzzle of Social Activity*. Dissertation No. 1019, Department of Computer and Information Science. Linköping: Linköping University.

Taxén, L. (2003). *A Framework for the Coordination of Complex Systems' Development*. Dissertation No. 800. Linköping University, Dep. of Computer & Information Science, 2003. Retrieved October 18, 2006, from http://www.diva-portal.org/liu/theses/abstract.xsql?dbid=5001

Taxén, L. (2004). Articulating Coordination of Human Activity - the Activity Domain Theory. In *Proceedings of the 2nd International workshop on Action in Language, Organisations and Information Systems (ALOIS-2004)*. Linköping University. Retrieved October 18, 2006, from http://www.vits.org/?pageId=37

Taxén, L. (2005a). A Socio-technical Approach Towards Alignment. *Software Process: Improvement and Practice,* 10(4), 427-439.

Taxén, L. (2005b). Categorizing Objective Meaning in Activity Systems. In G. Whymark, & H. Hasan (Eds.), *Activity as the Focus of Information Systems Research*. Eveleigh, Australia: Knowledge Creation Press.

Taxén, L. (2006). An Integration Centric Approach for the Coordination of Distributed Software Development Projects. *Information and Software Technology*, 48(9), 767-780.

Taxén, L., & Svensson, D. (2005). Towards an Alternative Foundation for Managing Product Life-Cycles in Turbulent Environments. *International Journal of Product Development* (IJPD), 2(1/2), 24-46.

Tuomi, I. (1999). Data Is More Than Knowledge: Implications of the Reversed Knowledge Hierarchy for Knowledge Management and Organizational Memory. In *Proceedings of the 32nd Hawaii International Conference on System Sciences* (pp. 1-12), Track 1, January 5-8, 1999.

Tuomi, I. (2002). The Future of Knowledge Management. *Lifelong Learning in Europe* (LLinE), VII(2), 69-79.

Virkkunen, J., & Kuutti, K. (2000). Understanding organizational learning by focusing on "activity systems". *Accounting, Management and Information Technologies*, 10(4), 291-319.

Vološinov, V. N. (1986). *Marxism and the Language of Philosophy*. London: Harvard University Press. Originally published in 1929.

Vygotsky, L. S. (1978). *Mind in Society—The development of higher Psychological Processes*. M. Cole, V. John-Steiner, S. Scribner, & E. Souberman, (Eds.). Cambridge MA: Harvard University Press.

Walsham, G. (2005). Knowledge Management Systems: Representation and Communication in Context. *Systems, Signs & Actions*, 1(1), 6–18. Retrieved October 18, 2006, from http://www.sysiac.org/

Wenger E (1998) *Communities of Practice. Learning, Meaning and Identity*, Cambridge UK: Cambridge University Press.

Wenger, E., McDermott, R., & Snyder, W. M. (2002). *Cultivating Communities of Practice: A Guide to Managing Knowledge*. Boston: Harvard Business School Press.

Zack, M. (1999). Developing a Knowledge Strategy. *California Management Review*, 41(3), 125-145.

Zinchenko, V. (2001). External and Internal: Another Comment on the Issue. In S. Chaiklin (Ed.), *The Theory and Practice of Cultural-Historical Psychology* (pp. 135-147). Aarhus: Aarhus University Press.

Örtenblad, A. (2005). Of course organizations can learn! *The Learning Organization*, 12(2), 213-218.

Additional Reading

Alavi, M., Leidner, D.E. (2001). Knowledge Management and Knowledge Management Systems: Conceptual Foundations and Research Issues, *MIS Quarterly.* 25(1), 107-136.

Augier, M., Shariq, S., Vendelo, M.T. (2001). Understanding context: its emergence, transformation and role in tacit knowledge sharing, *Journal of Knowledge Management*, 5(2), 125-136.

Bernstein, R.J. (1971). *Praxis and Action*, Philadelphia: University of Pennsylvania Press.

Bickhard, M.H., Terveen, L. (1995). *Foundational Issues in Artificial Intelligence and Cognitive Science: Impasse and Solution.* Elsevier Scientific, Amsterdam.

Bitici, U.S., Muir, D. (1997) Business process definition: a bottom-up approach, *International Journal of Operations & Production Management,* 17(4), 365-374.

Bowker, G.C., Star, S.L. (1999). *Sorting things out: classification and its consequences,* Cambridge, MA: MIT Press.

Brown, J.S.B., Dugiud, P. (2000). *The social life of information*, Mass. : Harvard Business School.

Burell, G., Morgan, M. (1979). Social Paradigms and Organization Analysis, Portsmouth, New Hampshire: Heinemann.

Cluts, M. (2003). The Evolution of Artifacts in Cooperative Work: Constructing Meaning Through Activity, *GROUP'03*, Nov 9-12, Sanibel Islands, Florida, USA, 144-152.

Duranti, A., Goodwin, C. (Eds., 1992). *Rethinking context: language as an interactive phenomenon*, Cambridge: Cambridge University Press

Earl, M. (Ed, 1996). *Information Management - The organizational dimension*, New York: Oxford University Press.

Gray, P., Meister, D. (2003). Introduction: fragmentation and integration in knowledge management research, *Information Technology & People*, 16(3), 259-265.

Heidegger, M. (1962). *Being and Time*, New York: Harper & Row. Originally published in 1926.

Hodge, R., G. Kress (1988). *Social Semiotics*, Ithaca, New York: Cornell University Press.

Jensen PE (2005). A Contextual Theory of Learning and the Learning Organization, *Knowledge and Process Management.* 12(1), 53–64.

Marjanovic, O. (2005). Towards IS supported coordination in emergent business processes, *Business Process Management Journal,* 11(5), 476-487.

Orlikowski, W. (2000). Using Technology and Constituting Structures: A Practice Lens for Studying Technology in Organizations, *Organization Science,* 11(4), July-Aug 2000, 404-428.

Morgan, G. (Ed., 1983). *Beyond method : strategies for social research,* In G. Morgan (Ed.), Beverly Hills, CA: Sage Publications.

Nardi, B. (1996). *Context and Consciousness: Activity Theory and Human-Computer Interaction.* In B. A. Nardi (Ed.), Cambridge, MA: MIT Press.

Schon, D. (1983). *The Reflective Practitioner. How Professionals Think in Action,* New York: Basic Books.

Searle, J. R. (1995). *The construction of social reality,* New York: The Free Press.

Searle, J. (1999). *Mind, Language and Society. Philosophy in the Real World,* Guernsey: Guernsey Press.

Shariq, S. (1999). How does knowledge transform as it is transferred? Speculations on the possibility of a cognitive theory of knowledgescapes, *Journal of Knowledge Management*, 3(4), 243-251.

Smircich, L. (1983). Concepts of Culture and Organizational Analysis, *Administrative Science Quarterly,* 28, 339-358.

Thayer, H.S. (1982). *Pragmatism- The classic writings*. In H.S. Thayer (Ed.), Indianapolis: Hackett Pub. Co.

uit Beijerse, R.P. (1999). Questions in management: defining and conceptualising a phenomenon, *Journal of Knowledge Management*, 3(2), 94-109.

Wertsch, J.V. (1998). *Mind as Action*, New York Oxford: Oxford University Press

Vygotsky, L.S. (1997). *The collected works of L.S. Vygotsky: Vol. 4. The history of the development of higher mental functions* (R.W. Reiber, Ed.; M.J. Hall, Trans). New York: Plenum Press. (Original work written 1931)

Vygotsky, L. S. (1986). *Thought and Language*. A. Kozulin (Ed.), Cambridge, MA: MIT Press. (Original work published in 1934)

Weick, K. (1993, December). The Collapse of sensemaking in organizations: The Mann Gulch disaster. *Administrative Science Quarterly, 38*(4), 628-645.

Weick, K. (1995). *Sensemaking in Organizations*, Thousand Oaks, CA: Sage Publications.

Weick, K., Sutcliffe, K.,M. (2005, July-August). Organizing and the process of sensemaking, *Organization Science, 16*(4), 409-421.

Yanow D. (2000, May). Seeing organizational learning: A 'cultural' View, *Organization*, 7(2), 269-276.

ENDNOTES

[1] In the literature 'knowledge strategy' is more or less used synonymously with 'knowledge management strategy'. In this contribution, we refer to 'knowledge strategy' as a strategy that is strongly linked to the business strategy in order to emphasize knowledge as a strategic resource (Zack, 1999). By 'knowledge management strategy' we indicate strategies for managing knowledge without a direct coupling to the business strategy.

[2] Malone & Crowston use the word 'activities'. We have replaced this with 'actions' to avoid confusion with our use of 'activity'.

[3] We have excluded the commercial and spatial schools since these are less relevant for our comparison.

Section IV
Selected Readings

Selected Reading I
Developing and Analysing Core Competencies for Alignment with Strategy

Keith Sawyer
Alpha Omega International, UK

John Gammack
Griffith University, Australia

ABSTRACT

Although it is widely accepted that alignment of knowledge with corporate strategy is necessary, to date there have been few clear statements on what a knowledge strategy looks like and how it may be practically implemented. We argue that current methods and techniques to accomplish this alignment are severely limited, showing no clear description on how the alignment can be achieved. Core competencies, embodying an organisation's practical know-how, are also rarely linked explicitly to actionable knowledge strategy. Viewing knowledge embedded in core competencies as a strategic asset, the paper uses a case study to show how a company's core competencies were articulated and verified for either inclusion or exclusion in the strategy. The study is representative of similar studies carried out across a range of organisations using a novel and practically proven method. This method, StratAchieve, was used here in a client situation to show how the core competencies were identified and tested for incorporation or not in the strategy. The paper concludes by considering the value of the approach for managing knowledge.

INTRODUCTION

Many companies have developed or adopted various knowledge management (KM) initiatives to try to surface and differentiate what they do know from what they need to know and also to identify the location of their knowledge gaps. Processes and tools that support efforts to capture knowledge are well known and widely used, such as expertise directories, intranets, communities of practice, knowledge audits, discussion forums, knowledge maps, building and documenting knowledge based and expert systems, storytelling, benchmarking, and the like. These efforts serve the strategy functions of organisations, aligning capability and know-how with strategic objectives.

Although the importance of strategic alignment is recognised, what is less understood is the practical means to determine what knowledge is strategically important and how this knowledge can be incorporated into the corporate strategy. Zack (1999) for example suggests that companies may have unique ways of doing this, (itself a competitive advantage) using techniques such as SWOT analysis. Zack's work, while providing a framework and some high-level questions, is light on actionable detail, and is silent on how the output of such efforts can be strategically assessed with sufficient reach to be implemented. The available literature on knowledge strategy alignment is generally very limited: although many documents refer to these issues, few go beyond noting the desirability of alignment, and even fewer provide any detailed methodological guidance. Few empirical studies appear to exist, and whilst academic comparison across unique cases is not always appropriate, the study reported in this paper describes a generic method that has also been used in several other organisations. The approach described here addresses *what* organisations know, and how it aligns with their wider strategy.

All organisations need to "know what they know" (and know what they don't know) to make strategic decisions on (for example) sourcing, customer satisfaction, recruitment and training, investment, and in identifying areas for process re-engineering, market development, or innovation. The familiar saying, "If only we knew what we know" is, however, flawed because it presumes that what exists as knowledge in organisations is always useful and needs to be formalised and actioned. More appropriate is to say "If only we knew what we need to know". This means that organisations must also know what they no longer need to know because it no longer has a sufficient impact on the corporate objectives. Similarly, organisations must know what knowledge is most important and determine whether they already have this knowledge or need to acquire it. Apart from the rather limited SWOT analysis, or proprietary methods (e.g., AMERIN, n.d.) that may or may not include tools that help identify knowledge gaps, there are few clear statements on how, in practice, strategy may be structured in actionable alignment with organisational knowledge.

Organisations must structure their strategy so that strategic decisions and actions can be made on a variety of fronts, such as retaining and growing profitable customers, selling the right products to the right market, and recruiting and developing staff. To achieve this, organisations must manage their knowledge effectively to ensure it is directly translatable into strategic actions. Without knowing how to effectively manage their own stock of intellectual capital, such decisions cannot be actioned nor can the company be properly valued[1].

When turnover or loss of key staff is potentially a consequential threat, failure to manage the implicit knowledge assets underpinning this value may be seen as negligent. Intellectual capital is the main source of value creation (Edvinsson & Malone, 1997) and thus strategically linked directly to the organisation's future. In larger organisations especially, formalisation of this activity is required, not only for internal purposes, but also externally, such as shareholder value creation and outperformance of competitors. Identifying, securing and managing the various forms of intellectual capital (human and structural) within an organisation has thus become a central theme for knowledge management research as well as for knowledge valuing and reporting.

KM initiatives typically centre on the personnel who embody and can apply their knowledge in project or other business activity settings, and often entail recording or abstracting from the traces of their contextualised activities. Such KM initiatives implicitly recognise the centrality of the competencies of individuals and groups in transacting the strategic aims of the organisation at operational levels, and in potentially identifying the specific knowledge and abilities that give comparative advantages. Rarely, however, are such initiatives directly linked to corporate strategy and are (often inappropriately) typically designed and implemented through the organisation's IT support function (Berkman, 2001). A focus on the competencies related to strategic objectives and alignment with operational competencies is vital and is addressed in the following case study.

If organisations are centrally reliant on their knowledge for their survival, value and prosperity, their knowledge management strategies must be fully congruent with wider corporate strategy. Hackney, Burn, and Dhillon (2000) note, however, that comments on implementing such congruence have been few, and there remains a "prevalent disconnect between (business) and IT strategies". Their analysis of contemporary business strategy implies a reappraisal of the conventional and rational assumptions implicit in strategic IS planning (SISP) and where installing an IT "solution" is insufficient without coherent linkage to business strategy.

Hackney, Burn, and Dhillon (2000) cite research suggesting a necessary relationship between innovation and organisational *competence* and see assessing organisational competencies as a critically relevant challenge for SISP. The terms *competences* and *competencies* are both used

in the literature to refer to such organisational abilities: we prefer to use *competencies* in this paper. The knowledge embedded in organisational competencies can be a key strategic asset, and conversely, strategy emerging from inherent capabilities and competencies provides flexibility and responsiveness. Identifying such competencies is prerequisite to their assessment, valuation, and incorporation into strategy. These competencies, which are typically knowledge based, can form the essence of a knowledge strategy embedded within a wider corporate strategy that is not simply cast in terms of KM technologies over some planning period.

A company's core competencies (Prahalad & Hamel, 1990) are the areas in which it has competitive strength and thus form a platform for its strategic thrusts. Not knowing or appreciating these means its strategies may fail and compromise proper valuation of a company's knowledge assets underlying the support, adaptation, and maintenance of its activities. Core competencies are the "cognitive characteristics of an organisation, its know-how..." (Hatten & Rosenthal, 2001, p. 50), that is, an organisation's collective (functional) expertise. Built on the skills and experience of individuals and teams, they are housed in characteristic business functions: examples Hatten and Rosenthal (2001) cite include McDonald's HR competency in recruiting, hiring, training, and retaining part time labour and Intel's technology competency in state of the art design of microprocessor chip families. Although such functions are not necessarily unique to an organisation, the know-how and processes involved in them may well be, thus conferring advantage.

Core competencies are necessarily part of a knowledge strategy which itself is part of the overall strategy. A focus on competencies (which implies active and generative abilities) rather than the knowledge traces itself is preferable, since in times of change, accumulated knowledge may be a hindrance to new thinking: what Leonard-Barton (1995) has called "core rigidities". To give a sustainable strategic advantage, competencies should be valuable, rare, hard to imitate or substitute, and ideally will confer a dominating ability in their area. Bollinger and Smith (2001) view the knowledge resource as a strategic asset, with the "collective organisational knowledge, (rather than that) of mobile individuals", that is the essential asset. This suggests a focal shift towards organisationally understood activity and process, not merely data and record storage requiring leverage by particular individuals for effectiveness.

In the knowledge based view, nicely contrasted with the conventional rational view of strategy by Carlisle (1999) the strategic focus is on value *creation* arising from uniquely effective internal capabilities and competencies, rather than value *appropriation*, which emphasises "optimisation" activity in imperfect markets. Although over time advantages may be eroded, organisations with developed "capabilities for managing knowledge creation and exploiting (its value) are better able to adapt by developing new sustainable core competencies for the future" (Carlisle, 1999, p. 24). Dawson (2000, p. 323) also notes "It is far more useful to think (about developing) dynamic knowledge capabilities than about knowledge as a static asset …to be managed".

The theoretical literature on core competencies does not however generally relate their development to concepts of knowledge management operation, nor to strategy implementation. Nor, although recognising that some competencies are more important than others, does it distinguish strategic from operational core competencies. Although the literature does not imply that strategic competencies arise from operational ones, we find it useful in practice to differentiate these since the only way strategy can be realised is at the operational level, by competent people performing activities that achieve strategic goals. For this to occur, an explicit linkage between strategic goals and operational activity, between strategic core competencies and their implementation (and

reciprocally between operational competencies and strategic objectives) must be articulated. This theoretical claim is demonstrated in the present case study.

Since contemporary thinking on strategy emphasises ability to respond to environmental changes quickly at all levels rather than planning in a controlled environment, an embedded knowledge strategy will act as the medium through which these levels can be brought into alignment and allow for emergent strategy to be developed across the organisation.

Klein (1998) asks the question "But how does a firm decide what set of operating-level initiatives would best meet its strategic goals?" and goes on to identify the "challenge of linking strategy with execution at the knowledge level" (p. 3) by a focus on various activities around intellectual capital. As an open research question however, specific implementation guidance is not offered, and associated literature (e.g., Graham & Pizzo, 1996) often notes only generic steps (identify strategic business drivers, determine business critical knowledge characteristics and locations, construct knowledge value chains, and find competency gaps).

Apart from private ownership tools, which may lack academic evaluation or an underlying original research base, there are few existing public domain management tools that offer help in modelling the different aspects a comprehensive knowledge-centric strategy development entails. These candidates include the "enterprise model" (Hatten & Rosenthal, 1999), later renamed the "action alignment (AA) model" and extended in Hatten and Rosenthal (2001); and more recently strategy maps (Kaplan & Norton, 2004). These generally provide broad areas for consideration, but give little or no guidance on strategy development or implementation beyond a flimsy structural outline. For knowledge strategy evaluation in financial terms, the KM valuation methodology of Clare and Detore (2000) applies, but this starts from a developed business strategy or KM project proposal.

The AA (action alignment) model is essentially a grid showing classical business functions (e.g., HRM, IT, and so on) crossed with business processes (e.g., order fulfilment) allowing visualisation of core junctures or problem (misaligned) areas, with supplementary tools to assess the fit or otherwise between customers and organisational capabilities and competencies. This appears to be essentially reactionary to the need for cross-functional alignment occasioned by new economy realities, but problematises the issue within an assumed industrial-era organisational structure of functionally defined silos, and without highlighting the knowledge activities required. The AA model has various other serious limitations in a knowledge-based view, in which traditional "Balkanised" organisational structures are considered obsolescent, and not conducive to the strategic planning and development of intangible assets and associated capabilities (Chatzkel, 2000).

The Balanced Scorecard (Kaplan & Norton, 1996) is a widely used performance measurement tool and has evolved since its origination in the early 1990s to more explicitly focus on strategy. Originally it aimed to address aspects of a company's performance not covered in simpler measures oriented primarily to financial performance. A customer perspective, an internal business perspective, an innovation and learning perspective, and a financial perspective provide a set of measures indicating aspects of performance relevant to various stakeholders. The strategy maps and supporting theory outlined in Kaplan and Norton (2004) are however very sketchy and conventional in relation to the knowledge based view — competency is effectively equated with job description (p. 225 et seq), and the references to the concepts of knowledge and KM are very shallowly treated. Furthermore, although the strategy maps show some linkages, the map's theoretical formulation is silent about the detailed linkages between these giving no guidance as to how the knowledge embodied in them can be identified, related to strategic competencies and

leveraged with respect to achieving financially quantifiable targets such as market share, net profit or shareholder value, or other non-financial performance measures. Tools such as Kaplan and Norton's strategy map thus do not explicitly address knowledge-centric strategy development and indeed a series of google searches in mid 2004 yielded few hits relevant to this aspect.

Yet an organisation's ability (or otherwise) to knowledgeably enact and leverage corporate processes and technologies is the essence of strategic competency. In a view of strategy that is not purely top down, but is essentially enacted dynamically by the knowledgeable activity of people in the "middle", it is crucial to reify these competencies in relation to strategy formulation. Current tools do not go far enough in guiding this, nor do they provide explicit methods for systematic engagement at this level.

THE CASE STUDY

Overview

We offer an approach addressing this by using a case study embodying action research techniques, beginning with a brief description of the organisation, its strategic position and the context of the fieldwork. A case study approach has been chosen since contemporary phenomena are being investigated in their real life context, with multiple variables of interest and converging sources of data; where the boundaries between the phenomena and the context are unclear and where the researcher has little control over behavioural events (Yin, 2002). The case study approach allows depth of understanding across many variables to occur. In this research an interpretivist position is adopted in which the organisation's own meanings and their negotiation are prioritised.

The case study reported here is of a UK accountancy company, and entailed the elicitation and reification of its hitherto poorly understood core competencies. The knowledge strategy was developed within a comprehensive corporate strategy overhaul and was built around the knowledge audit of its core competencies embodied in people and processes, supported by relevant technology.

The paper proceeds as follows. Having identified the need to provide detailed guidance on reifying an organisation's core competencies and to relate those effectively to knowledge strategy, we outline processes that address this weakness and show how they can be implemented within more generic strategic planning processes.

We illustrate these in the case study context to show how the organisation systematically identified its core competencies, as well as determining the core competencies that are no longer of strategic importance. In the process, learning that the company not only did not have the strategic competencies it thought it had, but that it had knowledge assets which it had not realised, provided the capability to explicitly incorporate the competencies into the strategy.

The result was an articulation of what the company "knew" as well as what it did not know but needed to know, both strategically and operationally. This enabled the company to consciously leverage its strengths but also identify areas in which it was deficient and therefore strategically vulnerable. The case study concludes by showing how the company had achieved a strong competitive position from which to strategically value its knowledge and other intangible assets in an informed manner for forward planning and reporting to shareholders and others. The detailing of this valuation is part of our ongoing research.

The Organisation

The UK accountancy company featured in this case study is involved in a broad range of financial services to a wide variety of customers, both large and small. For purposes of this paper, the company shall be called Target Accountancy. The company has 56 employees and has been existence since 1987. Staff turnover is low as a result of high loyalty and good conditions of employment.

Target Accountancy had never produced a formal strategy plan but realised it could not achieve the success it wanted without one. The saying "if you don't plan your company's future, it won't have one" was very pertinent in their case. The company possessed a rich abundance of talent but this was tacitly held in the minds of individuals; it wanted to be the formal owner of its capital knowledge. One of the aims of Target Accountancy was to verify whether the competencies it thought it possessed were being successfully engineered to generate the required competitive differentiators. There was thus a strong need to strategically specify and test the impact of its core competencies, to determine which were the most productive and identify gaps where new competencies were required.

The StratAchieve Method

One of us (Sawyer) was the external facilitator. The StratAchieve method[2] was chosen because of its proven capability in over 400 organisations to create and achieve strategies. Other tools currently on the market are geared either for helping to produce a strategy plan or to conduct project management, but not both. StratAchieve produces and combines the two, enabling iteration between the plan and implementation to take place.

The method is supported by software produced by Alpha Omega, which is used throughout the change programme. During a workshop session, a map is projected onto a screen and interactively developed through discussions, suggestions and learning from workshop delegates. An important aspect of the approach is its ability to integrate the various types of organisational strategies, such as customers, financial, HR, marketing, product, IS, and (crucially) knowledge, into a single, coherent corporate strategy.

The method enables organisations to determine, construct, legitimise, and achieve their strategy and conduct monitoring and controlling during implementation and provides the structure for all organisational strategic actions to be integrated. Thus, marketing, HR, finance, IT, and knowledge strategies are all holistically integrated into one coherent and comprehensive strategy. This will become apparent in the examples that follow.

The Strategy Tree provides the theoretical framework of the method (Sawyer, 1990) consisting of four or five layers of verb-fronted activities, logically related through *Why* and *How* connections. These Why and How relations provide a path that simultaneously justifies a given action at a higher level, whilst specifying an operational activity that achieves higher level aims. In discussions any given statement can be explored in either direction. For example rationale for the expressed operational competency *"Keep in regular contact with all clients"* was explored. The next higher-level activity was determined by asking, "why should we *Keep in regular contact with all clients"*? which elicited the response, because we want to *"Maintain excellent personal relationships with our clients"*. A further Why interrogation on this activity produced the parent, *"Retain our current clients"* and a further Why activity resulted in the parent *"Increase our revenues"*. A final Why activity generated the high-level statement *"Increase our gross margin"* linked directly to strategic mission. In this example, a set of Why interrogations produced the higher-level activities which linked to the pre-set vision (increase our gross margin). Conversely, How statements can be elicited by starting with a high-level aim, and identifying child activities that follow from it, as reversing the previous example shows. Turning a competence into verb-fronted form emphasises a capability focus for knowledge, and leads eventually to activity based costing and specific required operational actions. The software tracking the map thus developed shows what must be done,

when, how, why and by whom through specific supporting functions, and aids dynamic strategy construction.

Workshop Preparation

The process was initiated through a one-day workshop, attended by all senior members of Target Accountancy together with a range of staff from a variety of departments.

The Knowledge Positioning Matrix (KPM)

The KPM was developed to accommodate the core competency dimensions, as shown in Figure 1. The four quadrants provide a means for noting the knowledge that is strategically needed, and is already known; the knowledge that is required, but is not known; knowledge that is known, but not strategically required; and gaps in knowledge that do not bear on strategy anyway. Target Accountancy wanted to know whether its current set of core competencies were sufficiently robust to maximise their competitive performance. The company thus wanted to know what it *needed* to know (i.e., if only we knew what we needed to know) as opposed

Figure 1. The Knowledge Positioning Matrix showing examples from the workshop

	Do Know	Don't Know
Need to Know	Contact all our profitable customers monthly	Provide online accountancy services Provide hospitality packages
Don't Need	Provide doctoring services to ailing	✕

to the familiar saying "if only we knew what we know", to identify gaps in required knowledge, and to identify areas of knowledge that were no longer required. In other words, the company wanted to know which core competencies should be modified, deleted and created.

The StratAchieve Structure

The method naturally provides the structure and operations for the Knowledge Positioning Matrix. Figure 2 shows a four-level map. The *vision* is the prime focus of the organisation's strategy. Each successive level below the vision provides increased detail about the vision—what it is, what it means and how it can be achieved. The mechanism that does this is through top-down *How* and bottom-up *Why* explorations and checking.

The top-most activity of the tree represents the vision in the case of a company-wide strategy or the key objective of a department, division, or sub-strategy such as a marketing or a finance strategy. The levels below the top-most activity increase in specificity so that the day-to-day

actions can be specified and actioned. There is thus full alignment between the vision and the day-to-day operations.

The second level of the StratAchieve Map is occupied by the critical success factors (CSFs). CSFs are the vital factors that must be successfully actioned if the vision is to be fully achieved. The third level has the core competencies which in turn must successfully produce the CSFs. Traditionally, the number of organisational core competencies is suggested as five or six (Robson, 1994) at the maximum.

The top-down *How* and bottom-up *Why* structuring also provides the all-important alignment from the vision to the operational competencies on the lowest level of the StratAchieve Map. Only through this logical connectivity can alignment be achieved. This also provides a clear understanding to the fourth-level operational competencies. This also provides a clear understanding of what operational competencies must be actioned to achieve the core competencies, the CSFs and the vision. The process then provides for detailed operational specification of the requirement.

Figure 2. A four level StratAchieve map showing all four company csfs and two of the core competencies

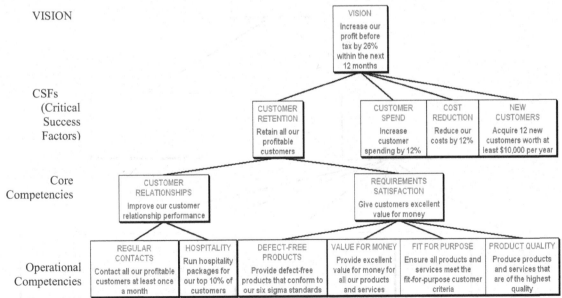

Knowing What We Need to Know

As mentioned, organisations need to "know what they need to know" (and know what they don't know) to make strategic decisions on various fronts. The first task in actioning the Knowledge Positioning Matrix is thus to establish "what needs to be known". From this capture, what is known and not known can then be determined.

To establish "what needs to be known", a set of core competencies was logically produced from the CSFs (top-down Hows) and verified through the operational competencies (bottom-up Whys). A fourth level of operational competencies were initially produced through logical How unpackings from the core competencies. Figure 2 shows two of the core competencies identified at the workshop, namely customer relationships and requirements satisfaction.

Although it would have been competitively desirable for Target Accountancy to action every operational competency, in practice this was not feasible through resource and time constraints.

In the course of establishing "what we need to know", it was found that two of the competencies were not distinct but instead were linked in a parent-child relationship. Figure 3 shows that two core competencies, namely Value for Money and Product Quality, share two child operational competencies. The more children that share the same two parents indicate the amount of overlapping of the parent activities. As a consequence of producing the StratAchieve Map, it was found that Product Quality should be a sub-set of Value for Money. Figure 4 shows how this competency structure was re-configured to account for the family resemblance.

Figure 3. Product quality shares child competencies fully with value for money which means product quality is a sub-competency

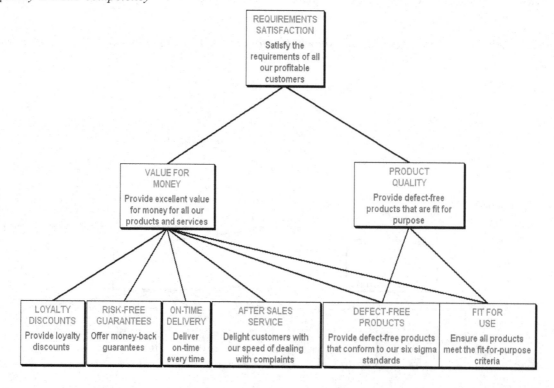

Figure 4. The revised structure showing product quality is a sub-set of value for money

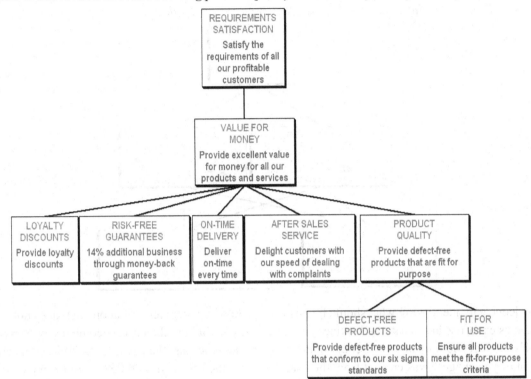

Figure 5 shows two core competencies, Customer Satisfaction and Product Quality. Each has a set of identical sub-activities. This duplication of sub-activities indicates that the two seemingly different core competencies are actually the same because they share exactly the same competency children. The degree of similarity between competencies is thus verifiable through the amount of shared sub-activities. Where there are no shared sub-activities, the core competencies are distinctly separate. The workshop delegates wanted to Product Quality to be featured on the StratAchieve Map and therefore showed it as a sub-activity. Alternatively, they could have eliminated the activity, and shown its two sub-activities under Customer Satisfaction.

Need to Know and Do Know

Once the set of core competencies were identified (need to know), the next stage was to identify which core competencies were known (available

expertise) and those that were unknown (unavailable expertise). Figure 2 shows how the CSF, *Customer Retention* was unpacked, first into the respective core competencies, and then into operational competencies.

At the workshop, delegates were asked to produce a knowledge map showing their key actions. A comparison was then made between the logically derived core competencies using StratAchieve and those competencies actually held by the individuals. Several competencies were matched while others were unmatched. Examples are shown in Figure 1.

Need to Know and Don't Know

The StratAchieve Why and How creations and connections produced the activity "use the Internet to increase sales". It was agreed that this activity was important enough to be regarded as a potential core competency, where new skills would be needed. The exercise thus identified a

Figure 5. Product Quality and Customer Satisfaction are semantic duplications

knowledge gap, identifying what should be possessed as expertise and what was lacking.

The logical operational competency "operate hospitality packages" was created from the core competency "improve our customer relationship performance". The workshop delegates agreed that this activity (operate hospitality packages) was an important competency that needed to be included in the strategy as part of the core competency "improve our customer relationship performance".

A further action the company took after the workshop was to determine which competencies they lacked and needed to purchase through recruitment and consultancy. The core competencies were also prioritised, based on agreed criteria such as contribution impact on the CSFs, resource demands (cost implications) and risk quantification. Through this process, it was possible to weight the core competencies and produce a ranked order of importance. Although supported within the method, this is not detailed further here.

Don't Need to Know and Know

The knowledge positioning matrix shows "provide doctoring services to ailing companies" as a known competency, but one that does not have any impact on the current company-wide CSFs. Thus is because there is no logical Why connection into the newly formed CSFs. For example, there is no *Why* connect to Customer Retention since once the customer's company has been restored it will cease to be a customer. With no logical connection for this in the developed map, it was thus excluded.

Don't Need to Know and Don't Know

It follows that not knowing what we do not need to know is a null set and therefore is left blank in the Knowledge Positioning Matrix.

CONCLUSION

This paper described the importance of core competencies and demonstrated the utility of the StratAchieve method for testing the validity of knowledge-laden core competencies for strategic goals. It has shown how to test core competencies for logical compatibility with the strategy plan as well as to identify core competencies that are essential for strategic success. The software support links these logically, and through separate functionality relates them to timescales, costing, human resources, and progress indicators for subsequent monitoring. In doing this, we needed to unpack the meaning of the word "know". For example, in the phrase *do we know what we need to know,* two uses of the term can be discerned, namely know-what and know-how respectively. Both relate to awareness, not necessarily the skills available.

The case study has demonstrated the formulation of a corporate strategy from a consideration of the core operational activities and associated knowledge competencies forming the organisation's intellectual capital resource. Meanings of the operational and other activities that produce the emergence of achieved strategic objectives have been systematically elicited, negotiated, and agreed within a multi-stakeholder framework, which explicitly links the strategic requirement to the necessary activities and identifies the knowledge requirements for each strategic objective.

Although simplified and indicative examples only have been shown here, linked and cohesive *Strategy Trees* for major business functions have been produced in a form that translates directly into actionable specifications, with a motivated logic chain of abstraction upwards towards, or implementation downwards from, strategic activities and competencies. Core strategic competencies, such as "contact all our profitable customers monthly" have been illustrated to show the alignment of activities, and how a competency at one level can provide an advantage at another. Equally less advantageous competencies, without strategic import, are highlighted by the method. An emphasis on the terminology and meanings understood within the company, and its reporting norms, helps strategy ownership and implementation. A sort of "mediated objectivity" applies, which explicitly links the strategic requirement to the necessary activities and identifies the knowledge requirements for each one.

By expressing the required activities in the structure the focus is shifted towards dynamic strategy achievement through knowledge capability, rather than merely managing the organisational resources and by-products of business activity. Evaluation of the strategy is provided for within the method, though beyond the scope of this paper to describe. Monitoring, activity based costing, resource allocation, and progress and performance indicators are all linked explicitly to the strategy model developed. During the case study, each core competency was analysed to determine its value and hence impact contribution on the company's goals and vision. This core competency valuation and ranking method has been the subject of ongoing research.

The case study reported in this paper is one of several conducted over a 15-year period with organisations large and small, public and private and whilst the case is unique, the methods involved are considered generic and stable. Individual studies such as this one lie within a "declared intellectual framework of systemic ideas, ultimately allowing general lessons to be extracted and discussed" as recommended by Checkland (1991, p. 401).

Although a case study does not aim at generalisation rich, contextual understanding and utility value are indicated. Apart from the direct pragmatic value to the organisation, the "story told" in reporting the notion of mediated objectivity may help convey insights that transfer to the understanding of similar situations. Results from action research studies can provide rich and useful descriptions, enhancing learning and understanding which may itself be abstractly transferable to other organisations, or provide an underpinning to future inductive theory development. This potentially allows further contextualisation of the work in the more nomothetic terms implicit in multiple case study research designs.

This case study has shown the development of strategy: further action research with the company will evaluate its impact and value. In general through work with this, and with other organisations we aim to develop a competency valuation method so that the value of operational competencies in relation to strategy may be assessed.

ACKNOWLEDGMENT

We thank the participants at Target Accountancy, three anonymous reviewers and the associate editors for constructive comments on earlier versions

REFERENCES

AMERIN Products. (n.d). *Creating value from intangible assets and human capital*. Retrieved July 12, 2005, from http://www.amerin.com.au/products.htm

Berkman, E. (2001). *When bad things happen to good ideas*. Retrieved July 20, 2004, from http://www.darwinmag.com/read/040101/badthingscontent.html

Bollinger, A. S. & Smith, R. D. (2001). Managing knowledge as a strategic asset. *Journal of Knowledge Management, 5*(1), 8-18.

Carlisle, Y. (1999). Strategic thinking and knowledge management. In *OU MBA Managing Knowledge Readings Part 1* (pp. 19-29). Milton Keynes: Open University Business School.

Chatzkel, J. (2000). A conversation with Hubert Saint-Onge. *Journal of Intellectual Capital, 1*(1), 101-115.

Checkland, P. B. (1991). From framework through experience to learning: the essential nature of action research. In H. E. Nissen, H. K. Klein, & R. Hirschheim (Eds.), *Information systems research: Contemporary approaches and emergent traditions*. Amsterdam: International Federation for Information Processing (IFIP).

Clare, M. & DeTore, A. W. (2000). *Knowledge assets*. San Diego: Harcourt.

Dawson, R. (2000). Knowledge capabilities as the focus of organisational development. *Journal of Knowledge Management, 4*(4), 320-327.

Edvinsson, L. & Malone, M. S. (1997). *Intellectual capital*. New York: Harper Collins.

Graham, A. B. & Pizzo V. G. (1996). A question of balance: Case studies in strategic knowledge management. *European Management Journal, 14*(4), 338-346. Reprinted in Klein DA (q.v.).

Hackney, R., Burn, J., & Dhillon, G. (2000). Challenging assumptions for strategic information systems planning. Theoretical perspectives. *Communications of the AIS, 3*(9).

Hatten, K. J. & Rosenthal, S. R. (1999). Managing the process centred enterprise. *Long Range Planning, 32*(3), 293-310.

Hatten, K. J. & Rosenthal, S. R. (2001). *Reaching for the knowledge edge*. New York: AMACOM.

Kaplan, R. S. & Norton, D. P. (1996). *The balanced scorecard*. Boston: Harvard Business School Press.

Kaplan, R. S. & Norton, D. P. (2004). *Strategy maps*. Boston: Harvard Business School Press.

Klein, D. A. (Ed.). (1998). *The strategic management of intellectual capital*. Boston: Butterworth-Heinemann.

Leonard-Barton, D. (1995). *Wellsprings of knowledge*. Boston: Harvard Business School Press.

Prahalad, C. K. & Hamel, G. (1990). The core competence of the corporation. *Harvard Business Review, 68*(3), 79-91.

Robson, R. (1994). *Strategic management and information systems*. London: Pitman.

Sawyer, K. (1990). *Dealing with complex organisational problems.* PhD Consortium, International Conference on Information Systems (ICIS), Copenhagen.

Sawyer, K. (1990). Goals, purposes and the strategy tree. *Systemist, 12*(4), 76-82.

Yin, R. K. (2002). *Case study research: Design and methods* (3rd ed.). Newbury Park: Sage.

Zack, M. H. (1999). Developing a knowledge strategy. *Californian Management Review, 41*(3), 125-145.

ENDNOTES

[1] The valuation of intellectual capital is significant: the most authoritative estimates typically suggest that around 75% of a company's value lies in its intangible assets (Handy [cited in Edvinsson & Malone, 1997; Kaplan & Norton, 2004, p. 4]).

[2] StratAchieve™ is a registered mark of Keith Sawyer.

This work was previously published in International Journal of Knowledge Management, Vol. 2, Issue 1, edited by M. E. Jennex, pp. 58-71, copyright 2006 by IGI Publishing, formerly known as Idea Group Publishing (an imprint of IGI Global).

Selected Reading II
Enhancing Performance Through Knowledge Management:
Holistic Framework

Anne P. Massey
Indiana University, USA

V. Ramesh
Indiana University, USA

Mitzi M. Montoya-Weiss
North Carolina State University, USA

ABSTRACT

Knowledge management (KM) has gained increasing attention since the mid-1990s. A KM strategy involves consciously helping people share and put knowledge into action. However, before an organization can realize the promise of KM, a fundamental question needs to be asked: What performance goal(s) is the organization trying to achieve? In this paper, we develop and offer a framework that provides a holistic view of the performance environment surrounding organizational knowledge work. We illustrate the KM framework using two organizational case studies. Then, based on the KM framework and further insights drawn from our case studies, we offer a series of steps that may guide and assist organizations and practitioners as they undertake KM initiatives. We further demonstrate the applicability of these steps by examining KM initiatives within a global software development company. We conclude with a discussion of implications for organizational practice and directions for future research.

INTRODUCTION

Knowledge management (KM) is a topic that has gained increasing attention since the mid-1990s. Knowledge about customers, products, processes, past successes, and failures are assets that may produce long-term sustainable competitive advantage for organizations (Huber, 2001; Leonard & Sensiper, 1998; Stewart, 2001). KM proponents argue that these assets are as important as managing other organizational assets like labor and capital. A survey conducted by *Knowledge Management* magazine and the International Data Corporation suggests that KM is evolving from a discrete undertaking to a strategic component of business solutions (Dyer & McDonough, 2001).

A KM strategy entails consciously helping people share and put knowledge into action by creating access, context, and infrastructure, and by simultaneously shortening learning cycles (Alavi & Leidner, 2001; Davenport, DeLong & Beers, 1998; Davenport & Prusak, 1998; O'Dell & Grayson, 1998). It takes place within a complex system of organizational structure and culture and is often enabled through information technology (IT) (Alavi, 2000; Alavi & Leidner, 2001). While technology drove the initial interest in KM, both academics and practitioners have begun to realize that effective KM initiatives and solutions will be based on a more holistic view of the knowledge work environment (Grover & Davenport, 2001; Holsapple & Joshi, 2002; Massey & Montoya-Weiss, 2002; Rubenstein-Montano et al., 2001). Specifically, before an organization can realize the promise of KM, a fundamental question needs to be asked: What performance goal(s) is the organization trying to achieve? Addressing this question will direct the organization to what knowledge should be managed and how it should be managed.

Improving customer service, shortening product development cycles, growing revenues, and improving profits are commonly cited as goals motivating KM initiatives. If the intent of a KM initiative is to enhance organizational performance, organizations first need to understand the performance environment surrounding and driving the underlying knowledge work. For example, improving customer service and shortening product development cycles require that firms look to their processes, which may be reengineered to capitalize on or to expand organizational knowledge resources and capabilities (Gold, Malhotra, & Segars, 2001; Hammer & Champy, 1993; Maier & Remus, 2001). Generating performance improvements via a KM initiative thus requires a deep understanding of how process work is organized, what knowledge is inherent to and derived from it, what factors influence knowledge workers, and how all of these factors relate to an organization's business environment (Massey & Montoya-Weiss, 2002).

In this paper, we offer a framework that provides a holistic view of the performance environment surrounding organizational knowledge work. The framework provides a useful means to identify, define, analyze, and address knowledge-based problems or opportunities relative to multi-level (business, process, and knowledge-worker) performance goals and requirements. Our perspective responds to a current call in the literature for KM frameworks that take a holistic, systems-oriented perspective by considering problems and opportunities in their entirety (Rubenstein-Montano et al., 2001; Senge, 1990). We draw from and integrate literature concerned with approaches to dealing with complexity and purposeful (i.e., performance-oriented) systems (Checkland & Howell, 1998), business process reengineering (Hammer & Champy, 1993), and human performance (Stolovich & Keeps, 1999). Rather than suggesting that KM requires a whole new perspective with its own special laws, our framework purports that KM sits well within our current understanding of what drives performance (Soo, Devinney, Midgley, & Deering, 2002).

We illustrate the efficacy of our framework to KM using case studies conducted at IBM and Nortel Networks. In addition, based on the framework and the insights we drew from our case studies, we offer a series of steps that can help direct organizations as they undertake KM initiatives. Finally, we illustrate the generalizability of these steps by demonstrating them in context of the software development process, using insights gained from a study with a software development firm. We conclude our paper with a discussion of broader implications for organizational practice and directions for future research.

BACKGROUND AND MOTIVATION

The general goal of KM is to capitalize on knowledge assets in order to achieve maximum attainable business performance (Barney, 1991; Becerra-Fernandez & Sabherwal, 2001; Davenport & Prusak, 1998). Organizations are faced with two key questions: What should an organization consider before undertaking a KM initiative? and How can KM become a strategic asset?

In a review of existing KM frameworks, Rubenstein-Montano and colleagues (2001) suggest that most frameworks to date have been prescriptive and focused primarily on knowledge flows. As such, they do not provide a comprehensive, holistic approach to integrate KM practices with strategic goals of the organization to realize potential for improving performance. Moreover, they do not consider non-task-oriented aspects that ultimately influence knowledge workers as they carry out business process activities. A further review of the literature suggests that KM has considered a broad array of issues and approaches, addressing things such as capturing and sharing best practices, building databases and intranets, measuring intellectual, establishing corporate libraries, installing groupware, enacting cultural change, and fostering collaboration (Ackerman, Pipek, & Wulf, 2003; Alavi & Leidner, 1999, 2001; Fahey

& Prusak, 1998; Grover & Davenport, 2001; O'Dell & Grayson, 1998; Stewart, 2001). Thus, while no generally accepted framework has been adopted, it seems that KM has involved all kinds of approaches, practical activities, measures, and technologies.

In order to make KM a strategic asset and to realize the potential for improving performance, there is a need for a unifying framework that considers KM relative to the entirety of the organizational system as well as its subcomponents (i.e., the business, its processes, and knowledge workers) (Soo et al., 2002). Such a framework should provide a general sense of direction (i.e., be prescriptive) for KM initiatives in order to ensure that the same general requirements are addressed across the organization, but it also should be descriptive in that it considers factors that ultimately influence KM success or failure (Rubenstein-Montano et al., 2001; Tsoukas, 1996).

A systems approach to KM can ensure a holistic and purposeful (performance-oriented) consideration of the interrelationships between the business, its processes, and knowledge workers (Ackoff & Emery, 1972). The objective is to enhance understanding of and responsiveness to a problem by examining relationships between various parts of the system (Checkland, 1981; Checkland & Howell, 1998; Gao, Li & Nakamori, 2002). A systems approach can enhance KM initiatives by examining and depicting the complex relationships among components such that an organization can ascertain where and how KM might respond (Rubenstein-Montano et al., 2001). In the following section, we develop and offer a holistic KM framework that considers the complex *interdependencies* among the business, its processes, and knowledge workers surrounding organizational knowledge work. When applied, the framework offers a systematic way to identify, define, and analyze performance problems or opportunities and their drivers and causes at multiple levels (business, process, and individual). By doing this, desired performance outcomes at all levels can be described, and behaviors that will produce those outcomes can be identified (Gordon, 1996). With this robust understanding, organizations can more precisely specify and implement interventions to address problems or capitalize on opportunities and ultimately improve performance (Gery, 1997; Massey & Montoya-Weiss, 2002; Rosenberg, 1995; Stolovitch & Keeps, 1999).

A HOLISTIC FRAMEWORK FOR KM

In Figure 1 we offer a framework to ensure that KM initiatives and multi-level requirements are addressed in a similar vs. an ad hoc fashion across the organization. Described next, the framework draws from and integrates literature concerned with approaches to dealing with complexity and purposeful (i.e., performance-oriented) systems (Checkland & Howell, 1998), business process reengineering (Hammer & Champy, 1993), and human performance (Rummler & Brache, 1992; Stolovich & Keeps, 1999). It possesses both prescriptive (task-oriented activities) and descriptive (consideration of factors that influence success or failure) elements, which, in turn, facilitate a holistic perspective. Importantly and consistently with a systems approach, the framework does not imply that the same methodologies will be used for all situations; rather, the framework facilitates a method to KM that is adaptive and responsive to different situations.

Since knowledge is context-specific, and since KM will be most powerful when applied to a specific domain (Sviokla, 1996), a component of our framework is its focus on core business processes. Thus, at the process level, we draw from the business process reengineering (BPR) literature, which is concerned with a fundamental rethinking of and redesign of business processes in order to achieve performance improvements (Hammer & Champy, 1993). Although BRP involves the analysis and design of workflows, it does not explicitly

consider the complex environment that influences knowledge workers (Davenport & Short, 1990). Without consideration of the human element in knowledge-intensive processes, BPR rarely will be successful. Therefore, by leveraging literature concerned with human performance (Stolovich & Keeps, 1999; Rummler & Brach, 1992), our KM framework includes factors that influence individual work behaviors and performance. It is likely that a KM initiative that only considers isolated subcomponents of the overall system will not enhance performance. Rather, success will hinge on understanding how each part — strategic goals, business process, knowledge workers — influences and interacts with other parts.

As illustrated, the external environment presents an organization with opportunities, pressures, events, and resources (Holsapple & Joshi, 2000, 2002). In response, an organization generates business and process requirements — a set of actions that allows the organization to capitalize on external opportunities and/or respond to threats. For example, to remain competitive, a strategic business performance goal may be to increase market acceptance of new products (Moorman & Rust, 1999). In a software-related business, the business-level requirement may be to increase the rate of new software introduction into the marketplace. This business requirement generates process-level requirements (e.g., the new product development process must produce a stream of continuous new products or services).

Gaps between current process capabilities and defined requirement(s) may force the organization to reengineer the business process such that the process performs at the required level of performance (Davenport, 1993; Hammer & Champy, 1993; Teng, Grover & Fiedler, 1994). Recognizing that processes are knowledge-intensive (Davenport, DeLong & Beers, 1998; Massey & Montoya-Weiss, 2002), reengineering efforts should focus on decomposing and structuring the process such that data, information, knowledge activities, and workflows between activities are clearly defined

Figure 1. A holistic framework for knowledge management (Adapted from Stolovich & Keeps, 1999; Rummler & Brach, 1992)

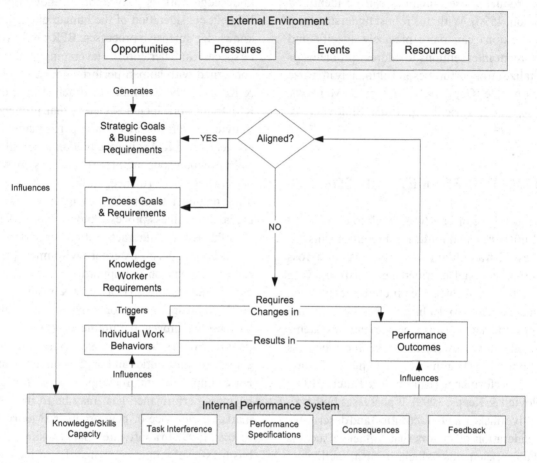

(Davenport & Short, 1990; Hammer & Champy, 1993; Teng et al., 1994). Importantly, structuring the process and identifying knowledge exchange activities inherent to the process will assist in identifying knowledge worker requirements (Leonard & Sensiper, 1998; O'Dell & Grayson, 1998). In particular, this involves defining what knowledge and what types of knowledge (i.e., tacit or explicit) are needed to accomplish activities. It also involves identifying who or what are the sources and receivers of knowledge (e.g., human, archives, etc.) as well as defining desired performance outcomes of process-level work. A purposeful and seamless flow of data, information, and knowledge — a defined knowledge cycle — then can occur among collaborating knowledge workers tasked with various process activities.

In addition to rethinking how a process work should be done via reengineering (Davenport, 1993; Hammer, 1990), it is important to consider the knowledge worker(s) who will be tasked with carrying out process activities. Thus, in addition to specifying the knowledge cycle, we must consider factors that influence the behaviors and performance of knowledge workers at the task/activity level (Checkland, 1981; Rubenstein-Montano et al., 2001; Rummler & Brache, 1992). As shown in Figure 1, the task/activity level factors are referred to as a knowledge worker's internal performance system. Here, it becomes important to recognize that individual (or often team) performance is not simply a function of knowledge, skills, or capacity. Rather, other factors influence performance, including: the nature and clarity of the business process work tasks and whether anything (e.g., lack of resources) interferes with task completion, clarity of performance specifications and goals, positive and negative work consequences, and performance feedback (Rummler & Brache, 1992). By taking a broader view of knowledge workers, cause(s) of poor performance and/or opportunities to enhance performance (beyond knowledge, skills, and capacity) can be identified.

As described previously, the framework enables a holistic examination of the interrelationships among multi-level goals and requirements that allows for the identification of problems or opportunities that should be addressed in order to enhance performance (Senge, 1990). In the following section, we illustrate the framework based on our work with IBM and Nortel. Our purpose is not to provide detailed case studies; rather, our intent is to illustrate key elements and interrelationships (see Massey, Montoya-Weiss, & Holcolm, 2001; and Massey, Montoya-Weiss & O'Driscoll, 2002 for further in-depth case studies).

PERFORMANCE-DRIVEN KM INITIATIVES

In the latter half of the 1990s, both IBM and Nortel Networks were facing significant external pressures. With regard to IBM, from 1986 to 1992, its market share dropped from 30% to 19%, with each percentage point representing $3 billion in revenues. Rather than paying attention to customer needs, IBM focused on its own financial needs and tried to reduce costs by cutting customer service staff and levels of support. In the end, customers were driven away. Thus, by the mid-1990s, the changing market environment and downsizing necessitated that IBM rethink the basic way they serviced customers in order to reduce customer defections and to increase sales. Throughout the 1980s and early 1990s, IBM's primary points of contact with its customers were through business partners, direct catalog, and the traditional "blue suits." Given that these points of contact were not supporting the business-strategic goals and requirements to remain competitive, an internal task force was charged with reengineering IBM's customer relationship management (CRM) process.

CRM involves attracting, developing, and maintaining successful customer relationships over time (Berry & Parasuraman, 1991; Day, 2000, 1994). At the core of CRM is the development of a learning relationship that engages customers in a two-way collaborative dialogue that is effective and efficient for both customers and the firm (Peppers, Rogers, & Dorf, 1999). When effective, this knowledge-based process leads to a relationship that gets smarter and deeper through every interaction. The task force charged with addressing the business problem recognized that

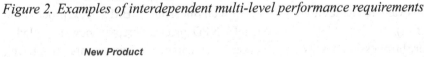

Figure 2. Examples of interdependent multi-level performance requirements

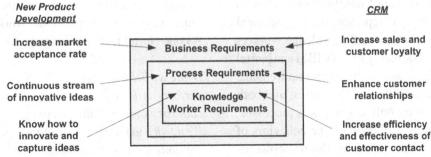

advanced information technology, the burgeoning Internet, and the emerging network-centric environment presented great opportunities for reengineering IBM's CRM process and leveraging its knowledge assets.

Similarly, at Nortel Networks, the Telecommunications Reform Act of 1996 produced intense competition in the telecom industry, yielding an explosion in the development of innovative telecommunications technology. The new rules of the deregulated telecommunications marketplace forced Nortel to recognize that differentiation through innovation was one of the few strategies that might allow the company to continue to succeed. Like IBM, an internal group was charged with the task of addressing this strategic business goal and requirement. After preliminary research, the group discovered that the generation and existence of innovative ideas within Nortel was not the issue. Rather, Nortel's existing new product development (NPD) process had no formal mechanism to systematically capture, develop, and manage internally generated ideas (i.e., ideas that could be developed into product or service concepts and evaluated for funding). Developing ideas and evaluating concepts is knowledge-intensive work based on the individual and collective expertise of employees. The Nortel task force set out to reengineer its NPD process in order to leverage its knowledge assets. As described, the efforts of both the IBM and Nortel initiatives were guided by strategic business goals and requirements that, in turn, led to them to focus on business processes most relevant to achieving desired performance (Figure 1).

As shown in Figure 2, core business processes like CRM and NPD represent the fundamental link between business and knowledge workers performance. The reality for both IBM and Nortel was that their respective business requirements would be achieved through processes, and both organizations were only as good as its processes, which ultimately depended on the behaviors of knowledge workers. Driven by this performance reality, IBM's reengineered CRM process was designed to enhance the customer relationship, while Nortel's reengineered NPD process was designed to produce a continuous stream of products and services. Although the specific details of the process reengineering efforts are beyond the scope of this paper (details are available upon request), both organizations structured their new processes by decomposing the process into knowledge-based activities, simultaneously identifying the required flows of data, information, and/or knowledge among activities and knowledge workers. The analysis led to the specification of the knowledge-based drivers (types, sources, and receivers) of each activity, decision, or information flow. In their reengineering efforts, both task forces went through several process prototype iterations (Davenport & Short, 1990), simultaneously considering whether (or not) the new process could, in fact, support business goals and requirements. As one IBM task force member put it:

We had done things the same way for so long. We realized early on that any changes to our [CRM] process had to demonstrate they would, in fact, improve business performance or nobody — our reps or our customers — would buy in. We continually asked ourselves whether the new process supported our business [level] goals.

This quote illustrates the strong link between business and process levels shown in Figure 1 and how important it is not only to decompose the levels but to integrate them, as well.

The reengineering of IBM's CRM process and Nortel's NPD process created new knowledge worker performance requirements, triggering requisite changes to individual work behaviors. As one Nortel task force member observed:

While we believed our new [NPD] process could perform as desired, we were not sure if our people could or would actually carry out the new process. We needed to gain a better understanding of their capabilities and motivations.

Given this, both organizations sought to understand the internal performance system of its various knowledge workers in light of the reengineered processes and requirements (see Figure 1). Specifically, did they possess the knowledge/skills/capacity to carry out reengineered or new process activities? Did they possess and/or understand the inputs required to carry out process tasks? Did anything exist that would interfere with task requirements? Did they understand the desired performance outcomes intended to support business and process requirements? What contextual factors would motivate or demotivate knowledge workers to share knowledge and carry out the new process (i.e., consequences and feedback)?

Answers to these questions enabled a collaborative learning relationship between IBM representatives and customers and a more collaborative relationship between the engineers and managers involved in the NPD process at Nortel. For example, Nortel's NPD process called for idea generators (often engineers) to develop a raw product or service idea into a robust concept along the lines of marketing, business, technology, and human factors (areas used by managers to make funding decisions). While engineers are technically knowledgeable, they typically do not possess sufficient knowledge in the other areas required in the new NPD process. This drove Nortel's team to consider interventions to support the specific knowledge gaps of workers engaged in this process activity. Similarly, IBM's team considered the factors that would influence the behavior of CRM knowledge workers. For example, IBM sales representatives felt threatened by the CRM reengineering effort, due to their perception that the customer relationships would be transferred largely from human contacts to technology. In response, IBM undertook efforts to show sales representatives that the new CRM process would, in fact, allow them to more proactively sell and market products and services.

Ultimately, both IBM and Nortel designed and implemented technology-based interventions to support the performance of knowledge workers. Drawing from the disciplines of KM and CRM, IBM developed an Internet-based system called *Inside IBM*. The system allowed customers to link directly to IBM's intranet and back-end, cross-functional, knowledge-based resources. Inside IBM was subsequently adopted as a corporate standard leading to IBM's *e-Services* as it is known today. Deploying artificial intelligence, information systems, and user-centered design, Inside IBM aggregated IBM's accumulated product support knowledge into a single system and enabled collection of information about its customers. IBM's efforts facilitated a collaborative and learning relationship between IBM and its customers. This led to improved decision making for both the customer and the organization's sales and service workforce, leading to increased sales and customer loyalty. IBM estimated that $525 million of incremental revenue and $50 million of productivity savings were realized over a three-year period as a result of this initiative (see Massey et al., 2001, for further details concerning IBM's initiative).

Similarly, Nortel developed a KM system called *Virtual Mentor*. Virtual Mentor supported both the performance of knowledge workers (engineers) engaged in developing raw ideas into robust concepts and decision makers (managers) tasked with making funding decisions. Virtual Mentor subsequently was integrated into a broader corporate time-to-market strategy that is in place today. Nortel's efforts led to decreased time-to-market, increased time-to-market acceptance, and improved funding decisions. Over a three-year period, Nortel's new product introduction rate increased by over 50% (see Massey et al., 2002, for further details concerning Nortel's initiative).

Clearly, the bottom line for IBM and Nortel was to increase profitability, sales, share, and return on investment by leveraging and managing its knowledge assets. As evidenced, IBM and Nortel's KM initiatives were guided by a holistic understanding of interdependent multi-level (business, process, knowledge-worker) performance goals and requirements. This facilitated problem/opportunity identification and definition, diagnoses of the changes required, and the subsequent design of suitable interventions needed to affect the performance of knowledge workers tasked with process activities. Addressing *what to do* from a performance perspective drove the reengineering of two knowledge-intensive business processes. Both processes called for improvements to cross-functional coordination, collaboration and learning, and knowledge exchange in business, technology, and marketing (and other relevant areas). Considering *how to do it* and simultaneously understanding the behavioral factors that influenced knowledge workers informed the development and implementation of interventions designed to enhance performance. In the end, both IBM and Nortel were directed by a deep understanding of the complex interdependencies inherent to their organizational systems. In their respective efforts, they not only decoupled the organizational environment into its smaller parts (business, process, knowledge worker), but also continually considered how the parts were linked in hierarchies to form the whole performance environment.

In the following section, we present a series of steps that underlie our framework and provide direction for KM initiatives. We then illustrate the efficacy of our approach in a software engineering context. Our data in this context are based on interviews with managers and developers regarding KM systems currently in use at TechCo (a pseudonym), a well-known Indian software development firm that has several centers certified at Level 5 of the Capability Maturity Model (Paulk, Weber, Curtis, & Chrissis, 1995).

STEPS FOR KM INITIATIVES

Step 1: Select a Target Business Process. Once an organization has identified its business goals and

requirements, a KM initiative then must identify the firm's key leverage points for achieving business results. As noted earlier and as evidenced at IBM and Nortel, since knowledge is context-specific (Sviokla, 1996), KM likely will be most powerful when it addresses a particular domain, such as new product development, operations, sales, and customer service. Organizations should start where advocacy exists for doing something different. Processes such as those targeted for improvement by the organizations we studied is where work is accomplished. Once the process is identified, establish a process and project owner and ensure that the new initiative is managed as a business change project, not an information technology project (as many early KM projects were managed). In this step, it is also important to establish performance measures for the business case. Demonstrating success with a single process may lead to acceptance for other processes.

Step 2: Model the Process. This step requires that the inherent, underlying process structure be found or defined in order for an initiative to move forward. Oftentimes, process activities and the data, information, and knowledge flows among activities are poorly defined. Clarifying activities and promoting an integrative view of the whole process is the starting point for managing knowledge and improving performance. For example, in the front end of the NPD process, idea-to-concept development and concept selection activities often are called the *fuzzy*, because they involve ill-defined activities and ad hoc decisions carried out by multiple and diverse stakeholders (Cooper & Kleindschmidt, 1995). Via careful analysis and benchmarking, Nortel reengineered and enhanced the front end of its NPD process by defining a consistent and structured approach for developing, screening, and cataloging new product ideas.

Step 3: Identify Activity-Based Knowledge Exchange Processes. This step requires understanding the context of work (i.e., the knowledge needs associated with each process activity defined in Step 2). For example, in IBM's CRM process, in order for customer representatives to target sales and marketing proactively, they had to determine how to acquire knowledge concerning customer requirements. Similarly, at Nortel, different knowledge workers and functions had different pieces of data, information, and knowledge relevant to the NPD process. These pieces needed to be exchanged in order to create a common and logically organized bank of knowledge about a product or service concept. The objective of this step is to identify the knowledge exchange processes that are or must be in place to support value-creating activities.

Step 4: Identify Desired Knowledge Exchange Performance Outcomes. When individuals or teams exploit knowledge in a business process, it is reflected in the quality of a valued outcome that benefits the organization. This step involves specifying the performance outcomes that should be derived from the knowledge exchange processes identified in Step 3. For example, in Nortel's NPD process, one desired outcome was that a decision maker (manager) could make an informed decision regarding further funding for product development. Another was when the right combination of product-related data (e.g., marketing, business, and technology) needed to be readily accessible in the right format for different tasks and functional areas. Alternatively, in IBM's CRM process, a desired outcome was that the right people, information, and services would be readily accessible to the customer.

Step 5: Identify the Knowledge Drivers of Each Process Activity, Decision, and Information Flow. This step requires the identification of the types of knowledge required, the sources of that knowledge (internal and/or external people, archived data), and the receivers of knowledge (people, other databanks). In Nortel's case, this step required identification of the specific knowledge required by an idea generator (i.e., an engineer or knowledge worker source) so he or she could develop a raw idea into a robust concept in the areas of marketing, business, human factors, and technology. With this knowledge, a raw idea could be developed into a complete and robust concept so that decision makers (i.e., manager or knowledge worker receiver) could evaluate the concept and make a funding decision.

Step 6: Identify and Develop Interventions. In concert, Steps 2 through 5 specify the knowledge inputs, exchange processes, sources and receivers, and desired outcomes associated with the targeted and defined business process. The factors that influence individual work behaviors (i.e., the internal performance system of knowledge workers) also must be considered to ensure that desired performance outcomes are achievable. With this holistic understanding available, an organization now can specify more precisely its KM interventions or solutions in order to support individual and/or teamwork. Interventions reflect both responses to identified causes of performance problems and opportunities for improving performance. Potential interventions could include the development of individuals or teams (e.g., training) or solutions that focus on rewarding performance (e.g., incentive/reward systems). Interventions also may include information technology-based KM systems (Alavi, 2000; Alavi & Leidner, 2001; Gery, 1997; Hinds & Pfeffer, 2003; Rosenberg, 1995). Intervention selection should be done in light of appropriateness (internally and externally), economics, feasibility (given organizational constraints or barriers to implementation), and acceptability to the organization and knowledge workers. Again, by taking a holistic view and understanding the performance environment first rather than starting with a solution looking for a problem, interventions can be identified more appropriately and precisely.

One key issue to be considered when supporting activities within a business process context is the issue of language translation. Knowledge workers deploy local languages relative to their areas of expertise. Thus, successfully enabling the flow of data, information, and knowledge between process activities and diverse knowledge workers may require language translation. For example, as noted earlier in our Nortel case, we found that idea generators (engineers) did not speak the language of decision makers (managers). Nortel's KM solution, Virtual Mentor, thus was designed to depict and translate knowledge in forms that were appropriate for different audiences (engineers, managers, process owners). For example, through concept development and rating forms designed in the language of engineers, idea generators provided knowledge concerning a new concept and its potential application(s). Virtual Mentor then translated the contextual structure of this concept information into a form so decision makers could conduct a SWOT—strengths, weaknesses, opportunities, threats—analysis. Virtual Mentor enabled collaboration by supporting the local languages of disparate knowledge workers who must exchange knowledge in order to improve decision making. Another issue that needs to be dealt with is the differential navigational needs of the various stakeholders. As an example, the navigation needs of a customer representative in the CRM process seeking to acquire customer requirements differs significantly from the needs of a customer seeking information.

AN APPLICATION OF THE STEPS FOR KM INITIATIVES

In this section, we provide further evidence that demonstrates the validity of our holistic framework and underlying steps identified in the previous section. Here, we describe the path taken by TechCo in arriving at the KM solutions in

use today. TechCo is one of the leading software services and consulting organization in Southeast Asia, providing systems development and integration services to Global Fortune 500 clients.

During the 1990s, TechCo saw a significant increase in competition in the offshore software development arena. With a business goal of maintaining its position as one of the market leaders in this arena, TechCo sought to gain a competitive edge by focusing its efforts on improving the quality of its core software development processes. This effort was very similar to Nortel's efforts described earlier, which focused on enhancing its NPD process.

Software development, by its very nature, is a knowledge-intensive process that involves many people working on several different activities and phases (Rus & Lindvall, 2002; Ward & Aurum, 2004). Success hinges on the creation, acquisition, identification, adaptation, organization, distribution, and application of knowledge within and between projects. It is also a dynamic process, evolving with technology, organizational culture, and development practices (Ward & Aurum, 2004). Inherent to software development is knowledge embedded in products and meta-knowledge concerning not only the products but also the development processes (Rus, Lindvall, & Sinha, 2001). While individuals engaged in software development projects make decisions based on personal knowledge, the sharing of this knowledge historically has been limited to informal means (Rus & Lindvall, 2002) (see Rus et al., 2001, for a review of KM and software engineering).

TechCo's focus on process improvement initiatives was driven by a desire to provide a measure of control and accountability within complex software development projects. Example processes that could be targeted in a software lifecycle context include the requirements analysis, software development and software maintenance processes, as well as more managerial processes, such as the project management or change management process (Jalote, 2000; Rus et al., 2001). TechCo sought to address several of these processes through its efforts to achieve the Carnegie Mellon Institute's Capability Maturity Model Level 5 certification (Paulk et al., 1995).

Having identified a set of target processes to reengineer (Step 1 of our checklist), TechCo began to specify and document the standard activities and information flows for each major process in the software development life cycle. This activity (a requirement in order to be certified at Level 3 of the CMM) helped TechCo to achieve the objectives stated in Step 2 of our KM checklist. Each process was broken down into stages consisting of activities that, in turn, were divided into subactivities. Key participants for each stage also were identified as part of the process definition. For example, the requirements analysis process was divided into the activities of preparation, eliciting requirements, analyzing requirements, and so forth. Examples of subactivities that were identified for the requirements analysis activity included the creation of logical data models and process models.

Steps 3 and 4 of our KM initiative checklist were achieved as a natural consequence of Tech-Co's efforts to detail the activities that comprised each process. TechCo used the ETVX (Entry, Task, Verification, and eXit) model (Radice, Roth, O'Hara & Ciarfella, 1985) to define the details of each stage in a process. The entry criteria and input specification together defined the primary knowledge inputs to each activity, while the exit criteria and associated metrics defined the knowledge exchange outcomes associated with each activity.

Step 5 of our checklist deals with the identification of the knowledge sources and receivers for each activity. At TechCo, the knowledge sources and receivers for each activity were defined in the process definition handbooks. These handbooks contained generic guidelines for performing activities such as group reviews, defect prevention, and so forth, as well as detailed checklists for ac-

complishing activities such as high-level design, functional design, code review, and so forth. In addition, TechCo created a series of templates for producing various types of documents generated during the software development process (e.g., requirements specification, unit test plan, and acceptance test documents). Specifying these items to a sufficient level of detail such that every project could follow the guidelines as well as produce documents in a standardized fashion was a key step in helping TechCo achieve Level 5 certification. These templates represented a codification of knowledge that then could be exchanged among the various sources and receivers.

Having defined in detail its software engineering processes, TechCo began to examine the best mechanism by which it could support the activities of the knowledge workers executing these processes (Step 6 of our checklist). It is well known that software development requires coordination and collaboration among various stakeholders (Kraut & Streeter, 1995) (i.e., project leaders, module leaders, analysts, developers, and members of quality assurance groups). Armed with an understanding of the individual tasks performed by each knowledge worker, the types of knowledge exchanged among the various stakeholders and the coordination and communication needs of knowledge workers during each phase of the life cycle, TechCo was able to design a project level KM system, the Project Reporting and Management System (PRMS). PRMS facilitates efficient knowledge sharing among the workers by providing support for essential collaborative activities, such as (1) configuration management of work products (e.g., documents and code); (2) division, scheduling, and assignment of subactivities to various knowledge workers; (3) support for testing and problem reporting; and (4) change management. In addition, PRMS captures various metrics relating to defects per stage, effort spent per stage, and so forth. In essence, PRMS is a project-level KM that serves as a one-stop shop for sharing key knowledge related to a given project, including informal knowledge generated during the course of the project.

By achieving the high level of process maturity and control over its software development processes and the use of tools such as PRMS, TechCo was able to maintain its competitive edge in the marketplace. However, it still did not have any organization-wide mechanism in place to facilitate knowledge sharing across various projects. This often resulted in wasted effort and costly mistakes in personnel and time estimation. For example, there was no easy mechanism to solve the problems related to the "who knows what" issue that plagues large organizations. Moreover, no mechanisms for sharing knowledge regarding best practices and processes were in place.

To address these problems, TechCo developed and deployed an organization-level KM system in the form of an electronic knowledge asset library (KAL). This system served as a repository for knowledge about its software development process (i.e., guidelines, checklists, templates, etc.). TechCo organized knowledge generated from prior projects based on two criteria: industry vertical (e.g., manufacturing, pharmaceutical) and technology characteristics (e.g., languages, tools, databases). Detailed knowledge from each project (captured in the PRMS) in the form of all final documents produced during the various phases of the lifecycle (e.g., requirements documents, high-level design documents, program code, and records of quality assurance reviews, was stored in this system. Furthermore, because of its highly mature processes, TechCo was also able to capture quantitative information (e.g., effort and defects per stage) in the system. This system also served as a forum for posting white papers and tutorials on emerging technology topics. Each knowledge item in the system had associated with it a contact person's information, thus creating knowledge about where expertise resides within the organization.

The knowledge captured in KAL is accessible to all users in the organization. Access to the library

is provided through a groupware system based on Lotus Notes® technology. Common navigation functionality, such as ability to search projects based on keywords and other criteria, is provided. Thus, using this system, a project leader initiating a project using J2EE technology in the financial industry can retrieve documents related to prior J2EE projects in the financial industry and use the knowledge in the system to estimate the manpower and time needed to execute the new project successfully. The project leader is able to find and communicate with other project leaders with experience in that domain and to make requests for software engineers, who have performed well in a specific domain. At the same time, a developer can read tips on how to develop wireless applications using J2ME. Similar systems (i.e., the process asset database [PDB] and Knowledge Map) are in use at Infosys, one of TechCo's chief competitors (Ramasubramanian & Jagadeesan, 2002). To encourage the sharing of knowledge via these KM systems, TechCo linked knowledge worker financial incentives to systems use, which TechCo believes led to performance improvements.

Through the use of these KM systems, TechCo has been able to deliver consistently high-quality software products by reducing the barriers of time and space associated with virtual software development (Carmel & Agarwal, 2001). It is worth noting that the process of accomplishing the six steps has taken more than five years. TechCo's efforts were spent on defining and refining the details of the software development processes (Steps 1 through 5) and the needs and motivations of its knowledge workers prior to considering and designing the subsequent technology-based KM system interventions. In the end, TechCo's efforts reflect its response to external competitive pressures and desire to improve interdependent, multi-level (business, process, and knowledge worker) performance (Figure 1). The fact that TechCo has been able to maintain its leadership position in an extremely competitive IT outsourcing/offshoring space provides evidence of the value of the KM initiatives. Thus, the TechCo case reiterates the importance of taking a holistic, performance-centric view of KM.

IMPLICATIONS FOR PRACTICE AND RESEARCH

Successful organizations like IBM, Nortel, and TechCo are searching for ways to improve performance by leveraging knowledge assets more effectively. New products, services, and customer relationships are key drivers of growth for sales and profitability, particularly for firms facing intense competition and rapid technological change (Alavi, 2000; Huber, 2001). Viability often hinges directly upon the competitive quality and exploitation of a firm's underlying knowledge base. Relative to their own environment, every organization will respond differently to the fundamental question posed earlier in this paper: What performance goal(s) is the organization trying to achieve by managing its knowledge assets? While KM cannot be applied generically, we have provided an overseeing framework and underlying steps that may assist organizations in addressing this question (Rubenstein-Montano et al., 2001; Tsoukas, 1996).

For practice, our perspective is both adaptive and responsive to different situations. Importantly, our approach considers the entire KM process—strategic objectives, operational factors, the role of technology, and people/culture—as well as underlying knowledge types, flows, tasks, and learning that must to be considered when considering the fit of a KM initiative to a particular organization. As evidenced in our cases, any KM initiative must be aligned with the existing strategic environment (Liebowitz & Beckman, 1998). An organization should assess the relationship of the initiative to current value chain processes, the level of change, the resources required to implement the envisioned solution, and the level of senior management support. Senior level support establishes an appreciation of knowledge assets and is essential for the ongoing funding and investment for necessary human and technical resources (Holsapple & Joshi, 2000). A KM initiative must fit with the operational environment. Interventions may change workflow and interpersonal relationships and thus may necessitate new roles and/or skills for knowledge workers. Deploying information technology in the form of a KM system also requires consideration of the existing technical environment (Flanagin, 2002; Holsapple & Joshi, 2002; Huber, 2001). The solution must be compatible with networks and platforms, and the organization must be ready to deal with the level of investment and change necessary to implement desired technical functionality. Perhaps the most challenging issue is the assessment of the fit between a KM initiative and the cultural environment. Creating a culture of knowledge sharing is critical to success (Davenport et al., 1998; Fahey & Prusak, 1998; Grover & Davenport, 2001). Given this, an organization needs to assess incentive and reward systems and identify internal inconsistencies. Understanding the internal performance system of a knowledge worker will assist in identifying factors that positively or negatively influence the behavior of knowledge workers.

For researchers, while we recognize the limits of a case study approach to generalizability, we maintain that the very nature of our framework requires holistic study of its application. This suggests a need for additional qualitative case studies conducted in collaboration with organizations that have engaged in or that are considering KM initiatives. It is only when a sufficient amount of systematic qualitative case study research has been conducted that themes and relationships inherent to our framework can be validated further via quantitative research methods.

CONCLUSION

A KM strategy entails developing a portfolio of strategically focused initiatives required to achieve business results. Organizations must prioritize these initiatives based on business value, enterprise support, and funding. As such, holistically and systematically understanding the performance environment surrounding organizational knowledge work takes on heightened importance (Massey & Montoya-Weiss, 2002; Rubenstein-Montano et al., 2001). With both prescriptive and descriptive elements, the framework and associated steps developed and offered in this paper should guide future research and assist organizations interested in undertaking and leading KM initiatives.

ACKNOWLEDGMENT

The authors gratefully acknowledge the research funding provided by the Advanced Practices Council of the Society for Information Management (SIM) and the Center for Innovation Management Studies, as well as the practical insights of their respective members. We also acknowledge the input and support of IBM, Nortel, and TechCo personnel.

REFERENCES

Ackerman, M., Pipek, V., & Wulf, V. (2003). *Sharing expertise: Beyond knowledge management*. Cambridge, MA: MIT Press.

Ackoff, R.L. & Emery, F.E. (1972). *On purposeful systems*. Chicago, IL: Aldine Atherton.

Alavi, M. (2000). Managing organizational knowledge. In R.W. Zmud (Ed.), *Framing the domains of IT management research: Glimpsing the future through the past*. Cincinnati, OH: Pinnaflex Educational Resources.

Alavi, M. & Leidner, D. (1999). Knowledge management systems: Issues, challenges, and benefits. *Communications of the Association for Information Systems, 1*. Retrieved from *http://cais.isworld. org/articles/1-7/article.htm*

Alavi, M. & Leidner, D. (2001). Review: Knowledge management and knowledge management systems: Conceptual foundations and research issues. *MIS Quarterly, 25*(1), 107-136.

Barney, J.B. (1991). Firm resources and sustained competitive advantage. *Journal of Management, 17*(1), 99-120.

Becerra-Fernandez, I. & Sabherwal, R. (2001). Organizational knowledge management: A contingency perspective. *Journal of Management Information Systems, 18*(1), 23-55.

Berry, L.L. & Parasuraman, A. (1991). *Marketing services*. New York: Free Press.

Carmel, E. & Agarwal, R. (2001). Tactical approaches to alleviating distance in global software development. *IEEE Software, 18*(2), 23-29.

Checkland, P.B. (1981). *Systems thinking, systems practice*. Chichester, England: Wiley.

Checkland, P.B. (1998). *Information, systems and information systems: Making sense of the field*. New York: John Wiley & Sons.

Cooper, R. & Kleindschmidt, E. (1995). An investigation into the NPD process: Steps, deficiencies, impact. *Journal of Product Innovation Management, 12*, 374-391.

Davenport, T.H. (1993). *Process innovation: Reengineering work through information technology*. Cambridge, MA: Harvard Business School Press.

Davenport, T.H., DeLong, D.W., & Beers, M.C. (1998). Successful knowledge management projects. *Sloan Management Review, 39*(2), 43-57.

Davenport, T.H. & Prusak, L. (1998). *Working knowledge: How organizations manage what they know.* Boston, MA: Harvard Business School Press.

Davenport, T.H. & Short, J.E. (1990). The new industrial engineering: Information technology and business process redesign. *Sloan Management Review,* 11-27.

Day, G.S. (1994). The capabilities of market-driven organizations, *Journal of Marketing, 58*(4), 37-52.

Day, G.S. (2000). Managing marketing relationships. *Journal of the Academy of Marketing Science, 28*(1), 24-31.

Dyer, G. & McDonough, B. (2001, May). The state of knowledge management. *Knowledge Management,* 31-36.

Fahey, L. & Prusak, L. (1998). The eleven deadliest sins of knowledge management. *California Management Review, 40*(3), 265-276.

Flanagin, A.J. (2002). The elusive benefits of the technology support of knowledge management. *Management Communication Quarterly, 16*(2), 242-248.

Gao, F., Li, M., & Nakamori, Y. (2002). Systems thinking on knowledge and its management: Systems methodology for knowledge management. *Journal of Knowledge Management, 6*(1), 7-17.

Gery, G. (1997). Granting three wishes through performance-centered design. *Communications of the ACM, 40*(7), 54-59.

Gold, A.H., Malhotra, A., & Segars, A.H. (2001). Knowledge management: An organizational capabilities perspective. *Journal of Management Information Systems, 18*(1), 185-214.

Gordon, J. (1996). Performance technology. In D. Zielinski (Ed.), *The effective performance consultant* (pp. 1-7). Minneapolis, MN: Lakewood Publications.

Grover, V. & Davenport, T.H. (2001). General perspectives on knowledge management: Fostering a research agenda. *Journal of Management Information Systems, 18*(1), 5-21.

Hammer, M. (1990). Reengineer work: Don't automate, obliterate. *Harvard Business Review,* 104-112.

Hammer, M. & Champy, J. (1993). *Reengineering the corporation: A manifesto for business revolution.* New York: Harper Collins.

Hinds, P.J. & Pfeffer, J. (2003). Why organizations don't "know what they know": Cognitive and motivational factors affecting the transfer of expertise. In M. Ackerman, V. Pipek, & V. Wulf (Eds.), *Sharing expertise: Beyond knowledge management* (pp. 3-26). Cambridge, MA: MIT Press.

Holsapple, C.W. & Joshi, K.D. (2000). An investigation of factors that influence the management of knowledge in organizations. *Journal of Strategic Information Systems, 9,* 235-261.

Holsapple, C.W. & Joshi, K.D. (2002). Knowledge management: A three-fold framework. *The Information Society, 18*(1), 47-64.

Huber, G.P. (2001). Transfer of knowledge in knowledge management systems: Unexplored issues and suggested studies. *European Journal of Information Systems, 10*(2), 72-79.

Jalote, P. (2000). *CMM in practice: Processes for executing software projects at Infosys.* Reading, MA: Addison-Wesley.

Kraut, R.E. & Streeter, L. (1995). Coordination in software development. *Communications of the ACM, 38*(3), 69-81.

Leonard, D. & Sensiper, S. (1998). The role of tacit knowledge in group innovation. *California Management Review, 40*(3), 112-132.

Liebowitz, J. & Beckman, T. (1998). *Knowledge organizations: What every manager should know.* Bacon Raton, FL: St. Lucie/CRC Press.

Maier, R. & Remus, U. (2001). Towards a framework for knowledge management strategies: Process orientation as strategic starting point. In *Proceedings of the 34th Hawaii International Conference on System Sciences.*

Massey, A.P. & Montoya-Weiss, M. (2002). Performance-centered design of knowledge intensive processes. *Journal of Management Information Systems, 18*(4), 37-58.

Massey, A.P., Montoya-Weiss, M., & Holcom, K. (2001). Re-engineering the customer relationship: Leveraging knowledge assets at IBM. *Decision Support Systems, 32* 155-170.

Massey, A.P., Montoya-Weiss, M., & O'Driscoll, T. (2202). Knowledge management in pursuit of performance: Insights from Nortel Networks. *MIS Quarterly, 26*(3), 269-289.

Moorman, C. & Rust, R.T. (1999). The role of marketing. *Journal of Marketing, 63,* 180-197.

O'Dell, C. & Grayson, C.J. (1998). If only we knew what we know: Identification and transfer of internal best practices. *California Management Review, 40*(3), 154-174.

Paulk, M., Weber, C.W., Curtis, B., & Chrissis, M.B. (1995). *The capability maturity model for software: Guidelines for improving the software process.* Reading, MA: Addison-Wesley.

Peppers, D., Rogers, M., & Dorf, R. (1999). *The one-to-one fieldbook.* New York: Currency and Doubleday.

Radice, R.A., Roth, N.K., O'Hara, A.C., & Ciarfella, W.A. (1985). A programming process architecture. *IBM Systems Journal, 24*(2), 79-90.

Ramasubramanian, S. & Jagadeesan, G. (2002). Knowledge management at Infosys. *IEEE Software, 19*(3), 53-55.

Rosenberg, M. (1995). Performance technology, performance support, and the future of training. *Performance Improvement Quarterly, 8*(1), 12-20.

Rubenstein-Montano, B. et al. (2001). A systems thinking framework for knowledge management. *Decision Support Systems, 31*(1), 5-16.

Rummler, G. & Brache, A. (1992). Transforming organizations through human performance technology. In H.D. Stolovitch & E.J. Keeps (Eds.), *Handbook of human performance technology: A comprehensive guide for analyzing and solving performance problems in organizations* (pp. 32-49). San Francisco, CA: Jossey-Bass.

Rus, I. & Lindvall, M (2002). Knowledge management in software engineering. *IEEE Software, 19*(3), 26-38.

Rus, I., Lindvall, M., & Sinha, S.S. (2001). Knowledge management in software engineering. DACS State of the Art Report (SOAR). Retrieved on April 10, 2005, from *http: www.dacs.dtic. mil/techs/kmse/kmse.html*

Senge, P.M. (1990). *The fifth discipline.* New York: Doubleday.

Soo, C., Devinney, T., Midgley, D., & Deering, A. (2002). Knowledge management: Philosophy, processes, and pitfalls. *California Management Review, 44*(4), 129-150.

Stewart, T. (2001). *The wealth of knowledge: Intellectual capital and the twenty-first century organization.* New York: Doubleday.

Stolovitch, H.D. & Keeps, E.J. (1999). What is human performance technology? In H.D. Stolovitch, & E.J. Keeps (Eds.), *Handbook of human performance technology: Improving individual and organizational performance worldwide* (pp. 3-23). San Francisco, CA: Jossey-Bass.

Sviokla, J.J. (1996). Knowledge workers and radically new technology. *Sloan Management Review,* 25-40.

Teng, J.T.C., Grover, V., & Fiedler, K.D. (1994). Business process reengineering: Charting a strategic path for the information age. *California Management Review, 36*(3), 9-31.

Tsoukas, H. (1996). The firm as a distributed knowledge system: A constructionist approach. *Strategic Management Journal, 17.*

Ward, J. & Aurum, A. (2004). Knowledge management in software engineering: Describing the process. In *Proceedings of the 2004 Australian Software Engineering Conference*. IEEE Computer Society. Retrieved on April 10, 2005, from http://csdl.computer.org/comp/proceedings/aswec/2004/2089/00/20890137abs.htm

Selected Reading III
Challenges in Developing a Knowledge Management Strategy for the Air Force Materiel Command*

Summer E. Bartczak
Air Force Institute of Technology AFIT/ENV, USA

Ellen C. England
Air Force Institute of Technology AFIT/ENV, USA

ABSTRACT

It is widely acknowledged that an organizational knowledge management strategy is a desired precursor to the development of specific knowledge management (KM) initiatives. The development of such a strategy is often difficult in the face of a lack of organizational understanding about KM and other organizational constraints. This case study describes the issues involved in developing a new KM strategy for the Air Force Material Command (AFMC). It centers around the AFMC KM program manager, Randy Adkins, and his challenges in developing the future KM strategy direction for the AFMC enterprise. The case study begins with a description of the history of the AFMC KM program and the existing KM system, but then focuses primarily on issues to be considered in future strategy development, such as maintaining top leadership support and understanding, conflict with the IT organization, funding cuts, future KM system configuration needs, and outsourcing of KM. The intent of this case study is to demonstrate, using Randy Adkins and AFMC as an example, many common issues that can be encountered as leaders struggle to develop viable KM strategies.

BACKGROUND

The Air Force Material Command

The Air Force Material Command (AFMC) is one of the Air Force's nine major commands (Figure 1). It is headquartered at Wright-Patterson Air Force Base in Dayton, Ohio, and employs 85,000 military and civilian employees across the globe. The primary mission of AFMC is to "develop, acquire, and sustain the aerospace power needed to defend the United States and its interests . . .

today and tomorrow" (HQ AFMC PA, 2001a). As such, it has cradle-to-grave oversight for the Air Force's aircraft, missiles, and munitions (HQ AFMC PA, 2001a). Key mission essential tasks supported by AFMC include product support, supply management, and depot maintenance (see Appendix 1 for a further breakdown).

According to the AFMC Public Affairs Fact Sheet (HQ AFMC PA, 2001a), AFMC fulfills its responsibilities through organizations that serve as product centers, research laboratories, test centers, air logistic centers for maintenance, and

Figure 1. US Air Force Major Commands

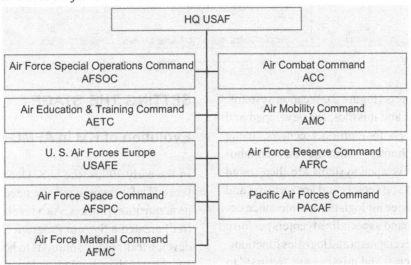

Figure 2. Air Force Material Command Organization

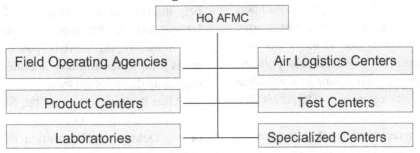

Figure 3. HQ AFMC Organization and Directorates

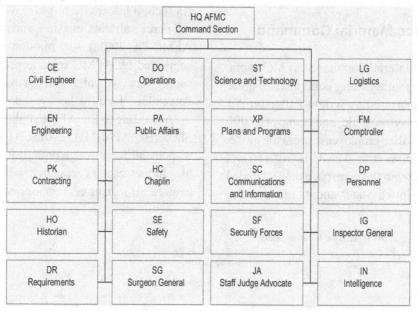

specialized centers (Figure 2). Weapon systems, such as aircraft and missiles, are developed and acquired through four product centers, using science and technology from the research laboratories. These weapon systems are then tested at AFMC's two test centers and are serviced and repaired at its three air logistics maintenance depots. The command's specialized centers perform various other development and logistics functions. Eventually, aircraft and missiles are "retired" to its Aircraft Maintenance and Regeneration Center in Tucson, Arizona.

AFMC's central governing organization, Headquarters (HQ) AFMC (Figure 3), consists of all the functional areas that provide support for command organizations. The Directorate of Requirements (DR)—the focus of this case study—is the command's focal point for policies, processes, and resources that support the product and information services mission (HQ AFMC PA, 2001b) and is the home of AFMC's Knowledge Management program which has the official name, Air Force Knowledge Management (AFKM).

SETTING THE STAGE

Evolution of KM in AFMC

In the early 1990s, the U.S. Department of Defense (DoD) recognized the need to streamline its acquisition process. As a result, the Air Force (AF) created a System Program Office (SPO) to develop technology solutions to help achieve that end. One such technology solution was called the AF Acquisition Model. Initially, this information system included an online repository of all acquisition regulations, step-by-step processes for conducting acquisitions, and miscellaneous help information such as points of contact and lessons learned. Although the technology used was immature, this digital repository was a first of its kind in the military and an idea quickly copied by the other services.

After its initial success, the SPO proposed the same idea to the Office of the Under Secretary of Defense for Acquisition Technology for possible implementation across the DoD. The proposal was approved in 1998 and the resulting effort became known as the Defense Acquisition Deskbook program. Now, as a DoD-level project, the program (and the accompanying information system) was to be managed and developed by an interservice Joint Program Office. As such, major Deskbook activities were transferred to the Joint Program Office and AFMC/DR personnel were assigned the remaining task of keeping the AF's Deskbook documents that resided on the system updated and current. Although the Joint Program Office retained oversight responsibility for the Deskbook program, a yearly funding stream of $1.5 million remained to support AFMC/DR's portion of the effort. Of this $1.5 million budget, only $500,000 was committed to maintenance of the Deskbook program. As such, AFMC/DR found itself asking, "What can we do with an extra million dollars?"

The answer came quickly in the form of an AF Inspection Agency study that identified a need for an overarching "lessons learned" program for the AF. While the need was AF-wide, the AFMC/DR Deskbook Team decided to use its own expertise and excess funding from the Deskbook program to address the problem for the AF. As a result, it produced a formal requirement to develop an information system-based AF Lessons Learned pilot program. Using the AFMC Deskbook system design as a foundation, the Deskbook Team added additional capabilities that allowed the capture and dissemination of "lessons learned" information.

While researching and developing the Lessons Learned pilot program, the Deskbook Team decided that the new business concept touted as "KM" captured the essence of what they were doing. The Team's understanding of KM was that it should be used to enhance organizational performance by explicitly designing and implementing tools, processes, systems, structures, and cultures to improve the creation, sharing, and use of knowledge that was critical for decision making. With this understanding, the Team felt that the goals of KM and the goals of the Deskbook and Lessons Learned projects were consistent. The Team also strategized that if it labeled its efforts as KM, it was possible the Team could receive more leadership support and funding. From that point forward, AFMC/DR Deskbook Team approached its projects and proposals from a KM perspective.

In addition to the Deskbook and Lessons Learned projects, the AFMC/DR Deskbook Team had also developed Web-based acquisition training to educate the acquisition workforce in lieu of sending them to classroom training. Randy Adkins, a civil service employee with 20 years of experience in various positions at Headquarters AFMC, was in charge of the development of this Web-based training program. At the same time, Robert Mulcahy, the deputy director of AFMC/DR, expressed concern with the impending retirement-driven talent drain that was soon to affect his organization as well as all of the AFMC enterprise. Previous studies both inside and outside the AF indicated that more than 50% of the AF's civilian acquisition personnel would be eligible to retire by 2005 (Cho, Jerrell, & Landay, 2000). Unless this issue was immediately addressed, Mulcahy knew that the acquisition workforce would lack the talent, leadership, and diversity needed to succeed in the new millennium. In searching for a solution, he recognized the value of KM concepts as they applied to his organization. He soon became a KM champion and pushed for a merger of the Deskbook, Lessons Learned, and Web-based training programs. He felt these programs, and the information systems that comprised their foundation, were synergistic and could be used in tandem to help capture and disseminate the knowledge of the rapidly retiring civilian workforce. In early 1999, Mulcahy turned to Adkins to spearhead the consolidation which would result in a new combined effort called the AF Knowledge Management (AFKM) program. Together, he believed they could bring KM to AFMC.

Developing the AFKM Program

Randy Adkins worked tirelessly to educate himself on KM and to develop an overarching strategic direction for the many existing elements of the AFKM program and AFKM system. His initial efforts in developing the AFKM program were aimed primarily at applying commercial KM processes and technologies to solve specific business problems. In doing so, his focus was on identifying, capturing, and leveraging knowledge and expertise within the organization. The ultimate goal of the AFKM program was to design information system solutions so that AFMC users could share information and knowledge and, at the same time, create a supportive, collaborative, and information- and knowledge-sharing culture (HQ AFMC/DRI, 2001).

The AFKM "System"

Under Adkins' direction, the Deskbook Team, deemed the AFKM System Development Team 1999, continued to grow the Web-based system beyond its original three components (Lessons Learned database, DoD Acquisition Deskbook, and Web-based training). The AFKM System Development Team structure is shown in Appendix 2. By mid 2000, the AFKM system was comprised of five basic components (Figure 4)—the Lessons Learned database, the AFMC portion of the DoD Acquisition Deskbook, the AFMC Virtual Schoolhouse (Web-based training), the AFMC Help Center module, and a Community of Practice (CoP) collaboration workspace module.

The AFKM home page (Figure 5) described the functionality of the AFKM system as follows:

Air Force Knowledge Management is the place to go to find out what you need and to share what you know. . . . [It] applies commercial knowledge management concepts and technologies to address AF business problems. It includes: collaborative workspaces for communities of practice, high-value Internet links, Internet-based learning technology to provide training via the Web, and a repository of lessons learned, best practices, and other bits of usable knowledge. The objective is to make our jobs easier and to enhance job performance by integrating organizational lessons learned, community wisdom, training and collaborative technology to support current and future projects. (AFKM Home Page, 2001)

The AFKM system was designed to be used as a portal. The main portal entry point is the AFKM Hub (or AFKM home page) which includes access to Lessons Learned, DoD Acquisition Deskbook, AFMC Help Center, Virtual Schoolhouse, and CoP workspaces. The AFKM Hub evolved from the original Lessons Learned Web site and now serves as the access point to a range of knowledge

Figure 4. AFKM system components

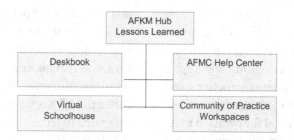

Figure 5. AFKM home page

and information resources. The DoD Acquisition Deskbook provides a variety of documents describing the laws, directives, policies, and regulations related to DoD acquisitions. The AFMC Help Center provides an English-language search engine for both AFMC and other customers to find information or documents that may reside on any of the many AFMC Web sites. The Virtual Schoolhouse delivers over 20 online courses for AF acquisition training. And finally, the CoP workspaces allow for information exchange, collaboration, and problem solving. The specific functions of each of these portal components is further described in Appendix 3.

CASE DESCRIPTION

It wasn't long after Adkins had taken charge of the AFKM program that he realized it was approaching a crossroads. Specifically, a strategic vision and plan for the future of the program and underlying system was lacking. With strong lead-

ership support and sufficient funding, the AFKM program and system had grown; however, there were now a variety of emerging issues that had to be considered in any future KM strategy development. Some of these key issues are discussed.

Leadership Support

As the deputy director of AFMC/DR, Robert Mulcahy had been a staunch supporter and champion of AFMC's KM efforts. It was his vision that had brought the program together under Adkins. He knew the value of creating the AFKM program and understood the benefits it could bring to AFMC, the AF, and the DoD. Mulcahy had protected and given support to the AFKM System Development Team so that it could expand and explore new opportunities. He believed all of AFMC, not just the headquarters organization, could benefit from KM. Mulcahy was a key reason the AFKM program was successful.

Upon Mulcahy's departure to a new job in early 2000, David Franke was appointed as his replacement. Major General Michael Wiedemer had also become the new Director of Requirements. Both were very open to KM concepts and the AFKM program, but neither was as educated or enthused about KM as Mulcahy had been. Franke, to whom Adkins primarily reported, was not sure that KM should be a centerpiece of AFMC strategy. Franke saw the primary benefits of KM as coming from the building "of" and participation "in" communities of practice. While encouraging Adkins and the AFKM Team to continue their pursuits, he did not have a firm vision for KM or the AFKM program in the future. He was also not sure that AFKM could compete with other programs for additional resources given all the other AFMC priorities. All in all, it was Adkins' assessment that Franke simply didn't see KM as needing emphasis above and beyond other programs. As a result, Adkins predicted that he might have increased difficulty getting the backing and exposure for AFKM that it needed to compete with other AFMC programs for scarce resources.

Conflict with AFMC's IT Organization

Dealing with the headquarters' information technology (IT) organization, referred to as the Directorate of Communications and Information, was a continual challenge. This organization saw many conflicts between its responsibilities and the direction being pursued by the AFKM System Development Team. The Directorate saw its role as providing technology solutions; AFKM was also providing technology solutions. Although the conflict had not escalated to an intolerable level, Adkins noted that his Team and the IT folks "just didn't talk anymore."

Within HQ AFMC, the Directorate of Communications and Information had primary responsibility for command, control, communications, computer, and information (C4I) issues and execution. As such, it possessed sole authority for policy, procedures, and standards with respect to C4I systems and programs. As the AFKM System Development Team expanded its efforts, a con-

flict had arisen regarding collaboration software tools. The IT organization had mandated and implemented LiveLink® software as the only authorized collaboration tool. This action not only conflicted with the AFKM System Development Team's work on CoP workspaces, but appeared to be, in the Team's estimation, a much more sophisticated collaboration tool than was needed by the average customer. Based on the AFKM Team's in-depth experience, Adkins had tried to convince the IT folks that an AFMC-wide LiveLink® implementation would be a waste of money at this point. Although Adkins had hoped to work with the IT organization on KM issues, this "disagreement" had driven them farther apart. Adkins stated:

We've had numerous discussions, but we have never been able to partner. So they're off getting everybody to do LiveLink®, trying to force everybody to do LiveLink®. I'm off trying just to get people stuff to help them do their jobs better.

Knowledge of the conflict with the IT organization was not limited to the HQ either. When asked by Adkins about his experience with LiveLink®, one of his CoP customers had remarked, "I will tell you . . . you are on the radar warning receiver. They know you're out there and you are a huge threat to them."

Although Adkins had been able to continue the AFKM efforts, he knew the conflict with the IT organization, regarding LiveLink® and other information system issues, was not going away. Since both organizations claimed a role in providing and establishing KM systems, disputes would be ongoing. While Adkins and his Team had a wealth of KM knowledge and system development expertise, the IT organization was still the authorized policy maker. If conflicts continued, the AFKM program and system risked being changed, dismantled, or simply "taken over." This, too, was something that weighed heavily on Adkins' mind.

Funding Cuts

It was Adkins' understanding that a $600,000 budget cut was in the offing for 2001. Such a cut would force him to make hard choices that would affect the AFKM program's future. In practical terms, the budget cut would require Adkins to let go of six AFKM System Development Team contractor personnel. If cuts did come to pass, he knew he would have to reassess, reprioritize, and reorganize the current AFKM system development workload distribution.

Adkins was also worried about the impact on AFKM system customers. From its inception, the AFKM program had attempted to serve a wide range of customers. Whether it was supporting DoD-wide efforts such as Deskbook, AFMC internal efforts such as the Help Center, or outside command efforts such as the Engineering and Technical Services CoP for Air Combat Command, the AFKM System Development Team had eagerly built new applications. While some of the projects had been fully funded by the requesting customers, many had been accomplished on an as-can-pay basis or without funding support at all. Adkins knew that without AFKM program funding assistance, some customers would never be able to get their KM efforts off the ground. With the budget cuts looming, customer support practices would have to be reevaluated as well.

AFKM System Usage Concerns

Despite rave reviews about the usefulness of the AFKM system from customers, Adkins was disturbed by low use, or "hit" rates. Simple system access metrics showed that, although use continued to rise, it was only a small portion of what it could or should be. To counter this phenomenon, Adkins and the AFKM System Development Team attempted to improve awareness with a series of road shows. They traveled to many AFMC bases to market the AFKM system's many capabilities. While this effort had increased usage somewhat, overall AFKM usage was still low. From a macro view, Adkins understood that KM and the AFKM system tools were still in their infancy. However, the low usage statistics did not help the AFKM System Development Team justify the benefit or the budget. Adkins was glad that his superiors had supported the Team's efforts on intuition and common sense; however, he also understood that he could be asked at any time to measure the true impact and return on investment. Remarking about the necessity of good metrics, Adkins said, "we had a budget drill not too long ago where I lost a little bit of money and some people . . . that reinforced the fact that I needed better metrics." In preparation of such requests, Adkins needed to seriously consider how he could improve results.

Lack of Understanding about KM

Adkins constantly encountered a lack of knowledge about KM. Few individuals, at any level across AFMC, had much idea of what KM was all about. Adding to the confusion was the fact that there seemed to be no accepted standard definition for KM. While it was easy to communicate the importance of individual KM applications, such as lessons learned databases, document repositories, and electronic yellow pages for experts, it was much more difficult to explain the more comprehensive KM concepts. This made it hard to get people interested in the purpose and goals of the AFKM program. Adkins realized that "learning about KM" took time, but also understood that ignorance by those whom he relied on for support could threaten the AFKM program's survival before it really had a chance to prove itself on a large scale. Again, any strategy for the future of AFKM had to address an education element.

Technological Challenges

The AFKM System Development Team was facing technological challenges even though it was very skilled in responding to the fast-paced changes in technology. In the past, it had Web enabled all of its products, making extensive use of technologies such as HTML, java script, active server pages, and so forth. After the Deskbook, Lessons Learned, and Help Center products achieved stability, the Team continued development efforts and had found a niche in developing CoP workspaces for customers. The Team became so efficient in developing workspaces that it could hand over a "CoP in a box" with a few minor customer-specific tweaks in only a few days' time. Instead of providing content, as it had done with Deskbook and Lessons Learned systems, the Team now simply provided the software framework and the customer became responsible for adding the information and knowledge. Actually, the CoP workspace component had been an important addition to the AFKM system as it had resulted in immediate benefits to various customers and helped to spread the word about the AFMC KM efforts. Adkins believed that continued development of CoPs might, in time, provide a central focus for the AFKM System Development Team's development efforts.

Along with this development, however, another technological challenge had arisen with the development of the AF portal. The new AF portal was to be, by decree, the de facto "single access point" for all AF information and knowledge. This raised a key question of how to design future AFKM system applications. Adkins acknowledged that his team was still heavily involved in the "technology piece" of building CoPs, but saw that the capabilities of the AF portal might eventually change that. Because the AF portal offered some "community" features, he saw the technical nature of the AFKM Team's work on CoPs possibly changing. As such, he now had to consider yet another host of issues such as how should AFKM products tie in to the AF portal? How could the AFKM Team take advantage of AF portal capabilities? Would the AFMC-centered KM system lose its identity and mission with

the establishment of the AF portal? Would the AF Portal provide new collaboration tools that would conflict or supersede those developed by the team at AFMC? These questions, again, made a clear future strategy very difficult for Adkins to envision.

The AFKM Name

Another issue for consideration in AFKM strategy development involved the AFKM name. When the AFKM Team began the Deskbook and Lessons Learned initiatives, there were no other known KM programs in the AF. This situation, combined with the fact that the Lessons Learned tool was originally designed to serve the entire AF, gave cause for the Team to label the program "AF" KM instead of "AFMC" KM. As time passed, however, KM initiatives began popping up across the service and the "AF" KM label seemed suddenly inappropriate. A representative from the AF chief information officer's office, who was heading the AF-wide KM movement, had even called Adkins to insist that his program's name be changed to avoid confusion with what would become the real AF-wide KM program.

Adkins realized this was not a simple name change from "AFKM" to "AFMC KM" — it had significant implications for his organization. On the positive side, Adkins thought a name change might actually be a good thing. With other KM initiatives surfacing throughout the AF and with the advent of the AF portal, he had found that the title "AFKM" was no longer descriptive of what his Team was providing. His thoughts were that the specific AFMC KM system and products had to be identifiable, especially now that they would be "buried" behind the AF portal. He used the following example:

And so, if I was Joe Blow out there at Ogden Air Logistics Center and I open the [AF] Portal and I happen to see this link [AFKM Hub], I wouldn't click on it . . . because I don't have any idea [of what it is] unless I happened to have that wonderful briefing we gave them.

On the negative side, Adkins knew a name change wasn't that simple. In addition to generating confusion among existing customers, a name change could signal a reduction in program scope and applicability, which might ultimately impact leadership support at the highest levels and funding.

Outsourcing AFKM Strategy

Since the initial collection of programs and systems (e.g., Deskbook and Lessons Learned) had been brought under the AFKM umbrella, Adkins had lacked a coherent strategy to guide future developments. Although most of the previous work of the AFKM Team had been technology-oriented, Adkins realized that a more comprehensive KM strategy that also addressed people and cultural issues was needed. So far, most AFKM program and system development priorities had been opportunistically selected depending on funding source and visibility potential, but were not consistent with an overall objective or strategy. However, with so many issues developing that could ultimately impact AFKM's existence, Adkins realized that a strategic vision, and ultimately an implementation road map, were needed to guide future AFKM developments and to help him make "hard decisions."

Not confident that he or the existing AFKM System Development Team had the expertise or time to develop a comprehensive strategic plan and roadmap on their own, Adkins contracted to AeroCorp[2] to lead the development. Although AeroCorp contractor personnel had composed a portion of the AFKM System Development Team all along, Adkins had only recently selected them as the primary contractor due to their growing KM expertise. To their credit, AeroCorp, with more than 5,000 employees nationwide, had successfully completed other government KM projects since 1997. In outsourcing to AeroCorp, Adkins justified his decision by saying,

We find AeroCorp provides unique benefits to the government and is the best value for the technical services required. AeroCorp rates are competitive with the other contractors reviewed; AeroCorp is a highly regarded supporter of KM at the OSD [Office of the Secretary of Defense] level; AeroCorp is the developer of the AFKM Virtual Schoolhouse; and AeroCorp has proven integration expertise. In addition, AeroCorp rated extremely high in the area of customer service and past performance.

Although the final statement of work for the AeroCorp contract reflected a number of specific deliverables (see Appendix 4) that ranged from strategic visioning to deployment plan and execution, Adkins' foremost concern was the development of the AFKM strategic vision and plan (or roadmap). These documents would be key in helping him to decide the future direction of AFKM. With a strategic vision and road map, he would have at least a starting point for decision making.

CURRENT CHALLENGES/PROBLEMS FACING THE ORGANIZATION

Randy Adkins had hoped that by outsourcing the AFKM strategy development to AeroCorp that resolution of major issues associated with the evolution of the AFKM program and system would be addressed. The statement of work outlined that it was AeroCorp's job to do the following (HQ AFMC/DRI, 2000):

1. Help AFMC management define a strategic vision for KM to support the AF acquisition community mission.
2. Integrate the AFKM Lessons Learned database, AFMC Help Center, and the Virtual

Schoolhouse into a single dynamic system based on this strategic vision.

3. Provide support to these existing systems throughout the integration effort and ultimately for the integrated AFKM system.

AeroCorp's initial deliverable was to build an AFKM strategic vision and plan within 60 days. According to the statement of work, this plan should incorporate both the cultural and technical aspects of the acquisition environment. The resultant document was to include a road map of how to proceed from the current business environment to the envisioned environment (HQAFMC/DRI, 2000).

Consequences of Outsourcing KM Strategy Development

The first action taken by AeroCorp under the new contract was to conduct both a cultural and technical needs assessment "snapshot" of AFMC with respect to KM. These needs assessments were to provide the "as is" picture of AFMC's environment while providing recommendations for the "to be" vision and the necessary supporting policies and processes. Actual completion of the needs assessments went rather quickly and were presented to Adkins in early 2001. Each report included both specific, one-liner recommendations for transitioning from the "as is" state to the "to be" state, and an additional section provided an even more in-depth description of recommendations of what needed to be done to achieve the "to be" state. These assessments with the final recommendation descriptions are detailed in Appendix 5. On the whole, the assessments were comprehensive and surfaced many technical and cultural issues that had to be addressed if AFMC was to transform itself into a true knowledge-sharing organization. These final reports, however, were not what Adkins had expected the strategic vision and plan document to be. The recommendations captured the complicated nature of the current AFMC en-

vironment yet, while providing a good road map for the future, were so broad and involved that it was difficult to determine a starting point. To further compound his disappointment, Adkins also learned that AeroCorp considered completion of the assessment reports as having not only fulfilled deliverable #1, the AFKM Strategic Vision and Plan, but also deliverable #2, the AFKM Integration Recommendations Document. He was baffled.

Although Adkins had not gotten exactly what he expected from AeroCorp, the company was allowed to continue work on the remaining deliverables. Adkins hoped that the subsequent documents would make things clearer. Deliverable #3, the AFKM Integration Blueprint, which AeroCorp referred to as a KM methodology, took much longer to produce than the assessments. Delays resulted, first of all, from the turnover of two AeroCorp program managers during early 2001. The current program manager, Mike Lipka, though very knowledgeable about KM, was relatively new to AeroCorp and had to get up to speed on the AFKM project. The key delay, however, stemmed from the fact that AeroCorp had difficulty developing a concise KM methodology or "blueprint" that could address the enormity of what AFMC needed to do to develop a comprehensive KM program that would help it evolve into a true knowledge-sharing organization.

Although the initial assessment and recommendations documents had stated that a systems engineering approach would be used to design the "integration blueprint," the use of integrated definition (IDEF) process modeling methodology surprised Adkins and Lipka. Neither Adkins, nor his superiors, were familiar with this methodology. Lipka, having not been the program manager when the decision to use IDEF was made, had not seen it applied to KM before. Developed for use in systems engineering, IDEF modeling had been around for quite a few years. Its primary users had been the DoD and other large organizations. IDEF had originated with the AF's Integrated

Computer Aided Manufacturing (ICAM) program in the mid 1970s, but had evolved over the past six or seven years to also address modeling enterprise and business areas. As such, it was used for modeling "as is" enterprise processes and defining information requirements for improved planning. On the whole, there were 14 separate methods being developed within the IDEF family for use in business process engineering and reengineering, software process definition and improvement, and software development and maintenance areas. It provided a multitude of viewpoints required to describe business area processes and software life-cycle processes and activities. As such, it stood that IDEF could be appropriate for modeling an enterprise approach to KM and subsequent KM systems development, but it did not appear to be a really usable methodology for the average customer. After seeing the initial draft of the high-level IDEF model (Figure 6), neither Adkins nor Lipka were satisfied. Lipka expressed his opinion thus: "I think we have too much methodology for what we need . . . I think it's [been] a little overengineered."

No one was more frustrated, however, than Adkins. After almost a year of working with AeroCorp and waiting patiently for a strategic vision and plan he could really use to press forward, what he had now was a cultural and technical needs assessment, some recommendations for transitioning AFMC into a knowledge-sharing organization, and a road map (or methodology) for doing so that was too unfamiliar and complicated for him or others to practically implement. And faced with the impending budget cut, it did not appear that AeroCorp would have the opportunity to make needed changes. Adkins knew, however, as the AFKM program lead he was still responsible for the strategic direction and success of the AFKM program. He was unsure exactly what to do next, but he knew the responsibility for a solution was his alone. He began to ponder the facts and options. Would he ever get a document from AeroCorp that would provide a KM strategy and vision for AFMC? Had he made a mistake in outsourcing AFKM strategy development? If not, would there be time and money for AeroCorp to prepare something that was more practical? What

Figure 6. AeroCorp's Proposed KM Blueprint (IDEF model)

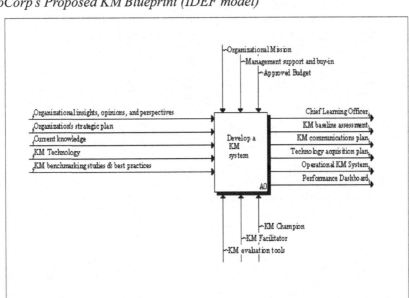

parts of the needs assessments and strategic plan were usable? In absence of a clear KM strategy for AFMC, what was the right direction for his AFKM Team to take? How did the AFKM effort now fit (technically and conceptually) into the evolving AF-level KM approach? Would his AFKM program and Team survive? At this point, Adkins had no good answers. The only thing he knew for sure was that there had been and would continue to be many challenges in bringing KM to AFMC, but it was he, if anyone, who still had the opportunity to make it a reality.

REFERENCES

AFKM Home Page. (2001). Information Page. Retrieved August 7, 2001, from *https://afkm. wpafb.af.mil/ASPs/Tabs/Entry_Subject.asp* [only accessible from .mil domains]

Cho, G., Jerrell, H., & Landay, W. (2000). *Program management 2000: Know the way how knowledge management can improve DoD acquisition.* Fort Belvoir: Defense Systems Management College.

HQ AFMC/DRI. (2000). *Statement of work.* Wright-Patterson AFB, OH: Air Force Knowledge Management Integration and Support.

HQ AFMC PA. (2001a). Air Force Material Command fact sheet. Retrieved October 17, 2001, from *www.afmc-pub.wpafb.af.mil/HQ-AFMC/ PA/fact_sheet/afmcfact.htm*

HQ AFMC PA. (2001b). HQ AFMC/DR home page. Retrieved October 17, 2001, from *https:// afkm.wpafb.af.mil/ASPs/Tabs/Entry_Subject.asp* [only accessible from .mil domains]

ENDNOTES

* The views expressed in this case study are those of the authors and do not necessarily reflect the official policy or position of the Air Force, the Department of Defense, or the U.S. Government.

[1] Information for this case, except where stated otherwise, is based on personal interviews conducted in October 2001.

[2] Pseudonyms have been used to protect the confidentiality of the contract organiza-

APPENDIX 1: AIR FORCE MATERIAL COMMAND MISSION ESSENTIAL TASKS AND OBJECTIVES

Tasks	Objectives
Product Support	To provide world class products and services, delivering dominant aerospace systems and superior life cycle management.
Information Services	To develop, acquire, integrate, implement, protect and sustain combat support information systems for the USAF and DoD customers.
Supply Management	To provide and deliver repairable and consumable items (right product -- right place -- right time -- right price).
Depot Maintenance	To repair systems and spare parts that ensure readiness in peacetime and provide sustainment to combat forces in wartime.
Science and Technology	To develop, demonstrate and transition affordable advanced technologies to achieve AF Core Competencies.
Test and Evaluation	To provide timely, accurate and affordable knowledge and resources to support weapons and systems research, development and employment.
Information Management	To provide secure, reliable, interoperable communication and information services/access anytime, anywhere, to AFMC customers, partners and employees.
Installations and Support	To provide base support services, property management and environmental protection at AFMC installations.
Combat Support	To provide the trained and equipped expeditionary combat support forces and capabilities to meet worldwide taskings.

(HQ AFMC PA, 2001a)

APPENDIX 2: AFKM TEAM AND STRUCTURE

Throughout the history of the AFKM program, contractors played a key role. Although final authority was always vested in a military officer or civil service employee assigned to AFMC/DR, most programming and technology for the AFKM System came from contractors. The primary contractor for the DoD Acquisition Deskbook development had been Company A². With additional projects, Company B² and Company C² joined the team. The specific responsibilities and tasks varied from year to year as projects evolved and as the contracts were renewed and renegotiated. The resulting AFKM program organization is shown in the Figure 1 below. AeroCorp was charged with establishing the basic AFKM program by bringing together the existing AFKM Lessons Learned database, AFMC Help Center, and Virtual Schoolhouse. Most of the AFKM System Development Team's work was split between maintaining and updating existing functions and developing new applications. A majority of the new applications focused on building workspaces for CoPs. Each contractor used a number of personnel to work on projects—some personnel worked on AFKM projects exclusively while others came in and out of the projects as necessary. Prior to the 2001 budget cuts, with AeroCorp acting as the lead contractor, 41 personnel had been assigned to the AFKM Team.

Figure 1. AFKM Team Structure

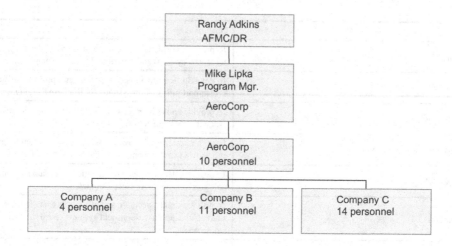

APPENDIX 3: EXPLANATION OF AFKM SYSTEM COMPONENTS

AFKM Hub. What is now the AFKM Hub was originally the primary website for the AF Lessons Learned utility. Although the website has evolved, the Lessons Learned are still the centerpiece of the Hub (Figure 1). Lessons Learned have been captured and categorized by subject area and provide valuable knowledge about past processes and events. The AFKM Hub also acts as a portal for all other AFKM components and, as such, it also serves as the default AFKM home page. The AFKM Hub provides a conduit to select relevant information and knowledge resources and provides an avenue for creating a knowledge-sharing organization.

Figure 1. AFKM Hub

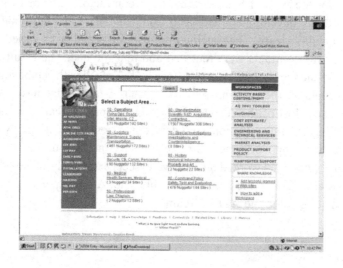

Figure 2. Defense Acquisition Deskbook

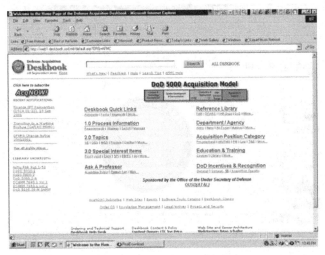

Deskbook. The DoD Acquisition Deskbook (Figure 2) is an automated reference tool that provides the most current acquisition information for all DoD Services and Agencies. Deskbook simplifies the acquisition process by maintaining a single source of up-to-date reference material on acquisition policy and practices.

AFMC Help Center. The AFMC Help Center (Figure 3) allows AFMC customers to perform a natural language or keyword search of over 130 AFMC websites and selected databases. It connects AFMC customers throughout the AF and DoD with the appropriate

AFMC information source or point of contact. The search engine used dynamically creates a unique results page separated into four categories:

- Ranked list of related web documents and links
- Top priority Major Command issues
- Bulletin board discussion entries
- Contact information for the AFMC command liaisons and topic area points of contact.

Figure 3. AFMC Help Center

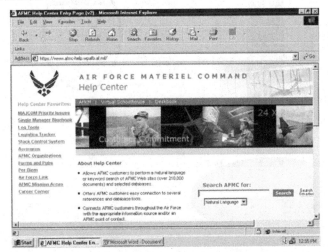

Figure 4. Virtual Schoolhouse component

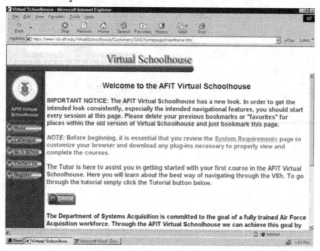

Virtual Schoolhouse. The Virtual Schoolhouse (Figure 4) is a cooperative effort between AFMC/DR and the AF Institute of Technology (AFIT). The Virtual Schoolhouse provides an integrated Web-based learning management system with over 20 on-line courses. Its purpose is to support the goal of a fully trained AF acquisition workforce.

CoP Workspaces. A community of practice (CoP) is a network of people who share a common goal. CoP workspaces are virtual environments where members of these CoPs can exchange information to complete work tasks and solve problems. Each CoP serves a specific customer set. The AFKM Hub provides workspaces (Figure 5) for a variety of CoPs.

Figure 5. Community of practice workspaces

APPENDIX 4: AEROCORP'S CONTRACT DELIVERABLES

1. **Deliverable 60 days:** AF Knowledge Management Strategic Vision and Plan
   - **Description:** A document that should incorporate both the cultural and technical aspects of the acquisition environment and include a "roadmap" from the current business environment to the envisioned environment.

2. **Deliverable 120 days:** AFKM Integration Recommendations Document
   - **Description:** An integration plan that should define user operational requirements with detailed cultural and technical consequences as well as time and material requirements to implement the recommendations.

3. **Deliverable:** AFKM Integration Blueprint
   - **Description:** Based on the approved integration plan, the blueprint document should show how the three existing knowledge management systems will operate in the new integrated environment.

4. **Deliverable:** AFKM Integrated Products
   - **Description:** The result of the contractor integrating the three AFKM systems using a phased approach. Each integration effort should provide a working product that can be accessed by the acquisition users in the organizational environment.

5. **Deliverable:** AFKM Deployment Plan and Execution
   - **Description:** The plan should support the deployment of the AFKM system. It should identify user support; and release change management support, including training, communications, and measurement, as well as time and material requirements.

6. **Deliverable:** On-going AFKM Sustainment Support
   - **Description:** Sustainment support should be provided for all AFKM elements. The contractor should provide all the functional and technical support necessary for the maintenance and upkeep of the Lessons Learned, Help Center, and Virtual Schoolhouse components.

7. **Deliverable:** Contractor's Progress, Status, and Management Report
   - **Description:** The contractor should use a management and cost tracking system to support the AFKM effort and ensure technical and funding requirements are accomplished on time and on budget. The contractor should also maintain a continuing dialog with the government program manager to ensure that schedule and budgetary requirements are met and potential problems are proactively addressed. The contractor will prepare and submit monthly progress and financial reports summarizing the technical accomplishments and expenditures for each task.

8. **Deliverable:** Weekly / Monthly Functional Analysis Support Analysis Reports
   - **Description:** The contractor should provide fielded system product support analysis and readiness assessments as directed by HQ AFMC/DR based upon immediate supportability concerns of the command.

9. **Deliverable:** 180 days After Receipt of Order (ARO), Market Research Decision Support Tool
   - **Description:** The contractor should provide a Web-based decision support tool integrated within the Market Research Post Tool.

APPENDIX 5: AEROCORP CULTURAL AND TECHNICAL NEEDS ASSESSMENT AND RECOMMENDATIONS

Cultural Needs Assessment: Recommendation Descriptions

1. Design a KM Action Plan that combines the results of the Cultural Needs Assessment with the results of the Technical Needs Assessment. Data from both assessments will be used to design a "track to action" plan that includes:
    *   Methodology and systems engineering
    *   Project management procedures
*   Top business technical process needs to streamline for efficiency
2. Create a KM communications plan with a centralized formulation strategy. Establish a clear roadmap so that the big picture can be articulated to all groups; this includes leadership support of the decisions communicated. The communications plan should clearly define why a project is being done and the benefits to the employees. This should support the mission/vision of AFMC in regards to process improvement. Document the strategy and create a plan to achieve the strategy and explain how each project supports the mission/vision. Establish a clear vocabulary for communication of ideas across teams; standardization of vocabulary for communication of ideas across groups is essential. Initiate team building/communication activities to foster relationships across the organization (dialogue, inquiry versus advocacy). Balance being a visionary against execution of jobs.
3. Perform an Organizational Cultural Inventory (OCI) across AFMC. The OCI expands the point-in-time picture of the AFMC culture collected in this report to include a broader pool. The OCI pinpoints 12 specific types of behavioral norms which focus on behavioral patterns that members believe are required to accommodate the expectations of the organization. Norms are organized into three general clusters that distinguish between constructive cultures, passive/defensive cultures, and aggressive/defensive cultures. In addition to measuring shared behavioral norms, the OCI will also identify the ideal operating culture within an organization, providing an opportunity for quantitative data collection on information about the organization's culture at multiple levels and add additional confirmation to this qualitative Cultural Needs Assessment. This cultural alignment tool will determine the cultural issues prevalent within AFMC.
4. Develop a KM transition plan from current practices to the new KM system. Create a plan of action identifying those items that are helping and hindering AFMC from moving toward their business direction; determine the present state of organization, the desired state, and what must occur during the transition from one to the other. This transition plan should include both internal and external changes within the organization and do the following:
    *   Create or incorporate a change management plan that focuses on cultural (and technical) issues within AFMC. A great deal of disillusionment, discouragement, and resistance may need to be overcome. Include a cohesive story of where the group is going and what it is doing. Consider projects that empower people more with authority and accountability for measurable results.
    *   Establish clear documentation, which defines roles, responsibilities, and boundaries within AFMC. Create a detailed corporate plan on how business is to be conducted in AFMC and with its customers.

- Establish priorities with specifics that provide needed direction to be executed effectively. Have project contacts to call as subject matter experts. Establish clear transition points of projects between groups. Require that decisions be discussed at the appropriate leadership level prior to being evaluated to upper levels of leadership.
- Identify and change business processes that need to be changed so that business can be run more effectively and efficiently.
- Provide extensive training for all aspects of developed KM protocols.

5. Create an AFMC Knowledge market. The AFMC knowledge market concept has knowledge "buyers" (seekers of specific knowledge) and "sellers" (suppliers of specific knowledge) who negotiate to reach a mutually satisfactory price for the knowledge exchange. Knowledge "brokers" (people who know who in the organization possesses the information sought) would make connections between buyers and the sellers. Knowledge transactions occur because people expect that knowledge helps them solve problems and succeed in their work. The knowledge market design puts into perspective the sharing culture and provides a framework for formulating actionable steps for building each category within AFMC. In addition, the knowledge market will work more efficiently if places are created where people can meet to buy and sell knowledge. Establish "talk rooms" where researchers are expected to spend 20 to 30 minutes casually discussing each other's work. Several organizations have held "knowledge fairs" at which sellers display their expertise for others in the organization. Intranet discussion groups provide an electronic gathering place for people to share knowledge.

6. Establish a multidisciplined AFMC KM integration team. This team will work on organizational and KM technical and continuous improvement teams. The initial tasks assigned to the team will be to do the following:
- Organize in such a way that all AFMC interests and disciplines are represented.
- Determine clear and measurable business and technical processes.
- Identify areas where activities overlap and create a business plan which includes management and technical requirements, with metrics to measure the success or failure of the effort. The metric system will be aligned directly with the business case issues and the KM requirements such that it will access and demonstrate incremental progress being made across the AFMC organization.
- Develop a reporting mechanism for continuous improvement item tracking to keep record of items that have been successfully identified (based on data collections) and resolved. Report the findings to AFMC management. Establishment of a clearly defined measurement process will provide the momentum and sustainment of the KM program.
- Foster a workplace that lends itself toward continuous improvement versus policing or auditing of organization information. The ideal workplace would be where people's growth and participation occur within the framework of open teamwork, collaboration, and open flow of new ideas. This way, a link exists between the bottom and top of the organization. Address leadership styles and determine which leadership style is appropriate for which situation (situational leadership).

7. Create a KM Executive Board to oversee KM implementation activities. The KM Executive Board will include community-wide members whose major role is to define the AFMC KM requirements. Create a KM Executive Board Charter. Start a focused pilot (business case development, lessons learned deployment, strategy, etc.). AFMC leadership needs to know and participate on the Board,

chaired by the Deputy AFMC Commander. The AFMC Chief Learning Officer (CLO) should serve as the liaison between the integration team and the KM Executive Board. The responsibilities of the Board should include:

- Endorsing mechanisms for transferring knowledge within the organization, including creating a knowledge map, providing mentoring programs, encouraging job transfers, and holding knowledge fairs.

7A. Approving the use of Rapid Improvement Teams (RITs) to work complex issues that the community is either unable to agree on a remedy or for which attempted remedies have not worked. The integration team should recommend RIT campaigns as a part of its activities. The CLO would serve as the RIT sponsor and bring RIT recommendations to the KM Executive Board for approval.

8. Launch a reshaping mission by the AFMC Commander that links the KM strategy to the AFMC Acquisition and Sustainment Strategic Vision and Plan. The architecture for the KM capability must be explicitly linked to the business processes that are required to implement the AFMC KM Strategic Plan. Without this linkage, one of these two planning elements becomes irrelevant as a guide for achieving AFMC's long-term interests. Establish a task force consisting of representatives from SAF/AQ, AFMC, and each center that will report to the Executive Board. The task force would rely on the collective ideas of many people throughout the AF community, using a number of approaches to obtain input from industry, academia, other federal agencies, members of the acquisition workforce, and employee unions. The task force deliverable should outline initiatives to make it easier and more efficient to manage, reshape the acquisition workforce, and advance the current AFMC program to share best practices within the AFMC acquisition workforce. By documenting the deficiencies in the availability of core knowledge; the effectiveness of knowledge capture, storage, and retrieval systems; and the adequacy of personnel skills and attitudes; AFMC will be able to establish tailored remedies that will provide the most efficient knowledge management capability to its members, partners, and customers. The task force should work in concert with the AFMC internal KM team's objectives.

9. Establish a rewards and incentive policy for sharing knowledge. To ensure that such people will share their expertise, AFMC management must make sharing more lucrative than hoarding knowledge. To establish value, evaluation criteria should be established, written, and eventually incorporated in the Human Resources evaluation process so as to provide direct evidence of AFMC employees being rewarded for sharing knowledge. The reward policies should be valuable, such as substantial monetary awards, high recognition, salary increases, or promotions. Such incentives promote a shift in behavior toward nurturing a sharing culture.

Technical Needs Assessment: Recommendation Descriptions

1. Develop a technology evaluation and approval mechanism that explicitly links requirements for new information technology to process improvements that impact mission accomplishment and customer satisfaction. As organizations have begun to recognize the value of KM to their future well–being, technology providers have been scrambling to recast their data warehousing, intranet, document management, workflow, etc., products and the ultimate KM solution. All of these providers fall short in that KM solutions are not "one size fits all" but, rather, organization specific. Without a business strategy, there is no rational basis to evaluate the various technology solutions and craft a KM toolkit that delivers value to the organization and its customers. Organizational

evaluation, then, needs to start with an assessment of the mission and business strategy. Value chain activities (research, develop, test, acquire, deliver, and support) should be used as the first level of indenture for evaluating AFMC's KM system.

2. Review AFMC Web sites and identify improvements to increase their effectiveness in making knowledge available to the users. When Web technology was new and viewed as a supplement to accomplishing work, efficiency did not seem very important. Web engineers were more concerned with the eye appeal and user friendliness of the site than whether it provided valuable information. Users readily accepted the fact that they would be directed through several Web sites before accessing any meaningful information. Today, however, the Web is becoming a key work tool for many of AFMC's personnel. For this reason, reduction in search and retrieval time and one-click access to information is no longer an option, but a necessity. All AFMC Web sites should be reviewed for their ability to provide value-added knowledge to the workforce.

3. Establish a working group to reduce redundancy in transactional databases. Much of the KM literature is focused on collaboration and the extraction of tacit knowledge. However, the foundation of an organization's knowledge and the source of many of its business metrics are found in its rather mundane workhorse transactional data systems. Several of the interviewees for this assessment commented on their inability to trust the data without independent validation. They reported that the same data element could be found in multiple sources with different values. Technology in and of itself cannot fix this problem, but enforcing the rules of good data management can go a long way to establishing trust in the data. Among these rules is assigning responsibility for ensuring the validity of each data element to the maximum possible extent. Each AFMC CoP should form a working group comprised of its database managers to address issues of data accuracy, replication transparency, and report validity.

4. Establish a task force to improve the capture of tacit knowledge from CoP designated experts. Each CoP has its own set of expert and tacit knowledge that should be captured and put in the organization's knowledge repositories. The pervasive dilemma is that expert knowledge is the most difficult to obtain because it often is ill-defined (knowledge holders do not know what they should be contributing) and difficult to provide (experts are usually too busy to provide this knowledge).Every CoP has its novices, apprentices, masters, and gurus. Each of these experience levels has an expectation for the knowledge that is required to perform work. An effective KM system should capture knowledge from the top of the experience pyramid and pass that knowledge down and across the CoP. Learning tools, such as the Virtual Schoolhouse, could provide training to knowledge workers on how to determine what constitutes value-added knowledge.The second important aspect of this recommendation is how to influence the collection of this kind of subjective knowledge. It is important that this not be viewed as an additional duty but as a routine and fundamental part of the job. Performance metrics should include contributions to the knowledge base. Technical equipment (e.g., electronic notes and journals) or personal whiteboards may make it easier to contribute.

5. Develop a plan for reducing restricted access to data and data repositories.An effective KM system is open to all participants. Though we are all familiar with the phrase "knowledge is power," many organizations have cultures that treat knowledge as political capital—something to be hoarded and shared only when it is deemed advantageous. If KM is to flourish, that cultural value needs to change from "having knowledge" to "sharing knowledge." Therefore, AFMC should review

internally imposed firewalls and password protections to determine those that are needed for security or sensitive data reasons. AFMC should also consider using software that reduces the need for blanket restrictions.

6. Create a metadata-tagging plan to improve AFMC's ability to search and retrieve stored knowledge. AFMC currently uses user profile metadata to improve ease of access to Web-enabled search engines. However, user profiles are limited if the desired data files are not also tagged. It is relatively easy to issue a policy that requires all new data files to be appropriately marked. The real question is "How much of the legacy data can AFMC afford to retroactively tag?" This raises the economic questions of return on investment. AFMC should create a plan that provides the necessary guidelines for tagging data files.

7. Require each AFMC CoP to develop a collaboration plan. Knowledge-based activities related to innovation and responsiveness are highly collaborative. The attention that AFMC pays to collaboration can be attributed to its role in leveraging the expertise that is often distributed throughout the organization. Frequently, a CoP—the epitome of a collaborative body—cuts across formal organizational boundaries. A CoP often extends across departments and into other organizations, including customers, allies, partners, and sometimes competitors. The range of collaboration enabling technology can present a daunting task to the people responsible for selecting the best solution for their organizations. Additionally, collaboration needs might vary from one CoP to another. AFMC should require each of its formally recognized CoPs to develop a collaboration plan that describes how that community intends to foster collaborative activity and the recommended technology to enable that collaboration.

SUPPORT MATERIAL: QUESTIONS AND ANSWERS

1. **What was the overall problem in this case?**

    The overall problem in this case was that Randy Adkins saw the need to develop a comprehensive vision and strategy to guide AFMC KM efforts. He felt that without such a vision and strategy he could not adequately guide and the lead the AFKM program and systems development for which he was responsible.

2. **What were the issues that affecting the central problem in this case?**

    The issues impacting this problem were many. They included loss of leadership support and funding, conflict with the IT organization, technological changes, "AFKM" program name legitimacy, lack of KM understanding and expertise, and the consequences of outsourcing KM strategy development.

3. **What grade would you give Randy Adkins as the AFKM Team Leader? Why?**

    Although this case seems to portray Randy Adkins as not having made much progress, he had been key in bringing KM to the forefront in AFMC. Not only was he very educated about KM, but also enthusiastic and evangelistic. He knew the benefits KM could yield to AFMC, even if he didn't exactly know how to make it happen. Because he and his AFKM Team were "buried" at the lowest levels of the AFMC hierarchy makes what they accomplished even more remarkable. Early leadership support from his boss, Mulcahy, was very important, but Adkins continued to carry the torch after he was gone. Adkins may have made some errors in judgment associated with outsourcing AFKM, but worked diligently and made significant progress in bringing KM to all of AFMC through the AFKM System.

4. **How did Randy Adkins and his Team describe the concept of KM? What was the primary focus of the AFKM System Development Team in providing KM to AFMC?**

    The AFKM Team conceptualized KM as practices that should be used to enhance organizational performance by explicitly designing and implementing tools, processes, systems, structures, and cultures to improve the creation, sharing, and use of knowledge that was critical for decision-making. With this concept in mind, the AFKM System Development team focused on "designing and implementing tools" aspect which resulted in development of the five-component AFKM System.

5. **What do think about Adkins' decision to outsource the AFKM Strategy Development?**

    Adkins didn't have the expertise to build a KM strategy that addressed the whole of the AFMC enterprise as well as the particulars of the AFKM Program (and system) he was responsible for. It was a huge task that required skill, expertise, and time he did not have which why he hired AeroCorp. The first lesson learned, however, was that a statement of work for any contract was only as good as expertise held by its authors. In the case of outsourcing to AeroCorp, the statement of work did not adequately define what Adkins needed. The second lesson learned was that with outsourcing, when the money runs out the project stops. Adkins began to question his decision early on as the contract deliverables were not met.

6. **What final solution would you recommend to Adkins at this point?**

    First of all, Adkins has to decide whether to continue with the decision to outsource strategy development or take some other approach. AeroCorp has done some valuable work, but the general recommendations and IDEF modeling have had no practical application for Adkins and his team. Secondly, given that he still has no strategic vision or plan, Adkins must decide what to do in the short term. He has some of the following choices:

    a. *Given additional funding, push AeroCorp to deliver a more concise vision and strategic plan.*

    b. *Develop his own strategy limited in scope to the AFKM Team. As such, the Team can continue maintaining existing AFKM systems and/or expand the community of practice focus.*

    c. *Continue to push for high-level AFMC and AF leadership support for AFKM and other KM initiatives.*

    Given the current political situation and lack of funding, it would appropriate for Adkins to focus on those issues under his direct control (i.e. the AFKM Team). He could push AeroCorp for a better strategy product, but that would be at the expense of other things his Team could accomplish on its own. To increase the AFKM System capabilities, such as an expanded CoP component, to better serve a larger customer base could build support for KM from the bottom-up while Adkins and the AFKM Team continue to champion KM from the top-down.

Epilogue and Lessons Learned

Epilogue

At the end of the time period discussed in this case Randy Adkins was truly at a crossroads. He was convinced of the value of KM and the AFKM System for AFMC and the AF as a whole, but was wisely concerned that many others were not. He understood, given the many issues that could potentially threaten the existence of the AFKM program, that he needed a strategic vision and plan to guide the future direction and decision-making, When his attempt to outsource AFMC KM strategy development met with limited success, he decided to re-scope his efforts. Instead of trying to lead the development of a KM strategy for all of AFMC, which required levels of leadership support he had not yet been able to gain, he made a conscious decision to focus the AFKM Team's work on a few key areas under their immediate control. From 2002 forward Adkins and his AFKM Team have focused on: 1) promoting communities of practice (CoPs) as a key technique for KM across the AF 2) providing an enterprise web search capability across AFMC and selected AF sites, and 3) using a process approach in delivering CoP capability. The AFKM Team's strategy ultimately became one of building momentum across the AF by providing KM services lightning fast (by developing "CoPs in a box") and following up with service support in terms of training and implementation guidance. As stated by Adkins himself, "We decided on our own to seek leadership support at the AF level as we determined there was a vacuum we could fill by demonstrating success at the grassroots level that leadership could observe for themselves" (R. Adkins, personal communication, September 13, 2004). Since the turn in strategy direction, Adkins and his team have had remarkable success. The AFKM website, now called AF Knowledge Now, continues to expand in both capability and customer base. Also, in early 2004, Adkins garnered key leadership support for the AFKM Team's efforts with recognition by the AF Chief Information Officer (AF CIO). The AF CIO recognized Adkins and his Team (AFMC/DR) as the AF Center of Excellence for Knowledge Management as well as made the decision to integrate AF Knowledge Now into the AF portal.

AFMC Case Lessons Learned

1. **KM is hard to define and communicate.** This case demonstrates, yet again, the recognized fact that no standard definition exists for KM. Although the case identifies a holistic working definition for KM used by the AFKM Team, it is apparent that much of their initial efforts were focused on the technology elements only. Additionally, because many KM concepts are hard to grasp, Adkins found it hard to communicate the elements and benefits of KM to superiors as well as to potential AFKM users. The case notes how Adkins consistently encountered a lack of understanding about KM which made it extremely hard for him to gain either bottom-up or top-down support.

2. **KM initiatives must be championed and supported at the highest levels of any organization.** Although Adkins had staunch leadership support early on, the situation changed with leadership turnover. Without top-level backing and involvement, he found it increasingly difficult to maintain adequate funding or get the necessary visibility to expand the AFKM effort across AFMC and the AF. The success of the many bottom-up KM initiatives, especially CoPs, have been a boon to the AFKM effort, but if KM is to be addressed at the AFMC enterprise level, the top-level leadership must be involved, supportive, and be ready to provide necessary resources.

3. **KM strategy development is not easy, yet critical.** The need for a KM strategy to guide organizational KM efforts is well-recognized. In this case, Adkins identified the need for an over-arching KM strategy for his Team's efforts as well as for AFMC early on. He saw a KM strategy as a necessary foundation for the decisions about AFKM's future he would have to make. KM strategy development requires time, expertise, and a keen knowledge of the business at hand. As demonstrated in this case, Adkins felt lacking in these areas so he outsourced the task. There are many recommended methodologies for developing a KM strategy, but whichever one is chosen must be appropriate for the organization and issues involved. AeroCorp had proven KM expertise, but did not understand how to develop a KM strategy that could address the complexity of the

AFMC enterprise and still be understandable and useful for the relatively small AFKM Team to implement.

4. **Outsourcing KM is risky.** Despite Adkins' attempt to outsource KM strategy development to a well-known, well-qualified contractor, he learned very quickly that there were pitfalls in such an approach. First of all, developing an accurate and robust statement of work is extremely challenging, especially for KM, when the expertise does not already exist in-house. Unless both parties are absolutely clear on the language and requirements (which has already been identified as a problem in this case), there is a great opportunity on both sides for disappointment with the outcome. Adkins was not satisfied with and could not use a majority of the products delivered to him by AeroCorp. Secondly, Adkins discovered he did not have much recourse when the contract did not go as expected. He certainly did not get the strategic vision and plan document that he desired, yet to have AeroCorp continue to work on the document and other contract deliverables would mean a commitment of more time and money he simply did not have. Finally, it became apparent to Adkins that AeroCorp did not have the intimate knowledge of the AFMC environment that was needed to provide a workable plan. As a contractor, AeroCorp could develop plans and methodologies for execution but was not in a position to implement. This led to a gap between recommendations from AeroCorp about what to do and what was actually feasible within the current AFMC context.

5. **Focusing on specific KM efforts is important.** By selecting specific KM initiatives that could easily demonstrate a return on investment, Adkins was eventually able to convince senior leadership of the benefit of KM. Prior to downscoping the original focus of his Team's efforts, Adkins was not able to concentrate attention and resources on a few key initiatives or to demonstrate significant impact. Once his refined strategy was in-place, he and his AFKM Team remained primarily focused on technology support of the KM effort. In doing so, it was easier to adapt appropriate implementation methodologies for each of the initiatives as well combine them into an integrated KM system.

List of Additional Sources

Books/Papers to Read:

Bartczak, S. E. (2002). *Identifying Barriers to Knowledge Management in the U.S. Military*, (Doctoral dissertation, Auburn University, 2002). Auburn, AL: Dissertation Abstracts International, 63, 4002.

Cho, G., Jerrell, H., & Landay, W. (2000). *Program Management 2000: Know the Way How Knowledge Management Can Improve DoD Acquisition*. Fort Belvoir: Defense Systems Management College.

Firestone, J. M., & McElroy, M. W. (2003). *Key Issues in the New Knowledge Management*. Boston: Butterworth-Heineman.

Havens, C., & Knapp, E. (1999). Easing Into Knowledge Management. *Strategy and Leadership*, *27*(2), 4-9.

Liebowitz, J. (Winter 2003-2004). A Knowledge Management Strategy for the Jason Organization*: A Case Study. *Journal of Computer Information Systems*, *XLIV*(2), 1-5.

Tiwana, A. (2000). *The Knowledge Management Toolkit*. Upper Saddle River: Prentice Hall PTR.

Zack, M. H. (1999). *Knowledge and Strategy*. Boston: Butterworth-Heinemann.

Web Sites to Visit

Air Force Knowledge Now Website (limited to .mil domain users) https://afkm.wpafb.af.mil/

Air Force Material Command Knowledge Now article http://www.afrlhorizons.com/Briefs/Dec02/HE0212.html

A Learning Transformation: The Eglin Learning Organization, Defense AT&L, (2004) http://www.dau.mil/pubs/dam/07_08_2004/dwye-ja04.pdf

Selected Reading IV
Measuring Organizational Readiness for Knowledge Management

W. A. Taylor
University of Bradford, UK

M. A. Schellenberg
University of Bradford, UK

ABSTRACT

While organizations continue to grapple with the implementation of knowledge management, there remains a need for empirical research into the practical difficulties they encounter. In this chapter, we investigate the challenges faced by one multinational telecommunications company in a post-merger environment. We develop an instrument to evaluate the knowledge-sharing culture and information infrastructure and, by using qualitative and quantitative data from a survey of five European sites, we illustrate how managers can measure gaps between the effectiveness of current practices and their importance, and decide whether to direct resources toward changing employee attitudes, organizational practices, or knowledge-management infrastructure. More significantly, we highlight the need for senior managers to be in agreement about the strategic direction of their business and the strategic alignment between business strategy and knowledge-management strategy. Without such consensus, knowledge management is likely to remain, at best, a series of fragmented and unrelated initiatives at local levels.

BACKGROUND

In today's knowledge economy, it is often asserted that for organizations to compete effectively they need to focus on creating and using intellectual assets (Grant, 1996; Murray, 2002). Ask most business leaders if knowledge is important to their company's future and they will say yes without hesitation. Ask them why it is so important, or how they plan to harness their organization's knowledge for competitive advantage, and the answers will be less convincing (Pollard, 2000). The key transition is from appreciating the importance of knowledge to being capable of managing it or, perhaps more accurately, being able to create the organizational conditions that facilitate the generation, sharing, and application of knowledge (Alavi & Leidner, 2001; Collison & Parcell, 2001). Defining these appropriate organizational conditions is still a focus of research and subject to much debate. The problem is exacerbated by the fact that implementation of knowledge management is context dependent, such that there is no universal recipe or methodology (Coakes, 2003; Probst, Raub, & Romhardt, 2000).

This chapter investigates the implementation of knowledge management in a global telecommunications company that provides data network services to multinational clients. We examine the challenges of managing knowledge in a post-merger environment. In particular, our results illustrate the practical difficulties in creating a conducive knowledge-sharing culture in such a merged organization, especially when it is organized around a business unit structure. We also show how the information infrastructure assumes critical significance in underpinning knowledge-sharing efforts, particularly to move beyond localized knowledge sharing and maximize the benefits of global organizational knowledge.

Especially since the Telecom Reform Act of 1996, the telecommunications industry has been experiencing intense competition, with several competitors facing serious financial difficulty, bankruptcy, and even break-up. Coupled with the rapid rise of hybrid networks, the challenge for many surviving network providers is to maintain profit margins through efficient asset management of their physical products while migrating to a more services-oriented business model, where additional revenues derive from enhanced network solutions, integration services capabilities, and telecommunications consultancy. This places greater emphasis on the importance of managing knowledge to support and secure such a change in strategic intent (Figure 1).

Figure 1. The role of knowledge in asset utilization and service-based business models

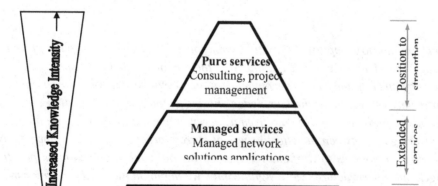

Our research in the focal firm was motivated by the need to investigate the preconditions that influence the implementation of knowledge management (Alavi & Leidner, 2001; Gold, Malhotra, & Segars, 2001; Walczak & Zwart, 2003). Only a few approaches to this are emerging from the current literature (Bock & Kim, 2002; Holt, Bartczak, Clark, & Trent, 2004), and this is recognized as an important research theme (Kim, Yu, & Lee, 2003). In practical terms, we developed this notion into three related questions:

1. Where is the company now, in terms of its culture and information infrastructure and its current methods for sharing and accessing knowledge? To address this question we used an employee survey.
2. Where is the company going with regard to its business strategy? Answers to this question are necessary to ensure the correct focus for knowledge management efforts to support the strategic intent (Hansen, Nohria, & Tierney, 1999). We interviewed three senior executive vice presidents in the firm to explore this issue.
3. What should be done to improve the firm's business transformation through knowledge management? The answers to the preceding questions provide fertile clues regarding whether the focus of change and improvement should be on employee attitudes, organizational practices, or knowledge-management infrastructure. We consider this more fully in our discussion of results.

In the next section, we review the pertinent issues for improvement of knowledge-management practice in multinational organizations. We then outline our research methods for investigating the focal firm, before presenting results of a survey of the organization's knowledge workers in five European countries. These results are contrasted with our findings from key informant interviews with three executive vice presidents. We conclude by discussing the significance of the findings for research and management practice.

ENABLERS OF KNOWLEDGE MANAGEMENT

From the extant literature, there is consensus that Knowledge Management (KM) requires a parallel focus on people, processes, and technology (Massey, Montoya-Weiss, & O'Driscoll, 2002; Tiwana, 2002), but that technology should only be seen as a fundamental support element. At best, IT only makes connection possible but does not make it happen (O'Dell & Grayson, 1998). While KM cannot be implemented without technology (Malhotra, 2000), the bottlenecks are usually psychological and organizational. The inherent danger is to place information technology at the center of KM implementation, endeavoring to *push* information and knowledge toward employees rather than creating the *demand-pull* for knowledge by enthusing employees with a desire for knowledge (Kluge, Stein, & Licht, 2001).

In a recent survey of KM practices, one of the most recurring weaknesses was that companies lacked the right cultural context to nurture reciprocal trust, openness, and co-operation (Kluge et al., 2001). To create such cultures, companies need to build social capital (Ghoshal & Naphiet, 1998) such that employees feel interconnected through their personal networks. In essence, connecting employees is more about building personal relationships and the development of a knowledge-friendly culture (Davenport, DeLong, & Beers, 1998; Walczak & Zwart, 2003) than the physical connections afforded by IT systems.

However, in a global organization, face-to-face relationships are not always possible, giving rise to difficulties in accepting knowledge from unknown outsiders—the "not-invented-here" syndrome (Kluge et al., 2001). Instinctively, employees tend to rely more heavily on "nearest" knowledge from physically proximate colleagues, perceiving such knowledge to be more dependable (Thomas, Kellog, & Erickson, 2001). In multinational companies, organizational structure is also important for leveraging knowledge assets (Abell & Oxbrow, 1997; Gold et al., 2001). When structured into business units, inter-unit rivalry and competition can impede collaboration and knowledge sharing, reflecting the "tyranny" of the business unit structure (Prahalad & Hamel, 1990).

Undoubtedly, personalization strategies (Hansen et al., 1999) that include, for example, "Yellow Pages" directories can help to connect people in an organization, yet it is far from easy to construct such systems (Stewart, 2001). Equally, *high-touch* collaborative technology environments that enable virtual communities do not necessarily lead to collaborative cultures (Tissen, Andriessen, & Deprez, 2000). Technology-mediated communities of practice may be a constructive way to build relationship capital (Wenger & Snyder, 2000), and circumvent the barriers of a business unit structure, but there is, as yet, very little empirical evidence of their effectiveness (Lesser, 2001).

As with most new organizational initiatives, the role of senior managers is crucial. They are responsible for identifying and communicating the role of knowledge management within the organization's strategic business plans, and for ensuring that the business strategy and knowledge strategy are in close alignment (Abou-Zeid, 2003; Zack, 1999). All too often, this link is relatively weak and poorly understood (Davenport, 1999; Davenport et al., 1998). Clear definition of the contribution of knowledge to the achievement of business strategy is essential in order to specify which knowledge must be managed and which measures are needed to assess performance improvement (Holsapple & Joshi, 2000; Treacy & Wiersema, 1996). Senior managers also influence the prevailing organizational culture and the commitment of resources to the implementation of KM practices (Bukowitz & Williams, 1999).

In this chapter, we assess the effectiveness of knowledge-management capability in the focal

organization and the importance that employees assigned to knowledge management for the future success of the organization. We also compare these findings with results from interviews with senior executives in the firm, contrasting the dichotomous perceptions between these two groups. Our method is outlined below.

RESEARCH METHOD

Research Setting and Sample Selection

The focal firm is one of the largest global telecommunications companies, with around 12,000 employees in more than 100 countries. Its core products are global data networks and related services, and its market focus is multinationals in the Global 2000 list of firms. The company has requested anonymity and therefore cannot be identified.

The employee sample was drawn from the Marketing and Sales Departments in five European countries of the focal firm, namely, Switzerland, United Kingdom, Germany, The Netherlands, and Belgium. The sample frame comprised of 389 knowledge workers, excluding clerical and administrative staff, and a random sample of 102 participants was selected. Each person was telephoned to establish willingness to participate in the survey. Key informant interviews were also conducted with three senior executives responsible for professional services, strategy, and product marketing, respectively.

Instrument Development

The survey instrument used items derived from previous surveys of KM (Davis, McAdams, Dixon, Orlikowski, & Leonard, 1998; KPMG, 1999). Item statements were modified to suit the specific context of the focal firm and the questionnaire was pilot tested prior to distribution. The survey was structured into five sections dealing with employees' perceptions of:

- The knowledge sharing culture;
- The information infrastructure;
- Current sources of information and knowledge;
- Usefulness of knowledge-sharing methods; and
- The most appropriate incentives for stimulating knowledge sharing.

Items were ranked on a 5-point Likert scale in terms of (a) the importance for the future success of the organization, and (b) the effectiveness of current practices, each anchored by 1 = strongly disagree and 5 = strongly agree. Each section included open questions to permit further comment and opinion. We also gathered categorical data on respondents, including their country, department, and position in the organization. The survey was distributed by e-mail, with 90 completed questionnaires returned, representing a response rate of 88%.

The interviews with senior executives explored their views of the long-term goals and strategies of the firm and their personal commitment to knowledge management in this context. We were particularly interested in the degree of consensus regarding the need to change the business model from a focus on effective asset management to a true value-added services orientation. All interviews were tape-recorded and transcripts analyzed for key themes.

Data Analysis Procedures

First, we used the chi-square test of significance to test for differences based on country, department, or position. No significant differences were detected. We then used t-tests to evaluate differences in item means for importance and effectiveness, where the presence of significant

negative scores represents employees' thirst for a better knowledge culture and infrastructure and a *demand-pull* for improvement. Conversely, a significantly positive score would indicate an activity where management was doing more than employees believed to be necessary. The sample size did not permit the use of advanced statistical analysis due to the low case-to-variable ratio. However, for an exploratory study, we believe that analysis of the differences in mean values for the ratings of the importance and effectiveness of each item gives a good initial indication of issues worthy of deeper investigation.

RESULTS

We firstly present data that indicates the current effectiveness of the knowledge-sharing culture and the support provided by the information infrastructure, together with employee perceptions of the importance of these dimensions. In each table, we also include the gap between the mean values for importance and effectiveness.

Knowledge-Sharing Culture

There were ten statements in this section, covering issues concerned with learning, knowledge sharing, and the openness and helpfulness of employees (Table 1).

Clearly, the results in Table 1 suggest that there is a significant gap between the importance (I) assigned to each of these behaviors and the effectiveness (E) of current levels of practice. The largest gaps relate to:

1. The time available for creative thinking, which is eroded by spending too much time on "firefighting" problems;
2. Having a process to avoid re-inventing the wheel by being able to re-use and build upon the work of others;

Table 1. Gaps in knowledge sharing culture

Item	Importance	Effectiveness	Gap
Time is allowed for creative thinking (versus always firefighting)	4.38	2.47	-1.91
Looking for best practices or work that can be re-used is a natural standard process	4.54	2.70	-1.84
Considerable time and attention is given to learn from failures and errors	4.70	3.06	-1.64
A climate of openness and trust permeates the organization	4.52	3.19	-1.33
People are responsive (e.g. emails and voice mail get answered in a timely manner	4.28	3.08	-1.20
Recording and sharing knowledge is routine and second nature	4.16	2.98	-1.18
All employees are ready and willing to give advice or help on request to anyone else on the organization	4.38	3.48	-0.90
Employees take responsibility for their own learning	4.05	3.23	-0.82
Informal networks across different parts of the organization are encouraged	4.03	3.26	-0.77
We have un-restricted access to non-confidential or personal information	3.74	3.35	-0.39
Overall	4.05	3.23	-0.82

(n = 90) 1 = strongly negative 5 = strongly positive

3. Giving more time and attention to learning from mistakes and failures;
4. Developing a more trusting and open climate in the organization; and
5. Being more responsive to requests from others.

Employee responsiveness is not only about willingness to reply, but also about the support mechanisms to enable communication, particularly the information infrastructure.

Information Infrastructure

A similar pattern emerged for the assessment of the importance and effectiveness of the information infrastructure, as illustrated in Table 2.

All items in Table 2 display large gaps between what users expect and the current reality of information provision.

We also explored employee's views about their preferred ways of accessing knowledge and information and their perceived usefulness of a range of access methods available in the organization.

Importance of Knowledge and Information Sources

Currently the most important sources of knowledge are from local sources within the respondents' own departments (Figure 2).

There is also a considerable amount of learning by doing and learning through contact with other local departments in each country. Noticeably, inter-country learning is of significantly lower importance. This finding about inter-country learning is complemented by the findings relating to the usefulness of knowledge-sharing methods, as discussed in the next section.

Table 2. Gaps in information infrastructure

Item	Importance	Effectiveness	Gap
We can rapidly find necessary information on our IT systems	4.59	2.72	-1.87
Our IT system provides excellent ease of access to information	4.56	2.86	-1.70
We have up to date information from our IT systems	4.58	3.01	-1.57
Our IT infrastructure is an excellent source of information and knowledge	4.47	3.10	-1.37
We can trust the information in our IT systems	4.59	3.24	-1.35
IT is a key enabler of efficient knowledge sharing	4.22	3.11	-1.11
Overall	4.50	3.01	-1.49

(n = 90)   1 = strongly negative   5 = strongly positive

Figure 2. How important are the following knowledge/information sources

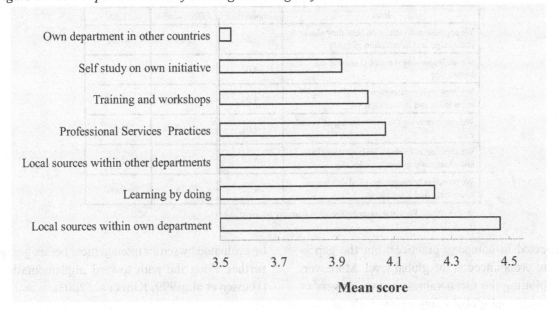

Knowledge-Sharing Methods

In Figure 3 we can see that the most useful methods for sharing knowledge and information are face-to-face and via the company intranet. Respondents' comments made it clear that product information was shared through the intranet, while face-to-face communication facilitated local knowledge sharing within their own departments and geographically adjacent departments.

We explored this further by asking about the importance and effectiveness of local, within-country knowledge sharing compared with global, inter-country and inter-business unit sharing (Table 3).

These results suggest that the largest gaps between importance and effectiveness of current practices exist at the global level of knowledge sharing. Overall, these respondents attach more importance to knowledge sharing than is currently

Figure 3. How useful are the following knowledge/information methods

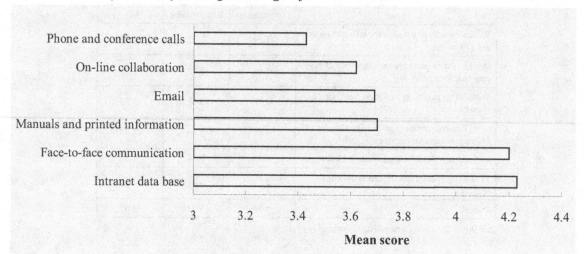

Mean score

Table 3. Gaps in sharing local and global knowledge

Item	Importance	Effectiveness	Gap
We appraise individuals on how they share knowledge and information globally	3.66	2.14	-1.52
We are improving the global sharing of knowledge	4.08	2.64	-1.44
We proactively encourage global sharing of knowledge and information	4.24	2.86	-1.38
We are improving the local sharing of knowledge	4.01	2.89	-1.12
We appraise individuals on how they share knowledge and information locally	3.69	2.62	-1.07
We proactively encourage local sharing of knowledge and information	4.32	3.36	-0.96

(n = 90)   1 = strongly negative   5 = strongly positive

reflected in company practices, but the gap is more pronounced at the global level. Moreover, by plotting the mean values for the answers to the local and global items respectively, we can see that, although the firm is viewed as being better at managing local knowledge, the overall gap between global and local knowledge sharing is not as significant as the overall improvement needed in effectiveness (Figure 4).

The preceding results provide a way to assess an organization's current state of readiness to implement knowledge-management practices. These methods provide answers to our first research question: "Where are we now?" and should

be evaluated by senior management before going further along the path toward implementation (Hansen et al., 1999; Kim et al., 2003).

Strategic Intent: Where Are We Going?

We now consider the interviews with the three senior executives in the focal firm to compare their understanding of the strategic direction of the firm and the consequent implications for knowledge management (Table 4). The interviews revealed significant disparities in the three respondents' views across each of the themes contained in

Figure 4. Overall gap between local and global knowledge sharing

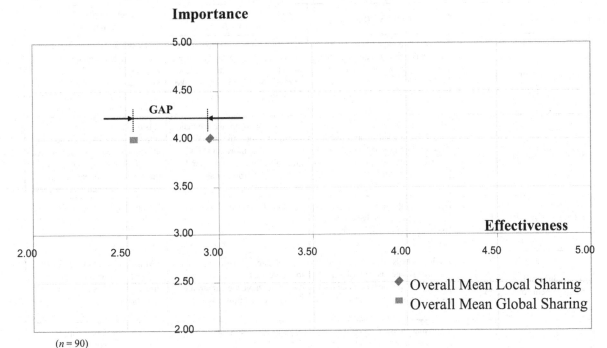

($n = 90$)

Table 4. For example, in relation to most desirable business model, the strategic direction of the organization, and the urgency for changing, the executives were polarized, with *in extremis*, the Executive VP of Strategy espousing the status quo, whereas the Executive VP of Professional Services advocated an immediate and proactive shift away from current products toward a value-added services portfolio. Similarly, while they all acknowledged the importance of knowledge management, they differed on its strategic priority. This lack of strategic consensus was also mirrored in their views about the need for top management commitment, inter-country knowledge sharing, culture change, and employee incentives.

Therefore, in relation to the second fundamental question, "Where are we going?," this firm appears not to be ready to adopt knowledge management because of its inability to articulate a clear and shared strategic direction, from which a knowledge-management strategy should be derived (Massey et al., 2002). These executives'

views contrast sharply with our earlier results, which highlighted the gaps in the current culture and IT infrastructure. In particular, employees reflected a strong requirement for a change to a more open, creative, and learning-oriented culture and much better access to accurate information to enable their sharing of knowledge. Our findings are further emphasized by the employees' views about the kind of incentives they believe would stimulate them to share knowledge (Figure 5).

Incentives for Knowledge Sharing

The results in Figure 5 indicate that respondents regard non-financial incentives as more useful. Their supplementary comments suggested that the incentives should become embedded in the company culture to avoid knowledge sharing becoming a "mercenary action for money." Comparing these results with the related comments from our interviews with senior managers in Table 4, it appears that senior executives are not

Table 4. Selected quotations from interviews with executive vice presidents

	Executive VP (Strategy)	Executive VP (Professional Services)	Executive VP (Products / Marketing)
Business model	We need to expand our core of network products, and we are basically happy with what we sell today	Not everybody at the top agrees with the current strategy, but we need to move to getting 40% of our revenues from services like IBM do	You can't draw a nice black and white line between networks and services. Wisdom is that you should choose one or the other but I think we need to be in the middle
Clarity of strategy	I don't see a fundamental shift away from what we are doing today. Doing a better job on what we offer today is central to our future strategy	It is unclear where we are making most of our margin. We have to focus more on skills and value-added service, and see network products as commodities	It is difficult to know. It is important to make a choice. If all senior executives agreed, we would not have to worry about the decision. We can still grow the scale of our current business
Urgency of moving to knowledge-intensive services	I'm probably not as focused on moving to knowledge intensive services as our Professional Services VP.	We have to shift right now	Eventually, economic logic will push us
Importance of Knowledge Management for the firm	While KM is important, what we really need is better internal measures and performance data - product statistics, network costs etc	Knowledge is absolutely crucial to where we need to go, but we do not yet have a clear strategy for managing knowledge	KM is no silver bullet. We need strategy, commitment and direction and I don't think we have that today
Top management commitment	Top management recognize the need for more complete and accurate internal data and better information systems to make the right decisions	Beyond endorsing the investment, I don't think we need them	You ask if KM will happen. You ask me to predict the weather!
Inter-country sharing	I have no specific view about this - it is not my responsibility	We don't share well yet, but we must. We are not yet where we need to be	There should be a view that we are a global company, and that information should be available globally, but not yet.
Culture change for KM	There is very little we can do to change our culture because we have over 100 cultures in the different countries	We should not only define the framework of the things to do, but also the dimensions of the culture we want to create	It is not a priority for many managers or employees. We are still focused on assets, processes and economics.
Employee incentives for sharing knowledge	We could mandate knowledge sharing in job descriptions	We need to find a mechanism to motivate people, but I don't know if they need to be financial or something else	This is not a problem. There is no blockage to sharing information.

in close-enough touch with employees' views and do not understand the importance of one of the key levers for effective knowledge sharing.

DISCUSSION

We set out to investigate the current status of knowledge-management capability in the focal firm. In both the knowledge-sharing culture and the information infrastructure, there were significant gaps between the effectiveness of current levels of practice and the importance assigned to these practices. These gaps represent the latent employee expectations for improvement in these key areas and are guidelines as to where management needs to focus its efforts. If the importance scores had been lower, then there would also have been a need for managers to stimulate more awareness of the need for knowledge management by stressing its business value. In the following sections, we review our findings and use illustrative quotations from the qualitative data in the survey.

Figure 5. Which incentives would be most effective in stimulating knowledge sharing?

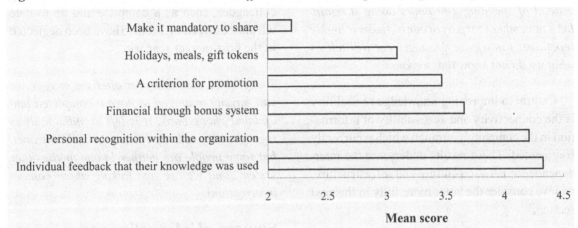

Knowledge-Sharing Culture

The results in Table 1 indicated several areas where the organization needs to close the gap between current practices and employee expectations. One of the most important areas for improvement is the climate of openness and trust throughout the organization. Several respondents commented on this lack of openness and attributed it primarily to the competition and rivalry between the organization's business units.

Business units have been trained to be protective of their knowledge. Competitive behavior is built into the organization mainly because of the current sales incentive plan.

Again and again business units fight over who will get a particular customer. I have lived through cases where this fight took up to 80% of the time available to answer a proposal, and then we have to finally rush an answer.

Another reason given for low levels of openness and trust was the recent merger.

Trust has partially broken down since the merger, and has since then not been fixed. What we need to achieve is to make employees feel they belong to something more than their business unit. We need to create communication channels across business units that break down the silo structure that prevents knowledge flowing efficiently across the organization. The thirst for knowledge should become more powerful than the influence of the silo guardians.

It appears that there is a significant thirst for knowledge, as evidenced by the scores for the importance of the ten cultural items, and that management needs to develop a cross-cutting communications infrastructure that enables interconnection across temporal and geographical boundaries.

A second area for improvement is the ability to re-use and build upon the work of others to avoid re-inventing the wheel. In this regard, we cite two pertinent respondents' comments below:

I know that there's not a day or a week that passes where we are not working on a new proposal that might be relevant somewhere else in the organization. Often, what enables us to win a new proposal is not just the features and functionalities of our services, which we have in boilerplates, but mainly the knowledge of where we have done it before and the type of people we can direct to that sort of project. If we look at our re-use of knowledge globally on a scale of 1 to 10, we are probably around 2.

We have to re-use what somebody else has learned instead of spending 100 hours doing it again. Let's remember that part of our business is highly repetitive; Knowledge Management will tell us what we do not know that we know.

Central to improving knowledge re-usability is the connectivity and accessibility of information in the company's intranet, which is currently fragmented. These results underscore the interdependence between culture and infrastructure, and we consider the latter more fully in the next section.

Information Infrastructure

The information infrastructure was also shown in Table 2 to be deficient in terms of the reliability and timeliness of information and ease of system use. The following comments give additional insights into the nature of the disparities.

We have too many information sources and a huge amount of data resulting in difficulties finding the right information. On Lotus Notes, we have 12589 databases and who knows how many on the Intranet. Probably 90% of the databases are dead.

Access to codified information was not the only problem. Respondents also commented on the difficulty of connecting with a key contact in another country. This can be a particular hindrance for sales and marketing staff who are often at customer sites.

Finding information produced in another country can be very difficult. I was recently looking for a proposal made in the UK, and it took me approximately an hour before I found the person that was able to help me. Unfortunately he was in his car and could not mail me the proposal, and there was no other way to get it.

Even fundamental mechanisms for contacting colleagues, such as a complete and up-to-date telephone directory, seem to have been neglected in the post-merger scenario.

Today, more than one year after the merger, we still haven't managed to have a completed and updated phone book. It is left to individuals to register either in Lotus Notes and/or the intranet, but some people are neither in one or the other system (and we are just talking about contact information).

Sources of Information and Knowledge

We then investigated the respondents' most valued sources of information and knowledge, highlighting the relative lack of importance given to sources in other geographical units of the organization. These findings were complemented by the results for the perceived usefulness of knowledge-sharing methods, where there was comparatively little perceived value in knowledge sources in respondents' own departments in other countries. It may be that employees have not yet recognized or do not believe in the benefit of working with colleagues in other countries. Such reliance on immediate coworkers is not uncommon (Alavi & Leidner, 2001), but it does limit the potential for exposure to new knowledge, since individuals in the same group tend to possess similar information (Robertson, Swan, & Newell, 1996) and can be subject to groupthink (Janis, 1982).

From the qualitative comments, many respondents cited reasons that were again concerned with inter-business unit rivalry, erosion of trust after the merger, and the difficulties of knowing who to contact and how to contact them. This lack of regard for organizational information and knowledge beyond respondents' own geographical unit was underlined by the results relating to local versus global knowledge sharing (Table 3), where the largest gaps existed at the global level.

Development of an effective communications infrastructure would provide a baseline for addressing these barriers, including a comprehensive telephone directory, a "Yellow Pages" catalog of experts, and, possibly, communities of practice that link experts in common fields across the business units, potentially circumventing what one respondent referred to as the "silo guardians."

Incentives for Knowledge Sharing

It is unquestionably important to create an environment wherein employees are stimulated to share knowledge (Szulanski, 1996). Mere exhortations to share are rarely sufficient, while mandating it is unlikely to succeed (Huber, 2001). Management practitioners and some researchers often advocate the use of financial incentives as extrinsic motivators of knowledge-sharing behaviors (Ba, Stallaert, & Whinston, 2001; Koudsi, 2000), founded on the notion of rational self-interest, yet there is substantive evidence that extrinsic rewards are, at best, short-term incentives that can undermine intrinsic motivation to share knowledge (Bock et al., 2002; Moore & Birkinshaw, 1998; Osterloh & Frey, 2000). Conversely, others cite intrinsic stimuli such as recognition, personal pride, or desire to be perceived as a thought leader as the key to develop sharing behaviors (Pfeffer, 1998; Rappleye, 2000). Taken as a whole, the literature on appropriate incentives for knowledge sharing is incongruent and inconsistent, and "our ignorance in these matters is considerable" (Huber, 2001).

Our interviews with senior executives underpin this conclusion and highlight the lack of understanding of this complex issue in the focal firm. One of the interviewees did not recognize the need for incentives, anticipating that knowledge sharing would happen spontaneously, while another thought that mandating sharing behaviors in job descriptions would be an adequate solution. The third interviewee at least recognized the need to find appropriate motivators but admitted ignorance as to what they might be. The most logical action would be to ask employees, which in this case revealed a diverse set of responses (Figure 5). While the respondents were most positively disposed to non-financial rewards associated with self-esteem and recognition, these factors were closely followed by financial motivators such as promotion and bonus payments.

These findings have two practical implications for senior managers. First, top management should explore employees' views about the most important incentives for knowledge sharing and understand what is most likely to engender desired behaviors. Second, where employees express preferences for a mixed-economy of financial and non-financial rewards, there is clearly no straightforward solution. While this endorses the complexity and ambiguity in the literature, it poses a challenge for management that is difficult to resolve. Nonetheless, to be aware of what matters to employees is a first and vital step toward effective knowledge sharing.

Strategic Alignment

Finally, we explored the strategic direction of this telecommunications company and the perceived importance of KM to support the strategy. We discovered a lack of clear consensus among senior executives, and this is perhaps the most significant of our findings and the one with the most serious ramifications. We echo Davenport's (1999) observation that for knowledge management to succeed, it must "affect the most important areas of the business, improve the firm's most critical objectives, and be viewed as an integral part of strategic business objectives." The danger for companies such as this is that when faced with survey evidence that there are significant gaps in the culture or IT infrastructure, improvement activities can be sanctioned under the umbrella of knowledge management without having clarity or consensus about the underlying purpose or desired outcomes (Abou-Zeid, 2003; Kim et al., 2003; Zack, 1999). Clear business strategies are critical to ensure that knowledge management activities support business drivers and performance objectives (Murray, 2002; Poage, 2002). One employee's comments seem especially apposite: "Management should be aware that we are all sitting in the same boat and that it is very exhausting to paddle while the cox is always changing direction, hoping to find the right way."

CONCLUSION

As a contribution to research, the chapter adds to the small number of empirical case studies of knowledge-management practices. The approach used in this research provides managers with a tool to evaluate their organizations' current knowledge-management capability, both in terms of the culture and supporting infrastructure. By measuring gaps between perceptions of current practices and their importance, managers can identify areas for improvement and decide whether to direct resources toward changing attitudes, practices, or infrastructure.

Taken together, these results illustrate the challenges facing a telecommunications company operating in a highly competitive and rapidly changing environment. In such markets, there are inevitable pressures on time, such that unless the organization recognizes the need to set aside time for creative thinking and learning from failures and errors, this will not happen. Moreover, while mergers are common occurrences, senior managers need to address their potential impact on knowledge-sharing capability and ensure that, at least in the short term, the disruption of a merger does not erode personal networks of contacts or the openness of the merged organization to share with new colleagues.

Our data suggests that the knowledge-sharing support platform inadequately satisfies the knowledge appetite of respondents. Harmonizing the information infrastructure of a merged organization can be a critical challenge, not only to reconcile a plethora of databases, but also to provide a comprehensive "Yellow Pages" facility to facilitate contact with key people. Our results also underscore the longer-term challenge to enhance the effectiveness of a business unit structure by ensuring that inter-unit rivalry does not inhibit global knowledge sharing.

Perhaps most strikingly, the interview data revealed how important it is to achieve consensus among senior managers about strategic direction, without which knowledge management is likely to remain, at best, a series of fragmented and unrelated initiatives at local levels.

REFERENCES

Abell, A. & Oxbrow, N. (1997). People who make knowledge management work: CKO, CKT, or KT? In J. Liebowitz (Ed.), *Knowledge management handbook*. Chapter 4. Boca Raton, FL: CRC Press.

Abou-Zeid, S. 2003. Developing business aligned knowledge management strategy. In E. Coakes (Ed.), *Knowledge management: Current issues and challenges*, (pp.156-172). Hershey, PA: IRM Press.

Alavi, M. & Leidner, D. E. (2001). Review: Knowledge management and knowledge management systems: Conceptual foundations and research issues. *MIS Quarterly, 25*(1), 107-136.

Ba, S., Stallaert, J., & Whinston, A. B. (2001). Research commentary: Introducing a third dimension in information systems design - The case for incentive alignment. *Information Systems Research, 12*(3), 225-239.

Bock, G. W. & Kim, Y.-G. (2002). Breaking the myths of rewards: an exploratory study of attitudes about knowledge sharing. *Information Resource Management Journal, 15*(2), 14-21.

Bukowitz, W. R. & Williams, R. L. (1999). *The Knowledge management fieldbook*. London: Pearson Education Ltd.

Coakes, E. (2003). Preface. In E. Coakes (Ed.), *Knowledge management: Current issues and challenges*. Hershey, PA: IRM Press.

Collison, C. & Parcell, G. (2001). *Learning to fly: Practical lessons from one of the world's leading knowledge companies*. Albany, OR: Capstone Publishing Ltd.

Davenport, T. (1999). Knowledge management and the broader firm: Strategy, advantage and performance. In J. Liebowitz (Ed.), *Knowledge management handbook*. (2.1-2.11). Washington, DC: CRC Press.

Davenport, T. H., DeLong, D. W., & Beers, M. C. 1998. Successful knowledge management projects. *Sloan Management Review, 39*(2), 43-57.

Davis, S., McAdams, A., Dixon, N., Orlikowski, W., & Leonard, D. (1998). *Twenty questions on knowledge in the organization*. London: Ernst & Young Center for Business Innovation.

Ghoshal, S. & Naphiet, J. (1998). Social capital, intellectual capital and the organizational advantage. *Academy of Management Review, 23*(2), 242-266.

Gold, A. H., Malhotra, A., & Segars, A. H. (2001). Knowledge management: An organizational capabilities perspective. *Journal of Management Information Systems, 18*(1), 185-214.

Grant, R. M. (1996). Toward a knowledge-based theory of the firm. *Strategic Management Journal, 17*(Winter Special Issue), 109-122.

Hansen, M.T., Nohria, N., & Tierney, T. (1999). What's your strategy for managing knowledge? *Harvard Business Review, 77*(2), 106-116.

Holsapple, C. W. & Joshi, K. D. (2000). An investigation of factors that influence the management of knowledge in organizations. *The Journal of Strategic Information Systems, 9*(2-3), 235-261.

Holt, D. T., Bartczak, S. E., Clark, S. W., & Trent, M. R. (2004). *The development of an instrument to measure readiness for knowledge management*. Paper presented at the 37th Hawaii International Conference on System Sciences, January 5-8, Hilton Waikoloa Village, Island of Hawaii (Big Island), IEEE Computer Society.

Huber, G. P. (2001). Transfer of knowledge in knowledge management systems: Unexplored issues and suggested studies. *European Journal of Information Systems, 10*, 72-79.

Janis, I. L. (1982). *Psychological studies of policy decisions and fiascoes* (2nd Ed.). Boston, MA: Houghton-Mifflin.

Kim, Y.-G., Yu, S.-H., & Lee, J.-H. (2003). Knowledge strategy planning: Methodology and case. *Expert Systems with Applications, 24*, 295-307.

Kluge, J., Stein, W., & Licht, T. (2001). *Knowledge unplugged: The McKinsey & Company survey on Knowledge Management*. New York: Palgrave.

Koudsi, S. (2000). Actually, it is like brain surgery, *Fortune*, March 20, 233-234.

KPMG (1999). Knowledge management research report, 20. London: KPMG Consulting.

Lesser, E. L. (2001). Communities of practice and organizational performance. *IBM Systems Journal, 40*(4), 831-841.

Malhotra, Y. (2000). Role of organizational controls in KM: Is KM really an oxymoron? In Y. Malhotra (Ed.), *Knowledge management and virtual organizations*. (pp. 245-257). Hershey, PA: IRM Press.

Massey, A. P., Montoya-Weiss, M. M., & O'Driscoll, T. M. (2002). Knowledge management in pursuit of performance insights from Nortel. *MIS Quarterly, 26*(3), 269-289.

Moore, K. & Birkinshaw, J. (1998). Managing knowledge in global service organizations: Centers of excellence. *Academy of Management Executive, 12*, 81-92.

Murray, P. (2002). Knowledge management as a sustained competitive advantage. *Ivey Business Journal* (March-April), 71-76.

O'Dell, C. A. & Grayson, C. J. 1998. *If only we knew what we know: The transfer of internal knowledge and best practice*: Free Press.

Osterloh, M. & Frey, B. S. (2000). Motivation, knowledge transfer and organizational forms. *Organization Science, 11*, 538-550.

Pfeffer, J. (1998). *The human equation: Building profits by putting people first*. Boston, MA: Harvard Business School Press.

Poage, J. L. (2002). Designing performance measures for knowledge organizations. *Ivey Business Journal* (March-April), 8-10.

Pollard, D. (2000). Becoming knowledge powered: Planning the transformation. In Y. Malhotra (Ed.), *Knowledge management and virtual organizations*. (pp.196-213). Hershey, PA: IRM Press.

Prahalad, C. K. & Hamel, G. (1990). The core competence of the corporation. *Harvard Business Review, 68*(3), 79-91.

Probst, G., Raub, S., & Romhardt, K. (2000). *Managing knowledge: Building blocks for success*. London: John Wiley & Sons.

Rappleye, W. C. (2000). Knowledge management: A force whose time has come. *Across the Board: The Conference Board Magazine*, January, 59-66.

Robertson, M., Swan, J., & Newell, S. (1996). The role of networks in the diffusion of technological innovation. *Journal of Management Studies, 33*, 335-361.

Stewart, T. A. (2001). *The wealth of knowledge: Intellectual capital and the twenty-first century organization*. New York: Doubleday.

Szulanski, G. (1996). Exploring internal stickiness: Impediments to the transfer of best practice within the firm. *Strategic Management Journal, 17*(Winter Special Issue), 27-43.

Thomas, J. C., Kellog, W. A., & Erickson, T. (2001). The knowledge management puzzle: Human factors in knowledge management. *IBM Systems Journal, 40*(4), 863-884.

Tissen, R., Andriessen, D., & Deprez, F. L. (2000). *The knowledge dividend: Creating high-performance companies through value-based knowledge management*. Harlow, UK: Financial Times Prentice-Hall.

Tiwana, A. (2002). *Knowledge management toolkit: Practical techniques for building a knowledge management system* (2nd Ed.). Saddle River, NJ: Prentice-Hall PTR.

Treacy, M. & Wiersema, F. D. (1996). *The discipline of market leaders*. Reading, MA: Addison-Wesley.

Walczak, S. & Zwart, D. (2003). Organizational knowledge management: Enabling a knowledge culture. In *Proceedings of the Information Resources Management Association International Conference*, Philadelphia, 18-21 May, pp. 670-673.

Wenger, E. C. & Snyder, W. M. (2000). Communities of practice: The organisational frontier. *Harvard Business Review, 78*(1), 139-145.

Zack, M. H. (1999). Developing a knowledge strategy. *California Management Review, 41*(3), 125-145.

This work was previously published in Advanced Topics in Information Resources Management Volume 4, edited by M. Khosrow-Pour, pp. 93-114, copyright 2005 by IGI Publishing, formerly known as Idea Group Publishing (an imprint of IGI Global).

Selected Reading V
Alignment of Business and Knowledge Management Strategies

El-Sayed Abou-Zeid
Concordia University, Canada

INTRODUCTION

The role of knowledge as a crucial asset for an enterprise's survival and advancement has been recognized by several researchers (e.g., von Krogh, Ichijo & Nonaka, 2000). Moreover, by having knowledge (intellectual resources), an organization can understand how to exploit and develop its traditional resources better than its competitors can, even if some or all of those traditional resources are not unique (Zack, 1999).

However, realizing the importance of organizational knowledge and its management in creating value and in gaining competitive advantage is only the first and the easiest step in any knowledge management (KM) initiative. The second and almost as important step is to answer how and where to begin questioning (Earl, 2001). In fact, "many executives are struggling to articulate the relationship between their organization's competitive strategy and its intellectual resources and capabilities (knowledge)" (Zack, 1999). As Zack (1999) argued, they need pragmatic yet theoretically sound model. It has been highly ac-

cepted that a pragmatic and theoretically sound model should meet at least two criteria. First, it should explicitly include the external domains (opportunities/threat) and internal domains (capabilities/arrangements) of both business (B-) and knowledge (K-) strategies and the relationships between them. Second, it should provide alternative strategic choices.

In order address this issue a KM strategic alignment model (KMSAM) is presented. It stems from the premise that the realization of business value gained from KM investment requires alignment between the business (B-) and knowledge (K-) strategies of the firm and is based on the Henderson-Venkatraman SAM for IT (Henderson & Venkatraman, 1993).

Overview of the Henderson-Venkatraman Strategic Alignment Model

The KM strategic alignment model is based on the theoretical construct developed by Henderson and Venkatraman (1993). In their model business success is viewed as the result of the synergy between four domains. The first two, the external domains, are business strategy and information technology (IT) strategy. The strategy domains are described in terms of (business/technology) scope, (distinctive business/IT systemic) competencies and (business/IT) governance. The second two, the internal domains, are organizational infrastructure and processes and IT infrastructure and processes. Both internal domains are described in terms of (administrative/IT) infrastructure, (business/IT) processes and (business/IT) skills. This synergy is achieved through two types of relationship:

- **Strategic fit** emphasizes the need for consistency between strategy (external domain) and its implementation (internal domain).
- **Functional integration,** which has two modes, extends the strategic fit across functional domains. The first mode, *strategic integration,* deals with the capability of IT functionality both to shape and to support business strategy. The second mode, *operation integration,* focuses on the criticality of ensuring internal coherence between organizational infrastructure and processes and IT infrastructure and processes.

Figure 1 shows the elements of the IT strategic alignment model (ITSAM).

Figure 1. IT strategic alignment model (Henderson & Venkatraman, 1993)

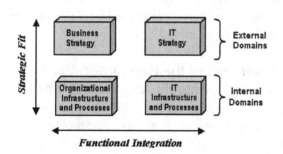

KM Strategic Alignment Model (KMSAM)

The premise of the original ITSAM is that "the effective and efficient utilization of IT requires the alignment of IT strategies with business strategies" (Henderson & Venkatraman, 1993). In parallel way, the premise of KMSAM, in which knowledge strategy replaces IT strategy, is that "the effective and efficient use of organizational knowledge requires the alignment of knowledge strategies with business strategies". Since strategy, whether business (B)-strategy or knowledge (K)-strategy, can be seen as a balancing act between the *external domain* (opportunities/threats) and the *internal domain* (capabilities/arrangements) of the firm (strengths and weaknesses) (Henderson & Venkatraman, 1993; Zack, 1999), the external and internal domains of K strategy have first to be defined.

K-Strategy External Domain

In the case of K-strategy, the *external domain* involves three dimensions: *K-scope* (what the firm must know), *K-systemic competencies* (what are the critical characteristics of the required knowledge) and *K-governance* (how to obtain the required K-competencies). The first dimension, K-scope, deals with the specific domains of knowledge that are critical to the firm's survival and advancement strategies. Survival strategies aim at securing current enterprise profitability, while advancement strategies aim for future profitability (von Krogh et al., 2000).

Determining the K-scope can be achieved by constructing a business (B-) domain/ Knowledge (K-) thing matrix that documents the current and required state of organizational knowledge concerning some or all business domains. The first group of elements that constitute this matrix includes the list of B-domains (B$_j$). The second group of elements includes the K-things (K$_j$) that describe the current state of knowledge associated

Figure 2. The generic form of B-things/K-things matrix (Abou-Zeid, 2002)

	Survival Knowledge			Advancement Knowledge		
B1	KS11 (Current/Required States)	....	KS1n (Current/Required States)	KA11 (Current/Required States)	....	KA1m (Current/Required States)
B2	KS21 (Current/Required States)	....	KS2k (Current/Required States)	KA21 (Current/Required States)	....	KA2l (Current/Required States)
....	....	....	....	....	....	....
BN	KSN1 (Current/Required States)	....	KSNk (Current/Required States)	KAN1 (Current/Required States)	....	KANl (Current/Required States)

with each of the relevant B-domains. To relate this knowledge to enterprise business strategies, K-things are further classified according to the roles they play in such strategies. Von Krogh et al. (2000) have suggested that there are two types of strategies: survival and advancement. Survival strategies aim at securing current enterprise profitability, while advancement strategies aim for future profitability. Therefore, organizational knowledge, and consequently K-things, is classified into two categories: survival (K_S) and advancement (K_A). Figure (2) shows the generic form of this matrix.

The second dimension of the K-strategy external domain is K-systemic competencies. The focus of this dimension is the set of utilization-oriented characteristics of knowledge that could contribute positively to the creation of new business strategy or better support of existing business strategy. This set includes characteristics such as:

- *Accessibility,* the extent to which organizational knowledge is made available to its members regardless of time or location (Buckman, 1998);
- *Transferability,* the extent to which the newly acquired knowledge can be applied in other contexts, for example organizational, cultural (Grant, 1996);
- *Appropriability,* the extent to which knowledge can be imitated. Things are said to have "strong" appropriability if they are difficult to reproduce by another organization. The

converse is "weak" appropriability. A related concept is that of "sticky/slippery"; that is, sticky knowledge is such an integral part of a regime that it cannot be extracted in a meaningful whole (Grant, 1996; Narasimha, 2000);
- *Depth and breadth* (Narasimha, 2000);
- *Compositionality,* the amenability of knowledge to be synthesized from existing knowledge; and
- *Integrateability,* the extent to which the newly acquired knowledge can be integrated with existing knowledge.

Finally, K-governance dimension deals with the selection and use of mechanisms for obtaining the required K-competencies. The following are examples of some "acquisition mechanisms" (Probst, Raub & Romhardt, 2000):

- Bringing experts to the firm by recruiting specialists as full-time or temporary staff. Temporary hiring is becoming an increasingly interesting alternative.
- Tapping knowledge held by other firms through different inter-organizational co-operation forms such as joint ventures or strategic alliances.
- Utilizing the knowledge of stakeholders, for example, customers, suppliers, employees and owners. For example, involving customers early in the product-development process could generate valuable information about their needs.

- Acquiring knowledge products such as software, patents, and CD-ROMs.

K-Strategy Internal Domain

In the case of K-strategy, the internal domain involves three dimensions: *knowledge (K)-processes, knowledge (K)-infrastructures,* and *knowledge (K)-skills.*

Knowledge (K)-processes, the first dimension of the K-strategy internal domain, can be classified into two main categories: K-manipulating processes and K-enabling processes. The first category, K-manipulating processes, includes all the organizational processes needed to change the state of organizational knowledge such as K-generation, K-mobilization and K-application (Abou-Zeid, 2003). The second category, K-enabling processes, includes organizational processes that support K-manipulating processes such as managing conversation, mobilizing knowledge activists, creating the right context, and globalizing local knowledge (von Krogh et al., 2000).

Organizational knowledge processes are socially interaction-intensive. They involve social interactions and direct communication and contact among individuals and among members of "communities of practice". Therefore, they require the presence of social capital. Social capital is "the sum of actual and potential resources embedded within, available through, and derived from the network of relationships possessed by a social unit" (Nahapier & Ghoshal, 1998). Recognizing the importance of social capital, Gold et al. (2001) have identified three key K-infrastructures, the second dimension of the K-strategy internal domain, that is, technical, structural and cultural, that enable social capital. The *K-technical infrastructure* includes IT-enabled technologies that support KM activities such as business intelligence, collaboration and distributed learning, K-discovery, K-mapping, opportunity generation and security. The *K-structural infrastructure* refers to the presence of enabling formal organi-

zation structures and the organization's system of rewards and incentives. Finally, the *K-cultural infrastructure* involves elements such as corporate vision and the organization's system of values (Gold et al., 2001).

The last dimension of the K-strategy internal domain is K-skills. KM processes are by their very nature multifaceted. They involve many dimensions such as technical, organizational and human. This characteristic of KM processes reflects on the nature of skills required to perform them. For example, Malhotra (1997) defines a senior knowledge executive, such as a chief knowledge officer (CKO) or an organizational knowledge architect, as the person who should have the combined capabilities of a business strategist, technology analyst, and a human resource professional. The ability to facilitate the ongoing process of knowledge sharing and knowledge renewal, the ability to develop the human and cultural infrastructure that facilitates information sharing, and the ability to utilize the available technologies for serving the creation, sharing and documentation of knowledge are some examples of the required skills.

The Dynamics of KM Strategic Alignment Model (KMSAM)

Effecting a change in any single domain may require the use of three out of the four domains to assure that both strategic fit and functional integration are properly addressed. Therefore, applying KMSAM requires the identification of three domains: pivot, anchor and impacted (Luftman, 1996). The pivot domain is the weakest and offers the greatest opportunity for improvement. The anchor domain is the strongest and will be the driver of change. Finally, the impacted domain is the area affected by a change to the pivot domain. Figure 3 shows the dynamics of the strategic alignment process.

Based on this distinction, different perspectives of strategic alignment can be identified. Each perspective represents a pattern of linkages

Figure 3. The dynamics of the strategic alignment process

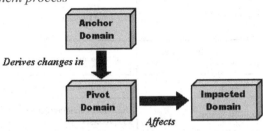

between at least three elements of the four elements of KMSAM, that is, the two external domains (business strategy and knowledge strategy) and the two internal domains (organizational infrastructure and processes and knowledge infrastructure and processes). By identifying the strongest (anchor) domain and the *adjacent* weakest (pivot) domain, it becomes possible to identify the area that will be affected by the changes (the impacted domain). The direction the perspective flows is based on which domain is the strongest and which is the weakest.

For example, Figure 4 shows knowledge potential perspective in which business strategy, the strongest domain, derives changes to the adjacent weakest domain, knowledge strategy, and these changes will impact knowledge infrastructure and processes. In general, each alignment perspective has to include two types of relationships. The first is between external and internal domains of

Figure 4. Knowledge potential perspective

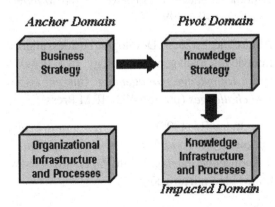

Figure 5. K-infrastructure fusion perspective

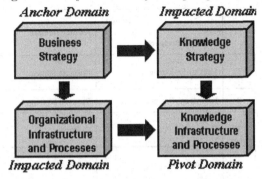

its business and knowledge components, that is, strategic fit. The second is the functional integration between business and knowledge domains. Eight single-path alignment perspectives can be then identified, namely: from anchor domain to adjacent pivot domain to impacted domain.

When the pivot and the anchor domains are not adjacent to one another, but rather across from each other on the diagonal, there will be two possible "paths" from the anchor domain to the pivot domain. This yields four fusion perspectives that result from fusing two of the eight single-path perspectives (Luftman, 1996). For example, Figure 5 shows K-infrastructure fusion perspective in which business strategy derives changes to the K-infrastructure and processes domain through organizational infrastructure and processes, and K- strategy domains.

Table 1 summarizes the 12 alignment perspectives.

CONCLUSION

Based on the premise that the realization of business value from KM investments requires alignment between the business and knowledge strategies and on the IT strategic alignment model (SAM) developed by Henderson and Venkatraman (1993), a KM strategic alignment model (KMSAM) is developed. Moreover, it provides executives with a logical framework for analyzing

Table 1. KM strategic alignment perspectives

Strategic Perspective / Domain	Anchor Domain	Pivot Domain	Impacted Domain
1 Strategy Execution	Business Strategy	Organizational Infrastructure and processes	K-Infrastructure and processes
2 Knowledge Potential	Business Strategy	K-Strategy	K-Infrastructure and processes
3 Competitive Potential	K-Strategy	Business Strategy	Organizational Infrastructure and processes
4 Service Level	K-Strategy	K-Infrastructure and processes	Organizational Infrastructure and processes
5 K-/Organizational Infrastructure	K-Infrastructure and processes	Organizational Infrastructure and processes	Business Strategy
6 K-Infrastructure/ K- Strategy	K-Infrastructure and processes	K-Strategy	Business Strategy
7 Organizational/ K- Infrastructure	Organizational Infrastructure and processes	K-Infrastructure	K-Strategy
8 Organizational Infrastructure/ Business Strategy	Organizational Infrastructure and processes	Business Strategy	K-Strategy
9 K-Infrastructure Fusion (Perspectives 4 + 7)	Business Strategy	K-Infrastructure and processes	• Organizational Infrastructure and processes • K-Strategy
10 Organizational Infrastructure Fusion (Perspectives 1 + 5)	K-Strategy	Organizational Infrastructure and processes	• Business Strategy • K-Infrastructure and processes
11 Business Strategy Fusion (Perspectives 3 + 8)	K-Infrastructure and processes	Business Strategy	• Organizational Infrastructure • K-Strategy
12 K-Strategy Fusion (Perspectives 2 + 6)	Organizational Infrastructure and processes	K-Strategy	• Business Strategy • K-Infrastructure and processes

and assessing alternative strategic choices with regard to aligning K-strategy and B-strategy.

Extension of this work would move in two directions. The first would be to use KMSAM in cross-sectional study of KM initiatives in order to identify the dominant patterns of K-strategy and B-strategy alignment. As "strategic alignment is not an event but a process of continuous adaptation and change" (Henderson & Venkatraman, 1993), the second direction would be a longitudinal study of each enterprise cycle around the alignment perspectives and how the adopted perspective is related to the degree of maturity of the KM initiative.

REFERENCES

Abou-Zeid, E. (2002). A knowledge management reference model. *Journal of Knowledge Management, 6*(5), 486-499.

Abou-Zeid, E. (2003). Developing business aligned knowledge management strategy. In E. Coakes (Ed.), *Knowledge management: Current issues and challenges* (pp. 156-172). IRM Press.

Buckman, R. (1998). *Lions, tigers and bears: Following the road from command and control to knowledge sharing.* White Paper. http://www.knowledge-nurture.com/

Earl, M. (2001). Knowledge management strategies: Toward a taxonomies. *Journal of Management Information Systems, 18*(1), 215-233.

Gold, A., Malhotra, A., & Segars, A. (2001). Knowledge management: An organizational capabilities perspective. *Journal of Management Information Systems, 18*(1), 185-214.

Grant, R. (1996). Toward a knowledge-based theory of the firm. *Strategic Management Journal, 17*(Winter Special Issue), 109-112.

Henderson, J., & Venkatraman, N. (1993). Strategic alignment: Leveraging information technology for transforming organization. *IBM Systems Journal, 32*(1), 4-16.

Luftman, J. (1996). Applying the strategic alignment model. In J. Luftman (Ed.), *Competing in the information age* (pp. 43-69). Oxford University Press.

Malhotra, Y. (1997). Profile of the ideal knowledge manager/architect. *http://www.brint.com/wwboard/messages/273.html*

Nahapier, J., & Ghoshal, S. (1998). Social capital, intellectual capital, and the organizational advantage. *Academy of Management Review, 23*, 242-266.

Narasimha, S. (2000). Organizational knowledge, human resource management and sustained competitive advantage: Toward a framework. *CR, 10*(1), 123-135.

Probst, G., Raub, S., & Romhardt, K. (2000). *Managing knowledge: Building block for success.* John Wiley.

von Krogh, G., Ichijo, K., & Nonaka, I. (2000). *Enabling knowledge creation: How to unlock the mystery of tacit knowledge and release the power of innovation.* Oxford University Press.

Zack, M.H. (1999). Developing knowledge strategy. *California Management Review, 41*(3), 125-145.

KEY TERMS

Anchor Domain: The area that provides (drives, catalyzes, or enables) the change forces applied to the pivot domain.

Impacted Domain: The area affected by a change to the pivot domain.

K-Systemic Competencies: The set of utilization-oriented characteristics of knowledge that could contribute positively to the creation of new business strategy or better support of existing business strategy.

Pivot Domain: The problem or opportunity being addressed.

This work was previously published in Encyclopedia of Information Science and Technology, edited by M. Khosrow-Pour, pp. 98-103, copyright 2005 by Information Science Reference, formerly known as Idea Group Reference (an imprint of IGI Global).

364

Compilation of References

Aamodt, A., & Nygård, M. (1995). Different roles and mutual dependencies of data, information, and knowledge: An AI perspective on their integration. *Data and Knowledge Engineering, 16,* 191-222.

Aamodt, A., & Plaza, E. (1994). Case-based reasoning: Foundational issues, methodological variations, and system approaches. *AI Communications, 7*(1), 39-59.

Abell, A. & Oxbrow, N. (1997). People who make knowledge management work: CKO, CKT, or KT? In J. Liebowitz (Ed.), *Knowledge management handbook.* Chapter 4. Boca Raton, FL: CRC Press.

Abell, A., & Oxbrow, N. (1999). *Skills for knowledge management.* London: TFPL Ltd.

Abell, D.F. (1993). *Managing with dual strategies: Mastering the present, preempting the future.* New York: The Free Press.

Abou-Zeid, E. (2002). A knowledge management reference model. *Journal of Knowledge Management, 6*(5), 486-499.

Abou-Zeid, E. (2003). Developing business aligned knowledge management strategy. In E. Coakes (Ed.), *Knowledge management: Current issues and challenges* (pp. 156-172). IRM Press.

Abou-Zeid, E. (2005). Alignment of business and knowledge management strategies. In M. Khosrow-Pour (Ed.), *Encyclopedia of information science and technology* (Vol. 1, pp. 98-103). Hershey, PA: Idea Group Publishing.

Abou-Zeid, S. (2003.) Developing business aligned knowledge management strategy. In E. Coakes (Ed.), *Knowledge management: Current issues and challenges,* (pp.156-172). Hershey, PA: IRM Press.

Abou-Zeid, E.-S. (2002). An ontology-based approach to inter-organizational knowledge transfer. *Journal of Global Information Technology Management, 5*(3), 32-47.

Achterbergh, J., & Vriens, D. (2002). Managing viable knowledge. *Systems Research and Behavioral Science, 19,* 223-241.

Ackerman, M., Pipek, V., & Wulf, V. (2003). *Sharing expertise: Beyond knowledge management.* Cambridge, MA: MIT Press.

Ackoff, R.L. & Emery, F.E. (1972). *On purposeful systems.* Chicago, IL: Aldine Atherton.

Adamides, E., & Karacapilidis, N. (2005). Knowledge management and collaborative model building in the strategy development process. *Knowledge and Process Management, 12*(2), 77-88.

Adamides, E.D., & Karacapilidis, N. (2006). Information technology support for the knowledge and social processes of innovation management. *Technovation, 26,* 50-59.

Adamides, E.D., Stamboulis, Y., & Kanellopoulos, V. (2003). Economic integration and strategic change: The role of managers' mental models. *Strategic Change, 12,* 69-82.

AFKM Home Page. (2001). Information Page. Retrieved August 7, 2001, from *https://afkm.wpafb.af.mil/ASPs/Tabs/Entry_Subject.asp* [only accessible from .mil domains]

Ahuja, A., & Katila, R. (2004). Where do resources come from? The role of idiosyncratic situations. *Strategic Management Journal, 25*(8/9), 887-907.

Ahuja, G., & Lampert, C.M. (2001). Entrepreneurship in the large corporation: A longitudinal study of how established firms create breakthrough inventions. *Strategic Management Journal, 22*(6/7), 521-543.

Akgün, A.E., Lynn, G.S., & Byrne, J.C. (2003). Organizational learning: A socio-cognitive framework. *Human Relations, 56*(7), 839-868.

Alavi, M. & Leidner, D. (1999). Knowledge management systems: Issues, challenges, and benefits. *Communications of the Association for Information Systems, 1.* Retrieved from *http://cais.isworld.org/articles/1-7/article.htm*

Alavi, M., & Leidner, D. (1999). Knowledge management systems: Emerging view and practices from the field. In *32nd Proceedings of the Hawaii International Conference on System Science.* January 5-9, Maui.

Alavi, M. & Leidner, D. E. (2001). Review: Knowledge management and knowledge management systems: Conceptual foundations and research issues. *MIS Quarterly, 25*(1), 107-136.

Alavi, M. (2000). Managing organizational knowledge. In R.W. Zmud (Ed.), *Framing the domains of IT management research: Glimpsing the future through the past.* Cincinnati, OH: Pinnaflex Educational Resources.

Alavi, M., & Leidner, D.E. (2002). Experiences into the practice of knowledge management systems. In S. Barnes (Ed.), *Knowledge management systems: Theory and practice* (pp. 17-40). New York: Thomson Learning.

Allweyer, T. (1999). A framework for redesigning and managing knowledge processes. Retrieved May 22, 2007, from http://www. processworld. com/ content/ docs/8. doc/

Alonso, G., Casati, F., Kuno, H., & Machiraju, V. (2004). *Web services: Concepts, architectures and applications.* Berlin: Springer.

Alvesson, M. (2000). Social identity and the problem of loyalty in knowledge-intensive companies. *Journal of Management Studies, 37,* 1101-1111.

American Management Association (AMA). (1999). *Knowledge management* (Research Report). New York: Author.

AMERIN Products. (n.d). *Creating value from intangible assets and human capital.* Retrieved July 12, 2005, from http://www.amerin.com.au/products.htm

Amin, A., & Cohendet, P. (2004). *Architectures of knowledge: Firms, capabilities, and communities.* Oxford, UK: Oxford University Press.

Ancona, D., & Caldwell, D. (1992). Bridging the boundary: External activity and performance in organizational teams. *Administrative Science Quarterly, 37*(4), 634-665.

Anderson, J., & Gerbing, D.W. (1988). Structural equation modelling in practice: A review and recommended two step approach. *Psychological Bulletin, 103,* 411-423.

Anderson, P. (1999). Complexity theory and organization science. *Organization Science, 10*(3), 216-232.

Andersson, U., Forsgren, M., & Holm, U. (2002). The strategic impact of external networks: Subsidiary performance and competence development in the multinational corporation. *Strategic Management Journal, 23*(11), 979-996.

Andreu, R., & Ciborra, C. (1996). Organisational learning and core capability development: The role of IT. *Journal of Strategic Information Systems, 5,* 111-127.

Andreu, R., & Sieber, S. (2005). Knowledge integration across organizations: How different types of knowledge suggest different "integration trajectories". *Knowledge and Process Management, 12*(3), 153-160.

Appleyard, M. (2003). The influence of knowledge accumulation on buyer-supplier co-development projects.

The Journal of Product Innovation Management, 20(5), 356-373.

APQC. (2001). *Embedding KM: Creating a value proposition.* TX: Author.

April, K. A. (2002). Guidelines for developing a k-strategy. *Journal of Knowledge Management, 6*(5), 445-456.

Argote, L. (1999). *Organizational learning: Creating, retaining, and transferring knowledge.* Norwell, MA: Kluwer.

Argote, L., & Ingram, P. (2000). Knowledge transfer: A basis for competitive advantage in firms. *Organizational Behaviour and Human Decision Processes, 82*(1), 150-169.

Argyris, C. (1992). Why individuals and organizations have difficulty in double loop learning. In *On organizational learning* (pp. 7-38). Cambridge: Blackwell Publishers.

Argyris, C., & Schön, D. (1978). *Organizational learning: A theory of action perspective.* New York: McGraw-Hill.

Armstrong, J.S. (2001). *Principles of forecasting: A handbook for researchers and practitioners.* Boston: Kluwer.

Arrow, K. (1962). The economic implications of learning by doing. *Review of Economic Studies, 29*(3), 155-173.

Ashiem, B.T., & Coenen, L. (2005). Knowledge bases and regional innovation systems: Comparing Nordic clusters. *Research Policy, 34*(8), 1173-1190.

Asociación Española de Bioempresas (ASEBIO). (2002). *Informe Asebio 2001.* Madrid: Author.

Asoh, D. A. (2004). *Business and knowledge strategies: Alignment and performance impact analysis.* (Doctoral Dissertation, UMI ProQuest Dissertation Publication Reference # 3134655). University at Albany, Albany, NY.

Asoh, D. A., Belardo, S., & Duchessi, P. (2003). *Alignment: The missing link in knowledge management research.*

Paper presented at the 4th European Conference on Knowledge Management, Oriel, Oxford.

Assudani, R.H. (2005). Catching the chameleon: Understanding the elusive term "knowledge". *Journal of Knowledge Management, 9*(2), 31-44.

Audretsch, D.B., & Stephan, P.E. (1996). Company-scientist locational links: The case of biotechnology. *American Economic Review, 86*(3), 641-652.

Augier, M., & Vendelo, M.T. (1999). Networks, cognition and management of tacit knowledge. *Journal of Knowledge Management, 3*(4), 252-261.

Autant-Bernard, C. (2001). Science and knowledge flows: Evidence from the French case. *Research Policy, 30*(7), 1069-1078.

Axelrod, R.M. (1976). *Structure of decision: The cognitive maps of political elites.* Princeton, NJ: Princeton University Press.

Ba, S., Stallaert, J., & Whinston, A. B. (2001). Research commentary: Introducing a third dimension in information systems design - The case for incentive alignment. *Information Systems Research, 12*(3), 225-239.

Baden-Fuller, C., & R, G. (2004). A knowledge accessing theory of strategic alliances. *Journal of Management Studies, 41*(1), 61-84.

Bagozzi, R.P. (1981). Evaluating structural equations models with unobservable variables and measurement error: A comment. *Journal of Marketing Research, 18,* 375-381.

Baird, L., & Henderson, J. C. (2001). *The knowledge engine.* San Francisco: Berret-Koehler Publishers, Inc.

Baldwin, C.Y., & Clark, K.B. (2000). *Design rules: The power of modularity (Vol. 1).* Cambridge, MA: MIT Press.

Banathy, B.H. (1996). *Designing social systems in a changing world.* New York: Plenum Publishing Co.

Barclay, D., Higgins, C., & Thompson, R. (1995). The partial least square (PLS) approach to causal modeling:

Personal computer adoption and use as an illustration. *Technology Studies, 2*(2), 285-309.

Barclay, R.O. (1997). *The CKO: Vision, strategy, ambassadorial skills, and a certain je ne sais quoi.* Retrieved May 17, 2007, from *http://www.ktic.com/*

Barnatt, C. (1998). Virtual communities and financial services: On-line business potentials and strategic choice. *International journal of Bank Marketing, 16*(4), 161-169.

Barnes, S. (Ed.). (2002). *Knowledge management systems: Theory and practice.* New York: Thomson Learning.

Barney, J. B. (1991). Firm resources and sustained competitive advantage. *Journal of Management, 17*(1), 99-120.

Barney, J.B. (1986). Organizational culture: Can it be a source of sustained competitive advantage? *The Academy of Management Review, 11*(3), 656-665.

Baron, J., & Spranca, M. (1997). Protected values. *Organizational Behavior and Human Decision Processes, 70*(1), 1–16.

Barr, P.S., & Huff, A.S. (1997). Seeing isn't believing: Understanding diversity in the timing of strategic response. *Journal of Management Studies, 34*(3), 337-370.

Baum, J., Xiao-Li, S., & Usher, J. (2000). Making the next move: How experiential and vicarious learning shape the locations of chains acquisitions. *Administrative Science Quarterly, 45*(4), 766-801.

Becerra-Fernandez, I. & Sabherwal, R. (2001). Organizational knowledge management: A contingency perspective. *Journal of Management Information Systems, 18*(1), 23-55.

Bedny, G., & Meister, D. (1997). *The Russian Theory of Activity: Current Applications to Design and Learning.* Mahwah, NJ: Lawrence Erlbaum Associates.

Beinhocker, E. (2000). On the origin of strategies. *The McKinsey Quarterly, 4*, 167-176.

Beinhocker, E.D. (1999, March). Robust adaptive strategies. *Sloan Management Review,* p. 22.

Belardo, S., & Belardo, A. W. (2002). *Innovation through learning: What leaders need to know in the 21st century.* Albany, NY: Whitston Publishing Company, Inc.

Bender, S., & Fish, A. (2000). The transfer of knowledge and the retention of expertise: The continuing need for global assignments. *Journal of Knowledge Management, 4*(2), 125-137.

Benjamins, V.R., Fensel, D., & Gómez Pérez, A.G. (1998). Knowledge management through ontologies. In *Proceedings of the 2nd International Conference on Practical Aspects of Knowledge Management (PAKM98) (pp. 5.1-5.12).* Basel, Switzerland.

Ben-Porath, Y. (1980). The f-connection: Families, friends, and firms and the organization of exchange. *Population and Development Review, 6*(1), 1-30.

Berger, P., & Luckmann, T. (1991). *The Social Construction of Reality.* London: Penguin Books. Original work published in 1966.

Bergmann, R., Althoff, K., Breen, S., Göker, M., Manago, M., Traphöner, R., & Wess, S. (2003). *Developing industrial case-based reasoning applications* (2nd ed.). Berlin: Springer-Verlag.

Berkman, E. (2001). *When bad things happen to good ideas.* Retrieved July 20, 2004, from http://www.darwinmag.com/read/040101/badthingscontent.html

Berry, L.L. & Parasuraman, A. (1991). *Marketing services.* New York: Free Press.

Bhagat, R.S., Kedia, B.L., Harveston, P.D., & Triandis, H.C. (2002). Cultural variations in the cross-border transfer of organizational knowledge: An integrative framework. *Academy of Management Review, 27*(2), 204-221.

Bhatt, G.D. (2001). Knowledge management in organizations: Examining the interaction between technologies, techniques and people. *Journal of Knowledge Management, 5*(1), 68-75.

Bhatt, G.D. (2002). Management strategies for individual knowledge and organizational knowledge. *Journal of Knowledge Management, 6*(1), 31-39.

Bierly, P. E. (1999). Development of a generic knowledge strategy typology. *Journal of Business Strategies., 16*(1), 1-26.

Bierly, P. E., & Daly, P. (2002). Aligning human resource management practices and knowledge strategies. In C. W. Choo & N. Bontis (Eds.), *The strategic management of intellectual capital and organizational knowledge* (pp. 277-295). Oxford: Oxford University Press.

Bierly, P., & Chakrabarti, A. (1996). Generic knowledge strategies in the US pharmaceutical industry. *Strategic Management Journal, 17*(Winter), 123-135.

Bierly, P., & Chakrabarti, A. (1999). Generic knowledge strategies in the U. S. pharmaceutical industry. In M. H. Zack (Ed.), *Knowledge and strategy* (pp. 231-250). Boston: Butterworth Heinemann.

Bishoff, L., & Allen, N. (2004). *Business Planning for Cultural Heritage Institutions*. Washington, D.C.: Council on Library and Information Resources.

Blackler, F. (1995). Knowledge, Knowledge Work and Organization: An Overview and Interpretation. *Organization Studies*, 16(6), 1021-1046.

Blumentritt, R., & Johnston, R. (1999). Towards a strategy for knowledge management. *Technology Analysis & Strategic Management, 11*(3), 287-300.

Bock, G. W. & Kim, Y.-G. (2002). Breaking the myths of rewards: an exploratory study of attitudes about knowledge sharing. *Information Resource Management Journal, 15*(2), 14-21.

Bodhanya, S.A. (2005, June). *Strategy making: Traversing complexity and turbulence*. Paper presented at the 7th International Conference on Foresight Management in Corporations and Public Organisations—New Visions for Sustainability, Helsinki, Finland.

Boland, R.J. (1996). Why shared meanings have no place in structuration theory: A reply to Scapens and Macintosh. *Accounting, Organizations and Society*, 21(7/8), 691-697.

Bollinger, A.S., & Smith, R.D. (2001). Managing organizational knowledge as a strategic asset. *Journal of Knowledge Management, 5*(1), 8-18.

Bonner, D. (2000). Enter the chief knowledge officer. *Training & Development, 54*(2), 36-41.

Bourdieu, P. (1997). *Outline of a theory of practice*. Cambridge, UK: Cambridge University Press.

Braithwaite, V.A., & Law, H.G. (1985). Structure of human values: Testing the adequacy of the Rokeach Value Survey. *Journal of Personality and Social Psychology, 49*, 250-262.

Brancheau, J.C., & Wetherbe, J.C. (1987). Key issues in information systems management. *MIS Quarterly, 11*(1), 22-45.

Brancheau, J.C., Janz, B.D., & Wetherbe, J.C. (1996). Key issues in information systems management: 1994-95 SIM Delphi results. *MIS Quarterly, 20*(2), 225-242.

Breschi, S., & Lissoni, F. (2001). Localised knowledge spillovers vs. innovative milieux: Knowledge "tacitness" reconsidered. *Papers in Regional Science, 80*(3), 255-273.

Bresman, H., Birkinshaw, J., & Nobel, R. (1999). Knowledge transfer in international acquisitions. *Journal of International Business Studies, 30*(3), 439-462.

Breu, K., Grimshaw, D., Myers, A. (2000). *Releasing the value of knowledge: A survey of UK industry*. Cranfield School of Management.

Bright, J.R. (1979). Technology forecasting as an influence on technological innovation: Past examples and future expectations. In M.J. Baker (Ed.), *Industrial innovation* (pp. 228-255). Basingstoke, UK: The Macmillan Press Ltd.

Brown, J.S., & Duguid, P. (1991). Organizational learning and communities-of-practices: Toward a unified view of working, learning, and innovation. *Organization Science, 2*(1), 40-57.

Bruner, J. (1990). *Acts of Meaning*. Cambridge MA: Harvard University Press.

Büchel, B., & Raub, S. (2002). Building knowledge-creating value networks. *European Management Journal, 20*(6), 587-596.

Buckman, R. (1998). *Lions, tigers and bears: Following the road from command and control to knowledge sharing*. White Paper. http://www.knowledge-nurture.com/

Buckman, R.H. (1998). Knowledge sharing at Buckman Labs. *The Journal of Business Strategy, 19*(1), 11-15.

Bukowitz, W. R. & Williams, R. L. (1999). *The Knowledge management fieldbook*. London: Pearson Education Ltd.

Bunnell, D. (2000). *Making the Cisco connection: The story behind the real Internet superpower*. New York: John Wiley.

Burgelman, R.A., Maidique, M.A., & Wheelwright, S.C. (1996). *Strategic management of technology and innovation* (2nd ed.). Boston: Irwin/McGraw-Hill.

Burstein, F., & Linger, H. (2003). Supporting post-Fordist work practices. A knowledge management framework for supporting knowledge work. *Information Technology & People*, 16(3), 289-305.

Caloghirou, Y., Aimilia, P., Yiannis, S., & Lefteris, P. (2004). Industry versus firm-specific effects on performance: Contrasting SMEs and large-sized firms. *European Management Journal, 22*(2), 231-243.

Caloghirou, Y., Kastelli, I., & Tsakanikas, A. (2004). Internal capabilities and external knowledge sources: complements or substitutes for innovative performance? *Technovation, 24*(1), 29-39.

Camagni, R. (1991). *Innovation networks: Spatial perspectives*. London: Belhaven Press.

Camisón, C. (2002). *A proposal of conceptualization for organization distinctive competences stock* (Working Paper No. 3-02). Castellón: University Jaume I, Research Group on Strategy, Knowledge Management and Organizational Learning.

Camisón, C. (2004). Shared, competitive, and comparative advantages: A competence-based view of industrial-district competitiveness. *Environment and Planning A, 36*, 2227-2256.

Capshaw, S. (1999, July). Spotlight on knowledge leadership, where's the CKO? *Inform*, pp. 20-21.

Carley, K., & Palmquist, M. (1992). Extracting, representing, and analyzing mental models. *Social Forces, 70*(3), 601-636.

Carlile, P.R. (2002). A pragmatic view of knowledge and boundaries: Boundary objects in new product development. *Organization Science, 13*(4), 442-445.

Carlisle, Y. (1999). Strategic thinking and knowledge management. In *OU MBA Managing Knowledge Readings Part 1* (pp. 19-29). Milton Keynes: Open University Business School.

Carmel, E. & Agarwal, R. (2001). Tactical approaches to alleviating distance in global software development. *IEEE Software*, 18(2), 23-29.

Cascella, V. (2002, November). Effective strategic planning: Processes, measurements and accountability are keys to success. *Quality Progress*, pp. 62-67.

Castells, M. (1996). *The Rise of the Network Society*. Oxford: Blackwell.

Castells, M. (2000). Materials for an exploratory theory of the network society. *British Journal of Sociology, 51*(1), 5-24.

Castillo, J. (2002). A note on the concept of tacit knowledge. *Journal of Management Inquiry, 11*(1), 46-57.

Cavusgil, S.T, Calantone, R.J., & Zhao, Y. (2003). Tacit knowledge transfer and firm innovation capability. *The Journal of Business & Industrial Marketing, 18*(1), 6-22.

Chae, B., & Bloodgood, J.M. (2006). The paradoxes of knowledge management: An eastern philosophical perspective. *Information and Organization, 16*(1), 1-26.

Chan, Y. (2002). Why haven't we mastered alignment? The importance of the Informal Organization Structure. *MIS Quarterly Executive,* 1(21), 76-112.

Chan, Y. E. (1992). *Business strategy, information systems strategy, and strategic fit: Measurement and performance impact* (Dissertation Summary). London, Ontario: University of Western Ontario.

Chan, Y. E., Huff, S. L., Barclay, D. W., & Copeland, D. G. (1997). Business strategic orientation, information systems strategic orientation, and strategic alignment. *Information Systems Research, 8*(2), 125-150.

Chan, Y. E., Sabherwal, R., & Thatcher, J. B. (2006). Antecedents and outcomes of strategic IS alignment: An empirical investigation. *IEEE Transactions on Engineering Management, 53*(1), 27-47.

Chandler, A. (1966). *Strategy and Structure.* Garden City, N.Y.: Doubleday & Company.

Charney, M., & Jordan, J. (2000). The strategic benefits of knowledge management. Serviceware Technologies.

Chase, L. R. (1997). The knowledge-based organization: An international survey. *Journal of Knowledge Management, 1*(1), 38-49

Chattopadhyay, P., Glick, W.H., Miller, C.C., & Huber, G.P. (1999). Determinants of executive beliefs: Comparing functional conditioning and social influence. *Strategic Management Journal, 20,* 763-789.

Chatzkel, J. (2000). A conversation with Hubert Saint-Onge. *Journal of Intellectual Capital, 1*(1), 101-115.

Checkland, P. B. (1991). From framework through experience to learning: the essential nature of action research. In H. E. Nissen, H. K. Klein, & R. Hirschheim (Eds.), *Information systems research: Contemporary approaches and emergent traditions.* Amsterdam: International Federation for Information Processing (IFIP).

Checkland, P., & Holwell, S. (1998). *Information, systems and information systems.* Chichester, UK: Wiley.

Checkland, P.B. (1981). *Systems thinking, systems practice.* Chichester, England: Wiley.

Child, J. (1972). Organizational structure, environment and performance: The role of strategic choice. *Sociology, 6,* 1-22.

Chiles, T.H., Meyer, A.D., & Hench, T.J. (2004). Organizational emergence: The origin and transformation of Branson, Missouri's musical theaters. *Organization Science, 15*(5), 499-519.

Chin, W. W. (2006). *PLS-Graph (Version 3. 0).* Soft Modeling Inc.

Chin, W. W., & Todd, P. A. (1995, June). On the use, usefulness, and ease of use of structural equation modeling in MIS research: A note of caution. *MISQ,* pp. 237-246.

Chiva, R., & Alegre, J. (2005). Organizational learning and organizational knowledge: Towards the integration of two approaches. *Management Learning, 36*(1), 49-68.

Cho, G., Jerrell, H., & Landay, W. (2000). *Program management 2000: Know the way how knowledge management can improve DoD acquisition.* Fort Belvoir: Defense Systems Management College.

Choi, B., & Lee, H. (2003). An empirical investigation of KM styles and their effects on corporate performance. *Information and Management, 40,* 403-417.

Choo, C.W. (1998). *The knowing organization: How organizations use information to construct meaning, create knowledge, and make decisions.* New York: Oxford University Press.

Christensen, C.M. (1997). *The innovator's dilemma: When new technologies cause great firms to fail.* Boston: Harvard University Press.

Ciborra, C.U. (1996). The platform organization: Recombining strategies, structures and surprises. *Organization Science, 7*(2), 103-118.

Ciborra, C.U. (1998). Crisis and foundations: An inquiry into the nature and limits of models and methods in the information systems discipline. *Journal of Strategic Information Systems, 7,* 5-16.

Cilliers, P. (1998). *Complexity and postmodernism.* London: Routledge.

Clare, M. & DeTore, A. W. (2000). *Knowledge assets.* San Diego: Harcourt.

Coakes, E. (2003). Preface. In E. Coakes (Ed.), *Knowledge management: Current issues and challenges.* Hershey, PA: IRM Press.

Coakes, E., Willis, D., & Clarke, S. (2002). Introduction. In E. Coakes, D. Willis & S. Clarke (Eds.), *Knowledge management in the socio-technical world: The graffitti continues* (pp. 1-3). London: Springer-Verlag.

Codet, M. (2000). The art of scenarios and strategic planning: Tools and pitfalls. *Technological Forecast and Social Change, 65,* 3-22.

Cohen, W., & Levinthal, D. (1989). Innovation and learning: The two faces of R&D. *Economic Journal, 99*(397), 569-586.

Cohen, W., & Levinthal, D. (1990). Absorptive capacity: A new perspective on learning and innovation. *Administrative Science Quarterly, 35*(1), 128-152.

Cohen, W., Nelson, R., & Walsh, J. (2002). Links and impacts: The influence of public research on industrial R&D. *Management Science, 48*(1), 1-23.

Collins, J.C., & Porras, J.I. (1996, September-October). Building your company's vision. *Harvard Business Review,* pp. 65-88.

Collis, D. J., & Montgomery, C. A. (1999). Competing on resources: Strategies in the 1990s. In M. H. Zack (Ed.), *Knowledge and strategy* (pp. 25-40). Boston: Butterworth Heinemann.

Collison, C. & Parcell, G. (2001). *Learning to fly: Practical lessons from one of the world's leading knowledge companies.* Albany, OR: Capstone Publishing Ltd.

Combe, I.A., & Greenley, G.E. (2004). Capabilities for strategic flexibility: A cognitive content framework. *European Journal of Marketing, 38*(11/12), 1456-1480.

Conner, K.R., & Prahalad, C.K. (1996). A resource-based theory of the firm: Knowledge versus opportunism. *Organization Science, 7*(5), 477–501.

Cook, S.D.N., & Brown, J.S. (1999). Bridging epistemologies: The generative dance between organizational knowledge and organizational knowing. *Organization Science, 10*(4), 381-400.

Cooper, R. & Kleindschmidt, E. (1995). An investigation into the NPD process: Steps, deficiencies, impact. *Journal of Product Innovation Management, 12,* 374-391.

Cooper, R. G. (1987). Defining the new product strategy. *IEEE Transactions on Engineering Management, EM-34*(3), 184-193.

Corcoran, M., & Jones, R. (1997). Chief knowledge officer? Perceptions, pitfalls, & potential. *Information Outlook, 1*(6), 30-36.

Couger, D.J. (1988). Key human resource issues in IS in the 1990s: Views of IS executives versus human resource executives. *Information & Management, 14*(4), 161-174.

Cowan, R., David, P.A., & Fory, D. (2000). The Explicit Economics of Knowledge Codification and Tacitness, *Industrial and Corporate Change,* 9(2), 211-253.

Cragg, P., King, M., & Hussin, H. (2002). IT alignment and firm performance in small manufacturing firms. *Journal of Strategic Information Systems, 11,* 109-132.

Crawford, C. H., Bate, B. P., Cgerbakov, L., Holley, K., & Tsocanos, C. (2005). Toward an on demand service-oriented architecture. *IBM Systems Journal, 44*(1), 81-107.

Crosby, L.A., Bitner, M.J., & Gill, J.D. (1990). Organizational structure of values. *Journal of Business Research, 20*(2), 123-134.

Croteau, A. -M., & Bergeron, F. (2001). An information technology trilogy: Business strategy, technological deployment and organizational performance. *Strategic Information Systems, 10,* 77-99.

Cummings, J.L., & Teng, B.-S. (2003). Transferring R&D knowledge: The key factors affecting knowledge transfer success. *Journal of Engineering and Technology Management, 20*(1/2), 39-68.

Cusumano, M., & Nobeoka, K. (1998). *Thinking beyond lean*. New York: The Free Press.

Cyert, R., & March , J. (1963). *A behavioural theory of the firm*. Englewood Cliffs, NJ: Prentice Hall.

Daft, R.L., Sormunen, L., & Parks, D. (1988). Chief executive scanning, environmental characteristics, and company performance: An empirical study. *Strategic Management Journal, 9*(2), 123-139.

Daghfous, A. (2003). Uncertainty and learning in university-industry knowledge transfer projects. *Journal of American Academy of Business, 3*(1/2), 145-151.

Daghfous, A. (2004). Organizational learning, knowledge and technology transfer: A case study. *The Learning Organization, 11*(1), 67-83.

Dalkey, N.C., & Helmer, O. (1963). An experimental application of the Delphi method to the use of experts. *Management Science, 9*(3), 458-467.

Darr, E.D., & Kurtzberg, T.R. (2000). An investigation of partner similarity dimensions on knowledge transfer. *Organizational Behaviour and Human Decision Processes, 82*(1), 28-44.

Darroch, J. (2003). Developing a measure of knowledge management behaviours and practices. *Journal of Knowledge Management, 7*(5), 41-54.

Davenport, T. (1999). Knowledge management and the broader firm: Strategy, advantage and performance. In J. Liebowitz (Ed.), *Knowledge management handbook*. (2.1-2.11). Washington, DC: CRC Press.

Davenport, T. H. (2005, June). The coming commoditization of processes. *Harvard Business Review, 83*(6), 101-108.

Davenport, T. H., & Glaser, J. (2002). Just-in-time delivery comes to knowledge management. *Harvard Business Review*(July 2002), 5-9.

Davenport, T. H., DeLong, D. W., & Beers, M. C. (1998). Successful knowledge management projects. *Sloan Management Review, 39*(2), 43-57.

Davenport, T. H., Jarvenpaa, S. L., & Beers, M. C. (1996). Improving knowledge work processes. *Sloan Management Review, 37*(4), 53-65.

Davenport, T.H. & Prusak, L. (1998). *Working knowledge: How organizations manage what they know*. Boston, MA: Harvard Business School Press.

Davenport, T.H. & Short, J.E. (1990). The new industrial engineering: Information technology and business process redesign. *Sloan Management Review*, 11-27.

Davenport, T.H. (1993). *Process innovation: Reengineering work through information technology*. Cambridge, MA: Harvard Business School Press.

Davenport, T.H. (1997). *Secrets of successful knowledge management*. Austin, TX: Quantum.

Davenport, T.H. (1997). Ten principles of knowledge management and four case studies. *Knowledge and Process Management, 4*(3), 187-208.

Davenport, T.H. (1999). Knowledge management and the broader firm: Strategy, advantage, and performance. In J. Liebowitz (Ed.), *Knowledge management handbook* (pp. 1-11). Boca Raton, FL: CRC Press.

Davis, S., McAdams, A., Dixon, N., Orlikowski, W., & Leonard, D. (1998). *Twenty questions on knowledge in the organization*. London: Ernst & Young Center for Business Innovation.

Dawson, R. (2000). Knowledge capabilities as the focus of organisational development. *Journal of Knowledge Management, 4*(4), 320-327.

Day, G.S. (1994). The capabilities of market-driven organizations, *Journal of Marketing, 58*(4), 37-52.

Day, G.S. (2000). Managing marketing relationships. *Journal of the Academy of Marketing Science, 28*(1), 24-31.

Dayasindhu, N. (2002). Embeddedness, knowledge transfer, industry cluster and global competitiveness: A case study of the indian software industry. *Technovation, 22*(9), 551-560.

De Geus, A. (1988). Planning as learning. *Harvard Business Review, 66*(2), 70-74.

De Geus, A. (1997). *The living company: Habits for survival in a turbulent business environment.* Boston: Harvard Business Press.

De Long, D. W., Fahey, L. (2000). Diagnosing cultural barriers to knowledge management. *Academy of management executive, 14*(4), 113-127.

DeCarolis, D.M., & Deeds, D.L. (1999). The impact of stocks and flows of organizational knowledge on firm performance: An empirical investigation of the biotechnology industry. *Strategic Management Journal, 20*, 953-968.

DeLurgio, S.A. (1998). *Forecasting principles and applications.* Boston: Irwin/McGraw-Hill.

Dennis, A., Vessey, I. (2005). Three Knowledge Management Strategies: Knowledge Hierarchies, Knowledge Markets, and Knowledge Communities. *MIS Quarterly Executive, 4*(4), 399-412.

DeSanctis, G., & Poole, M.S. (1994). Capturing the complexity in advanced technology use: Adaptive structuration theory. *Organization Science, 5*(2), 121-145.

Deutschman, A. (1994, October). The managing wisdom of high tech superstars. *Fortune, 17*, 197-206.

Dexter, S.A., Janson, A.M., Kiudorf, E., & Laast-Laas, J. (1993). Key information technology issues in Estonia. *International Journal of Information Management, 2*(2), 139-153.

Dey, A.K., & Abowd, G.D. (2000). *Towards a better understanding of context and context-awareness.* Atlanta: Graphics, Visualization and Usability Center and College of Computing, Georgia Institute of Technology.

Diakoulakis, I.E., Georgopoulos, N.B., Koulouriotis, D.E., & Emiris, D.M. (2004). Towards a holistic knowledge management model. *Journal of Knowledge Management, 8*(1), 32-46.

Dibella, A., & Nevis, E. (1998). *How organizations learn: An integrated strategy for building learning capacity.* San Francisco: Jossey-Bass.

Dickson, G.W., Leitheiser, R.L., & Brancheau, C.J. (1984). Key information systems issues for the 1980's. *MIS Quarterly, 8*(3), 135-159.

Dierickx, I., & Cool, K. (1989). Asset stock accumulation and sustainability of competitive advantage. *Management Science, 35*, 1504-1513.

Dillman, D.A., Sinclair, M.D., & Clark, J.R. (1993). Effects of questionnaire length, respondent-friendly design, and a difficult question on response rates for occupant-addressed census mail surveys. *Public Opinion Quarterly, 57*(3), 289-304.

Dodgson, M. (1993). Organizational learning: A review of some literatures. *Organization Studies, 14*(3), 375-394.

Doke, E.R., & Swanson, N.E. (1995). Decision variables for selecting prototyping in information systems development: A Delphi study of MIS managers. *Information & Management, 29*(4), 173-182.

Dollinger, M.J. (1984). Environmental boundary-spanning and information processing effects on organizational performance. *Academy of Management Journal, 27*, 351-368.

Dommeyer, C.J., & Moriart, E. (2000). Comparing two forms of an e-mail survey: Embedded vs. attached. *International Journal of Market Research, 42*(1), 39-50.

Dose, J.J. (1997). Work values: An integrative framework and illustrative application to organizational socialization. *Journal of Occupational and Organizational Psychology, 70*, 219 -240.

Dose, J.J., &. Klimoski, R.J. (1999). The diversity of diversity: Work values effects on formative team processes. *Human Resource Management Review, 9*(1), 83-108.

Drew, S. (1999). Building knowledge management into strategy: Making sense of a new perspective. *Long Range Planning, 32*(1), 130-136.

Drucker, P. (1959). *Landmarks of tomorrow*. New York: Harper.

Drucker, P. F. (1994). The age of social transformation. *The Atlantic Monthly, 274*(5), 53-80.

Drucker, P. F. (2002, August). The discipline of innovation [Special issue: The Innovative Enterprise]. *Harvard Business Review*, pp. 95-102.

Drucker, P.F. (1993). *Post-capitalism society*. Oxford: Butterworth Heinemann.

Drucker, P.F. (1996). *Managing in a time of great change*. Boston: Butterwort-Heinemann.

du Toit, A. (2003). Knowledge: A sense making process shared through narrative. *Journal of Knowledge Management, 7*(3), 27-37.

Duffy, J. (2001). The tools and technologies needed for knowledge management. *The Information Management Journal, 35*(1), 64-67.

Dushnitsky, G., & Lenox, M. (2005). When do firms undertake R&D by investing in new ventures? *Strategic Management Journal, 26*(10), 947-965.

Dyer, G. & McDonough, B. (2001, May). The state of knowledge management. *Knowledge Management*, 31-36.

Dyer, G., & McDonough, B. (2001, May). The state of KM. Communicator eNewsletter. Retrieved May 16, 2007, from http://http://www.destinationcrm.com/km/

Dyer, J.H., & Nobeoka, K. (2000). Creating and managing a high-performance knowledge-sharing network: The Toyota case. *Strategic Management Journal, 21*(3), 345-367.

Earl, M. (2001). Knowledge management strategies: Toward a taxonomy. *Journal of Management Information Systems, 18*(1), 215-233.

Earl, M. J. (1989). *Management strategies for information technology*. New York: Prentice Hall.

Earl, M.J., & Scott, I.A. (1999). What is a chief knowledge officer? *Sloan Management Review, 40*(2), 29-38.

Eden, C., & Ackermann, F. (1998). *Making strategy: The journey of strategic management*. London: Sage.

Eden, C., & Ackermann, F. (2000). Mapping distinctive competencies: A systemic approach. *Journal of Operational Research Society, 51*, 12-20.

Edvinsson, L. & Malone, M. S. (1997). *Intellectual capital*. New York: Harper Collins.

Eisenhardt, K. (1989). Making fast strategic decisions in high velocity environments. *Academy of Management Journal, 32*(3), 543-576.

Eisenhardt, K.M., & Brown, S.L. (1999). Patching: Restitching business portfolios in dynamic markets. *Harvard Business Review, 77*(3), 72-82.

Eisenhardt, K.M., & Martin, J.A. (2000). Dynamic capabilities: What are they? *Strategic Management Journal, 21*, 1105-1121.

Ellis, R.K., & Hall, M.L.W. (1994). Systems and values: An approach for practical organizational intervention. *Proceedings of the ISSS, 94*.

Elmes, M.B., & Kasouf, C.J. (1995). Knowledge workers and organizational learning: Narratives from biotechnology. *Management Learning, 26*, 403-422.

Engeström, Y. (1999). Activity theory and individual and social transformation. In Y. Engeström, R. Miettinen, & R. L. Punamäki (Eds.), *Perspectives on Activity Theory* (pp. 19-38). Cambridge UK: Cambridge University Press.

Eppler, M., Seifried, P., & Röpnack, A. (1999). *Improving knowledge intensive processes through an enterprise knowledge medium*. Paper presented at the 1999 ACM SIGPR CONFERENCE, New Orleans, Louisiana.

Ettlie, J., Bridges, W., & O'Keefe, R. (1984). Organizational strategy and structural differences for radical vs. incremental innovation. *Management Science, 30*(6), 682- 695.

Fahey, L. & Prusak, L. (1998). The eleven deadliest sins of knowledge management. *California Management Review, 40*(3), 265-276.

Fairlough, G. (1982). A note on the use of Weltanschauung in Checkland's systems thinking, systems practices. *Journal of Applied Systems Analysis, 9,* 131-132.

Fayard, P. (2003). Strategic communities for knowledge creation: A Western proposal for the Japanese concept of Ba, *Journal of Knowledge Management,* 7(5), 25-31.

Fernandes, K.J., & Raja, V. (2002). A practical knowledge transfer system: A case study. *Work Study, 51*(2/3), 140-148.

Ferstl, O. K., & Sinz, E. J. (1995). Der Ansatz des Semantischen Objektmodells (SOM) zur Modellierung von Geschäftsprozessen. *Wirtschaftsinformatik, 37*(3), 209-220.

Flanagin, A.J. (2002). The elusive benefits of the technology support of knowledge management. *Management Communication Quarterly,* 16(2), 242-248.

Flash, C. (2001, May). Who is the CKO? *Knowledge Management Magazine.* Freedom Technology Media Group. Retrieved August 31, 2007 from http://www.destinationkm.com/articles/default.asp?ArticleID=232

Fleming, L. (2001). Recombinant uncertainty in technological search. *Management Science, 47*(1), 117-132.

Florida, R. (1995). Toward the learning region. *Futures,* 27(5), 527-536.

Foote, N.W., Matson, E., & Rudd, N. (2001). Managing the knowledge manager. *The McKinsey Quarterly, 3,* 120-129.

Fornell, C. (1982). *A second generation of multivariate analysis. Volume 2: Measurement and evaluation.* New York: Praeger Publishers.

Frank, K.A., & Fahrbach, K. (1999). Organization culture as a complex system: Balance and information in models of influence and selection. *Organization Science, 10*(3), 253-277.

Frappaolo, C., & Capshaw, C. (1999). Knowledge management software: Capturing the essence of know-how and innovation. *Information Management Journal, 33*(3), 44-48.

Friedman, B. (1997). *Human values and the design of computer technology.* Cambridge, UK: Cambridge University Press.

Frishammar, J., & Horte, S. (2005). Managing external information in manufacturing firms: The impact on innovation performance. *Journal of Product Innovation Management, 22*(3), 251–266.

Fritzsche, D.J. (1995). Personal Values: Potential Keys to Ethical Decision Making, *Journal of Business Ethics,* 14, 909-922.

Gaines, B.R., & Shaw, M.L.G. (1986). A learning model for forecasting the future of information technology. *Future Computing Systems, 1*(1), 31-69.

Gamble, P.R., & Blackwell, J. (2001). *Knowledge management: A state of the art guide.* London: Kogan Page.

Gao, F., Li, M., & Nakamori, Y. (2002). Systems thinking on knowledge and its management: Systems methodology for knowledge management. *Journal of Knowledge Management,* 6(1), 7-17.

Garavelli, C.A., Gorgoglione, M., & Scozzi, B. (2002). Managing knowledge transfer by knowledge technologies. *Technovation, 22*(5), 269-279.

Garshol, L.M. (2002). What are topic maps? Retrieved May 22, 2007, from http://www.XML.com

Garud, R., & Nayyer, R. (2004). Transformative capacity: Continual structuring by intertemporal technology transfer. In K. Starkey, S. Tempest & A. McKinlay (Eds.), *How organizations learn* (pp. 137-165). London: Thompson.

Gefen, D., Straub, D. W., & Boudreau, M. -C. (2000). Structural equation modeling and regression: Guidelines for research practice. *Communications of the Association for Information Systems, 4,* Article 7, 1-77.

Geletkanycz, M.A., & Hambrick, D.C. (1997). The external ties of top executives: Implications for strategic choice and performance. *Administrative Science Quarterly, 42*(4), 654-681.

George, J.M., & Jones, G.R. (1997). Experiencing work: Values, attitudes, and moods. *Human Relations, 50*(4), 393-417.

Gerencser, M., Napolitano, F., & Van Lee, R. (2006). The megacommunity manifesto. Retrieved May 20, 2007, from http://www.strategy-business.com/resiliencereport/resilience/rr00035

Gery, G. (1997). Granting three wishes through performance-centered design. *Communications of the ACM, 40*(7), 54-59.

Geschka, H. (1992). The strategic aspect in the process of innovation. In H. Geschka & H. Hubner (Eds.), *Innovation strategies: Theoretical approaches - experiences - improvements* (pp. 69-78). Amsterdam: Elsevier Science Publishers.

Gherardi, S. (2000). Practice-based Theorizing on Learning and Knowing in Organizations. *Organization, 7*(2), 211–223.

Gherardi, S., & Nicolini, D. (2000). To transfer is to transform: The circulation of safety knowledge. *Organization, 7*(2), 329-348.

Ghoshal, S. & Naphiet, J. (1998). Social capital, intellectual capital and the organizational advantage. *Academy of Management Review, 23*(2), 242-266.

Giddens, A. (1979). *Central problems in social theory: Action, structure, and contradiction in social analysis.* London: MacMillan Press, Ltd.

Giddens, A. (1984). *The constitution of society: Outline of the theory of structuration.* Berkeley, CA: University of California Press.

Ginsberg, A., & Baum, J.C. (1994). Evolutionary processes and patterns of core business change. In J.C. Baum & J. Singh (Eds.), *Evolutionary dynamics of organizations* (pp. 127-151). New York: Oxford University Press.

Gloet, M., & Berrell, M. (2003). The dual paradigm nature of knowledge management: Implications of achieving quality outcomes in human resource management. *Journal of Knowledge Management, 7*(1), 78-89.

Goffman, E. (1974). *Frame analysis: An essay on the organization of experience.* Boston: Northeastern University Press.

Goh, S. C. (2002). Managing effective knowledge transfer: An integrative framework and some practice implications. *Journal of Knowledge Management, 6*(1), 23-30.

Gold, A. H., Malhotra, A., & Segars, A. H. (2001). Knowledge management: An organizational capabilities perspective. *Journal of Management Information Systems, 18*(1), 185-214.

Goldkuhl, G., & Röstlinger, A. (2003). The significance of work practice diagnosis: Socio-pragmatic ontology and epistemology of change analysis. In *The International workshop on Action in Language, Organisations and Information Systems (ALOIS-2003).* Linköping University. Retrieved October 19, 2006, from http://www.vits.org/?pageId=161

Gordon, J. (1996). Performance technology. In D. Zielinski (Ed.), *The effective performance consultant* (pp. 1-7). Minneapolis, MN: Lakewood Publications.

Gorelick, C., & Tantawy-Monsou, B. (2006). For performance through learning, knowledge management is the critical practice. *The Learning Organization, 12*(2), 125-139.

Gottschalk, P. (2000). Studies of key issues in IS management around the world. *International Journal of Information Management, 20*, 169-180.

Graham, A. B. & Pizzo V. G. (1996). A question of balance: Case studies in strategic knowledge management. *European Management Journal, 14*(4), 338-346. Reprinted in Klein DA (q.v.).

Granger, C.W.J. (1989). *Forecasting in business and economics.* San Diego: Academic Press.

Granovetter, M. (1985). Economic action and social structure: The problem of embeddedness. *The American Journal of Sociology, 91*(3), 481-510.

Grant, R. (1996). Toward a knowledge-based theory of the firm. *Strategic Management Journal, 17*(Winter Special Issue), 109-112.

Grant, R. G. (1997). The knowledge-based view of the firm: Implications for management practice. *Long Range Planning, 30*(3), 450-454.

Grant, R. M. (1999). The resource-based theory of competitive advantage: Implications for strategy formulation. In M. H. Zack (Ed.), *Knowledge and strategy* (pp. 3-23). Boston: Butterworth Heinemann.

Grant, R.M. (1991). The resource-based theory of competitive advantage: Implications for strategy formulation. *California Management Review, 33*(3), 114-135.

Grant, R.M. (1996). Prospering in dynamically competitive environments: Organizational capability as knowledge integration. *Organization Science, 7*(4), 375-387.

Grant, R.M. (2003). The knowledge-based view of the firm. In D.O. Faulkner & A. Campbell (Eds.), *The Oxford handbook of strategy* (pp. 203-229). Oxford, UK: Oxford University Press.

Grant, R.M., & Spender, J.C. (1996). Knowledge and the firm: Overview. *Strategic Management Journal, 17*(Winter Special Issue), 5-9.

Green, A., & Price I. (2000). Whither FM? A Delphi study of the profession and the industry. *Facilities, 18*(7/8), 281-292.

Grover, V. & Davenport, T.H. (2001). General perspectives on knowledge management: Fostering a research agenda. *Journal of Management Information Systems, 18*(1), 5-21.

Gruber, T. R. (1993). A translation approach to portable ontology specifications. *Knowledge Acquisition, 5*(2), 199-220.

Gulati, R., & Gargiulo, M. (1999). Where do inter organizational networks come from? *American Journal of Sociology, 104*(3), 1439-1493.

Guns, B. (1998). The chief knowledge officer's role: Challenges and competencies. *Journal of Knowledge Management, 1*(4), 315-319.

Gupta, A.K., & Govindarajan, V. (1991a). Knowledge flows and the structure of control within multinational corporations. *Academy of Management Review, 16*(4), 768-792.

Gurteen, D. (1999). Creating a knowledge sharing culture. *Knowledge Management Magazine, 2*(5). Retrieved May 16, 2007, from http://www.kmmagazine.com

Guzman, G.A.C., & Wilson, J. (2005). The "soft" dimension of organizational knowledge transfer. *Journal of Knowledge Management, 9*(2), 59-74.

Habermas, J. (1984). *The Theory of Communicative Action*, Polity Press.

Hackney, R., Burn, J., & Dhillon, G. (2000). Challenging assumptions for strategic information systems planning. Theoretical perspectives. *Communications of the AIS, 3*(9).

Hagedoorn, J. (1993). Understanding the rationale of strategic technology partnering: Inter-organizational modes of cooperation and sectoral differences. *Strategic Management Journal, 14*(5), 371-385.

Hagedoorn, J., & Schakenraad, J. (1994). The effect of strategic technology alliances on company performance. *Strategic Management Journal, 15*(5), 291-309.

Hair, H.F., Anderson R.E., Tatham, R.L., & Black, W.C. (1999). *Multivariate analysis*. New York: Prentice Hall.

Håkanson, L. (2001). The rediscovery of articulation, *European Business Forum*, 5, 29-36.

Hall, E.T. (1959). *The Silent Language*, Anchor Books, New York.

Hall, M. -J. (2002, Summer). Aligning the organization to increase performance results. *The Public Manager*, pp. 7-10.

Hall, R. (1993). A framework linking intangible resources and capabilities to sustainable competitive advantage. *Strategic Management Journal, 14*, 607–618.

Hall, R. (1999). The strategic analysis of intangible resources. In M. H. Zack (Ed.), *Knowledge and strategy* (pp. 181-195). Boston: Butterworth Heinemann.

Hall, W. (2005). Biological nature of knowledge in the learning organization. *The Learning Organisation*, 12(2), 169-188.

Halliday, M. (1975). *Learning How to Mean*. London: Edward Arnold.

Hambrick, D. C., & Fredrickson, J. W. (2001). Are you sure you have a strategy? *Academy of Management Executive, 15*(4), 48-59.

Hambrick, D.C., & Mason, P.A. (1984). Upper echelons: The organization as a reflection of its top managers. *Academy of Management Review, 9*, 193-206.

Hamel, G., & Prahalad, C.K. (1994). *Competing for the future*. Boston: Harvard Business School Press.

Hammer, M. & Champy, J. (1993). *Reengineering the corporation: A manifesto for business revolution*. New York: Harper Collins.

Hammer, M. (1990). Reengineer work: Don't automate, obliterate. *Harvard Business Review*, 104-112.

Han, J., & Kamber, M. (2001). *Data mining: Concepts and techniques*. San Diego: Academic Press.

Hansen, M. T., Nohria, N., & Tierney, T. (1999, March-April). What's your strategy for managing knowledge. *Harvard Business Review, 680-689*.

Hansen, M. T., Nohria, N., & Tierney, T. (2001). What's your strategy for managing knowledge? *Harvard Business Review on Organizational Learning*, 61-86.

Hargadon, A., & Fanelli, A. (2002). Action and possibility: Reconciling dual perspectives of knowledge in organizations. *Organization Science, 13*(3), 290-302.

Hatten, K. J. & Rosenthal, S. R. (1999). Managing the process centred enterprise. *Long Range Planning, 32*(3), 293-310.

Hatten, K. J. & Rosenthal, S. R. (2001). *Reaching for the knowledge edge*. New York: AMACOM.

Havens, C., & Knapp, E. (1999). Easing into knowledge management. *Strategy Leadership, 27*(2), 4-9.

Hayes, N., & Walsham, G. (2003). Knowledge Sharing and ICTs: A Relational Perspective. In M. Easterby-Smith, & M. Lyles (Eds.), *The Blackwell Handbook of Organizational Learning and Knowledge Management* (pp. 54-77). Blackwell Publishing.

Hayes, R.H., & Pisano, G.P. (1994). Beyond world-class: The new manufacturing strategy. *Harvard Business Review, 72*(1), 77-86.

Hazlett, S.-A., McAdam, R., & Gallagher, S. (2005). Theory building in knowledge management: In search of paradigms. *Journal of Management Inquiry, 14*(1), 31-42.

Hearn, G., Rooney, D., & Mandeville, T. (2003). Phenomenological turbulence and innovation in knowledge systems. *Prometheus, 21*(2), 231-245.

Hedlund, G. (1994). A model of knowledge management and the N-form corporation. *Strategic Management Journal, 15*(Special Issue), 73-90.

Heisig, P. (2001). Business process oriented knowledge management. In K. Mertins, P. Heisig & J. Vorbeck (Eds.), *Knowledge management: Best practices in Europe* (pp. 13-26). Berlin: Springer.

Helfat, C.E., & Eisenhardt, K.M. (2004). Inter-temporal economies of scope, organizational modularity, and the dynamics of diversification. *Strategic Management Journal, 25*, 1217-1232.

Henderson, J. C., & Venkatraman, N. (1999). Strategic alignment: Leveraging information technology for transforming organizations. *IBM Systems Journal, 38*(2/3), 472-484.

Henderson, J., & Venkatraman, N. (1993). Strategic alignment: Leveraging information technology for transforming organization. *IBM Systems Journal, 32*(1), 4-16.

Henderson, R., & Cockburn, I. (1994). Measuring competence? Exploring effects in pharmaceutical research. *Strategic Management Journal, 15*(Winter Special Issue), 63-84.

Herschel, T.R., & Nemati, R.H. (1999). CKOs and knowledge management: Exploring opportunities for using information exchange protocols. *Proceedings of the 1999 ACM SIGCPR conference on Computer personnel research* (pp. 42-50).

Heusinkveld, S., & Benders, J. (2001). Surges and sediments: Shaping the reception of reengineering. *Information & Management, 38*(4), 239-251.

Hildreth, P. M., & Kimble, C. (2002). The duality of knowledge. *Information Research*, 8(1). Retrieved October 18, 2006, from http://informationr.net/ir/8-1/paper142.html

Hilgard, E.R. (1980). Consciousness in contemporary psychology. *Annual Review of Psychology, 31*, 1-26.

Hill, Q.K., & Fowles, J. (1975). The methodological worth of the Delphi forecasting technique. *Technological Forecasting and Social Change, 7*(2), 179-192.

Hinds, P.J. & Pfeffer, J. (2003). Why organizations don't "know what they know": Cognitive and motivational factors affecting the transfer of expertise. In M. Ackerman, V. Pipek, & V. Wulf (Eds.), *Sharing expertise: Beyond knowledge management* (pp. 3-26). Cambridge, MA: MIT Press.

Hitt, M.A., & Ireland, R.D. (2002). The essence of strategic leadership: Managing human and social capital. *The Journal of Leadership and Organizational Studies, 9*(1), 3-14.

Hitt, M.A., Hoskisson, R.E., & Harrison, J.S. (1991). Strategic competitiveness in the 1990s: Challenges and opportunities for U.S. executives. *Academy of Management Executive, 5*(2), 7-22.

Hoetker, G. (2006). Do modular products lead to modular organizations? *Strategic Management Journal, 27*, 501-518.

Holsapple, C. W. & Joshi, K. D. (2000). An investigation of factors that influence the management of knowledge in organizations. *The Journal of Strategic Information Systems, 9*(2-3), 235-261.

Holsapple, C.W. & Joshi, K.D. (2002). Knowledge management: A three-fold framework. *The Information Society, 18*(1), 47-64.

Holt, D. T., Bartczak, S. E., Clark, S. W., & Trent, M. R. (2004). *The development of an instrument to measure readiness for knowledge management*. Paper presented at the 37th Hawaii International Conference on System Sciences, January 5-8, Hilton Waikoloa Village, Island of Hawaii (Big Island), IEEE Computer Society.

Holtshouse, D. (1998). Knowledge research issues. *California Management Review, 40*(3), 277-280.

Hoopes, D.G., & Postrel, S. (1999). Shared knowledge, "glitches", and product development performance. *Strategic Management Journal, 20* (9), 837-865.

Hoskisson, R. E., Hitt, M. A., & Ireland, R. D. (2004). *Competing for advantage*. Australia: Thompson South-Western.

HQ AFMC PA. (2001). Air Force Material Command fact sheet. Retrieved October 17, 2001, from w w w . *afmc-pub.wpafb.af.mil/HQ-AFMC/PA/fact_sheet/afmcfact.htm*

HQ AFMC PA. (2001). HQ AFMC/DR home page. Retrieved October 17, 2001, from *https://afkm.wpafb.af.mil/ASPs/Tabs/Entry_Subject.asp* [only accessible from .mil domains]

HQ AFMC/DRI. (2000). *Statement of work*. Wright-Patterson AFB, OH: Air Force Knowledge Management Integration and Support.

Huber, G.P. (1991). Organizational learning: The contributing processes and the literatures. *Organization Science, 2*(1), 88-115.

Huber, G.P. (2001). Transfer of knowledge in knowledge management systems: Unexplored issues and suggested studies. *European Journal of Information Systems, 10*(2), 72-79.

Huxham, C., & Vangen, S. (2000). Leadership in the shaping and implementation of collaboration agendas: How things happen in a (not quite) joined-up world. *Academy of Management Journal, 43*(6), 1159-1175.

Huysman, M.H., Fischer, S.J., & Heng, M.S.H. (1994). An organizational learning perspective on information systems planning. *Journal of Strategic Information Systems, 3*(3), 165-177.

Ingram, P., & Roberts, P. (2000). Friendships with competitors in the Sydney hotel industry. *American Journal of Sociology, 106*(2), 387-423.

Ingwersen, P. (1992). *Information retrieval interaction.* London: Taylor Graham Publishing.

Inkpen, A. (1996). Creating knowledge through collaboration. *California Management Review, 39*(1), 123-140.

Inkpen, A.C., & Tsang, E.W.K. (2005). Social capital, networks, and knowledge transfer. *Academy of Management Review, 30*(1), 146-165.

Ipe, M. (2003). Knowledge sharing on organizations: A conceptual framework. *Human Resource Development Review, 2*(4), 337-359.

Israel, J. (1979). *The language of dialectics and the dialectics of language.* New York: Humanities Press.

Jackendoff, R. (1983). *Semantics and Cognition.* Cambridge, MA: MIT Press.

Jackson, M.C. (2003). *Systems thinking: Creative holism for managers.* Chichester: John Wiley & Sons.

Jalote, P. (2000). *CMM in practice: Processes for executing software projects at Infosys.* Reading, MA: Addison-Wesley.

Janis, I. L. (1982). *Psychological studies of policy decisions and fiascoes* (2nd Ed.). Boston, MA: Houghton-Mifflin.

Jasimuddin, S.M., Klein, J.H., & Connell, C. (2005). The paradox of using tacit and explicit knowledge: Strategies to face dilemmas. *Management Decision, 43*(1), 102-112.

Johnson, D.G. (1997). Is the global information infrastructure a democratic technology? *ACM SIGCAS Computers and Society, 27*(3), 20-26.

Jones, N.B., Herschel, R.T., & Moesel, D.D. (2003). Using "knowledge champions" to facilitate knowledge management. *Journal of Knowledge Management, 7*(1), 49-63.

Jones, O. (2006). Developing absorptive capacity in mature organizations: The change agent's role. *Management Learning, 37*(3), 355-376.

Jones, P.H. (2000). *Embedded values in innovation practice: Toward a theory of power and participation in organizations.* Ann Arbor, MI: Dissertation Abstracts International.

Jones, P.H. (2002, June). Embedded values in process and practice: Interactions between disciplinary practice and formal innovation processes. In *Proceedings of the 11th International Forum on Design Management Research,* Boston, Massachusetts.

Jones, P.H. (2002). When successful products prevent strategic innovation. *Design Management Journal, 13*(2), 30-37.

Joreskog, K., & Sorbom, D. (2002). *LISREL (Version 8. 52).* Lincolnwood, IL: Scientific Software International, Inc.

Jöreskog, K.G. (1971). Simultaneous factor analysis in several populations. *Psychometrica, 57,* 409-426.

Junginger, S., et al. (2000). Ein Geschäftsprozessmanagementwerkzeug der nächsten Generation - adonis: Konzeption und Anwendungen. *Wirtschaftsinformatik, 42*(5), 392-401.

Kahneman, D., & Tversky, A. (1979). Prospect theory: An analysis of decision under risk. *Econometrica, 47*(2), 263-291.

Kalling, T. (2003). Organization-internal transfer of knowledge and the role of motivation: A qualitative case study. *Knowledge and Process Management, 10*(2), 115-126.

Kalthoff, O., Nonaka, I., & Nueno, P. (2001). *The light and the shadow: How breakthrough innovation is shaping European business.* Oxford: Capstone Publishing Ltd.

Kaplan, R. S. & Norton, D. P. (1996). *The balanced scorecard.* Boston: Harvard Business School Press.

Kaplan, R. S. & Norton, D. P. (2004). *Strategy maps.* Boston: Harvard Business School Press.

Kaplan, R. S., & Norton, D. P. (2001). *The strategy-focused organization.* Boston: Harvard Business School Press.

Karim, S. (2006). Modularity in organizational structure: The reconfiguration of internally developed and acquired business units. *Strategic Management Journal, 27,* 799-823.

Katila, R. (2002). New product search over time: Past ideas in their prime? *Academy of Management Journal, 45*(5), 995-1010.

Katila, R., & Ahuja, G. (2002). Something old, something new: A longitudinal study of search behaviour and new product introduction. *Academy of Management Journal, 45*(6), 1183-1194.

Keeble, D., & Wilkinson, F. (1999). Regional networking, collective learning and innovation in high-technology SMEs in Europe. *Regional Studies, 3*(4), 295-400.

Keeble, D., Lawson, C.B.M., & Wilkinson, F. (1999). Collective learning processes, networking and "institutional thickness" in the Cambridge region. *Regional Studies, 33*(4), 319-332.

Keller, A. (2001). Future development of electronic journals: A Delphi survey. *The Electronic Library, 19*(6), 383-396.

Kelly, D., & Amburgey, T.L. (1991). Organizational inertia and momentum: A dynamic model of strategic change. *Academy of Management Journal, 34*(3), 591-612.

Kidwell, J.J., Vander Linde, K.M., & Johnson, S.L. (2000). Applying corporate knowledge management practices in higher education. *Educause Quarterly, 4,* 28-33.

Kiesler, S., & Sproull, L.S. (1986). Response effects in the electronic survey. *Public Opinion Quarterly, 50*(3), 402-413.

Kim, Y.-G., Yu, S.-H., & Lee, J.-H. (2003). Knowledge strategy planning: Methodology and case. *Expert Systems with Applications, 24,* 295-307.

King, A.W., & Zeithaml, C.P. (2003). Measuring organizational knowledge: A conceptual and methodological framework. *Strategic Management Journal, 24,* 763-772.

Kivijärvi, H. (2004). Knowledge Conversion in Organizational Contexts: A Framework and Experiments, *Proceedings of the 37th Hawaii International Conference on System Sciences.* Retrieved August 23, 2007 from http://csdl2.computer.org/comp/proceedings/hicss/2004/2056/08/205680242a.pdf

Klein, D. A. (Ed.). (1998). *The strategic management of intellectual capital.* Boston: Butterworth-Heinemann.

Kling, R. (1996). The centrality of organizations in the computerization of society. In R. Kling (Ed.), *Computerization and controversy: Value conflicts and social choices* (2nd ed., pp. 108-112). New York: Academic Press.

Kluge, J., Stein, W., & Licht, T. (2001). *Knowledge unplugged: The McKinsey & Company survey on Knowledge Management.* New York: Palgrave.

Knoll, K., & Jarvenpaa, S. L. (1994). Information technology alignment or "fit" in highly turbulent environments: the concept of flexibility. In *Proceedings of the 1994 computer personnel research conference on Reinventing IS* (pp. 1-14). Alexandria, Virginia, United States.

Kodama, M. (2005). Knowledge creation through networked strategic communities: Case studies on new product development in Japanese companies. *Long Range Planning, 38*(1), 27-49.

Kogut, B., & Zander, U. (1996). What firms do: Coordination, identity and learning. *Organization Science, 7,* 502-518.

Kogut, B., Walker, G., & Shan, W. (1994). Interfirm cooperation and startup innovation in the biotechnology industry. *Strategic Management Journal, 15*(5), 387-394.

Kogut, B.M., & Zander, U. (1992). Knowledge of the firm, combinative capabilities, and the replication of technology. *Organization Science, 3*(3), 383-397.

Kogut, B.M., & Zander, U. (1995). Knowledge and the speed of the transfer and imitation of organizational capabilities: An empirical test. *Organization Science, 6*(1), 76-92.

Kolb, D. A. (1984). *Experiential Learning: Experience as the Source of Learning and Development.* Englewood Cliffs, New Jersey: Prentice Hall.

Koput, K. (1997). A chaotic model of innovative search: Some answers, many questions. *Organization Science, 8*(5), 528-542.

Kosík, K. (1976). *Dialectics of the concrete.* Dordrecht: Reidel.

Kostova, T. (1998). *Success of the transnational transfer of organizational practices within multinational companies* (Working Paper No. 98-4). Carnegie Bosch Institute.

Kostova, T. (1999). Transnational transfer of strategic organizational practices: A contextual perspective. *Academy of Management Review, 24*(2), 308-324.

Kotabe, M., Martin, X., & Domoto, H. (2003). Gaining from vertical partnerships: Knowledge transfer, relationship duration, and supplier performance improvement in the U.S. and Japanese automotive industries. *Strategic Management Journal, 24*(4), 293-316.

Koudsi, S. (2000). Actually, it is like brain surgery, *Fortune,* March 20, 233-234.

KPMG (1999). *Knowledge management research report, 20.* London: KPMG Consulting.

KPMG (2000). *Knowledge management research report 2000.* London.

Krafzig, D., Banke, K., & Slama, D. (2005). *Enterprise SOA: Service-oriented architecture best practices.* Upper Saddle River, NJ.

Kraimer, M.L. (1997). Organizational goals and values: A socialization model. *Human Resource Management Review, 7*(4), 425-447.

Kraut, R.E. & Streeter, L. (1995). Coordination in software development. *Communications of the ACM, 38*(3), 69-81.

Kumar, K., & Bjorn-Anderson, N. (1990). A cross-cultural comparison of IS designer values. *Communications of the ACM, 33*(5), 528-538.

Kurtz, C.F., & Snowden, D.J. (2003). The new dynamics of strategy: Sense making in a complex and complicated world. *IBM Systems Journal, 24*(3), 462-483.

Lahti, R.K., & Beyerlein, M.M. (2000). Knowledge transfer and management consulting: A look at "the firm". *Business Horizons, 43*(1), 65-74.

Landry, R., Amara, N., & Lamari, M. (2001). Utilization of social science research knowledge in Canada. *Research Policy, 30*(2), 333-349.

Larsen, E., & Lomi, A. (2002). Representing change: A system model of organizational inertia and capabilities as dynamic accumulation processes. *Simulation Modelling: Practice and Theory, 10,* 271-296.

Larsson, R. (1990). *Coordination of Action in Mergers and Acquisitions - Interpretative and Systems Approaches towards Synergy.* Dissertation No. 10, Lund Studies in Economics and Management, The Institute of Economic Research. Lund: Lund University Press.

Laursen, K., & Salter, A. (2003). Searching low and high: What types of firms use Universities as a source of innovation? (Working Paper Series). Danish Research Unit for Industrial Dynamics (DRUID).

Laursen, K., & Salter, A. (2006). Open for innovation: The role of openness in explaining innovation performance among UK manufacturing firms. *Strategic Management Journal, 27*(2), 131-150.

Lave, J., & Wenger, E. (1991). *Situated learning: Legitimate peripheral participation.* Cambridge, UK: Cambridge University Press.

Lavis, J.N., Toss, S.E., Hurley, J.E., Hohenadel, J.M., Stoddart, G.L., Woodward, C.A., & Abelson, J. (2002). Examining the role of health services research in public policymaking. *The Milbank Quarterly, 80*(1), 125-154.

Lei, D., Hitt, M.A., & Bettis, R. (1996). Dynamic core competences through meta-learning and strategic context. *Journal of Management, 22*, 549-569.

Lemke, J. L. (1993). Discourse, Dynamics, and Social Change. *Cultural Dynamics* 6(1), 243-275. In *Language as Cultural Dynamic*, M.A.K. Halliday (Ed.) Leiden: Brill. Retrieved October 18, 2006, from http://academic.brooklyn.cuny.edu/education/jlemke/cult-dyn.htm

Lenz, M., Bartsch-Spörl, B., Burkhardt, H., & Wess, S. (1998). *Case-based reasoning technology: From foundations to applications.* Berlin: Springer-Verlag.

Leonard, D. & Sensiper, S. (1998). The role of tacit knowledge in group innovation. *California Management Review, 40*(3), 112-132.

Leonard-Barton, D. (1995). Core capabilities and core rigidities: A paradox in managing new product development. *Strategic Management Journal, 13*(2), 111-126.

Leonard-Barton, D. (1995). *Wellsprings of knowledge.* Boston: Harvard Business School Press.

Leont'ev, A. N. (1978). *Activity, consciousness, and personality.* Englewood Cliffs, N. J.: Prentice-Hall. Original work published 1975. Retrieved October 18, 2006, from http://lchc.ucsd.edu/MCA/Paper/leontev/

Lesser, E. L. (2001). Communities of practice and organizational performance. *IBM Systems Journal, 40*(4), 831-841.

Levinthal, D., & March, J. (1981). A model of adaptive organizational search. *Journal of Economic Behaviour and Organization, 2*, 307-333.

Levinthal, D., & March, J. (1993). The myopia of learning. *Strategic Management Journal, 14*(2), 95-112.

Levitt, B., & J, M. (1988). Organizational learning. *Annual Review of Sociology, 14*(1), 319- 340.

Lewin, A.Y., & Volberda, H.W. (1999). Prolegomena on coevolution: A framework for research on strategy and new organizational forms. *Organization Science, 10*(5), 519-534.

Li, M., & Gao, F. (2003). Why Nonaka highlights tacit knowledge: A critical review. *Journal of Knowledge Management, 7*(4), 6-14.

Liebeskind, J. (1996). Knowledge, strategy, and the theory of the firm. *Strategic Management Journal, 17*(Winter Special Issue), 93-107.

Liebeskind, J.P., Oliver, A.L., Zucker, L.G., & Brewer, M.B. (1996). Social networks, learning and flexibility: Sourcing scientific knowledge in new biotechnology firms. *Organization Science, 7*(4), 428–443.

Liebowitz, J. & Beckman, T. (1998). *Knowledge organizations: What every manager should know.* Bacon Raton, FL: St. Lucie/CRC Press.

Liebowitz, J. (1999). The new star in organizations: The chief knowledge officer and the knowledge audit function. *Proceedings of the 1999 ACM SIGCPR conference on Computer personnel research* (pp. 11-13).

Liebowitz, J. (Ed.). (2000). *Knowledge management handbook.* Boca Raton, FL: CRC Press.

Liebowitz, J., & Wilcox, L.C. (Eds.). (1997). *Knowledge management and its integrative elements.* Boca Raton, FL: CRC Press.

Lieibold, M., Probst, G., & Gilbert, M. (2002). *Strategic management in the knowledge economy: New approaches and business applications.* Erlangen, Germany: Publicis Corporate Publishing and Wiley-VCH-Verlag.

Lindkvist, L., Soderlund, J., & Tell, F. (1998). Managing product development projects: On the significance of fountains and deadlines. *Organization Studies, 19*(6), 931-951.

Lomas, J. (2000). Using linkage and exchange to move research into policy at a Canadian foundation. *Health Affairs, 19*(3), 236-240.

Lord, M.D., & Ranft, A.L. (2000). Organizational learning about new international markets: Exploring the internal transfer of local market knowledge. *Journal of International Business Studies, 31*(4), 573-589.

Louis, M.R. (1980). Surprise and sense making: What newcomers experience in entering unfamiliar organizational settings. *Administrative Science Quarterly, 25*, 226–248.

Lovas, B., & Ghoshal, S. (2000). Strategy as guided evolution. *Strategic Management Journal, 21*, 875-896.

Luftman, J. (1996). Applying the strategic alignment model. In J. Luftman (Ed.), *Competing in the information age* (pp. 43-69). Oxford University Press.

Luftman, J. (2003, Fall). Assessing IT/business alignment. *Information Systems Management*, pp. 9-15.

Luftman, J. N., Lewis, P. R., & Oldach, S. H. (1993). Transforming the enterprise: The alignment of business and information technologies strategies. *IBM Systems Journal, 32*(1), 198-221.

Luftman, J. N., Papp, R., & Brier, T. (2002, September). Enablers and inhibitors of business-IT alignment. *IBM Advanced Business Institute (ABInsight)*, pp. 1-26.

Lusti, M. (2002). *Data warehousing und data mining: Eine Einführung in entscheidungs-unterstützende Systeme*. Berlin: Springer-Verlag.

Lyles, M., & Schwenk, C. (1992). Top management, strategy, and organizational knowledge structures. *Journal of Management Studies, 29*, 155-174.

Lynn, G.S., Skov, R.B., & Abel, K.D. (1999). Practices that support team learning and their impact on speed to market and new product success. *The Journal of Product Innovation Management, 16*(5), 439-454.

MacNeil, C.M. (2003). Line managers: Facilitators of knowledge sharing in teams. *Employee Relations, 25*(3), 294-307.

Mahoney, J.T., & Sanchez, R. (2004). Building new management theory by integrating processes and products of thought. *Journal Of Management Inquiry, 13*(1), 34-47.

Maier, R. & Remus, U. (2001). Towards a framework for knowledge management strategies: Process orientation as strategic starting point. In *Proceedings of the 34th Hawaii International Conference on System Sciences*.

Maier, R. (2004). *Knowledge management systems: Information and communication technologies for knowledge management* (2nd ed.). Berlin: Springer-Verlag.

Maier, R., & Peinl, R. (2005). Semantische Dokumentbeschreibung in Enterprise Knowledge Infrastructures. *HMD - Praxis der Wirtschaftsinformatik*(246), 84-92.

Maier, R., & Remus, U. (2002). Defining process-oriented knowledge management strategies. *Journal of Process- and Knowledge Management, 9*(2), 103-118.

Maier, R., & Remus, U. (2003). Implementing process-oriented knowledge management strategies. *Journal of Knowledge Management, 7*(4), 62-74.

Maier, R., Hädrich, T., & Peinl, R. (2005). *Enterprise knowledge infrastructures*. Berlin: Springer-Verlag.

Maitlis, S. (2005). The social processes of organizational sensemaking. *Academy of Management Journal, 48*(1), 21-49.

Malhotra, Y. (1997). Profile of the ideal knowledge manager/architect. *http://www.brint.com/wwwboard/messages/273.html*

Malhotra, Y. (2000). Role of organizational controls in KM: Is KM really an oxymoron? In Y. Malhotra (Ed.), *Knowledge management and virtual organizations*. (pp. 245-257). Hershey, PA: IRM Press.

Malhotra, Y. (2004). Why do knowledge management systems fail? Enablers and constraints of knowledge management in human enterprises. In M.E. Koenig & T.K. Srikantaiah (Eds.), *Knowledge management lessons learned: What works and what doesn't* (pp. 87-112). Silver Spring MD: Information Today (ASIST Monograph Series).

Malhotra, Y. (2005). Integrating knowledge management technologies in organizational business processes: Getting real time enterprises to deliver real business performance. *Journal of Knowledge Management, 9*(1), 7-26.

Malone, D. (2002). Knowledge management: A model for organizational learning. *International Journal of Accounting Information Systems, 3*, 111-123.

Malone, T., & Crowston, K. (1994). The Interdisciplinary Study of Coordination. *ACM Computing Services, 26*(1), 87-119.

March, J. (1991). Exploration and exploitation in organizational learning. *Organization Science, 2*(1), 71-87.

March, J. (1994). *A primer on decision making.* New York: The Free Press.

March, J. (1999). *The pursuit of organizational intelligence.* Malden, MA: Blackwell Publishers.

March, J. G., & Simon, H. A. (1958). *Organizations,* 2nd edition. Cambridge, Massachusetts, USA: Blackwell Publishers.

Markus, M.L. (2004). Fit for function: Functionalism, neofunctionalism and information systems. In J. Mingers & L. Willcocks (Eds.), *Social thinking and philosophy for information systems* (pp. 29-55). Chichester, UK: Wiley.

Martino, J.P. (1983). *Technological forecasting for decision making.* New York: Elsevier Science Publishers.

Maskell, P. (2001). Knowledge creation and diffusion in geographic clusters. *International Journal of Innovation Management (Special Issue), 5*(2), 213-238.

Maslow, A.H. (1965). *Eupsychian management: A journal.* Homewood, IL: The Dorsey Press.

Maslow, A.H. (1971). *The farther reaches of human nature.* New York: Viking Press.

Massey, A. P., Montoya-Weiss, M. M., & O'Driscoll, T. M. (2002). Knowledge management in pursuit of performance insights from Nortel. *MIS Quarterly, 26*(3), 269-289.

Massey, A.P. & Montoya-Weiss, M. (2002). Performance-centered design of knowledge intensive processes. *Journal of Management Information Systems, 18*(4), 37-58.

Massey, A.P., Montoya-Weiss, M., & Holcom, K. (2001). Re-engineering the customer relationship: Leveraging knowledge assets at IBM. *Decision Support Systems, 32* 155-170.

Massey, A.P., Montoya-Weiss, M., & O'Driscoll, T. (2002). Knowledge management in pursuit of performance: Insights from Nortel Networks. *MIS Quarterly, 26*(3), 269-289.

Mathiassen, L. (1996). Information Systems Development: Reflections on a Discipline. *Accounting, Management and Information Technologies, 6*(1/2), 127-132.

Maxfield, R.R. (2003). Complexity and organization management. In D.S. Alberts & T.J. Czerwinski (Eds.), *Complexity, global politics and national security.* Washington, DC: National Defence University. Retrieved May 15, 2007, from http://www.ndu.edu/inss/books/books%20-%201998/Complexity,%20Global%20Politics%20and%20Nat'l%20Sec%20-%20Sept%2098/index.html

McConnell, J., & Nantell, T. (1985). Corporate combinations and common stock returns: The case of joint ventures. *Journal of Finance, 40*(2), 519-536.

McDermott, R. (1999). Why information technology inspired but cannot deliver KM. *California Management Review, 41*(4), 103-117.

McElroy, M.W. (2000). Integrating complexity theory, knowledge management and organizational learning. *Journal of Knowledge Management, 4*(3), 195-203.

McEvily, S., & Chakravarthy, B. (2002). The persistence of knowledge-based advantage: An empirical test for product performance and technological knowledge. *Strategic Management Journal, 23*, 285-305.

McKeen, D. J., & Staples, D.S. (2001). *Knowledge managers: Who they are and what they do* (pp. 1-17). Kingston: Queen's School of Business.

Meadows, D.H., & Robinson, J.M. (2002). The electronic oracle: Computer models and social decisions. *System Dynamics Review, 18*(2), 271-308.

Mehta, R., & Sivadas, E. (1995). Comparing response rates and response content in mail versus electronic mail surveys. *Journal of the Market Research Society, 37*(4), 429-439.

Mertins, K., Heisig, P., & Vorbeck, J. (Eds.). (2001). *Knowledge management: Best practices in Europe.* Berlin: Springer-Verlag.

Meyer, M., & Lehnerd, A. (1997). *The power of product platforms.* New York: The Free Press.

Meyer, M., & Seliger, R. (1998). Product platforms in software development. *Sloan Management Review, 40*(1), 61-74.

Miles, G., R. E., Perrone, V., & Edvinsson, L. (1998). Some conceptual and research barriers to the utilization of knowledge. *California Management Review 40*(3), 281-292.

Miles, R. E., & Snow, C. C. (1978). *Organizational strategy, structure, and processes.* New York: McGraw-Hill.

Miller, D. (1992). Environmental fit versus internal fit. *Organization Science, 3*(2), 159-178.

Mintzberg, H. (1975, July-August). The manager's job, folklore and fact. *Harvard Business Review, 53*, 49-61

Mintzberg, H. (1983). *Structures in Fives: Designing Effective Organizations.* New Jersey: Prentice-Hall.

Mintzberg, H. (1990). The design school: Reconsidering the basic premises of strategic management. *Strategic Management Journal, 11*, 171-1965.

Mintzberg, H. (1994). *The rise and fall of strategic planning.* New York: Free Press.

Mintzberg, H., & Lampel, J. (1999). Reflecting on the strategy process. *Sloan Management Review, 40*(3), 21-30.

Mintzberg, H., Ahlstrand, B., & Lampel, J. (1998). *Strategy safari: A guided tour through the wilds of strategic management.* New York: The Free Press.

Mitchell, W., & Singh, H. (1996). Precarious collaboration: Business survival after partners shut down or form new partnerships. *Strategic Management Journal, 17*(2), 99-115.

Moody, K. W. (2003, Fall). New meaning to IT alignment. *Information Systems Management*, pp. 30-35.

Moore, K. & Birkinshaw, J. (1998). Managing knowledge in global service organizations: Centers of excellence. *Academy of Management Executive, 12*, 81-92.

Moorman, C. & Rust, R.T. (1999). The role of marketing. *Journal of Marketing, 63*, 180-197.

Morel, B., & Ramanujam, R. (1999). Through the looking glass of complexity: The dynamics of organizations as adaptive and evolving systems. *Organization Science, 10*(3), 278-293.

Morgan, G. (1997). *Images of organization.* Thousand Oaks, CA: Sage Publications.

Morgan, K. (1997). The learning region: Institutions, innovation and regional renewal. *Regional Studies, 31*(5), 491-503.

Murray, P. (2002). Knowledge management as a sustained competitive advantage. *Ivey Business Journal* (March-April), 71-76.

Mu-Yen, Ch., & An-Pin, Ch. (2006). Knowledge management performance evaluation: A decade review from 1995 to 2004. *Journal of Information Science, 32*(1), 17-38.

Nadkarni, S., & Narayanan, V.K. (2004). *Strategy frames, strategic flexibility and firm performance: The moderating role of industry clockspeed* (Academy of Management Best Conference Paper 2004, BPS:U1-U9).

Nadkarni, S., & Narayanan, V.K. (2005). Validity of the structural properties of text-based causal maps: An empirical assessment. *Organizational Research Methods, 8*(1), 9-40.

Nadler, D., & Tushman, M. (1999). The organization of the future: Strategic imperatives and core competences for the 21st century. *Organizational Dynamics, 28*(1), 45-60.

Nadler, D.A., & Tushman, M.I. (1989). A model for diagnosing organizational behavior, Applying congruence perspective, In D.A. Nadler, M.L. Tushman & C. O'Reilly, (Eds), *The management of organizations: Strategic, tactics, analyses*, (pp. 91-106). Harper & Row, New York

Nahapier, J., & Ghoshal, S. (1998). Social capital, intellectual capital, and the organizational advantage. *Academy of Management Review, 23,* 242-266.

Narasimha, S. (2000). Organizational knowledge, human resource management and sustained competitive advantage: Toward a framework. *CR, 10*(1), 123-135.

Nardi, B.A., & O'Day, V.L. (1999). *Information ecologies: Using technology with heart.* Cambridge, MA: MIT Press.

Neely, A., Filippini, R., Forza, C., Vinelli, A., & Hii, J. (2000). A framework for analyzing business performance, firm innovation and related contextual factors: Perceptions of managers and policy makers in two European regions. *Integrated Manufacturing Systems, 12*(2), 114–124.

Neilson, R.E. (2000). Knowledge management and the role of the chief knowledge officer. Retrieved May 17, 2007, from *http://www.ndu.edu/ndu/irmc/km-cio_role/km-cio-role.htm*

Nelson, R.R., & Winter, S.G. (1982). *An evolutionary theory of economic change.* Cambridge, MA: Belknap Press.

Nicolini, D., & Meznar, M. (1995). The Social Construction of Organizational Learning: Conceptual and Practical Issues in the Field. *Human Relations*, 48(7), 727-746.

Niederman, F., Brancheau, J.C., & Wetherbe, J.C. (1991). Information systems management issues for the 1990s. *MIS Quarterly, 15*(4), 474-500.

Nielson, B.B. (2005). Strategic knowledge management research: Tracing the co-evolution of strategic management and knowledge management perspectives. *Competitiveness Review, 15*(1), 1-13.

Nissen, M., Kamel, M., & Sengupta, K. (2000, January-March). Integrated analysis and design of knowledge systems and processes. *Information Resources Management Journal, 13*(1), 24-43.

Nonaka, I. (1990). Redundant overlapping organization: A Japanese approach to managing the innovation process. *California Management Review, 32*(3), 27-39.

Nonaka, I. (1991, November-December). The knowledge-creating company. *Harvard Business Review*, pp. 14-36.

Nonaka, I. (1994). A dynamic theory of organizational knowledge creation. *Organization Science, 5*(1), 14-38.

Nonaka, I. (1996, February 23). *Knowledge has to do with truth, goodness, and beauty: A conversation with Professor Ikujiro Nonaka.* Claus Otto Scharmer. Tokyo.

Nonaka, I., & Konno, N. (1998). The concept of "ba": Building a foundation for knowledge creation. *California Management Review, 40*(3), 40-54.

Nonaka, I., & Nishiguchi, T. (2001). *Knowledge emergence: Social, technical, and evolutionary dimensions of knowledge creation.* Oxford, UK: Oxford University Press.

Nonaka, I., & Takeuchi, H. (1995). *The knowledge creating company: How Japanese companies create the dynamics of innovation.* New York: Oxford University Press.

Nonaka, I., & Toyama, R. (2003). The knowledge-creating theory revisited: knowledge creation as a synthesizing process, *Knowledge Management Research and Practice*, 1(1), 2-10.

Nonaka, I., Toyama, R., & Konno, N. (2001). SECI, Ba and Leadership: A Unified Model of Dynamic Knowledge Creation, In I. Nonaka, & D.J. Teece, (Eds.), *Managing Industrial Knowledge* (pp. 13-43). Sage Publications, London.

Normann, R., & Ramirez, R. (1993, July-August). From value chain to value constellation: Designing interactive strategy. *Harvard Business Review*, pp. 65-77.

Novo, J. (2001). The source of customer value: Customer knowledge. Retrieved May 19, 2007, from http://www.ckm-forum.com

O'Dell, C. & Grayson, C.J. (1998). If only we knew what we know: Identification and transfer of internal best practices. *California Management Review, 40*(3), 154-174.

O'Dell, C., & Grayson, C.J., Jr. (1999). Knowledge transfer: Discover your value proposition. *Strategy & Leadership, 27*(2), 10-15.

O'Hare, M. (1988). *Innovate! How to gain and sustain competitive advantage*. Oxford: Basil Blackwell Ltd.

OCDE. (1996). *The knowledge-based economy*. Paris: Author.

Oestereich, B., et al. (2003). *Objektorientierte Geschäftsprozessmodellierung mit der UML*. Heidelberg: dpunkt.

Offsey, S. (1997). knowledge management: Linking people to knowledge for bottom line results. *Journal of Knowledge Management, 1*(2), 113-122.

Oliver, B.L. (1999). Comparing corporate managers' personal values over three decades, 1967-1995. *Journal of Business Ethics, 20*(2), 147-161.

Oppermann, M. (1995). E-mail surveys: Potentials and pitfalls. *Marketing Research, 7*(3), 28-33.

Ordóñez de Pablos, P. (2002). Knowledge management and organizational learning: Typologies of knowledge strategies in the Spanish manufacturing industry from 1995 to 1999. *Journal of Knowledge Management, 6*(1), 52-62.

Orlikowski, W. (2002). Knowing in practice: Enacting a collective capability in distributed organizing. *Organization Science, 13*(3), 249-273.

Orlikowski, W.J. (1992). The duality of technology: Rethinking the concept of technology in organizations. *Organization Science, 3*(3), 398-427.

Orlikowski, W.J. (2000). Using technology and constituting structures: A practice lens for studying technology in organizations. *Organization Science, 11*(4), 404-428.

Orlikowski, W.J., & Robey, D. (1991). Information technology and the structuring of organizations. *Information Systems Research, 2*(2), 143-169.

Örtenblad, A. (2005). Of course organizations can learn! *The Learning Organization, 12*(2), 213-218.

Österle, H. (1995). *Business engineering: Prozeß- und Systementwicklung. Band 1: Entwurfstechniken*. Berlin et al.

Osterloh, M. & Frey, B. S. (2000). Motivation, knowledge transfer and organizational forms. *Organization Science, 11*, 538-550.

Palacios, D., & Garrigós, F. (2005). A measurement scale for knowledge management in the biotechnology and telecommunications industries. *International Journal of Technology Management, 31*(3/4), 358-374.

Pan, S.L., & Scarbrough, H. (1998). A socio-technical view of knowledge-sharing at Buckman Laboratories. *Journal of Knowledge Management, 2*(1), 55-66.

Papazoglou, M. P., & Georgakopoulos, D. (2003). Service-oriented computing. *Communication of the ACM, 46*(10), 25-28.

Papert, S. (1980). *Mindstorms: Children, computers, and powerful ideas*. New York: Basic Books.

Paulk, M., Weber, C.W., Curtis, B., & Chrissis, M.B. (1995). *The capability maturity model for software: Guidelines for improving the software process*. Reading, MA: Addison-Wesley.

Peltonen, T., & Lämsä, T. (2004). 'Communities of Practice' and the Social Process of Knowledge Creation: Towards a New Vocabulary for Making Sense of Organizational Learning. *Problems and Perspectives in Management, 4/2004*, 249-262.

Penrose, E.T. (1959). *The theory of the growth of the firm*. New York: Wiley & Sons.

Peppers, D., Rogers, M., & Dorf, R. (1999). *The one-to-one fieldbook*. New York: Currency and Doubleday.

Pfeffer, J. (1998). *The human equation: Building profits by putting people first*. Boston, MA: Harvard Business School Press.

Pfeffer, J., & Sutton, R., (1999). Knowing what to do is not enough: Turning knowledge into action, *California Management Review, 42*(1), 83-108.

Pine, B.J. (1993). *Mass customization: The new frontier in business competition*. Boston: Harvard Business Press.

Poage, J. L. (2002). Designing performance measures for knowledge organizations. *Ivey Business Journal* (March-April), 8-10.

Polanyi, M. (1961). Knowing and Being, *Mind*, New Series, 70(280), 458-70.

Polanyi, M. (1962). *Personal Knowledge*, University of the Chicago Press, Chicago.

Polanyi, M. (1966). *The Tacit Dimension*, Doubleday & Co., Reprinted Peter Smith, Gloucester, Massachusetts.

Polanyi, M., & Prosch, H. (1975). *Meaning*, The University of Chicago Press.

Pollard, D. (2000). Becoming knowledge powered: Planning the transformation. In Y. Malhotra (Ed.), *Knowledge management and virtual organizations*. (pp.196-213). Hershey, PA: IRM Press.

Popper, K.R. (1979). *Objective Knowledge*, Oxford University Press, Oxford.

Porter, M. (1979, March/April). How competitive forces shape strategy. *Harvard Business Review, 57*(2), 137-144.

Porter, M. E. (1996). What is strategy? *Harvard Business Review, 74*(5-6), 61-78.

Porter, M.E. (1980). *Competitive strategy: Techniques for analyzing industries and competitors*. New York: Free Press.

Porter, M.E. (1998). *Competitive advantage: Creating and sustaining superior performance*. New York: Free Press.

Powell, T. C. (1992). Organizational alignment as competitive advantage. *Strategic Management Journal, 13*(2), 119-134.

Powell, W. W., Koput, K. W., & Smith-Doerr, L. (1996). Interorganizational collaboration and the locus of innovation: Networks of learning in biotechnology. *Administrative Science Quarterly, 41*(1), 116-145.

Prahalad, C. K. & Hamel, G. (1990). The core competence of the corporation. *Harvard Business Review, 68*(3), 79-91.

Prahalad, C., & V., R. (2000). Co-opting customer competence. *Harvard Business Review, 78*(1), 9.

Prahalad, C.K., & Bettis, R.A. (1986). The dominant logic: A new linkage between diversity and performance. *Strategic Management Journal, 7*, 485-501.

Price, I. (2004). Complexity, complicatedness and complexity: A new science behind organizational intervention? *E:CO, 6*(1-2), 40-48.

PriceWaterHouseCoopers. (2000). *Technology forecast: 2000*. Menlo Park, CA: Author.

Probst, G., Raub, S., & Romhardt, K. (2000). *Managing knowledge: Building blocks for success*. London: John Wiley & Sons.

Prusak, L. (1997). *Knowledge in organizations*. Boston: Butterworth-Heinemann.

Puschmann, T., & Alt, R. (2005). Developing an integration architecture for process portals. *European Journal of Information Systems, 14*(2), 121-134.

Pyke, F., G, B., & W, S. (1990). *Industrial districts and inter-firm cooperation in Italy*. Geneva: International Institute for Labour Studies.

Radice, R.A., Roth, N.K., O'Hara, A.C., & Ciarfella, W.A. (1985). A programming process architecture. *IBM Systems Journal, 24*(2), 79-90.

Ragu-Nathan, B., Ragu-Nathan, T. S., Tu, Q., & Shi, Z. (2001). Information management (IM) strategy: The construct and its measurement. *Journal of Strategic Information Systems, 10*, 265-289.

Ramasubramanian, S. & Jagadeesan, G. (2002). Knowledge management at Infosys. *IEEE Software, 19*(3), 53-55.

Rappleye, W. C. (2000). Knowledge management: A force whose time has come. *Across the Board: The Conference Board Magazine*, January, 59-66.

Rasmus, D. (2000). How to make the chief knowledge officer (role) work. *Giga* (p. 6).

Rastogi, P.N. (2000). Knowledge management and intellectual capital: The new virtuous reality of competitiveness. *Human Systems Management, 19*, 19-26.

Rath, H.H., & Pepper, S. (1999). Topic maps: Introduction and Allegro. In *Proceedings of the Markup Technologies, 99*. Philadelphia, USA.

Reagans, R., & Zuckerman, E. (2001). Networks, diversity, and performance: The social capital of corporate R&D units. *Organization Science, 12*(4), 502-517.

Real, J., Leal, A., & Roldan, J. (2006). Determinants of organisational learning in the generation of technological distinctive competencies. *International Journal of Technology Management, 35*(1-4), 284-307.

Reger, G. (2001). Technology foresight in companies: From an indicator to a network and process perspective. *Technology Analysis & Strategic Management, 13*(4), 533-553.

Reger, R.K., & Huff, A.S. (1993). Strategic groups: A cognitive perspective. *Strategic Management Journal, 14*, 103-123.

Reger, R.K., & Palmer, T.B. (1996). Managerial categorization of competitors: Using old maps to navigate new environments. *Organization Science, 7*, 22-39.

Regev, G., & Wegmann, A. (2004). Remaining Fit: On the Creation and Maintenance of Fit. In *The 5ᵗʰ BPMDS Workshop on Creating and Maintaining the Fit between*

Business Processes and Support System (pp. 131-137). Riga, Latvia.

Reix, R. (1995, September/October). Savoir tacite et savoir formalisé dans l'entreprise. *Revue Française de Gestion*, 105, 17-28.

Remus, U. (2002). *Prozessorientiertes Wissensmanagement, Konzepte und Modellierung.* PhD thesis, University of Regensburg, Regensburg.

Remus, U., & Schub, S. (2003). A blueprint for the implementation of process-oriented knowledge management. *Journal of Process- and Knowledge Management, 10*(4), 237-253.

Riempp, G. (2004). *Integrierte wissensmanagement-systeme—Architektur und praktische anwendung.* Berlin: Springer.

Riesbeck, C.K., & Schank, R.C. (1989). *Inside case-based reasoning.* Hillsdale: Lawrence Erlbaum Associates.

Ringland, G. (2002). *Scenarios in business.* West Sussex: John Wiley & Sons.

Robertson, M., Swan, J., & Newell, S. (1996). The role of networks in the diffusion of technological innovation. *Journal of Management Studies, 33*, 335-361.

Robson, R. (1994). *Strategic management and information systems.* London: Pitman.

Rogers, E.M., Takegami, S., & Yin, J. (2001). Lessons learned about technology transfer. *Technovation, 21*(4), 253-261.

Rogers, P. R., & Bamford, C. E. (2002). Information planning process and strategic orientation: The importance of fit in high-performance organizations. *Journal of Business Research, 55*, 205-215.

Rokeach, M. (1973). *The nature of human values.* New York: Free Press.

Rollet, H. (2003). *Knowledge management: Processes and technologies.* Dordrecht: Kluwer.

Rose, J., & Scheepers, R. (2001). Structuration theory and information systems development; frameworks for practice. In S. Smithson and S. Avgerinou (Eds.), *The 9th European Conference on Information Systems* (pp. 217-231). Bled, Slovenia, June 27-29, 2001.

Rosenberg, M. (1995). Performance technology, performance support, and the future of training. *Performance Improvement Quarterly, 8*(1), 12-20.

Rosenkopf, L., & Nerker, A. (2001). Beyond local search: Boundary-spanning, exploration and impact in the optical disk industry. *Strategic Management Journal, 22*(4), 287- 306.

Rowley, J., & Slack, F. (2001). Leveraging customer knowledge: Profiling and personalisation in e-business. *International journal of Retail and Distribution Management, 29*(8/9), 407-415.

Roy, M., Guindon, J.C., & Fortier, L. (1995). *Transfert de connaissances: Revue de littérature et proposition d'un modèle* (Rapport R-099). Montréal: IRSST.

Rubenstein-Montano, B. et al. (2001). A systems thinking framework for knowledge management. *Decision Support Systems, 31*(1), 5-16.

Rumbaugh, J., Blaha, M., Premerlani, W., Eddy, F., & Lorensen, W. (1991). *Object-Oriented Modeling and Design*. New Jersey: Prentice-Hall International, Inc.

Rummler, G. & Brache, A. (1992). Transforming organizations through human performance technology. In H.D. Stolovitch & E.J. Keeps (Eds.), *Handbook of human performance technology: A comprehensive guide for analyzing and solving performance problems in organizations* (pp. 32-49). San Francisco, CA: Jossey-Bass.

Rus, I. & Lindvall, M (2002). Knowledge management in software engineering. *IEEE Software, 19*(3), 26-38.

Rus, I., Lindvall, M., & Sinha, S.S. (2001). Knowledge management in software engineering. DACS State of the Art Report (SOAR). Retrieved on April 10, 2005, from *http: www.dacs.dtic.mil/techs/kmse/kmse.html*

Rynes, S.L., Bartunek, J.M., & Daft, R.L. (2001). Special research forum: Knowledge transfer between academics and practitioners. *The Academy of Management Journal, 44*(2), 340-355.

Saaty, T.L. (1980). *The Analytic Hierarchy Process*, McGraw-Hill, New York.

Saaty, T.L. (1994). *Fundamentals of Decision Making and Priority Theory with the Analytic Hierarchy Process*. Pittsburgh: RWS Publications.

Sabherwal, R., & Chan, Y. E. (2001). Alignment between business and IS strategies: A study of prospectors, analyzers, and defenders. *Information Systems Research, 12*(1), 11-33.

Sabherwal, R., & Kirs, P. (1994). The alignment between organizational critical success factors and information technology capability in academic institutions. *Decision Sciences, 25*(2), 301-330.

Saint-Onge, H. (1999). Tacit knowledge: The key to strategic alignment of intellectual capital. In M. H. Zack (Ed.), *Knowledge and strategy* (pp. 223-230). Boston: Butterworth Heinemann.

Salton, G., & McGill, M.J. (1983). *Introduction to modern information retrieval*. New York: McGraw-Hill.

Sanchez, R. (1995). Strategic flexibility in product competition. *Strategic Management Journal, 16*(5), 135-159.

Sanchez, R. (2002). Modular product and process architectures: Frameworks for strategic organizational learning. In C.W. Choo & N. Bontis (Eds.), *The strategic management of intellectual capital and organizational knowledge* (pp. 223-231). New York: Oxford University Press.

Sanchez, R., & Collins, R.P. (2001). Competing—and learning—in modular markets. *Long Range Planning, 34*, 645-667.

Sanchez, R., & Heene, A. (2004). *The new strategic management: Organization, competition and competence*. New York: Wiley.

Sanchez, R., & Mahoney, J.T. (1996). Modularity, flexibility, and knowledge management in product and organization design. *Strategic Management Journal, 17*(Winter Special Issue), 63-76.

Sanderson, S.W., & Uzumeri, M. (1997). *Managing product families*. New York: McGraw-Hill.

Satorra, A., & Bentler, P.M. (2001). A scaled difference chi-square test statistic for moment structure analysis. *Psychometrika, 66*, 507-514.

Sawhney, M. (2002). Don't just relate: Collaborate. *MIT Sloan Management Review, 43*(Spring), 96.

Sawhney, M., & Prandelli, E. (2004). Communities of creation: Managing distributed innovation in turbulent markets. In K. Starkey, S. Tempest & A. McKinlay (Eds.), *How organizations learn* (pp. 271-301. London: Thompson.

Sawyer, K. (1990). *Dealing with complex organisational problems*. PhD Consortium, International Conference on Information Systems (ICIS), Copenhagen.

Sawyer, K. (1990). Goals, purposes and the strategy tree. *Systemist, 12*(4), 76-82.

Scarbrough, H., Bresnen, M., Edelman, L., Laurent, S., Newell, S., & Swan, J. (2004). The process of project-based learning: An exploratory study. *Management Learning, 35*(4), 491-506.

Schaefer D.R., & Dillman, D.A. (1998). Development of a standard e-mail methodology: Results of an experiment. *Public Opinion Quarterly, 62*(3), 378-397.

Schatzki, T. R. (2001). Introduction: Practice theory. In T. R. Schatzki, C. Knorr Cetina, & E. von Savigny (Eds.), *The practice turn in contemporary theory* (pp. 1-14). London: Routledge.

Scheepers, R., Venkitachalam, K., & Gibbs, M.R. (2004). Knowledge strategy in organizations: Refining the model of Hansen, Nohria and Tierney. *Journal of Strategic Information Systems, 13*, 201-222.

Scheer, A. (2000). *Aris: Business process modelling* (3rd ed.). Berlin.

Schein, E.H. (1985). *Organizational culture and leadership*. San Francisco: Jossey-Bass.

Schiller, D. (1999). *Digital capitalism: Networking the global market system*. Cambridge, MA: MIT Press.

Schilling, M.A. (2000). Toward a general modular systems theory and its application to interfirm product modularity. *Academy of Management Review, 25*(2), 312-334.

Schilling, M.A., & Steensma, H.K. (2001). The use of modular organizational forms: An industry level analysis. *Academy of Management Journal, 44*(6), 1149-1168.

Schmidt, R., Lyytinen, K., Keil, M., & Cule, P. (2001). Identifying software project risks: An international Delphi study. *Journal of Management Information Systems, 17*(4), 5-36

Schmidt, R.C. (1997). Managing Delphi surveys using nonparametric statistical techniques. *Decision Sciences, 28*(3), 763-774.

Schoemaker, P.J.H. (1995). Scenario planning: A tool for strategic thinking. *Sloan Management Review, 36*(Winter), 25-40.

Scholl, W., König, C., Meyer, B., & Heisig, P. (2004). The future of knowledge management: An international Deplhi study. *Journal of Knowledge Management, 8*(2), 19-35.

Schultze, U., & Stabell, C. (2004). Knowing what you don't know? Discourses and contradictions in knowledge management research. *Journal of Management Studies, 41*(4), 549-573.

Schwartz, P. (1998). *The art of the long view: Planning for the future in an uncertain world*. West Sussex: John Wiley & Sons.

Schwartz, S.H. (1994). Are there universal aspects in the structure and contents of human values? *Journal of Social Issues, 50*(4), 19-46.

Schwarz, M. (2003). A multilevel analysis of the strategic decision process and the evolution of shared beliefs. In B. Chakravarthy, G. Mueller-Stewens, P. Loramge & C. Lechner (Eds.), *Strategy process: Shaping the contours of the field* (pp. 110-136). Oxford, UK: Blackwell Publishing.

Sears, R. (2001). Managing the knowledge asset manager. *Knowledge Management Asia-Pacific, 1*(2), 8-10.

Seemann, P., De Long, D., Stucky, S., & Guthrie, E. (2000). Building intangible assets: A strategic framework for investing in intellectual capital. In D. Morey, M. Maybury & B. Thuraisingham (Eds.), *Knowledge management: Classic and contemporary works* (pp. 81-98). Cambridge, MA: MIT Press.

Segrestin, B. (2005). Partnering to explore: The Renault-Nissan Alliance as a forerunner of new cooperative patterns. *Research Policy, 34*(5), 657-672.

Semler, S. W. (1997), Systematic Agreement: A Theory of Organizational Alignment, *Human Resource Development Quarterly*, 8(1), 23-40.

Senge, P., Kleiner, A., Roberts, C., Ross, R., & Smith, B. (1994). *The fifth discipline fieldbook: Strategies and tools for building a learning organisation.* New York: Currency Doubleday.

Senge, P.M. (2006). *The fifth discipline: The art and practice of the learning organisation.* London: Random House.

Serban, A., & Luan, J. (2002). Overview of knowledge management. *New Directions for Institutional Research*, 113, 5-16.

Shah, S. (2005). Open beyond software. In C. Dibona, D. Cooper and M. Stone (Eds.), *Open Sources 2* (pp. 339-360). Sebastopol, CA: O'Reilly Media.

Shapiro, C., & Varian, H. R. (1999). *Information rules: A strategic guide to the network economy.* Boston: Harvard Business School Press.

Sharma, S. (1996). *Applied multivariate techniques.* New York: John Wiley & Sons.

Shimizu, K., & Hitt, M.A. (2004). Strategic flexibility: Organizational preparedness to reverse ineffective strategic decisions. *The Academy of Management Executive, 18*(4), 44-59.

Sidhu, J., Volberda, H., & Commandeur, H. (2004). Exploring exploration orientation and its determinants: Some empirical evidence. *Journal of Managment Studies, 41*(6), 913- 932.

Siegel, S. (1956). *Nonparametric statistics for the behavioral sciences.* New York: McGraw-Hill.

Simmonds, P.G., Dawley, D., Ritchie, W., & Anthony, W. (2001). An exploratory examination of the knowledge transfer of strategic management concepts from the academic environment to practicing managers. *Journal of Managerial Issues, 13*(3), 360-376.

Simon, H A. (1960). *The New Science of Management Decisions*, New York: Harper Brothers.

Simon, H. (1976). *Administrative Behavior*, Free Press, New York.

Simon, H.A. (1996). *The Sciences of the Artificial*, Cambridge, Mass. MIT Press.

Simon, H.A. (2003). The architecture of complexity. In R. Garud, A. Kumaraswamy & R.N. Langlois (Eds.), *Managing in the modular age: Architectures, networks, and organizations* (pp. 15-44). Oxford, UK: Blackwell Publishing.

Simonin, B. (1997). The importance of collaborative know-how: An empirical test of the learning organization. *Academy of Management Journal, 40*(5), 1150-1174.

Skyrme, D. J. (2000). *Knowledge networking: Creating the collaborative enterprise.* Oxford: Butterworth Heinemann.

Skyrme, D.J. (1997). Knowledge management: Making sense of an oxymoron. Retrieved May 17, 2007, from *http://skyrme.com/insights/22km.htm*

Slack, N. (1983). Flexibility as a manufacturing objective. *International Journal of Operations and Production Management, 3*(3), 4-13.

Smircich, L., & Stubbart, C. (1985). Strategic management in an enacted world. *Academy of Management Review, 10*(4), 724-736.

Smith, E.A. (2001). The role of tacit and explicit knowledge in the workplace. *Journal of Knowledge Management, 5*(4), 311-321.

Smolnik, S., Kremer, S., & Kolbe, L. (2005). Continuum of context explication: Knowledge discovery through process-oriented portals. *International Journal of Knowledge Management, 1*(1), 27-46.

Soo, C., Devinney, T., Midgley, D., & Deering, A. (2002). Knowledge management: Philosophy, processes, and pitfalls. *California Management Review, 44*(4), 129-150.

Spender, J.-C. (1994). Organizational knowledge, collective practice, and Penrose rents. *International Business Review, 3*(4), 353-367.

Spender, J.C. (1996). Making knowledge the basis of a dynamic theory of the firm. *Strategic Management Journal, 17*, 45-62.

Spender, J.C. (2005). Review article: An essay of the state of knowledge management. *Prometheus, 1*, 101-116.

Spender, J.C. (2006). Managerial practice: Shaping the reasoning and imagining of others (CIKM 2006 Working Paper Series). Retrieved May 19, 2007, from *http://www.cikm.ul.ie*

Srikantaiah, K.T., & Koenig, E.D.M. (Eds.). (2000). *Knowledge management for the information professional.* Medford, NJ: Information Today, Inc.

Stacey, R.D. (2003). *Strategic management and organisational dynamics: The challenge of complexity* (4th ed.). Harlow: Prentice-Hall.

Star, S.L. (1989). The structure of ill-structured solutions: Boundary objects and heterogeneous distributed problem solving. In L. Gasser & M.N. Huhns (Eds.), *Distributed artificial intelligence Vol. II* (pp. 37-54). London: Pitman Publishing.

Stenfors, T. (2003). Narrated knowledge: How to use stories for knowledge dissemination. In F. McGrath & D. Remenyi (Eds.), *Fourth European Conference on Knowledge Management* (pp. 853-860).

Sterman, J.D. (2000). *Business dynamics: Systems thinking and modeling for a complex world.* London: William Heinemann.

Stetsenko, A. (1999). Social Interaction, Cultural Tools and the Zone of Proximal Development: In Search of a Synthesis. In S. Chaiklin, M. Hedegaard, U. J. Jensen

(Eds.), *Activity Theory and Social Practice: Cultural-Historical Approaches* (pp. 235-252). Aarhus: Aarhus University Press.

Stewart, T. (1999). *Intellectual Capital, The New Wealth of Organizations,* Currency Doubleday, New York.

Stewart, T. (2001). *The wealth of knowledge: Intellectual capital and the twenty-first century organization.* New York: Doubleday.

Stewart, T.A. (1997). *Intellectual capital: The new wealth of organization.* Currency New York: Doubleday.

Stolovitch, H.D. & Keeps, E.J. (1999). What is human performance technology? In H.D. Stolovitch, & E.J. Keeps (Eds.), *Handbook of human performance technology: Improving individual and organizational performance worldwide* (pp. 3-23). San Francisco, CA: Jossey-Bass.

Stuart, T., & Podolny, J. (1996). Local search and the evolution of technological capabilities. *Strategic Management Journal, 17*(1), 21-38.

Suppe, F. (1974). *The Structure of Scientific Theories,* Urbana, IL: University of Illinois Press.

Susi, T. (2006). *The Puzzle of Social Activity.* Dissertation No. 1019, Department of Computer and Information Science. Linköping: Linköping University.

Sveiby, K.E. (2001). Knowledge management: Lessons from the pioneers. Retrieved May 20, 2007, from http://www.sveiby.com/Portals/0/articles/KM-lessons.doc

Sviokla, J.J. (1996). Knowledge workers and radically new technology. *Sloan Management Review,* 25-40.

Syed-Ikhsan, S.O.S., & Rowland, F. (2004). Knowledge management in a public organization: A study on the relationship between organizational elements and the performance of knowledge transfer. *Journal of Knowledge Management, 8*(2), 95-111.

Szulanski, G. (1996). Exploring internal stickiness: Impediments to the transfer of best practice within the firm. *Strategic Management Journal, 17*(1), 27-43.

Szulanski, G. (2000). The process of knowledge transfer: A diachronic analysis of stickiness. *Organizational Behaviour and Human Decision Processes, 82*(1), 9-27.

Szulanski, G. (2003). *Sticky knowledge: Barriers to knowing in the firm.* London: Sage Publications.

Szulanski, G., & Capetta, R. (2005). Stickiness: Conceptualizing, measuring, and predicting difficulties in the transfer of knowledge within organizations. In M. Easterby-Smith & M.A. Lyles (Eds.), *Handbook of organizational learning and knowledge management* (pp. 513-534). Malden, MA: Blackwell Publishing.

Tallman, S., Jenkins, M., Henry, N., & Pinch, S. (2004). Knowledge, clusters and competitive advantage. *Academy of Management Review, 29*(2), 258-271.

Taxén, L. (2003). *A Framework for the Coordination of Complex Systems' Development.* Dissertation No. 800. Linköping University, Dep. of Computer & Information Science, 2003. Retrieved October 18, 2006, from http://www.diva-portal.org/liu/theses/abstract.xsql?dbid=5001

Taxén, L. (2004). Articulating Coordination of Human Activity - the Activity Domain Theory. In *Proceedings of the 2nd International workshop on Action in Language, Organisations and Information Systems (ALOIS-2004).* Linköping University. Retrieved October 18, 2006, from http://www.vits.org/?pageId=37

Taxén, L. (2005). A Socio-technical Approach Towards Alignment. *Software Process: Improvement and Practice, 10*(4), 427-439.

Taxén, L. (2005). Categorizing Objective Meaning in Activity Systems. In G. Whymark, & H. Hasan (Eds.), *Activity as the Focus of Information Systems Research.* Eveleigh, Australia: Knowledge Creation Press.

Taxén, L. (2006). An Integration Centric Approach for the Coordination of Distributed Software Development Projects. *Information and Software Technology, 48*(9), 767-780.

Taxén, L., & Svensson, D. (2005). Towards an Alternative Foundation for Managing Product Life-Cycles in Turbulent Environments. *International Journal of Product Development* (IJPD), 2(1/2), 24-46.

Taylor, W.A. (2004). Computer-mediated knowledge sharing and individual user differences: An exploratory study. *European Journal of Information Systems, 13*, 52-64.

TechWeb (1999). *Sharing knowledge isn't easy yet.* Retrieved August 31, 2007 from http://www.informationweek.com/bizint/biz748/48bzshr.htm

Teece, D. J., Pisano, G., & Shuen, A. (1999). Dynamic capabilities and strategic management. In M. H. Zack (Ed.), *Knowledge and strategy* (pp. 77-115). Boston: Butterworth Heinemann.

Teece, D., Pisano, G., & Shuen, A. (1997). Dynamic capabilities and strategic management. *Strategic Management Journal, 18*(7), 509-533.

Teece, D.J. (1982). Towards an economic theory of the firm. *Journal of Economic Behaviour and Organization, 3*(1), 39-63.

Teece, D.J. (1984). Economic analysis and strategic management. *California Management Review, 26*(3), 87-110.

Teece, D.J. (1998). Capturing value from knowledge assets: The new economy, markets for know-how, and intangible assets. *California Management Review, 40*(3), 55-79.

Teece, D.J. (2000). Strategies for managing knowledge assets: The role of firm structure and industrial context. *Long Range Planning, 33*, 35-54.

Teece, D.J., Pisano, G., & Schuen, A. (1997). Dynamic capabilities and strategic management. *Strategic Management Journal, 18*(7), 509-533.

Teng, J.T.C., Grover, V., & Fiedler, K.D. (1994). Business process reengineering: Charting a strategic path for the information age. *California Management Review, 36*(3), 9-31.

Thierauf, R. J. (1999). *Knowledge management systems for business* (1st ed.). Westport: Quorum Books.

Thomas, J. C., Kellog, W. A., & Erickson, T. (2001). The knowledge management puzzle: Human factors in knowledge management. *IBM Systems Journal, 40*(4), 863-884.

Thomas, J.B., Sussman, S.W., & Henderson, J.C. (2004). Understanding "strategic learning": Linking organizational learning, knowledge management and sensemaking. *Organization Science, 12*(3), 331-345.

Thomas, L.G. (2004). Are we all global now? Local vs. foreign sources of corporate competence: The case of the Japanese pharmaceutical industry. *Strategic Management Journal, 25*(8/9), 865-886.

Tierney, T. (1999). What's your strategy for managing knowledge? *Harvard Business Review, 77*(2), 106-116.

Timbrell, G., Delaney, P., Chan, T., Yue, A., & Gable, G. (2005). A structurationist review of knowledge management theories. In *Proceedings of the 26th Annual Conference on Information Systems* (pp. 247-259), Las Vegas, Nevada.

Tissen, R., Andriessen, D., & Deprez, F. L. (2000). *The knowledge dividend: Creating high-performance companies through value-based knowledge management.* Harlow, UK: Financial Times Prentice-Hall.

Tiwana, A. (2002). *Knowledge management toolkit: Practical techniques for building a knowledge management system* (2nd Ed.). Saddle River, NJ: Prentice-Hall PTR.

Treacy, M. & Wiersema, F. D. (1996). *The discipline of market leaders.* Reading, MA: Addison-Wesley.

Tsai, W. (2001). Knowledge transfer in intraorganizational networks: Effects of network position and absorptive capacity on business unit innovation and performance. *Academy of Management Journal, 44*(5), 996-1004.

Tse, A.C.B. (1998). Comparing the response rate, response speed, and response quality of two methods of sending questionnaires: E-mail vs. mail. *Journal of the Market Research Society, 40*(4), 354-361.

Tsoukas, H. (1996). The firm as a distributed knowledge system: A constructionist approach. *Strategic Management Journal, 17.*

Tsoukas, H. (2003). Do we relay understand tacit knowledge, In M. Easterby-Smith & M. Lyles (Eds.), *The Blackwell Handbook of Organizational Learning and Knowledge Management* (pp. 410-427). Blackwell Publishing.

Tsoukas, H., & Chia, R. (2002). On organizational becoming: Rethinking organizational change. *Organization Science, 13*(5), 567-582.

Tsoukas, H., & Vladimirou, E. (2001). What is organizational knowledge? *Journal of Management Studies, 38*(7), 973-993.

Tsui, E. (2005). The role of it in KM: Where are we now and where are we heading? *Journal of Knowledge Management, 9*(1), 3-6.

Tuomi, I. (1999). Data Is More Than Knowledge: Implications of the Reversed Knowledge Hierarchy for Knowledge Management and Organizational Memory. In *Proceedings of the 32nd Hawaii International Conference on System Sciences* (pp. 1-12), Track 1, January 5-8, 1999.

Tuomi, I. (2002). The Future of Knowledge Management. *Lifelong Learning in Europe* (LLinE), VII(2), 69-79.

Tushman, M. (2003). Exploitation, exploration and process management: The productivity dilemma revisited. *Academy of management review, 28*(2), 238-256.

Uzzi, B. (1996). The sources and consequences of embeddedness for the economic performance of organizations: The network effect. *American Sociological Review, 61*(4), 674-698.

van den Hooff, B., Vijvers, J., & de Ridder, J. (2003). Foundations and applications of a knowledge management scan. *European Management Journal, 21*(2), 237-246.

Van der Heijden, K. (1998). *Scenarios: The art of strategic conversation.* Chichester: John Wiley & Sons.

Vanston, J.H. (1996). Technology forecasting: A practical tool for rationalizing the R&D process. *The New Telecom Quarterly, 4*(1), 57-62. Technology Futures Inc.

Venkatraman, N. (1989). The concept of fit in strategy research: Toward verbal and statistical correspondence. *Academy of Management Review, 14*(3), 423-444.

Venkatraman, N. (1989). Strategic orientation of business enterprises: The construct, dimensionality and measurement. *Management Science, 35*(8), 942-962.

Venkatraman, N., & Camillus, J. C. (1984). Exploring the concept of "fit" in strategic management. *Academy of Management Review, 9*(3), 513-525.

Venkatraman, N., & Prescott, J. E. (1990). Environment-strategy coalignment: An empirical test of its performance implication. *Strategic Management Journal, 11*, 1-23.

Venkatraman, N., & Tanriverdi, H. (2005). Reflecting "knowledge" in strategy research: Conceptual issues and methodological challenges. *Research Methodology in Strategy and Management, 1*, 33-65.

Vennix, J.A.M. (1996). *Group model building: Facilitating team learning using system dynamics.* Chichester, UK: John Wiley & Sons.

Vickers, G. (1983). *The art of judgment.* London: Harper and Row.

Vickers, G. (1984). *Human systems are different.* London: Harper and Row.

Virkkunen, J., & Kuutti, K. (2000). Understanding organizational learning by focusing on "activity systems". *Accounting, Management and Information Technologies, 10*(4), 291-319.

Vološinov, V. N. (1986). *Marxism and the Language of Philosophy.* London: Harvard University Press. Originally published in 1929.

Von Hippel, E. (1978). Successful industrial products from customer ideas. *Journal of Marketing, 42*(1), 39-49.

Von Hippel, E. (1988). *Sources of innovation.* New York: Oxford University Press.

Von Hippel, E. (1989). New product ideas from "Lead Users". *Research Management, 32*(3), 24-27.

von Krogh, G. (2003). Knowledge Sharing and the Communal Resource, In M. Easterby-Smith & M. Lyles (Eds.), *The Blackwell Handbook of Organizational Learning and Knowledge Management* (pp. 372-392). Blackwell Publishing.

Von Krogh, G., & Von Hippel, E, (2003). Open source software: Introduction to a special issue of research policy. *Research Policy, 32*(7),1149-57.

von Krogh, G., Ichijo, K., & Nonaka, I. (2000). *Enabling knowledge creation: How to unlock the mystery of tacit knowledge and release the power of innovation.* Oxford University Press.

Vygotsky, L. S. (1978). *Mind in Society—The development of higher Psychological Processes.* M. Cole, V. John-Steiner, S. Scribner, & E. Souberman, (Eds.). Cambridge MA: Harvard University Press.

W3C. (2004). Web services architecture requirements. Retrieved May 22, 2007, from *http://www. w3. org/TR/wsa-reqs/*

W3C. (2004). Web services glossary. Retrieved May 22, 2007, from http://www. w3. org/TR/2004/NOTE-ws-gloss-20040211/

Walczak, S. & Zwart, D. (2003). Organizational knowledge management: Enabling a knowledge culture. In *Proceedings of the Information Resources Management Association International Conference*, Philadelphia, 18-21 May, pp. 670-673.

Walsham, G. (1993). *Interpreting information systems in organizations.* Chichester, UK: Wiley.

Walsham, G. (2005). Knowledge Management Systems: Representation and Communication in Context. *Systems, Signs & Actions,* 1(1), 6–18. Retrieved October 18, 2006, from http://www.sysiac.org/

Walsham, G., & Waema, T. (1994). Information systems strategy and implementation: A case study of a building society. *ACM Transactions on Information Systems, 12*(2), 150-173.

Ward, J. & Aurum, A. (2004). Knowledge management in software engineering: Describing the process. In *Proceedings of the 2004 Australian Software Engineering Conference*. IEEE Computer Society. Retrieved on April 10, 2005, from *http://csdl.computer.org/comp/proceedings/ aswec/2004/2089/00/20890137abs.htm*

Waruszynski, T.B. (2000). *The knowledge revolution: A literature review*. Ottawa: Defence R&D Canada.

Watson, T.R. (1989). Key issues in information systems management: An Australian perspective. *The Australian Computer Journal, 21*(2), 118-129.

Weick, K. (1995). *Sensemaking in organizations*. Thousand Oaks, CA: Sage.

Weick, K.E. (1990). Cartographic myths in organizations. In A.S. Huff (Ed.), *Mapping strategic thought* (pp. 1-11). Chichester, UK: Wiley.

Weick, K.E., Sutcliffe, K.M., & Obstfeld, D. (2005). Organizing and the process of sensemaking. *Organization Science, 16*(4), 409-421.

Weisbord, M.R. (1992). *Discovering common ground*. San Francisco: Berret-Koehler.

Wenger, E. (1998). *Communities of practice: Learning, meaning and identity*. Cambridge, UK: Cambridge University Press.

Wenger, E. C., McDermott, R., & Snyder, W. M. (2002). *Cultivating communities of practice*. Boston: Harvard Business School

Wenger, E., & Snyder, W.M. (2000). Communities of practice: The organizational frontier. *Harvard Business Review, 78*(1), 139-146.

Wensley, K. P. A., & O'Sullivan, A. V. (2000). *Tools for knowledge management*. Retrieved August 30, 2007 from http://www.icasit.org/km/toolsforkm.htm

Wernerfelt, B. (1984). A resource-based view of the firm. *Strategic Management Journal, 5*(2), 171-180.

Whitley, B. (1996). *Principles of research in behavioral science*. Mountain View, CA: Mayfield Publishing Company.

Whitman, I.N. (1990). The Delphi technique as an alternative for committee meetings. *Journal of Nursing Education, 29*(8), 377-379.

Wiener, Y. (1988). Forms of Value Systems: A Focus on Organizational Effectiveness and Cultural Change and Maintenance, *The Academy of Management Review, 13*(4), 534-545.

Wiig, K. M. (1999). What future knowledge management users may expect. *Journal of Knowledge Management, 3*(2), 155-165.

Wilson, T.D. (2002). The nonsense of "knowledge management." *Information Research, 8*(1), paper 144. Retrieved May 21, 2007, from http://InformationR.net/ir/8-1/paper144.html

Winkler, I. (2006). Network governance between individual and collective goals: Qualitative evidence from six networks. *Journal of Leadership and Organizational Studies, 12*(3), 119-133.

Winter, S.G. (1987). Knowledge and competence as strategic assets. In D. Teece (ed.), *The competitive challenge: Strategies for industrial innovation and renewal*. Cambridge, MA: Ballinger Publishing Co., 159-184.

Wolff, E. N. (2005). The growth of information workers. *Communications of the ACM, 48*(10), 37-42.

Wordweb 1.63. (2001). *Fad entry*. Retrieved from http://wordweb.info/

Worren, N., Moore, K., & Cardona, P. (2002). Modularity, strategic flexibility, and firm performance: A study of the home appliance industry. *Strategic Management Journal, 23*, 1123-1140.

Wostenholme, E.F. (2003). Towards the definition and use of a core set of archetypal structures in system dynamics. *System Dynamics Review, 19*(1), 7-26.

Wu, I.-L. (2002). A model for implementing BPR based on strategic perspectives: An empirical study. *Information and Management, 39*(4), 313-324.

Yin, R. K. (2002). *Case study research: Design and methods* (3rd ed.). Newbury Park: Sage.

Zack, M. H. (1999). Developing a knowledge strategy. *California Management Review, 41*(3), 125-145.

Zack, M. H. (1999). Introduction. In M. H. Zack (Ed.), *Knowledge and strategy* (pp. vii-xii). Boston: Butterworth Heinemann.

Zack, M. H. (1999). Managing codified knowledge. *Sloan Management Review, 40*(4), 45-58.

Zack, M. H. (2002). Epilogue: Developing a knowledge strategy. In C. W. Choo & N. Bontis (Eds.), *The strategic management of intellectual capital and organizational knowledge* (pp. 268-276). Oxford: Oxford University Press.

Zack, M.H. (2005). The strategic advantage of knowledge and learning. *International Journal of Intellectual Capital and Learning, 2*(1), 1-20.

Zahra, S.A., & George, G. (2002). Absorptive capacity: A review, reconceptualization, and extension. *Academy of Management Review, 27*(2), 185-203.

Zand, D. (1997). *The leadership triad: Knowledge, trust, and power.* Oxford: Oxford University Press.

Zander, U., & Kogut, B. (1995). Knowledge and the speed of the transfer and imitation of organizational capabilities: An empirical test. *Organization Science, 6*, 76-92.

Zelewski, S. (2001). Ontologien—ein Überblick über betriebswirtschaftliche Anwendungsbereiche. In Workshop Forschung in schnellebiger Zeit", Beitrag 5, Appenzell.

Zellner, C., & Fornahl, D. (2002). Scientific knowledge and implications for its diffusion. *Journal of Knowledge Management, 6*(2), 190-198.

Zinchenko, V. (2001). External and Internal: Another Comment on the Issue. In S. Chaiklin (Ed.), *The Theory and Practice of Cultural-Historical Psychology* (pp. 135-147). Aarhus: Aarhus University Press.

Zollo, M., & Winter, S. (2002). Deliberate learning and the evolution of dynamic capabilities. *Organization Science, 13*, 339-351.

Zyngier, M. S. (2001). *Knowledge management strategies in Australia.* Caulfield East, AU: Monash University.

About the Contributors

El-Sayed Abou-Zeid is associate professor in the Department of Decision Sciences and MIS, John Molson School of Business, Concordia University. His current research interests include alignment of knowledge and business strategies, cultural aspects of knowledge of knowledge management processes, design theory for knowledge management support systems. His work has appeared in journals such as *Journal of Knowledge Management*, *Journal of Global Information Technology Management*, *Journal of Computer Information Systems*, *Knowledge Management Research & Practice* and others. In addition, he has published over 35 refereed conference papers in proceedings such as IFIP, HICSS, IEEE, IRMA and ISAT.

***

Emmanuel D. Adamides is a tenured assistant professor of operations and technology management in the Section of Management of the Department of Mechanical Engineering and Aeronautics of the University of Patras (Greece). Previously to joining the University of Patras he held academic and professional positions in Switzerland and Greece. He has published extensively in the areas of information systems engineering, operations strategy, strategy and knowledge management, and innovation and technology management. Adamides is a graduate of Democritus University of Thrace (Greece), the University of Manchester, and the University of Sussex (UK).

Derek A. Asoh is assistant professor in the School of Information Systems and Applied Technologies, College of Applied Sciences and Arts, Southern Illinois University (Carbondale). He holds an inter-disciplinary PhD in information science from the College of Computing and Information, State University of New York at Albany (USA); and has a background in information and computer science, educational research, business statistics, and management information systems. His research interests are in the areas of data mining, educational technologies, entrepreneurship, health informatics, information technology, knowledge management, systems management technologies, and statistical modeling. His publications have appeared in *Health Care Management Review* and *Methods of Information in Medicine*. Some of his recent research has also been presented at several conferences including European Conference on Knowledge Management (ECKM), Hawaii International Conference on Systems Sciences (HICSS), Information Resources Management Association (IRMA), and Systemic, Cybernetics and Informatics (SCI).

Salvatore Belardo is associate professor of management science and information systems at the University at Albany. He holds PhD in management information systems. Belardo has been a visiting professor at the Copenhagen School of Business, the University of Passau (Germany), the University of Del Salvador (Argentina), DUXX Graduate School of Business Leadership in Monterrey (Mexico), and the Graduate School of Business Administration in Zurich (Switzerland). Belardo has published widely in a number of top journals including *Management Science, Decision Sciences, IEEE Transactions on Systems Man and Cybernetics*, and the *Journal of Management Information Systems*.

Julie Béliveau is a DBA student at the Faculty of Administration, Université de Sherbrooke (Québec), undertaking her thesis on knowledge transfer in the health care industry. She is interested in the role of middle management in the transfer of humanistic practices in a regional institution for the rehabilitation of physical impairments. Prior to her academic career, Béliveau worked as a manager in the automobile sector.

Shamim Bodhanya, originally trained as a professional engineer, worked in the corporate sector for nearly 14 years, serving in a variety of functional, professional and managerial capacities before becoming an academic at the Leadership Centre, University of KwaZulu-Natal (Durban, South Africa). He is now actively involved in research, programme and course development, lecturing, facilitation and consulting. He has engaged in facilitation and consulted in a variety of contexts both for small and large groups in corporate, government and not-for-profit sectors. He is a founding member of Equilibria Consulting, and serves as a director of the Institute for Natural Resources. He is married and has three children.

Anne-Marie Croteau is associate professor of MIS at the John Molson School of Business at Concordia University. Croteau's research mainly focuses on strategic information technology alignment and impact of information technology on business performance. Her research has been published in *Journal of Strategic Information Systems, Journal of Information Technology, International Journal of Knowledge Management, Industrial Management & Data Systems*, and *Canadian Journal of Administrative Sciences* as well as in various national and international proceedings.

Peter Duchessi is associate professor and chair of the Information Technology Management Department of the School of Business, State University of New York at Albany. He holds a PhD in management information systems. He has published extensively in his research areas of business planning and transformation, operations management, and IT management. His latest book is entitled *Crafting Customer Value: The Art and Science*.

Fernando José Garrigós-Simón, is a associate professor in the Department of Management, University Jaume I (Spain). He received his degree in economic and entrepreneurial sciences from the University of Valencia (Spain) and his MSc in tourism management and planning, Bournemouth University (England). He was a visiting scholar at the International Centre for Tourism and Hospitality Research (Bournemouth University), a visiting fellow at Institute of Management Science, Walailak University (Thailand) and a visiting fellow at Miami University.

Marc Henselewski works as a consultant with Deloitte Germany in the area of CIO advisory services and IT strategy. He received a master's degree in information systems sciences from the University of Paderborn (Germany). Henselewski has been working within the research field of knowledge management throughout his studies and started to focus especially on knowledge management's role in technology forecasting and innovation management while developing his master thesis.

Peter H. Jones is a managing principal of Redesign Research, a consulting practice for interactive product design, customer research and innovation strategy, located in Dayton and Toronto. This practice supports a research agenda enhancing consultation with organizational and cognitive research. Jones publishes research in *Information Cognition, User Experience Design*, and *Organizational Values and Strategy*. His dissertation research (Union Institute, 2000) identified the organizational effects of embedded values in innovation processes, based on activity theory analysis of processes in large product organizations. His book, *Team Design* (1997, 2002), has found use in product design projects for nearly a decade.

Hannu Kivijärvi is a professor in information systems science at the Helsinki School of Economics. He received his PhD in management science. His research interests include knowledge management, decision support systems in financial, production and marketing planning, IT Governance, and investments in information systems. His publications have appeared in a number of journals, including *European Journal of Information Systems, European Journal of Operational Research, Journal of Decision Systems, Decision Support Systems, Managerial and Decision Economics, International Journal of Production Economics*, and *Interfaces*

Ronald Maier holds a PhD in management information systems from The Koblenz School of Corporate Management—Otto Beisheim Graduate School of Management (WHU) and a habilitation degree from the University of Regensburg. He worked as visiting assistant professor at the Terry College of Business, University of Georgia (Athens, GA) (1998-1999). Since 2002, he has been with the School of Business and Economics, Martin-Luther-University Halle-Wittenberg and holds a Chair in MIS, information systems leadership. He has published articles on knowledge management (systems) in a number of research journals, books and conference proceedings. His research interests include data management and business intelligence, business process management and knowledge management

Daniel Palacios Marqués is an associate professor in the Department of Management, Universitat Jaume I (Spain). he holds an engineering degree in computer science from the Polytechnic University of Valencia (Spain), a master's degree in information systems, Polytechnic University of Valencia (Spain). He was a visiting scholar at the International Centre for Information Technologies in Pisa (Italy) and the Department of Business in Saldford University (England). He has carried out several research projects supported by the Spanish government related to the introduction of knowledge management in the firm. He has also developed an intranet for knowledge management with consultant and software firms.

Fergal McGrath is director of the AIB Centre For Information And Knowledge Management at the University of Limerick. He established the centre in 1999 to address the issues around technology, information and knowledge in the changing world of the 21st century. His research focuses on the role of institutional economics in the new knowledge economy. He is currently head of the department of Management and Marketing at the Kemmy Business School and chair of the European Conference on Knowledge Management.

Robert Parent holds a PhD in human and organizational systems from the Fielding Graduate University in Santa Barbara (California) and conducts his teaching and research as a full professor of strategy with the Faculty of Administration at the Université de Sherbrooke (UdeS) (Québec). He also serves as Director of the Dynamic Knowledge Transfer Research Laboratory at the university. As a researcher with the Chaire d'étude en organisation du travail at the UdeS, he conducts research on how effective knowledge transfer contributes to a systems' competitive advantage. Prior to his academic career, Parent was president of an international consulting firm specializing in strategic management.

Nikolaos Pomonis has graduated from the University of Patras with an MEng in mechanical engineering (2002), and from the Athens Laboratory of Business Administration (ALBA) with an MBA (2003). Currently, he is a manager of Toyota Hellas SA, while working at the same time towards a PhD degree in the Section of Management of the Department of Mechanical Engineering and Aeronautics of the University of Patras (Greece). His research interests are in the areas of strategic management, system dynamics and game theory.

Rebecca Purcell is a research associate at the AIB Centre for Information and Knowledge Management, University of Limerick (Ireland). Having completed a BBS in the University of Limerick, Purcell has since pursued a PhD in knowledge management. Her research interests include external knowledge search processes and the impact of the extended enterprise on innovative performance.

Ulrich Remus studied management information systems (MIS) at the University of Bamberg (Germany). From 1996 to 1998 he worked for a large IT consulting company. He received his PhD in MIS (2002) from the University of Regensburg (Germany) in the field of process-oriented knowledge management. Before joining the AFIS Department at the University of Canterbury (New Zealand) in 2006, he was an assistant professor for IS at the University of Erlangen-Nuremberg(Germany). His research interests focus on process management and knowledge management and the development of enterprise portals.

Gerold Riempp is head of the chair of Information Systems 2 at the European Business School (EBS), Oestrich-Winkel (Germany). His main research focus comprises knowledge management, strategic IT management, and customer & supplier relationship management. He looks back on more than 14 years with experiences in consultancy and he has introduced knowledge management in many organizations. Riempp headed the competence center "Customer Knowledge Management" at the University of St. Gallen's Institute of Information Management in Switzerland from 2000 to 2002. Before, he was senior manager and leader of the overall project for knowledge management at PricewaterhouseCoopers in Germany.

Stefan Smolnik is a research director, senior lecturer, and project manager at the European Business School (EBS), Oestrich-Winkel (Germany). Smolnik received a master's degree in computer science as well as a Ph.D. in information systems from the University of Paderborn (Germany). He has been working in the research fields of knowledge management, semantic technologies, and collaborative computing for a couple of years. Smolnik is an international recognized specialist in the research domain of topic maps and has published several articles on the topics of knowledge and process management, and information visualization. He is currently heading the competence center "knowledge-oriented Business Performance Improvement" at EBS to establish a link between academics and practitioners of the information and knowledge management research domains.

Denis St-Jacques is a consultant and a research assistant with the Chaire d'étude en organisation du travail at the Université de Sherbrooke. He holds a master's degree in psychology and a master's in philosophy. Throughout his career he has conducted numerous literature reviews and research activities on knowledge transfer, semi-autonomous work groups, change management, and innovative union-management partnerships. He gained considerable practical experience over the years as a training and organizational development consultant in both the private and public sectors.

Lars Taxén received his MSc from the Royal Institute of Technology in Stockholm (1968). Between 1968 and 2003 he was employed at the Ericsson telecommunication company. He has held several positions such as line manager, technical manager, project manager, etc., in the areas of support for hardware and software design. From 1995 on he was engaged in the development and implementation of incremental development methods for large, globally distributed software development projects. The experiences from this work were reported in his PhD thesis *A Framework for the Coordination of Complex Systems' Development* (2003). He has published various conference papers, journal articles and book chapters. Taxén is a senior member of IEEE and is now active as a researcher and consultant. More details can be found on his personal homepage www.neana.se.

César Camisón Zornoza holds a PhD in economic and business sciences. He is the principal professor at University Jaume I (Spain). He has been visiting professor at the University of Texas, the Universitá Commerciale Luigi Bocconi de Milán, the University of Surrey, the University of Vienna, and the Université de Montpellier I. He is Director of the *Strategy, Knowledge Management and Organizational Learning Research Group (GRECO).* His specialization areas are strategic management and competitiveness, entrepreneurship (SME and familiar enterprises), knowledge management, strategic alliances and industrial districts.

Index

V

W